UNKNOWN SOLDIERS

G.I.s of the 45th Infantry Division in France try on new jackets, oblivious of their dead enemy. What the hell, who'll be next? (*Department of Defense*)

UNKNOWN SOLDIERS

Reliving World War II in Europe

Joseph E. Garland

Protean Press
Rockport, Massachusetts

Protean Press
37-J Whistlestop Mall
Rockport, MA 01966
www.ProteanPress.com

14 13 12 11 10 09   1 2 3 4 5 6
First Edition 2009

Library of Congress Cataloging-in-Publication Data

Garland, Joseph E.
Unknown soldiers : reliving World War II in Europe / Joseph E. Garland.
p. cm.
Includes bibliographical references and index.
ISBN 978-0-9625780-3-8 (hbk.)
1. Garland, Joseph E. 2. United States. Army. Infantry Regiment, 157th. 3. World War, 1939–1945—Regimental histories—United States. 4. World War, 1939–1945—Campaigns—Italy. 5. World War, 1939–1945—Campaigns— Western Front. 6. World War, 1939–1945—Personal narratives, American. 7. Soldiers—United States—Biography. I. Title. D769.31157th .G37 2008
940.54′12730922—dc22
2008023412

Manufactured in the United States of America

Text and cover design by Judy Arisman, arismandesign.com. This book was typeset in Vendetta by Anne Rolland and printed and bound by Sheridan Books, Inc. The author's journal entries are set in italics; all other extracts from interviews, books, and letters are medium weight.

Portions of this book and supplemental material are available at: www.UnknownSoldiersMemoir.com

Front endpaper: The 157th Infantry Regiment of the 45th Infantry Division at Camp Barkeley, Texas, during training in the early 1940s. (*Courtesy of William E. Woodhams*)

Back endpaper: The 157th passes in triumphal review in the historic Königsplatz of Munich, in 1945. (*U.S. Army Signal Corps*)

The author gratefully acknowledges the following for permission to reprint previously published material:

Quotes and excerpts from the *157th Infantry Association Newsletter*, by Felix L. Sparks. Copyright ©1982–1990 by the 157th Infantry Association. Reprinted by permission of the 157th Infantry Association.

United Press dispatch "Aschaffenburg's Major Tells Private: 'We Yield,'" April 5, 1945. Reprinted by permission of UPI.

Quotes and excerpts from *Brave Men*, by Ernie Pyle. Copyright, 1943, 1944 by Scripps-Howard Newspaper Alliance. First Edition copyright, 1944, by Henry Holt and Company, Inc. Reprinted by permission of Scripps Howard Foundation.

Extract from "Capture of 'Bloody Ridge' Told by Boys Who 'Dood' It," Associated Press dispatch July 30, 1943. Copyright © 1943 by the Associated Press. Used with permission of the Associated Press © 2007. All rights reserved.

Quotes and excerpt from *A General's Life: An Autobiography* by General of the Army Omar N. Bradley and Clay Blair. Copyright © 1983 by Omar N. Bradley and Clay Blair. Reprinted by permission of William Morris Agency, LLC on behalf of the Authors.

Excerpts from *The Links of the Chain (Les Maillons de la Chaîne)*, written by Henry F. Siaud in 1983 and reproduced privately. Translated by Joseph E. Garland and used with permission of Henry F. Siaud.

Excerpts from *Mein Kampf* by Adolf Hitler, translated by Ralph Manheim. Copyright © 1943, renewed 1971 by Houghton Mifflin Company. Reprinted by permission of Houghton Mifflin Harcourt Publishing Company. All rights reserved.

Quotes from "News From Old Friends," an editorial by Harold B. Johnson, July 16, 1943 in *The Watertown Daily Times*, Watertown, New York, p. 4. Copyright © 1943 by The Watertown Daily Times. Reprinted by permission.

Quote and excerpts from *Not So Wild a Dream* by Eric Sevareid. Reprinted by permission of Don Congdon Associates, Inc. Copyright © 1946 by Eric Sevareid, renewed 1974 by Alfred A. Knopf.

Excerpts from *The Patton Papers, Volume II*, edited by Martin Blumenson. Copyright © 1974 by Martin Blumenson. Reprinted by permission of Houghton Mifflin Harcourt Publishing Company. All rights reserved.

Quotes and excerpts from *The Rock of Anzio. From Sicily to Dachau. A History of the 45th Division*, by Flint Whitlock. First Edition originally published by Westview Press, A Division of HarperCollins Publishers, Inc. Copyright © 1998 by Westview Press, A Division of HarperCollins Publishers, Inc. Reprinted by permission of The Perseus Books Group.

Excerpt and quote from *Sicily—Salerno—Anzio: January 1943–June 1944*, History of United States Naval Operations in World War II, Vol IX by Samuel Eliot Morison. Copyright © 1954. By permission of Little Brown & Company.

"1. 'Vale' from Carthage (*for my brother, G.S.V. Jr., 1918–44, killed fighting the Nazis*)" from "Two Elegies" in Section Two of Part II Ore (Shorter Poems, Both New and Old). From *Tide and Continuities: Last and First Poems 1995–1938* by Peter Viereck. First Edition published by University of Arkansas Press. Reprinted by permission of Peter Viereck and the University of Arkansas Press.

Quotes and excerpt from *World War II Fighter-Bomber Pilot*, Second Edition by Bill Colgan. Copyright © 1988 by Sunflower University Press®. Reprinted by permission of William B. "Bill" Colgan.

Excerpts from *The Youngest of the Family* by Joseph Garland, M.D., pp. 5, 171, Cambridge, Mass.: Harvard University Press, Copyright © 1932 by the President and Fellows of Harvard College.

Images on pages 390, 401 and 405 are courtesy of the United States Holocaust Memorial Museum. The views or opinions expressed in this book and the context in which the images are used, do not necessarily reflect the views or policy of, nor imply approval or endorsement by, the United States Holocaust Memorial Museum.

Quotes and extracts of interviews conducted by the author for the purposes of writing this book are used with permission to reproduce, edit and publish their words as he sees fit, and have been edited as necessary for the purposes of clarity in the narrative. The interviewees are acknowledged by name on page 475. Archival audio recordings of these interviews are available online at www.UnknownSoldiersMemoir.com. Though the author strove to convey accurately in print the accents and word choices of the men, and to preserve the vernacular of the time, he has not added formal annotations such as ellipses and [*sic*] except where, in his judgment, this is necessary. Thus, the audio recordings and the printed book complement each other but are not exact word-for-word renderings.

To Monk,
Jerry, Jimmy and Doug.
And to the rest I know of,
departed,
yet with us still.

HERE RESTS IN HONORED GLORY
AN AMERICAN SOLDIER KNOWN BUT TO GOD

Tomb of the Unknowns
Arlington National Cemetery

GOTT MIT UNS
(GOD IS WITH US)

German soldier's belt buckle,
World War II

ONLY TAKE HEED TO THYSELF, AND KEEP THY
SOUL DILIGENTLY, LEST THOU FORGET THE THINGS
WHICH THINE EYES HAVE SEEN, AND LEST THEY
DEPART FROM THY HEART ALL THE DAYS OF THY LIFE:
BUT TEACH THEM THY SONS, AND THY SONS' SONS.

Deuteronomy 4:9

Contents

Up Front

The king is not bound to answer the particular endings of his soldiers,
the father of his son, nor the master of his servant; for they purpose not their death,
when they purpose their services.

The King, in Shakespeare's *Life of King Henry V*,
Act IV, Scene 1

EVEN AS I, AT EIGHTY-FIVE, close the book sixty-five years later, I confess in the recollection of it all to a tinge of what we now call post-traumatic stress disorder. No, none of us purposed our death when we purposed our services to President Roosevelt and to our country back in the 1940s.

This book was embarked upon in March 1943 in the form of a journal—a catch-as-catch-can record of whatever lay ahead of me, a bottom-of-the-pile volunteer in the United States Infantry when the USA was viewed as the last hope of a more or less civilized world grappling with the most evil force in the recorded history of mankind. Six months after I signed up for battle, not long after the Allied invasion of Italy, I landed in ravaged Naples with the first contingent of American casualty replacements in Europe and was assigned to the Intelligence & Reconnaissance Platoon of about thirty front-line scouts and observers in the 45th Infantry Division's 157th Regiment, already baptized in the battle to drive the Germans from Sicily after their expulsion from North Africa.

Soon after the nearly repelled landing of the Yanks and Brits in Salerno, Italy, I was cautiously up on the stalemated Winter Line in the almost straight-up steepness of the Apennine Mountains and incautiously under hit-or-miss enemy fire until January 1944. Then five months of leisurely twenty-four hour duty as target practice for the Krauts on the Anzio Beachhead; then the "Champagne Campaign" liberation of southern France; a bout with malaria; a leisurely AWOL return to the front; and a leg injury falling down a barn loft ladder during an enemy barrage that hospitalized me back to Italy as our Platoon approached the Vosges in northeastern France. My buddies went on to fight the desperate Battle of the Bulge, and finally, on the verge of the end of the war in Europe, to liberate Dachau, the prototype concentration camp, where they at the last moment saw and smelled what it was all about before carrying on to occupy the very Munich beer hall from which *der Führer* had loosed his Holocaust.

Over the course of the following months, as a field-hospital driver in the Volturno Valley east of Naples, I absorbed an Army manual on journalism as a postwar career, was hooked and mulled over the idea of a book about it all. My first attempt around 1947—after graduating from Harvard and getting a job with the Associated Press in Boston—I couldn't write myself into my first day in action.

Thirty years of journalism, free-lance writing and books, and in 1978, the haunting compulsion resurfaced. I realized that this was really the *collective* story of our Platoon and by no means mine alone. So I turned to my old comrades around the country, one leading to another, ferreting them out, interviewing them with my newshound know-how and with bottle and camera in hand, and discovering that few if any of us had talked of our war to anyone. Well, we old buddies, under the magic of our mutuality and lurking, unrecognized sense of guilt (for lack of a better word) over having survived while so many others hadn't, unloaded our burdensome memories and terror and denial, talked and talked and almost wept and laughed and roared. They granted me, every one, unreserved freedom of publication in the bargain. Ninety taped hours, much of it available on the *Unknown Soldiers* website (www.UnknownSoldiersMemoir.com) along with their friendly faces.

Yet, though I wrote and rewrote, I still could not get myself and our book past the roadblock of my first day in action. Why?

More productive years passed—but still no war book—until in 1994 Veterans Administration psychiatrist Jonathan Shay, MD, published his landmark study, *Achilles in Vietnam,* wherein he recognized virtually the identical psycho-emotional disorder among Vietnam vets and the survivors of the Trojan War in the twelfth century B.C. described by Homer. In an intense discussion at my home one evening, Doctor Shay helped me to project myself retrospectively from my particular rung on what he described as "the ladder of guilt" for surviving as one's buddies died.

That was the first step, and it enabled me to rear back, charge through my baptism of fire and write *our* book. But a more significant second step toward insight revealed itself to me recently as I awakened from a troubled night's sleep, and it harked back not to my first day in action but to my last, when I was hospitalized back to Italy for a cut on my left shin in a fall down a rickety ladder in a barn in France, trying to gain observations of the enemy under their artillery fire.

My "wound" wholly healed, and though entirely fit for return to action with my buddies in France, my sympathetic Army surgeon reclassified me as *unfit* for further combat, and I was reassigned to the Medical Corps as a driver in a station hospital in the countryside east of Naples, whose commander just happened to be an old medical friend of my influential doctor father back in Boston, as was another friend, the Chief of Surgery for the

European Theater of War. A third colleague of Pa, running an Army hospital in Naples, looked me up, congratulated me and declared that after nearly a year of it I'd had enough.

And dear old Jimmy Dowdall, ninety-six now and one of the last four of us left alive in our Platoon, was wounded in action three times before they declined to return him to his buddies.

So now at last, in this moment of revelation and with a lump in my throat, I hereby face up to what's *really* been gnawing at me for sixty-five years. Flat on a stretcher on the ambulance plane back to Italy, my first time aloft, I was overcome by dread that the symbolic loss of my helmet, which had disappeared somewhere between hospitals in France, would cost me my life if I returned to action. Now I realize that through my years of focusing on my helmet's loss I was only silently rationalizing the loving, but never revealed, undoubted intervention of my father to rescue me from my war.

Thus the letdown of my buddies back on the front, thus the "guilt," thus the book.

❖ ❖ ❖

And we Unknown Soldiers? The Greatest Generation? No, we occasionally pulled off what had to be done. My vote for "Greatest Generation"—with all respect, love and loyalty for my own—goes back to our Revolution of men and women who fought, sacrificed, suffered and died for their freedom from a distant, contemptuous, arbitrary and rather stupid emperor across three thousand miles of ocean. They were the generation that produced the most noble documents in human history, the United States Constitution and Bill of Rights, the generation of my particular forefathers here in Gloucester, Massachusetts, once the greatest fishing port in the New World, who met in Town Meeting on December 15, 1773, and voted as one: "If we are compelled to make the last appeal to Heaven, we will defend our resolutions and liberties at the expense of all that is dear to us."

And they did.

No one who hasn't been inside war, at war, down-to-the-dirt-and-shit of it can even vaguely imagine it. Those who have waged it and endured it from the ground down, any war, find it an overwhelmingly horrifying nightmare of inexpressible inhuman experience. The naked truth of humanity's (yes, *humanity's*) capability for beastliness is rarely conveyed person-to-person from one generation to the next, or even within its own. Thus each succeeding generation is denied the first-hand lesson of it. And thus this all-too-human urge for self-destruction of our species rebuffs prevention anew and persists in remaining a hidden mine shaft in the human experience known as the "passage to manhood."

This work, then, is an experiment in breaking through that void toward the expression of the duality of what we two-legged mammals regard so jealously, so fearfully, so vulnerably, so utterly humanly, as our *humanity*.

Joe Garland
Eastern Point
Gloucester, Massachusetts
August 2008

ACKNOWLEDGMENTS

To MA AND PA who rarely knew if I was still alive; and to my watchful buddy Jerry who saved my diary, the heart of this work, and has stuck with me ever since we shared a hole in the ground; and to my pal in the Army from Day One, Gareth Dunleavy, renowned literary scholar and avid supporter of our book, who died in 2004; to Jimmy Dowdall and the rest of us beloved "Ironheads," the particular unknown soldiers who are the very soul of this their memorial; to Monk, my guardian angel with the amusing nickname; to my step-daughter Ali whose brilliant major edit restored my faith in myself; to Doctor Jonathan Shay of the Veterans Administration in Boston, author of *Achilles in Vietnam*, who explained to me the now-familiar soldier's survivor's "guilt" syndrome that he recognized from antiquity, thereby freeing untold aging combat vets, including me from my writer's block; to Paul Bertrand, Max Dauphin, Mayor Jean-Pierre Goudal, André Salvetti, Germain Sauvaire, and especially to my old comrade Henry Siaud, for their assistance in reconstructing and memorializing the Varages ambush in which two of our buddies were killed; to Kirsten Sutton of The History Press, whose encouragement was invaluable when I sulked in the dark vales of rejection; to Fred Buck, who rendered every photo almost more real than its subject, and Erik Ronnberg, who made a proper map of our wintry trap; and finally to my publisher and savior Laura Fillmore, right in next-door Rockport all the while, and her superb editors, Elizabeth Foz and Karen Fuhrman, who rescued us Unknowns on the very brink of unknowability.

One and only furlough home. Private Joe Garland and Dr. Joe Garland. (*Collection of the author*)

COME BACK WITH THIS SHIELD,
OR ON IT

Fort Devens, Massachusetts, to Piedimonte d'Alife, Italy
March–October 1943

COLD, GRAY AND MISERABLY RAINY, New England was awash in the dregs of winter as I boarded the train from Boston's North Station with a mixed crowd of collegians for the hour's ride to the Army's induction center at Fort Devens. I was a Harvard junior of twenty on loan to my country, playing cool but nervous, poised on the brink of the Second of the Worst Wars, and about—not to be pushed—but to leap.

It was the eleventh of March, 1943. There were signs that the tide was beginning to turn against Germany, if not yet Japan. On the Eastern Front Adolf Hitler's Wehrmacht (War Power) was pressing on into the Soviet Union, but at the cost of a million men in four months. In the North African desert the dogged British were at last stopping the unstoppable German Afrika Korps with our help. And although the fearsome U-boat submarines of the enemy harassing our convoys at the rate of four ships sunk a day were as close as they would come to winning the Battle of the Atlantic, Europe remained in the iron grip of Nazi tyranny.

For six years during the Great Depression of the 1930s I had commuted from the Boston suburb of Brookline to the nearby Roxbury Latin School for boys, which since 1645 had been preparing us for nearby Harvard College. Our tall, bald, tweedy headmaster and my mentor, George Norton Northrop, a midwesterner with an Oxford education and accent, had been in infantry intelligence on the Western Front during the First War and never spoke of it. I was going on seventeen as Hitler was crushing Poland in September of 1939 the morning Baldy welcomed us back from summer vacation with "Before it's over, boys, you'll be over there fighting the Nazzis."

My first impression of old Fort Devens was that after only twenty-five years, here we go again, we progeny of the First Worst War, in the same bumbling, mixed-up snake-lines among the same rows of reactivated frame barracks, supply depots, motor pools, mess halls and shithouses, all dull, drab, chilly and drizzled-upon in the same gliding glop of mud. My father, a children's doctor, was worried that I hadn't brought along my rain rubbers.

The next morning a stripped and shivering line of us shuffled through our physicals under the disgusted gaze of the medical officer, who'd plainly initiated enough bathless ones in the fore-and-aft inspection to merit permanent return from private parts to private practice. Each mandatory viewing closed with a sigh and "All right, turn around, bend over and spread your cheeks."

Sensing that I might be off on something worth recording, I'd brought along a small notebook. Second night: "Called out of bed for some crazy fire alarm at eleven. Put on our neckties, wandered around in the barracks and went back to bed again." Third night: "Detailed as Night Fireman in charge of the coal stove. Almost all of us nearly asphyxiated with the smoke and gas from my brew. Opened door and all froze."

With the career expectations—real and presumed—of three generations of Doctor Joe Garlands hanging over me, I'd enrolled in the Harvard pre-medical courses as early as 1941, applied for admission to four medical schools and joined the Army's Enlisted Reserve Corps in the summer of 1942 as a junior to defer military service until I had my medical degree. Fortunately, destiny intervened, and I flunked the unfathomable but essential-to-pass pre-med course of organic chemistry with the spectacular grade of fourteen out of a hundred, quite possibly a record.

Meanwhile, the Allied invasion of Sicily was agreed upon in Casablanca by President Roosevelt and Prime Minister Churchill in January of 1943 as a cautious first step toward reclaiming Europe via "the underbelly of the Axis,"[1] as the PM airily dismissed Italy and Sicily with what would be written in bloodshed as one of the more unfortunate metaphors in the lexicon of military strategy. The Enlisted Reserve Corps, to which we had committed ourselves for scholastic deferment, was prematurely mobilized as a partial source of replacements for anticipated casualties. Many if not most of us collegians who entrained for war that March were not yet twenty-one, eligible to die in the cause of freedom but not to vote on the matter.

On our third day in the Fort Devens version of World War II, as nominal volunteers we were offered some choice as to the arm of the United States Army in which we desired to serve. "I told the interviewer," I wrote in my first letter home, "that I was interested in the Motorized Infantry. He didn't know the branch but suggested that perhaps the Mechanized Cavalry was like it. At any rate I am down for the former, or the latter as an alternative. Probably I stand a good chance of getting into this branch, where I understand that opportunities of advancement are among the highest."

The reaction of my parents, who, bless them, refrained from chiding me after such an irreversible plunge, could have been no less incredulous than the sergeant's—and I was in the infantry. Getting out in one piece was chancy, wherein of course lay the vaunted opportunities of advancement for the survivors, until the next action. As for the alternative, I would soon enough learn that "mechanized cavalry" meant tanks. The sort of impulsive young fool war thrives on, in exercising the one and only option of my nascent career in the military I swung from flunking pre-med at Harvard to flunking the first lesson of survival out there: never volunteer. No wonder soldiers are plucked young. About-facing from healing to homicide, I thought through the implications of neither.

In the distraction of war, that fortunate failure to launch upon the wrong career relieved me for the moment, anyway, of my generational baggage. For the first time in my young life I could do what I would with it—gamble it, lose it, but, by God, try making something of it on my own, as stripped of protections and impediments as when I shivered in that inspection line.

"You were the focus of awe and consternation among the rest of us," my Harvard ERC classmate Norman Byrnes would recall wryly sixty years later. He too was destined to be a foot soldier but not as a foolhardy volunteer.

And consternation if not awe since at least twelve years previously, when I was eight and my father, an eminent children's doctor, confided to his diary that I was "a considerable trial, and we devoutly wish that something would happen to change his attitude." Pa's child-rearing creed was there for all to read in the first of his guidebooks for parents, *The Youngest of the Family*.

> ... "Like father, like son" is an axiom that is as true as it is old, and we must remember that to the child the parent is the pattern of perfection. It is a tribute to us as well as a responsibility on us that we should be expected to provide the models on which our children would wish to mold their lives, and no greater success can come to the worthy parent than to raise a worthy successor by precept and example. The battle of Waterloo, history tells us, was won on the cricket fields of Eton, and the battle of life may be won or lost on the playground or in the nursery.[2]

Or on the field of battle?

Come back with this shield, or on it. How many times at the dinner table had Pa directed to me this Spartan command of the Spartan mothers bidding their sons off to battle and death? And why?

Doctor Joe's advice to mothers (including mine, I assume) was to curb the mothering. "It is in what he is to become that we are interested, even more than in what he is, and to the attainment of this end our early care and guidance must be aimed. Thus we refrain from picking him up and amusing him when he cries, no matter what maternal instinct dictates, because we know that such indulgence will tend to make him self-willed and irritable as he grows older."[3]

I was just sixteen when Pa grumbled to his diary that "Joey is frequently trying almost beyond one's ability to endure—uncooperative, impudent, rude and overbearing, but I suppose it is simply part of a particularly uncontrolled adolescent period. I hope he will outgrow it before too long. Some people never do."

Mira and Doctor Joe with their two-year-old, 1924 (*Collection of the author*)

Home on Brookline's "Pill Hill," a bastion of Boston doctors and Boston Symphony Orchestra musicians (*Collection of the author*)

Joey at sixteen with Ma, on the beach in ancestral Gloucester, Massachusetts, 1938 (*Collection of the author*)

Joe Garland: a kid in a big cap (*Collection of the author*)

"Arr, hold still and lemme knock that chip off yer shoulder," he'd growl, raising a fist in mock retaliation against some infuriating boyish hyperbole. "Square peg in a round hole"—"Agin' the government"—"Everybody's outta step but Joey."

Well, I suppose so. I loved and admired and resented him—charismatic, compassionate, brilliant, handsome, lyrical, whimsical, wise, obsessive and insecure. A "blue baby" long before there was surgical repair for his congenital heart defect of patent ductus arteriosis, patients and friends fussed over him, and his family revolved around him in reflexive dread of his sudden demise at any time of day or night.

My lovely mother, Mira Crowell, the belle of a rurally rooted New Hampshire family, was a vital and superb head nurse at the Massachusetts General Hospital in Boston during the influenza pandemic of 1918–19 when she and the handsome intern fell in love. From the day of their marriage in 1921 Ma was his home nurse/secretary, arranger of everything, and resident referee of the demands of her husband and the needs of her son and vice versa, always expressing far more on his behalf than on her own.

In September of 1942 I turned twenty. The Allies invaded French North Africa in November. President Roosevelt and Prime Minister Churchill agreed at their Casablanca Conference the following January that once driven from Africa, the Germans would be pursued up through Sicily and presumably the mountains of Italy, the PM's underbelly of Europe.

Casualty replacements would be required. That false haven for postponement of the fateful day, the Enlisted Reserve Corps, was placed on alert for active duty, and reality caught up with us on the eleventh of March, 1943, as a trainload of college boys clickety-clacked off on a wide-open and conceivably terminal change of careers.

Flouting the laws of chance as I had the rules of reason, I would survive my bravado, petulance, fantasy, foolishness, rebelliousness, recklessness, innocence, ignorance, patriotism, Harvard hubris and inherited Puritanism. Not to mention an occasional dip into the warm bath of self-pity; but never outright self-destructiveness. No, I was full of energy and excitement and on the very verge of learning for the first time in my cramped and limited experience what it was to love life.

As a schoolboy I knew that since Roman times it was the foot soldier who closed in hand-to-hand hacking with the designated enemy, took the ground inch by bloody inch and shaped the course of empire. But except for the passing shadow of the First War cast in 1930 by the staggering motion picture *All Quiet on the Western Front,* I was as ignorant of the trench warfare in the aftermath of which I'd been born, and of the literature and unlearned lessons it produced, as my country was barely brushed by it.[4]

Even as the events of September 1939 had portended the end of the economic Depression, they succored the ten-year depression of the American spirit with the ever-renewable antidote of war and the going-off to it. The intensity, the camaraderie, the manliness and the togetherness, the sweep of action, the hope and fear of heroism, the recruitment of the movies and the musicals, Kilroy, Bob Hope, the dramatics, the Americanism, the invention of the Home Front, the poignancy of sacrifice.

And always the poet Horace's immortal siren song to the Infantry of Rome: *Dulce et decorum est pro patria mori!* It is sweet and honorable to die for one's country.

Sweet indeed.

A mere twenty-five years after that first war to end all war my generation of Americans was insulated from it by the unspeakable and unspoken-of horror of it. Our fathers would not speak of it, the dead could not, and as for us, like the German youth, we would follow the preordained path.

I confronted neither the prospect of murdering another human being nor of objection to it, conscientious or otherwise, nor did the others. The only living thing beyond insect, fish or duck I'd wiped out was a squirrel once with a .22 rifle. Shooting someone in hot or cold blood? That's what they were brainwashing us for, beyond the horizon of our innocent imaginations three thousand miles across the sea.

Curious, because aggression was as unsublimated in us as compassion. I would discover that the great majority in this most personally confrontational of the armed services shared an abhorrence of violence and were foot soldiers by designation, not choice. Except that I was not the only uncertain one saved by harsh reality from learning too late that he had embarked on the wrong life course or from not learning that living was not the sole object of life, or sweetness and honor that of death by the sword.

Was it adolescent fascination with action and to hell with the consequences, a chosen rite of passage, off to the Foreign Legion of the psyche to prove strength and manhood? Was it penance in a far-off arena for the fear of a bruising on the football field, for shyness with the girls, for failing the father by faltering in the footsteps?

Impatient with my incautiousness, I'm sure my cautious father viewed this latest and possibly last display with mixed feelings. We didn't discuss the *risk factor,* a term of caution not yet current, nor is there a mention of my enlistment in his careful diary. Such indulgence was not for fathers and sons, though he must have agonized with my brave and duty-bound mother. Back in 1915, during his senior year at Harvard, medically ineligible for service and in revulsion against the carnage in Europe, he wrote six poems I discovered eighty-two years later and fifty-four years after my war, concluding with "Afterwards," which begins:

> A sovereign speaks a word; princes command,
> And war, black as the plague, spreads through the land

and ends:

> You are the pawn, moved by a mightier hand;
> You are the Christian martyr, living brand
> That lights the kingly orgy of that king
> To whom *you* homage bring.
> This is your lot, oh Common Man; is it your choice?
> When war takes all do *you* rejoice—

Father and brother, son and livelihood,
Leaving all evil where was once all good?
Another commands your destiny.
Are you less fitted for that task than he?
Freedom and life are offered you; now choose,
Nor overlong debate, nor yet refuse,
And when the stricken land raises its head,
May you, rising from burial of your dead,
Stand by your brother, teaching him to see—
YOU, the director of your destiny.

Pa's only brother, my equally handsome Uncle Kimball Garland, Harvard 1911, would serve as a young officer in the Army Engineers on the Western Front in France, of which I only recall his remarking that a shell fragment ripped across the front of his coat without touching him.

So here was I, oh Common Man, the director of *my* destiny.

Ten more days and we were in the all-white section of a segregated troop train bound for Camp Croft, outside Spartanburg, South Carolina, hotter by the mile, sleepless in our grimy seats, sweaty, choking and caked with soot and cinders that flew in the open windows from the chugging, smoking steam engine up ahead as we clattered over the tracks of the Southern Railway. Croft was a mold for reconstituting twenty thousand civilians, nearly all conscripted draftees, into the shape of infantry casualty replacements in exactly thirteen weeks. We were organized into oversize companies of four platoons of sixty men each, one platoon to a two-story frame barrack on stilts to keep out varmints, with tar-paper roof, latrine and showers.

Hardly was I made a temporary barracks squad leader under Corporal Mazurowski, a muscular, good-natured Polack who addressed us as "youse men" and tossed firecrackers at our tangled feet on the drill field, when I was hospitalized with a respiratory infection and fever of 104 and replaced. Abed, I read *All Quiet on the Western Front,* better or not late than never, and pondered this strange cousin of the North, the segregated South, and for all of us, white and black, the segregated United States Army. I wrote home:

> I don't know what to make of the Southerners I've seen so far. Many have more than
> a suspicion of good-natured laziness and unreliability in their appearance. As a rule,
> Yankees have little animosity toward the South. Perhaps we're more condescending
> than we suspect. Typically, Negroes are separated from Whites in the wards by par-
> titions. All the colored troops I've run across have been neat and clean, well-disci-
> plined, and look like splendid soldiers, which I understand they are.

Much of our equipment was left over from the last Great War and older than we were—canvas cartridge belts with attached first-aid kits, mess kits, canteens and their cups, canvas folding field packs and pup-tent shelter halves with wooden poles and pegs, and gas masks and canisters. Synthetics not having dawned on the military, wool and its itch kept us alert as well as warm, while the heavy cotton tans and green fatigues of spring and summer kept us sweating. Camouflage was unknown. Leggins, or canvas puttees, were still laced up the calf to enclose pants cuffs below the knee, sufficient insulation against the mud of Ypres a mere quarter-century before, and the flat-crowned helmets of World War I had only recently been turned in for the more enveloping contour adopted by Hitler's Wehrmacht.

Drill, drill, drill. Like scales to the musician, close-order drill came before all else in the rearrangement of youse men into dogfaces, first with tangled feet and arms askew, then with rifles, and then with the age-old manual of arms. And then one day we got it almost all together, the long and the short and the tall, the fat and the thin and the small, and sur-rendered to the primal swinging of a human centipede that lurched this way and that to the proud bark of its trainer as foot soldiers have been responding since the commands were roared out in Latin across the plains of Tuscany.

Lectures on sanitation, first aid, squad tactics, aircraft spotting, skirmishing, nomen-clature of the new M1 semi-automatic rifle, and the situation in North Africa. The obstacle course: "UP, UP, UP AND OVER, YOUSE MEN! DOUBLE TIME! JUMP!" And bayonet drill. We'd been ex-civilians for less than three weeks when we were issued World War I bayonets and instructed in hand-to-hand combat.

Great battle training for swinging on ropes under rifle fire, scaling fences under machine-gun fire, and dashing across fields of tires under tank fire (*From U.S. Army Publication* Camp Croft, South Carolina, *December 1941*)

"FIX BAYONETS!" We drew the blades from their scabbards on our belts and ran them onto the slides along our rifle barrels in a chorus of clink-clanks, then lunged like a chorus line at the straw-filled enemy. Our choreographer barked: "THE PARRY! THE PLUNGE!" And the clockwise twist to break the suction of flesh and blood. "Step back, withdraw, and smash down with your rifle butt precisely on the skull, so! UGH!"

Poison-gas drill came before almost all else at Camp Croft. Adolf Hitler had been temporarily blinded in 1918 during a British mustard-gas attack at Ypres. Memories on one side were as long as on the other, and both had immense stockpiles at the ready.

The size of a small portable typewriter and about as useful in the event of a gas attack, the gas mask and canister were slung from right shoulder against left waist, across from the rifle, wherever we were in the field, chafing the swinging left arm, and of course thousands of these detested lifesavers were "mislaid" upon arrival overseas. We were run through a tear-gas chamber, masked and unmasked, and touched on our forearm with a droplet of mustard gas that, untreated with the antidote in the kit, caused a suppurating abscess the faint scar of which I carry to this day.

A more present threat to the developing physiques of Croft's foot soldiers was venereal disease, which to a certain number of us innocents was as distant as its manner of transmission. Captain Day, our Regular Army company commander, an earthy double for Clark Gable who had risen through the ranks, lined us up one morning for a fatherly talk, concluding: "Now I want you men to know that as far as I'm concerned you ain't soljers until you've gone into town and got laid, but God help you if you come back with a dose!" No doubt he scared more of us than he challenged, which may or may not have been his object.

With the dousing of the lights each night, sleep embraced fatigue like a hot bath.

⁂

As the sun rose higher and red hotter over the red clay of the Old Confederacy, the noncoms got down to business. I unloaded on Pa:

> I don't feature this infantry training too much. The whole business is scaled to the level of a moron. Over and over again we have the simplest things explained to us even when only one or two men can't get it. The lieutenant comes up to you with the same dull stare with which he has faced hundreds of others, as if you were just another stupid fool, and when you suggest something that isn't in the books, he looks perplexed, and bawls you out because you aren't as literal-minded as he. The whole platoon has spent all evening cleaning its rifles over and over and over for our senior corporal who is one of the most sadistic maniacs I ever saw . . . I'm having a pretty good time here, really. I only get a little disgusted once in a while, as does everyone. On reading this over, I ask you to take it all with a grain of salt. I was only mad as hell at the corporal![5]

If short on Army experience, Pa was long on life and knew his son.

The chief danger you will run, I think, is that of not being aggressive enough in the promotion of your own interests; if you find yourself overlooked or snubbed or unfairly treated, you're a little too likely to retire into your shell and say "what the hell's the use; if they don't want to recognize a man they needn't." Thereby instead of getting even with the Army, which doesn't give a damn, you'll be simply putting J.E.G. behind the 8 ball.

Almost from our arrival at Croft we sensed that our particular destinies were being shaped. Our Second Platoon was a mix of Irish, Greek, Swiss, German, Polish, Portuguese, English, Jewish, French-Canadian, American Indian (no blacks in this successor to both the Union and Confederate armies), Yankee, collegian (balanced off with two or three illiterates), and such a predominance of Italian backgrounds as to suggest that the Army had something in mind.

Our early exposure to gas drill and the antique quaintness of our equipment evoked the trenches of France, and as our training progressed under conditions that might be encountered anywhere but in the jungle, it concentrated on the circumstances of battle that were familiar to the World War I veterans of France who shaped our curriculum.

"This is a rifle," the United States Army informed Private Girard with his gourmet's potbelly, his cigar, his dishwater hands, and his French accent, Girard who was said to have been J. P. Morgan's chef—and what the hell was HE doing in the Army? And a roly-poly stand-up comedian in another platoon, Sam "Zero" Mostel, who kept his barracks in an uproar of laughter, and a German Jewish refugee of twenty, Henry Kissinger, who doubtless didn't and who at Croft became an American citizen.

And gentle, sad-eyed Saul Goldfarb, untannably soft and white-skinned from hours and days and months at his diamond cutter's bench. A New York diamond cutter, a gem surgeon, in the infantry. We talked and talked about the fates and acts of willfulness that had brought us to this strange pass in our lives. Saul, did you survive?

All scooped up in the indiscriminate (but not color-blind) draft save for the Enlisted Reserve and a few fools like myself.

Off to the immense firing range in our green fatigues, day after day we swung along the coppery dirt road that wound through the peach groves of the soft Carolina countryside blossoming with the southern spring. The enemy was a row of two hundred targets raised and lowered from an abutment of concrete, steel and earth.[6]

From his tower the range officer roared through his megaphone: "READY ON THE RIGHT! READY ON THE LEFT! READY ON THE FIRING LINE!" In lots of two hundred we banged away with our M1 semi-automatic rifles from up to five hundred yards, sounding like Gettysburg. "CEASE FIRING!" Down dropped the targets out of sight, where the pitmen marked the bullet holes with colored disks according to their distance from the bull's-eye and hauled them up on their tracks so we could set down our scores. The waving of a red flag derisively called "Maggie's drawers" signaled an unscathed target.

Gas chamber No. 2 and other pictures from *Camp Croft, South Carolina*. Little did we know. (*U.S. Army, December 1941*)

Already pretty good with a .22-caliber, I qualified as an expert rifleman. They gave me a medal and put me to coaching such foxy duffers as big, gawky Omar Forand from Maine, who admitted neither to literacy nor to knowing left from right. Nor could he decide with which eye to aim, sometimes hitting his neighbor's target, which complicated the scoring. We prayed that he'd fight the war with a mop, which may have been his object.

Just as easily I qualified as expert with the old 1918 model Browning Automatic Rifle on its bipod that pumped out a clip of twenty rounds with a squeeze of the trigger. "There was a good deal of all-round chiseling with both," I admitted to my journal. When we moved on to another heirloom from the late war, the chattering light .30-caliber machine gun, it began to dawn that there were two sides to these Boy Scout medals for marksmanship. This time I merely qualified, having been tipped off by some alarmist that the machine gunner lives an average of nine seconds in battle, hyperbole enough to cloud the clearest eye on the range.

Then the 60-millimeter mortar whose smooth-bore barrel was supported on a ground plate by a pair of folding legs. Distance was determined by the angle of fire and the number of powder charges that ignited when the projectile was dropped down the muzzle onto a firing pin at the bottom that exploded a cap. More explicitly than appropriate I wrote Ma and Pa that "the shell explodes immediately upon contact, killing everything within a radius of fifteen yards and sending fragments as far as 200 yards. When you hear a mortar shell first in front, then in back, you'd better clear out in a hurry."

We learned how to pull the ring on the time fuse of the hand grenade, count out the seconds, hurl it not like a baseball but with a looping swing, and duck, but we never saw one explode. We set up a roadblock and an anti-tank barrier, and weeks later actually saw two tanks.

Marching through the sparse woods of the Old Confederacy, we Yanks crept with our rifles, fanning out in mock attack. We hit the red clay headfirst like sliding into second base, gun butt down to break the fall. Then a fast roll to be somewhere else when the first pre-tend bullets spat dust. We fired blanks at pop-up targets, strung barbed wire, buried dummy land mines but never watched one explode and blew up the enemy's with a banga-lore torpedo. We wired a booby trap but didn't trip it to see what it could do to flesh and bone and blood. We learned, if we could, to read a topographical map, use a compass, strike an azimuth and fumble and crash in the night from Point A to Point B and sometimes even back.

Of the Wehrmacht's huge tanks and their dreaded cannon that overpowered us in North Africa we were told nothing, for good reason. The old-style roadblocks and tank bar-riers of Camp Croft? Already useless even as we practiced erecting them. The sole anti-tank weapon available for training was an antiquated projectile lobbed from the muzzle of a rifle firing a blank round that we tried with dummies. We were shown the new American "secret weapon," the recoilless, shoulder-aimed rocket launcher (minus rocket) nicknamed the bazooka, which we never saw fired.

Our only anti-tank defense was the shovel strapped to our field packs, designed for digging a foxhole, the slightly safer if less sociable model of the trench in which countless had died a short generation earlier. We hiked out to a peach grove, dug holes, filled them in, hiked back and that was that.

City boys, country boys, we traded fat for fiber in the oven of the South, 115 degrees on the drill field by the end of May. Some crumpled in the midday dust. The medics brought them back to life and back to the hospital if need be, and a few never came back to us at all. First the blisters rubbing off the bleeding tenderfeet, and then the calluses on dogs so alienated by sundown that they cowered in your boots, and you wanted nothing more than to shove both foot and leather under the bunk for the night and crawl under the covers in your shinbones.

When every nerve had turned to wire, every muscle to thong, every bone to steel, then your feet, forever your feet, carried you along, left and right, day and night, over hill and dale, through rain and shine, dirt and mud. And you swung through Caroline, mile after mile in full field pack, rifle, gas mask and anything else they told you to carry until you knew every dirty stitch in the bouncing pack in front of you, every sweaty crease in the back of the flaming neck above it, every hitch in the swinging gait.

The sun burned down on the long column of soldiers-in-the-making, swinging and a-winding, tramp, tramp, tramping through the red dust raised on the country road to who knew where, and then was when the sing-song Irish tenor of Dougherty, just "Dockert" from

Brooklyn, the freckled scarecrow with the peeling, turned-up nose, called out clear as a rau-cous altar boy the songs to swing along to, "MacNamara's Irish Band" and "Old MacDonald Had a Farm" and "I've Been Workin' on the Railroad," "Allouette," "The Caissons Go Rolling Along" and "Who Threw the Overalls in Missus Murphy's Chowder?"

And when that magical voice rose like the voice of the albatross above the muffled march and cried out the lilting lyrics, how we threw out the choruses, and the pace picked up, and the aching shoulders lifted! The guns and the packs shed pounds, and for a few miles it all looked almost worth it, whatever it was, and not a bad way to go, wherever we were going.

Weekends our songbird would head for Spartanburg and roll back to the barracks, roaring drunk, provoking a different chorus: "DOCKERTY, SHADDUP!"

At half an inch over six feet, I did everything double-time, ate my way twice through every chow line and watched the scale hit 180 pounds. "I feel fine. Have a great sun burn/tan from my shoulders up and my wrists down. The rest of me is chicken-white since we always stay covered," I wrote home. Hard labor in the rough was my New Hampshire rock-farming heritage, clearing brush, splitting firewood, digging postholes, building stone walls, plowing, pitching hay, backpacking for a week at a time with my school buddy in the wilds of the White Mountains, football, soccer, wrestling, rowing and track.

Strong as a Storm Trooper. But as tough? Ah, we didn't talk about that at Croft.

The camp public relations officer chose Mother's Day, May the fourth of '43, to launch the *Camp Croft Spartan* featuring a homespun cartoon of Mom knitting in her rocking chair, photo of Son in uniform on the console radio at her elbow, Star in the window designating familial sacrifice. Recall the ancient Spartans, the guy wrote. Of course! *Spartanburg*, South Carolina!

The men were clean and courageous; the women brave and stoical. Historians tell us of the Spartan mother whose spirit has seldom been surpassed. As her youngest son set out to war she buckled on his shield and without tears or sighs admonished him: "Come back with this shield—or on it." No half-way exhortation this. Her son must fight to the finish. His shield, a symbol of honor, must be borne back in triumph or become a funeral chariot.

Like the Lacedaemonian mother of the past the mothers of fighting men through the ages have suffered in silence just as they are doing today. Each day some American mother equals or even surpasses the example set by her Spartan sister. Simply, they encourage their sons to fight to a triumphant finish, a glorious victory. It is fitting, therefore, to dedicate to the Mother of every Soldier the first issue of a newspaper which bears the title THE SPARTAN. Send this copy home to her, Soldier, so that she will know you are thinking of her!

There it is again. *Come back with this shield, or on it!* Damn!

To be double-sure we dunces got the point, the PR guy (who was never going to be within three thousand miles of the action) announced in an open letter "To the Best Mother in the World" that his Mother's Day gift was his $10,000 government insurance

CAMP CROFT SPARTAN

VOLUME ONE   CAMP CROFT, S. C., MAY 4, 1943.   NUMBER ONE

CROFT ENTERS THIRD YEAR OF TRAINING MEN

PROGRESS SHOWN

One year and five months after treachery struck the blow at Pearl Harbor that plunged the United States into a bloody war, Camp Croft is well into its third year. Under the able leadership of Maj. Gen Durward S. Wilson, commander of the infantry replacement training center, and Col. Frederick D. Griffith, Jr., post commander, Camp Croft has played an important part in the events which are graven across the pages of history in smoke and flame.

From December, 1940, when the first spadeful of earth was turned up on the site that was later to become one of the finest training camps in the country, the cantonment forged ahead weathering many storms during its period of construction. Then, March 27, 1941, the first group of recruits began to trickle in with Brig. Gen. Louis A. Kunzig in command of the post and entrusted with the task of turning civilians into soldiers steeled to the rigors of modern warfare.

Many changes in the command of the post took place in the ensuing months with Maj. Gen. Oscar W. Griswold, Maj. Gen. Alexander M. Patch, Brig. Gen. Clarence R. Hueber, and Maj. Gen. P. L. Ransom taking the reins in rapid succession.

For a year Camp Croft was a beehive of activity, turning out fighting men for America's armed forces, and then, on April 6, 1942, the citizens of Spartanburg were given the chance to see the results obtained when 1,000 Croft soldiers participated in an army day parade through Spartanburg's main street. April also saw the activation of the first negro regiment at Croft under Col. John D. Newton.

Expansion was still the order of the day when Croft added 1,849 acres of land the following month to take care of the rapidly growing population of South Carolina's "newest city." In June a new unit was added to the cantonment with the formal opening of the induction station near the station hospital.

The first big change in Camp Croft's headquarters set-up since the activation of the camp in September when the infantry replacement training center and the Fourth service command units were split into two distinct departments, with Maj. Gen. Charles F. Thompson named as commandant of the infantry replacement training center, and Col. Griffith designated as post commander. This month also saw Brig. Gen. Reginald W. Buzzell installed as assistant to General Thompson. General Thompson, however, held command of the infantry replacement training center for only two months before Maj. Gen. Durward S. Wilson took active command on Nov. 10, 1942.

On April 18, 1943 Brig. Gen. Francis V. Logan had been named assistant commander of the infantry replacement training center, replacing General Buzzell who had been transferred.

Camp Croft bears the name of the late Maj. Gen. Edward Croft, once chief of infantry, who was

MOTHER'S DAY — 1943

MOTHER'S DAY NOTED IN FIRST CROFT PAPER

SPARTAN PUBLISHED

As a form of tribute to Mother's Day, Sunday, May 9, this first edition of The Camp Croft Spartan makes its appearance as the official camp news organ.

Besides being dedicated to Mother's Day, this issue of The Camp Croft Spartan may be labeled a trial baloon or an experiment to continue the publication on a permanent basis, likely a weekly in an effort to establish a post media for dissemination of news of camp-wide interest.

It is not intended for this issue or any subsequent issue to supercede or interfere with post organizational papers now in existence; nor will this newspaper be a bar to the publication of a paper in the future by any unit.

The Camp Croft Spartan will operate on the policy that it is an enlisted man's paper edited by enlisted men, and be given camp-wide free distribution. No advertising will be carried in accordance to a war department regulation.

While it is sincerely hoped that each individual whose mother is living will make some effort to remember her on Mother's Day as well as others during the year, it is suggested that everyone mail this dedicatory issue to her.

Published by headquarters, Camp Croft, the paper is under the editorship of the post public relations office. The special service office is the financial sponsor of the publication.

Since only a limited amount of space was available for this edition, a considerable amount of articles contributed from various sources had to be held out. However, in the event that the paper is continued, reconsideration will be given these items for future publications. Fullest appreciation is extended to all those who submitted contributions.

The paper is Camp Croft's and consequently its success, if continued in the future, depends on cooperation of all organizations to assist in filling its columns. Write your opinions of this publication to the public relations office, post headquarters, building No. 13.

CITY, CAMP FIX SET TAXI RATE

Establishment of a set price for cabbies to tax patrons for trips to and from Spartanburg and Camp Croft recently was effected through a joint agreement between Spartanburg city council and camp officials. New set rates are:

From Spartanburg's Main and Liberty streets to Camp Croft with one to five passengers, in a 5-passenger cab, one dollar, with the same price holding from camp to aforementioned site in the city. Where a 7-passenger auto is used, the rate is $1.40 for one to seven riders. No charge is allowed for first piece of luggage, but a tax of 10 cents is fixed above one.

DELAWARE WOMAN WINS MOTHER'S DAY CROFT TRIP

Mrs. Grace M. Stigler of Wilmington, Del., is a very lucky mother. She is to spend Mother's Day with her 19-year-old son, Pvt. Charles L. Stigler, in Camp Croft.

It came about this way. Officers and men of Company "C", 26th battalion, figured that they could not get all their mothers here, so they did the next best thing. They pooled their assets and drew the name of one of the trainee's mother in true lottery style. To this mother went an all-expense paid trip to Camp Croft to see her son. Mrs. Stigler will represent all absent mothers and try to take their place at a special Sunday meal given in her honor.

Private Stigler came in the army last January 2. Prior to his coming into the service, Private Stigler worked in a shipyard in Wilmington, Del.

born and reared in nearby Greenville, S. C. The suggestion of the Croft name came from General Kunzig, first commander of the post, and currently post commander of Camp Blanding, Fla.

Mother's Day Dedication

Many centuries ago in the Ancient World the name of Spartan was one feared and respected by all civilized and semi-civilized nations. The men were clean and courageous; the women brave and stoical. Historians tell us of the Spartan mother whose spirit has seldom been surpassed. As her youngest son set out to war she buckled on his shield and without tears or sighs admonished him: "Come back with this shield—or on it." No half-way exhortation this. Her son must fight to the finish. His shield, a symbol of honor, must be borne back in triumph or become a funeral chariot.

Like the Lacedaemonian mother of the past the mothers of fighting men through the ages have suffered in silence just as they are doing today. Each day some American mother equals or even surpasses the example set by her Spartan sister. Simply, they encourage their sons to fight to a triumphant finish, a glorious victory. It is fitting, therefore, to dedicate to the Mother of every Soldier the first issue of a newspaper which bears the title THE SPARTAN. Send this copy home to her, Soldier, so that she will know you are thinking of her!

Post Public Relations Officer.

HOLY NAME TO HONOR MOTHERS

Camp Croft's Holy Name Societies will mark Mother's Day May 9, with a communion-breakfast in Spartanburg, with visiting mothers as special guests.

Mass will be celebrated on the lawn of St. Paul's Roman Catholic church and convent, North Dean street in Spartanburg, at 8 a.m., with the breakfast gathering fixed for the Cleveland hotel in the city. The latter event will begin shortly after 9 a.m. Reservations for the breakfast are limited to 200. Tickets may be obtained at the NCCS-USO hall, North Dean street.

As a feature of the breakfast program, special honor will be given the mother in attendance who has the most sons serving the colors.

The Croft Knights of Columbus group also is cooperating with the Mother's Day event.

You KNOW you are well, but your mother doesn't. Why not write and tell her so!

(U.S. Army)

policy so that "your little boy will know that if the worst happens, there will be a check for you as long as you live ... Give my love to Dad and tell him all the fellows' Dads are buying war bonds like he is so we will have something to fight with and to make the other fellow give his life for his country instead of us."

I don't know how my Ma reacted to the Mother's Day issue of the *Camp Croft Spartan*, but besides her son she gave twenty or thirty pints of her blood to her country, which was a hell of a lot more than he did.

In *Mein Kampf* Hitler had addressed the sons and mothers of the Fatherland in a similar vein just ten years previously:

> ... the folkish State has not the task of breeding a colony of peaceful aesthetes and physical degenerates. Not in the honest petty *bourgeois* or in the virtuous old maid does it see its ideal of humanity, but in the robust incorporation of manly forces and in women who in their turn are able to bring men into the world ...
>
> *It is precisely our German people, that today, broken down, lies defenseless against the kicks of the rest of the world, who need that suggestive force that lies in self-confidence. But this self-confidence has to be instilled into the young fellow citizen from childhood on. His entire education and development has to be directed at giving him the conviction of being absolutely superior to others. With his physical force and skill he has again to win the belief in the invincibility of his entire nationality.*[7]

Our assumption of our American invincibility had been shaken on February 20 when those manly other fellows out-gunned, out-armored, out-soldiered, and threw out our ill-prepared 34th Infantry Division from the Kasserine Pass in Tunisia. Although the outfit redeemed itself on Hill 609 on the first of May, the lesson was slow reaching home.

Discipline in the American Army continued to be consented to by civilians who tacitly relinquished their right of self-determination under the necessity of conducting a war against totalitarian enemies. Whether we fought more effectively under the terms of such a compact is arguable. Our brass persisted in underestimating the professionalism of the Germans and the fanaticism of the Japanese, and the discipline, will, skill and courage of both in the service of false idols.

On May 13 the last German and Italian troops in North Africa surrendered, and I wrote home that "here in camp the consensus of opinion seems to be that the victory in Africa will send us to combat sooner."

In ten more days the eight weeks allotted to transforming us from aesthetes, sissies and physical degenerates into conquerors of the invincible were completed. Soon enough we'd discover that the only real training ground for war is war. But give them credit; at Croft our teachers came as close as they dared, and it was something to write home about.

> Yesterday was the toughest day we've had so far. We rose at 5 and didn't get to bed until 12:30 the next morning—a good 20-hour day. In short, we went through the "Battle Inoculation Course" til supper, then went on a seven-mile hike. The course consisted of a bad obstacle course with lots of barb wire to be crawled under. Then we went through an hour of village fighting. Squads cleaned out a village of small frame houses equipped with surprise targets. We went through with rifles, B.A.R.s, carbines, machine guns—loaded and cocked. This was done under simulated battle conditions. Charges of dynamite went off under our noses, and our own men fired right by our heads!
>
> Then we went down to the demolition course, learned to use dynamite and make sticky bombs and booby traps. We made a sticky bomb from a sock filled with

three sticks of dynamite and coated with axle grease. We threw this at a double tree, and it split down the middle. Where it split was around three or four feet in diameter! Those things will blow the tracks off a medium tank and destroy the personnel. Then we went through a grenade course which consisted of crawling through the woods for an hour tossing dummy grenades at targets here and there.

Finally we went through the infiltration course. We lay in the first ditch. When the machine guns began firing we crawled out on our bellies with our rifles. There was a curtain of machine gun fire 36 inches above the ground and about two feet over us. When we reached the wire (strung about six inches off the ground), we rolled over on our backs and wiggled through it, holding each strand over ourselves as we passed under. Dynamite was being set off in the craters all the time, and we consequently got our faces full of dirt and well shaken up. The strip of wire was about ten yards long. Then we rolled over on our stomachs and crawled into the last ditch. When everyone was in the ditch we threw a stick of dynamite at the dummies. We were exhausted by supper but had to hike back for four hours in the dark.

From that day on at least, we were inoculated, if not with battle antibodies, then with the reflex to hug the ground at every big bang. A three-day walking bivouac of sixty miles capped a couple of more weeks of tactical exercises and hikes. I was a squad leader. Our company attacked three objectives through mud and brambles, and three twin-engine, twin-tailfin B-25s lumbered over our heads, threw a few random machine-gun bursts into the hillside beyond and bombed us with bags of flour.

Thus ended our formal training for battle. My new close buddy Gareth Dunleavy (a lanky student from Clark University, who'd volunteered for the infantry after failing the physical for the Marines and now cursed the military with every dragging step) would dismiss it all in retrospect as "nonsense cooked up by men who had never seen combat and had no idea what the real situation was like."

The shortcomings of our basic training were owing to lack of American experience in the field in the spring of 1943 and to the hard fact that our bunch from Croft were not to go into battle as a seasoned unit but as spare parts, casualty replacements generally denied opportunities for promotion and leadership, and destined neither to fight together nor die together.

Home in Brookline for a week toward the end of June on his only furlough of the war, G.I. Joe was made much of, striding around town in uniform. The old gang was gone. Ma's home cooking was all the *Spartan* said it should be. Son and father posed for a snapshot, son standing at parade rest, overseas cap the prescribed finger's width over the right eyebrow, necktie tucked in shirt just so, hands in back pockets, hoping he looked like a man to be reckoned with—father assuming a stance of stern approbation, hoping so too.

I'd hardly returned to Croft when on July 8 our Seventh Army under General George S. Patton and the British Eighth Army under General Bernard L. Montgomery, veterans of the North Africa war, invaded German-occupied Sicily in the first Allied landing on the European continent since its occupation by the Wehrmacht.

Second Platoon, Company C, 35th Infantry Battalion, Camp Croft, June 1943. Top row, fourth from left, Garland. Seventh from left, Dunleavy. Fourth row, in front of Garland, Goldfarb, then Furber. Below Dunleavy in the third row, Dave Goss. Standing, Corporals Mazurowski (*left*) and Magnuson (*right*). (*U.S. Army*)

As if on cue a hundred or so of us Crofters were on the train for Camp Rucker ("Fuckin' Rucker") outside Dothan in the southeastern Alabama rattlesnake and water-moccasin everglades, where we Yanks were loosely attached to the 134th "All Hell Can't Stop Us" Regiment of the southern 35th Infantry Division, in whose 129th Field Artillery Missouri Senator Harry Truman had served as a young captain in the Meuse-Argonne in 1918.

Our apparent mission: mark time until further orders, keep in condition and provide some diversion for the poor guys in their endless weekly maneuvers, when this chainless chain gang was marched out of camp to play war in country that combined the worst of the jungle with the worst of the desert, then marched back to captivity. Passes were regarded by the recipients as one-way tickets to as far away as possible and rarely issued. We tagalongs could only have added to their housekeeping problems, but misery will settle for almost any company.

One might wonder if Senator Truman had intervened to keep his old outfit out of harm's way. The 35th was said to have been on alert for overseas assignment since March and wouldn't fight its second war in Europe for another year, when the poor guys would post three thousand casualties at St.-Lô, Vire and Mortain.

Even as the brilliant withdrawal of the Germans toward Messina and escape to Italy was being hailed as a rout, I fretted for action. I wrote home that "I'm not so anxious to get a rating or commission as I am to get where I can feel that all my sweat is for a cause. I hope I can either join some volunteer outfit such as the Mountain Troops or Air Corps, or that all of us, either the new men or the whole 35th will be moved positively and decisively in the direction of combat."[8]

In mid-August, five days after it was decided that in September the U.S. Fifth Army, newly organized out of Patton's Third, would breach the continent of Europe south of Naples on the beach at Salerno, the last German safely crossed the Strait of Messina to Italy. Three more days and we Crofters were told to make our wills. I mailed mine home and raised the war-bond allotment to $6.25 out of my fifty-a-month pay.

Allied bombing was said to be retarding Germany's industrial output, and I thought it would be all over in a few months. Crushing the enemy beyond any ability to start a third world war, I wrote home, was the only answer.

> We must profit, in at least that respect, by Versailles. Cities must be leveled, armies crushed, and spirits utterly broken. I think Russia's claims at the peace will be limit-ed to the northern shores of the Black Sea, plus the Balkan States, plus part of Poland. They need a western seaboard and the protection against future European aggression the Black Sea affords. I think Russia basically desires only the security to develop behind a decent set of borders.
>
> We'll be doing a greater service for the postwar world if we set an example of what a really working democracy can do. Ever since we've been a world power, the tide of global fortunes has been governed by the state of American affairs. To settle the European mess is not our problem. Our duty must not be to police and mediate for the world, but for our hemisphere alone—to build our own fortress and to gov-ern our lives for ourselves without meddling with a parcel of squabblers who have brought us only grief in the past.

On August 24 we slung our barracks bags aboard the train for Camp Patrick Henry in Virginia, staging area for the port of embarkation of Newport News and overseas. Made an acting staff sergeant hopefully "in charge" of a Pullman carload of thirty-eight other replacements, I sewed on my stripes and thought it "a great bubble to be called sergeant by the men and other real NCOs" (noncommissioned officers). A bubble all right. "The train commander gave all acting NCOs recommendations as excellent noncommissioned officer material," I journaled. "There was a reorganization when we reached here, and I was reduced to acting corporal, mainly because I refuse to suck ass and also because I didn't happen to be around at the right time. Some of the acting NCOs now are perfect morons, so I don't mind so much." And though I was in the top 10th of the 250 in my company who took the Army Specialization Test, reassignment for special training was as remote as advancement. Camp Croft's monthly quota for Officers Candidate School was forty out of 20,000, and applications weren't being accepted.

So I was a buck-ass private in the infantry. No one talked about the casualty rate among second lieutenant platoon leaders. Fate had grinned at me.

Off on the first, the greatest, and what the hell, maybe the last (but who dared talk of *that?*) adventure of our endless young lives, how we were swept along! Scantily armored with the thin skin of untested fatalism, we many who tried to serve submitted our destinies to the frailties of the few who tried to lead.

As the sons of the generation of the self-styled lost, we were citizen-soldiers of a nation by turns euphoric, depressed, hopeful, cynical, idealistic, heroic, banal, self-centered and magnanimous. Now we were the Found Generation, off to shoot up the Bad Guys under FDR, the only Commander-in-Chief we'd ever known. About to get under way for Over There again, ever-zestful Yanks we were, but never again Yankee Doodle Dandies. Verdun, Versailles and Vermouth and their aftermath were our heritage, not Victoria and hers.

Beyond clinging to one another, what would sustain us? What faith? What hope? What symbol of permanence, or hint of immortality?

Well, our dog tags. With what concentrated self-identity we would invest this pair of sweat-corroded icons that hung by their rosary beads of brass from our scrimy necks. Into these ever-rattling talismans were stamped name and serial number, date of enlistment, blood type, faith or godlessness, next of kin and *their*, not *our*, home addresses—all that anyone, friend or enemy, would need to know or to remember, if one were salvaged from the battlefield ages after the mere neck it hung from had been stretched, severed or atomized. Good ole ASN 11081221.

Here in his clinking pair of dog tags was all the comforting faith or sustaining hope a dirty dogface needed ... always with him, unlike God, and only a heartbeat away.

On a gray pier beyond a wall of gray warehouses at the Newport News Port of Embarkation, a few gray Red Cross ladies served iced tea and cookies from the back of a station wagon to the dutiful strains of a minimal Army band as we dragged our barracks bags up the gangway of the dirty gray Liberty Ship *Samuel Ashe* as ignorant of our destination as steers in the stockyard. We knew it was the third of September 1943, the British Eighth Army had invaded Italy, this was a helluva chilly and cheerless way to remember the U S of A, we were being loaded onto a large target headed for war much too slowly on an Atlantic fraught with German U-boats and we had feathers in our stomachs.

Each of the 2,709 Liberties that supplied the war fronts of the globe had seven prefabricated holds welded together by housewives, clerks and such home-front heroes in assembly-line shipyards. The record was four days, fifteen hours and thirty minutes, and the more wonder that only a couple of hundred were lost. Fewer than half a dozen just split apart, odds immaterial to the five hundred of us packed in a hold fifty by seventy feet in five tiers of pipe berths stretched with dirty canvas, no room to sit up, in the bowels of the wracking, creaking *Samuel Ashe*.

With parting puffs of black smoke and a predawn twinkle of signal blinking among our naval escorts, our armada of fifty or sixty ships raised anchor on the fifth of September. As the *Ashe* rolled one way to the rising and falling of the oil-smooth ground swell, our stomachs rolled the other. Perhaps because I wasn't yet seasick my reduction from temporary staff sergeant to temporary corporal was sidetracked to temporary ship's steward and CQ (in charge of quarters) or boss of the hold. They told me to threaten with the brig anyone throwing stuff overboard, as telltale trails of trash for peeping periscopes were frowned upon. Since we were all virtually in the brig already, I could but appeal to common self-interest.

Though we'd been five days at sea, strangely south the convoy bore away to within eighty miles of the Bahamas, jet-blue ocean, flying fish leaping up on deck, sea turtles, semi-tropical sun, guys stripping to the waist, scarlet sunburns. The weather held. "Life at sea is humdrum," I noted in my journal. "No jitters except among the neurotic few, and it might be a pleasure cruise in any other ship." The *Ashe*'s shortwave radio reported that the Fifth Army was meeting "stubborn, perhaps overwhelming resistance, where a reported force of fourteen German divisions is making things hot. We may see battle sooner than we think."

Then we swung back into the mainstream turbulence of the North Atlantic. Porridge at ten in the morning, powdered eggs at four—vile dehydrated stuff it was, vilely prepared, vile going down, even viler coming back up. By now the stale bread doled out to us crawled with maggots. Calm or storm, a few poor souls threw up all over themselves, their berths and their buddies who were trying to sleep or didn't move fast enough. No showers. Reeking bodies and clothing, fresh and drying puke and shit, and oily, smoky, metallic, stomach-turning emanations from the bilge. The filth accumulated, and the stench thickened and clung and gagged.

The officers lived in staterooms and dined from the ship's mess, while down in our "Black Hole" we staged a demonstration, drew up our "Gripes of Wrath," and delivered them to the brass on high. A ringleader, I stood at the bottom of the companionway of our *Bounty* trying to be Clark Gable's *Mister* Christian. Framed against the sky, the officer in charge peered down into the malodorous mess, trying not to be Charles Laughton's *Captain* Bligh. He and we felt futile about the whole confrontation, since the cooks could do nothing with what they had. When cases of C rations were discovered in a cargo hold, we rejoiced.

The only escape for those still strong enough to stand the weather was topsides on a deck so crowded with crated and battened-down vehicles and guns and the other stuff of war that to find a spot to huddle in you had to beat the gang to it and camp there like a nesting gooney bird for the rest of the day, come what may.

Liberty Ship *Samuel Ashe* (*Courtesy of The Mariners' Museum, Newport News, VA*)

The enlisted men's head spanned the deck forward of the cabin, entered through doors at either end. The common drainpipe of a long row of filthy hoppers exited through the topsides, port and starboard, except when a hugely deep roll reversed the process with such hydrostatic force that seawater and everything with it geysered back up through the thrones to the mortification of any poor buggers seated thereon. One day as I lolled at the rail that rose and fell above and below the horizon with each mighty sea, my gaze fixed upon a pair of fugitive turds from one of these latrinal explosions, expelled through the door upon the deck, playing tag as they rolled back and forth, back and forth, athwartships with each stately roll, smaller and smaller until mercifully they disappeared. I gulped.

Up there in the weather we pressed shivering against the main cabin under the overhang of the lifeboat deck, passing by the crew's and officers' galley on the way to our steerage swill. Now and then a porthole would swing casually open, letting out a blast of warm and delicious air. A hand would thrust out a piping hot leg of fried chicken or a succulent lamb chop, a juicy little steak or a wedge of apple pie, to be grabbed by the closest and torn into with warning snarls as the round window snapped shut against the blast of wind and rain. We felt and looked and acted more like starved animals every day.

Besides good hot food, I fumed in my journal, "an AB [able-bodied seaman] in the Merchant Marine pulls $400 a month, $150 for every port reached, $5 a day in the Mediterranean, overtime and various other bonuses." The buck private lugging a rifle into battle got fifty bucks a month. Except that either way, dead was dead.

Mid-Atlantic. Gray seas and green gills, the dull drills in the everlasting life belts, the listless calisthenics, the endless crapshoots on the G.I. blankets that emptied fifty times as many pockets as they filled. Reading, bulling, dozing, daydreaming, watching the waves, or sick, sick, sick, and bitching and griping but scarcely any bemoaning. And a boxing ring, and Nathan Crystal, remembered by Dunleavy as from East Saint Louis. "Came up by way of the Golden Gloves. A gentle, decent, lovely guy. I think he won every bout on the ship."

Twelve days out we churned through bunker oil. A torpedoed tanker on the bottom below us? German subs around? The next day a Navy reconnaissance plane growled in from somewhere and circled the convoy reassuringly. A few seagulls flapped over. Gunnery and lifeboat drill were stepped up, and anti-aircraft practice from the puny bow and stern turrets, the slim Swedish Oerlikons POM-POM-POMMing like brisk popguns. The crew ran out the outriggers to tow the paravanes designed to cut enemy mines loose from their moorings. We were skeptical. Dun put his ear to the steel side of the ship and heard through the water the dull PING of exploding depth charges being dropped by our destroyers and for the first time was scared.

Italy had surrendered to the Allies on September 8, and the next day our Fifth Army landed at Salerno, meeting an inferno of fire. Over the shortwave crackled the news. "We've succeeded in establishing an air base in Italy," I journaled, "and the Germans are beating a stubborn withdrawal. Probably they intend to eventually sacrifice Italy and make a stand in the Alps."

Two weeks out. "A devil of a gale, the ship rolling like hell, and last night mess kits, bags and even men crashing to the floor. All of us are quite weak from malnutrition, for the food, in addition to being limited (supposedly) and poor, is now spoiling." But Dun was relieved that no torpedo could find us in the huge waves. The storm subsided.

And then: "There's something about the air that seems to spell Africa. Or am I just being picturesque? The clouds are heavy and panoramic, like a herd of elephants."

Early on September 22 we rendezvoused with a British convoy and its destroyer escort, and at 12:45 in the afternoon sighted land after twenty days on the Atlantic.

We've just passed Tangier, a white Spanish city slapped on close-cropped green hills. On our left is the Spanish coast, and on our right Spanish Morocco, and we're now entering the Straits, which are about twenty miles long and ten miles wide. The entire region is jutting with promontories and steep precipices, very hilly. Directly behind is a gorgeous sunset, a perfect scene from a travelogue, and ahead all is dark, cloudy and foreboding—a fitting enough commentary on what we're leaving behind and what we're about to enter.

Approaching Europe and World War II in the tightening clutch of anxiety and excitement, I struggled boyishly, manfully, with my feelings a week before my twenty-first birthday.

A few of us passing into the Strait of Gibraltar on a Liberty Ship are pretty thoughtful. Just what are we doing 4,000 miles from home? Are we defending something very real and personal or are we being sacrificed on the same old altar of greed and ambition? In this war the soldier has no choice but to do or die (I mean the soldier). Unhappy though his position may be through either our common negligence or the willfulness of a few, he must accept it with a shrug as perhaps his fate and prepare to fortify himself against the inevitable moral sabotage of war. The Pandoran box has hardly yet been opened for the fighting man. Before the shouts of exultation and tumultuous gratitude have died away he will be pounding the pavement, meeting good wishes but "sorry no vacancies," one of a vast Legion of Forgotten Men.

The problems in America will be a natural aftermath, and their solution to a great degree will depend upon the realization by the soldier that when he discards his martial garb and steps back into civilian dress he resumes all his dormant responsibilities and social obligations, regardless of his sacrifices, which are priceless and bear no relevance to his normal life and relationships. The great thing is that all of us are working together towards the winning of the War, and beside that goal everything that is petty and weak fades and diminishes.

Well, OK. So we were youth on the razor's edge of manhood, and life, and death.

Late the same evening our swollen convoy funneled from the Atlantic into the Mediterranean under the dark hulk of Gibraltar. Across the Strait to starboard, Ceuta was a small, smug string of neutral lights. All the next day, a red-hot North African roaster, we steamed through the blue and lake-like watering hole of western civilization as placidly as if nothing were amiss with the world, gliding along the Moroccan and then the Algerian coasts under the busy shepherding of our naval escorts.

Mid-morning of the twenty-fourth, twenty-two days from America, our flock was hustled without a lost sheep into the harbor of Oran. "Shaped like a huge horseshoe fringed

The crossing. Pencil sketches in the author's journal by Dave Goss.

with giant, straight ledges. We saw a tanker here with a gaping hole in her bow big enough to drive a launch through. Maybe that's where all the oil came from. This goddam ship is a bedlam tonight. Let's get the hell ashore!"

It was then that I noticed the penciling on the overhead near my berth: *Hier haben 480 deutsche Soldaten vom 21.7.43–10.8.43 gehungert.* "Here 480 German soldiers went hungry from July 21 to August 8, 1943." So it was nothing but a lousy swap. The gehungry Krauts were shot intact from the mouth of *their* cannon clear across the pond in *our* boat to the safety of *our* motherland, while we puking doggies were fed into the breech of *our* cannon for fodderization on the road to *their* Vaterland.[9]

We were ferried ashore in a beat-up grain barge, trucked straight through Beautiful Downtown Oran and dumped upon the superheated desert amid a scattering of tents grandiosely called the First Replacement Depot, "Repple Depple" to us repples. The sandstorms that turned clothing into sandbags, blackened skin and drove through the chow in our mess kits like birdshot forced us into goggles and even respirators. After three days of desert for dessert, 5,400 of us, mostly Yanks including the rest of the Croft contingent from our sister Liberty, boarded the 20,000-ton, 663-foot *Orontes*, a 1929 Pacific & Orient liner converted by the British to a troopship and recently back from Salerno, where she had taken on board a regiment of our 36th Infantry Division that got mauled in the landing.

Orontes wasn't as posh (*port out* to India, *starboard home* to England, the locations of the best cabins away from the sun) as when the P&O stood for elegance at sea. But we swung in clean hammocks in the main lounge, with portholes we could see out and breathe through, tables to sit down to, plenty of good chow, and cheerful banter with a contingent of British combat veterans resignedly headed back into it.

On the last day of September we pushed back into the Mediterranean from Oran in a small convoy. The pit of my stomach told me we were in for it now for sure, and the calendar reminded me I was now twenty-one. A man, at last, just like that!

We're under way this morning, making excellent time, and seem to be headed east by northeast. We all expect air attack within a day or two. The British Eighth and American Fifth Armies are closing on Naples and driving the Germans back with the help of the British fleet which is shelling the retreating Heinies. I really believe we'll be in the frontlines within weeks. There are 5400 British and Americans on board, mostly the latter. The British troops and sailors are a fine bunch. The troops are extremely well disciplined, clean and neat, and are far more cordial than I had expected, even volunteering to engage you in conversation. Most all are combat veterans, while the great part of Americans are green.

I find it hard to believe that 21 years could have been spent with so little to show, so many years wasted, so many opportunities left untouched, so many things unappreciated. I'm at a dead standstill, with no future ahead, nothing but dark days. Well, that's the way it seems, anyway. I wonder whether there's anything lower in America than a buck private in the Infantry. When I contrast myself with my Old Man, whom I have ever set as a standard for my actions and thinking, it makes me utterly ashamed to think that I have fallen so short.

Yeah, well, buck up, boy. If that Old Man of fifty was struggling with his own faith three thousand miles astern of his son, he didn't let on. Instead, practiced physician/poet that he was, he composed a sonnet in the Miltonic mode and mailed it to me:

Has he, then, come so soon to man's estate
Whom we half considered as a child,

Earnest in sports, with ancient books beguiled,
Yet conscious of the thunder at the gate?
And this brief day that we would dedicate
Finds him, to straitened freedom reconciled,
Holding his cherished idols undefiled,
Custodian of a larger freedom's fate.
For youth has gone to carry on the fight
In vine-choked jungle and on wind-swept hill
Where dawn reveals the everlasting snows;
And youth has gone to storm the starlit height,
While faith and patience are abiding still
With us, the keepers of the inner close.

First the bunker oil, then the eerie CLUMP of the depth charges, then the tanker with the hole big enough to float a landing barge through, and now we drew nigh indeed. I journaled:

Just passed three empty lifeboats, about a quarter mile apart. What they were doing or what had happened we don't know. Stuff keeps floating by. Four more lifeboats and three life rafts, riddled and splintered with machine gun bullets. Hatches, oars and even helmet liners have come by. One boat had an English fire extinguisher with a bullet hole in it. Probably air attack, and of course the survivors were machine-gunned in typical Heinie fashion. It's all in sight of Africa too. Perhaps the destroyers picked up survivors. As a matter of fact, they must have, since the boats are empty. From now on, wherever we go, we're due for action, and plenty…

Over the speaker tonight comes the news that the lifeboats were from two ships torpedoed last night at 11:30 by a U-boat. Bastards!

We awoke in the harbor of Bizerte, "thrown together on flatter ground than Oran, with the same black, barren hills, and subjected to such bombings that they say it's a pile of walls and rubble." We weren't let ashore to see for ourselves. Deservedly immortalized in the soldier's tune "Dirty Gertie from Bizerte," the city had fallen on May 7 to the Americans, even as the British walked into Tunis, in the Allied drive through the desert to the coast. Idling at the rail, we jeered as a tugboat churned by with a small Italian submarine in tow. Most of the Italian fleet had surrendered three weeks before. Maybe these guys had been out of contact. Maybe they heard about the capture of Naples the previous day and voted in favor of a return to civilian life. They should have jeered back. Like the *deutschen Soldaten* with whom we'd traded berths, they were out of it, and we were going in.

Our fourth morning locked up in Bizerte harbor a recently arrived hospital ship steamed out by us to pick up another cargo of the wounded from Italy. Lit up like a casino, the snow-white floating ambulance with the billboard-red crosses brought up the rear of a thickening trail of casualties, starting with that sea of bunker oil. And now we were officially in the war zone, although still three hundred miles from the front. What the hell were we waiting for?

For the harbor and docks of Naples, the great southern gateway port to Italy, to be cleared of enough sunken ships and debris for us to enter, we were told. This seized us with our first real taste of gut-wrenching apprehension, mixed with an edgy eagerness, as if we were slipping from the free-fall of the tedious, almost dreamlike sea voyage into a world where we were already beginning to accept that the insane was the normal. Already this exotic excitement was seducing us toward the realm of cautious recklessness that empowers the soldier to function, if not to survive.

At the break of dawn on October fifth *Orontes* joined the compact convoy steaming out of Bizerte's basinlike harbor into the rising sun. By mid-afternoon Sicily was low on the eastern horizon. We churned past an island. Pantelleria maybe? Next morning, end of voyage:

Here we are. Orontes *has just steamed by the Isle of Capri, and Mount Vesuvius looms up in a pall of haze, an ashy column of thick grey-white smoke blowing off the peak. The modern city of Pompeii lies at its base, barely discernible in the haze, while in the back are the excavated ruins of the ancient city which was completely buried two thousand years or more ago. I believe Naples stands on the other side of Vesuvius. Imagine landing some time today in a city which five days ago was in the hands of the enemy! Boy oh boy, we're headed straight for Hell! Why, twenty centuries ago Roman legions marched on this rocky coast, and Odysseus sailed up this water in a chip with a piece of canvas.*

With the exception of three on land we've been at sea thirty days. We're walking jellyfish. It tires me to climb the stairs or walk around the deck. Morale has been as low as it could be, and there's a good deal of resentment against the officers, who have traveled first class with sheets, pajamas, liquor and tablecloths. But now we're getting there. This is for keeps, and we all feel better about the whole thing. A squadron of bombers just flew over with one missing. The landing barges are oiling up and set for action with smoke bombs and guns standing ready. There's the first real tension in the air.

Orontes was the first large Allied ship in Naples and in the absence of cleared dock we anchored in the harbor. The grand sweep of the Bay, one of Europe's most majestic natural settings, was not lost on us, but we were preoccupied travelers.

The waterfront was demolished, a mass of debris. Ships lay on their sides or upright in perfect rows at the wharves, burned and ruined. The buildings along the whole stretch were mere piles of stone and dust, or bare skeletons. Already the engineers had cleared a small fraction of the docks and buoyed off sunken ships. The whole edge of the Bay had the aspect of absolute desolation, so well had it been barraged by the British fleet and the Germans.

We leaped in the landing barges and scanned the sky, earnestly wishing ourselves ashore. Two LCIs (Landing Craft, Infantry) lay abreast at the slip cleared by the Engineers, and three or four barges were ahead of ours, so we had to hop and climb and jump over and across half a dozen rails and cluttered decks to the dry land of Italy.

We took a long march north along the shore past miles of ruins, although as we progressed through narrow streets lined with hotels and villas there was less damage. Many citizens lined the streets and greeted us with Americanos, paesan (friend) or more often cigaretta [sic]. Once I shouted Viva Italia! as we passed a large group that returned the gesture with a tremendous uproar.

All the faces were war-weary. The Germans had had complete autonomy over the city. When they evacuated they destroyed everything of military value and much besides and took practically every article of food except some wine and apples. A large fraction of the people have mourning bands on their lapels. Demobilized Italian soldiers are everywhere, either idle or standing guard for us, working at the docks and manning anti-aircraft guns.

And so we marched, or tiptoed bug-eyed, into a war seemingly hyperbolized for us in *Life* magazine and the newsreels. It was as if the hopelessness of our Depression as projected, and in a similar sense distanced, by James Agee's prose and photography in *Let Us Now Praise Famous Men* had realized its Armageddon here in the very Europe that had given birth to the American Dream and whose war now was revalidating that dream, if only momentarily. How else explain how we innocents had hardly stepped into its desolation when the process of inurement to it that had set in so subtly with the sight of that undulating blanket of bunker oil was now pushing one booted foot so trudgingly after the other?

To the Neapolitans, half of whom had fled their city and were now drifting back to semi-starved liberation from their recent Axis partners, the destruction was all the same. We would learn that to this happiest and saddest of people there were no more friends and foes, only those who would bribe from them or extort from them their souls.

Naples liberated (*U.S. Army*)

What the Allied bombardment had begun, the Germans finished with wanton vengeance on the ally that had deserted them. As they departed to prepared positions in the mountains to the north they demolished the transportation and communications network of which Naples was the hub, poisoned the water supply, blew up power, water and sewer systems, fired coal stocks and destroyed oil storage tanks, blew up the spaghetti factories that were the populace's main source of food, crippled the huge port by ripping up railroads, blasting waterfront installations and scuttling every ship in sight, looted, torched or mined the principal hotels, and mined buildings. The main post office was blown apart by a time bomb the day we landed, killing and injuring a hundred or more. They found the villa to which the Italian government had moved the city's archive of documents dating back to medieval times for safekeeping, soaked them with gasoline and burned the lot.

We hiked as far as the Count Ciano College on the north side of Naples, where we doffed our packs for the night. Until a few days before, this attractive academic setting had been the headquarters for Hitler's elite Hermann Goering Division.

The outsides of all buildings except the church are very cleverly and completely camouflaged to represent a landscape—trees, bushes, sky and villas, the painted skyline blending with the real one.

The inside of every building is a mass of wreckage, bare except for the rubbish on the floor, covered with maps of North Africa and France, etc., pamphlets, magazines, letters, proclamations, signs, pictures of Hitler, swastikas, 88-mm. shells and smaller, clips and boxes of ammo, dozens and dozens of helmets. We have managed to clean up the place somewhat.

In back there are dugouts in the hill where we've found much ammo, artillery and mortar shells, etc. All around are huge charred piles of Italian equipment which has been burned—rifles, motor parts and various unidentified stuff.

The church near the college was a simple, high-arched chapel, with two belfries, the fourteen Stations of the Cross and a very simple, fine little altar. The Germans removed all the chairs and brought in acrobatic bars, etc., converting it into a gymnasium. When they evacuated they smashed most of the windows, tore up the latrine in back, ripped off the candles at the Stations of the Cross, and destroyed the altar, bearing away the Cross which was probably gold. One might be prepared for this in an enemy country, but for the Huns to do this to their allies?[10]

The Patron Saint of the Foolish was watching over us as we poked around the enemy's leavings like a troop of Cub Scouts. Four days later a time bomb or a huge mine exploded in an Italian Army barracks in another section of the city where veterans of the 82nd Airborne Division were quartered, killing eighteen and injuring fifty-six.

Next morning I slipped out past the guard with Frank Dupont, who was always good for a lark, and another young soldier.

We strolled down a beautiful lane towards Ricovero and came across a bridge which had been completely destroyed. To the left and perpendicular to the road was the high retaining wall of a cemetery

Pencil sketch and description in the author's
journal by Dave Goss

which had been partly exposed by the blast. The wall was a tremendous vault of built-in tiers of coffins, hundreds of them. Scores of skeletons and bodies lay there, bones hanging by a rag, skulls in violently outrageous positions and winding sheets all torn to shreds. It was the most gruesome, violent scene imaginable, so unbelievably strange in such a peaceful-looking country that again I had to blink my eyes.

Having been raised in a family that shrank from the open coffin, these were the first corpses I'd ever seen.

We bypassed the bridge and went down through the main street of Ricovero, which looked for all the world like the North End [Boston's Little Italy]*, but with hardly anything for sale. Crowds accumulated as we, the three solitary soldiers in the place, strolled through. As usual, they wanted cigarettes, chocolate and whatever we had. We took off down a side street and found a small liquor store on a corner. Cognac was six dollars so we didn't buy any, but we did get some nut brittle which was a treat.*

Months later an Italian explained hilariously that all those signs to everywhere and nowhere led to the air-raid shelter, *il ricovero.*

As evening descended the three of us, joined by Gareth Dunleavy and a fifth, followed the high road that twisted three or four miles up a steep hill to a pass cut in the slope just below the summit and sheltering two tucked-in, blacked-out little restaurants. Spread out way down below we could more sense than see the first great city to be liberated by the Allies in Europe, fated to be as troubled in its liberation as it had been tormented in its occupation by its Axis partner.

After checking out the steak, pasta and wine in the first ristorante on the height we paid our bill with grunts of satisfaction and moved on to the starlit terrace of the next, overlooking the Bay of Naples far below. A little old waiter who had served in London, Paris, Berlin, Rome and other places brought us another steak, more pasta and two bottles of the most exquisite Italian champagne.

Never could you expect to find a more Continental figure than the gnomelike old waiter, who was most obliging. To top it off we asked him for fried eggs. "No," he said, "we have no more, we're most distressed," etc. We insisted, and he went into a huddle back in the kitchen which was really a cave in the hill, and emerged with the announcement that they had just five eggs, and he would fry them. So they were served up fried, and we patted our bellies again, paid another bill and started our swaying journey back. The whole adventure seemed like a candle in a lost world.

A hole in the night, a luminous suspension of time and place and the dread of darkness. To this day the scene still conveys to me the quality of cinematic hallucination: the flicker of the candle, the dancing shadows, faces hardly seen, voices hardly heard, the low laughter, the tinkle of a glass, the blackness closing in.

How serenely, for once, we still-innocent ones caroused under the stars, high above the darkling plain, attended with such sad solicitude by our surrogate old grandfather, feasting on hoarded fare served up for the delectation of the still-brave New World from the depths and devastation of the Old.

Far below sprawled the silent city of sorrow in the embrace of its protective bay. Beyond, the hump of mythical Capri. Rising up on the south, the volcano, cradling, possessing, Vesuvian. Opposite, over the horizon to the north and west of the ancient Roman road to Rome, the momentarily stilled war into which we five young feasters were on the point of being injected, five more drops of fuel for the Death Machine as old as the cave from which it thundered.

Together we had put behind us the very liberty for which we now must be prepared to die. We had trained and conformed and ached and crossed the ocean, and wondered, and endured the loneliness of the unattached and the unidentified together. We had known all along in the pits of our forever-hungry stomachs that we would not kill together, suffer together, laugh uproariously together, survive together and die together. And so we had, 'til now, stuck together, as we yearned to, but kept some distance, as we had to. The moment of parting forever, of surely forever never knowing what might have been, was at hand.

The wizened old waiter is long in his grave. For all Gareth Dunleavy and I ever knew, only we two of the five came out of the war alive.

And the candlelit moment remains fixed in the secret notebook of a nervous but almost buoyant young soldier on his way to war.

❧ ❧ ❧

We'd been in Italy a week when we were hiked from Ciano College on October 13 to a racetrack a mile or so west of Naples built by Mussolini within an eroded volcanic crater at Bagnoli. Its hilly rim was intensely planted with vineyards and fruit trees. A grandstand ranged above the home stretch, ornamented midway with the dictator's source of legitimacy, the imperial crown of old King Vittorio Emanuele. Inside the oval we pitched our pup tents among a flock of sheep, some horses and a few farmers cutting hay. It was the first American casualty replacement depot on the continent of Europe.

North of us our Fifth Army was ranged before the Volturno River, having barely broken through the fearsome German resistance at Salerno that nearly pushed it back into the sea, and was rearing back to attack across and up into the Apennine Mountains where the enemy had used its masterful delaying action during the battle for Sicily to raise a formidable line of defense.

Close enough now for us to hear its roar and to shudder at the dancing reflection of its fire in the northern sky, the Death Machine shook the mountains up ahead. Searching through my gear I found my notebook, lest I forget.

To the north we constantly hear the rumble of artillery and see the flashes at night. The front is only twelve miles away, we hear. This very minute the sound appears to be growing. I wonder whether we're retreating or what. We have no news.

In from out of the blue next day sputtered half a dozen Piper Cubs back from above the German lines spotting targets for our artillery. One after another they bounced down on the home stretch in front of the grandstand. The pilots ambled over to us: "They're getting ready to jump off across the river up there. Probably gonna throw you guys into the bridgehead."

A major from the Rangers appeared, sizing up the rookies. The three battalions of the Ranger Force, patterned after the British Commandos by Colonel William O. Darby, had fought through Sicily and Salerno, going on to occupy Naples with the 82nd Airborne Division. The recruiter delivered a rip-snorting harangue to the effect that we were goddam yellow-bellies if we didn't sign up with him then and there.

Leon Domaszewicz, New Yorker Red Gillig and my fellow Enlisted Reserve Corps Harvardian George Furber fell for it. George had learned how to fire a machine gun while a bumptious kid under paternal sentence to a southern military academy. He never quite forgave the rest of us for not plunging with the three of them even deeper into limbo.[11]

Next day a couple of hundred of us Crofters climbed on trucks and roared out of Mussy's volcanic Racetrack to catch up with the 45th Infantry Division, of which we knew only that its "Thunderbirds" (for their spread-winged shoulder patch) were veterans of the Sicilian campaign and the landing at Salerno, that they were somewhere up there where the guns were rumbling, that they had to have had casualties for whom we were about to be their first replacements in Italy.

That night we slept in a vineyard and by dawn were rattling through Benevento, about thirty miles northeast of Naples, inhaling our first stench of slaughter from bodies still buried under the rubble in the wake of the advancing 45th.

A heavy fog shrouded the place, as though an unseen power were ashamed to let the world see what was there. At the edge of the city bulldozers had cleared a bumpy road out of piles of debris often 20 or 30 feet high. That section had been completely leveled by our bombers, I hear. It is impossible to describe the starkness of the scene; it was like gaunt dunes of broken rock, plaster and wood, more desolate than the worst smoking dump. Dazed citizens still wandered about, though the damage had been done days before. Thus Rotterdam and Coventry must have looked. It was most incongruous to pass the next minute into the countryside where fields of tobacco, vineyards and farms lay serene, green and untouched.

To this day I retain the fleeting image of a former homeowner carefully replacing a pane of glass in his only window in a fragment of his only wall, all that was left of his *casa*.

From the rubble of Benevento our truck convoy turned northwest into the Volturno River valley. It was the twentieth of October, and after forty straight days of fighting, the casualty-ridden 45th's dirty and dogtired dogfaces had come off the line for their first breather since landing on the beach at Salerno.

Our next stop was the Division field headquarters, where my big brooding pal Dunleavy was one of a dozen cut out as casualty replacements for the 45th Cavalry Reconnaissance Troop, which had long since traded hooves for wheels.[12]

Of the rest who were parceled out among the Division's three infantry Regiments—the 157th, 179th and 180th—around forty of us were told to pitch up our gear on trucks for the 157th and were dropped off near its Service Company in an olive grove potted with shell holes, the trees torn by shrapnel and bullets. Left on our own, we got rations, explored the countryside and helped ourselves to the wine cellar of an abandoned farmhouse. Soon enough we got used to the idea of being bivouacked on a fresh battlefield, whooping it up in a shattered olive grove or lazing around, wondering what the hell was coming next.

In the afternoon trucks came up and we were told to swing aboard with our barrack bags, that we were all assigned to Third Battalion and were going on the line that night as riflemen. But the captain told me to get on the back of the last truck, as I was to be let off on the way.

A couple of miles on we stopped, and I dropped off, and the truck roared away with its spare parts for the rifle companies. A jeep was waiting. Hey, pretty classy! I climbed in with my gear, and the driver took me up a dirt road to a vineyard where jeeps and trucks were parked in the shade, and a few guys were hanging around, weary and dirty.

The vineyard was in the outskirts of the ancient town of Piedimonte d'Alife, nestled against the steep foothills bordering the plain of Campania in the valley of the Volturno. My destination and my destiny was the Intelligence and Reconnaissance Platoon of front-line scouts and observers of Headquarters Company of the 45th Division's 157th Infantry Regiment—its "Eyes and Ears" that required two or three casualty replacements.

I&R Platoon Sergeant Jack Pullman and company Top Sergeant Bill Sevey had spotted *Harvard* on my service record as they were checking the roster of Crofters and at the last minute plucked me from my buddies. It was close. I know in my bones that if I'd gone on to a line company as a rifleman I'd not have come back alive. So I did get something out of my Harvard education after all.

45th INFANTRY DIVISION
14,250

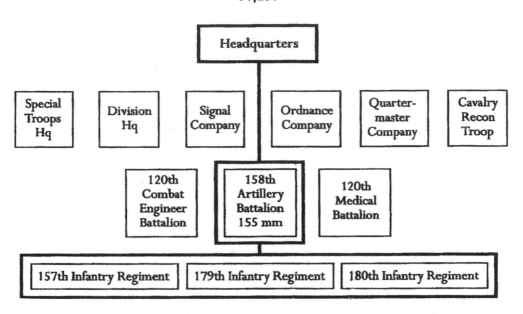

157th INFANTRY REGIMENT
3,250

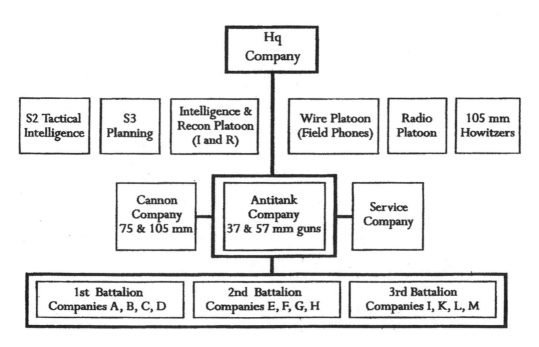

FIRST BATTALION
835

```
                    ┌─────────────────┐
                    │  Headquarters   │
                    └─────────────────┘
                             │
 ┌──────────┐  ┌──────────┐  │  ┌──────────┐  ┌──────────┐
 │ Antitank │  │   Mine   │  │  │  I & R   │  │  Ammo/   │
 │ Platoon  │  │ Platoon  │  │  │ Platoon  │  │ Pioneer  │
 └──────────┘  └──────────┘  │  └──────────┘  │ Platoon  │
                             │                └──────────┘
┌────────────────────────────────────────────────────────────┐
│ ┌──────────┐ ┌──────────┐ ┌──────────┐ ┌────────────────┐  │
│ │A Company │ │B Company │ │C Company │ │   D Company    │  │
│ │  Rifle   │ │  Rifle   │ │  Rifle   │ │Heavy machine guns│ │
│ └──────────┘ └──────────┘ └──────────┘ │  and mortars   │  │
│                                         └────────────────┘  │
└────────────────────────────────────────────────────────────┘
```

LINE (RIFLE) COMPANY
195

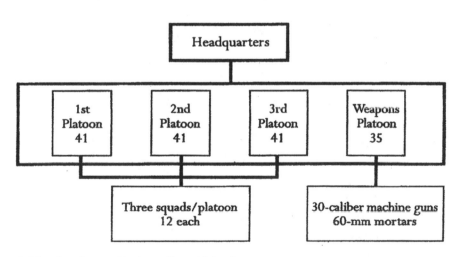

```
                    ┌─────────────────┐
                    │  Headquarters   │
                    └─────────────────┘
                             │
┌──────────────────────────────────────────────────────────┐
│ ┌──────────┐ ┌──────────┐ ┌──────────┐ ┌──────────┐      │
│ │   1st    │ │   2nd    │ │   3rd    │ │ Weapons  │      │
│ │ Platoon  │ │ Platoon  │ │ Platoon  │ │ Platoon  │      │
│ │    41    │ │    41    │ │    41    │ │    35    │      │
│ └──────────┘ └──────────┘ └──────────┘ └──────────┘      │
└──────────────────────────────────────────────────────────┘
        └──────────────┴─────────────┘        │
      ┌────────────────────────┐   ┌─────────────────────────┐
      │ Three squads/platoon   │   │ 30-caliber machine guns │
      │       12 each          │   │     60-mm mortars       │
      └────────────────────────┘   └─────────────────────────┘
```

(All charts by author's granddaughter Molly Spindel Flomer)

Thunderbird insignia of the 45th Infantry Division (*top*) and insignia
of the 157th Infantry Regiment (*bottom*) (*Department of Defense*)

＋＋＋ 2 ＋＋＋

Yeah, "Eager for Duty"

Fort Sill, Oklahoma, to Algeria
September 1940–July 1943

JACK PULLMAN HAD JUST TURNED NINETEEN and was hung over from a night in a
Denver, Colorado, barroom when he read in the newspaper on September 13, 1940, that
with the fate of western civilization in the balance, President Roosevelt had activated the
volunteer National Guard, including the 45th Infantry Division and its 157th Infantry
Regiment from Colorado that was about to head south to Fort Sill in Oklahoma for a year's
training. This was fifteen months before the Japanese attack on Pearl Harbor.

Jack, jes' plain Jack, was born in Idaho and raised in Kansas by his mother after his
father died in a mining accident in Nevada. He was lean and blond and talked sparsely in a
mountain drawl punctuated by a sardonic half-laugh, half-snort. He was about to spend as
much as he could get away with of his sophomore year at the University of Colorado ski-
ing in the Rockies when on an impulse he signed up with the 157th Infantry to get his year
of service behind him. Thought he was joining the field artillery until someone told him he
was a foot soldier.

Fort Sill had been imposed on the parched Oklahoma prairie near Lawton to keep the
Kiowa, Comanche and Apache Indians off their native turf. The recruits marched from the
train to the old Army post with three-story barracks and a parade ground. As Pullman
would tell me decades later:

> "Boy," we says, "this is gonna be real soldierin'." We marched on down to where the
> Oklahoma National Guard had their summer camp with mess hall, latrines and nice

concrete bases for tents, and thought, "Wal, this isn't gonna be too bad." So we marched on through that. Finally we got out to where you couldn't see a damn thing, and pretty soon here comes a stake in the ground that says Headquarters Company. That probably made the Regiment right there. Why, we were the best in the Division because we were the ones that had to rough it. They started building the camp right around us. We ate on the ground, including chocolate pudding that turned gray in the mess kit with that Okie dust.

Dirty pudding, and a dirty record that began with the militia back in 1864 when Colonel John Chivington, a racist former Methodist preacher, led a surprise militia attack on the federally protected village of the Cheyennes at Sand Creek in a massacre of entire families that resulted in a Congressional investigation. With statehood in 1875 the militia became the Colorado National Guard that in 1879 put down an uprising of White River Utes and the next year broke a Leadville mine strike in the first of many such goon-squad missions.

Tootling "There'll Be a Hot Time in the Old Town Tonight," their regimental march, the Coloradoans joined the force of eleven thousand that won the Battle of Manila with the loss of twenty American lives in the Spanish War of 1898 and were saddled by their brigadier with the rather arch motto "Eager for Duty."

Then when striking coal miners and their families and supporters pitched a tent colony at Ludlow, Colorado, in 1914, the owners called for help and the governor sent in the Guard. Strikers were killed, and eleven children and two women died when the tents were set afire in what would go down as the Ludlow Massacre in the annals of the state, though not of the Regiment, which expunged the entire nefarious record from its history.

Colorado's little army, federalized as the 157th Regiment of the 40th Infantry Division and sent to France in August 1918, was too late to see action as a unit, though many served as replacements in the trenches. In the reorganization of the National Guard in 1921, the 45th was created from the 157th, 179th and 180th Regiments from Oklahoma, and the 158th from Arizona and New Mexico that was later broken off and sent to the Pacific as an independent combat team in World War II.

The 45th's insignia was the fylfot, a three-legged cross hopping counterclockwise, a sun-god/good-luck symbol of the American Indians among other venerable peoples. No one seemed aware that in 1918 the growing anti-Semitic movement in Austria had added a fourth leg and reversed the direction to make of the fylfot the swastika that Hitler appropriated for his National Socialist party in place of the "decadent" Cross of Christ.

When the Nazi swastika fluttered over the Rhineland, and then Austria, the Sudetenland and Czechoslovakia in 1938 and 1939, and America began to stir, the 45th's innocent fylfot was ripped from every shoulder and replaced with the fierce American Indian Thunderbird—eyes flashing the lightning, overarching wings flapping the thunder, broad back balancing the lake up there somewhere—source of the rains in response to the prayers of the parched Southwest.

With President Roosevelt's mobilization in September 1940, the peacetime National Guard was shaken down and beefed up with Army Regulars and Selective Service recruits. For lack of a single basic infantry training camp, Fort Sill was taken out of the mothballs, and for Private Pullman so were a pair of rebuilt shoes, an oversize World War I choker blouse, canvas leggins, gas mask, bolt-action '03 Springfield rifle, washbasin helmet, mess kit stamped *1918*, and an ankle-length overcoat cut unhemmed so it wouldn't snag on the barbed wire at St.-Mihiel. But blitzkrieg was not the trenches, and the Army had twenty-two years of drowsing to catch up on.

By beating the draft, the Pullman kid who never heard of the Colorado National Guard was an instant good ole boy, qualifying as a topographical draftsman and vaulting from buck private to buck sergeant. When the 45th was trucked to Camp Barkeley outside Abilene, Texas, he was jumped up to staff sergeant with orders to make something of a new concept called the Regimental Intelligence and Reconnaissance Platoon.

The ABCs of the I&R

Richard "Dick" Beech (*Courtesy of Richard Beech*)   William "Bill" Caird (*Courtesy of William R. Caird*)

Jose Contreras (*Collection of the author*)

Harold Dibble and Stewart "Mickey" Smith (*Courtesy of Charles E. Nye*)

Vernon Dilks (*Courtesy of Vernon Dilks*)

James "Jimmy" "Doodle" Dowdall (*Courtesy of James J. Dowdall*)

Lester "Les" Gerencer (*Courtesy of Lester Gerencer*)

Herbert "Herb" Glover and Charles "Shorty" Nye aloft (*Courtesy of William E. Woodhams*)

Delmar "Griff" Griffith and his buddy Art Discoe at the entrance to their Colorado gold-mine shaft in 1936 (*Courtesy of Delmar W. Griffith*)

Herbert "Herb" Illfelder (*Courtesy of Charles E. Nye*)

Frank Merchant (*left*) with Mullenax and Beech
(*Courtesy of Charles E. Nye*)

Henry "Hank" Mills (*Courtesy of Dominick M. Trubia*)

Valen "Mohawk," "Big Mo" Mullenax and Jack
Pullman (*Courtesy of Charles E. Nye*)

Katie and Dave O'Keefe (*Courtesy of David J. O'Keefe*)

Jack Pullman (*Courtesy of William E. Woodhams*)

Stewart "Mickey" Smith (*right*) with Pullman (*left*) and Nye (*Courtesy of William F. Woodhams*)

Douglass "Doug," "Studie" Studebaker (*right*) with Dowdall (*Courtesy of Charles E. Nye*)

Dominick "Dom" Trubia (*Courtesy of Dominick M. Trubia*)

George Viereck (*Courtesy of Peter Viereck*)

Philipp "Phil" Vollhardt (*Courtesy of Philipp F. Vollhardt*)

William "Bill" Woodhams (*Courtesy of Charles E. Nye*)

Andrew "Andy," "Zapeck" Zapiecki (*Author photo*)

The other noncom in this paper platoon was Bill Woodhams, a bluff and rugged Guardsman of twenty-nine who wore a pair of metal plates in one leg from an old automobile accident ("couldn't run real fast, but it didn't affect my walking a damn bit") and had already put in his time with a rifle company in the 1930s. When he got out in 1936 he ran a movie house in Denver, then waterproofed miles of heating tunnels with asphalt at the new Lowry Air Force Base, only to be drafted and returned to a rifle company. Now married with one kid, he got himself transferred into the new platoon.

The I&R's mission was to gather intelligence on the strength, movement and, if possible, intentions of enemy units facing the regiment. The new platoon's scouts, with a few radio operators and jeep drivers, were to be organized in small, virtually autonomous crews to operate up at the front in concealment and to be prepared to be shot at by the enemy when discovered, but to stick to the job and not shoot unless actually attacked.

That spring of 1941 Sergeants Pullman and Woodhams coached their recruits to be the extended eyes and ears of the Regiment's commanding officer, Colonel Charles M. Ankcorn, a rock-featured ramrod of forty-seven who rose from Regular Army second lieutenant in 1917 to command the Colorado Guard when it was activated as the 157th in 1940.

Seemingly created the model "scout" in these early days was a rugged Colorado cowpoke with broad, weathered features and a moniker to match, Valen J. Mullenax, known early on as Mohawk, which was close enough, his Ma being part Cherokee from Oklahoma, as he explained it, and his Pa a not very successful Colorado flatland rancher. Mohawk was built and talked like a parked freight train with steam up and was on occasion as immovable, which is how he got tagged The Roadblock when fully armed.

Because he was born in their sod homestead on Saint V-fer-Valentine's Day, 1914, his folks jes' naturally called him Valen, and his younger brothers Vilo, Verlin and plain Vee when they came along. He started riding horses bareback when he was eight.

> The ole man says, "When you can ride bareback you can graduate to a saddle." I learned how to break horses when I was twelve, and my mother could break one better than he could. I learned more from her, time I was eleven years old, than I ever did from him. Carried a gun on the range since I was a kid. The old man never carried a six-shooter. He said if he lost his temper he'd be liable to kill somebody and he didn't want that on his conscience.
>
> Dad started another ranch at Haswell, where I stayed with him 'til I was fourteen, then worked for a neighboring ranch cowpunching, then one at Muleshoe 'til I was eighteen that extended from South Texas toward the Gulf clear up to West Texas and the New Mexico line and just about split Texas in half. Rode fence two or three days at a time and would stop overnight at a line shack where there was a man and his wife. Then on a smaller spread over the line in New Mexico where I wound up as foreman.
>
> During the Depression I was logging, laying sections on the Union Pacific, National Park work crew boss in the Civilian Conservation Corps (the "CCs"), and along about 1937 I was married for a few days to a big woman who ran a bar in

Carson City, Nevada. You might say an overnight binge, 'cause we was drunk, and she went back to her bar, and I never did see her again. In '38 I was a relief stationary engineer with the YWCA in Denver. Then I drove a big gasoline rig through the mountains outta Pueblo until my mother passed away of a double stroke two weeks apart. Then on a ranch with Vee and Verlin next to where our dad was. We all three went together into K Company on January the sixth of 1941, and then I qualified for the I&R.

Yeah, the Roadblock could have been sent over by central casting.

The Thunderbirds joined the biggest training maneuvers in history in the summer of 1941 as part of the Third Army of 270,000 (the Blues), against the Second Army of 130,000 (the Reds). Here in the miserable terrain of western Louisiana the military mind stirred from its interbellum snooze to the reality of modern war. The rude awakening was administered by General Tank himself, George S. Patton, whose clanking Second Armored Division was everywhere, covering hundreds of miles in astounding dashes and forays, encircling, striking here when they were supposed to be there, capturing opposing generals, and raising dust and hell amid bursts of Pattonic profanity.

But driving "Uncle Charley's Foot Cavalry," as they were calling themselves on the chessboard of the countryside, the 157th's commander outflanked Patton, and his boys "captured" 1,300 prisoners, gaining national attention and a new nickname for their

Colonel Charles M. Ankcorn
(*Department of Defense*)

Colonel, "Flank-'em Ankcorn." On one occasion, Pullman recalled, they cut off General Patton's supply train. "His tanks couldn't move. We had all their gasoline. Patton shoulda been captured. Somebody was shootin' blanks at a command car that turned around and took off. How do you capture a general in maneuvers if he doesn't wanna be?"

Late that year Congress voted to hold on to draftees under twenty-seven, which meant that more than half the Regiment would be eligible to go home. On Sunday, December 7, Bill Woodhams was writing his wife that he'd be out in about a month. Years afterward, he recalled: "We were on the rifle range when the news of Pearl Harbor came. The command was roared out: 'Ready on the right! Ready on the left! Ready on the firing line!' And up went the Jap flag, and we all fired on it! And I went back to the barracks and jest tore up the letter to Selma and threw it away."

In four more days Germany and Italy declared war on the United States. Congress extended the draft age to between twenty and forty-four, and the Bill Woodhamses were spun right back through the revolving door.

Eager for duty? Well, yeah, considering the alternative. Doug Studebaker's father had been out of work for two years in the early Depression when Ford Motor closed down the plant in Denver, finally got two jobs paying twelve bucks a week and signed up for the Colorado National Guard with the 157th Service Company, where he eventually rose to warrant officer. Son Doug enlisted at nineteen in Pa's unit for a year in September 1940, figuring there'd be more jobs when he got out. But along came Pearl Harbor and young Studie was locked in and then transferred out to the I&R in Bill Woodhams's crew with Mullenax.

After a year and a half in Texas and Louisiana the 45th entrained in April 1942 for the East Coast and Fort Devens, 25 miles west of Boston and 1,500 closer to Europe. Blown out of the trench mindset of the First War by the thunder of Hitler's lightning blitzkrieg, our brass had finally reexamined the rigidly square grid of the infantry division—two brigades of four regiments held together in the ancient matrix of the Greek phalanx by red tape and chains of command—and now reassembled it as a triangular pattern of mobile units and subunits of three, one of which at each level could be rotated out of action and into reserve at intervals for rest, replacements and refit.

Out of the chocolaty dust of Oklahoma a modern division of American infantry emerged on the rocky hillsides of Massachusetts. As war production shifted into high, the fast-firing M1s and the more enveloping German-style helmets replaced the hand-me-down Springfield single-shot rifles of 1903 and dishpan helmets of the "Over There" of the generation before. Civilian recruits who knew nothing of the old National Guard and the Regular Army were coming in, and those not regarded as fit for a real war were moving or being moved out. Promoted on the battlefield as General Pershing's youngest regimental commander in World War I, General Troy H. Middleton came in as Division commander from Louisiana State University where he had been a dean since his retirement in 1937. Now he had a student body of fourteen thousand.

Enter Corporal Andrew Zapiecki. Captain Ralph Krieger (German for "warrior"), the regimental intelligence officer, had heard about him and his uproarious ways, and out of mischief as much as intuition reached down into K Company and grabbed him for the I&R, bellowing in protest. Protest? Krieger probably saved his Polack neck.

This new old guy's father, Casmer Zapietski, emigrated from Poland to Pennsylvania, worked in the Frick coal mine in Mt. Pleasant twenty-eight years and never learned English. His mother came over separately with English and German, found work as a maid in New Jersey, met and married her countryman and bore him eight sons and a daughter. In 1920 the family left the mines for Toledo, Ohio, where an uncle and two of the sons had gone ahead and sent back money. Zapiecki now, Casmer got a job at Standard Steel and Tube in Toledo.

> Pa could say yes and no and didn't learn to write his name until he had to endorse his check, so I taught him how. We didn't know for thirty years that he could play a violin. My brother Walter played, and one day the Old Man says in a kidding way, "Here, lemme show ya." We all laffed. He whipped off a coupla tunes and give it back to him and never played again.
>
> When we got to Toledo Uncle Joe let my mother have fifteen hunnert dollars. She was the boss and bought a house for sixty-five hunnert. Six bedrooms. Biggest on the block in the Fourteenth Ward, one of the Polish districts. In 1924 it was paid off. She says to my older brothers and sister, "You can pay me ten dollars a week rent. I'll give you spending money, and I'll give you twenty-five hunnert when you get married." So, boy, give yer mother ten and don't bother me no more, and that's the way it was.
>
> When the stock market crashed in '29 the priest asked if anyone had any money they could lend the parish. Ma went down cellar. Fifteen hunnert dollars in jars wrapped in newspapers! We used to make sauerkraut there. We put the cabbage and stuff in a big box, and brother Bart, who was the smallest, took off his shoes and socks and washed his feet and got in and stomped, and then another brother would salt it down. And all that time we never paid no attention to Ma's jars full o' money wrapped in newspapers up overhead.
>
> Our family was one of the only ones that wasn't on relief on the whole street. Our block was split, half Polish and half German. Ma'd always listen to Hitler on the radio and get mad as hell.[1]

After his father died in 1931 Andy quit school and worked with a barrel and box company. In 1934 he volunteered, like Val Mullenax, for six months in the New Deal's youth work project, the Civilian Conservation Corps contingent at Yellowstone Park, then back to Toledo with the American Can Company as a double seamer, tester and trucker.

> I liked trucking better'n standing there staring at that machine. It was so loud I'd sing as loud as I could and nobody ever heard me except me and the machine. Cans come banging down the line, seven hunnert an hour, and you'd hafta put the ring on top, take and turn it over and double-seam the bottom, and then to a water tank where you tested 'em.

Lt. General Troy H. Middleton, the youngest
U.S. regimental commander in World War I
(*Department of Defense*)

About that time I fell in love, and then the girl says she don't love me no more, and bingo, she goes with another guy and gets married. But there's always a life-saver. March of 1941 I was inducted in the Army, age twenty-eight. We're taking the physical at Fort Thomas, Kentucky, bare-assed and carrying our clothes, and these guys are holding a shelter half [half a pup tent] and saying "Throw yer loose change and cigarettes in here!" And the guys are digging fer it, and I knew what the score was and says, "Don't do it!"

There's this sergeant, one o' those that says, "If yer don't like what we're doing, we'll go behind the barracks." Nobody wanted to fight. They were all new. I'd fought a little in the Three Cs, but mostly referee because I didn't wanna hurt nobody. A real husky guy and me put on a little show for the guys for about three rounds, and then we each fought three o' the guys for three rounds each. So when the sergeant comes around, well, "We'll let you know when we don't like sump'n, and if it's behind the barracks, we'll go behind the barracks." Man, after that you ain't seen a sergeant that treated guys as if they were long-lost buddies!

While we're taking basic at Walters they called me in. Do I wanna go to Officers' Training? I says, "If ya don't mind I'd like to talk it over with the guys." There's six Polacks lay right there in a row in the barracks, all from my neighborhood, and I told 'em what they said in the office, and one says, "Aw, gee whiz, I waited until you were inducted and I volunteered, and now yer gonna leave us!" So I says

OK, OK, OK, and I went back and says, "Naw, I come with these guys here and I wanna stay with 'em."

That sarge was so depressed at our leaving Walters that he went out and got drunk, stumbled back to the barracks, and passed out on his bunk. We nailed his shoes to the floor and tied his clothes in knots, and that's the last picture of him was when the truck was pulling out, and he was out there waving his fists and no clothes on. Didn't we fix his clock!

About now Zapiecki and two other guys from the Toledo area—Stewart "Mickey," "Smitty" Smith, as cool and low-key as Andy was hot and high, and Charles "Chuck," "Shorty" Nye, as cool and short as they were tall—landed in the 45th and were filtered down into the I&R. Mickey was twenty-three, born in Toronto, Canada, having made it on his own and since the death of his widowed mother when he was fifteen helped support his siblings in the U.S. by doing odd jobs, going to sea on the Great Lakes and working as an undertaker's helper. Shorty Nye, who couldn't have stood much more than five feet, was a skilled machinist from Fostoria and would prove that he could more than hold his own in any company, including unfriendly.

Fort Devens wasn't big enough for regimental maneuvers on a useful scale, and that summer of '42 the I&R was assigned to demonstrate small-unit tactics. They'd take on an "enemy" platoon in the morning. Zapiecki would slip out to a nearby grocery store for provisions, and they'd cook lunch in style. Then another "enemy" in the afternoon for dessert. For "how-not-to-do-it" demonstrations, Krieger put Andy in charge of the "Awkward Squad."

He had me creepin' an' crawlin' through where they had this dynamite buried and tole me the charge was on one side, but it blew up on the other. And they were making movies of it. I was supposed to demonstrate how not to use a compass. So I put on an act fumbling around with it, and somebody says, "Where did you say that guy was from?" And they said the I&R. And he says, "What dumb sonsabitches they got there!" Then three or four of us are crawling under the barbed wire at night, flares going up, did the wrong things naturally, and I got hooked up in it, and they yell, "OK, all clear you guys! Come on out!" And I'm stuck! The rest of Headquarters Company called us a bunch o' smart-asses.

Still not up to their TO (table of organization) of around thirty scouts, a half dozen easterners (some from the new I&R School at Camp Croft) arrived at Devens to swell the ranks of the Ironheads, as someone dubbed them (I and R heads—get it?): Dick Beech, Bill Caird, Jim Dowdall, Les Gerencer, Frank Merchant, Dave O'Keefe and Dom Trubia among others, of all of whom more in due course.

Sergeant Woodhams and Corporal Zapiecki brought up the rear of the roll call, but they led off the hikes through the autumnal hills and dales of Massachusetts. With his metal plates in his leg Uncle Billy (so called by Merchant, who regarded him with a degree of awe though Frank was seven months older), upped the pace with "The chicken that they give you, they say is of the best. We get the necks and assholes, and the officers get the rest," while the big Polack would roar out "The Open Road" and similar favorites from his repertoire of light opera.

Of the same vintage as this rollicking pair was Private James J. Dowdall, openfaced Galwayman by way of New York, ever-cheerful bachelor with a wit and a heart and a brogue as broad as his Irish grin, who from the day of his assignment to the platoon at Devens in September was adopted as its lay padre. Jimmy was born in Tuam and educated at Presentation Brothers College in Cork.

> You had to learn Gaelic and pass a written examination if you wanted to go into a civil-service job in Ireland, though nobody spoke it, and mathematics was compulsory, always me best subject. I was much too security-minded, no doubt due to the insecurities of early life, and should have pushed forward with academic education or even with a trade such as plumbing. I'd like to say that I had aspired for a profession, but I considered me schoolin' preparatory for the civil-service exam and didn't look much beyond that. I'm farseein' in hindsight. So I wound up a clerk in a grocery store in Dublin in 1930, a dollar a week in American money. I'd measure the tea in half- and quarter-pounds. Nobody was rich enough around that neighborhood to buy a pound.
>
> Me dad had gone to America in '29 and in '32 got me mother out fer a Christmastime visit. The travel agent in New York told him 'twould be very difficult to bring the family over. Dad said nobody over there is workin' to support themselves, and he had to send money home, so why couldn't he bring 'em over an' support 'em? The agent said that made sense. Me brother and me were minors. The American consul in Dublin decided that if we went to America, to support us would keep American money at home, an' that's what got us over.
>
> So we sailed from Belfast on the Cunard liner *California* and came into New York Harbor after dusk on May 6, 1933, in quarantine. I remember goin' up to the bow and lookin' at America, the skyline o' New York, and thinkin', "I wonder in that big city if there's a job fer me." I went from porter to dishwasher and so on, became a citizen, and wound up runnin' an elevator in Rockefeller Center before goin' in the Army in May o' 1942, the last month o' twenty-one dollars a month, and on June first it went up to fifty. England wasn't all that of a saint to me, bein' an Irishman, but I was an American citizen now, an' the only way, if a feller hits yer in the jaw or spits in yer face, is belt him back.

Frank Merchant was a teacher, poet and writer with a master's degree from Brown University in his native Rhode Island back in 1932. Pacifist and conscientious objector until Pearl Harbor, he enlisted in the Medics as soon as a couple of his amateur plays had been performed but was "shanghaied," as he put it, into the Infantry and then the I&R on the strength of his ability in French and German and even Italian. Corncob pipe clamped between bulldog brows and jutting jaw, ole Frank viewed the military as a dark farce, submitting his bearish bulk to its discipline reluctantly, his mordant tongue not at all, a misfit from academia pondering with bibulous bemusement what the hell he was doing as a foot soldier.

His German got Frank assigned to comb the 157th's records for candidates for the 45th's language school for interpreters, interrogators and translators, among whom was Private George Sylvester Viereck, Jr., a twenty-four-year-old magna cum laude graduate of Harvard who had volunteered for the Army and combat duty after two years of Harvard Law School. His older brother Peter, who taught at Harvard after graduating with highest honors in 1937, was also in the Army.

George's namesake father, born in Munich but educated in America, had been a pro-German propagandist during World War I and was at that moment under sentence for violation of the Foreign Agents Registration Act and under indictment for conspiracy to undermine the morale of the Armed Forces. A poet, historian, novelist, playwright and polemicist with a lifelong fixation on the supremacy of Germany under first the Kaiser, then Hitler and his propaganda minister Joseph Goebbels, whose pictures hung in his study, Viereck senior had been arrested in New York in 1941 on charges of withholding information about his propaganda activities from the State Department.

Merchant recalled of the son that "though attached to his father by affection, he was anti-Nazi, liberal, a Harvard intellectual, attractive, agreeable and very American." His mates thought him a good soldier but withdrawn and battling despondency; evidently he was hounded, even in the service of his country, by the F.B.I.

Adding irony to irony, Merchant's second German-speaking recruit was Herbert Illfelder, a Jew who before the war had escaped from Germany with his family to America barely ahead of the Gestapo, in his mid-twenties, reportedly related to a prominent New York City financial family. Thickset, strong but miserably coordinated, goodhearted, an intellectual—some said with a PhD—Herbie could hit the bull's-eye with the date of the Battle of Yorktown, but was helpless to take a rifle apart and put it back together.

Illfelder's hatred of military life was surpassed only by his detestation of the Nazis. Merchant, who thought it ironic that he was the butt of some anti-Semitism, found him one Saturday afternoon, "scrubbing away in the field kitchen, his fatigues covered with crap, an absolute mess, and he said to me, 'Dey alvayss giff me da shid, da shid details I get.'"

And one night the silence of the barracks was broken from his bunk. He was talking in his sleep. "PULLMAN! PULLMAN! You got one fugged-up oudfit!"

Herbie Illfelder's nightmares. The flight from Hitlerism. The crude hazing. Da shid details. Da fugged-up oudfit.

⁂ ⁂ ⁂

After nearly two years of shadowboxing the Thunderbirds trucked from Devens to Camp Edwards on the sands of Cape Cod for their first exposure to amphibious training, and for many, to the sea itself, across which lay shores to be liberated. It was a vacation of swimming, clamdigging and sunburning when not establishing shadow beachheads.

Descent from a towering deck down a net, hand-under-hand with rifle and full field pack into a bobbing landing craft was an unwelcome new sensation for all.

Hopes and fears that the Division would be in the first wave to wade ashore somewhere were dashed and calmed for the moment with the news that Allied forces in Operation Torch under General Eisenhower had landed at Casablanca, Oran and Algiers on November 8, 1942. By contrast, as the winds of autumn rattled the sered oak leaves, and the Bay State skies turned gray, woolen overcoats and galoshes were issued.

The 'Birds turned their shivering backs on Massachusetts, the sea and the war, and moved north to Pine Camp (later Camp Drum) near Watertown in upstate New York. As if on cue the snow rose to their cartridge belts and the mercury dropped to forty below. They had neither arctic clothing, skis nor snowshoes. Somebody in a warm armchair far to the south had goofed. They were frozen in.

The only recourse was to the warm bars of Watertown, which the Division attacked with the pent-up thirst and stored energy of cabin-feverish sourdoughs in town from the glaciers. Nineteen landed in the local tank one weekend. Then somebody shot somebody in the street. When two of their number were rolled in a gin mill, their enraged buddies surged into town, beat up the barkeeper, uprooted his bar from the floor and shoved it through the front window onto the sidewalk. Two other wild ones held up a local bank with their Thompson submachine guns; they were court-martialed and sent to Leavenworth for five years.

These high and low jinks seemed to confirm the rumor they brought with them from Devens that a playful pair of American Indians from the Division had cut off the ears of a patron in a Boston bar who laughed when they suggested he stand up while the jukebox was playing "Deep in the Heart of Texas." Pine Camp stamped the 45th as a bunch of crazy cowboys and wild Indians. Later, when it was revealed that they had descended on the island of Sicily, the *Watertown Times* expressed pride and relief:

> … They were a rugged, rollicking group. They made the 4th Armored, which had preceded them appear as docile as Dagwood Bumstead …
>
> Raw November and December weather never really cooled off their spirits. They cut high, wide and handsome capers on our streets. They broke up a tavern or two. They gave local police and the M.P.'s [military police] a real workout.
>
> Yet we look back with affection upon the 45th. They were fighting men. Woe to anyone who fell in their path … They will deliver any town, mussed up perhaps, but thoroughly conquered.[2]

Here amid the icy blasts of Pine Camp the Ironheads were joined by the frigid and fateful figure of Sergeant Delmar W. Griffith, for whom busting up the barrooms of Watertown and such frivolity had no place in the serious business for which the United States Government had gathered them all together.

And Philipp Frederick Vollhardt, Brooklyn-born of German immigrant parents.

Griff was bone-and-gristle Welsh stock, a hardheaded skinflint with words he rationed out in a nasal, Rocky Mountain sorta twang from between broadly angular jaws that had been known to crack a sardonic smile but never to have split into an outright hoss-laff. His restless forebears had pushed almost straight through from Wales to western Illinois and from there to homestead a poor half-section of eastern Colorado flatland where they built the sod house of his birth in 1911. When he was four, however, they gave it up and moved back to rural Illinois, where he went from high school to teaching thirty kids in eight grades. By 1935 he was ready to move on and took off for the West and a pretty luckless crack at old-style gold prospecting.[3]

Pushing thirty early in '41 he was packed off to Fort Sill in D Company with the first draftees from Colorado. With all that schooling and mining and bossing experience, it was a fast rise to regimental intelligence in charge of battle maps, and then to the I&R, and back to the action (he hoped) that his restless spirit yearned for.

Sergeant Griffith was the antithesis of Pullman and Woodhams, under whom and alongside he now served; it grated on him that Jack was ten years his junior, and he had his misgivings. The laxity, the jocularity, all the bullshitting and coffee-making and phonograph-playing and duffing off and profanity and obscenity—in sum, the rampant unmilitary individualism that at times approached operation by consensus—caused the new noncom considerable uneasiness.

Phil Vollhardt from Brooklyn, on the other hand, weighed two and a half pounds at birth ("when they made me they broke the mold") and was kept in a washbasket warmed by wine bottles of hot water under a pillow. His father was a butcher from Offenbach, his mother the daughter of a Frankfurt electrical engineer. Phil quit school at seventeen and learned tool and die making as an apprentice with Remington Rand, earning twelve bucks a week, two of which he turned over to his ma for rent. But the city wasn't for him, and he and his buddies hit the road backpacking in the Adirondacks whenever they could break loose. His mother was German through and through. Phil:

> Around '39 I bought a comic record that put Spike Jones and his band on the map, *Der Fuhrer's Face* satirizing Hitler. Ma didn't like that record and one day managed to sit on it. "Oh, I didn't *see* it on the couch." I was inducted in January of '42 at Camp Upton in New York. The sergeant lost my papers, and I've never liked sergeants since. Supposed to go Air Force but was shipped to Camp Croft, went through basic training and mechanics school, applied for Air Force, passed everything and astigmatism washed me out. Shipped to the 45th at Pine Camp, where everything I learned at mechanics school was wasted. Then I was accepted for OCS, the division was put on the alert, nobody left, and when they found I could read, write and speak German they switched me to the I&R.

With the decision in January of 1943 to invade Sicily in July, General Eisenhower was named Supreme Allied Commander in the Mediterranean, and the 45th was ordered to dig out of the snowdrifts of Pine Camp and on to Camp Pickett, Virginia, fifty miles southwest of Richmond. The Thunderbirds were disgusted. Griff, for one, was thirty-two and had already given up two years for a fight that seemed no closer than ever. "We were being trained to death. I felt I'd be relieved to get out of the States. Combat didn't hold the horrors that more training seemed to."

The scrawny Scripps-Howard correspondent Ernie Pyle, who more than any other was conveying the real war to the folks back home, wrote of the 'Birds that "everybody almost went nuts thinking they'd never get overseas." Getting himself assigned to cover them for the coming invasion, he cited a captain who wouldn't take a furlough the previous Christmas "because he was ashamed to be seen at home after spending two years in the Army and still not getting out of the United States. Then after he had leaped the overseas hurdle and felt qualified to go home he couldn't get there, of course."[4]

Pyle could have been writing about Henry Mills, the last and last-minute Stateside recruit to the I&R, the youngest just turning twenty, the wittiest, the sassiest, the scaredest and perhaps the bravest. A lightweight amateur boxer with a level, appraising gaze and an outthrust iron chin, Hank hailed from the railroad depot of Altoona, Pennsylvania, where his father was a yardmaster, and he had the fastest (the biggest to those not so fast) mouth in the Platoon. Back in '41 he'd enlisted in the 28th Division and quickly rose to buck sergeant. During the Louisiana maneuvers, and though under orders not to allow his squad to drink water in the midday heat, Sergeant Mills was observed by some chickenshit officer looking the other way while the guys slaked their thirst at a farmhouse. He was busted back to private and transferred to the 45th, where he talked himself into the I&R at Pickett and vowed surprise that everyone knew so much more than he did.

Down in the ranks the weeks dragged by, but not in the councils of those who send men and boys to war. On March 16 the Division staff was alerted top-secret for Operation Husky. The 45th had been rerouted from England where it was to have trained for the Normandy invasion, and would now hit Sicily instead on July 10 under Generals Bradley and Patton. The ascendancy of General Middleton to its command persuaded Bradley, his old admirer, that the 'Birds were ready to thunder.

Boredom and frustration gave way before the devil's brew of anxiety, excitement, dread and adrenaline that has juiced up men and boys facing their first taste of blood and flame since they crept from the caves ... *He shall baptize you with the Holy Ghost and with fire* (Luke 3:16) ... *GOTT MIT UNS* (Adolf Hitler).

Amphibious and mountain equipment materialized. The jeeps were crudely waterproofed by the Navy for an ocean voyage ending in a splash on someone's beach somewhere. The rope ladder and landing barge routine was resumed on Chesapeake Bay.

And as the outfit moved ever closer to its appointment with apocalypse, there was the matter of security. In his search of the files for interpreters and interrogators Frank Merchant had stumbled on evidence of an internal spy system under regimental intelligence on the lookout for, as he put it, "expressions of disloyalty, disaffection and radicalism. Griff was one of them." Such recruitment of vigilantes was evidently unknown to Sergeant Pullman but not to his right-hand man, Sergeant Woodhams:

> Griff and me were both in the Army Counter Intelligence Corps. The guy says, "You will pick a man outta each company in the Regiment and appoint him to the C.I.C. You will give him these stamps, and he will write to this address to this shoemaking company in Texas, and they'll report what they think is any subversive activity." We used to kid about it and call each other the spies. You'd get the goofiest reports. Some guy had it in for so-and-so—"He has four extra pairs o' shoes"—stuff like that.

Old Merchant's resort to bibulosity as an antidote for his alienation from all matters military had already been responsible for his banishment down to B Company at Pine Camp; someone had relented, however, perhaps Uncle Charley himself, and he was reprieved. But now he got the boot again, and he thought he knew why: "My long, unpleasant monologue about our officers one night in the barracks was reported and apparently stimulated Colonel Ankcorn to return me to B Company."

Private Merchant suspected he'd blown the cover of the C.I.C. and had the impression the spying was abandoned before the Division went overseas. Like a kid benched before the Big Game, he would follow the fortunes and misfortunes of the Ironheads, and muse upon the comradeship, for the rest of his days. "We were away from the National Guard denigration of easterners, radicals and intellect in the rifle companies. Notice Pullman's regard for bright guys, a general alleviation of disciplinary meanness or racial prejudice (albeit anti-Semitism was there, perhaps unconsciously supported from above). Life in the Platoon was quite different from servitude in the rifle companies. It prided itself on being weird and not truly G.I. [mass-produced Government Issue, specifically a buck private in the Infantry]. Its spirit was its shared, saving sense of humor, which kept those of us who are still alive, alive."

Comradeship yes, but what of love, the absence of which makes the heart grow fonder, love left behind in the going-off to war? Few in the Platoon were married; fewer still would risk the fondness lest the absence be forever. Helen Weiler had taught Phil Vollhardt to dance so she could take him to her junior prom and wanted to tie the knot before he boarded the boat. Not until he was home safe, he told her.

Only two dared take the step as each step took them closer to the parting.

Dave O'Keefe would rush out of Devens for Connecticut and home by bus, taxi, train or thumb to pay court to Katie Colerick, then back for the Monday morning bugle. It was a last-minute, picture-book wedding (*see page 42*).

Mickey Smith and Edith Moore met in her parents' home while she was patriotically entertaining a couple of the boys from Devens. They canoed on the Charles River in Boston, danced at Norumbega Park and took in the springtime concerts of the Boston Pops Orchestra. When he was moved on to Pickett, Edie joined him; they married and were together three more times. She got the word to him before he sailed that she was pregnant. The Xs for the kisses in his letters were blacked out by the censor just in case it was some kinda code.

The last 125,000 of General Erwin Rommel's almost invincible Afrika Korps and about as many Italian soldiers surrendered to an Allied force of veteran British Desert Rats and American G.I.s rapidly becoming so, led by Generals Montgomery and Patton. Africa was at last rid of the odious Axis presence.

Sergeant Pullman was given an unidentifiable contour map of the beach the Regiment was to hit and made a scale model on a sand table for his men to commit to memory. Where? He guessed Sardinia, maybe Spain.

On the first of June they rolled out of Pickett for the ride to Camp Patrick Henry, and then to Newport News, where they boarded the transports, twenty-eight of them carrying the entire Division with a pair of cruisers and eighteen destroyers as escorts. A week later, after thirty-three months overpreparing for it, they steamed off to World War II. Two more weeks, and we replacements-to-be completed our thirteen of basic at Camp Croft, all the training we ever got, and the 45th arrived in the harbor of Oran.

Bathless and shirtless under the baking Oranian sun, fourteen thousand Thunderbirds crowded the rails to watch the Navy gobs in their whites pile into the landing barges for a taste of the dubious delights ashore. In the predawn of the twenty-fifth of June, after two more tantalizing days, Cent Force weighed anchor, steamed along the barren Algerian coast to the east, and without explanation came to a stop off a stretch of beach even more forlorn than the rest.

The only route ashore for the wobbly 'Birds, by now three weeks at sea, was over the side and down the chain ladders, with rifles and full field packs banging and battering, and into the landing barges. As they grounded in the waist-deep water they were opened up on by a splatter of overhead machine-gun fire and an orchestrated charade of dynamite explosions, flying sand and flares before they stumbled up the beach into an entanglement of barbed wire.

They'd been set up for a sucker-punch by their old friendly foe from the war games back in the States, the 36th Division, shipped over ultimately to fight but meanwhile to be sparring partner for combat units arriving at the Advanced Amphibious Training Base.

The 157th came ashore where it was supposed to, but the Navy landed the 179th and 180th miles off target. Watching the debacle, General Omar Bradley, to whose Second Corps of General Patton's Seventh Army the 45th had been assigned, was aghast and expostulated to General William Kean, his chief of staff, "Good Lord! Suppose they miss it by that much in Sicily?" Kean did not reply. "It was too grim to contemplate," thought Bradley.[5]

Fortunately not in the first wave ashore, under Sergeant Pullman's laid-back supervision the I&R Platoon encamped in the desert with the rest of regimental HQ near Arzou, twenty miles east of Oran.

Later General Patton reflected to the assembled officers of the Division:

Battle is the most magnificent competition in which a human being can indulge. It brings out all that is best; it removes all that is base.

All men are afraid in battle. The coward is the one who lets his fear overcome his sense of duty.[6]

Somebody told the recently anointed Ironhead Henry Mills, as cocky in his way, that Blood and Guts also swore that day that "if he knew the Forty-fifth was comin' over, and that they were so goddam bad, he'da turned the boats around and sent 'em back because he didn't want 'em. Patton knew that was horseshit. In fact he'd asked for the Forty-fifth. And there was two guys ridin' by in a jeep hollered at him, 'Blow it out yer ass!'"

At 1630 on the fifth of July Cent Force sailed again, carrying the Division as battle-ready as it would ever be. Back on the Mediterranean a few thousand copies of *The Soldier's Guide to Sicily* were handed around.

Buried in Andy Zapiecki's jeep somewhere in the hold of the transport *Susan B. Anthony* was a hand-cranked Victrola and a box of records he'd been lugging around for eight months. When the turntable lost a ball bearing and wouldn't turn, Phil Vollhardt, the

The transport *Susan B. Anthony* at Oran, Algeria, July 5, 1943 (*U.S. Navy. Now in the collections of the National Archives.*)

mechanical whiz, fixed it with a brass bead from his dog-tag chain. Armed with that kind of ingenuity, the Ironheads were obviously ready for come what may.

An ocean away, having completed our basic infantry training back at Camp Croft, as if on cue we replacements-to-be boarded the train for maneuvers at Fuckin' Rucker in the asshole of Alabama, not in the least ready for come what may.

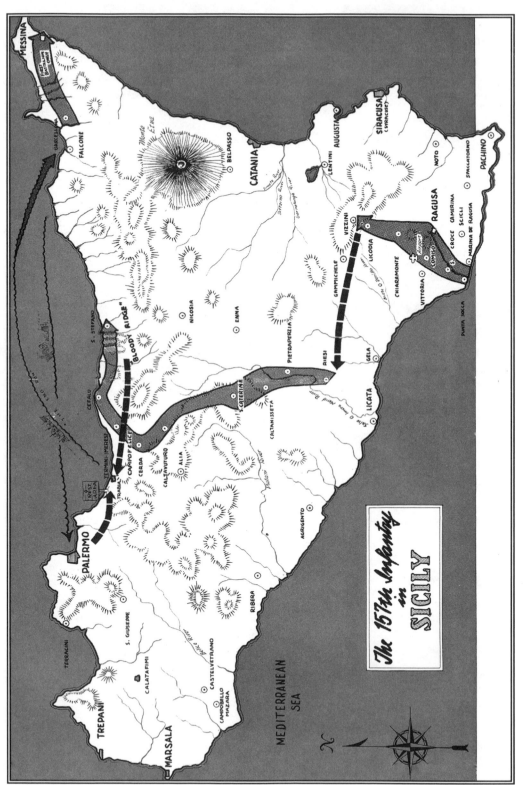

The 157th Infantry in SICILY

(Department of Defense)

❧ 3 ❧

OPERATION BARN DOOR

Sicily: Santa Croce Camerina to Messina
July–August 1943

AFTER WEEKS OF IDEAL INVASION WEATHER, the wind rose on the eighth of July and overtook the Allied convoy creeping as stealthily toward the island of Sicily as 580 ships could creep. By nightfall 228,000 stomachs were rolling and pitching in a roaring gale.

Could they even reach the beaches? General Eisenhower anxiously fingered his seven lucky coins. General Bradley was in sick bay, under the knife for an acute attack of piles and was miserable at both ends. General Patton felt the shortness of breath that was usual before a polo game.

And what if they did? Doug Studebaker, who stuck with his pals when the discovery of a hernia just before leaving the States would have disqualified him for combat if he chose, had read that life expectancy in the trenches of the previous war was about eight minutes and figured he wasn't gonna come back anyway. "It didn't make me reckless, but I didn't worry as much. I did worry that I'd screw up or run like hell."

At 2230 (10:30 PM), with four hours to go, the gale moderated, but not the seas. Admiral Alan Kirk had to hold back the ships carrying the 45th as the storm bore them toward the coast in the blackness to avoid tangling with the convoy bringing in the First Canadian on his right, delaying H-hour until 3:45 AM.[1]

Scout boats nearly swamped in the westerly-driven surf crashing high on the sandbars off the beaches and were slewed away from their objectives by a stiff alongshore current, some missing their assigned landing sectors entirely. Then the softening-up bombardment from the cruisers and destroyers lying offshore shattered the night, and then the eerie drone of our bombers approaching from North Africa, and the CRACK, CRACK, CRACK-CRACK, CRACK of their payloads smashing into the sand and soil of Sicily.

Transport Division 5, carrying the 45th Division's 157th Infantry Regiment, anchored in parallel lines four or five miles off the southwest coast of the island and was attacked for almost an hour just before dawn by thirteen high-flying Italian bombers and a squadron of torpedo planes that failed (or perhaps declined) to make a direct hit on the ships.[2]

The men were ordered belowdecks, where there was some protection from bombs and falling flak, and earnestly wished themselves ashore. Jimmy Dowdall was at a table "downstairs" in the *Susan B. Anthony* awaiting the on-deck call when the first bombs dropped. "One we heard pretty close. An' gosh, we're tryin' to be nonchalant, but our knuckles were showin' white on the table. Next one dropped on the other side, farther away, an' then they got more distant, an' there was a little sigh."

And then it was over the side with Private Dowdall and the rest:

> I was one of the first down the cargo nets. I hit the landing craft around the middle and went to the stern, and then the wave lifted it up to the rail o' the ship, and everybody steps on except one guy. He delays too long, the boat's goin' down, and he jumps and lands in the middle. His rifle bangs against his head, his helmet goes one way, and the helmet liner another, and he's on his hands 'n' knees lookin' up, and the lieutenant says, "Don't you DO that again!" I got a fit o' laughin', and everybody looked at me strangely. I was afraid, but there was somethin' inside me that kinda detached itself.

Hundreds of the flat-bottomed landing craft swamped in the surf or came in miles from their assigned beaches, breaking up units as no hostile fire could have. Twenty-seven men from E and F Companies, weighed down with full equipment, drowned when their boats collided on unexpected rocks off Punta Braccetto. Plenty more would have been Thunderbird soup had they faced Germans. As it was, a handful of stunned Italian coastal units offered less than token resistance and surrendered at the convenience of their liberators.

Winston Churchill's brainchild, Operation Husky, had been commanded by British General Sir Harold R. Alexander but dominated strategically, psychologically and numerically by General Montgomery, whose Eighth Army was mainly responsible for expelling the Germans from North Africa. The Brits remained skeptical of Yank fighting ability. General Patton was a grandstander, and the 45th had never been in battle, so his Seventh Army was assigned to secure the west of the island and Palermo, while Monty would take the glory road to Messina. There the script called for his Desert Rats to cut off the escape of the German and Italian armies across the Strait to the toe of Italy in a repeat of the encirclement of a million prisoners that ended the North African campaign.

In fact, both British and American staff considered the invasion of a classically defensible mountainous island a dubious strategy further skewed by Montgomery's ambition for another personal triumph. By vetoing the logical landing at Palermo, which would have secured that port for the mass transit of supplies, he forced Husky's entire support to come in over the beaches the hardest way so that he could strike directly up the island at Messina, the only feasible escape hatch to Italy for the Axis troops. Bradley, commanding Patton's

Landing craft of the 45th ride the surf or swamp. (*Department of Defense*)

Sixth Corps, thought the landings should have been at Calabria, the toe of Italy, blocking the Axis escape from Sicily by way of Messina—except that the Allies had agreed not to think about an Italian mainland invasion for the moment.

In his Seventh Army Patton had the Third Division from the North African fighting and two Ranger battalions on the left. The First Division (the Big Red One) from Africa, another battalion of Rangers, and a combat team from the Second Armored Division were in the center. On the right was the 45th Division, combat-loaded from the States. Regimental combat teams from the Second Armored and First Divisions were in floating reserve. In all, 228,000 Americans were in the Western Task Force, 580 ships and 1,124 on-board landing craft.

Patton regarded the 45th's as his key landing because its first objectives were the Comiso and Biscari airports, reportedly unusable by the enemy, though Bradley had misgivings about throwing a green division into the first major amphibious landing of the war, albeit "there was probably no better group of guinea pigs."[3]

Yet it was the Navy that scattered the Division's 180th Regiment over ten miles into the sectors of its 179th and the First Division; the Hermann Goering Panzer Division counterattacked and captured most of the Regiment's Second Battalion before its tanks were stopped by rallying resistance and naval gunfire within a mile of the beach.[4]

So far, pretty tough on the guinea pigs.

The 157th got ashore almost unopposed, with a breather to reassemble and match landscape to maps before pushing the four miles inland to its first objective of the war, Santa Croce Camerina. Its First Battalion moved up to overlooking high ground behind a reassuring artillery barrage, unaware that a battalion of the 505th Paratroopers was moving in on the other side of the town. They spotted each other barely in time to avoid a clash. Five hundred prisoners were taken. An Italian battery that might have raked the beach was found to consist of captured French guns for which the gunners had no shells. Close too.

Casualties—and replacements (*Department of Defense*)

Upon making the beach, the I&R Platoon didn't immediately assume a heroic posture. Corporal Dominick Trubia's patrol drew some sniper fire and retired to a barn where they shot a hole in a cask of red wine and passed out in their first encounter with what they denounced upon regaining consciousness as the purple death, worse than death itself. Thus did Dom celebrate his return to the land of his parents, who had emigrated to a farm colony of fellow-Sicilians around Mount Morris in upstate New York.

Playing it safe in the confusion of the landing, Henry Mills found and stuck with the regimental sergeant-major.

> I mean I'm a twenty-year-old kid. He can't be wrong. Next morning we're sitting on this intersection, and here come two of our columns up each side of the road. The company commander in the lead says, "What the hell are you guys doin' here?" I

says we been here all night; we understood this was taken. "Hell," he says, "this is the point [of the advance guard]. Nobody's been ahead of us."

Meanwhile Sergeant Bill Woodhams was in the regimental command post (CP) in a farmhouse when a plane roared over.

I fell on the floor with everybody else except this big, tall figure of Charley Ankcorn with those ice-blue eyes, looking right at me—laying on my belly on the floor and looking back up—as if to say, "You stupid jerk!" I wasn't afraid of gitting hit with a bomb. I was afraid of gitting hit with a airplane!

Mid-summer heat, the shimmering, scraggly Sicilian hillsides, the parched vineyards, the winding dirt roads turned to dust as fine as flour, the invading Americans sweat-and-saltwater-caked with it, and startling, repelling, swelling, sweet-stinking corpses, gray with it, sprawled in the ditches.

The second day found the 157th coming up on its next objective, the airfield six miles through the hills beyond Santa Croce Camerina and the town of Comiso. Woodhams took his crew of Doug Studebaker, Mohawk Mullenax, and Dick Bashore, his raggedy-Andy, hard-drinking jeep driver from Colorado, up a hill overlooking the airfield from which they watched German fighters escaping off the supposedly "unusable" runway ahead of the attacking Americans. One climbed past so close that Bashore gave him a burst from his BAR (Browning Automatic Rifle). The pilot swung around and roared by again, leaned over, and thumbed his nose.

Colonel Ankcorn called for support. Our tanks clanked up to the airport and knocked out five Italian tanks. Behind the eerie, exciting, whistling crack of our 105-millimeter howitzer artillery and singing mortar shells, the very nervous men of the Third Battalion moved in, and the defending Italians, strengthened now by Germans, pulled back across the airfield to a group of buildings.

From a ditch on the edge of the runway, Sergeant Jack Pullman fired into the buildings, and when they were taken, walked over and found a dead German whom he may or may not have killed. From a pocket he liberated some snapshots of the Russian Front and cut the Hermann Goering Division patch from the blouse. The first spoils of war.

From another hill Corporal Zapiecki and his crew descended to the airfield, where they had their first close-up of a German, one of Hitler's men, albeit a captured one.

Here's this dejected soldier sitting down. That sonofabitch was way over six feet and weighed about two hunnert and fifty. I'd been reading about the Afrika Korps, and here's this guy in this Kraut helmet, and his face is bulging out of it, and I says, "Boy, I better get the hell outta here if they got some more like that!"[5]

Comiso Airport was the Division's first major prize. Although a few flew the coop, 25 intact enemy planes were taken, with 500 bombs, 200,000 gallons of aviation gasoline, and 450 prisoners. The brass called it the "Fort Benning attack" as if it were an exercise at the Officers' Training School, because it didn't feel so different from the Blues versus the Reds in Louisiana, except that the few dead and wounded really were.

Still, it was into the skies, in the first hours, that the invaders glanced over their shoulders with the greatest apprehension. Phil Vollhardt was on a patrol with Mullenax, who had armed himself with a BAR from a dead G.I., bandoliers of ammunition crossed over his broad shoulders, and a brace of captured Italian .44-caliber revolvers with only twelve shots between them. Suddenly a German fighter plane was on top of them. Instead of thumbing his nose he dropped a bomb.

> We hit the dirt. Mullenax was up on the ridge, and it blew him into a crack in a rock. He disappeared. Where's Mullenax? We looked around, and there he was, wedged in the rock. It took two of us to haul him out, and he wasn't even scratched.

That night naval shells whirred and crackled over their heads, red-hot against the blackness of the sky, reaching for the apex, gathering speed in the fading earthward plunge that ended in mushroom lightning flashes and crumps of thunder bouncing between the hills.

During the second day the Germans intensified their bombing and strafing of artillery batteries, command posts, the beaches and the ships offshore. There was a rumored alert that enemy paratroopers might be dropped behind the lines. But the real alert—that 144 *American* planes from Tunisia were about to fly over the 45th's sector and drop 2,000 paratroopers from the 82nd Airborne Division behind the German lines in front of the First Division—didn't arrive until late that evening.

Zapiecki was at the regimental CP beyond Comiso:

> The I&R had the job o' passing down the message to the battalions that the paratroopers were gonna be dropped from planes and hold yer fire. It was about ten o'clock. But by the time we got there, here come the planes from Africa. What we didn't know was that the Germans at the same time were coming over to bomb the ships. They musta met each other right about there.

They almost did. The Germans hit the Navy with a heavy raid just before 10 PM and blew up an ammunition ship that gave them a spectacular torch to bomb by. The ships and anti-aircraft batteries on the beach responded with everything they had. Just as the raiders took off, the first of our low-flying C-47s packed with the jittery 82nd droned over. Although the Navy had promised to reserve a fire-free corridor for the flyover, word of the drop was still filtering haphazardly down through the troop echelons on shore.

Zapiecki had a ringside seat.

> The ships started firing, and in the confusion the paratroopers didn't know what was going on. A new soldier's gonna shoot at anything that moves, these guns are

blazing away at the sky, and all the guys on shore are shooting machine guns, fifty-caliber, everything, at the German bombers and the American paratroopers, and they're scattered all over Sicily. So they blame us for it.

Somewhere in the middle of it all Trubia was lying up against a stone wall with his BAR.

> Every time I'd see a parachute go across the moon I'd spray it. I was plenty frightened to see all these chutes coming down on us. But we never got any return fire. I think they landed far enough ahead of us that by the time they reorganized and morning came we could see what a horrible mistake we'd made.

The warning never reached the 45th's artillery either. One gunner was mistaken in the darkness for an enemy paratrooper and killed by his buddies.

Some of the crippled C-47s were ditched in the sea. A few made it back to Africa. Others speeded up and overran their drop by miles. Twenty-three were shot down. The crew of the *Susan B. Anthony* got one as it crossed their bow. Thirty-seven other C-47s were shot up. Eighty-one paratroopers were killed, 132 wounded, sixteen missing.[6]

Pushing on, Third Battalion attacked the town of Licodia Eubea, about twenty-five miles inland, and ran into roving elements of the Hermann Goering Division, whose abandoned quarters we Crofters would occupy in Naples. Here the Thunderbirds came under the flat-trajectory fire of the dreaded 88-millimeter guns that would dog them for the rest of the war. Originally a high-velocity anti-aircraft (flak) gun, the 88 was a lethally accurate cannon employed so successfully for ground warfare in Africa that it was adapted as an artillery piece and anti-tank and anti-personnel weapon, principally mounted on a tank. The high-powered shell screamed in like a banshee, could knock out a tank over a mile off and terrorized us with its direct ground fire and timed air bursts over our heads.

The Hermann Goerings threw in heavy artillery and fought through the streets with machine guns and flame-throwers before withdrawing. Third Battalion lost twenty men killed and forty wounded. Andy and his crew nervously went in, doorway to doorway.

> Some guys had come into the town square in a half-track. One burst of a flame-thrower, and the only one that come out of it was Riggs. The rest of 'em were burned to a crisp. They were always knocking Riggs back in the States and didn't wanna promote him. "Boy," he says, "in combat I'll show 'em! I'll show 'em!" And there he was, laying in that ditch. I rolled him over, and it was him. He got hit once. The bullet split his head all to nothin'.

And there in the streets of Licodia a sniper got Herb Glover in the chest, the loftiest target in the Regiment, a pipe-smoking young farmer from Lamar, Colorado. The Platoon's first casualty was about to throw a grenade when he was shot and shoved the pin back so it wouldn't explode before the medics took him away.

⁂ ⁂ ⁂

The Yanks were meeting stiffening resistance in their push up through the low, rolling, desolate ridges and valleys of the interior of Sicily while the Brits were stalled in the malarial Catania Plain leading up to the two-mile-high bulk of Mt. Etna athwart the coast road to Messina. When a limited flanking attempt around the defending Germans failed, Montgomery pulled what Bradley in outrage called "the most arrogant, egotistical, selfish and dangerous move in the whole of combined operations in World War II."[7]

Without any notice the Eighth Army commander shifted the First Canadians and 51st British Highlanders west along Highway 124, directly across the front of Bradley's Second Corps. His object was simply to bypass Catania and Etna—and his rival Patton—with a knockout left hook to Messina. After the fact, he informed Alexander, who then informed his Allies of the switch. Patton uncharacteristically bit his lip and kept his counsel.

The 157th was only a thousand yards from Highway 124. Bradley had no choice but to halt the advance of the 45th toward Vizzini while the British crossed its front in the sights of the American artillery that was about to fire on a gaggle of enemy tanks and vehicles beyond the highway, nixing the barrage while the Germans had a free breather to shift tactics. Later General Bradley wished he'd balked at Patton's acquiescence in this British arrogance. Had the Seventh Army not been forced to hike left to make room for the Eighth, he believed, it would have dashed north to the coast and east to Messina, relieving Montgomery to break through the Catania Plain, and shortening the campaign by weeks.

The vino hunters Val Mullenax, Bill Woodhams, Herb Glover and Dick Bashore (*Courtesy of William E. Woodhams*)

Beyond Caltanissetta the 45th hikes northward. (*Department of Defense*)

However, two could play this game. Patton fired off the Third Division to take Palermo and with sudden swiftness made his response to Montgomery, sideslipping the entire 45th behind the First Division fifty-eight miles west to Riesi. There, the next day—July 18—the 157th led the race to cut the Palermo–Messina road along the north coast.

The first objective was Caltanissetta, a rail center and den of Fascist operations in Sicily, so heavily bombed that most of the civilian population of sixty thousand had fled into the countryside. Bypassing a knocked-out bridge, the Regiment crossed the Salso River and took the city with hardly a shot. Here for the first time the dogfaces saw and smelled what soldiers can do to civilians. Les Gerencer, the skinniest guy in the Platoon, who before the Army worked as an industrial molder for forty cents an hour in Phillipsburg, New Jersey, walked through Caltanissetta with a rifle company. "All you could smell was the dead in the rubble, and the people on the side looking at you like you was some kinda bug."

Patton drove through and wrote in his diary:

> ... we killed at least 4,000 civilians by air alone and the place smelled to heaven as the bodies are still in the ruins. I had to feel sorry for the poor devils. [8]

He wrote his wife:

> Of all the countries I have ever been in, this is the most utterly damned. Dust, filth, bugs, and natives.

. . . The people are just on the verge of starving and look utterly hopeless, but don't like us and there is a lot of sniping which is bad for us but worse for the snipers . . . [9]

Back of my house is a little court yard. Yesterday I counted eleven children, eight goats, five dogs, and a horse, also a flock of chickens minus tails. The children were competing with the other animals for scraps of food . . .

I feel terribly sorry for the poor things. Wherever you pass them, they beg for food, but I suppose they are natural beggars.[10]

As the 157th pushed through the rugged hills of mid-Sicily toward Alimena, the lead company was pinned down by a battery of Italian artillery. An I&R crew prowling the front spotted them through the sharp eyes of Jose "Joe" Contreras, wiry Guardsman from the flatland around Bovina, Colorado, one of the earliest recruits to the Platoon, who radioed their position to the regimental artillery liaison officer, who got the commander of the 157th's supporting 158th Field Artillery Battalion of 105-millimeter howitzers, Colonel Dwight Funk, on the field phone.

The artillery relied for its targets on an elite of forward observers, or FOs, who knew more of trigonometry and the art of gunnery than the gunners themselves and like the I&R sought exposed observation posts (OPs) on the front. From these lookouts hopefully hidden from the enemy, usually miles ahead of their batteries, they would search for an enemy target, phone or radio back the position on the map and call for a white phosphorus smoke shell as a visual marker, instructing the gunners that it landed so many yards over or under and to the right or left of the target. This zeroing-in procedure was repeated until the white puffs were close enough to call for "fire for effect" with a lethal barrage of high explosives.

Infantry directing artillery fire was just not done, but here was a battery of enemy guns holding up the advance, and the I&R had them in its sights.

"OK, if Contreras can see it, let him fire it," said Colonel Funk.

Smiling and soft-spoken Joe had the instincts of an old-time cavalry scout and the eyesight of a prairie hawk. He called for a round of smoke. In a minute or so they heard the distant boom of the gun and the sighing whistle of the shell arcing overhead. A white puff blossomed out of the landscape a couple of hundred yards beyond the enemy guns, then the CHUNK of the exploding shell. Joe radioed back the yardage of the overshoot, the piece was lowered a hair, and the second smoke popped up, short a hundred yards. Another correction, and the third phosphorus was within fifty.

"Closer!" Contreras radioed.

"Whaddya want us to do, put 'em down their barrels?" the gunners relayed back. "We're firin' for effect!"

The 105s poured it on and knocked out the entire enemy battery. The liaison artillery officer claimed it was the first time ever that the infantry directed artillery fire. Seems unlikely, but from that day on the Ironheads were ad hoc forward observers for the big guns whenever they spotted "targets of opportunity," in the lingo of the gunners.[11]

Uncle Charley's Foot Cavalry were relieved by the 180th on July 20 and got off their dogs after eleven days of walking, shooting and getting shot at. For two more it was the grapes, peaches, watermelons and figs of the Sicilian countryside washed down with purple death—and out by the other G.I.s, the gastro-intestinal variety, or more graphically, the shits. Then back on their blisters for a hike-and-truck shuttle of thirty miles through the hills to Cerda, five miles short of the coastal road to the east of Palermo over which the enemy was methodically falling back toward Messina.

The Second Armored and Third Infantry Divisions occupied Palermo and the coast earlier the same day. Patton's strategy had worked. Monty's left hook flying past his nose had been no more effective than the stalled right jab in Catania, and Alexander now had no choice but to let the American swaggerer loose on the coast road in an all-out race of the egos for Messina.

The 157th reached the sparkling Tyrrhenian Sea, swung east along Highway 113 and took Cefalù, a picture-book port nestled between its small harbor and a sheer headland 1,200 feet high. The 180th again passed through the 157th, which paused for a weary moment. Meanwhile belief in the accuracy of Allied precision bombing had led to the first air raid on Rome on July 19. A thousand tons of bombs were dropped by 560 planes on the central rail yards. Some fell wide, killing two thousand civilians, it was claimed, injuring many more, and heavily damaging public and historic buildings.

The day after this terrifying strike against his capital, old King Victor Emmanuel called in the ailing and shaken Italian dictator and tried to persuade him to break with Hitler before all of Italy tasted more of such bitter fruits of its misalliance. The Grand Council of

Cefalù, Sicily (*Collection of the author*)

the Fascist Party toppled Mussolini on July 26, put him under house arrest, and replaced him with the moderate Marshal Pietro Badoglio. Hitler ordered his divisions across the Alps. Italy would be a battleground in the defense of Germany.

That night the 157th resumed leading the Division along the coastal highway toward Messina. The 179th was on the right, while fifteen miles over the mountains to the south, the First Division advanced in parallel.

Cut in and out of cliffs that rose straight up from the sea and intercepted by a deep corduroy of ravines and high, rocky ridges, Highway 113 twisted in precarious company with the railroad poking through tunnels that penetrated a series of promontories over a distance of about nine miles east of Cefalù. The Germans had armed this succession of blind corners with machine-gun ambushes and mortars zeroed in on minefields.

As the Regiment passed through the 180th, the Platoon encountered the chilling work of one such ambush on a motor recon patrol from the 180th's I&R, four men in an amphibian—one of the oversized, overrated jeep/boats Jack Pullman in disgust had traded in for jeeps before leaving the States. Mullenax was enraged: "Four good men lost because they couldn't git that damn thing turned around in the road and got shot to pieces."

A lesson here. With no armor, a jeepload of guys up on the front relied on speed, a tight turning radius, and a laid-back driver the likes of the sardonic New Jerseyite Vernon Dilks:

> When I went on patrol with Mickey Smith in the front seat, the two scouts would sit on one cheek in the rear, and as soon as they heard shooting, ZOOM—right off the back. And I'd have to stop the thing and try to get off myself. With the sandbags on the floor against land mines, you had to drive with your toes, your heels way up in the air, and you gotta clutch and brake.
>
> First time under fire, like everybody else you're scared, but you figger you're in it so you hope for the best. A lotta times on those ole winding roads, the Krauts would let us go up there. Coulda cut us in half if they'd wanted to, but they wouldn't open fire 'cause they knew we was gonna go back and report no resistance, and then when the rifle companies come up they'd get the hell cut outta them. They were masters at camouflage. You could walk by three feet away and never know. And they knew the terrain 'cause they were there long before us.
>
> At night it wasn't too bad when you could run that big ole blackout light on the left fender. But a lotta places all you could use was those lil-biddy lights, and on those black roads you couldn't see nothin' unless the moon was out. You'd be driving along in a convoy with the companies moving up, and a truck up ahead would stop, and the next thing you'd hear would be clunk, clunk, clunk, right on down the line like dominoes.
>
> The driver stayed with the jeep. You took water, food, mail up to the guys for the OPs. They wanted that jeep back. They didn't care whether they got you back.

As for the riflemen up ahead, Jim Dowdall was hurrying along the dusty coastal road between columns of them, on a mission to the lead battalion. The midday heat was a cooker.

The engineers precariously repair Highway 113 on the north coast, blown up by the methodically retreating Germans. (*U.S. Army*)

'Twas a ten-minute break around lunch. They had their rations. Some o' the guys took off their boots, called for the medics, took off their socks, an' the heels an' soles o' their feet were so blistered the medics had to let the water out. The poor medics didn't get any break. Here they were on their lunch, an' there were so many o' these guys. As I walked on, the order came, "On yer feet! Ready to roll! On yer feet! On yer feet!" An' these guys started to scream, "Wait a minute! Can't get my socks on! Can't get my boots on!"

And they pulled on their socks, and struggled into their boots. And they stood up, put their rifle butts on the ground to give 'em support, slung 'em, took a few steps with the pain, and settled into that peculiar shuffle o' the riflemen, and kept goin'. And to go through that, and perhaps git shot an' killed or wounded, 'twas a fantastic thing.

Farther along, where the road edged close to the sea, Dowdall was now in the back seat of a jeep with a recon patrol heading east.

> I noticed two or three of our guys walkin' up the slope from the shore with their helmets full o' seashells, and thought to myself, "They're crazy to go to all that trouble for souvenirs, kinda asinine."
>
> Comin' back, here's this little rise off the road, and this new grave with a neat border o' seashells around it, and I think a crude cross. And I felt about an inch high on account o' me first thought.

By the next morning the Thunderbirds had reached the high ground above the west bank of the Tusa River, twelve miles east of Cefalù. Their objective was Santo Stefano, only five miles farther, but on the other side of a roller coaster of ridges of which the rockiest and ruggedest was Motta d'Affermo.

A fortnight into their dogged withdrawal toward their escape hatch of Messina, the Germans were digging in for their crucial time-buying stand athwart the most formidable of the mountain ridge barriers to the Seventh Army's advance along the north coast. Like a pair of reinforced gateposts, Motta d'Affermo rose steep above the Tusa River and the coastal highway before the 157th, while twenty-five miles southeast across the roadless ridges, the mountain fastness of Troina stalled the First Division. As long as the enemy gateposts held, the gate would not swing open.

Scaling those rocky, open ridges with rifle and pack was a mountaineer's work; with machine guns, heavy mortars, ammunition, water and rations it was a mule's. Cowpokes and miners notwithstanding, there were mighty few muleskinners in the outfit. Sicilian and U.S. Army, some of the gallant little beasts of burden were driven so hard by well-intentioned dudes that they dropped dead, and some just balked. Others were killed or were wounded and shot. A frustrated platoon sergeant calling the roll was answered from the darkness: "Two four-legged mules, sarge, and forty-two two-legged ones."

Bill Woodhams took Mullenax and Studebaker up on the ridge west of Motta d'Affermo, overlooking the heat-parched bed of the Tusa River, and spotted several Germans on their hands and knees way down below, laying charges under the bridge. Before they could call down the artillery on them, the bridge exploded.

The riflemen of First Battalion led off the attack up through the sharply terraced olive and lemon groves northeast of Motta on the morning of July 28, ran into a storm of fire and took cover. Thus began the Battle of Bloody Ridge.

Colonel Ankcorn had sent Woodhams and his crew back up the mountain to follow the action and set up an observation post, cautioning them to take care, that he expected a big fight up there. They gained the terraces on the northern flank, overlooking the sea.

> Studie and Mullenax were farther back than I was when I heard this German machine gun go off. Sounded like it was right underneath me. I got my field glasses off and set down on the edge of the terrace and looked over. I thought I could drop

a grenade on it. And then the damn thing cut loose, and boy, laid a string o' lead right alongside o' my rear end. I thought I was hit, the rocks stung so bad. I fell over the edge, lost my cartridge belt and everything else, and ran around back down the terrace and dropped down a coupla more, and here was Studebaker pressed in against the wall. "Git down, git down!" he said. "They're shootin'!" So I jumped in with him, and where's Mohawk?

The big guy was still one or two terraces above them, standing there, when the machine-gun bullets spattered toward him. Studie yelled, "Mohawk, they're shootin' at you, goddammit, get down!" Turning around, Mullenax yelled back, "I know it, goddammit!" Then he jumped down and joined them, exclaiming that he could see two hundred Germans attacking. As they leapt down over the terraces, they heard a RAT-TAT-TAT-TAT above them. Somebody had a BAR, and it was music to Studie's ears:

WHAM WHAM WHAM, like a poke in the snoot. And they come bouncing down the terraces after us, a squad from B Company. They had two prisoners and had left two of their wounded up there. The kid with the BAR was right outta Hollywood, the typical towheaded, all-American boy, had a scratch on his hand and a handkerchief wrapped around it with a few beautiful drops of blood coming out, nothing big, but picturesque as hell, and he was really excited. His adrenaline was up. "I musta killed twenty o' them sonsabitches!" Christ, he may not have hit anybody, but he was really high.

The trail was real tortuous coming down, and in some places you had to hang on to the bushes. The prisoners weren't all that sure of their guard. He was a boy who probably had a beautiful sense of humor and wouldn't hurt a fly, but he had a scar on one corner of his mouth that pulled it up and made him look meaner'n hell. He kept poking at 'em with his bayonet, and they went down that mountain without taking their hands off their heads.

As both sides dug in, the casualties included some of the illusions each had about the fighting abilities of the other. At the end of the first day, the Regiment counted 108 of its men dead, wounded or missing, the highest toll of the campaign.

What came to be expected as the inevitable German counterattack crashed down the slopes the second morning but was repulsed with great difficulty, confusion and more heavy losses. A knot of dogfaces digging into their K rations waved and yelled at what they thought was a column of very startled G.I.s moving along the slope to the south of them and received rude bursts of Schmeisser machine-pistol fire in response.[12] As darkness descended, the Second Platoon of A Company attacked, only to meet fire that seemed to be coming from the First Platoon advancing some distance over on its right, whereupon radio communications between the two failed.

Zapiecki and his crew came tumbling down the hill.

We come off there, an' they got their asses knocked off. The Krauts could see 'em from on top an' were rollin' hand grenades down the slope. Our artillery laid a

rolling barrage in there, an' we were tellin' 'em how far up the hill it was goin', up
an' up an' up. Ankcorn was bawlin' the shit outta Major Moore, in charge o' supplies. "Those guys want food an' ammo, an' you get it up there if you hafta carry it
yerself!"

But we couldn't get no trucks across this dry river bed. Three German tanks
come outta that curve in the road an' fired, but we were behind the hill, too far away
to get mortar fire, an' we didn't worry about flat trajectory from the tanks. The guys
had been pushed down to the bottom o' the Ridge, an' they rustled up trucks with
food an' ammo an' everything. The one who was directin' traffic there useta sing,
"Oh, the pale moon was she-eye-ning o'er the green moun-tin-a!"

So we were taken off. I was tired, an' they had little shallow holes dug in the CP
where you could rest up. I'm sleepin', covered with a blanket, an' someone comes an'
says, "Hey Andy! Here's Patton!" I says, "Aw, piss on him. I wanna sleep." An' I
looked up an' saw them pearlhandled revolvers. Patton was standin' about four or
five yards away, an' he says, "Don't wake up the colonel if he's sleepin'." An' this guy
says the colonel's been up there on the hill for two or three hours.

"All the men steal looks at me," the General had confided to his diary, "it is complimentary but a little terrible. I am their God or so they seem to think."[13]

This was probably when Patton drove to the CP as the First Battalion was attacking. "I
talked to the men and said, 'I hope you know how good you are, for everyone else does. You
are magnificent.' I also told the engineers what fine work they have done. They have, but
love to be told."[14]

What he told General Middleton, however, was that he looked tired and his Division
looked "sticky." The Seventh Army commander had the boss of the 45th in mind for a corps
if he ever got a new army for the Normandy invasion, but didn't hesitate to prod him now:
"This is a horse race, in which the prestige of the U.S. Army is at stake. We must take
Messina before the British. Please use your best efforts to facilitate the success of our
race."[15]

Correspondent Quentin Reynolds dropped in at the regimental aid station to check
out the costs of the race of the egos and reported from Palermo:

The boys lay there after their wounds were dressed, smoking, usually, and not saying much, because they were still a bit dazed from the pounding they had taken at
Bloody Ridge, and the noise of the guns still rang in their ears.

I asked one of them how he had got it.

"This morning," he drawled in his Colorado accent, "we took that damn ridge,
and then they counter-attacked like they always do and kicked us out. We went back
at them and they raised a white flag. Of course, we thought they were surrendering.
We should have known better after Tunis, where they used their own dead as booby
traps, so that when we went to bury them, we would get blown to pieces.

"Anyway, we went up the hill and we were halfway up when they pulled down
the white flag and let us have it. They killed sixteen of us. Nice guys, these Nazis! The

British are right about them. They say the only good German is a dead German. There's no rules in this war. Well, if they want to fight it like that, it's okay with us."[16]

Prisoners and the Geneva Convention?

Two weeks earlier a rifle company of the 180th was ambushed by snipers near the mountain town of Butera. Thirty-eight Germans in uniform and five in civilian clothes were smoked out and captured. An overwrought young captain lined them all up against a barn and ordered them shot. About the same time a sergeant with a detail taking thirty-six German prisoners to the rear, fearing, he claimed later, that they'd overpower his men in the gathering darkness, ordered them mowed down by the side of the road.

The massacres came to the attention of General Bradley, who reported them in horror to Patton, who told him to order the two admitted perpetrators to claim the murdered prisoners were shot in self-defense or while attempting to escape. Patton made it clear to Bradley that he did not want bad press or to anger the public.[17] Patton's own opinion was that "both men were crazy."[18] Bradley ignored such "absurd instructions"[19] and had the two court-martialed.

During their trial the defendants argued that Patton had encouraged the Thunderbirds to kill prisoners, that "if the enemy resisted until we got to within 200 yards, he had forfeited his right to live," and that he had told them that snipers should be destroyed. Credit Patton's pep talk to the officers and noncoms in North Africa.[20]

According to Albert Wedemeyer from Operations Division:

> ... He admonished them to be very careful when the Germans or Italians raised their arms as if they wanted to surrender. He stated that sometimes the enemy would do this, throwing our men off guard. The enemy soldiers had on several occasions shot our unsuspecting men or had thrown grenades at them. Patton warned the members of the 45th Division to watch out for this treachery and to "kill the S.O.B.'s" unless they were certain of their real intention to surrender.[21]

Now Patton himself was investigated by the Army Inspector General. Bradley was furious. Had not the whole dirty affair been kept from the press, it would have disgraced Patton and the High Command and had unthinkable consequences for Americans captured by the Germans. "I inwardly boiled with anger. Patton's big mouth had us dancing on yet another griddle."[22] Eisenhower, boiling too, told him he talked too much, but Patton remained as unrepentant as ever, writing his wife:

> When I addressed the 45th Division in Africa just before sailing for Sicily, I got pretty bloody, trying to get an untried division to the sticking point ... However, I made no statements by which the wildest stretch of the imagination could be considered as directing the killing of prisoners ...[23]
>
> Some fair-haired boys are trying to say that I killed too many prisoners. Yet the same people cheer at the far greater killing of Japs. Well, the more I killed, the fewer

men I lost, but they don't think of that. Sometimes I think that I will quit and join a monestary [*sic*].[24]

Did the captain and the sergeant, new to combat, simply lose control of themselves over the enemy's heavy toll of their First Battalion? How about the G.I.s who carried out their orders? The two were found guilty, given suspended sentences, and returned to their units, where both were killed in action.

The evidence, and so the real extent of the wanton murder of soldiers, prisoners of war and civilians by both sides during World War II, is buried with them and can never be known.[25]

The night fighting on Bloody Ridge was so close and confused that dawn revealed to an A Company officer that what he had thought to be one of his own men sleeping beside him was a dead German. Live ones awoke in the hands of the Americans. The Germans counterattacked again, and the Second Platoon held its fire, thinking they were the First Platoon. As the Battalion was forced back, four of its machine gunners were killed covering the withdrawal.

On the fourth day the Germans dropped back to the next ridge above the town of Reitano. Three correspondents wanted to see the battleground. Hank Mills, who had just been driven off the Ridge by shellfire, drew the guide duty.

> I didn't wanna go back, but I told 'em to take their insignias off so they wouldn't reflect from the sun. It was pretty quiet. I'm sittin' on the river bank. They'd blowed the bridge, and a coupla our half-tracks come along, and one runs over a mine. They had all their C rations in there, and all I could see was cans o' C rations flyin' twenty-five feet up in the air. We got up there and was talkin' with some guys from A Company, that I'd been in before the I&R. Their first sergeant was killed there.

The Mills family clipped the dispatch of the Associated Press reporter from their paper and mailed it to their boy Henry.

> The capture of "Bloody Ridge," an almost perpendicular hill mass barring the American advance east along the northern coast toward the mountain village of Santo Stefano, is an epic battle of the brief Sicilian campaign.
>
> This natural rock-studded fortress held by Germans entrenched with machine guns in protecting draws and ravines was stormed and taken yesterday in blinding heat.
>
> Officers of American outfits who fought in North Africa said that the taking of "Bloody Ridge"—the nickname given it by the boys who fought there—was comparable to the seizing of formidable Hill 609 in Tunisia whose fall paved the way to the capture of Mateur in the closing days of the campaign.
>
> Here is the story of "Bloody Ridge" told to me by the boys who captured it. I met them while climbing up its frowning skirts on the rocky, tortuous trail which would break the heart of a mountain goat and which is strewn with the shoes thrown by pack mules:

Slipping and sliding through loose gravel and holding onto clumps of long grass and tough bushes, Pvt. Jerry Wolfe, (905 West End Avenue, New York City), worked his way down the slope for a drink. He was dripping sweat like a faucet.

"It was tough taking, but we took it and we will kick hell out of anybody who tries to take it from us," he said. He looked at my military guide, Pvt. Henry Mills (208 Fourth Avenue, Altoona, Pa.) and said, "You were up here yesterday, weren't you?"

Mills nodded.

"Well, then, you know how it went. We started up with a battalion yesterday morning and got driven off. Then we came back up again and got bounced right off. We came up a third time yesterday—and now we're here to stay."

As we moved up the twisting path, we passed German helmets, ammunition, pieces of uniform, all abandoned. There was a heavy burnt smell still lingering from grass fires started by American artillery fire which had blackened most of the countryside. Two soldiers came down the trail leading a pack mule—the only way water, food and other supplies can reach the troops on the top except on their own backs.

"We are lucky any of us are alive—we were up here the whole day under heavy fire, without food or water," said Pvt. Frank Larosa (231 Smith Street, Brooklyn, N.Y.).[26]

Sergeant Bill Mauldin, the cartoonist then creating the classic dogfaces of World War II, Willie and Joe, as composites of his buddies in the 45th, hiked up on the Ridge and came down with a sketch of five men from the 157th clambering over the rocks, one firing a rifle grenade at an enemy position, another hauling on a balky mule, the other three lugging the supplies two dead mules had been carrying. The "babyfaced" (as the correspondents called him) New Mexican, not yet twenty-two, had been with the Thunderbirds since September 1940. He was a rifleman in the 180th for a year before his passionate rendering of the forever unshaven, sodden, scrimy, scraggly, stoical essence of the American foot soldier put him where he belonged on the staff of the *45th Division News*, the first Army newspaper of the war and now the first in the European Theater, and in the pantheon of the great chroniclers of war.[27]

After the Germans withdrew, the Woodhams crew returned and set up an OP on Motta d'Affermo. They saw enemy vehicles going in and out of a command post in a grove, but beyond the reach of the artillery. A naval liaison officer at the CP relayed their radioed fire orders to a cruiser offshore that laid in a few salvos on this beehive. When they spotted gun flashes, Woodhams sent Studebaker off a ways to get a divergent compass fix so they could pinpoint the enemy position, then posted Bashore back to the jeep for water.

In a while here comes Bashore screaming at the top of his lungs with a can full o' water, a rifle in the other hand and a bayonet, jest coming through the brush like a wild man. He says, "I'll kill that goddam Studebaker!" And I says, "What's the matter with him?" And he says, "He's up there settin' next to a dead German, and he won't pay any attention to me, won't even speak to me!" Studebaker was that way. These dead guys fascinated him.

A night or two later a few of the guys were talking about the death all around them, and Studie said he didn't like to see dead Germans any more than dead G.I.s, but there you were.

Yeah, there was a dead German near me in a slit trench. One of our mortars had hit and opened up his stomach. He'd stuffed a towel all the way in. The body started swelling and took up the towel, except the fringes that protruded. He was in a lot of pain, because you could see where he'd been scratching the ground before he died.

Bashore came up with the mail. I had the radio and was all alone. He saw this dead Kraut and was bug-eyed and went down raving that "that goddam Studebaker says he doesn't like to see dead Krauts, but he's up there not paying any attention to one!" He thought I was very callous.

On the outside chance of intercepting the enemy withdrawal along the coast, Colonel Ankcorn sent Second Battalion on a cross-country flanking movement south around the unfriendly ridges west of Santo Stefano. Sergeant Griffith took a crew to keep radio contact with S2, the regimental intelligence section. But they were seen more than they saw. Intermittent machine-gun fire and shellfire kept driving the column into the ditches. For a while they knew when they were about to get it when someone stumbled on the radio wavelength being used by the German artillery observers.

Eventually they lost contact with the CP behind the intervening ridges. Pullman loaded a mule with telephone wire and set off with a crew in search of the lost battalion. "It

Bill Mauldin could be dead serious, as in this stark early sketch of combat in the Battle of Bloody Ridge. (*Copyright 1943 by Bill Mauldin. Courtesy of the Mauldin Estate.*)

was darker'n hell and very steep. Luck was with us. We were at it all night, and along about dawn we found 'em."

In dropping back from their northern gatepost of Motta D'Affermo, the Germans merely made another of the next major ridge east, above Reitano, while beating off all efforts of the First Division to dislodge them from their stronghold of Troina to the south.

To see for himself, Colonel Ankcorn led an early-morning patrol to reconnoiter Highway 113, which snaked and tunneled between the sea and the ridges. The Germans had planted thousands of land mines in the road and along the sides and around springs bubbling from the hillsides that would attract thirsty Yanks, as they had in the North African desert. The large Teller anti-vehicular mine would blow a track off a tank. The smaller anti-personnel S-mine was called Bouncing Betty because when you stepped on one buried in the ground it shot up two or three feet, after a couple of seconds exploded and drove ball bearings into your backsides and balls like bullets.

Dowdall was bringing up the rear. As they picked their way around a bend where the Germans had blown the road out of the cliff, someone up ahead stepped on a Bouncing Betty that flew up but dropped back without going off. A dud. Bad business, this road, so Ankcorn took them down a short distance to follow the railroad until he'd satisfied his curiosity about the territory and turned back, sticking to the tracks. Last in, first out, Dowdall was now the point man as he led the patrol into a short tunnel.

The sun was on me back, shinin' through the tunnel, and as I went forward me shadow was blackening the ground in front o' me. I stumbled a coupla times on the loose stones between the ties, and then I heard that POP again. I threw meself down! Waitin' for the thing to go off, every fraction of a second seemed like an hour, and I started to pray. I was wearing what the Catholics call a miraculous medal. I looked back and could see the guys silhouetted at the end o' the tunnel.

Suddenly BOOM, flame and dust and smoke all over! I stayed exactly where I was, and somebody hollered "Are you all right?" but I wasn't stirring until I could see good. "I'm all right!" I was alive! And I felt this rock that fell from the tunnel on me thigh. When the smoke and dust had finally cleared I stood up and faced the sunlight very cautiously. By God, 'twas salted with mines! They had dug up the stones between the ties and put the mines down.

I was sweatin'. How'm I gonna get out? I didn't know but what they'd put them under the ties. Me best bet was to walk the rail out. The sweat was running down me legs. I put my hand back here, and it come away with blood. Hey, I've been hit! So I walked the rest o' the rail out, and there was a jeep—I think it was Ankcorn's—and the driver was told to bring me back to the hospital.

'Twas the funniest way ever a guy rode in a jeep, because I was kneeling in the front seat, holding up me backsides. 'Twas a hospital outfit from Boston. The doctor took it out and said, "You can have it back, but I'd like it as a souvenir." 'Twas a ball bearin', more or less antiseptic until afterwards, when they put all kinda stuff in these Bouncin' Bettys, broken glass, nails, gravel. And then they had the one that shot straight up, the castrator mine. I never saw one o' them.

A professional soldier before most of his men were born, but never before in battle, the 157th commander was everywhere. Bill Caird, one of the I&R drivers, was jeeping up to Second Battalion with more maps, and there he was with a couple of officers leaning up against the road bank. The CO told him when he turned the next bend to drive like hell and don't stop.

Now at twenty-nine, Bill was one of the older easterners from Connecticut, where he'd worked in the New London sewage-treatment plant, a curious occupation for a mild, unflappable fellow with his long nose and polite smile. Amidst the chaotic filth of war, he was as careful and neat in his personal habits as a neurosurgeon.

Outrunning bullets wasn't quite his line, but Caird had his orders.

I revved up the jeep, and after we got around the bend, there was machine-gun fire right above our heads up on the cliff. "Well jeez, that sonofabitch sent us up here and knew they was gonna fire at us!" When we come back the Colonel says, "I wasn't worried. I knew they'd fire at you, but I knew they couldn't hit you."

Not so the commanding general of the Seventh Army. Trubia was with a line company following along the coast road when they bumped into an ambush that sent them all into the ditches.

Patton came right up the road. He was on foot with a coupla aides. I was the last man in line. I told him, "Sir, you'd better get down in the ditch. This road's covered by fire." He said, "Are they firing now?" I said, "Nossir." He said, "Then get the hell outta there and start fightin'!" I said I was told to stay here.

He went up to the head o' the column and talked to the officer and ordered him to advance and then went back to the rear. I'm sure the Germans didn't shoot at him because they felt he was a high-ranking officer and would order us to advance, and the minute we got back on the road they'd open up on us. They saw him all right. We got the word to get outta the ditches, started up the road, and the minute we did they opened up on us again. They'd blown the bridge and had machine guns over on the other side. We got back in the ditch, and a tank come up and started shooting across the bridge. They left in a hurry.

Or were they simply dumbstruck by the spectacle of a three-star American general swashbuckling up to the head of a column of soldiers flat on their faces?

Not Hank Mills on another occasion:

There was a bunch o' brass, and I'm standin' right in back o' Patton. He had the pink britches and the boots you could see to shave in and them two pearlhandled pistols and the varnished helmet with the stars on it, just a beautiful man. And they're all introducin' themselves, "I'm Colonel So-and-So, such-and-such outfit," you know, and I turned to the guy standin' next to me and says, "I'm Private Mills, 157th Infantry."

Omar Bradley, the Soldier's General, was something else. The day he turned up at the CP, Hank heard him telling Colonel Ankcorn that

> General Patton was very pleased with the performance of the 45th, and he wanted him to keep up the good work. I know it was Bradley because I'd seen him when he commanded the 28th Division in Louisiana. I went through the obstacle course crawlin' about five feet away from him.

With his tanks next to useless among these bloody ridges of northern Sicily in his personal horse race with Monty, Patton put it on the foot soldiers and now ordered Bradley to drive all-out *even if you've got to spend men to do it.* His corps commander was shocked. "The orders sickened me. I ignored them. I continued to maneuver and refused to waste lives merely for the sake of winning a meaningless race."[28]

But there it was. Although Bloody Ridge had fallen to the Regiment by the fifth morning of the battle on July 30, the Germans still hung on to the Reitano heights to the east and the coast road; to the south they continued holding against the First Division at Troina and the Eighth Army on the right in a coordinated delaying tactic that was paying off in bonus days to evacuate Sicily and reinforce the defensive backbone of mainland Italy.

After a naval and artillery barrage on Reitano ridge, the men of First Battalion got out of their holes and climbed again into an often man-to-man battle that rocked back and forth all that day and into the night. Mullenax was nearby with a crew and heard a bayonet fight on the ridge next to the water in an orchard, and blood-curdling screams.

Before dawn the lost-and-found Second Battalion emerged on the coast road. But the 29th Panzer Grenadiers, having held as a human wall for four days and nights, had eluded flanking and slipped away, leaving behind thirty-eight dead. More were killed, but few were taken, and the civilians said that every *Tedesco* (German) walking out of the hills was helping a wounded *Kamerad*.

At 7:15 on the morning of July 31, after plodding into one more minefield, the exhausted 157th shuffled into Santo Stefano. Its objective had been gained, and the 45th was relieved by the Third Division. The Germans had traded a few worthless acres for five priceless days, and kept open the way out to Italy.

Respite was only momentary. Termini Imerese on the Gulf of Termini, twenty miles east of Palermo, a watering spot for the conquering Romans and before them the conquering Carthaginians, was now resorted to by the conquering Yanks. The battle-weary warriors of the 157th backtracked forty miles of hard-won coast to rejoin the rest of the Division in the groves above the beaches that had refreshed the battle-weary for 2,350 years.

The engineers had cleared the German mines from seven miles of Sicilian sand for the boys but had neglected to do anything about the infamous undertow that grabbed several of the Ironheads who were among the first to shed their filthy uniforms and was in a fair way of dragging them out to sea before they struggled back to the beach or were rescued.

You might get it anywhere, on or off the battlefield. Half a dozen Cannon Company gunners were under the green camouflage netting draped over their self-propelled 75-

millimeter cannon, making a stew out of foraged onions and tomatoes, when an Ordnance man came up to check a problem with the firing mechanism. Zapiecki was taking a nap in his tent.

> They claimed it was stuck. Instead o' waitin' to unload the gun, somebody pulled the lanyard, an' SSSSPOOONG, the shell hit the tree above 'em where they were fixin' their lunch, exploded an' killed 'em all.

Still in hospital after stepping on the land mine, Jim Dowdall was replaced by the Platoon's first college graduate, a tall and ruddy New Hampshireman whose service record revealed that while recently at Dartmouth College he had taken a map-reading course. Jeremy Waldron admitted to having volunteered for the Infantry and was headed for a rifle company. His ruddy, open face, with his explosive Teddy Roosevelt laugh and mouthful of gleaming teeth to match, was a study in youthful idealism, good humor and absence of pretense. Suffice it that the father he deeply admired, a municipal judge in Portsmouth and a former New Hampshire attorney general, had enlisted in the First War as a bugler, achieved a commission in the engineers, volunteered for Infantry duty in the trenches, and fought in the Meuse-Argonne.

Next to arrive during this rest period was Herb Glover, who only a couple of weeks earlier had gotten it in the chest from a sniper. Walking AWOL out of the hospital in North Africa, the big guy found his Regiment and his Platoon, and was showing one and all where the slug entered his chest, missed a lung and emerged from his back. He had been fashioning

Jeremy Waldron (*Collection of the author*)

knives from German bayonets, kept one under his shirt and one tucked inside each boot, sharpened them every day, and swore revenge.

And then Jimmy Dowdall himself was "home" from the hospital, to carry on side by side with his replacement Waldron, for home to the Irishman was the Platoon, and his family the Ironheads.

What drove or drew wounded men back into the thick of it? So wondered the soldiers' pal Ernie Pyle, hospitalized himself in the 45th's clearing station with "a combination of too much dust, bad eating, not enough sleep, exhaustion, and the unconscious nerve tension that comes to everybody in a front-line area."[29] He was amongst litter cases from our 180th Regiment and wrote:

> Those wounded Oklahomans were madder about the war than anybody I had seen on that side of the ocean. They weren't so mad before they went into action, but by then the Germans across the hill were all "sonsabitches"...[30]
>
> It was flabbergasting to me to lie there and hear wounded soldiers cuss and beg to be sent right back into the fight. Of course not all of them did that; it depended on the severity of their wounds and on their individual personalities, just as it would in peacetime. But at least a third of the less severely wounded men asked if they couldn't return to duty immediately.[31]

From his stretcher Pyle watched a harried chaplain pause to pray with a Thunderbird who tried in vain to gasp out the words with him before the padre moved on to the next one.

> The dying man was left utterly alone, just lying there on his litter on the ground, lying in an aisle, because the tent was full. Of course it couldn't be otherwise, but the aloneness of that man as he went through the last few minutes of his life was what tormented me. I felt like going over and at least holding his hand while he died, but it would have been out of order and I didn't do it. I wish now I had.[32]

At the other end of the command chain General Patton couldn't allow himself the luxury of such compassion, which was why he was the general and Ernie Pyle and Bill Mauldin the only friends the foot soldiers thought they had. In a field hospital Patton saw one of his men who "had the top of his head blown off and they were just waiting for him to die. He was a horrid bloody mess and was not good to look at, or I might develop personal feelings about sending men to battle. That would be fatal for a General."[33]

Two days into the First Division's bloody assault on the southern gatepost of Troina, which was now holding him up in his vicarious foot race with Monty for Messina, the commanding general of the U.S. Seventh Army was leading the infamous patrol of brass through the 15th Evacuation Hospital when he came to the rifleman who had been returned from the lines with battle fatigue, the "shell shock" of World War I. Suddenly Patton saw yellow. Beside himself in the presence of an apparently intact "coward" amongst row upon row of broken "heroes," he slapped him with his gloves, cursed him, and threw

Ernie Pyle, "Friend of the
Infantry" (*Department of Defense*)

him out of the hospital tent. The kid, had he inquired, was not only diagnosed psychoneu-
rotic but had chronic dysentery, malaria, and a fever of 102.

The hospital personnel and most of the patients were outraged. Such abuse of an
enlisted man was a violation of Article 95 of the Articles of War governing Conduct
Becoming an Officer and a Gentleman, which called for court-martial and, on conviction,
dismissal from the Service. The perpetrator, however, was the boss of all American forces in
Sicily, and the medical officers swallowed hard. Back at his HQ Patton fired off an order
that soldiers trying to resort to the hospital on the pretext that they were nervously inca-
pable of combat were to be court-martialed on the spot for cowardice in the face of the
enemy.

Troina fell on August sixth after a six-day battle. Trying to make up for the delay in his
personal race agenda, Patton put a battalion of the Third Division on boats to land at
Sant'Agata di Militello, in the rear of the 29th Panzer Grenadiers Division that was withdrawing from Troina. They were put ashore on the wrong beach. The Germans fought them
off and continued their pullback.

The strain of the game was getting to the General. Three days later he stormed into the
93rd Evacuation Hospital looking for another scapegoat. He found an artilleryman in
severe shock, huddled and shivering on his bunk from the aftereffects of shellfire.

"Your nerves, Hell, you are just a goddamned coward, you yellow son of a bitch!"
screamed Patton. "You're a disgrace to the Army and you're going right back to the front to
fight, although that's too good for you. You ought to be lined up against a wall and shot. In
fact, I ought to shoot you myself right now, goddam you!"

Pulling out one of his pearlhandled pistols, he waved it at the quivering patient, and
struck him across the face with his other hand, bellowing high-pitched curses. As he
stomped out he turned and saw the soldier crying. Rushing back, Patton gave him a blow
that sent his helmet liner rolling outside the tent. "I won't have those cowardly bastards

hanging around our hospitals," he squealed at the hospital's stunned commanding officer. "We'll probably have to shoot them sometime anyway, or we'll raise a breed of morons!"[34]

Within hours Patton ordered a second end run that night with the same unit, this time twenty miles around the coast to the beach at Brolo. General Bradley, and General Lucian K. Truscott of the Third Division, protested that not enough progress had been made to back up such a landing and pleaded for delay, but he angrily overrode them. The amphibians again embarked, this time in the grip of premonitory fear.

They landed undetected until dawn, when they were hit by dive bombers, tanks, artillery and infantry. They lost radio contact and in total confusion were bombed by their own air support. At the last minute they were rescued by a sister battalion coming up the coast road. The cost: 177 casualties, including a hundred dead. And again the Panzer Grenadiers escaped.

In his paranoid obsession with beating Montgomery to Messina, the American General cared not how many of his countrymen he "spent" to do it. He ordered the 157th back into action for a third, spectacular, outrageous end run of a hundred miles almost the entire length of the coast of Sicily from its rest area at Termini Imerese to Spadafora, only ten miles short of Messina.

Bradley and Truscott were aghast: The landing might very well be on top of the Third Division instead of the Germans, risking a battle between the Americans because of the secrecy required for the operation. Patton's reaction: So what? He'd be augmenting his force at the gates of Messina, and hell, it would be great publicity.

All were on edge as they boarded the troopships, LCIs and LSTs (in the nomenclature of the Navy, "Landing Ship, Tank"; in the jargon of anyone aboard in a combat zone, "Large Slow Target") the night of August fifteenth and put to sea—all except Jack Pullman, so sick with an infected mouth from a tooth extraction that nothing mattered.

Off Spadafora, instead of sending the men in a troopship down the net into their waiting landing barge, the Navy loaded from the rail and lowered away. A cable snapped, dumping a C Company platoon into the sea. The boat crashed down on them, and twenty-one were drowned, the only casualties of the operation. "We landed in the Third Division's service area," remembers Hank Mills, "and captured their supplies. We never lived it down."

Under orders to hold up until Patton arrived to lead them personally into Messina, the riflemen of the Third and 45th Divisions watched from the hills above the port as the last Germans, way down below, crossed the three miles of the Strait of Messina to Italy.

On the morning of August 17 Griffith and Studebaker rode with a B Company platoon and beat Patton himself into the center of Messina, where the overjoyed citizens told them the last of the *Tedeschi* had left four hours before. Two hours later a column of Eighth Army tanks clanked in. The battle for Sicily was over. The Regiment got back on the boats and returned to Termini.

In a campaign General Bradley would call "an abysmal tactical failure,"[35] the Americans, British and Canadians lost 5,532 killed, 14,410 wounded, and 2,869 missing in action. The 45th's share was 302 killed (including 121 on Patton's feckless end runs), 717 wounded and 167 missing, a total of 1,186 casualties; the Division took 10,977 prisoners.

German casualties were approximately 12,000 dead and captured, Italian 147,000 dead, wounded and, overwhelmingly, captured.

Mainly during the final six days of a skillful defensive strategy, using ferries and mosquito boats in the face of ineffective Allied naval and air interdiction, the Axis evacuated 39,569 German soldiers (including 4,444 wounded); 62,000 Italian soldiers; 9,833 vehicles; 47 tanks; 135 pieces of artillery; more than 2,000 tons of ammunition and fuel; 15,000 tons of equipment and stores; enormous quantities of supplies; and twelve mules.

The Germans, with only two divisions in southern Italy, could never understand why the Allies hadn't invaded Calabria in the first place and denied them the use of the Strait.

Nor could Admiral Morison, historian of the Navy in the war.

> . . . I cannot avoid the conclusion that the entire HUSKY plan was wrong; that we should have attacked the Messina bottleneck first. After a severe and prolonged air bombing of both shores, the Western Naval Task Force might have sailed around the western end of Sicily and landed the Seventh Army near Milazzo, while the Eastern Task Force landed the Eighth Army on both sides of the Strait, which was not nearly so strongly defended on 10 July as it eventually became a month later. The enemy, whose dispositions had been made to meet landings elsewhere, would have been completely surprised and his communications with the mainland severed. His forces could then have been rolled up into western Sicily and forced to surrender, and in less time than it took to push them out of Sicily into Italy, where they "lived to fight another day."[36]

Word of General Patton's bullying attack on psychoneurosis, battle fatigue, shell shock or cowardice spread like a flash fire through his army. One correspondent said there were fifty thousand soldiers in Sicily who'd shoot him if they had the chance. The medical officers of the 93rd Evac Hospital pulled off an end run of their own and bucked their shock and dismay clear up to General Eisenhower, who reacted with mixed feelings.

> . . . to assault and abuse an enlisted man in a hospital was nothing less than brutal, except as it was explained by the highly emotional state in which Patton himself then existed. His emotional tenseness and his impulsiveness were the very qualities that made him, in open situations, such a remarkable leader of an army. In pursuit and exploitation there is need for a commander who sees nothing but the necessity of getting ahead; the more he drives his men the more he will save their lives. He must be indifferent to fatigue and ruthless in demanding the last atom of physical energy.[37]

So Ike persuaded all sixty key correspondents in the Mediterranean Theater to sit on this sensational story and thereby saved Patton's career; not for another three months did Drew Pearson break their self-imposed embargo over the radio. Instead of court-martialing him, Eisenhower put Patton on probation with a reprimand and ordered him to apologize to the soldiers he had abused, to the personnel of the hospitals he had violated, and finally

General Patton presents his philosophy of war to the commissioned and noncommissioned officers of the 45th Division. (*Department of Defense*)

to each of the divisions in his Seventh Army. Patton repaid the best friend he ever had by talking patronizingly about him behind his back.

One brilliantly sunny day at the end of August, Blood and Guts summoned the officers and representatives of the enlisted men of the Thunderbird Division to an easily sloping hillside east of Palermo, where they sat massed around him on the ground in a roped-off semicircle. He faced them in the shade of a gnarled olive tree with a microphone, Prussian-straight, helmet gleaming, hands clasped behind his back.

True to the fraternity, the unit historians recorded neither the occasion for this gathering nor whether, indeed, the General apologized as ordered by his savior. The closest he may have come, as Bill Woodhams vividly remembered, was: "I've kicked a lot of asses in my time, but for every ass I've kicked I've patted a hundred backs." And his exhortation: "It doesn't make a damn bit of difference whether you come out of this war or I come out of this war, just so we kill plenty of Germans so that when we reach Valhalla or Hell, wherever we go, we'll have plenty of servants."

For the record, however, General Patton concluded his Caesarean harangue, and his relationship with the Thunderbirds, as follows:

> You are still up against a resourceful enemy, but you, as Americans, are his superior. When you meet him, as you will someday, on the plains of Europe, you may expect him to throw large masses of armor at you. He will seek to drive through your

center with a point of armor and once through will attempt to fan this point out, exploit it and strike at your flanks and rear installations. But, by god, this point will not get through you! When it strikes at you, you must be ready and strike it first— blunt it—hit it from both sides—knock the hell out of it—take the initiative—hit and hit again until there is no point and nothing behind the point to oppose you. Your Division is one of the best if not the best division in the history of American arms. I love every bone in your heads—, but, be ever alert. Do not go to sleep at the switch—or, someone's liable to slip up behind you and hit you over the head with a sock-of — (left blank for the reflections of those who heard the speech) and that's a hell of an embarrassing way in which to die.[38]

The other side of the twin bill for the Thunderbirds that day was the comedian Bob Hope, on USO tour with movie actress Frances Langford. Old Ski-nose joked about how scared he was during a night bombing raid on Palermo, and when they flocked around him after the show said *he* should be the one asking for the autographs.[39]

Hope, Langford and Patton. Or was it Patton, Langford and Hope?

In Sicily the Ironheads learned they weren't much use to their Regiment unless they stuck their necks out. Their jeeps could carry them only so far, and sometimes into an ambush. To see the enemy, they had to get close enough and exposed enough to be seen themselves, and they rapidly discovered that a line of sight in one direction was a potential line of fire from the other. Likely observation posts, therefore, were almost routinely shelled by both sides. Rations, water, clothing, bedding, packs, arms, ammunition, spotting scopes, field glasses, compasses, maps, and radio or telephone and wire, chewing gum, cigarettes and bungwad had to be backpacked up to the OP, often under fire.

As since time immemorial, communications were war's worst headache. The old cavalry radios they took into Sicily stood on rods that were meant to be detached from a horse's stirrup carrier and stuck in the ground. "From one side of a tree you couldn't hear the other," said Dowdall.

The "horse radios" gave way to more powerful backpacks with channel inserts that were shuffled frequently to keep the enemy (but too often our own people) guessing. Zapiecki was on the air when a guttural voice broke in with "'one, two, three, four,' an' up to ten, an' then 'nine, eight, seven'—an' I says 'Get off the line!'—I didn't know he was a Kraut jammin'—an' somebody says, 'Ask him how are things on the Russian Front!'"

Where land masses blocked the weak signal, the I&R relied when possible on the field telephone of the First War. From the battalion CP if there was a drop available on the switchboard, or even all the way from Regiment, a reel of two-strand wire had to be run out cross-country to the hand-cranked magneto phone in its leather carrying case on the OP. Shells, bombs, bullets, rocks, boots, mules, tanks, trucks, and acts of God and the Devil knocked out the wire, which had to be followed from one end or the other, in darkness by feel alone, to find the break and splice it, not infrequently under fire.

But when the field phone worked it worked, and it remained the way of talking, of necessity if not always of choice, throughout the war, especially in the mountains.

Their first brush with Jerry behind them, hard-bitten Delmar Griffith thought a little better of his platoonmates. "We felt pretty cocky, like we can handle any situation. It was kind of a proving ground. We were lucky we didn't get into an engagement we couldn't handle. That happened to some new troops who hit a catastrophe from the start and never recouped."

Jack Pullman's abscessed jaw was giving him hell, and he was sent back to the hospital in North Africa. His "boys" (he being nearly the youngest) had done OK. "Of course the Sicilians hoped they were gonna be the forty-ninth state, because every family had relatives in the U.S. But they were anti. They didn't like Italians, didn't like Germans, and if we'd stayed there much longer, they wouldn't have liked Americans."

≈ ≈ ≈

Loafing in the shade one afternoon after Jack had gone back sick, waiting for what's next, the Ironheads picked up Axis Sally, the Nazi radio propagandist with the sexy American voice, beaming in on the Thunderbirds from Rome, and purring: "Why aren't you boys home eating watermelons instead of risking your lives over here?"

"An' whaddya know?" says Dowdall with that twinkle, "that's jist what we were doin'—eatin' watermelon!"

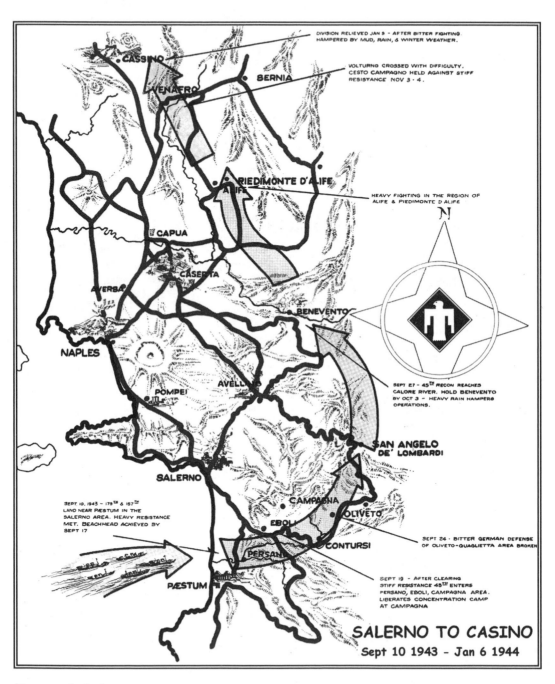

DIVISION RELIEVED JAN 9 - AFTER BITTER FIGHTING.
HAMPERED BY MUD, RAIN, & WINTER WEATHER.

VOLTURNO CROSSED WITH DIFFICULTY.
CESTO CAMPAGNO HELD AGAINST STIFF
RESISTANCE NOV 3 - 4.

HEAVY FIGHTING IN THE REGION OF
ALIFE & PIEDIMONTE D'ALIFE

SEPT 27 - 45TH RECON REACHES
CALORE RIVER. HOLD BENEVENTO
BY OCT 3 - HEAVY RAIN HAMPERS
OPERATIONS.

SEPT 10, 1943 - 179TH & 157TH
LAND NEAR PÆSTUM IN THE
SALERNO AREA. HEAVY RESISTANCE
MET. BEACHHEAD ACHIEVED BY
SEPT 17

SEPT 24 - BITTER GERMAN DEFENSE
OF OLIVETO-QUAGLIETTA AREA BROKEN

SEPT 19 - AFTER CLEARING
STIFF RESISTANCE 45TH ENTERS
PERSANO, EBOLI, CAMPAGNA AREA.
LIBERATES CONCENTRATION CAMP
AT CAMPAGNA

SALERNO TO CASINO
Sept 10 1943 - Jan 6 1944

CASSINO
VENAFRO
ISERNIA
PIEDIMONTE D'ALIFE
ALIFE
CAPUA
CASERTA
AVERSA
BENEVENTO
NAPLES
AVELLINO
POMPEI
SAN ANGELO DE' LOMBARDI
SALERNO
CAMPAGNA
OLIVETO
EBOLI
CONTURSI
PERSANO
PÆSTUM

N

(Department of Defense)

4

SURE, GENERAL, YOU BASTARD, FIVE DAYS TO NAPLES

Italy: Salerno to Piedimonte d'Alife
September–October 1943

NOT UNTIL THE GERMANS WERE EVACUATING Sicily with most of their Wehrmacht intact did the Allied brass decide to land on the boot of Italy itself only six weeks hence, first with the British Eighth Army on the toe as a diversion, and then below Naples on the smooth arc of the Gulf of Salerno with the still-forming Fifth Army, to which the 45th Division was being transferred.

Within five days the elusive enemy would be trapped by the converging armies, Naples would fall and code name "Avalanche" would roar on through Rome to liberate Italy, whose surrender and betrayal of its Axis partner following the fall of Mussolini was as secretly in the works (so it was believed) as the Grand Plan itself.

Created under U.S. General Mark W. Clark in North Africa, the Allied Fifth Army was made up of the American Sixth Corps (the Third and 45th Infantry and 82nd Airborne Divisions from the Sicily campaign and the 34th and 36th Infantry and First Armored Divisions from North Africa) and the British 10th Corps (the veteran 46th and 56th ["Black Cats"] Infantry Divisions from the desert), with more units to come.

The Sixth Corps was to land on the beaches of Salerno on the right, the 10th on the left. Clark was spared only enough assault craft from the buildup for the Normandy invasion (though nine months away) for the Sixth to land but two regiments of a single division. He chose the untested 36th, which had extended such an unexpected mock greeting to the 45th on its arrival at North Africa. A bare two battalions of the 45th's 157th Regiment and the 179th would have to be held in floating reserve while the rest of the Fifth Army not in the first assault waited until transport was released after Montgomery's beachhead to the south had been secured or the port of Naples was taken.

The British 10th Corps was to land to the north of the American Sixth, while the American Rangers and British Commandos on the extreme left were to take the town of Salerno and the passes through the mountainous Sorrento Peninsula ("There's a sunset in So-rren-to / Deep-er than the redd-est wine … Come back, oh come back …") that divides the Gulf of Salerno from the Bay of Naples.

Generals Patton and Bradley were shifted to England to plan the Normandy invasion, put off until 1944 at British insistence over American reluctance. Bradley thought the Avalanche plan "ripe for disaster." He liked neither the idea of the joint command (with recent memories of Sicily) nor the tall and prepossessing Clark—"false somehow, too eager to impress, too hungry for the limelight, promotions and personal publicity." According to Bradley, "Patton didn't trust him either" and thought Clark was too focused on his own ambitions.[1]

While his gunners and bombers raked the deserted beaches of Calabria, Montgomery held up landing his unopposed Eighth Army for four days until September 3, thereby holding up transfer of his landing craft to back up the Salerno operation. "A gift to the Axis," smiled Generalfeldmarschall Albert Kesselring when he heard about it. Two weeks earlier "Smiling Albert" had assigned his 10th Army to General der Panzertruppen Heinrich Gottfried von Vietinghoff genannt Scheel, an unsmiling Prussian with a Hitler mustache; the 10th was being assembled from units from North Africa, Sicily and the Russian Front, where he had commanded a corps.

Laying odds that his enemies would land in the Naples-Salerno area, Vietinghoff three days before Avalanche moved the 16th Panzer (armored) Division to the Salerno plain to reinforce the Italian 222nd Coastal Division (or to take over altogether if need be) and began loading his airfields with Luftwaffe (air force) fighter-bombers.

Thus was the scene laid for the second attempt of the Allies in a generation to wrest Europe from the iron grip of Germany.

Generals Albert "Smiling Albert" Kesselring (*left*) and unsmiling Heinrich Gottfried von Vietinghoff (*right*) (*Department of Defense*)

Behind its arc of beaches the plain of Salerno is divided by the gently converging valleys of the Sele and Calore rivers but girdled from one end of its bay to the other by a battlement of small, abruptly rising mountains. "Blue Salernian bay / With its sickle of white sand," the poet Longfellow rejoiced when he saw it.[2] Yes, a smooth ramp to land upon from the sea, a flat table to attack across, given the small matter of taking those hills. So the planners of Avalanche saw it.

Viewed from the mountains from which every move of the unsuspecting invaders could be spied out, however, the plain was a shooting gallery. And these were the mere foothills of the Apennines, among the craggiest fastnesses on the Continent.

For the 16th Panzers, textbook stuff. They rolled in their artillery and zeroed in fields of fire behind the beaches, set up infantry strongpoints, machine-gun nests and roadblocks, strung barbed wire and laid mines down to the water's edge (the bay was already thick with them), dug in anti-aircraft batteries, and warmed up more than a hundred tanks. When the commander of the Italian division balked at taking orders from his Axis ally, he was invited on a short walk and shot.

Back in the arid seaside groves of Termini and Trabia the Sicilian summer baked and buzzed on from August into September, and the Thunderbirds sweated, and sweated it out. Then on the eighth about half of the 45th filed aboard the row of LCIs and LSTs nosed up on the Mediterranean beach. With them were the Ironheads of the 157th, minus Sergeant Jack Pullman, still in hospital. Under cover of a flight of P-37 fighter-bombers roaring overhead, they embarked on their second big beach party.

The green 36th, on which the day depended, was already under way from Oran. As the four convoys converged on their rendezvous toward evening, Ike's reassuring Kansas twang

Thunderbirds at Palermo boarding LSTs for the invasion of Italy (*Department of Defense*)

crackled over hundreds of Navy radio loudspeakers with the sensational news that Italy had just surrendered and joined the Allies.

The effect of this orchestrated thunderclap was the opposite of that intended. The Texans about to be in the assault wave were afraid the war was over and felt cheated of their one shot at glory. Even the veterans of Bloody Ridge, before whom the Italians by the thousands had laid down their arms, fell for the wishful thinking that Italy out of it wouldn't be any more of a factor than Italy in.

But not Hitler, who'd been planning for a month to use as much of Italy as he needed for a battleground. Vietinghoff had been tracking the Allied convoy and on hearing of the deal with Marshal Badoglio ordered the 26th Panzer Division to disengage the slow-moving Eighth Army and make for Salerno, which he now felt sure was the real target.

As for Mussy's now-former soldiers, upon learning of their country's overnight switch of partnership, they turned instant civilians and melted into the hills. The *Tedeschi* quietly took over their positions, peered seaward, and waited.

Bracing themselves for the naval and air bombardment that would precede the first assault waves, the Germans could see the flashes to the north where the 10th Corps was hammering away with British thoroughness before landing, and hear the cascading rumble of guns and bombs. Yet directly in front of them, where the Americans were dropping into the landing craft in the early dawn, all was strangely silent. Why?

The 36th's General Fred Walker had convinced himself and then Mark Clark, the boss with whom he aspired to immortality, that if the game weren't given away by the preliminary fireworks, an armada of metal motorboats, loaded to the gunwales with thousands of jittery and seasick soldiers who'd never before been in combat, and jammed with rattling vehicles and guns, could leave a convoy that had been sailing for two days over a thousand square miles of ocean, chug six miles through thickly mined seas, avoiding uncharted sandbars, fetch up in the dark on two miles of strange beach, deposit his rightly scared-to-death boys ashore in full battle panoply, and so catch the defenders napping, if there were any.

As documents revealed years later, Walker believed that it would be immoral to bombard the Italian defenders if they still held their positions after news of the "armistice"; that if the defenders were Germans they might be shifting their tanks to the 10th Corps sector in reaction to the British bombardment; and from aerial photos, that enemy defenses were practically nonexistent anyway.

So nary a bomb dropped upon the waiting Germans that night, nor did a friendly shell whistle across the Salernian bay over the flotillas of frail craft feeling their way toward the wave-lapped white sand that marked the American sector, even as the thunder preceding the assault of the British 10th Corps to the north rolled across the dark waters.

Expecting nothing more exciting than a few excited Italians waving welcome, the first innocent wave of dogfaces of the 36th washed unsteadily into the beach at 3:30 in the black of the moonless predawn.

Precisely on signal, an explosion of flares streaked up into the sky, freezing every leaping silhouette in phosphorescent ghastliness, and *der Führer's* 16th Panzer Division opened up with everything it had.

Surprise had been achieved indeed, etched for eternity on the faces of the boys wading in from the sea, who now littered the beach with their bodies.

Back on the fantail of their Large Slow Target where they slept because there was no room belowdecks, the Ironheads watched and listened in wonder as the flares whitened the night and German guns split the air, followed after what seemed an eternity by the shocked Navy's first answering broadsides. The replacement Jerry Waldron had nothing to fall back on but boyhood experience in New Hampshire.

Whether it's a basketball game or whatever, you don't sleep so well before. You wonder what it's about, like going into a black void without knowing the checkpoints or ramifications. And then, gosh, they're coming over! My first thought was how interesting! And I'm trying to figure out from all the aircraft silhouettes I've seen in training, when all of a sudden right off the fantail this plane comes in, and it isn't fun and games anymore. There's a big splash over here, and about the time they put one on the other side of the boat, you think, ohmygosh, they're coming back! And then you know fear for the first time. They hit one of the ships, and it went up.

I was scared to death because I'd never been in combat and couldn't move around and protect myself. I wished I was on shore. There was no place to hide.

The anti-aircraft guns on the ground were ack-acking away at the dive bombers, tracking them right down over the dark ocean. Dom Trubia crouched behind a steel ladder as if it could offer some protection against the flying flak.

A German plane dove on them. Zapiecki could think only that here he was on an amphibious operation and couldn't swim. What if they got hit and were in the water? He huddled with Dowdall next to a stack of empty five-gallon cans. Jimmy: "Trow 'em in, an' jump after an' hold on." Andy: "We played a nice tune on those cans when the bombs were droppin', we were shakin' so hard. We lay there side by side, an' then EEERRRR-WWWWHAM!"

Hank Mills was belowdecks with "five hunnert guys tryin' to come up the ladder and six hunnert tryin' to go down. They dropped a few bombs on each side o' the ship, close, but close ones don't count, only in horseshoes—until the guy tells us we're loaded with five thousand gallons o' high-octane airplane fuel, an' I says, 'Jesus Christ, that's enough to blow you onto the beach without even goin' in the barge!'"

By the evening of D-day the surviving Texans of the 36th Division were off the beach and stumbling inland through withering enemy fire behind a rolling naval and air bombardment and the support of the first of their artillery to get ashore. Their fingerhold, four miles deep, clutched at the Roman town of Paestum and clawed partway up the seaward slopes of Mount Soprano and Mount Soltano. Of five hundred casualties, a hundred lay dead.

To the north, the Brits of the 10th Corps had it better after the pounding their guns gave the defenders but ran into stiffening tank and infantry opposition and had no more than a bare grip themselves, while the Commandos and Rangers barely gnawed out quarter-moons around the town of Salerno and the Amalfi–Maiori crescent on the canyon-like

Sorrento coast. That night the Germans deftly eased up on the battered 36th in order to shift more weight against the British threat to Naples, the port that could supply the entire Allied invasion.

Mark Clark awoke on the second morning to his worst nightmare, had he even anticipated it. A gap, indeed a corridor, had been left between his Sixth and 10th Corps, seven miles wide along the twisting valleys of the Sele and Calore rivers, a no-man's-land that broadened as the enemy engaged the beachhead of each corps away from these valleys where they diverged inland. All the Fifth Army commander had in reserve were the 157th and 179th Regiments of the 45th that had been floating offshore under sporadic air attack for more than thirty hours. To make room for them on his situation map, he shifted the boundary between his two corps north four miles from the Sele River and ordered the 'Birds ashore.

First on the beach early in the morning of the second day, the 179th came up with a deuce of naive mistakes in its attempt to clear the Germans from the south bank of the Sele. The Regiment bypassed the key crossroad town of Persano and craggy Altavilla overlooking the Corridor it was supposed to help the embattled 36th take. Beyond Persano, however, the Germans counterattacked the 179th's rear and threatened to cut the Regiment off altogether, while the Altavilla end run ran headlong into an armored roadblock that bounced them back three miles before they could dig in for the night. Some hard lessons were being learned about the penalties for avoidance.

Meanwhile, with its Second Battalion back in Sicily still waiting for a ride, the 157th was to land in the Sixth Corps sector expanded by Clark north of the Sele River that afternoon, push along the left side of the Corridor for ten miles, and take Eboli, from which the Germans were giving both his corps serious trouble. But Admiral Hewitt was so hot to get his landing craft in and back out from under fire on the beach that he dumped the First and Third battalions south of the Sele, evidently unaware that Clark wanted them on the north and that the Germans had blown up the bridge in between. Another hard lesson, this time in interservice communications.

Evidence of the 36th Division's first cruel taste of battle everywhere confronted the Ironheads as they chugged into the beach between Paestum and the Sele River. The landing area was still under intermittent artillery fire and air attack from the Germans, who from the hills could observe the movements of the invaders as if under a microscope.

Les Gerencer was in Mickey Smith's squad reconnoitering up the road on foot to what looked like a picnic ground. "Around it there was a irrigation ditch. You could smell the dead where they got hit in there, the 36th, and the smell o' gunpowder." Zapiecki couldn't even see the end of a line of bodies laid out by the Graves Registration guys. Everywhere sprawled the debris of war among the clutter of G.I.s, vehicles, supplies, fuel, guns, ammunition, food coming in from the sea, swamped and riddled landing craft crippled in the tide, shouting men, roaring engines, crashing guns, the scream of incoming shells.

The Platoon spent its first night in Italy under the stars, not far in from the beach near the railroad alongside Highway 18. Mills thought they were dug in behind one of the battalions, because he saw the battalion commander up in a tree looking around. "And he's up there with binoculars, and some Kraut with a gun's clippin' the bark off below his feet, PK-WHRRR! And the guys are tellin' him, 'If ya don't get outta that tree they're gonna saw it out from underneath ya!'"

Dilks listened on his jeep radio to men hollering for a medic.

Zapiecki watched a Kraut fighter plane get hit and go down in smoke. He was sent out to investigate.

> The jeep hit a hole in the road and set off a rifle in the box in back. They all thought somebody was shootin' at 'em, and everybody was takin' potshots at the pilot comin' down with his parachute. Holy smokes! Somebody said "Stop it" and they stopped. All he had was a cut from where the automatic seat flipped him out of his cockpit. We got there to the hole where the plane nose-dived in the ground.

The third morning of the invasion the 157th crossed the bridge thrown across the Sele by the engineers, with the object of hitting the rear of the enemy attack that was giving the 179th so much trouble. Its initial objective was a tobacco warehouse, five large stone buildings in an extensive near-circle on a dominating swell, or rise of ground, near the west bank of the Sele and almost across from Persano. A natural stronghold, the "Tobacco Factory" commanded a small river plain, the Grataglia, and the road crossings that led up the Corridor to Highway 19—the enemy's best route between Battipaglia, Eboli, Altavilla and Highway 91, their main supply and escape road.

Of course what we could go up, they could come down. By the time the decision was made to throw the 45th into the breach, the Corridor was recognized by both sides as a chute from the inland heights for a counter-Avalanche of Panzers to the sea right through the middle of the already split Fifth Army.

By the fourth day of Avalanche the entire Fifth Army front was stalled. The Hermann Goering and 15th Panzer Divisions had been brought up and had the 10th Corps at a standstill. The link-up of the Sixth Corps with the Eighth Army from the south that was intended to trap the Germans between and behind the two had been stopped cold. Vietinghoff was rushing extra fuel down for the 29th Panzer Grenadiers, the defenders of Bloody Ridge, to roll north and augment the 16th Panzers against the 36th Division, which was desperately trying to hang on to the Altavilla heights on its right and a piece of the Sele/Calore Corridor on its left. Ominously rising enemy firepower knocked the 45th's 179th back from the south bank of the Sele and stopped the 157th's First Battalion at the hamlet of Bivio Cioffi on Highway 18, from which a key gravel road took off to the east for what we called The Farm, a large, three-story building half-enveloping a recessed court under the rear of the second floor.

Over the tenuous sea-borne supply lines the Luftwaffe had unveiled its new secret weapon, a devastating radio-controlled glider bomb. Under orders from Hitler to liquidate the invasion, Kesselring and Vietinghoff built up their strength, probing the stretched-out Allied lines for weak spots with tanks and motorized infantry, holding here, pulling back a little there, always keeping the invaders guessing.

The Tobacco Factory, German stronghold and key to the Beachhead (*Department of Defense*)

Facing A and B Companies dug in below the Tobacco Factory on their left, the Germans moved out of Persano during the night of September 11, relieving their flanking pressure on the 179th, which moved in. On the left a battalion of the Division's 36th Combat Engineers relieved Company C at Bivio Cioffi. When A and B Companies climbed out of their holes and reached the Factory through heavy artillery, tank and small arms fire, it was deserted; the Germans had pulled back up the Eboli road.

Early next morning the engineers made contact with British patrols groping from the right flank of the 10th Corps into the Corridor. For a firmer feel of the Corps on the left and the enemy in the valley served by the gravel road between Bivio Cioffi and the Factory/Farm sector, the I&R was called on for a reconnaissance patrol.

From its formation in 1941 the Platoon had seen a succession of second lieutenants come and go as its nominal commanding officer, albeit the leadership and responsibility in fact was left to Staff Sergeant Jack Pullman, its youthful organizer. The most recent of them, amiable Lieutenant Charles Edwards, was elevated after the Sicilian campaign to the position of S2, regimental intelligence officer, but with Pullman still in hospital, the command of the Platoon's first full-fledged recon mission of the war fell to Edwards's replacement, Francis Patrick "Pat" Farley, an easygoing young lieutenant from Massachusetts with neither I&R training nor combat experience.

So four jeeploads of Ironheads drove north on Highway 18 to Bivio. No G.I.s were seen, only a British motor patrol that warned them not to go on; Germans were to the north and east.

But Farley carried on, and there the enemy could be seen, about a thousand yards down the gravel road at the crossing of the railroad that paralleled Highway 18. Ignoring or forgetting his orders to radio the situation back to the Command Post when they reached Bivio and hold up for instructions, and seeing merely a few figures in the dusty distance, the new lieutenant in the passenger seat of the second jeep beside driver Norby "Dan" Boone, a rangy, good-natured country guy from Santa Rita, New Mexico, exclaimed the words immortalized in the lore of the I&R: "Let's get foolish! Let's go get 'em!"

Andy Zapiecki had dismounted from the fourth jeep and came up in time to hear Corporal Cyril "Tex" Reynolds say, "Now look, Jose [Contreras] here says there's Germans all along that railroad track." Then Farley: "I'm givin' the orders here!" And Tex: "All right, you give the orders, but when I go down this road I ain't stoppin' 'til we hit Germans."

Reynolds was a compact, ex–oil-rig roustabout with eyebrows that met over crinkly eyes and a small nose, one cheek forever bulging with a chaw, and a Texas drawl. Good observer and map man.

Orders were orders, asinine or not. The canvas tops of the jeeps were off, windshields folded flat over the hoods to avoid giveaway reflections. Narrowly crowned between deep drainage ditches, the gravel road was almost one-way, and the open jeeps kept close, as if for comfort—too close for comfort. The guys stuck up like dominoes.

Tex's jeep was about a third of the way to the clearly visible railroad when a German leaped into view and dashed toward a small station. The column halted. Lieutenant Farley climbed out and told Mills to come over and check the map with him. Hank leaned his M1 against the jeep:

> All of a sudden they give us a burst from a machine gun outta the upstairs window o' the station. I'm standin' right beside Farley, lookin' over his shoulder, and they shot him through the knee, and it come out the other side, and I never got a scratch. All I heard was these bees buzzin' around me. I go headfirst into the ditch and my rifle's laying on the road.

Harold Dibble, a quiet, steady guy from Connecticut, dropped his gun and dove for the ditch. Jerry Waldron, reacting reflexively to his inexperience and instinct in his first action, hung on to his:

> The German we saw had got to the machine gun and fanned it. My rifle was knocked outta my hand. I dove into about six inches of putrid water, looked at my gun, and about an inch and a half of wood was gone near the butt along the bottom.

Back in the fourth jeep, Corporal Zapiecki saw it all up ahead.

> Farley's dancin' around an' yellin', "Let's get the hell outta here!" HE wants to get outta here! That was the first time I was foolish. I was safe in that ditch, but when I put my head up them goddam bullets come down above my helmet. They were in

that railroad station an' in a house on a little knoll on the left an' had a nice cross-fire. How the hell did they miss us?

Like Waldron, Sergeant Griffith's first reaction was to fire back. He dragged a BAR off the jeep, except that the machine-gun bullets were kicking up so much dust in front of him that he couldn't see where to fire.

Beech and I took off down the ditch. My first intention was to save my hide. There was a lot of fire coming down the road. We crawled back until we got behind a hedge and made it back to a farmhouse.

Beech was a lean Pennsylvania farmer with hawknosed, Indianlike features and an experienced outdoorsman who shared Griff's reserve and dutiful attitude toward duty. The last jeep in the advance was now the first in flight. Mickey Smith and Les Gerencer crawled out of the ditch and jumped in the back, Zapiecki in front. As Dilks the driver gunned it in reverse back where they came from, they heard the PLINK of a bullet that nicked Smitty's helmet. In the shelter of a rise, they got turned around and took off.

Next in line, chubby Emmett Oman slipped back into his driver's seat and exploded in reverse after Dilks. Likewise Danny Boone, the wounded Pat Farley's driver, perforce leaving Mills and Dibble in the ditch. Dib crawled back through the filthy stagnant water until he got behind some brush, then ran, crouching low.

Mills slithered far enough out of the ditch to grab his rifle from the road.

I crawled down that ditch full o' alkali, and the Krauts were takin' the weeds off around my head. I had a habit o' rollin' my sleeves up, and when I got to the end I didn't have no skin left up to my elbows. Every time I'd stick my head up this guy in the upstairs window would give me a burst.

So this Italian comes along on a bicycle, and he stopped, and I pulled him over and took his hat and coat an' put 'em on and said, "Well, it's now or never." And I walked down the road. And the guys seen me coming, and they said "Jesus Christ!"

That left Bill Caird's lead jeep, with Waldron and Trubia in the ditches. Getting no return fire, the Germans ran up and captured it, with guns, a case of cigarettes and a box of Zapiecki's treasured phonograph records.

Having abandoned his men to manage for themselves, the not seriously wounded Pat Farley sped back to the CP, presumably with the intelligence that he had met the enemy in his first action and that his men were pinned down in the ditches. He was taken to an evacuation hospital, and a detachment from the Third Battalion was sent to attempt to rescue what was left of his patrol and dislodge their presumed captors from the railroad.

The ignominy of the I&R's first experience of real trouble as a platoon marked the beginning of its real closeness. Trying to establish himself with soldiers already growing battle-wise, Pat Farley invited disaster, and fortunately for all paid the price himself and was out of their hair for a while. Lucky the Krauts didn't bring up mortars.

Thus ended the baptism of Jerry Waldron, the stinking, sweating, shaken young Dartmouth grad from Portsmouth, New Hampshire, dragging his ass in the footsteps of his father.

> I got back, I don't know how. I had a gun with a piece shot out of it, and I laid back against a barn, and that's where I spent the night. I'm going to war, and for the first time in my life I don't have anything to my name except a wounded gun that's been through the water. So I cleaned it.

While the Third Battalion drove the ambushers of the hapless Ironheads from the rail-road embankment, the First expelled the 16th Panzers from the Factory. An hour later eight tanks and a battalion of German infantry bounced them back out, and after another hour's occupancy withdrew again, as if to say what a cinch it was to move in and out at will. By evening the G.I.s were back in.

All along the front the signs multiplied that the Germans were positioning themselves for a major counterattack down the Sele/Calore Corridor. Mark Clark decided that the 36th Division had to retake the heights of Altavilla that dominated the Corridor, and that he'd have to move the 179th from between the 157th and the 36th over to the left of the former to strengthen the Corridor defense—a shift that of necessity would leave the already weak-ened and exhausted Texans stretched like a rubber band along an impossible front of thirty-five miles, while attacking uphill against a strongpoint on their right.

With a stream of 29th Panzer Grenadiers arriving from the stalled Eighth Army front to the south, and no additional Fifth Army reserves ashore, the Germans on the night of September 12 turned the 36th's assault on Altavilla into the makings of a rout and evicted the British from the key supply and attack crossroad of Battipaglia on the other side of the Corridor.

Came daybreak of the thirteenth of September that would darken into what the sur-viving Thunderbirds would remember for the rest of their lives as Black Monday. With the coming of the dawn came the full realization for General Vietinghoff that the Sele/Calore valley was held only by the 45th at less than two-thirds strength, with a five-mile gap on its left in the nominal possession of a few roaming British patrols, and the thin and harassed line of the 36th on its right, still in the shadow of Altavilla.

Concluding that the Fifth Army might actually be preparing to evacuate the Beachhead, the German commander advanced his timetable and reared back his forces to hurl a flying wedge of Panzer steel from Eboli down the Corridor to the sea that would split and shatter his enemy and wrap up the remnants before they could escape in their boats.

It was all as General Patton had predicted, studying the maps a week before the land-ings. General Alfred Gruenther, the Fifth Army Chief of Staff, had asked him his opinion of the invasion plans. Patton recalled their conversation in his diary:

... I was very tactful, but could not help calling his attention to the fact that the plan uses the Sele River as a boundary between the British X Corps and the U.S. VI Corps, with no one actually on, or near, the river. I told him that just as sure as God lives, the Germans will attack down that river.

He said their plans provided for ample artillery to be ashore by 0630 on D Day to stop any German counterattack.

Of course plans never work ... especially in a landing. I suggested this, but it did not register.

I can't see why people are so foolish. I have yet to be questioned by any planner concerning my experience at Torch [the North African invasion], yet Torch was the biggest and most difficult landing operation attempted so far.[3]

So Sergeant Woodhams mustered a few veterans of the previous day's near-fatal fool-ishness for a return to Bivio Cioffi, a clear spotting scope shot up the Corridor to Eboli, the largest town around, on Highway 19 that skirted the base of the mountain, clear 88 shot down the Corridor to the beach, and the scene of intense German activity as the sun rose. He picked one of several evacuated houses on the east side of Highway 18 just south of the intersection. They found a ladder, climbed up on the east pitch of the tile roof, and mount-ed their telescope barely behind the chimney. Portions of the Eboli road stretched beyond the tops of the Factory buildings that could be seen over an intervening rise.

Doug Studebaker spotted what might be a German tank in a patch of woods, but the early light was poor. They radioed the map coordinates back to artillery and called for a round of smoke. It was long. The next one hit a tank that burned and lit up three others right around it. "On target! Fire for effect!" The shells whistled overhead, right in on them. Woodhams and Griff watched a tanker climb out of the turret of one, bent over and hold-ing his stomach. He staggered over to a tree and seemed to collapse against it.

As the morning wore on, First Battalion moved out of the Factory into a line of woods and was stopped by enemy fire. It was more imperative by the minute to get clear observa-tion up the Corridor to Eboli, where something was brewing.

At midday Woodhams was taken off his roof and sent with a two-jeep crew to recon-noiter the Factory, just previously found eerily empty by Zapiecki except for American and German dead. The I&R crew was then to continue another three-quarters of a mile and set up an OP in the Farm, which looked to have a good view of the Corridor. He took Dom Trubia, big Herb Glover, Bill Caird and Dick Bashore.

The embattled semicircle of warehouses was still deserted save for the dead. No sign of Germans. On to the Farm. They parked one jeep here and the other out back near one belonging to two artillery forward observers already in residence.

Woodhams left Caird and Trubia on the ground floor to watch for any surprises direct-ly in front of them, Glover on the second covering the intermediate terrain. With his Tommy gun and a bazooka, he and Bashore with a BAR took their places at a third-floor window to search the distance.

Sergeant Griffith and a crew in the meantime had set up an OP in a house on the Bivio road where they'd been ambushed; they spotted tanks and armored troop carriers coming

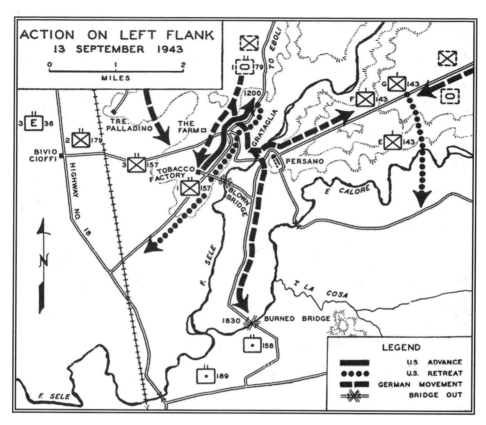

Penetration of the German armored wedge to split the Beachhead. The Farm where Woodhams and his crew confronted the unfriendly tanks on this day is north of the Tobacco Factory. (*Department of Defense*)

down from the Eboli heights along the road to the Corridor and the Factory and radioed their position back to the regimental command post. Through a captured German scope Woodhams had also seen the Jerries cranking up and was already calling for artillery.

Six German tanks had moved down and were now firing on A and B Companies dug in north of the Factory. Vietinghoff's counterattack had begun.

By 3:15 fifteen more tanks and a battalion of Panzer Grenadiers towing field artillery were advancing down the road from Eboli against the right flank of the First Battalion, which was pinned down by their supporting shellfire. Fifteen more minutes, and the all-out German drive to split the Salerno Beachhead was in high gear, with another column charging down from the northeast onto the thin line to the right of the 157th held by a single battalion of the 36th Division's 143rd Regiment.

Studebaker was back at the CP in radio communication with Woodhams when at four he got a report, probably from Griff's OP, of tanks approaching the Farm.

I tried to warn Bill on the radio without telling the Germans we knew they were there. I said something about Charlie Chaplin's kiddie cars are coming or some goddam thing [a reference to Chaplin's spoof of Hitler in his film *The Great Dictator*]. I don't know if he got it or not. This was just seconds before the tanks got there, because he said, "I can't see anything"—and then—"By God, one's right in front of us now!" I said, "Well, whaddya gonna do?" And he said, "I guess we gotta shoot our way out."

How could enemy armor have appeared out of nowhere? Jerry Waldron recalled Dom Trubia telling him right after the action that

since only one man can look through a scope at one time, it was necessary for the other three to pass the time of day in some way. One or more became explorers, and eventually an excellent wine cellar was found. Certain of the contents were transported to the OP level, and a sampling of the vintages was undertaken with the result that after a while no one was using the scope because apparently everyone was fairly well plastered. Such failure to observe allowed an armored German scouting party to come down from Eboli along the north–south road and turn west toward Bivio Cioffi. Naturally the noise alerted the revelers, and they began observing south instead of north. While the I&R was never supposed to stand and fight, the courage gained from the wine cellar dictated otherwise.

Whatever the exact circumstances, Sergeant Woodhams with his rocket-launching bazooka was the only one on the scene with any anti-tank capability.

The first thing I know is ole Bashore grabbed me and says, "Jesus Christ, Bill, looka there!" And here sets these two Mark IV tanks and three armored troop carriers. Hell, they were right there, because with that bazooka I took a hundred-yard elevation on that tank, and I went clear over the top o' that damn thing with the first round. So I lowered it to fifty yards.

That German gunner and me pulled the triggers jest BANG at the same time, and I hit him the classic shot, right at the junction o' the turret, and he hit the edge o' the window right alongside o' where I was shooting out, and the wall come down, and a rock or something hit me on the knee.

When all this banging back and forth started there, these Germans would jest select a window and POW POW POW. Those artillery observers jest went nuts when they saw the tanks and ran. We started down the stairs, and the other tank put a shell right through that damn wall and wiped the stairs out from under our damn feet. We jumped out of a big hole in the back o' this house where a shell had gone right through, and I gotta hand it to ole Dick Bashore. We couldn't git our jeep. It had been caved in on under the house when a shell hit. But the other one was setting at the back, and by that time Caird and Trubia had taken off for parts unknown.

Bashore hit the ground first and got the jeep turned around, and I jumped and got halfway in. We were going across this plowed field, and Bashore was trying to keep the Farm between us and these troop carriers. I was half in and half out on one foot going across this damn field, and we come to this fence. Dick had to turn to go through a gate, and it threw me off. I landed right on top o' my head. He stopped, and I ran and got in, and away we went back to the CP.

When the shooting started, Trubia yelled at Glover, "Let's get outta here!" But with a recent bullethole in his chest from Sicily and possibly a bellyful of dago red vino, the biggest guy in the Regiment shook his head: Naw, he had a score to settle, and he was staying. Giving up on him, Trubia and Caird fled out the back past some tank destroyers that Caird recollects were preparing to take off too. As frequently occurs when time narrows the windows of memory, Dom Trubia remembered only his own part in their escape.

> I just took off lickety-split across the field. The Krauts were right on me. That tank just sat there with its machine gun and shot at me and shot at me and shot at me. Those bullets whizzed by my ears, and I never got a scratch. [Coming to a wooden fence he dared not go over, as Waldron later recalled that Trubia had told him, Dom hit the dirt, whereupon the gun cut a gap in it, and he lurched through.] The last time I turned around and looked, I was outta their range. I had one rest in a little ditch not much more than three or four inches deep. The tanks were at the Farm, a good three hundred yards away. They'd already taken it. Then I got up again and ran like a scared deer down the road back to the CP.

And what about the big guy waiting with a score to settle? He wasn't seen again—not for many years, anyway, when Bill Woodhams ran across Master Sergeant Herb Glover, Regular Army, and asked whatever happened to him on Black Monday. Bill recounts the story Herb told him:

> When they started putting these shells in, there was a vegetable cellar a coupla feet deep, and Herb crawled down into it. He no more got in there when they put a round through the house and caved in the wall on the cellar door, and after a few more rounds he heard someone yell, "Let's get the hell outta here!" Within practically ten seconds the Germans were in that house, and they put a machine gun right on top o' him and were shooting around there. They were there for a day or two. He couldn't git a damn drink o' water or nothin' else and was practically dying.
>
> Finally a shell come into the house and killed this machine-gun crew and blew the rocks offa this root cellar in the floor so he could git out. He remembered there was a bathroom upstairs, and he got up there, and the water was still running, and he jest filled his helmet full o' water and drank it, and it knocked him out. When he come to, there was a German sergeant standing there kicking him in the ribs, and Herb opened his eyes, and the guy said, "Come on, bud, let's go." They captured him and marched him up through there, and that's the story he tole me.

And a bizarre story it is. But there was never any doubt about the dimensions of the main event at the Farm that day. Nine months later Sergeant William Woodhams was awarded the first of the Platoon's five Silver Stars for valor. He told a newspaper reporter how a round from the second tank covered their jeep with debris. "Burned me up. They not only beat up our German scope, but they buried all that good coffee we had in the truck."

✤ ✤ ✤

A storm of German armor and infantry on Black Monday afternoon roared down the Corridor out of Eboli onto Avalanche. The counterblitz was everywhere and on top of everybody at once. Corporal Shorty Nye had a crew on an OP in a house somewhere in the path of the blitz, but no bazooka.

> We was on the top floor and seen a tank and called it in on the radio. It was just like across the street from us and pointed that ole gun muzzle up, and I says, "Everybody down!" We got down one flight o' stairs and looked up. KER-BOOOMM! There went the top floor. He lowered that ole thing a lil bit. I says, "Everybody down!" We went down to the next floor, and there went the second floor. And I looked out again, an' there he was lowerin', and I says, "Everybody out the back door!" There was a ditch, and we went down that ditch and back, and left everything.

The German "avalanche" hit First Battalion and rolled the boys back, almost getting around behind A Company until Third Battalion came to the rescue with tanks and artillery and a covering smokescreen from the chemical mortars.

In a couple of hours First Battalion had been knocked a mile and a half behind the Factory, which gave the enemy the crossroads and the bridge, and they clanked over the Sele River into Persano again. One German column turned back northeast between the Sele and the Calore, aiming to get behind the strung-out 36th Division and link up with a column attacking down the Corridor from the heights of Altavilla, while Vietinghoff's main force rumbled on through Persano and down the middle of the Corridor toward the junction of the rivers.

Ahead were Fifth Army headquarters and Generals Clark and Dawley making contingency plans to evacuate the entire Sixth Corps sector of the Beachhead and consolidate what was left with the 10th for a desperate stand at the water's edge. All that stood between the blitz and the beaches was the disrupted 157th and two battalions of 45th Division artillery. The Germans had broken through exactly where Patton had warned they would a week before the landings.

As the Ironheads were shelled off the OPs by the onrush, they gathered at the CP, which was wherever Colonel Ankcorn was. Dibble was sure they were going to be knocked clear back into the Tyrrhenian Sea.

> Most of the tank fire was hitting in front of us where the rifle companies were. Guys were running everywhere, streaming back from the line. Ankcorn gets up there, and he says, "STAY THERE! Don't move an inch! This is as far as we're going!" They were going back to the beach. It was bad, the only time I ever saw guys run, really run from something.
>
> These tanks were coming right outta the woods, CHOOOMM, right at 'em. It was mass panic. The officers weren't with 'em. I don't know how the guys got away from the officers. Ankcorn told the officers there, "You stop those troops, and if they

don't, SHOOT 'EM! STOP!, no matter what!" They finally got 'em simmered down so they stopped running.

Jimmy Dowdall wondered what could be expected of the dogfaces when the tanks were turning tail too. "Ankcorn wanted to know who's in charge? An' they got the guy, an' he says, 'Git those things off the road! They're demoralizin' the men!'"

The pandemonium of Black Monday engulfed Fifth Army headquarters at Albanella Station, just below a bend in the Sele River. Watching American tanks rumble off to battle and roar back in panic, Norman Lewis, a green British officer serving mainly as an interpreter, crouched in his slit trench, fearful of being shot by hysterical G.I.s firing at anything that moved, including each other.[4]

Directly in the path of the counterattack, a few hundred yards south of a burned-out bridge over the Calore, were ranged the 105-millimeter howitzers of the 157th's backup 158th Field Artillery, and on their left the batteries of the 189th behind the 179th Infantry. Gun crews had been stripped down to the minimum, and gunners taken off their posts had been sent up with whatever weapons could be collected and told to dig in on the forward slope above the river crossing where the engineers had been working on a new bridge.

Late in the afternoon the pilot of the 158th's observation Piper Cub swooped down and yelled out his window that twenty-five German tanks were approaching the river. And then they were there. Both artillery battalions and their hastily dug-in skirmish lines opened up. Depressed like rifles and sighted down the barrels as if they were Revolutionary War cannon, the 105s belched death. Time after time the tanks approached the river only to be driven back by a storm of fire such as they hadn't faced since Stalingrad.

Echoes of Patton. *But, by God, this point will not get through you! When it strikes at you, you must be ready and strike it first—blunt it—hit it from both sides—knock the hell out of it!*

Five volleys of 105s leveled a house occupied by forty Germans; seven were seen to escape. A single barrage knocked out five of a group of six Panzers. After another, forty enemy dead were counted only by identifying dismembered limbs on the ground. At the worst of it, each gun was throwing a round every seven seconds onto the river crossing and the road beyond. Trubia watched the sweating crews drape their red-hot barrels with burlap and pour water over them and keep firing. The batteries of the two battalions sent 3,650 shells across the Calore before the Germans withdrew at sunset. As darkness descended on the battlefield, a scene was seared into Andy Zapiecki's memory. Colonel Ankcorn was standing by a stone wall at the edge of a field.

He's lookin' out an' says, "They're really pourin' it on us." We'd even been shelled by our own artillery. I'm standin' right next to him, and I'm wonderin' what the hell are we gonna do? I was really scared. I says, "Colonel, it looks like it's the end o' the war." "Well," he says, "it looks pretty bad." An' he's lookin', an' he's lookin', and it's gettin' dusk.

Then he calls these lieutenants. "YOU get shovels. YOU get everyone you can find. Take 'em off the jeeps an' the trucks. Bring in the accordion wire. Bring in the mines an' go out there." An' he tole 'em where he wants 'em laid out. "GET this! GET that! Take yer gun an' go there." An' our tanks were comin' back. An' when the guys were dug in, he's tellin' the officers, "Don't let 'em come out fer nothin' during the day. See they got enough rations, an' if they wanna crap to stay right in the hole an' crap in a K-ration box."

They were passing out bandoliers of extra rifle ammunition and shouting to the men, among them Jerry Waldron, "'We hold at the canal.' And somebody says, 'Where's the canal?' And he says, 'Right there.' And it was behind us."

Trubia was digging in when a lieutenant drove by, throwing off bandoliers and shouting, "This is where we're gonna die. There's no place to go." With no time to bury land mines in front of them, the Engineers just scattered them on the ground.

Thought Zapiecki the nonswimmer, holed up with his crew in a farmhouse a few hundred yards from the beach: "Oh God, don't let 'em make me go in the water!"

Their backs to the sea, the brass huddled at Sixth Corps HQ. There was no room left on the map. In Sicily General Patton swam and sailed in a boat he rented from a nobleman and chafed over the news of disaster impending, dreaming in a letter to his wife: "I may get in yet as a relief, who knows."[5]

It was all up to the dogfaces. Bill Caird was listening as Mark Clark sought out Colonel Ankcorn.

> Clark lets out a little laugh and says, "One thing's for sure. We can't fall back any farther because we're almost on the beach already." I guess they were making plans to get as many people off as they could, because it was touch and go.

Not Middleton and Ankcorn. The Division commander then and there said it for all: "Put food and ammunition behind the Forty-fifth. We are going to stay here."

Black Monday night was a void of standoff fraught with tricks and deceptions, alarms and silent shiftings, as each side dressed its wounds, collected its dead, wondered about the other, and awaited the light of dawn.

Griff:
Ankcorn sent men around in kind of a circle so that the Germans could observe a certain point, thinking that there was a continuous procession of troops being brought up when it was only a company.

Dowdall:
There was a woods shaped like me finger goin' around me thumb, with a wide expanse o' field between. In the daytime Uncle Charley had watch-outs, an' at night he pulled 'em back when the German patrols would be comin' through an' moved machine guns up on both sides. Next day, thinkin' there was nothin' there, they attacked right through the open space. We held our fire and then opened up an' cut 'em to pieces.

And he had the Engineers plant mines on the banks of the road comin' down from the Factory, an' at a certain point across the road. So this column o' German armored vehicles come barrelin' through. The first one hit the mines in the road. The others all stopped an' reversed an' backed into the banks where the other mines were. An' he destroyed ten or twelve.

With Teutonic promptness, at 8:00 on the misty morning of September 1, roving German tanks and infantry probed for every possible soft spot in the line. But the dogfaces were dug in, ammoed and rationed and backed by layers of armor compressed against the beaches, by pulverizing air strikes and naval bombardment, and by the most devastating shellfire of the Beachhead—10,786 rounds sent whistling over their helmets by the 45th's and 36th's artillery.

Herbert L. Matthews of the *New York Times*, who had landed with the 157th and was sticking with the Regiment though sick with dysentery, wrote of "that tremendous double-crack over our heads of the naval shells making sleep impossible as they split the heavens . . . the rolling thunder of our bombs as the terrain on the northern edge of the beachhead took a tremendous, incessant pounding from the air."[6]

Bill Caird watched the B-25s come in from Africa—"BUM BUM BUM BUM BUM— those bombs landing one after the other." Zapiecki saw Germans caught on a road. "The P-38s would dive on 'em, strafin' an' bombin', an' sometimes it looked like they were a hunnert feet from the ground, maybe less, when they pulled outta that dive."

With a crew crouching behind a stone wall, Phil Vollhardt peered helplessly at four Panzers in the distance clanking across a field toward them.

At the last minute we called in the P-38s. First time I ever saw air-ground coordination. They saved our bacon. They come in, knocked out two of the tanks, and the other two spun right around and took off.

Matthews of the *Times* was with the regimental commander at about noon when General Clark came out to check the situation: "'Now, there is no falling back,' he said. 'Hold that line.' I heard him, a little later, say to the 179th commander, 'If you go back any more we won't have any beachhead.' Ankcorn later muttered to me that he did not have to be told such things. The lines held."[7]

It was the 157th Infantry and the 45th Division artillery, in the opinion of the veteran war correspondent, that turned the Avalanche against the Germans. The factor that "proved to be the decisive one, was that the 157th Regiment, along the north bank of the Sele, had stood its ground."[8]

General Vietinghoff lost nearly half his armor trying to smash the Allied Beachhead. The Thunderbirds knocked out seventeen enemy tanks on that day alone.

Uncle Charley Ankcorn and his foot cavalry had been responsible for his share, and Uncle Billy Woodhams got his.

Consistent with the screwed-up planning of Avalanche, reinforcements arrived at Salerno a few hours after the skeleton assault forces, with their backs to the beach, had fought the German counterattack to a halt, and with them Platoon Sergeant Jack Pullman, back from the hospital to the relief of his men.

By then the worst was over. The Corridor had been closed. The tide of reinforcements along the beach was finally on the flow. The heavy bombing and naval shelling of enemy lairs up in the hills intensified, and patrols of the plodding Eighth Army made contact with the right flank of the Fifth. Montgomery claimed he'd saved the show, but the 'Birds knew different.

On September 17 General der Panzertruppen Gottfried Heinrich von Vietinghoff genannt Scheel set in motion a counterclockwise pivot of his entire 10th Army on the axis of the Sorrento Peninsula. His orders from Marshal Kesselring were to hold off both Allied armies from coast to coast while successive fallback defense lines were established and everything in Naples that might make the port useful to the Allies as the transportation and communications center of southern Italy was blown up.

The abrupt German pullout from the savagely contested Sele/Calore Corridor the day after left a bloody, empty countryside into which the Thunderbirds tottered like the punchy winners of a split decision in the ring. And the next day they were picking their way through the rubble of Eboli on the heights from which the Jerries had hurled their Panzers. Overnight, the Salerno plain had changed hands.

The Third Division landed from Sicily and took the place of the mangled 36th that in twelve days had lost 267 killed, 679 wounded and 984 missing and would be out of action for two months.

Now on the Fifth Army's right flank, the Thunderbirds were on the move again, no time to look back, except momentarily as did Andy Zapiecki, ascending the slow rise from the flat of the Beachhead to crumpled Eboli from which Vietinghoff had loosed Hitler's iron wedge.

> We come to this little stream. I remembered readin' about Caesar crossin' the Rubicon, and I says, "Here we are, crossin' this stream. You better look back, and you'll see it for the last time." The Tobacco Factory was behind us, and we went through Eboli with the stink.

Eboli with the stink, where an unposted letter back to the Fatherland was found on a soldier's body.[9]

> My dearest little wife—
>   You will be amazed to read about our bitter fighting in the official Wehrmacht communiques. We are fighting in the Eboli sector. Casualties are ever increasing. To add to the terror, the enemy Air Forces are bombing us relentlessly and atrociously. And with all that, an uncanny and perpetual artillery fire is scoring hits. Our fight against the Anglo-Americans requires more strength from us than our fight against the Russians. Many of us are longing to get back to Russia, even longing for conditions as they were at Stalingrad.

Eboli, the last bastion of Christendom—so they said before its bloody parapets— before the desolate Lucanian wilderness in the interior swallowed all who dwelt therein, all who came thereto. Among those who did, in handcuffs one August day in 1935, was Carlo Levi, the anti-Fascist writer/doctor/painter who dared oppose Benito Mussolini's barbarous war upon the pitiful Ethiopians. *Il Duce* mercifully banished him to the village of Gagliano, perched in poverty near Eboli upon a saddle of clay above dank and malarial ravines.

After his triumph over the tribesmen the next year, the dictator proclaimed his magnanimity and freed his political prisoner, while the captives by birth remained, having nowhere to go. What Carlo Levi wrote of the inescapable incarceration within their own country of his countrymen in *Christ Stopped at Eboli* a few months after its "liberation" applied as hopelessly to all those paesans imprisoned by blood and history throughout the remote southern Apennines, never more so than in this year of Christ 1943. Now, even in death, there was no release from the rubble.

> ... Christ never came this far, nor did time, nor the individual soul, nor hope, nor the relation of cause to effect, nor reason nor history ... No one has come to this land except as an enemy, a conqueror, or a visitor devoid of understanding. The seasons pass today over the toil of the peasants, just as they did three thousand years before Christ; no message, human or divine, has reached this stubborn poverty.[10]

From the stink of Eboli the messengers from America turned northward, hiking ever higher into the mountains, flank-to-flank with their brothers of the Eighth who were carefully shinnying along the backbone from the south. To surmount the insurmountable, these ant trails of antiquity doubled on themselves, creeping over streams on bridges set stone-upon-stone in times as medieval as they remained the day of their downfall. On that

Eboli
(*Department of Defense*)

day, as in Sicily, the methodical Huns from the north dynamited the aged arches into the waters below, planted their crops of mines in the most attractive turf, and emplaced as slyly as ancestral crossbows their crossfiring machine guns and snipers hidden on the bumpy slopes to await the traffic jam they were creating. Around the unexpected bend they concealed a self-propelled 88 here, a tank there, with flash-hiders over their muzzles, so methodically—as with everything—zeroed in on the target moving within range.

When confusion, casualties and delay had been achieved, and the shaken survivors, hanging on to bushes, were dragging themselves up the steep slopes to outflank them, the barbarian rear guard—that job done—dropped back to the next preset trap. Then the radio crackled, and our combat engineers, always in double jeopardy, rushed up to bulldoze a ford or nail together a span of stilts under a spatter of mortar shells lobbed over from the other side of the ridge.

Beyond Eboli and Contursi, on the twisting way to Oliveto, the Germans could look down on the whole 45th so doggedly advancing up on them. It was the twenty-second of September, the anniversary of his father's death, and Zapiecki felt a foreboding. He asked Ralph Krieger, who'd plucked him out of K Company and now commanded First Battalion, if he knew what was up ahead. The reply: "Your guess is as good as mine. You guys will just have to go up there." That should teach him not to ask dumb questions. Next he knew, he was in a jeep with a crew looking for a way around the next blown bridge.

> We found where there was a battle. Equipment strewed along, all these dead soldiers that was trapped on the hillside, and the Germans shot 'em just as if they were at a trap shoot. A real scary place, trees all cut and nicked. Some outfit had gone up, got hell, and pulled back, and then we went up, and the Krauts had pulled back. I didn't have nothin' to eat and found a can o' C-ration hash somebody'd thrown away. There was a bridge across the river that the Germans blew, and these guys was trapped. We was goin' down the road, bodies here, an anti-tank gun there, and on this hillside on the right you'd see a body here and a body there. That was one stink alley I'll never forget.

Not far from this grisly scene K Company was moving up on the village of Colliano. Corporal James D. Slaton was lead scout of a squad assigned to knock out Germans on the flank pinning down two attacking platoons.

> . . . Working ahead of his squad Corporal Slaton crept upon an enemy machine gun nest and assaulting it with his bayonet succeeded in killing the gunner. When his bayonet stuck he detached it from the rifle and killed another gunner with rifle fire. At that time he was fired upon by a machine gun to his immediate left. Corporal Slaton then moved over open ground under constant fire to within throwing distance, and on his second try scored a direct hit [with a grenade] on the second enemy machine gun nest killing two enemy gunners. At that time a third machine gun fired on him 100 yards to his front, and Corporal Slaton killed both of these gunners with rifle fire. As a result of Corporal Slaton's heroic action in immobilizing three enemy

machine gun nests with bayonet, grenade, and rifle fire, the two rifle platoons which were receiving heavy casualties from enemy fire were enabled to withdraw to covered positions and again take the initiative. Corporal Slaton withdrew, under mortar fire, on order of his platoon leader at dusk that evening. The heroic actions of Corporal Slaton were far above and beyond the call of duty and are worthy of emulation.

Jim Slaton's Congressional Medal of Honor citation[11]

And then there was another Smitty Andy heard about, always gnawing on a mouthful of chewing tobacco.

They was guardin' a road, and here comes a German on a motorcycle. This guy with him was gonna knock him off, but Smitty says, "No! Wait 'til he comes closer! I want that motorcycle!" An' that Kraut fooled him. He just bent over and pressed the trigger on his gun, and split Smitty and killed him. And he turned around and got away. The other guy coulda knocked his ass off with one shot.

Uncle Charley's boys drove the Germans out of Colliano and pushed on above the east bank of the Sele, edging around a 1,500-foot mountain past the hamlet of Valva on the road to Laviano on September 24. At every turn enemy observers brought down shellfire. Early in the morning Colonel Ankcorn called Jack Pullman over.

Griff was ahead a coupla miles following the battle, and I could talk to 'em by radio. The plan was that he was gonna go one way, somebody else from the Platoon another way and maybe me with 'em. We could see the battle going on. Our artillery was shelling tanks, and they had one of 'em burning. Ankcorn wanted to get up there, but he didn't want to go clear around, so he cut off up this road. I told him that as far as I knew—I'd just talked to somebody there—everything's clear.

Well, it was, except he hit a mine. He could have said, "Take the jeep and go ahead," but he wasn't that way. I must have been one of the last people to talk to him outside of his driver.

Like all the jeeps around the front lines, the floor of Flank-'em Ankcorn's was sandbagged as protection of sorts against an exploding land mine from below. Such a stickler was he for keeping your feet on those bags that he'd busted a sergeant back at Devens for riding with his leg cocked out on the right fender, cowpoke style, and within days he'd reamed out a couple of I&R drivers for letting their passengers ride the same way.

Do as I say, not as I do. Ankcorn was relaxing in the forbidden position while being driven up to see how his boys were doing when the right front wheel rolled over a land mine. The explosion tore his right leg apart and tossed him in the ditch. His driver and bodyguard were hardly hurt. He reached the hospital just as word reached his CP that he had been awarded the DSC (Distinguished Service Cross) for bravery in Sicily and the star of a general officer.

The surgeons amputated. The war for which General Ankcorn had been preparing for twenty-six years was over for him in two months. By January the amputee was on crutches on a ship for home, grinning at the Signal Corps cameraman. On the last day of 1944 he was retired from the Army at fifty-one.

Sergeant Pullman spoke for his noncoms:

I loved the man. He was one of the best, an infantryman in the mode of Stonewall Jackson, one of the very few who really knew how to use infantry. Move 'em fast and get your superiority at a given point, which is what war's about anyway. I'm convinced if this hadn't happened he'd have ended up a four-star general.

Corporal Zapiecki spoke for his men:

When you'd get some little bit of information back to S2, they always gave it to him. He knew how to use it, and he'd always piece things together. When he got hit I never felt so sorry for a man in my life. I says, "Who the hell's gonna replace him?" I felt as if the war was over, and I didn't think I could trust another man.

And Herbert Matthews spoke for the war correspondents:

... To me, the great privilege and satisfaction of those anxious days was to be always at the elbow of one of the greatest soldiers it has been my pleasure to watch in four wars, Colonel (now Brigadier-General) Charles M. Ankcorn. He was then a veteran of twenty-six years' service in the Regular Army and I saw him at his best—calm, wise, and brave, and adored by his troops who would have followed him anywhere.[12]

But the battlefield is not for irreplaceability. Shocked at the loss of his most brilliant field commander, General Middleton turned over the 157th to Colonel John H. Church, the Division's fifty-two-year-old chief of staff since Camp Barkeley. The Pennsylvanian had enlisted as a reserve lieutenant in the infantry from New York University in 1917. He got the chance Ankcorn didn't and was twice wounded with the 28th Infantry Regiment in France. From the Army of Occupation in Germany he rose through the Regular Army until his assignment to the 45th at Fort Sill in October 1940 and was promoted up to colonel neck-and-neck with his predecessor.

Their styles were opposite. Church was a seemingly mild, careful gentleman/soldier with a quiet sense of humor, a competent tactician and administrator. He left as many of the field decisions as he could to his deputies and kept his eye on the situation from his command post where, as conditions allowed, his creature wants were attended to by his devoted Chinese orderly and houseboy.

The first order of leftover business remained the capture of Laviano. The line companies moving along Highway 91 were now under unremitting artillery and machine-gun fire. Pullman sent up a recon patrol under Zapiecki, who followed a rolling barrage up into the town and reported the Germans gone. Doug Studebaker, now a crew leader, took Dave

Newly starred General Charles M. "Uncle Charley" Ankcorn homeward bound (*Courtesy of Delmar W. Griffith*)

O'Keefe and Phil Vollhardt along another road with the advance point of a rifle company that had run into small-arms fire. Off on the left the company commander set up his CP with radio and aid station in a ravine. Studebaker walked forward to check the enemy machine-gun positions on the map with the lieutenant so he could radio back to regiment for artillery fire.

Right then a cluster of enemy mortar shells hit up ahead. Momentarily gripped by one of those premonitory feelings of battlefield dread that is part of survivorship as three more bracketed him, Dave O'Keefe ran and crawled into a culvert under the road. The mortars got both Studebaker and Vollhardt. The road had no ditch, only a slight depression for runoff that was paved up to a low stone wall, and Studie dove for it.

> I didn't know I'd been hit, but when I got over there I looked down and saw my shirt was slit along my chest. I opened it up and saw a little cut in there and I thought "Boy, you lucky sonofabitch, a coupla weeks in the hospital, warm food, clean sheets, Purple Heart." That shell got me in the face, the chest, the right upper thigh, and probably I had a small piece of shrapnel sticking in my belly like a thorn.
>
> The next one hit in back of me and tore my left foot pretty good and probably put a piece in my right arm. The main damage was from the concussion that traveled across the crown of the road and entered the radial nerve of the arm and paralyzed it. Scared hell outta me. I felt my foot was hurt and thought I'd been hit by a rock.

157th commander Colonel (later
General) John H. Church (*Department
of Defense*)

There was an overhang in this cliff and I tried to get over this wall to it. I was
holding my helmet in my left hand. My right hand was just hanging, and before I
stood I didn't feel any sensation in the arm. A couple of days before, I'd seen where
a German had his right arm blown off across a fence, and the thought flashed
through my mind that I'd lost my arm.

I determined that if the arm was off I didn't wanna live. I didn't wanna go back
with a stub. I thought if it's off, I'm just gonna stand up and let 'em finish me off.
When I finally got enough courage to look down, by God it was there! My foot was
starting to hurt, and as I started over the wall I stepped on my right hand and
thought how goddam dumb can you be? I got up under this overhang. There was
some other guy there who'd been injured probably more than I, and somebody on
top was really moaning.

It was bleeding more, wasn't spurting or anything, but I didn't know how much
blood I had to lose. I stuffed a dirty finger in the wound. I saw the shoe was separated. The shrapnel sawed right through it. Good English came into play. I yelled, "Is
there a medic available?"

I guess he thought it was the colonel. He came across the road double-time. If
I'd just yelled "medic!" he might not have moved as fast. He led me around in back
where there was better cover and started treating my wounds. You get awfully greedy
instantly. He checked the foot, and I said, "Do you think you can save it?" He said,
yeah, he thought so. And I said, "How about the toes?" Well, he couldn't tell at that
point.

The shrapnel had entered from the bottom and grooved along the axis and
came out and cut off the top of the third toe, and there was a fracture of the whole
metatarsal area. The result was that the tendon grew down into the fracture area and
pulled the second toe down into a hammer toe. They decided to take that off at the
hospital and took some meat off to fill in the groove at the bottom. It's worked fairly well. I was in the hospital for quite a while. They said the radial nerve had been
pinched by the concussion wave as if by a pair of pliers. I was babying that arm, had

it in a sling, and one day this big blonde nurse asked me why, and I said I couldn't straighten it out. She said, "Yes you can!" CRRRAAANNK! And she did me the favor of my life!

Vollhardt was standing on the left side of the road when the second arcing flight of mortar shells whispered down.

The road ahead dropped down to a plain, and the mortars musta been up in the hills above it. They had the range all zeroed in and dropped in a cluster, shwish-shwish-shwish-shwish-shwish. Couldn't hear 'em above the rustle of these Italian poplars that were waving in the wind.

First thing I knew, the road blew up in front o' me. They were daisy-cutters—hit and spread. Sump'n hit me in the side, and I started getting mad and cussing. I hit the dirt. A coupla more come in. One got Doug, and I got shrapnel through the legs. I was pissed off. I got up and said to myself, "Don't stay here, ya dumb shit! Yer gonna get plastered again!" I was bleeding bad. I ran back maybe fifty or a hundred yards to the aid station in the ravine.

The aid men sprinkled sulfanilamide powder in his torn abdomen and bandaged him. He was triaged back to a field hospital in North Africa, on the way getting separated from Studebaker.

The first piece took a chunk outta my left side and went through, but it musta hit a rib and been deflected and cut a vein in the abdomen. They didn't know anything about it 'til they got me down to the hospital, when I started doubling up the next day. The doc says it looks like appendicitis. They took me into the OR and gave me a spinal, opened me, and the appendix was fine, so they sewed that up.

The doc says, "You got a bleeder in there. Sump'n cut a vein. What happened?" I told him. He says, "All right, I'm gonna look for it," and they knocked me out. He clipped off the vein and took out the shrapnel. The abdominal cavity was flooded with blood. They hadda bail it out, and I was nauseous and puking but feeling better in a coupla days. Sixty-three stitches.

Phil Vollhardt was still in the hospital in North Africa for Christmas; they made a tree out of a native thorn bush and decorated it with all they had, candy Life Savers. Months later, reclassified unfit for further combat, he was assigned to the Ninth Evacuation Hospital near Naples as a ward boy. It was a shame to lose a tool and die maker who could fix a phonograph with a bead from a dog-tag chain.

The annoying Germans pulled back to the next mountain station on their timetable, and the next day Zapiecki and crew drove into the next little town to the cheers of the paesans. Somehow they were the first Americans. Where the hell were the rifle companies? Their radio wasn't working. They pushed on. Late in the afternoon the fall rains of Italy descended, drips into rivulets. The dust they'd been living with for three months turned more or less to peanut butter.

They pulled over and slept by the side of the road under an abandoned German tent flap. In the morning they drove cautiously on along Highway 91 and entered a town near the junction with Highway 7 coming up from the south to Naples. There were few civilians, and Zapiecki smelled trouble. "Musta been Germans nearby because pretty soon planes come wigwaggin' their wings, the signal for the G.I.s not to fire on 'em, an' all of a sudden the bombs come down!"

Out of contact, Zapiecki couldn't know that Woodhams and his crew had been sent to observe the effects of this same bombing mission on enemy reported around the highway junction and got caught in "friendly" shellfire that was failing to clear the crest. They pulled back as fast as Woodhams could limp along on the knee he'd injured during his duel with the tank. Bill:

> We got up another hill, and here come these six planes. I called back on the radio, and those babies winged over, and down they come and dropped their bombs. But they weren't hitting this junction. They were hitting another back whar the Second Battalion was strung out. The bombs were coming so straight they didn't look like they was moving, they were jest getting bigger. I called this guy on the radio. "My God! They're hitting on this road whar Second Battalion is!" He says, "Don't git excited. We'll git ahold o' them and tell 'em not to do it anymore." About five minutes later here come six more planes, and they winged over, and bombed all along here agin'.

It was no mere dozen planes that the two horrified crews watched going awry, but twenty-four A-26 dive bombers. They hit both Second and Third Battalions, wounded two men and destroyed two mortars. Lucky their aim was so lousy.

In unrelieved pain, Woodhams dragged himself up a hill next day, staked out an OP for his boys, hobbled back down and threw in the towel with the Medics. Three months later he and his old buddy Studebaker were on a hospital ship for home, one still with the same metal plates in his leg from the prewar auto accident, the other with the same hernia he came over with. The Army surgeons had to remove Uncle Billy's kneecap. "It didn't affect my walking a damn bit, but they kept me in a cast so long that my left foot turned in pigeon-toed, and the leg is partly stiff. Once in a while a bone chip breaks loose and hurts like hell. They've gone in thar five times since."

Northwestward from Lioni the 45th's objective was the transport center of Benevento on the Calore, where the river curlycued among the hills towards its merger with the Volturno, the major valley of Campanian Italy. The Germans were making a time-buying moat of the meandering stream while they forged a chain of mountain redoubts across the Apennines that would be their strongest defenses of the war. The going now was a mucky plod and slide through chilling autumnal rain, the Krauts taking potshots over their shoulders at the plodding dogfaces at every bend in the beastly roads. Once off the black-top, vehicles slid sideways as if on sheer ice or bogged down about as much as they churned forward.[13]

For the Ironheads now, observation sites were few, and the weather was against seeing much anyway. Down four wounded, injured or captured, they welcomed the chance to keep a low profile during the somber change of regimental command.

Naples fell to the British and the rage of the Germans, I entered manhood and the war zone, and the 45th approached flattened Benevento on October 2, holding up until the Engineers brought up bulldozers to clear through the rubble, stinking with corpses, that we replacements would be trucked through twelve days later. And Pullman encountered the results of an ambush of a 34th Division regimental CP that had moved up alongside the 45th.

I almost fell on my butt. The pavement was just covered with blood. They were sacking up G.I.s in mattress covers. They'd come around that corner in a close column, and tanks were sitting across the valley, and let 'em get in there and killed fifty or sixty of 'em with direct fire. There was a gin factory in town, and the whole Regiment got dead drunk. The Germans could have come in and taken everybody.

Leaving Benevento to its ruins and its despair, the 45th crossed the Calore and attacked northwest through the river valley. Not far along the road Zapiecki had a close one looking for a spot for an OP.

We come across a half-track that can't get through because there's a car there with no wheels, on cement blocks, blockin' the road. We said, "Let's give the guys a hand." I grabbed one o' the axles, the other two grabbed the other. HEAVE! HEAVE! HEAVE! The damn thing wouldn't go. Hey, wait a minute! No wonder! There's a tree there! We worked around it, and the half-track got by.

Then a guy says, "Get away from the car!" "Whatsa matter?" "Take a look!" Right underneath the axle is this German potato masher grenade. It had a wire attached to it, and every time I hauled on that axle there wasn't quite enough tension to pull that pin out. So I called back on the radio to have somebody come out from the mine squad.

We go on, and about ten minutes later we hear on our radio that an Italian came along and reached in there and pulled it out, and that was it. He got killed, and the guy with him lost his arm.

The 45th was being pushed by Fifth Army Headquarters to step on it for the twenty-two miles from Benevento along the narrow valley of the Calore to its junction with the Volturno flowing southwest to the sea. With the impending attack of the main body of the Sixth Corps across the Volturno, the right flank of the 34th Division would be vulnerable to an enemy flanking movement unless the Thunderbirds drove hard along the east bank of the river and turned the German flank on itself.

With the taking of Pontelandolfo on October 9, the 157th settled gratefully into Division reserve, a fretful day to day wait for the whistle to blow again while the 179th and 180th struck off to the west toward the Calore–Volturno river junction.

During these rare regimental respites, chickens and eggs, and grapes—whenever possible fermented—vied with mail call. Cleanliness was confined to the volume of a helmet, godliness to whatever consolation the chaplains could offer the inconsolable, and *la bella signorina* by her *mamma* to her *casa*.

Anything would do to relieve the drearily minimal sameness of field rations C and K. The foraging *Tedeschi* in their withdrawal had left little more than the countryside's own minimal sameness. The common misery of the dirty dogface and the dogged paesan established a scroungy, bottom-of-the-pile bond between these foot soldiers in their respective fields.

So the chicken, the egg, the grape, the can of Spam, the cigarette, the shave, the haircut, the shoeshine, and the "Hey Joe, you wanna nice girl?" were adopted as the common currency of those who lived hand-to-trigger or -mouth. For the most part, however, Pullman's Ironheads chose to chase chickens and eggs and the hell with the girls, of whom there were none at hand anyway, and with the Germans, of whom there were too many.

Chasing the lingo, Jimmy Dowdall found his broad Celtic grin an asset, his native brogue a confusion.

> When I went out to bargain rations for eggs, I said the word, an' to be sure, with me brogue, would draw a picture, because Italian for egg is *uovo* and for grape is *uva*. I was very unlucky. They always wanted to give me grapes, an' I always wanted eggs.

The Platoon had settled in on the second floor of a building in Pontelandolfo (Ponte for short), and the cylindrical Coleman gasoline stove was hissing away under a pot of water when Corporal Zapiecki, Commander-in-Chief of the Chicken Patrol,

> sent Hank Johnson and a little guy with a squeaky voice out to get a coupla chickens. They had to ford a stream to where this farmer was at. They tied the chickens up and threw 'em in back with the radio and come back across the stream.
>
> But they lost the place where they forded on the way over and got in the deep water, and the radio was soaked. They come up to the room, and this little guy was laffin' like hell and sayin' "The chickens got drowned! The chickens got drowned!" And Pullman coulda killed 'em because the radio was ruined. And I coulda killed 'em because we had everything fixed up, the water boiling, and the chickens got drowned in the river.

Uovo and *uva* were a harmless enough mix, but *uovo* and *vino* had explosive possibilities. Some of the guys were lying around in a field near Ponte when Mullenax and his sometime buddy Bashore came rolling over with a helmetful of the one they had foraged between snootfuls of the other. Hank Mills was watching.

> They're countin' the eggs, separatin' 'em, and got into a heated argument. It was the middle of the day, and they were really gooned. Mullenax hit Bashore and knocked him down. It was like Rocky Marciano puttin' down a flyweight. CRUNCH, and

down he went. Mohawk was great on bein' armed, and Bashore grabbed a grenade offa him. I don't think he intended to more than throw it at him like a stone, but not to pull the pin. Everybody dove for cover.

Mohawk reached down and was pullin' him up, and what was goin' through my mind was that if he hits him again he may kill him or hurt him real bad, and he's gonna be sorry because they were really friends. So I got in between 'em and told Bashore to give me the grenade, and he did. The ironic thing is that if Mullenax woulda punched me I woulda been in the same position Bashore was. Bashore was on the ground sayin' "Thanks Hank, fer savin' my life!" He figgered if Mullenax hit him again he might put his lights out permanent. I guess I saved him from a lickin'. I looked over, and they're sittin' there smokin' and gigglin' and countin' the eggs out like nothin' ever happened.

On its fifth day of rest the Regiment was awakened by eruptions of lightning and rolling thunder along the western horizon. "More rain, dammit," was the grumbling first reaction out of that half-sleep of the foot soldier. Not rain, but the rumble and flashes of the great artillery barrage that preceded the coming attack of the Sixth Corps across the Volturno. In the early morning hours of October 15 the doggies moved out in the dark and drizzle through the mud-bedraggled positions of the 180th. As dawn broke, a downpour descended that had nothing to do with the booming and echoing crescendo of the barrage ahead except to fall equally on all the foot soldiers facing off, to whomever their sodden bodies belonged.

The Third Division led the amphibious crossing of the Volturno with a brave and bloody beachhead that would have been even costlier except for the feint of its commander, General Lucian Truscott, with a distracting left hook that relieved some of the enemy resistance frontally and against the 34th on its right. Yet in the plain between Capua and the sea on the left, the three divisions of the British 10th Corps swept across the river with hardly a hitch.

Once the Fifth Army had breached the Volturno, the Germans were forced to protect their vulnerable left flank while falling back, squareheaded as ever, from the expanding beachhead of the 34th in the crook of the river's right-angle bend. General Vietinghoff had assured Marshal Kesselring that he would hold the Volturno line until October 15, and he was on the mark, thanks to the 26th Panzers and Mount Acero, dominating the Calore–Volturno junction where the 157th now returned to action.

The men Colonel Church inherited forced the Jerries back to the west slope of Acero while the 179th enveloped the mountain from the east. The 180th moved west to the Volturno, then north along its shore. The Panzers withdrew, guns blazing. That first night back on the line the 157th took Faicchio, due north of the mountain.

But five more days were consumed hammering only eight more miles to Piedimonte d'Alife at the base of the Matese Mountains through harrowing conditions that failed to stall roving Mark IV and Tiger tanks, or dampen constant enemy shellfire, or bog down fierce rear-guard infantry attacks, or even ground the Luftwaffe. General Middleton pleaded for air support for his Willies and Joes and got nothing but excuses from the Air Force.

Screaming Meemie, the German six-barrel
rocket launcher (*U.S. Air Forces*)

Tank country. With the Apennines looming up in the distance, the broad valley of the
Volturno afforded the last chance for either side to use tanks for much more than artillery
in Italy for the rest of the year. Nothing was as fearful to a foot soldier, as Bill Woodhams
and his crew had discovered at Salerno, as the sudden emergence over a hill or around a
bend or out of the woods of a roaring, clanking German behemoth with its pistol-pivoting,
fast-firing, sharpshooting 88.

The 34th Division was following the Volturno on the 45th's left. On their right the
Eighth Army had captured the strategic Foggia airfields and was pushing on as the
Germans dropped back to the mountains. Facing them, the 26th Panzers were trading
acres for hours to forge a chain of strongpoints in the Apennines at their backs. Time for
another secret weapon to scare hell out of the decadent dogfaces of democracy.

For the Russian Front the Germans had developed a heavy mortar that lobbed a pattern of smoke rockets to screen an attack or retreat. Six barrels, each about six inches in
diameter, were aimed in a circle on a two-wheeled carriage to be rotated and fired rapidly
by remote electric control. When they realized its powerful psychological effect they
replaced the smoke with high-explosive rockets fitted with tail assemblies that emitted
insanely scary shrieks as they descended one after another. The launching made so little
noise it was nigh impossible to locate from the sound alone.

They called it *der Nebelwerfer*, the smoke mortar. The 'Birds called it Wailing Willie,
Screaming Meemie, or the Six-Barrel Organ Playing the Purple Heart Blues, and first
danced to its tunes on the fifteenth of October. The Division was attacking Faicchio from
both east and west. Twenty German planes dropped out of the sky, bombing and strafing.
Tanks firing from its right stopped the 179th, while heavy artillery pinned down the Third
Battalion of the 157th on the left. As usual, Zapiecki was there when something screwy was
about to happen.

That night we were in a little cave. I was madder'n hell because I couldn't get a fire started to make some coffee. Then come these things. Man, they made the weirdest sound! We were wonderin' what the hell's goin' on. BUM BUM BUM BUM BUM BUM when they hit this field. The first thing I hit when I went down was a patch o' cactus, and bingo! I'm outta there fast!

The Germans had a lotta hired hands in their line, alternating 'em, and this guy comes dashing up there, wavin' his arms, and somebody's gonna take a potshot at him, but they said, "Don't shoot! He's a prisoner," an' then somebody says, "This is for you, Andy!" He was a Polack, told me they'd been advancing him toward the front, and he figgered that when they got him up on the line he'd escape.

I know a little Polish, but I couldn't think what to say for "pipe." I'm rackin' my brains, and this guy's sayin' to me, "Whaddya wanna know? Whaddya wanna know?" So I start showin' him. He says, "Oh, mortars, with *sechs* ["six" in German] somethin' barrel mortars." That was the word I couldn't get for pipe. "Oh," he says, "the Germans were afraid of 'em. They'd put 'em inside a hole and have a real long wire, go way back in another hole and set 'em off. Sometimes they'd explode right there."

That scream. They musta done somethin' to make 'em more terrifying. They had a big field, with no particular accuracy, though if you got hit you'd think it was accurate enough. Maybe they figgered if they fired six and got one guy it was worth it.

One more ho-hum rear-guard delaying action, as the papers back home were by now reporting, and the Germans pulled out of Faicchio late on October 15. Three more days to slug eight miles to the outskirts of stone-and-stucco Piedimonte d'Alife, clinging to the sharply rising lap of the rugged Monti del Matese in a corner of the Volturno plain, thirty-five miles north of Naples.

The next day, October 19, the Regiment occupied Piedimonte, dominated by its outsized cathedral at the high end of its echoing cobbled piazza, and the doggies rested on their arms, as had Caesar's men on theirs, in the surrounding countryside. Having fought up from Salerno for forty straight days and nights, the hardened and weary veterans of the 45th were relieved by the fresh 34th and sank with a groan into corps reserve for their first real rest since sailing from Sicily, for rehabilitation, and for a massive blood transfusion (almost literally) of casualty replacements.

Naples was supposed to have fallen in five days. Tell that to the families of the 2,000 Allied soldiers killed, the 7,000 wounded, and the 3,500 missing so far in the campaign— and to the Germans, maybe half that, maybe less.

Up ahead, the Apennines loomed almost vertically and more than a mile high, dark with menace and the coming of a winter that would exact a bitter toll of thousands upon thousands more.

The 157th Regiment's Front
November–December 1943

179th Regiment attacks Hill 769 11/11,
finally occupies it 12/6

First Battalion (157th) is repulsed from Hill 640 12/15

Third Battalion attacks Hill 460 11/12,
is thrown off it 11/13 and occupies Hill 470.
Repulsed again from Hill 460 11/21, 12/11
and 12/13, and from Hill 470 on 12/15.
Enemy withdraws from Hills 460, 470 and 640 on 12/17

Sleeping family killed

First Battalion (157th) occupies
Mt. Cavallo 12/18

Second Battalion attacks Mt. Fialla
and Hill 770 12/15 and is repulsed.
Enemy withdraws 12/17

First Battalion occupies Hill 759 11/11,
is relieved by Second Battalion 11/13

SCALE OF MAP
HEIGHTS IN METERS

DEL. E.R., 2008, AFTER DWG. BY J.E.G.

POZZILLI
CAVE OF THE IRONHEADS
No. 85
BLOWN BRIDGE
VENAFRO
No. 85
CEPPAGNA
S. PIETRO
VOLTURNO RIVER
M.S.CROCE
CP 2 BN
HAMLET
M. CODNO
CONCA CASALE
FIALLA
OP
M.CAVALLO
VITTICUSO
M. MARTINO
GERMAN 44TH INFANTRY DIVISION
CASALE
ACQUAFONDATA
TO S. ELIA
LAGONI
640
670
769
460
759
770

(Map by the author, drawn by Erik Ronnberg)

··· 5 ···

THE UNDERBELLY

The Winter Line
November 1943–January 1944

THE REGIMENT ENCAMPED for three weeks on the verge of the Campanian plain, resting after saving the Salerno Beachhead from Vietinghoff's Panzers and replenishing itself with casualty replacements, of which I was one.

After forty days of it, the Thunderbirds turned over the fighting to the 34th Division, which with the Third butted across the valley of the Volturno, first against the impromptu Barbara Line's roadblocks, strongpoints and blown bridges, then bang into the Bernhardt Line the Germans had been digging and blasting into the rocky crests of the Apennines that rose like brooding thunderheads before the slogging doggies.

The bountiful bottom land around Piedimonte d'Alife, however, was as salubrious a respite for the touring Americans of '43 as it must have been for the Samnite conquerors of the fifth century B.C. Abruptly plucked from nowhere and dropped into a platoon of fagged-out veterans as their third youngest at barely twenty-one, I remember but dimly those days of restless pause for them and easy transition for me.

A *signora* who'd picked up some English in Canada swapped Andy Zapiecki a couple of chickens for a G.I. shirt or two and a change of underwear and had just cooked these *galline* for his crew, "and Joe, that's where you come in. I was shavin', and Jack introduced you."

It was not to the madcap corporal that Jack consigned me, however, but to the custody of the schoolmasterish Sergeant Griffith and my fellow Ivy Leaguer Jerry Waldron—Dartmouth and Harvard, old rivals tenting together at last, so far from home. "The men seem a smart bunch," Harvard logged two days later. "They're somewhat reserved in their relations with me. I suspect they're waiting to see really what kind of a joker I am when it comes time to hit a ditch."

Two more nights, and "a couple of Jerry planes came over to case our anti-aircraft fire. We all jumped in the ditch, but nothing came of it." First hurdle: Harvard knew how to hit a ditch. The rest was not so easy. In training we had all been civilians turning soldier. Over here I was an untested recruit among veterans, and a raw one at that.

Along with the red-and-gold Thunderbird patch for my left shoulder came a lifesaving reclassification. No longer a *rifleman* (745) at the bottom of the Army's pile, I was upgraded to *scout* (761) with the rest of the Platoon who weren't drivers, evoking the image of a monosyllabic frontiersman combing through the still-warm campfire ashes in the forest primeval. Or more exactly, *Scout: One sent out to obtain and bring back information, as about the position and movements of an enemy.*

How to go about such a daunting mission, I had no idea. There being neither field manual nor any hands-on instruction in the vineyards of Piedimonte, I inferred what I could from the anecdotes of my new platoonmates. This was going to be on-the-job training. I was struck by their independence from the rest of an informally held together Regimental Headquarters Company that was responsible directly to Colonel Church and his staff. Here was a freedom to come and go that was of necessity restricted in the rifle companies and undreamed of deep in the bully-brass chickenshit we'd left behind in the States.

A clique of smart individualists noisily loosened by Zapiecki and laconically led by Pullman, these Ironheads struck me as a laid-back, anti-military fraternity of scruffy, often outrageously funny, or strangely quiet and introspective free-wheelers, which I came to learn was the whole idea behind Intelligence and Reconnaissance, whatever that was meant to be. In short, good scouts. And after the departure of Lieutenant "Let's Get Foolish" Farley for the hospital, uniquely and thankfully brassless, though I suppose most all of us were qualified.

For all, however, the Italian campaign just begun was already a strange and otherworldly experience shot through with irony, compassion, frustration, embarrassment, tragedy, mystery and fear. Fresh on the scene and perplexed, I was already overloaded with a kaleidoscope of images since we jeered the surrendered Italian submarine in Bizerte harbor and hiked blinkingly through Naples in the wake of the rampaging Hermann Goering Division. Now I was in the countryside amidst the rubble of our gang's turn at trashing, journaling my first taste of the side of the ancient civilization that would be most ravaged by the war.

Every Italian field has a jackass, and there is nothing quite so plaintive as the braying hee-haw of the sturdy little eunuch. As different from the ancient Roman is the modern "Dago" as the puling jackass from the snorting charger that drew a racing chariot into battle. How a nation can degenerate! From a roaring, battling celestially-minded empire that was the very revolving point of the universe Italy has turned into a collection—I hate to call it nation—of tourist accommodators, balcony worshippers who have lost all self-respect and seem to be held together by a common spirit of opportunism. The price of an apple went from one tenth of a lira to two liras in two days. Walk down the street, and four out of five people you pass beg "cigaretta? [sic]" Yet mention Mussolini and they give you the slit-throat sign.

To them we're not soldiers, not conquerors, I wonder whether even saviours. We're American tourists, suckers. It's easily seen that they treated the Germans to the same ingratiating smiles.

My first contemptuous impression was similar to the early, bitter, Willy-and-Joe cartoons of the 45th's Bill Mauldin. Compassion overtook most of us gradually and painfully as with deepening experience of the war we saw civilians and soldiers on both sides as compromised and degraded victims of human designs at their most base.

Such was the insight of a British officer who with a sergeant had for eighteen months been a prisoner of the Italian army in northern Italy and escaped upon learning of the Italian surrender. Working south, the two snuck through the enemy lines to one of our forward positions and were brought back to the CP for debriefing, the thrust of which was that the German defenses were so impregnable that they believed we'd be in the mountains all winter. Driver Dan Boone and I took them back to Division HQ for more debriefing. As I recorded in my notebook:

During the drive they were almost childlike in their joy to get back to friends. The Captain exclaimed, "By God, it's hard to believe we're free!" They were full of plans about their homecoming to England. He observed that the "Eyetie" farmer is most sturdy, independent, industrious, and freedom-loving. It is through his isolated position and his lack of union that he's been unable to exert any political power. If he could have presented a united front and an effective bloc in the years preceding the war, a great disaster for Italy might have been avoided. As is only too evident to all of us here, the result was tragic. The government saw the handwriting on the wall and in haste turned upon its partner. Ever since, the Germans have wreaked their rage upon the mass of innocents who had little to do with either the union or the breach. Perhaps we're prone to judge too hastily at that.

Like the begging. The proud paesans begging? At every meal they showed up around our chow line until it even got to Dowdall, the most charitable of all.

> *Mangiare, mangiare* all the time. One mornin' we're all preoccupied wid shavin', takin' a bath out of a helmet, writin' letters. Bashore's the only one talkin', talkin' about these beggin' bastards, you know, all the time beggin'. Then this girl comes along with a baby in her arms an' goes up to him an' says, *"Mangiare, bambino!"* There's no sound from the guys. Dick goes into the tent an' gets out some K rations an' gives 'em to her. Still not a word. An' then he starts talkin' to everybody—"I had to give her somethin', she had a baby, they were hungry."

They were hungry all right, hanging around our garbage pit, intercepting our leftovers. Trying to swap a pair of shoes for a pair of chickens with a couple of kids, we found they had to steal them first.

I'd been a Thunderbird for two weeks when the Regiment was ordered back into action on November 7. The 179th and 180th Regiments had by then fought across the Volturno and were dug into the mountains, stopped cold and soaking wet against the Bernhardt Line.

"Every time the Division moves it rains," groaned Zapiecki. "It HAS to or there can't be no move." Twenty-seven soaking miles in an open jeep bumping across the streaming, muddy plain toward that ever-rising wall of mountain brought the reverberating booming of the artillery closer and heightened the throat-tightening mixture of excitement and dread and aloneness and inevitability that had taken possession of me from the moment we boarded the *Samuel Ashe* two months before at Newport News.

Moving back into action, the veteran Regiment was a blunted triangle whose broadening bulk shoved its cutting edge of riflemen against the enemy's, kept them energized and

Venafro, the mountains and the enemy (*U.S. Army Signal Corps*)

honed and backed with supporting fire, reabsorbed their broken and dead bodies and exchanged them for fresh replacements, a sort of mobile killer anthill.

Out of the gashed and torn plain the stolid bulk of the Apennines loomed ahead and to the right and left, east and west, as far as we could see until it disappeared in the rain and gathering dusk. At the pontoon bridge over the Volturno the convoy was telescoped. Up there the Germans, down here sitting ducks huddled in our jeeps, dripping in the downpour, keeping our distance in case a Focke-Wulf fighter plane popped in from over the mountain crest, already almost too miserable to be nervous as we waited our turn.

At last the Platoon rattled across the bridge and joined the Regiment moving north on Route 85 to Venafro, through the hollow-echoing main street of the bombed and shelled old town, and onto the dirt road that followed the base of the mountains.

About a mile beyond, we turned off to the left and up into a steeply sloping olive grove that Colonel Church had chosen for his command post, a sandbagged tent. Aroundabout were the vehicles of Headquarters Company as its specialized components staked out their ground. The rest of the Regiment was strung along the road. I still drip and shiver through that first night just below the front in the downpour and the blackness, curled up on the hood of the jeep in my raincoat, soaked and shivering, the rivulets streaming down amongst the olive trees, and I still hear the roar and rumble of the guns.

The rain lifted enough next morning to reconnoiter for the enemy line of defense in the dark ridges up there above us and check out corresponding heights on which to perch a couple of observation posts, hopefully with one-way views. We knew only that they'd had months to entrench themselves and were waiting for us.

As the tenderfoot I was invited along, probably in Griffith's crew, to find a likely lookout from which to observe our coming attack to the northwest, somewhere on a ridge above the road that twisted higher and higher through narrow valleys from Pozzilli eight or ten miles to the mountain town of Acquafondata, the 157th's objective.

Instead of tackling the mountainside looming up to the north, we followed the road that hugged its base to Pozzilli and took to the slope past a couple of companies from our 179th Regiment pinned down on our right by unfriendly German snipers on Hill 769, so designated in meters on our crude old Italian contour map with its roads and trails poorly or wrongly marked if at all, mountain peaks and hills all jumbled together. The Apennines reminded me vaguely of the White Mountains of New Hampshire where I'd backpacked in the thirties. But, as I would write home,

they can't begin to compare in beauty. Generally they have only a low, insignificant scrub at their bases, are very much rockier and have few commanding peaks. Olive groves are usually terraced part way up the base. The "paesans" select the most precipitous and tortuous route up to the barest peak they can find, then scratch out a town at a grade of about sixty degrees, miles from nowhere, bleak, unproductive, almost devoid of quaintness. Sometimes in a little saddle way up in the hills a paesan will cultivate about an acre, a tiny spot of life in a barren nest of rock.

Some "soft belly" (*Joint Intelligence Collecting Agency*)

We were hiking along just below the crest of the ridge when enemy mortar fire just cleared it and landed in the draw below. "I hit the dirt," I journaled later, "and hard. Farther on, both going and coming, a sniper fired on us as we came to a certain exposed spot. The bullets sounded like the crack of a whip, but the range was pretty far, and he didn't come too near."

✥ ✥ ✥

The going was rocky, steep, unexpectedly exposed and unpredictably mined. Snipers watched and waited with their Schmeisser burp guns whose BRRRRP and deceiving echo made them hard to place by sound—yet no more chilling than the choral sighs and zooms of a cluster of German mortar shells looping overhead to explode and splatter their shrapnel around.

As I recorded in my journal, on the way back through Pozzilli, where the Regiment's forward CP was being set up as close as caution dictated behind the expected action,

I saw some of the boys who've been taken down from the hills, mostly shrapnel. One had his legs blown up by a mine. One lad came down with shell shock. He was whimpering and shivering like a dog. A couple

of prisoners went by, and about a half dozen Empire-builders [Italians] *came running along, armed with clubs, pitchforks and knives. They were going to "chop them up and eat them." One old guy went after them with his fork. The guard kicked him in the pants. "You're not gonna run away with my first prisoner!"*

Down in the CP in the pup tent I shared with Jerry Waldron I wrote with studied understatement: "My first day was not uneventful. I wasn't as disturbed under fire as I thought I might be. The Army has given me a certain stoic philosophy, I guess."

Not yet. Stoicism, like cynicism, cannot be conferred, only earned. Homeward I wrote with studied casualness. "I've been under fire—nothing much—and learned how to love Mother Earth with a zeal unequalled by even such an ardent agriculturalist as Dad. I've seen Germans and find most of them hardly more than kids, but great fighters. At that we're a match for any two of them. They're terrified by our artillery, and their foxholes look like mining shafts."

Such foolish hubris. I'd soon enough learn.

We set up our observation post on the right of the regimental sector on a ridge about a mile across a creek valley from Hills 460 and 470 held by the enemy. Its distinguishing feature was a rough stone shepherd's hut with a thatch roof that formed the corner of one of the myriad terraces by means of which the farmers clawed enough rough level out of the mountainsides for grazing and agriculture. We could slip in and out through an opening at the rear and out of sight, we hoped, of the eyes of the Third Reich.

Down along the ridge a couple of hundred feet, crouching out of sight the last few yards, we could walk most of the way to a stone wall two or three feet high that afforded a sweeping view across the valley to Hills 460 and 470 and a portion of the Pozzilli–Acquafondata road. Nearby was a hollow in a boulder that collected rainwater where we made a pass at washing above the neck. We shared the OP with a bunch of artillery observers, which would prove to be too much of a good thing.

Mine detectors sweep the way to the body of a G.I. killed stepping on an enemy ground mine. (*Department of Defense*)

We had binoculars, a monocular spotting scope of about twenty power, and hand-held azimuth compasses. Because our radios were useless in the mountains, we relied on a leather-cased field telephone that rang up with a hand crank. This primitive device was connected through vulnerable miles of wire laid beside the trail from Second Battalion CP in a small commandeered farmhouse in a small hamlet that clung to the soaking hillside a couple of miles back down the mountain, thence down to the Regimental switchboard.

Herbie Illfelder, the refugee from the Gestapo, the awkward intellectual, the practical joke butt who'd transferred out of the Platoon in the States, was by now in the small intelligence section of Second Battalion housed in this hamlet. Not far above, the Germans periodically shelled an exposed stretch of the trail where it branched off to our OP. His friend Frank Merchant was back in hospital with trench foot when he heard what happened:

> Herbie had been sitting on the edge of his foxhole when they brought down some prisoners, and he was interrogating one in his usual methodical manner when mortar shells started coming in. He, as very often, paid no attention. They said the prisoner slid into his hole, and Herbie sat there and kept on with his job and got a whole bunch of shrapnel in his back. Within a day or two he died.

That rocky, slippery, treacherous, shelled and sniped-at route that was our life support by back and mule pack would be our main highway to hell and heaven. Beside it, farther up the slope, was a grave with a cross, and a German helmet on it. Within burp-gun range at the end was the southernmost parapet of Hitler's Fortress Europa.

Buying time to build the Bernhardt Line in depth from the mouth of the Garigliano through the mountains in which we were stalled, while slowing the Fifth Army's advance from Naples, the 14th Panzer Corps had first set up the Barbara Line of temporary outposts from the west coast into the Matese Mountains in the Volturno region.

This Winter Line, as we were soon enough calling it, followed the ridges from the Tyrrhenian Sea through the broad Liri Valley, dominated by the formidable bulk of Monte Cassino, and into the mountains along the Garigliano and Rapido rivers. Straight up the Liri corridor ran the only road from Naples to Rome, the Allied objective fifty miles north, on the bed of the Appian Way built by the Romans 2,200 years before. Monte Cassino and the namesake town at its base, crowned by the ancient and world-famous abbey founded by Saint Benedict in 529 upon its crest, commanded the valley, anchored the defense of the mountains, and in the months ahead would determine the fate of the war in Italy.

The abbey, wrote historian Martin Blumenson, "looked to the south with hypnotic gaze, all-seeing, like the eyes in a painting that follow the spectator wherever he moves. To the Allied soldiers on the plain below, the glistening white abbey on the peak watched them with German eyes from which there was no concealment."[1]

East of Cassino the Apennines interlocked in a continuous fastness to the Adriatic. Foothills, high hills and peaks from 1,500 to 3,500 meters were jumbled together, weathered bald above the bush line, affording nary an opening for advance except through twisting valleys, or ridge by jagged ridge, all reprogrammed into a mosaic of death.

(*U.S. Army Signal Corps*)

Blending with the slope of Mount Lungo, a German "pillbox" looks down on uphill assault.
(*U.S. Army Signal Corps*)

Bridges and culverts were blown up and bypass sites mined methodically by the Germans. Machine-gun and mortar positions were dug and sometimes blasted into rock with crossfires sweeping narrow valleys, stream beds and slopes, while unoccupied areas were covered by artillery and mortars. Snipers with burp guns were stationed at vantage points. Mines were laid on key trails, narrow passages and fields, and in strategic locations with rolls of concertina barbed wire and log-and-earth bunkers. The Germans' dugouts were furnished with mattresses and blankets, hams, potatoes, fresh bread, and preserves— hot meals, even, brought up from the headquarters mess.

From the OPs we never knew how much we couldn't see. One day we checked out a stretch of the Pozzilli–Acquafondata road the Germans had given up. I was mightily impressed with "a remarkable job of camouflage," as I described it in my notebook. "The road is cut into the hillside, and Jerry had stood long tree trunks at 30-foot intervals along the outside of the highway. He had then strung trees along supporting wires for hundreds of yards. At intervals he had strung wire across the road and hung branches on it. Thus the road seemed part of the hillside, particularly when shadows fell across it."

Enemy howitzers and long-range guns were often self-propelled and didn't have to be hauled, and with tanks were well defiladed behind ridges. Having long since occupied the high ground before the Allied landing in Italy, their forward observers and air reconnaissance watched everything we did by day if the weather favored, and brought down uncannily accurate shellfire on our front lines, trails, roads, bivouacs and installations. One day two flights, each of a dozen Focke-Wulfs, bombed and strafed the 45th sector. Generally we had to move by dark while they maneuvered at will and supplied their lines from the closed-in valleys at their rear. On clear nights they achieved accurate counterbattery fire against our artillery with advanced sound-and-flash ranging units.

To add to the frustration, their binocular range-finders shamed our primitive spotting scopes, and it was a big bonus for the I&R the day we captured one.

With a window in the weather on November 11, the 45th went on the attack, as recounted in its official history, *The Fighting Forty-Fifth*:

> Those moving on Hill 460 were halted twice by mortar and machine gun fire. Those fighting their way toward the 179th Infantry Regiment sector encountered rough action all the way.
>
> Division artillery fired 2,475 rounds on November 12 . . . One battery of the 189th Field Artillery Battalion lost all but one of its prime movers and much ammunition in a shelling by enemy artillery . . .
>
> . . . enemy infantry supported by artillery counterattacked three times to regain possession of Hill 460 during the day and night and was thrown back each time.
>
> One company of the 157th Infantry Regiment attempted to move from Hill 460 to Hill 470 and was hit by two counterattacks, which were beaten off. Extremely heavy artillery concentrations lasting for two hours caused heavy casualties and the company withdrew to Hill 460 and to the base of Hill 769 . . .

During the night of November 12–13 the enemy assembled approximately 100 men on the reverse slope of one peak and 200 on the reverse of another. They were still in possession of most of the peaks and slopes of the defense ridge.

A heavy artillery and mortar preparatory barrage was placed upon the Division positions between 0600 and 0645. Six hundred rounds dropped in Vallecupa within the hour.

At 0645, with the artillery still firing, a part of the German force attacked fiercely, swinging to the left up the ridge. At the same time, the group of 100 Germans on the other peak swung south down the ridge. Both the left and right flanks of the Division were forced to give ground. The center remained firm.

Division artillery fired extremely heavy concentrations on the enemy forces, and eventually the attack was broken up.

The Germans attacked in waves of skirmishes, with men carrying mortars and machine guns following in the wake of each attacking wave. When enemy soldiers were hit, the groups following would pick up their weapons and continue the advance . . .

By 1045 the attack had spent its fury and the arrival of another reinforcing company eased the situation.[2]

Up on the OP Dave O'Keefe was on the scope when he saw two or three Germans at the bottom of the valley below and as many dogfaces behind a stone wall on Hill 460, about a mile away. When he heard shots he looked back again, and the doggies were no longer there. Half an hour later he watched the Germans walk up to the wall, look over, and shoot down behind it. He figured our guys must have been wounded in the skirmish and got finished off, and he felt lousy watching it all from afar, so helpless.

If I hadn't been hauled off the truck of replacements headed for Third Battalion three weeks earlier, I'd have been over there with a rifle instead of on the OP trying to figure out what was going on a mile away. November 17 journal:

It's been raining steadily for four days, bringing operations to a standstill, converting the terrain into a sea of mire and swelling dry river beds with rushing torrents. Hitler has told his soldiers to hold their line until January. Terrain is much in favor of the Germans, and their defenses are complete and well dug in. As usual they hold the high ground and hope to draw us through the valleys as at Kasserine Pass, but we're hitting the high spots and pounding them with artillery and mortars. Their withdrawal has all the signs of being orderly and planned long in advance. Many of their dead have marked graves (is it true that every Jerry has his cross already lettered?), and they are covering their retreat by laying extensive demolitions and mine fields, by leaving tanks and 88s to cover the hills and valleys, and by dotting the hills with machine guns with communications.

The British Eighth, with less opposition, is broadening its front and consequently narrowing our sector while we turn west to Rome. Enemy morale is reported to be low, and Goebbels has announced that if Great Britain and the U.S. fail to make separate peace with Germany and bring about her downfall, Europe will be overrun by the "Bolshevist Terror." The Russians, in precipitate advance, are less than 50 miles from Poland.

OP work has been difficult of late. Griff has been unable to report anything because of weather, though he has excellent observation, and the enemy generally has OPs which can overlook ours.

Saw my first dead Jerry on this hill. It was approaching twilight, and he had been stretched out there for several days. He was a redhead, just a kid, and had been in the act of bandaging his hands when a mortar shell fragment took the top of his head clean off. His helmet was lying at some distance, and his shoes were gone, probably taken by his comrades. He lay there, a bloody but bloodless picture of frozen action, stiff and solitary. Around him were German foxholes, looking as though they had been blasted out of the rock. Terraces had crumbled and scattered under our fire, branches were ripped away, and the soil was gashed where fragments had torn their way through. Farther up we saw our foxholes, scratched into the earth with typical abandon when we occupied the hill. All about them were discarded equipment, K-ration boxes and cans, playing cards, and even a little gilt statuette of the Virgin Mary. All that remained of the struggle was the sprawling, redheaded body.

About this time we passed a G.I. overcoat, muddy and torn by shrapnel, draped over a bush by the trail, and shook our heads over the poor bastard who got it where X marked the spot.

The goddam mountains of the underbelly again. I'd been hearing all the stories about Bloody Ridge in Sicily, but that had to be flatland compared to this.

Faced with the problem of supply in these hills, we've requisitioned a number of mules to carry food, water and ammo to the troops. I'd heard they were going to do this back at Naples. QM [Quartermaster] *is going to be besieged by Guineas with slips of paper saying "IOU One mule. John Doe."*

The Platoon drew an old nag named or rechristened Marco, and for a few weeks the honor of muleskinning was reluctantly divided amongst Hank Mills, Vern Dilks, Les Gerencer, Bill Caird, myself and perhaps one or two other dudes under the direction of cowboys and farmers like Mullenax, Contreras and Beech. Mule tales tended to be grim and weighed down with black humor. Knowing neither mules, tack nor Italian, we overloaded and misloaded the poor beast. Having no idea how to flatter and persuade him on the level, let alone on a rocky, muddy, slippery trail a yard wide up a 45-degree slope—burdened with a couple of five-gallon cans of water, rations, blankets, bungwad, clothing, letters and Christmas packages from home, guns and ammunition—we whacked and cussed Marco with predictable results.

Ah, the morning back at the CP I fed him a huge breakfast of damp green baled hay. What did I know about damp green baled hay, let alone mules? Looked almost tasty enough to munch myself. Then I loaded him and of course cinched him up tight with the belly strap, and we set off on the trail up to the OP, Marco farting green-hay flatulus in my face with every step all the way up, and then all the way back down. Naturally I had to keep cinching up that strap around his bloated belly as the trail steepened and his load lurched around, and the more I cinched the more he farted, and the more I cinched.

Dilks, the sourpuss driver, claimed "there was a certain way you had to hit Marco in the belly with yer knee when you drew those straps up, except that we didn't know how to

A 157th Infantry Regiment "pack train" picks its way along a rare level trail. (*U.S. Army Signal Corps*)

Above Venafro mule #1 barely plods along under the burden of an 81-mm mortar while behind him a frustrated 'Bird hauls on balking #2 loaded down with the weapon's ammo. (*U.S. Army*)

do that, and he'd take a deep breath first and go about five feet, and the whole load would slide off."

His buddy Hank Mills's mule technique was as distinctly Mills:

> Caird and I were goin' up there with Marco. He wouldn't go so I stretched his neck about four feet. I believe that was the closest I come to gettin' killed—by a mule kickin' me. I'm standin' behind. A guy's comin' down leadin' a mule. The path was narrow, with a helluva drop, so when he went by, this dizzy bastard hollered, "Give it to him!" An' I turned around, and that goddam mule o' his kicked both feet straight back. Honest to God, I could feel the wind, it was that close. Another inch and he'da kicked my face flat.

The Regiment's lifeline mule trail was up to five miles long, with stretches so steep that only a guy with a packboard could barely get through. There never was enough gear, and our Army issue was too heavy for the Italian mules and further reduced their normal load of 220 pounds. From the *History of the 157th Infantry Regiment*:

> ... Trails were narrow and fell away to sickening depths. They were always wet, sometimes coated with ice. Usually the patient mules were loaded in the late afternoon at supply and ammunition dumps and led up the trails in darkness. It was slow, nerve-wracking business, inching up the mountains in the black of night. Occasionally, mules fell to their deaths, kicking and screaming through the air to the rocks hundreds of feet below.[3]

The Thunderbirds tackled the mountain with thirty-two mules, and in a few weeks four hundred wouldn't be enough.

A week after the 157th rejoined the front and on the fourth day of our attempt to break the Bernhardt Line, November 14, the battle subsided in mutual exhaustion. Late that day the rains returned. Without shelter on the ridges, the dogfaces were huddled under intermittent gunfire as it poured and poured. In many areas it was all they could do to scratch pitiful holes through the dirt, if there was any, until ledge was struck, then pile loose rocks, if they could find any, around the perimeter to the bare height of a shallow coffin. Icy rivulets of rain twisted through their scattered and lonely positions under the crests of these miserable mountains and streamed down the trails, making the job of bringing up supplies and evacuating casualties under always-unpredictable fire merely another nightmare, only of a movable sort.

For winter mountain clothing: long cotton underwear, wool "OD" (olive drab) pants and shirt, lightly lined OD field jacket, OD cotton socks, World War I-vintage leather boots that no amount of dubbin could render waterproof, perhaps OD puttees, heavy OD wool overcoat (unwaterproofable), light OD raincoat, light OD woolen gloves, OD woolen cap, OD cotton handkerchief, plastic helmet liner and dark OD steel helmet. Shelter halves for pup tents and to cover foxholes were of light OD canvas. The entire infantry outfit was

Stuck in grave-like "foxholes" of piled-up rocks and exposed to wind, cold and driving rain with no cover but their canvas tent shelter halves, the dogfaces of the 157th are somewhat safer from enemy artillery, but not from mortar fire looping down on them from over the mountaintop. (*Department of Defense*)

designed to blend with the trenches of France in another war twenty-six years gone by, and to hell with the poor bastards.

Up front the fare—morning, noon and night—was occasionally the sumptuous two-can C rations but basically the compact K ration in the thickly waxed, OD cardboard container about half the size of a cigar box which, I wrote home, consisted of "two packages atrocious dry biscuits, atrocious corn and pork loaf or some such, atrocious dextrose tablets, coffee extract or atrocious lemon or bouillon powder, stick of gum." I forgot to mention the packet of four of five atrocious cigarettes, invariably some off-brand such as Raleigh or Viceroy.[4] And how cleverly were untold thousands of us hooked on the habit by the so-generous tobacco companies.

Down in the regimental CP on the lower slope of Monte Santa Croce and below on the flat, the rain swelled the waters of the Volturno until it carried away all four of the Division's vital pontoon bridges. The rich mud of the valley, churned up by thousands of wheeled and tracked vehicles and shellfire and bombs, was a foot to three feet thick; it gave the entire support system of the miserable fighters up on the ridges a case of chronic constipation all the way back to Naples reminiscent to senior field officers like our Colonel Church of the worst of the trenches of France. It was further mucked by bogdowns and breakdowns that tied knots at crossroads under daytime enemy observation, with the inevitable shellfire interdiction when there was a rare break in the weather. What agony, crawling through one of these bull's-eyes tended by some poor, sodden MP trying to keep it all moving, holding your breath that suddenly out of the sky wouldn't burst that shattering staccato of

ZZZZZEEEEWWOW-WHAM-WHAM-WHAM-WHAM-WHAM

We dogfaces didn't know it, but at least one of our life-and-death big bosses truly felt for us. The corncob pipe-smoking General Lucas, commander of our Sixth Corps, wrote in his diary in mid-November that in addition to days of rain "it is cold as hell. I think too often of my men out in the mountains. I am far too tender-hearted ever to be a success at my chosen profession ... I don't see how our men stand what they do ... They are the finest soldiers in the world and none but an humble man should command them. My constant prayer to Almighty God is that I may have the wisdom to bring them through this ordeal with the maximum of success and the minimum loss of life."[5]

Still, up and down the mountain to the line, and on and off the OPs, the luck of the I&R held, the blind luck to stumble on the ultimate in simple but secure accomodations for the American unavoidably detained in southern Italy—a cave. Indeed, The Cave.

Someone came upon this hole in the hill in an old olive grove a short climb above the CP, which was known wryly up around the foxholes as "back at Regiment." One had to stoop to get through the entrance, which was four or five feet wide and looked south over the Volturno Valley. It was impervious to shellfire coming over Monte Santa Croce, and in the remote event a visitor from the Luftwaffe spotted it or even thought it worth the bother, he would have to roar up low from the valley on his way home over the mountain and send his message through a keyhole.

Once, to elude our anti-aircraft fire, a Heinie did take this route back from a mission in the valley. Supply Sergeant Benjamin leaped to the .50-caliber machine gun mounted on his truck and BAM-BAMMed away, following the plane lower and lower up the slope

"Hit th' dirt, boys!"

(Copyright 1943 by Bill Mauldin.
Courtesy of the Mauldin Estate.)

until he was clipping off the olive branches over our heads, provoking a general rush for the Cave. And more than once. But WHISH, der Kraut vass gone, and Benjy never did bag one.

The extent of our cavern was probably not much more than fifteen feet in width by twenty front-to-back. We found neither bones, artifacts nor representations of bison, though it must have been a place of refuge for hunter and prey since the Stone Age, level enough for human habitation, with not much more than headroom anywhere, even way back when heads were so much lower. This made little difference to us because whoever happened to be in residence kept a green wood fire going that produced a breathtaking stratum of nose-and-eye-level smoke at the mere cost of the owner's ever-diminishing olive grove.

At first, the coziness of the Cave had little appeal; claustrophobia perhaps, and the probability that the Krauts looking down at us hadn't gotten around to marking the CP for harassment. The arrival of the first few shells lobbed haphazardly into our general midst, not to mention Benjy's frenzies with his machine gun, capped by the mid-November rains on our scattering of pup tents, aroused more interest in domestic spelunking.

MUD (*U.S. Army Signal Corps*)

Major General John P. Lucas
(*Department of Defense*)

Mills was paired with Dilks sleeping out in the open where "there was a big tree maybe thirty feet away with a Y in it, and the Krauts dropped a mortar shell in the middle and split it. Dilks and me woke up. The tree was hangin' there, and we gathered everything up and headed for the Cave." Hank had a sixth sense about stuff coming in, and we swore he could hear the lanyard being pulled on an 88 three miles away. Jerry Waldron was nearby outside the Cave one day, "and Hank says 'Jesus, they're comin!' I says, 'What're you talkin about?' And they lobbed one over, but he was up in the Cave by then."

Pullman's two replacements, Waldron and I, and a few others stuck to our pup tents at the remote risk of a stray shell. "What a feeling of utter helplessness overcomes one in a tent with shells dropping a quarter of a mile away!" I wrote to myself. "And yet get out of the tent, escape from that suffocation of canvas, and you think nothing more of it." A miss was as good as a quarter of a mile, as I would soon learn.

Cold and wet, but thank God for the guy back at that Replacement Depot we'd set up in Mussy's Racetrack outside Naples, the one who got clothes and bedding up to the front by giving every replacement or dischargee from the hospital circulating through a barracks bag of gear including three wool blankets to lug back. A couple of Ironheads were in their tent close by Colonel Church's, and Waldron heard one ask "'Should we sleep with nine blankets over and twelve under, or twelve over and nine under?' And the Colonel's standing there, just shakin' his head."

When not up on an OP most of us spent our idle hours and evenings in the Cave, sitting on our haunches on our inverted helmets around the fire, the sharp rims cutting off the circulation to our butts but never mind, the light of the flames dancing in the circle of faces, smoking, endlessly smoking, coffee steaming (there was no wine or liquor, ever), some kind of slumgullion in the pot that somebody had scrounged, maybe toasting the cheese from the K ration, or passing around cookies or a fruitcake from home.

Or on the verge of passing out from the blend of various smokes, crude attempts at cuisine, stale straw brought in for bedding, exhalations of carbon dioxide and flatus, bodies unwashed for weeks, and the accumulated aromas of the centuries of inherited ambience of a genuine, unspoiled Campanian cave amidst the ambience of marathon coffee, marathon smoking, marathon cribbage and marathon argument.

"Dilks beat Zapiecki five straight at cribbage," recalls Waldron, always strong on sports stories, "and that wasn't possible, so Andy insisted on playing me, and I beat him five straight, which upset him so much he took on Garland, who was only learning the game and beat him five straight."

The colloquy around the fire, with revolving participants like a never-ending poker game, analyzed the strategic conduct of the war and the global politics of it all; morality in conflict situations; the locally perceived demographics of southern Italy in World War II; the hierarchy of sonsabitches in the Regiment past and current; who was the Oklahoma Indian who got drunk and backtalked Uncle Charley back in the States; just what bullshit did Patton give the Division that day in Sicily; and exactly where was Woodhams when he knocked out the tank?

As the Harvard boy who was bound to make an impression, next to Mills I was the youngest and brashest, facing off with Mullenax, who would expound doggedly on some point of history, politics or military tactics and was often maddeningly wrong, or with Dave O'Keefe, who was maddeningly right, or with one and all, wrong or right. Dave was a smart civil engineer from Derby, Connecticut, whose father was the street commissioner and his uncle the mayor. His cherubic smile betrayed his joy in adopting the most contrary

Tent City at the 157th command post, sketched in my notebook November 29. Not pictured, our cave is in the rising slope a few yards to the right. (*Author*)

possible stance in any multiple argument from which he predictably emerged with a technical knockout.

Beyond the fire, an oxygen-starved candle in a far corner flicked angular shadows on the black walls. Dilks and a couple of other grumps lounged in their sacks, launching from afar their wisecracks when the talk lapsed, fending off the response with a grunt and retreating into the murk.

Way back somewhere under his blankets lurked Les Gerencer, the Thin Man a.k.a. Meatless Tuesday (Meet Les, of course—so dubbed by Mills), Bread and Butts from his eating and smoking habits, and the self-styled second-toughest guy on his block back in the factory town of Phillipsburg, New Joisey, where his parents met after fleeing Hungary just ahead of the First War. His father opened a poolroom and his mother worked as a maid in a brownstone mansion. When the kid was two Pa died and Ma took over what was now their neighborhood grocery until the repeal of Prohibition, when she built a brick house next door, moved her brood of four in upstairs and opened a street-floor beer joint.

Chilled to his thin bones in the damp cold, Bread and Butts wore three shirts over his long underwear and worked a routine of feigned courtesy when in a group, withdrawing from the outermost pocket a pack of scorned Raleigh cigarettes that he passed around with much solicitous show and then replaced. The amenities satisfied, he'd thrust two willowy fingers down through his shirtneck and deftly withdraw a universally coveted Lucky Strike from an inside pocket and stick it with sheepish diffidence between his lips, where it took its place as part of his bony, smirking countenance, not to be removed, an inch or so of ash miraculously intact, until it expired.

Cigarette glowing and the firelight twinkling in the steel-rimmed glasses through which he peered at his comrades with feigned buglike innocence, Meatless would demonstrate that he was hungry or thin enough to squeeze out of any fix.

What talk, what stories, what nonsense!

Mills:
I was standin' by the kitchen one day, beside the stone wall, talkin' to the guy cleanin' a chicken, and a shell come in and he threw the chicken straight up in the air and run like hell.

Waldron:
Colonel Church's Chinese houseboy wrote a letter to Mrs. Church every week on her orders. The Old Man starts to go out of his tent one day, and you hear this guy singin' out, "Colonel, come back and put your rubbers on!" When his boss keeps on goin' he says, "I'll tell Mrs. Church!"

Mills:
I got up in the middle of a real dark night to take a leak an' didn't see him an' pissed all over Army Joe [Milton Armijo, a CP guard], who was layin' there asleep in his bedroll. Next mornin' he gets up an' feels his blanket an' says "Jeez, I didn't know it rained last night."

Nary an Ironhead admitted to acquaintance with a musical instrument, and anyway, why lug a harmonica through World War II when all the music anyone wanted, and sometimes more, squawked ever more scratchily from Zapiecki's hand-cranked phonograph, as much a fixture of the Cave as Andy himself? They echo now, "Buckle Down, Winsocki," Nelson Eddy and "Song of the Open Road," John McCormack and "Danny Boy," "The Gypsy Baron," forgotten snatches of grand opera, Victor Herbert, Sigmund Romberg, and an uproarious rendering of "The Biggest Aspidistra in the World" by that wild British comic Beatrice Lillie. A polka perhaps, but nary a bar of Goodman, Dorsey, Miller, Waller or Armstrong, not for the Polack.

And every time the 105s down in the valley fired a mission, and one of the great shells sighed up and over the peaks ahead toward the fated target, the compression wave rolled up the slope, and the "shelter" half of a canvas pup tent, hung across the entrance to keep the warmth and light in and the cold out, would go WHOOSH.

If there was a drawback it was the fleas, but as Mills said, "between gettin' bit by a flea and hit by a artillery shell, you had to take the fleas. I didn't think they lived in November. I guess we kept 'em warm with our body heat."

Where they came from nobody could say. Bill Caird thought they were indigenous to the streets and leaped on his pants as he hiked through liberated towns. "They never really bothered me. Probably I didn't shower enough. Ernie Pyle said if you didn't shower the fleas wouldn't bite you." Dom Trubia was "one bloody mess" around his belt line and boot tops, and Gerencer would sleep on the straw and in the morning be red with bites. I wrote home at the end of December that "I'm practically crawling with fleas. I usually change my clothes only when I take a bath, which I do about once a month if I'm lucky."

On the lookout for filthier and cozier quarters, maybe our fleas deserted Marco or the stray mongrel we adopted around mid-November as our beloved Platoon mascot, a black bitch with four white paws, hence "Boots." Whatever their origin, the Cave was jumping with them—not the infamous cooties or body lice of the trenches of the Previous War, but genuine fleas, maybe even German fleas.

Sergeant Shorty Nye disdained the Cave for all but supper and socializing, preferring tenting in the diminishing olive grove, aware that his famous luck was in inverse proportion to his size as a target. As he recalled during a group interview with Caird, Zapiecki and Dilks:

> I put my tent up and measured about four or five inches inside an' dug my hole with plenty o' room, then dug a ditch around the outside so's to drain the rain, and had a lil Coleman lantern for writin', readin' or what have you. Our topkick Bill Sevey jumped in on top o' me during a barrage once, all squinched up an' said, "Dig a decent hole, dammit, not with a lil ole teaspoon!" I said it was all right for me.
>
> An' I had my lil black bag, and when you got that you had everything. Everybody tried to root around in it. They useta steal stuff and I'd steal it back. My best friend was the cook, whoever he was, anybody, I didn't care. I could talk anything outta anybody. Anybody needed anything, always go to the lil black bag. I had ways. I'd take my rations an' exchange sump'n nobody liked for sump'n everybody liked.

Caird:
One time somebody crawled under Nye's jeep to fix something and found a can o' bacon taped to the frame. He would never go hungry.

Zapiecki:
No matter how bad it was, you knew if you was with Nye you'd get some real coffee, maybe a little bacon, some little goodie. If he was there we'd never starve, but if he wasn't, just think how many guys would have to go out lookin' for grub.

Caird:
He carried four or five pairs o' boots because they were so small he could never get any, four-and-a-half or five shoe.

Nye:
Five E E.

Zapiecki:
Mine were eleven E E E.

Nye:
Big shithouses are built on big foundations.

Dilks:
He kept three or four pair under the back seat o' the jeep. I was drivin' him somewhere, and this Italian couple invited us for dinner. Didn't have much, rabbit or sump'n, but we appreciated it. One o' the daughters had real small feet and was walkin' around barefoot, so I went out an' dug around an' picked out a nice pair o' his shoes an' give 'em to her. Ole Nye was gonna call the MPs tryin' to find out where them shoes went. I tole the ole guy, who could speak English, to hide 'em if the MPs come around or they'd take 'em right off her.

Mills, in a separate interview:
Shorty was givin' out the Raleighs to everybody and keepin' the Luckies for himself. It'd be his turn to go on the OP and he'd say to me before he left the CP, "Now you watch my stuff. Somebody's stealin' my cigarettes." He comes back and some are gone and he says, "I thought I tole you to watch." I says, "I can't be there all the time. They must be waitin' 'til I leave." Little did he know it was me stealin' his Lucky Strikes. He got to be the Platoon commissary. Helluva good guy but a little bit on the tight side. When his kid was born I was bunkin' with him, an' they nicknamed the kid Chucky Joe, an' he was givin' Madge, his wife, hell in a letter for spendin' too much on baby oil. Hard little customer. Well put together. Strong.

All five-foot-two or -three of the little sarge was as good for morale in his way as Zapiecki and Mills. You got the laffs outta Andy and the wisecracks outta Hank, and with Nye you knew it was possible, in spite of all the crap flying around and the misery and the lousy K and C rations, to live like half a human being as long as he had his lil black bag. He looked out for his crew, did his job, took no more chances than he had to, and was lucky as hell. And except for a couple of times, his luck rubbed off.

As the weeks of deadly deadlock passed, our Cave—with its warm fire, the anonymity conferred by its veil of smoke, and the conviviality of the Ironheads—attracted visitors who'd as soon have waited out the war in a hole in a hill above the Volturno.

Growled Mills: "They were comin' from everywhere hidin' out. We shoulda took rent. One guy was AWOL from a line company, from West Virginia, but we called him Tex. About every ten minutes he'd break into 'San Antonio Rose.' I wanted to tell him, hey, no more. He just disappeared like all of 'em."

Some men from Cannon Company moved in for a while, and some from the 106th Ack-Ack. A self-styled line company "BARman" from Tinnissee who'd been hit and was returning from the hospital, being in no hurry to get back, dropped in for a while with a story on himself of being on an outpost up a ridge above us one night, hearing a noise out in front of him and opening up with his BAR. A voice in the darkness shouted "Who the hell are you shootin' at, you sonofabitch?" Tinnissee yelled back "I'm shootin at you, you sonofabitch!"—still too shaken to realize it was his buddies returning from a patrol.

Gerencer reminded me that "you and Pullman went out on a patrol and Tinnissee volunteered to go with you, and Jack tells him no, you better not."

By the smoky glow of the olivewood fire (it burned as readily and dirtily as pine), I scrutinized, and submitted to the scrutiny of, the men with whom my existence was becoming entwined as with none before or since. In eight months I'd been bent from college boy to enlistee to trainee to replacement to soldier under fire in a deadlocked battle.

And Mark Clark was promising his wife Maurine that he was going to give her Rome for a Christmas present. Or so it was said up on the line. Such asininity would have been in character. Although Martin Blumenson, the official historian of the campaign, doesn't mention it in his damn-with-faint-praise biography, he notes that after the fall of Naples Clark wired her: "I give you Naples for your birthday."[6]

A couple of miles to the west of our Cave, in the sector of the First Ranger Battalion on the 45th's left flank, about fifty German soldiers on the steep slope of a pass near the mountain village of Conca Casale had made a seemingly impregnable strongpoint of a similar cavern whose entrance was shielded by enormous boulders. Over a span of days, one by one the Rangers stealthily lugged blocks of TNT over a trail to a precarious point just above this Berchtesgaden of the Bernhardt. One rainy night they lowered their eight-hundred-pound bomb by ropes to just over the entrance and detonated it. The explosion rocked the Volturno Valley. Nothing was ever found of the men trapped inside.[7]

A few days after staking out observation on the right sector Pullman struck off about a mile and a half to the west through the mountains with another crew and a reel of telephone wire. After another stiff climb they set up a second OP on Hill 1010 that more or less overlooked hills occupied by the enemy on our left front from the southeast toward Conca Casale on the south to the stronghold of the small town of Viticuso to the northwest, headquarters of the German 44th Infantry Division, and a valley to the north.

"The best OP in the pleasant hills of sunny Italy," Jack thought, because of its over-look, because he and his crew kept strictly out of sight when there was visibility, and because the heavy-gauge phone wire they strung was rarely if ever cut by enemy shellfire. They directed even more firing missions than the artillery forward observers. They knew that if they could see the Germans they could be seen back, so they took care to dig in their position during the night behind well-camouflaged rocks, and to eat and sleep in a thatched shack down a short way on the reverse side of the ridge where they kept a small fire whose smoke blended unsuspiciously (they hoped) into the dreary hillscape.

Zapiecki, Mullenax, Contreras, Nye, Griff, O'Keefe, all experienced observers, were brought up at various times by Pullman. The captured binocular scope and range finder returned the Krauts some of their own medicine, most effectively at night, when it provid-ed an exact compass reading on enemy gun flashes. Then you could get a fair fix on the dis-tance by counting off the seconds elapsed from seeing the flash of the gun to hearing the report at about 1,000 feet a second—one hippopotamus, two hippopotamus and so on.

On this OP Andy met up with his famous farmer and his cow, and for years his telephone greeting to an old buddy would be: "Has anybody seen mine cow?"—which translates:

> This paesan would hike up to the shack and wanna know, has anybody seen mine cow? There was a grassy plateau way below us to the north where his cow would go, and he'd come up and have us look for her from the OP. And there she'd be, and he'd go out and get her, and neither of 'em ever hit a mine.
>
> The people lived in Viticuso and had farms they'd go out to in the valley. They figgered they weren't in the war, like this guy lookin' for his cow every morning. We were laying down there in the shack one rainy night, and we hear cryin', and here come a guy and a woman. Their son got in a minefield, and they wanted us to go out there and get him out. The guy with the cow was tryin' to explain that they should wait until morning because he knew where the mines were.

During rare breaks in the rainy mist that hung over the valley they'd spotted Jerries around one of these small, isolated stone farmhouses, possibly using it as an OP, and had called for gunfire on it several times without any direct hits. Pullman:

> One morning the ever-present fog tunneled out briefly and we had direct observa-tion, almost like looking down a tube, just as a Kraut came out of this house facing us to take a shit, because of course all he could see was fog. We had the house zeroed in, just had to call for a number, and got the 155s [heavy artillery] because the 105s were on another mission. Over the phone you could hear 'em go off, then pretty soon you'd hear the shells go over, and this Kraut, he could hear it too. He pulled up his pants and ran around the house to meet his appointment. The shells lit right where he was going. Later somebody said they saw a cross there.

We'd been giving the Germans a hard time from the most perfect OP in sunny Italy for about a week when around November 17 they spotted where it was coming from, handed

Top: A 45th Division artillery or I&R forward observer (FO) has spotted through his field glasses an enemy position on Hill 769, located the hill on his relief map and relayed this information via his field phone and as much as a mile or more of wire (note at lower left) laid by hand back to our 105-mm howitzer battery. (Our portable field radios were especially no damn good in the mountains, and the wire was at best a tenuous link subject to break by enemy shellfire, men, mules, vehicles, etc.) *Bottom:* The battery has in turn mapped the target and just zeroed in on it with a trio of white phosphorus smoke shells easily seen by the FO, who calculates and phones how far and in what direction they're off. Back at our battery, lateral and vertical corrections are made in the aim of the gun or guns, the observer instructs "Fire for effect!" and a cannonade of shellfire hopefully eliminates or cripples the German position. Unfortunately, hand-to-hand fighting was required to take Hill 769. The 105 firing here near Venafro aims skyward at the expense of some accuracy to clear the looming mountaintops up ahead. The 105s were the infantry's best support. (*U.S. Army Signal Corps, U.S. Army*)

to them on a platter with a red ribbon around it. Pullman, eagle-eyed Joe Contreras and Shorty Nye were on the ridge observing when right up the slope and profiled against the sky trooped a crew of observers from Cannon Company who'd found the OP simply by following the phone wire.

Jack knew that was it. Their cover was blown. It seemed less than a minute before the first shells whined and whammed in around them, mortars probably. The Jerries ran them all right off the ridge, and they took off toward the shanty and what slight protection the terraces afforded. Jose and Shorty were together a couple of levels below Jack, and they all hit the dirt. One shell struck the lower edge of the terrace above the two and a fragment got Contreras in the shoulder, leaving Nye untouched.[8]

As for Pullman,

> Mine just cleared the top of the terrace above me and knocked me out, and when I came to I put my hand out into this hot crater. It hit on the same level I was, so close it cleared me. Would have blown me to pieces if I'd been farther away. Second Battalion was all around on the ridges. The Krauts laid on the whole area, and there were a lot of casualties just from this stupidity. I don't know what happened to the people from Cannon Company except that they survived. Ran into one of 'em later, and he apologized profusely for what happened.
>
> Joe got a bad fragment right in the shoulder. Somebody put a compress on my head. I walked down, dazed, couldn't even hear my own voice. I just got it in the face and a tiny piece in my knee. I found a hole in my drawers but never could find one in my pants. Scared as hell. You know you're not going to live forever because you almost bought it right now; it's happened to everybody in the infantry.

Contreras walked himself back down to the CP and showed Zapiecki his shoulder. Andy said that was the first time he ever saw bone, "just as if somebody had cut the meat off with a knife, and the bone was busted. He had the biggest grin you ever saw and said, 'Hey Andy, my million-dollar wound!'"

I was at the CP when our wounded and still-shaking Platoon Sergeant stumbled in, and I can still see the dried droplets of blood and speckling of embedded bits of dirt and pebbles that had been driven into his pale, haggard face by the blast that came so close to blowing him off the terrace. I felt a wave of dread, that death had brushed close by and so barely missed taking the guy who had so recently given me a last-minute lease on life.

Everybody felt good about Contreras. One of the best, and we'd miss that pair of eyes and friendly grin, but he was just badly enough messed up to be out of it for sure, while Pullman, the glue that held us together, had been knocked for a loop up on the terrace, and we were afraid we'd never see him again, until damned if he didn't show up AWOL from the hospital, shaky and half-deaf.

Back at the station hospital he'd hung around all evening while they worked on the more seriously wounded.

Finally about four in the morning this doctor, dead-tired, said come on in. I told him to put it off 'til morning, and they showed me a canvas cot. The tent had been leaking and the ward boy dumped the water out of it. I asked where's the latrine? He said, down at the end of the street. I just kept going and caught me a ride back up to the outfit. Couldn't hear right for a long time.

It had been rain, rain, rain with bouts of thick fog, only three days all month it didn't rain during the daytime, often with violent gales that blew down tents and soaked everything that wasn't soaked already. Day by day the slippery, sliding, sucking mud grew deeper. "It has resolved itself into the static warfare of twenty-five years ago," I lamented to my journal. "Mud has almost stopped operations; consequently nearly all the action has consisted of patrolling and artillery duels"—the gist of the ever-briefer news accounts of the almost-forgotten war.

"Apparently we're waiting for the great pincers on our flanks to close in [it would be a long wait]. The Germans threw over about 44 out of 50 [shells] as duds the other night. We call them ones from the Poles [slave labor in the munitions plants]. There's a fair bit of risk involved in being shaved in Venafro, as Jerry periodically shells the place, and the paesans are extremely jumpy." No wonder. By now four thousand vehicles a day were funneling through the town with supplies and matériel.

President Roosevelt had promised us Thanksgiving dinner. I wrote home that "FDR and the mess sergeant did well by us. We had turkey, gravy, cranberry sauce, olives, walnuts, and blueberry pie! A meal fit for a king. Yes, we eat pretty well in HQ Co."

Up front it was maybe cold turkey sandwiches if they made it that far, and if not, K's and C's, and heat your powdered coffee and lugged-up water in your canteen cup over strips of the waxed cardboard of your K-ration box that didn't send smoke signals.

A couple of more days came my turn at roulette. I recorded it in my journal:

With about ten artillery observers up there sticking their heads over the top, Jerry caught sight of our shack and decided to shell us while we were in it. It must have been a tank that gave it to us for an hour, and they came so close we couldn't move out. One piece of shrapnel came through the roof and hit a guy in the back pocket where his wallet was. During a lull we managed to escape, going all the way around the hill, under enemy observation for another hour, shelled all the way. That night we sneaked back to the shack, which had since received a large hole in the roof, and smuggled out our equipment. We were all pretty shaky for quite a spell after.

Shaky? That stuff was coming in all around us. ZZZZEEEEEWWWWW WHAM! ZZZZZEEEEEEWWWWWW WHAM! ZZEEWW WHAM! ZEW-WHAM! WHAM! Shell fragments flying high and low YOYOYOYOYOYOYOYOYOYO in every direction. The air filled with dirt and rocks. That satanic, heart-pounding perfume of burnt cordite, the combination of smokeless powder, nitroglycerine and mineral oil that exploded an 88-millimeter steel projectile when it hit at 2,000 feet a second.

Death rode every breath that afternoon. The next one, the very next, was going to be the last, just HAD to be. I'd never, ever, been so scared and haven't been since. There would be plenty of worse barrages, but the first was the worst.

Dom Trubia was with me, shaky too, but an old hand with this sort of shit by now. He'd directed tank fire on a house the Krauts were spotted around and figured maybe it was they who saw so many of us milling around the OP. Like he said, the forward artillery observers thought it was Times Square up there. They must have been pretty green. The tanks were doing artillery duty because they were immobilized by mud up to their bogie wheels. When the Germans came running out of the house, the FOs called in the 105s. The Krauts hit the ground and tried to get cover. Then the 105s dropped aerial bursts over their heads. Jimmy Dowdall said somebody heard screams, but maybe that was another time. Not long after that we got it from the tank.

Back at the CP on November 29: "I wonder how much longer my luck will hold out after that. I felt as though I used up nine lives. Since then I've been somewhat out of use, as the soles of both my boots have come off, and the heels are tearing apart."

Less than three weeks on the front and I'd already gone through a cat's luck and a pair of boots. Benjy the supply sergeant didn't have my size, bless his heart, so I made do by wrapping layers of tape around what was left and clumping about the CP in the mud on odd jobs and hiding out in the Cave while my footwear was back-ordered.

From there I wrote Pete Sax, my Roxbury Latin School buddy, now a Harvard Medical School student.

Things are muddy, dark, unwashed here in the seat of the Classics. Travel, my friend, is not what it's cracked up to be by those dwellers on Main Street who toured the world's capitals first class. To really appreciate, move as I do. See the heart of the people; perhaps the romance in your soul will be supplanted by a feeling of helpless cynicism and revulsion at the sordid stupidity. Often I wonder whether a faith in human nature is not simply an admission that the main difference between man and animal is that man can tie a knot. You know that I am manifestly unsentimental as most of us go, Pete, but I've come to be amazed at the level of life in the States, and I've seen enough to have a deep-felt faith in and admiration for the American soldier.

After five or six bootless days *hors de combat* I was hospitalized with dysentery, which cleared up quickly but had the effect of about a cup of castor oil, eating areas of my intestinal lining to shreds. Between everybody shitting in open slit trenches when available, no sanitary facilities, cold, mud, rain and the strain of battle, there was plenty of wildly contagious amoebic dysentery around. Mullenax had it too, presenting an alarming appearance evacuating the Cave on the run, with the runs, pants down, evacuating all the way. But Mohawk was damned if he'd raise the dirty flag. I did, probably because I was from a medical family. Unable as I was to climb to an OP with boots that were disintegrating, I experienced for the first time the all-too-common feeling of shame that I was letting my new buddies down by my absence.

In the hospital I ran across Dougherty, our carrot-topped tenor of the Camp Croft marches, sent back for the second time with what the Army shrinks were diagnosing as battle fatigue but what anyone who had survived a few barrages called simply the same old shell shock of the First War. Dock had heard that Dave Goss, the artist, was headed home with the same thing and trench foot, and that Duart, a friend of ours who'd been sent to a Third Division line company, was killed by a direct hit his first day in action.

Did they send you back up again, Dock? And did you make it? I would never know.

A couple of days before I went on sick call, on December 2, an armada of 105 JU-88 night bombers struck the Adriatic port of Bari and sunk sixteen of a brilliantly lighted Allied fleet of thirty ships carrying 38,000 tons of cargo, including a mammoth load of mustard-gas shells should Corporal Hitler take a notion to get back at his old enemies for his gassing the first time around. Fortunately the wind was offshore and carried the fumes out to sea, but at least 125 sailors and merchant seamen were killed.[9]

We never heard a whisper of it. "It would have been indeed difficult to explain," wrote Eisenhower in *Crusade in Europe*. On the close outskirts of Naples I was aghast to ride by a dump, acres big and stacked with thousands of gas shells for our 4.2 chemical mortars, just in case. Jesus, what if the Krauts hit it during an air raid, or blew it up by sabotage, and the wind was fair for Napoli or anywhere! Another gas war, and all of us had long since dumped our gas masks.[10]

In a few days I was back, writing home, "Mud, mud, mud—that's all the news. We wonder when the war will end. Perhaps an invasion of France will do it. Perhaps Russia, perhaps the winter. Surely a combination. We think that if they last the winter they'll last the summer, too. Whether the 45th will be demobilized at the Armistice is an unanswered question. I can barely see the paper, it's so dark and rainy outside the cave."

Privately: "Went to Naples for an afternoon. Didn't get to Pompeii. Shopped on the Via Roma. Pimps, ½ dozen/block, offering 'beefsteak, spaghetti, nice girl.'"

Innocent and unsullied—not so unusual in those days even for an alien foot soldier treading where Legions had trod before him—I politely declined all invitations.

Second- or fiftieth-hand sex in Napoli following the departure of the rampant Master Race had even more than the ancient city's age-old risks, as did life up on the line. And while a dose was less desirable but more preventable than the dysentery, a prophylactic visit to one of the Allied Military Government's handy "pro stations," before or after the sin, was somehow more unthinkable to me and not a few other country-type city boys than the prospect of the sin itself. Hell, there I was, a foot soldier barely twenty-one on the verge of death before I'd hardly lived, barely having summoned the courage to touch trembling lips with a girl, in the grip of my rock-farming, Bible-thumping New Hampshire ancestors enjoining me across 3,000 miles of time and cold salt water: NO SCREWING BEFORE MARRIAGE, and don't you ever use that word, and no necking, no petting—and a kiss is the first slip on the slippery road to SEX!

Such was the lot of the stinking dirty, unshaven, worn-down, shell-shocked front-line dogfaces, Mauldin's Willie and Joe at the bottom of the military pile in twice-ravaged Italy. At the bottom of the civilian pile in grieving Naples were the desolate, ravaged sisters, daughters and wives selling their bodies and their souls and being sold by brothers, fathers and husbands for a few cigarettes and for the sake, God knows, of mere existence.

Sold for whatever they could trade in the rampant black market supplied with goods stolen from the Army and run by the rear-echelon goldbricks and suckass bastards who were supposed to be the backup of the poor buggers doing the dying. But no, they were strutting up and down the Via Roma with the high-priced *signorinas* they kept in their fancy apartments, swaggering through the great glass-roofed Galleria in the shiny new, buckle-top combat boots designed for us doggies, OUR boots they had stolen en route to the front, while the junk we wore fell apart in the shell holes, and we bound our shivering legs in canvas puttees left over from the previous intervention to save Europe from itself.

As for our opposite serial numbers, I reported to Pete Sax that "progress in the hills is slow and tough. Jerry seems determined to resist, though I think (or rather, I know) the only thing that is keeping him from returning to his 'kleine Frau' is the magnificent discipline of his Army. Our artillery pounds him constantly, and it gets so that, like the hum of traffic, I can hardly sleep unless I am under the noses of the big guns."

Across the stream bed from our OP on the right, Third Battalion tried again on December 11 to take Hills 460, 470 and 640 that commanded the 157th's drive through twisting Purple Heart Valley from Pozzilli toward its objective of Acquafondata. On 460 the men were under murderous fire from three sides, but kept trying for 470 between heavy covering barrages. One patrol made the hill and found "arms and legs but no personnel," but the enemy was back the next day, and fought off our night attacks of the thirteenth and fourteenth and our daylight try on the fifteenth with the addition of First Battalion and tanks.

Working to get around behind 470, C Company lost a platoon cut off. Lucky we didn't take the hill; a squadron of A-36s bombed the bejesus out of the Germans on it by mistake. On the same day, the 15th, Second Battalion on the left attacked Fialla less than a mile south of our OP, was forced off by German artillery, regained it that night and barely escaped encirclement, with heavy losses. G Company attacked Hill 770, a few hundred yards south of the OP.

This must be the action Andy witnessed in horror.

These guys on the hill didn't have no helmets. I says to this one next to me from Second Battalion, "Do you see what I see?" An' he says, "Gimme those glasses. Those aren't Americans, they're Germans." They were wearin' their caps with those visors and had their helmets by their sides; when they went into combat they took 'em off and put on the helmets. So we call the CP and say they look German. Captain Edwards says the hill had been captured. So we let the fight go until that night. The commanding officer come in and says we're supposed to be on such an' such a hill. Everybody's lookin' at one another. "Hey, we thought you guys were on that hill." He says "We just came in!" And nobody said a word after that. We could see the Germans on the opposite side of the hill.

Our guys advanced and fired a few shots and these Krauts were supposed to come out. But at a given signal they came from behind the trees, bingo, and dropped to the ground with their guns and just laid our guys out. So right after that they were sayin' whenever a German gives up don't ever leave your place where they can't see ya, and wait 'til they advance right toward ya.

Company G was forced back to Hill 759, having lost half its men and all its officers.

"Still haven't done any work," I told my notebook on the eve of this ambush. Within a day or two, however, we were issued the new winter "combat suit," a heavy khaki, zippered, one-piece Doctor Denton patterned on the Air Force's and so well insulated, as we discovered, that during a climb up the ridges in the bitterest weather you had to loosen the zipper to cool off. And Supply finally tracked down a new pair of the old-fashioned WWI-style boots my size (not the notorious noncombat "combat" boots) I took to the cobbler in Venafro to stitch on thin leather tops of another four or five inches, the best a few of us with access behind the front could do against the rain and mud.

Going on six weeks after the 45th was committed to the mountains, I noted on December 14 that "the lines have moved only a few hundred yards. The main Army objective is Cassino, 72 miles from Rome, and the Cassino road to Rome. The 8th Army is expected to take Pescara on the Adriatic before it makes its marked pivot west. They have been reinforced by Indians and New Zealanders, while we've been joined by Moroccans and Italians. It's said that the Moroccans slip through the lines and cut the throat of the man who sleeps in the middle in the German tent."

The Second Moroccan Division of General de Gaulle's French Expeditionary Corps from North Africa, composed of Arab enlisted men—the celebrated *goums* or *goumiers*—under French officers, had relieved our 34th Division on our right on the eighth of December. Missing a recon unit that went to the bottom during a bombing raid as they were landing in Naples, the Moroccans were loaned the services of the 45th's Cavalry Reconnaissance Troop to which my training and overseas buddy Gareth Dunleavy had been assigned.

The day after my journal entry of the fourteenth, Dunleavy's platoon volunteered to take supposedly lightly defended Hill 895 about two miles northeast of Purple Heart Valley. Gareth:

> We'd gone two-thirds of the way up when we met this awful fire coming from both flanks. Our officers just weren't there, and I don't think I'd have come out of it if not for our Indian Sergeant Scott, the only one who knew what we'd run into and by hand signals and waving orchestrated a sensible withdrawal.
>
> Littlefield, a great gawky guy with glasses, and I covered our retreat with a light machine gun, kept moving it back and forth across the top of the ridge, couldn't see if we were hitting anyone but tried to hold down their fire. He and I just kinda bolstered each other. I kept yelling, "You sonofabitch, ya want more ammunition? Here's more, just pull the goddam trigger!" ... "The barrel's hot!" ... "Never mind the fuckin' barrel, just pull the goddam trigger!" A concussion grenade intended for us landed between Scottie's legs and blew him three feet in the air, yelling "My God, they've shot my balls off!" He died in the hospital and should have got the Silver Star.
>
> Next day the *goums* went up the hill with the French officers walking beside them with their canes, and I heard them shouting *"En avant! En avant! En avant!"* and the Germans opening up with everything they had, and then hearing *"Au secours! Au secours! Au secours!"* The *goums* knew the words to yell for help in French, because the medics were French. Twenty dead and forty wounded. The Germans never saw the bottom of the hill. All died.[11]

A week before the Hill 895 action, the 36th Division, now reorganized after its horrible clobbering at Salerno, had moved up on our left and relieved the veteran Third Division, our constant companions through hell and fire, only to be plunged into one of the Italian campaign's bitterest, the battle for the town of San Pietro, a key stronghold of the Bernhardt Line. For ten days the Germans beat back everything we could throw at them while the dauntless John Huston directed and narrated probably the starkest combat film of the war. Finally budged a week before Christmas, the enemy withdrew in their usual orderly fashion from bloody San Pietro and Hills 460, 470 and 640 in our sector to well-fortified fallback positions and prepared to celebrate the birth of our mutual Guide to Humanitarian Behavior.

The Third's assistant commander, General William W. Eagles, replaced our General Middleton, ill and worn out, who had come out of retirement to shape up the Thunderbirds back in the States. It was now my turn, with my new boots and my combat suit, to emerge from semi-retirement.

Pullman led a recon patrol, my first experience of such derring-do, to check out whether the Viticuso Valley, beyond the OP on the left, had been vacated by the enemy on the seventeenth. Mullenax was along, and perhaps Hank Mills. The circumstances are long forgotten except our cautious foray beyond our lines and down into no-man's-land where we approached with rising trepidation a small stone farmhouse that stood by itself in this sweep of the valley. The ridges rising a few hundred yards to the northeast may or may not have been enemy-occupied. To the south was Hill 1010 and our OP from which our artillery had been directed that mucky day when Jack, through the tunnel in the fog, caught the lone German taking a crap out in front of this very house.

Jack and I approached gingerly with our guns at the ready, the others covering us. The area around the lonesome farm cottage had been hit with shellfire all right. We snuck up and listened. No sound but the breeze and sporadic chatter of gunfire off in the hills. We kicked open the door.

There in a shrapnel-torn room sprawled the family on their beds, father and mother and four or five children and babes, greenish and bloated in death, covered with gray palls of plaster dust from the explosion of the shell that had torn through the wall by the ceiling. The hole faced our lines. Nothing we could do. It had all been done. We got the hell out.

We had seen how the country people, like Zapiecki's old paesan who had nowhere else to go and was forever looking for his cow in this same valley, tried to convince themselves that this was not their war. They had nowhere else to go, whether they lived in the cities, in the towns, in the hamlets up in the hills, or on the isolated farms. Especially in the mountains the paesans scratched out a subsistence with a few remote vineyards and olive groves, and lived, as they had since Caesar's time, in poverty and in the grip of a lifelong acceptance of the inevitable.

However they got it, and from whom, it's clearer now than then that this family must have stuck to their land and their home as the war rolled over them simply because they had nowhere to go. Their neighbors were in the same fix, and Viticuso was being flattened. Maybe they and the Germans figured that if they laid low except at night and in the fog we

Medics enter what's left of San Pietro. (*Department of Defense*)

softies wouldn't shell the place as long as we thought it was occupied by civilians. Maybe they tried to sleep during the day.

My first inkling that our platoon might have been responsible for these murders was Pullman's account thirty-five years later of firing through the tunnel of fog at the Kraut taking a crap some weeks earlier. This jogged Dowdall's memory:

> On the OP on the right we could see this house, an obvious place fer the Germans to be on account o' the situation an' terrain. Nobody could be sure. Nobody saw any. One of our tanks across the valley on the Pozzilli road saw this house an' fired point-blank into it. The shell had got through the wall an' wiped out the family.

After thirty-nine years it was left to Mullenax, upon our meeting again, to produce a version that rings true (although it's unlikely the Germans would have located an OP except on the heights) if less literally than metaphorically, with the poignant tragedy and irony of the war in Italy:

> Our own artillery did it. I directed it. There was a German OP right behind that house. From where we was in that OP behind the rock fence on the hill, that farmhouse was settin' at the base of the hill right across the valley on the range where the Germans had their front line, about two-thirds of the way down a kind of flat plateau, in the open.
>
> This OP was what was giving us the trouble in holding the hill where I Company was at. We had already lost about half of I company as the result of that OP. We seen 'em all the time for two or three days. I kept callin' it back, and they said, "Well, why don't you call some artillery on it?" An' I says, "I don't wanna do that. I

think there's some kids in there too." So I didn't ask for it. I Company got kicked offa there about twice. About the third day I says it's us or them, and I called for the artillery, and that's what happened, and the 105s plastered it. But I don't think they got one damn German. I think they'd all pulled out. I was with you on that patrol, and I was the one that had called that in. It was jest a matter of we were going to wipe their OP out or they was gonna wipe us out.

It sure turned my stomach when I looked at those children and that man and wife. That was on my mind for years. I drank a quart o' whisky for about ten years and nobody ever knew I was drunk. It stuck in my mind, that family I called the artillery on, and I still to this day think that maybe they was working with the Germans, but I dunno. But to kill innocent children bothered me to beat the devil. The Germans was either holding them hostage or they were cooperating with 'em. We didn't have much choice. We had to wipe that thing out.[12]

Terrible as it was, for whatever reason I made no record of the ghastly tableau. But I couldn't expunge it from my mind's eye through more than half of a century that would see the eradication of millions of other innocents. Without doubt this family that clung to its home and patch of land, in the eye of a holocaust it had nothing to do with, was murdered by us.

Tens of thousands of their countrymen suffered the same fate simply by being in the way of the grappling armies let loose on this ancient and beautiful land by the vanity and weakness of the posturing dictator who sold his soul and his nation's to the Huns from the north.

Poor ole Mohawk. Was he the one who took aim and called down the fire? Even if he didn't and as time went by assumed the burden for us all, he suffered as much as if he had.

Jack Pullman never volunteered his men for anything, and that went double for patrols. "The weather was nasty, and things were stable. If we could have one OP let's try to stay out of patrols as much as possible. I felt that anything we did was really not going to do much for anybody."

Our Platoon Sergeant was right. But on the eighteenth of December, Division intelligence wanted to know if the Germans in their withdrawal of the previous day had pulled out of their stronghold of Viticuso, and Colonel Church passed the assignment on to us. Jack picked Dom Trubia and me, and off the three of us hiked, our fate strangely in the hands of a local Italian kid, "a little wispy thing in dark black shepherd's clothes and slouching hat." I sorted it out in my journal the next day:

We were to go through our lines to about two miles behind the theoretical German lines. The Guinea was to slip into the town and report back to us. We were at H Company's mortar positions. If there were Jerries, hunky-dory, we'd go back. If there weren't we'd have to go into town and investigate further, following him along a trail which would undoubtedly be mined and trip-wired [for booby traps].

We waited all day for him to return and then went back to the CP to find that he'd been back all afternoon and reported no Germans. He'd gone to his mother's house three miles out of town, and she'd told him that the Tedeschi *left four days before. So he probably sidetracked us intentionally, since he knew that if he told us he'd have to go into town with us. I suppose it's just as well that he missed us, because there surely would have been a half-dozen or so Jerries to knock off the first patrol and then scram. A three-man patrol in there would have had a damned hard time getting out.*

Looking back, Trubia, who spoke Italian, wondered "how could the town be evacuated if there were still Krauts up on the line? When we got up into H Company I told the kid to go on by himself and come back and report to us. I think he was a little liar. I think the Germans were in the village all right, and I'm just as happy we didn't go in."

Too late to do us any good, aerial reconnaissance photos taken the same day indeed revealed German positions in the area.

Two days later Jack got the order to do a repeat. He latched onto me again, and a line company sergeant remembered as Montgomery, who'd somewhat mysteriously been transferred into the Platoon. My private after-action report:

Night before last [December 21] went on another patrol with Jack and Montgomery. We managed to get about one half to two thirds of the way down the valley towards Viticuso, spent about three hours behind the German lines, didn't find out a thing. It was raining and you couldn't see ten feet in front of you. We could have walked right up to an enemy and not have known he was there. Our biggest worry was mines and, of course, the chance of being taken prisoner. Shrapnel from enemy shelling of our lines actually was most of the excitement we had. Coming back, black as pitch, Jack fell about five feet into one of our foxholes. There was much scrambling and cussing by both Jack and the occupant, whereupon I slipped and fell on top of them. We picked ourselves up and beat a hasty retreat, expecting to have rocks bounced off our heads any second.

Jack reflected in long retrospect: "I think when I started out I had no intention of going into that town at night. I think I faked some of that patrol because I figured the Germans were in there, which they may very well have been."

⁂ ⁂ ⁂

Yuletide drew nigh, and here we all were in the mountains of southern Italy, stopped colder by the day by the impenetrable German Winter Line. Our disappointment over failing to deliver the Holy City to Mrs. General Clark for Christmas as directed failed to cast a pall over prospects of an otherwise joyous celebration of our own. Of course General Patton, who had wanted the Fifth Army himself and had little use for our boss, knew it had been in the cards all along and wrote his wife Beatrice, back when we butted the mountains in November, that "we are fiddeling [*sic*] while Rome burns, but only in metaphor, for I doubt if she burns—not for quite a while any how."[13]

And here we were, still fiddeling. "My first Christmas away from home!" Then, with the dreary conscience embedded in my genes: "Spent to good purpose, I hope."

Not so Zapiecki. Sick with jaundice and a stomach ulcer, existing on quarts of coffee, persecuted by his huge flat feet on the rocky trails, he'd dropped forty pounds, and looking lousy was triaged back to hospital on the twenty-third. Well, he was an old man; he'd just turned thirty-one.

Truckloads of packages arrived from home, sent weeks before. If sturdily enough wrapped, brownies and fruitcake survived the long ocean crossing best, while anything that was oblong and gurgled when shaken, like the bottle of Scotch from my beloved Aunt Betty, must have been regarded with suspicion by some teetotalling mail clerk because it never reached me. From Pete Sax, for light reading in the current Roman war, Virgil's *Aeneid* with a Latin dictionary, Ibsen's plays and Laurence Sterne's rollicking eighteenth-century novel *Tristram Shandy*, whose old ex-soldier uncle Toby and his imaginary campaigns put me in mind of Winston Churchill in his bombproof cellar and our own Uncle Mohawk holding forth on infantry tactics in the Cave.

Christmas was a dream of family and fireside so impossible that it invaded and departed the consciousness in the guise of a nightmare. But one had to keep the upper lip stiff, and I informed the home front that "it isn't raining yet, though it is cloudy, and there has been no truce declared as in the last War. This morning for breakfast I had an egg, my second in four months! We'll have turkey and whatnot for dinner. I've even heard beer rumored, but I don't know about that." One 'Bird brought a bottle of Coke back from Naples and raffled it off at a dollar a chance.

The peak of the Yuletide had to be Vernon Dilks's present to General Clark. Ours to the jolly squareheads on the other side was 2,055 rounds of artillery. Dilks was the usual imperturbable Dilks:

> Mark Clark was comin' up to have Christmas afternoon dinner with Colonel Church at the forward CP in Pozzilli, which was a helluva place to get into. The food was bein' cooked in the rear CP an' brought up 'cause they didn't have no room there right on the side of the mountain, no flat part to it or nothin'. Seems to me it was jes' an ole shepherd's house up there, maybe two an' a half or three miles.
>
> With the four-wheel drive and chains that jeep just barely pulled out in that mud. These three CP guards were in the trailer. The road went this way an' then way over to the right, real steep, and then you hadda make another turn where they'd busted the stone outta an old stone fence, an' these CP guards was on the left side of the trailer, where it was way down.
>
> I shoulda had enough sense to tell 'em to git on the other side or git off the damn thing, but I didn't, an' I kept goin', an' the next thing I know that trailer went over an' threw 'em clean down the side of the mountain. I couldna gone no slower, had my foot on the brake, all four wheels locked, but it was so steep we jes' slid down in the mud. The trailer upset an' dumped the food. Some o' the containers, the lids stayed on, some hit so many rocks an' bounced so bad the lids blew out an' it was a mess.
>
> We was right there at the forward CP when it happened, the cooks standin' there waitin'. Course they went barrelin' down the mountain tryin' to git some o' the containers. I guess they recovered enough food to make a halfway meal out of it, I dunno. I hope the Colonel got enough to eat anyway. I felt real bad 'cause it wasn't

just the officers, there was a lotta men up there, an' this was their Christmas dinner for the whole bunch.

No Rome in Mrs. Clark's stocking that day. And no Second Front, but not far off, I wrote the Home Front hopefully, and when it comes "the Italian Front (which as nearly approaches the warfare of the last war as any) will be dwarfed by its big brother, and we hope some opposition will be withdrawn." Vain hope indeed.

But first there was still Viticuso. This time Griff led the patrol, with me, and again Monty, the new sergeant. We left the CP at daybreak on December 27. It was snowing, with two or three inches on the ground already. In our shit-drab clothing we kept fifty feet or so of distance between us. To a German in his reversible brown/white winter uniform on a long-since dug-in OP on one of those ridges, we were three black bugs crawling across a blank sheet of paper, or as I wrote Pete, "like a flea on my long johns."

In my journal:

When we had gone about a half a mile beyond our lines we noticed that Monty, who had been holding the rear, was nowhere to be seen. After waiting for a half hour, we went on. We moved along a hillside, carefully observing the town. Seeing not a thing, living or dead, except what appeared to be a woman in a window, we moved down the hill and across a hundred yards of open terrace, making our way into town. I covered Griff as he led the way.

There wasn't a house left untouched, and only two or three were liveable. Shelling and bombing had left it little more than a heap of rocks and mortar. There were fresh footprints going out, but that's all we saw. Viticuso is about two miles in front of our lines, and the enemy seems to keep popping in and out. First they're there, then they're not. Then they're there again. Undoubtedly we were observed for at least three or four hours, but their idea probably was to let us get through, see the town was deserted, send a force in, and get hell knocked out of them by a combat patrol they would later bring in.

Griff and I were both taking a crap in a stable with our pants down around our ankles when we heard a rattling outside. We duck-waddled across the floor and trained our guns outside, but it was only the wind shaking a broken gutter. We must have been a strange sight, ready for action with our pants down. We left the town without mishap, having the distinction of being the first Americans in there. I think there was something fishy about its emptiness though, because the Guineas generally come whooping back as soon as they know the Heinies have gone for good. I'll bet there are Jerries there now. It was a terrifically long chance for us to take; I wonder how much longer our luck will hold.

Monty came back today [December 28] *and said he went to Viticuso. I think he got cold feet, backtracked and hid out for a while.*

We all had cold feet, but Monty, the getaway man supposed to be covering us and our rear, had the coldest. Later he changed his story and claimed he lost us and turned back. But Griff's and mine were the only tracks in the snow. The poor guy was out of the Platoon fast. One of the values we learned if we lived was that the line between carrying on and losing your nerve as time went on stretched thinner and thinner and had nothing much to do with courage and cowardice, however they might be defined in Pattonic terms or otherwise. Just as likely that a battle-fatigued Monty got moved up to the I&R for a "rest," only to find himself out on a goofy recon patrol in broad daylight and snow, and panicked.

The year stalled to a standstill. On the final two days our artillery fired 11,518 shells on the 45th's front. Two battalions of the 180th attacked through the high ground north of Purple Heart Valley toward Monte Rotondo against hardly a shot until the waiting Jerries had them in their sights and opened up. The guys were forced back, and roll call revealed the rifle companies were down to an average of 66 men from a full combat strength of 160.

"This is the last day of the Old," I kicked good-bye to '43, "and I think the New holds Victory in Europe." Homeward I wrote on the first of '44: "Today we had a terrific blizzard, and the hills are covered with snow, while last night the New Year was ushered in by a slight barrage from the Jerries. We have a good fire in our cave, so have warmth and shelter. Turkey this noon."

Up in their holes that New Year's Day, with no protection against the blizzard except maybe a flapping shelter half, under intermittent fire, drenched to the bone, blue and shaking with the cold, were the young Americans an ocean away from home, the limping wounded, the stretcher wounded, the dying wounded, the dead wounded. And the trench-foot cases, frostbitten feet in filthy wet socks that swelled so grotesquely the wet boots had to be cut away with a knife as their half-alive owner was rolled onto a stretcher or over a mule's back to get him down the mountain in a race with gangrene and death.

Joints stiffened and ached. Swollen and frostbitten hands puffed with piercing pain. Racked by colds, grippe, pneumonia, pleurisy, dysentery and fever, yellow with jaundice from the cold. Solidified, indigestible fat forced down from almost frozen cans of C-ration hash and beans.

A lot of good it did the guys who were left up there, eight days on the line and four off, when it took one of the four to hobble down to the rest area and another to climb back up, and lucky to have a full day left to half-thaw out.[14]

On the ninth of January the Third French Algerian Division, a new unit, moved into the line beside the Second Moroccan and relieved the 45th after seventy days of continuous combat, said at the time to be the longest ever recorded for an American infantry division.

In their turbans and colorful cloaks and washbasin helmets, dark and black-bearded and fierce and friendly and shy, these fresh goums offhandedly cooked their native fare over their open fires under clouds of smoke, and even walked barefoot through the snow— quaint colonial customs we figured they'd get over in a hell of a hurry.

Jerry Waldron got a grim charge out of the French company commander.

> He boasted that his men would go out in combat patrol strength tonight and straighten things out in Viticuso, and they got the living bejabbers kicked out of them, though they went quite a distance before they had to withdraw. They found that Andy's paesan's "mine cow" had been hit wandering around, and in half an hour it was in steaks. They didn't think much of our OP because they couldn't get their German scope with the four-foot legs in the hole with them. So they stood it up on the ridge line, where they soon found the observation worked both ways. Before we left, both mine cow and the OP were gone.

So we bid *arrivederci* to our Cave and to what was left of the paesan's olive grove and of Marco our mule. We packed into the jeeps with Boots, our whitefooted regimental bitch dog, and Andy's Victrola and records, and Shorty's lil black bag, and retraced our tracks back through the mud and across the Volturno to Piedimonte, except this time to the inauspicious luxury of pyramidal tents and the by no means intriguing mystery of whatever was to come—more fighting on this front, or on another.

In a day or two all of us in Headquarters Company stripped and rejoiced in the luxuriously hot and insecticidal showers of the Fifth Army's portable delousing unit, which fortunately for us cave-dwellers did not discriminate against fleas. Every stinking stitch of rotten clothing so foul that the pants stood up by themselves was exchanged for brand-new, or at least laundered, issue. "My first bath in over a month!" I exulted.

Of course no one could top our trumpet-lunged Zapiecki, off to a hospital in North Africa and sorely missed, who had already undergone his cleansing while on a brief rest in Naples. "The MPs were keepin' us in line and takin' us to the showers and gonna give us new uniforms, and these dagoes are throwin' rocks at us, thinkin' we're German prisoners, that's how dirty we were."

☙ ☙ ☙

In the two months since it came up short against the frozen affability of Smiling Albert Kesselring, the grand Churchillian strategy to pierce the European underbelly had died in the Apennines, taking with it enough mules and more than enough soldiers and *Soldaten* on both sides of the Bernhardt Winter Line. We Ironheads, on the other hand— having singularly free-wheeling options to live to fight another day, and a leader who was willing for the sake of his boys to sort of partially fake a patrol that had no chance of learning anything anyway—came through with no casualties but Jose with his million-dollar wound and our leader with his faceful of sand.

As for me (the I&R's second replacement), Jerry Waldron (its first) conceded that "they really worked you over when you came in. At Harvard you probably didn't know the guy down the hall. It was rugged, and you gave back as good as you got. You'll never agree, but you went right across full pendulum, and that's why you're a halfway decent guy now."

My own take on myself on the eighteenth of January, 1944, ten days into our rest period:

Lately the diary has become rather sketchy. Perhaps I'm more and more preoccupied with my work, and perhaps I'm changing myself. I'm much less concerned with introspection and philosophy than I used to be. My life revolves increasingly around immediate matters of expediency—eating, drinking and merrymaking, living from one day to the next, in large part due to the constant presence of hazards and dangers, the chance that life may be snipped off in a minute, with no opportunity to compose oneself and to make one's peace with his Maker.

Any thoughtful person must try to turn his thoughts from himself and to consciously avoid any form of self-analysis. It isn't healthy, for one idea leads to another, and pretty soon you're no good for anything. Of course there is the old adage, "There are no atheists in foxholes." Perhaps not, but I know that in moments of extreme danger I was too terrified to think of anything but saving myself. Too many times a man should be acting instead of praying. As far as luck allows, his life is in his own hands, and only a fool would sit back and rely on God to break the fuse to that shell or jam that burp gun, which goes for prayer in general too.

Nevertheless, recollection of a really narrow escape convinces one strongly of some Divine Power, particularly if one seems to have a string of luck. Thinking of the day at Salerno when Jerry had the base of his rifle stock knocked off by small-arms fire, and the time we were shelled out of the shack, I'm sure that perhaps something beyond our comprehension may intervene to snatch us from death. I guess I feel a little sheepish about it, but it's only a vague notion I can't get out of my mind.

I have.

Bearing our wounded back. Mules carry the dead. The mountains held by the Germans are steep, rocky and virtually impervious to attack. (*Department of Defense*)

ALLIED STRATEGY IN ITALY
January 1944

ALLIED FRONT LINE 15 JANUARY
GUSTAV LINE
Units as of 15 January

ELEVATIONS IN METERS

0   200   600 1000 1600 and above

10   0   10   20
MILES

(Department of Defense)

⇢ 6 ⇠

Whale on the Beach

Anzio

January–February 1944

ALL WE KNEW AS WE SLUMPED down exhausted in the frozen fields of Piedimonte was that Italy was the forgotten war—all mud, mountains, mayhem, misery and death, forsaken by God and Country.

So anything for a laff. Henry Mills is lounging on his straw-stuffed tick in our pyramidal tent after the 45th's seventy-two days on the line, smoking and waiting for the Coleman stove to boil the water in a number-ten coffee can. Hank is gonna make real coffee from real ground coffee he's scrounged from the cooks, not the powdered piss we'd been poisoning ourselves with up there on the front.

> I thought I'd finish the cigarette and then put the coffee in and pour in a half a canteen o' cold water around the edge to settle the grounds. This replacement, Jim Buckley, about six feet two, had swiped a loaf o' bread from the kitchen and is down on his hands and knees, and his foot keeps creepin' back toward the stove, and I'm watchin' it like I'm enchanted.
>
> Next I know, the can tips off an' lands within inches o' my crotch an' burns the hell outta me, both legs but mostly on the bottom. I jump up an' pull my pants off, an' my buddy Vern Dilks is layin' over on his sack laffin' an' laffin' an' says, "Well, I didn't know you was hurt, and it was damn funny, you tryin' to get your pants off!"[1]
>
> So I went to the Medics. The only guy on duty was a dentist, an' he put some thick ointment on my legs an' wrapped 'em tight with gauze. Ambulance to the field hospital, then the hospital train to the general hospital in Naples. They carried me on the litter up to the fourth floor, an' the guy says, "Your bed's over there." So I got off an' walked over, an' he says, "If you could walk why the hell didn't ya tell us?" Never dawned on me.

The bandages the dentist put on me with the ointment set up like concrete. The doctor slit 'em down the side, told me to hold on to the head o' the bed, an' ripped 'em off an' took half the skin on my legs with 'em.

So scratch Mills for a while. But on the plus side, sort of, Staff Sergeant Jack Pullman, who had organized the Platoon before Pearl Harbor when he was twenty, got a battlefield commission as second lieutenant and was made platoon leader in place of the wounded Farley. An honor and sort of an embarrassment for Lieutenant Pullman, but where it counted he remained one of us.

Delmar Griffith was jumped to the new platoon staff sergeant, Corporal Mickey Smith to buck sergeant and Mullenax and Trubia to corporal, and a few new guys came in, including a couple of doozies.

Bob "Dynamite" Thatcher was a wiry runt from Lancaster, Pennsylvania, who claimed not to have found enough excitement as a rifleman in A Company and volunteered for the Third Battalion Rangers, an impromptu commando-type outfit organized in Sicily. After around 115 patrols, mostly in the mountains, they transferred him to us for a rest. I sized him up in my journal as "a blond shrimp with a goofy little turned-up nose, a wispy blond mustache that took 110 days to grow, and twinkling eyes. He imitates playing a fiddle when somebody gets corny, will follow the leader anywhere, and is fearless even when afraid. Above Venafro he had his overcoat completely blown off him by a smoke shell and wasn't scratched."

Bob Winburn, Bob "Dynamite" Thatcher and Griff (*Courtesy of Lester Gerencer*)

Walter Wolff in German helmet struts his former stuff. (*Courtesy of Lester Gerencer*)

Dynamite swore that was his shredded overcoat on the bush we passed that day on the trail from Pozzilli to the OP. Could be.

The other one-of-a-kind was Walter Wolff, a spare, intense young German with angular features and a high-pitched accent who'd fled Berlin with his family in the late thirties on a supposed vacation to England. "Looks like one of these Kraut kids we capture. Loves music, very opinionated, and rattles off big words in English, not always sure of their meaning. His main usefulness lies in his knowledge of the Wehrmacht and his recent training in interrogation. He admits that in his youth he fell hook, line and sinker for Party Doctrines. He has barriers to break down and a lot to put up with, but he takes it all in his stride with never-failing good humor and generally gives back better than he takes."

It seems that Walter had been a thoroughly indoctrinated member of the *Hitler Jugend*, the Nazi Youth Movement, when one day he was jammed into a crowd cheering a military parade in Berlin, awaiting the passage of the beloved *Führer*. He'd brought his camera. Here comes the big open Daimler and Hitler himself! Walter raises his camera to snap his hero—and is clubbed to the pavement by an SS trooper, just in case it's loaded with something instead of film. The boy's worship turns to fear and hatred, and the Wolffs take the first chance to get out.[2]

In contrast to the constant rain, deepening mud, penetrating cold and finally the blizzards of the mountains, the reappearance of the famous Italian sun and the surprising mildness of the January weather down on the Campanian plain restored the old American bounce, with some help from Hollywood.

Joe E. Brown, the comedian with the bullfrog grin, turned up on a makeshift stage with a piano and a mike and worked his pitcher's pantomime before a few thousand doubled-over Thunderbirds squatting on a slope that formed a natural amphitheater. A couple of days later Humphrey Bogart tried a few jokes, but "not too hot," I reported home. "They should send over only comedians. We're making coffee now, eating bread and apple butter, and as soon as I finish this I'm going over to eat an egg (oh, rarest of things!), which can be had, four for a bar of soap."

Back in the fields of Piedimonte we played soccer and cribbage and loafed and heard the distant gunfire, but we knew nothing beyond surmise, and I wrote home a few hours before the resumption of our destiny:

> It's a beautiful day, quite mild, and I'm in the best of health except for a tenacious cough which seems to be due to the charcoal fires in our tents and the cold nights. Literally every other native is a barber, and I rarely have to shave myself. Costs 10 liras, or cents. Sometimes it's risky business if there is any excitement going on, as they are very demonstrative and will like as not slit your throat while showing what they would do to a German. A good part of our time is spent trying to avoid work, another in trying to loaf when it can't be avoided, and finally in regretting that we worked as hard as we did.
>
> On one side of our area is a flock of goats and sheep. The paesans drive them over the hills by going brrrr or ahhhh or zzzz. By our kitchen we have a small town, and at every meal about fifteen dozen kids collect around with tin cans and fight for our garbage. There are even a couple of very old women out there. Most of the kids are very ragged, thin and dirty. Some even have red networks all over their legs, due to cold or disease. I hear they get enough to eat just the same, though it probably wouldn't come close to feeding American kids.
>
> Their mules are not like ours, much smaller and therefore unable to carry the load. The Italians treat them cruelly when they're working, beating and kicking them, even hitting them in the mouth. But they take pretty good care of them when they're resting. Like the women, the mules carry terrific loads. Oxen are used to draw very heavy loads, and in the field to plow. They drive the mules and oxen like the goats, by going brrr or ahhh at them. As Ernie Pyle says, it sounds as though they were freezing to death.

Hitler's resolve to make a stand in the mountains north of the Volturno had been evident by late October. Encouraged by a small Eighth Army end run at Termini on the east coast a few weeks earlier, General Alexander directed the Fifth Army on November 8 to prepare a similar waterborne hop on December 20 to the seaside resort of Anzio, to be called "Shingle," the quaintly British word for a stony beach. But when Mark Clark found there weren't enough landing craft for even this one-division operation, it was scratched just two days short of H-hour. However, the plan appealed to Winston Churchill, who was just then meeting at Carthage with Generals Alexander and Eisenhower, whom he swept along with his vision of a bigger Shingle to cut off the Germans' supply lines to the mountains to the south and liberate Rome in one stroke.

The Prime Minister threw himself into his latest enthusiasm, and President Roosevelt agreed reluctantly on December 28 to a further delay in shifting shipping to Britain for the Normandy invasion, the specter of which understandably gave the PM the willies. Alexander and Montgomery, jealously guarding the Mediterranean Theater as a British prerogative on behalf of the boss as if in the days of Empire, were convinced the Germans couldn't handle a two-front war in Italy, and Clark—stuck in the Winter Line, put down by the Brits and hungry for the redemption and glory that would come his way with the liberation of Rome—was ordered to revive Shingle, in corps strength this time, for around January 20. That allowed only three weeks for planning.

In one of those fortunes of war, General John P. Lucas, who'd succeeded Dawley as Clark's Sixth Corps commander after Salerno, was haunted by nightmares of being pushed back to the sea by the Panzers at Salerno. Older, cautious by nature, having a weakness (suspect in a general) for sparing his men, and faced with insufficient forces, guns, landing craft and time for planning and rehearsal, he confessed to his diary that he "felt like a lamb being led to the slaughter."[3]

Like Salerno but more so, this latest objective was a plain overlooked by semicircular hills—here the Alban Hills, which were traversed by the main supply route of the Germans to the Winter Line—that must be wrested from the enemy as the first objective. Yet Lucas's recurrent Salerno nightmare bade him first build up the strength to repel the inevitable German counterattack before pushing forward to this high ground. Knowing his military history, he bemoaned to his diary on January 10 that "this whole affair had a strong odor of Gallipoli and apparently the same amateur was still on the coach's bench."[4]

The nervous general was referring to the strategy embraced by Churchill as First Lord of the Admiralty in January 1915, when the Brits mounted an amphibious landing at Gallipoli on the western shore of the Dardanelles designed to divert the Turks from their pressure on the Russians in the Caucasus. A test of the British contention that an offensive against the Central Powers in the Balkans stood a greater chance of success than an outright assault on the Western Front, it cost 100,000 casualties before it was abandoned, a classic case of incompetent execution more than faulty strategy in the view of most historians—including Churchill.

The Anzio assault would be made by our Third Division, which had been resting and replenishing since it was relieved on the Winter Line on November 17 by the rested and replenished 36th; an armored battalion; a paratroop regiment and battalion; two battalions of Rangers; and the veteran British First Division, with a regiment of tanks and two Commando battalions. This was the largest possible waterborne force with the available landing craft that would have to return to Naples and load up the 45th Division and most of the First Armored for the second round.

As the assault forces were practicing landings—the Yanks above Naples, the Brits around Salerno—the weather turned foul, and the Navy dared not close in on the beaches in the heavy seas. Forty-three Third Division landing craft were swamped, an undisclosed number of men drowned, and about thirty artillery pieces were lost. A bad omen.

"Shingle is pretty dubious as the beaches are bad and largely unknown," General Patton, now in England, wrote in his diary. "At a rehearsal some nights ago, 40 Dukws were lost ... If the thing is a success, Clark will get the credit. If it fails, Lucas will get the blame ... It seems inconceivable that the Boche will not guess that we are coming but he has made so many foolish mistakes that we may get ashore unopposed after all."[5]

On the night of January 20, two days before the landings behind the German lines at Anzio twenty-six miles below Rome, the grand strategy called for the 36th Division to breach the Winter Line with a crossing of the swift-flowing, steep-banked and dominatingly defended Rapido River, six miles west of ill-fated San Pietro. Thus with a one-two punch, according to the script, the Germans would be fighting a two-front war in Italy. The trouble was that practically every square inch of the 36th's sector on the Winter Line was under the scrutiny of the German observers on Monte Cassino.

So for the third time under Generals Clark and Walker the dice were loaded against the Texans. They walked and swam into a trap and were drowned and cut to pieces. In two days the hapless division suffered 1,681 casualties, including 500 captured.

H-hour for the landing at Anzio was two in the morning of January 22. To gain surprise, air strikes effectively grounded enemy air surveillance, and instead of a softening-up naval bombardment, a dummy operation was directed at Civitavecchia sixty-five miles farther up the coast. A heavy rocket barrage preceded the landing. The defenders had evacuated and had nothing but an understrength battalion of the 29th Panzer Grenadier Division blowing up the waterfront, a few tanks and some artillery in the area.

The landing was close to a total surprise, and by late the next day the British on the left and Americans (by then including the 45th's 179th Regiment) on the right, virtually unopposed, had reached the predetermined line, about seven miles inland and fifteen wide from shore to shore, that was the most the initial force was expected to be able to hold. There, instead of lancing combat patrols into the undefended Alban Hills to cut the enemy lifelines to the southern front, they were ordered by General Lucas, haunted by his close shave at Salerno, to wait for reinforcements.

On the day of the invasion the 157th and 180th were alerted to move to a staging area at Naples, and I rejoiced over radio reports that Shingle was already ten miles inland and had "trapped two Panzer Divisions while the Air Corps bombed hell out of them. [Somebody's fabrication, of course.] Events have taken a wonderful turn. Perhaps we're going to hit the South of France."

Not for two more days did Lucas feel ready to get on the move again, and by then it was too late. Amazed at his enemy's failure to push on with a good chance of taking Rome and cutting off the south, Kesselring had elements of eight German divisions rushing in and brought General von Mackensen's 14th Army headquarters down from the north to manage the containment. Shingle was stopped in its tracks before it ever got reshingled.

The I&R shifted to the staging area and the secret was out. We'd be boarding a cavernous LST for a cruise up the coast, bypassing Monte Cassino, and disembarking on the Beachhead. "May my first landing be as near a dry run as possible!" was as close to praying as I could achieve.

Three nights later we embarked in the LSTs for a sleepless voyage of eighty-five miles. Any illusions as to what lay ahead had vanished. Approaching the plateau spread out below its parapet of hills already swarming with enemy, we felt all over again the same rising anxiety that gripped us that direful day back in November as we trucked through the rain and mud toward the looming mountains from which we just knew they were looking down our throats.

On the morning of January 29, 1944, with the rest of the 157th, the Platoon hustled off the boats at the small port of Nettuno, a couple of miles east of Anzio, and beat it as fast as we could from the logistic bustle of the harbor, which was loaded with sitting ducks, because the Luftwaffe was always somewhere there over the horizon. The Regiment hiked and rode rapidly north on the short road to the Padiglione Woods, where we dug in for the night on the southern edge of the only substantial cover on the Beachhead.

Of Anzio we knew nothing except that once again the Germans were up there looking down on us. Twenty-three hundred years before our arrival, Antium, as it was then known, lost out in its wars with Rome and was absorbed in the early empire. Inevitably it was adopted as a favorite resort for emperors and rich Romans, achieving a certain distinction as the birthplace of both Caligula and Nero, alongside whom Benito looked benign. I suppose if you shed your toga and stuck to the Tyrrhenian beaches, the sea breeze blew away the malaria mosquitoes.

"Definitely we're in the Pontine Marshes," I wrote in my journal. "Miles and miles of absolutely flat, drained land—one of *Il Duce's* better ideas—and bare except for occasional areas that are very thickly scrubbed. Most foxholes take water in the bottom."

Foxholes were wells because much of the plain behind Anzio and Nettuno was barely above sea level, fed by underground springs and from the hills. Periodic attempts had been made to drain the Pomptine (so-called originally) Marshes since the Emperor Appius Claudius built the Via Appia through them from Rome to the south in 312 B.C., but success awaited Mussolini's dictatorial drive that reclaimed fifty thousand acres for cultivation by 1932 by means of a canal system to which he deigned to give his name. The draining materially reduced but failed to dry up the standing water that bred the malaria-bearing *Anopheles* mosquito—hence the preventative Atabrine pills we popped daily during our sojourn on what might more aptly have been called the Pontine Beachhead.

At dusk and again near midnight came 110 Luftwaffe bombers. And we dug, man, did we dig! Not for five days could I find a break to write home with something the censor would pass.

I will tell you something about the beauty of a night air raid. The Luftwaffe, of course, is rarely to be seen, but they come over in small force occasionally. We have a tremendous amount of A-A [anti-aircraft] protection, and it is a fascinating sight to see great threads of tracers crisscrossing or paralleling each other up into the sky, moving back and forth slowly as they follow the planes. The din is terrific, and now and then a flare goes up or comes down, giving the countryside for miles around a ghostly complexion. The terrific flashes and "crump" of the bombs make the whole thing fascinating though terrible.

But in my journal:

They came in, a plane at a time. The sky was filled with red streaks of tracers and ack-ack, really terrifying. We saw what appeared to be planes that had been hit heading for the harbor. Later they told us they were magnetic glider bombs released by enemy planes which are attracted by the ships. At least three ships were hit. How helpless I felt in my foxhole, seeing the whole thing come off before my eyes!

No magnetic glider bomb, this was Hitler's latest secret weapon, the Henschel Hs 293, a pioneering guided missile with wings, first deployed at Salerno. Rocket-driven and weighing 2,870 pounds including a 725-pound warhead, this infernal flying machine was launched from an aircraft and steered by radio for up to ten miles to the target at a speed of 375 miles an hour. Vern Dilks saw one that landed and didn't explode and said it looked like a toy airplane.

We must have mistaken the rocket blast for a hit and a fire. One of the ships that got it in Anzio harbor that night was the British cruiser *Spartan*, anchored close inshore, which capsized and was a total loss. Then the Liberty Ship *Samuel Huntington*, loaded with ammunition and gasoline; they fought the fires until the skipper ordered abandon ship, and in a few hours the *Huntington* blew up and sank—probably what I took to be the third hit.

Dilks heard that the ammo ship had been blessed by an Italian priest, presumably in Naples, a day or two before sailing. Could the Krauts have been tipped off about its cargo via their spy system? The Luftwaffe needed no spies on the night of the twenty-fourth when it attacked three brightly lit hospital ships in the harbor, sinking the *St. David* with some lives lost. "This infuriated the assault forces as did no other act of the enemy during the operation," commented the official historian Admiral Morison.[6]

Those in the air thanked the heavens they weren't down there with no place to hide, while we who were immobilized targets on land or sea wished ourselves anywhere else, but certainly not up there when two days after the initial landing thirty German planes jumped eight P-40s from the 79th Fighter Group based in Naples. Flight Commander Bill Colgan recalled being suddenly in the midst of combatants

all over the sky, from about 5000 feet on down to the deck [ground], going in all directions and with heavy streamers [vapor trails] rolling from their wingtips.

One Me 109 tried to turn with two P-40s and was losing, but the enemy pilot hiked the nose almost straight up and corkscrewed up on the inside to escape, where another P-40 was in position to run the Me 109 back down to the deck and start a turning fight all over. A few of our pilots had enemy fighters suddenly pop up in front of them, which was good. More of our pilots had enemy fighters pop up behind *them*, which was bad.[7]

Abruptly out of the free-for-all, six Focke-Wulfs charged Colgan's flight. "Starting with a head-on shootout, the next several moments involved a very small piece of the sky, but that piece was crammed rather full of cannon shells, tracers, and streamers."[8] Then along came some more patrolling P-40s and RAF (Royal Air Force) Spitfires and chased the Jerries back to Rome and beyond. No Allied planes were lost, and the Luftwaffe was kept from attacking the Beachhead.

Leading eight P-40s on patrol the day before we landed, Colgan spotted twenty enemy planes headed for our ships offshore. As they closed on the dozen FWs while other patrols took on the Messerschmitts (Me-109s), the floating targets cut loose. He made the tough decision to pursue the enemy fighter-bombers into the intense friendly fire.

It was thick and all around us. The heavy bursts were bigger but did not seem as bright a fireball as the German 88s, and they left a large, nasty-looking brownish smoke glob instead of the oily black of an 88 ... When the FW 190s went into their dive-bomb run, we went down with them into a sky solid with smaller, whiter bursts of antiaircraft fire. I guessed that was our automatic stuff, 40mm and 20mm on ships. The whole mixture wasn't too different from German flak but it was thick and intense over these ships. I had some second thoughts about my decision to fly into Allied antiaircraft fire, but one thing looked promising: If the FWs made it out of the Navy fire, they were not all going to get away. We made it out and they didn't all get away by any means. On their attempts to withdraw, both the FW 190s and Me 109s were swarmed over by Allied fighters.[9]

One brilliant morning on the ground we watched transfixed as a mile above us, against an azure sky, a Spitfire hung on the tail of a German fighter squirming to elude it when suddenly our anti-aircraft batteries picked up the chase, puncturing the blue with cotton puffs of airbursts as they tracked the twists and turns of the prey. Alas, our ground fire lagged just enough for the dogged Brit to dive into it on the very verge of his kill; he took a hit, burst into smoke, spiraled down and bought it; for we saw no parachute flutter open.

Thank God for the flyboys.

By the morning of January 30 the Sixth Corps had 61,330 men ashore facing an estimated 71,500 Germans, and Lucas launched his second attack. The British and our First Armored Division were to smash up Via Anziate, the main highway from Anzio that joined Highway 7 from the south to Rome, while on the right the Third Ranger Battalion would infiltrate the weakly defended town of Cisterna to the northeast and the Fourth would sweep around and bottle them up, opening a wedge for our Third Division to exploit and go on to cut Highway 7 and the enemy lifeline to the southern front.

The Brits rammed a narrow salient up the Anziate beyond the "Factory" (or Aprilia, actually a model farm settlement created by the Fascists) but were stopped beyond at the Campoleone rail junction by an impenetrable enemy defense. The Sherwood Foresters Battalion on our right was reduced to eight officers and 150 men.[10]

The worst of it was that what looked like good tank country proved the opposite. Our First Armored, trying to swing around to their left in support, bogged down in the fields, mushy and crossed by numerous draws, or "wadis," as the Eighth Army chaps remembered them ruefully from the North African campaign, sometimes holding water and fraught with tangles of brush. Thus, as the Germans were the first to realize, command of the hard ground of the highway and the assembly points of the Factory and the rail station of Carroceto on the west side opposite where the track paralleled the highway was vital to both sides.

Meanwhile, to their right, my Croft buddy George Furber, in B Company of the Fourth Rangers since we parted that day in Mussy's Racetrack, had a view from the inside. Evidently nobody had tipped them off that they were up against the Hermann Goering Division. They walked right in and got knocked right out.[11]

On the first of February, the day after the ghastly failure of the Rangers' attempt at a breakout, the 157th relieved the 36th Engineer Combat Regiment, which fought as infantry when they weren't building or destroying something under fire, truly the worst of both worlds; they were dug in from the extreme left of the Beachhead on the coast along the

The Factory at Anzio (*Department of Defense*)

diminutive Moletta River to the sector held by the British First Division. Our First Battalion took the coast and coast road, then there was a broad stretch of woods considered to be more or less impenetrable and scarcely defended at all, with our Third Battalion on the right next to the Second North Staffordshire Regiment. Our Second was back in reserve.[12]

Facing us was the German Fourth Parachute Division—one tough bunch of Squareheads, the Engineers warned us as they pulled out for the rear with relief.

That may have been the night Colonel Church sent Jack and Dom Trubia out to take a prisoner for interrogation or, failing that, to capture some mutton for his table from a small flock of sheep that a farmer was herding suspiciously close to our lines as if to signal the *Tedeschi* just where we were. Or, failing that, maybe grab the farmer himself.

They found sheep but neither shepherd nor paratrooper, so Dom, who was raised on an upstate New York farm and knew about such things, took over:

> I grabbed one sheep for the Colonel and one for the Platoon. I don't think he was too happy with him, a poor old broken-down ewe, but I couldn't catch a lamb. I dropped one off there with his Chinese cook and cut its throat, and got the other back to the Platoon, the only fresh meat we had on Anzio. I made a cut on the inside knee and took a tire pump and blew him up and separated the hide from the carcass just as easy as anything. Then we boiled him in a five-gallon can we got from the kitchen, the only way we could cook him.

Thus fortified, I wrote home that "life worms its mouldy and rather hectic way through the spiritless stratum of war as usual. The other day we raided a flock of sheep and had some quite good lamb chops to go with our K rations. Our dog Boots has been gnawing on the bones."

We'd inspected a Messerschmitt 109 knocked down in a nearby field. The bloody remains of the pilot were splattered around the cockpit. I enclosed in the letter a clean piece of fabric I cut from the fuselage.

The smashing repulse of our twin attempts at a breakout was followed by the inevitable lull when you just knew that no good was brewing over there. But where, and when? The word came down from Division that G2, the 45th's intelligence section, had to have a prisoner for interrogation, and the arm was put on the I&R.

So on the night of the second of February Lieutenant Pullman rounded up all of us he could find, and we headed out to First Battalion CP, checked in, and from there to B Company CP at the edge of the woods. From here we prepared to move out through our lines as a combat patrol and find and attack an enemy outpost that was known to be off in the dark somewhere—the first time the Platoon had ever been told to start a fight. To make it quicker and quieter, it was decided to limit the action to Mickey Smith, Griff, Jim Dowdall, me and maybe another. Jerry Waldron wanted to go but had to stay behind lest a stray flash of light in his eyeglasses give us away. It was three days before I had the chance to record in my little black notebook what happened:

Just before we were about to leave there was a burst of burp-gun fire and a few rifle shots to our left front. The artillery forward observer, surmising a counterattack, radioed in the concentration and had a couple of dozen rounds thrown in. A few minutes later two men brought in a sergeant wounded by burp-gun in arm and leg who said that his outpost had been sitting around talking when they saw two or three men appear about twenty-five yards in front of them. He challenged three times, and the third time one of them opened up with his Schmeisser, whereupon he shot him through the chest. Then came the artillery.

We decided to go out and try to bring in a man from the patrol, wounded or not. Of course we didn't know how big the patrol was, how many were still alive, whether they were being reinforced, or what. We sneaked out, found the remaining man on the outpost scared as hell, went a little farther and found two dead Germans. We searched them, and Smitty was commencing to cut the pockets of a third who was apparently dead, when he sat bolt upright, his hands in the air. So there was I&R's first prisoner.

That box barrage the FO called for in fact landed behind us as "friendly fire" between wherever we were in no-man's-land and our lines. An unpleasant sensation to be out there in front of your own shellfire. Dowdall was sweating it.

> I went out ahead about twenty yards farther, layin' as close to the ground as I could, prayin' "Hurry up Mickey! Hurry up!" because at the end o' this field was a row o' bushes, an' I was thinkin' mebbe the Jerries are comin' up from there. Then, "He's alive! Thank God, thank God! Get him on his feet, let's go, get him on his feet!" I've never been so scared. Me mind was racin', but me body was actin' calmly.

On our way back I paused over the paratrooper who'd burp-gunned the sarge who shot him dead through the chest. He'd fallen forward on his Schmeisser. I rolled him over and almost without thinking grabbed his gun and caught up with the others. No use leaving it there for one of his *Kameraden* to recycle against us, and besides, what a trophy! It felt wet. I peered at my hands in the dark. They were soaked with his blood.

Back at our CP I scrubbed myself and cleaned and scrubbed my spoil of war, and showed it off to the guys. Jack thought he might arrange for me to send it home somehow (fat chance), so I recorded the serial number, 2092f, and stashed it away in our supply tent.[13]

Our prisoner, one tough Kraut, was passed back to Division for interrogation. Trubia heard they put him in a locked room with a big MP who was going to use his fists to get him to talk—and our paratrooper beat the MP up. So they bucked him back to Corps, Waldron heard, where "they tried to break him down by making him dig his own grave, and I'll be a son-of-a-gun if he didn't escape with knowledge of the location of all of our positions!"

"Oh, I felt so mad about that," steamed Dowdall, "because I remembered the fear I had, bein' out there, to go through all that trouble an' all that fear, an' those *bastards* [strong language for Jimmy] back there lettin' him git away!"

Anyway, he was our first prisoner without our firing a shot, so our hands (except mine) were clean, nor was it ours he slipped through.

The grinning Kraut on the left is holding the fearful "burp gun." (*Collection of the author*)

Next day the only OP we had out was pulled in, I journaled succinctly, "as the enemy hit its house three times." That night the German 14th Army attacked with a pincer against the British salient on the Anziate highway in heavy rain that grounded our planes, infiltrating either side and coordinating their attack on the flanks with their frontal assault. The salient was eliminated, with 1,400 British casualties, mostly captured. It was bad. Mark Clark ordered a final Beachhead defense line prepared.

While the Devil was loose on our right, eleven of us were sent up, as I put it wryly, "to patrol a 1000-yard gap between First and 3rd Battalions while 2nd came up to relieve the First. We contented ourselves with staying at the edge of the woods until one."

Some contentment. Ninety-one yards of the Allied second front in Italy apiece. If the paratroopers across the river bed over there in the dark had known that a handful of jumpy *amerikanischen Dummköpfe* without even a machine gun and no hand-to-hand combat experience were all that stood between them and the breach of a half-mile front, what a party!

The burp gun, or German Schmeisser MP40 (*Courtesy of Digger History www.diggerhistory.info*)

The *History of the 157th Infantry Regiment* dismissed such an invitation to disaster with these words: "Between lay a 1,000-yard gap but it was heavily wooded and the few men defending it furnished adequate protection against a breakthrough." Bull. Adequate because there was no breakthrough. The woods were some way behind us. A very hairy night.[14]

By the next day, the fourth of February, the Sixth Corps had nearly 100,000 men bottled up on the Beachhead by an estimated 110,000 Germans with armor and artillery building day and night. Churchill rumbled with Olympian discontent, "I had hoped we were hurling a wildcat onto the shore, but all we got was a stranded whale."[15] General Lucas, by now the universal scapegoat, was on the verge of despair.

Maybe it was too quiet in our sector. The next night our nervous S2 intelligence officer told Pullman to check out the paratroopers on the other side of the Moletta River bed. Sergeant Mickey Smith, the cool, slow-talkin', slow-grinnin' sorta Gary Cooper of the Platoon, was given the job, with Mullenax and me and maybe a fourth. I journaled:

The patrol was a recon, but we were supposed to get a prisoner if we could. Ha! We went up a draw parallel to and in front of the lines, reached the end of it, a clearing, heard Germans and vehicles moving along the dry river bed about 300 yards ahead and parallel to the gully. Smitty looked around, heard lots of Jerries, and we headed back. Undoubtedly they saw him and would have fired if we'd all gone across the clearing. Going back we followed a trail through the middle of the gully. Mohawk missed stepping on a carefully laid mine by about six inches, so we had a pretty good report to turn in.

Carefully laid all right. Right on his heels, I spied the mine just in time to miss tramping on it myself. We got off the trail fast. How we avoided them going up, their *Gott* must have been *mit uns* that night. If Mickey was so sure they'd spotted him, why didn't they

The immense "Anzio Express" railroad gun (*U.S. Air Forces*)

charge the draw and eliminate an American recon patrol? Maybe because of whatever
stayed Griff's hand in this sector when, as he recalled, "concealed on one side of a hill in the
brush, we picked up what we thought was an enemy OP, a soldier sitting there with field
glasses. I thought about taking a shot at him or calling some artillery but decided he was-
n't a worthwhile target."

Nowhere was safe, from the front lines back to the shining Tyrrhenian. From their
bleachers up in the hills our enemies observed us like fleas on a map at their leisure and
every day accumulated more artillery coordinates of our significant installations, daily
updated by the Luftwaffe whose recon planes, circling high above like lone hawks, attracted our futile ack-ack fire.

Nothing was beyond their reach, from mortars to the "Anzio Express," the giant railroad gun outside Rome that hurled 280-millimeter, 11-inch-diameter, 550-pound shells
from a 70-foot barrel up to thirty or so miles sighing high over our heads to explode with
titanic devastation in the rear areas and among the ships unloading in the harbor, or without a hint of warning on top of us at the front.[16]

As its daylight bombing diminished somewhat with our increased air cover and anti-
aircraft fire from the ground, the Luftwaffe took to the night all the more, as on the ninth
of February, when I observed to my notebook that "things have been pretty hot around the
CP. We're close to the lines, and something like eight TDs [armored tank destroyers], two
tanks and six artillery pieces have moved right in next to us. At five the other morning several Jerries came over and dropped 'butterfly' bombs over us, and they've sent a few shells
in occasionally. Consequently we have all dug in, and my shelter seems to be the best of all.
It gives protection against about everything except a direct hit."

The anti-personnel butterfly bomb was another work of the Devil of the Night, a bath-
tub-sized canister parachuted from a Junkers Ju-88 or Heinkel He-111 bomber toward the
target by the fierce white light of a parachuted flare that seemed to strip us naked to the
enemy looking down. A timed charge blew open the sides at the optimum altitude for scattering scores of offspring like a flight of deadly butterflies that exploded with a storm of
fragments. Pullman parked his boots outside his hole one night, and they were riddled.

The menace of a Heinkel approaching with a load of butterfly bombs before our ack-
ack had got wind of it haunts the memory of the howling crescendo

EEERRRROOOWWWWOOOOWWWEEERRROOOOWWWW

of the slightly out-of-synch engines up there in the darkness that in the recalling sends the
same shivers as ever up my neck.

One of *der Führer's* more quixotic scientists conjured up the "Goliath," a miniature
unmanned tank about two feet high that was supposed to lumber along toward our lines
with two hundred pounds of explosive, guided remotely by a couple of thousand feet of
trailing wire, to be detonated at its destination. Drawback: the Doodlebug, as the dogfaces
derided it, could be stopped by rifle fire.[17]

I penciled for home a cross-sectional sketch of the major hole I excavated with
Waldron's skeptical assistance: "Jerry and I have dug into the side of a hill and pitched a

A Brit stands by a butterfly bomb
(*Department of Defense*)

beautiful tent over the dugout. It's like a cathedral; your voice almost echoes ... had the time of my life opening packages in it last night. The one with Wordsworth's poems came, minus, strangely, your '4 tins of food.' Some hungry mail clerk must have intercepted 'em." A few days later: "It collapsed in the rain and Jerry spent a whole day digging out my stuff." And from him in a letter to my father: "Relations became a bit strained recently due to the fact that Joe enlarged our foxhole while I was on an OP and the hole fell in on top of me while he was on an OP."

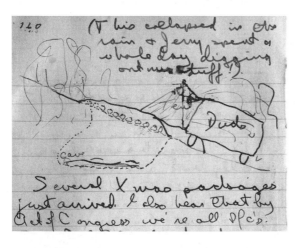

Jerry's and my dugout
drafted in my journal

Two weeks of deadlock while his enemies strengthened their Beachhead by the day, and Adolf stamped his foot. This cancer on the shin of his Fortress Europa must be removed:

> ... the landing at Anzio marks the beginning of the invasion of Europe planned for 1944. Strong German forces are to be tied down in areas as far as possible from the bases in Britain where the majority of the invasion troops are still stationed. The object of the Allies is to gain experience for future operations.
>
> Every soldier must, therefore, be aware of the importance of the battle which the Fourteenth Army has to fight.
>
> It must be fought with bitter hatred against an enemy who wages a ruthless war of annihilation against the German people and who, without any higher ethical aims, strives for the destruction of Germany and European culture.[18]

For the first week of February following our commitment to the line on the left we were lucky. The weather wasn't bad, and the thrust of German intentions was clearly coalescing down the Anzio highway against the British on our right. Then on February 7 it rained all day, and that night enemy infantry again infiltrated around the British flanks and after a heavy barrage attacked from the rear, and head-on with tanks. The rain stopped, and the moon came out. The Second North Staffordshires were driven back from the key high ground of Buon Riposo Ridge west of Carroceto. On the British left the Germans smashed over our Third Battalion. Major John Boyd, its commanding officer, was killed, and his men spent a three-day supply of machine-gun ammunition and over 5,600 rounds of mortar shells with the support of an intense concentration of artillery. General Penney of the British First pleaded for relief, but Lucas insisted he had virtually none available.

In two more days, on February 9, the Germans attacked again and drove the exhausted and depleted Brits from the Factory. The pressure was intensifying. This was the date of my last journal entry and letter home for three weeks, with a P.S.: "I hear that by Act of Congress we're all Pfc's." A singular, and my single, promotion of the war—by legislative fiat to all privates first class in combat.

Next day the British were pushed out of Carroceto. General Penney's men were taking the whole brunt of the building German offensive, and once again he pleaded for help. Lucas at last agreed to commit the 45th's 179th and a few tanks from the First Armored Division; their counterattack on the Factory was repulsed. The Engineers moved back up on the left, relieving our Second and Third Battalions, leaving only the First in the line.

In Britain Patton chafed to his diary: "If we lost that beach, it will be bad, but so much sloth, or timidity, was shown at the start that the thing was doomed. Only 8 miles in 12 days. I would have been in Rome."[19]

Not until February 29 (this was a leap year), more than two weeks after the fact, was I able to record my next near-demise when it was all too clear that both armies were bracing for what was to come. The upper windows of isolated stone houses as close to the front as we could get provided almost our only chance to spy on the enemy. Of course if we could see them, as we'd learned in the mountains, they could see us back. We were in the left coastal sector at the time. From my journal:

Went out on an OP in a big two-story house in plain view of the enemy. Observation was perfect. We found one CP where there must have been at least a company of Germans. We saw a camouflaged gun there, scores of jeeps [perhaps Volkswagens], *ammo carriers, command cars, large trucks, half-tracks, motorcycles, even a man on horseback. The first day we saw a train moving in the distance. Reported it and next day the Air Force bombed it.* [A day or so later they'd repaired the track, someone said with American POWs, and the train was back running.] *Saw the Jerry ack-ack knock down two of our B 25s and saw the men that survived float to earth.* [I have a vivid memory of a crippled Flying Fortress going down over the Velletri area on this or another occasion.]

On our right I saw a camouflaged tank or self-propelled gun. In back of it was a house and road where we saw vehicles and columns of men. I fired two missions on it with the 105s. Got three rounds within four or five yards of the tank and the rest dispersed around the house and road. Caught a Kraut taking a shit and saw him run for it when the first round came in, pants around his knees.[20]

Our last day there the English came to take over, and Jerry [the enemy] *must have spotted them. He hit the houses across the road from us with what must have been at least a 170-millimeter gun, moved down the road, scored a direct hit on the house next to us, and then hit the road 75 yards from our house. We dove into a ditch next to the foundations in back, about ten men still in the house. He put one about ten yards in back of the house, and the Limeys decided to come downstairs. Next one was a direct hit on the peak of the roof, knocking off the roof and the entire upper story, damaging the first, covering us with plaster and landing rocks as big as trunks two feet from our heads. We got out of there FAST. Thus ended, quite conclusively, a good OP.*

The road behind what was actually a modest villa paralleled the front and was reached by a driveway of a couple of hundred feet through a field. The British crew swung off this road and up the drive as jauntily as if crossing Piccadilly Circus, arms flailing in the fashion of the King's Own, in plain view of any Kraut with a pair of binoculars, and of course had to have a jolly outdoor howdjado with us, much to our discomfiture. Soon after, in roared the big shells, curtains for one of our hottest windows on the show, a latter-day example of how the Redcoats lost the American Revolution.

No sooner had we climbed out of the ruins and got to the end of the drive than a German fighter plane, an FW or Me-109 following the road low on the lookout for targets, roared in on us, guns blazing, and we threw ourselves in the ditches. A wonder they hadn't long since given this and a few other isolated landmarks a dose of preemptive shellfire, unless they assumed we'd hardly be so rash as to use them.

The next day, February 15, marked the onset of irony enough on both sides to illuminate the somber lines from "Dover Beach" by Matthew Arnold, who never went to war but must have listened to those who had, writing of it as a "darkling plain, / Swept with confused alarms of struggle and flight, / Where ignorant armies clash by night."[21]

Overriding the misgivings of his generals that such a tactic would concentrate too much of their forces in too narrow a sector, Hitler ordered Kesselring and Mackensen to drive the 14th Army's climactic Beachhead-splitting attack down the Via Anziate like a spear of Siegfried, the lightning point of which should be his favorite Berlin-Spandau Lehr

Our observation posts just behind the front line offered enemy gunners easy targets ranging from our Sherman tank (nigh useless against the German armor) to a clump of five tempting farm structures already under fire, to a guy peering over a haystack while his buddies loiter in more or less plain view, to a shell hole for catching a glimpse of our enemies until the next round brings what's left of the building down around our ears. (*Department of Defense*)

Regiment of "demonstration" troops who in fact had never fought a battle and were rushed to Italy with scarcely a briefing as to what they were being thrust into.

Our Intelligence indicated that the blitz was poised for the morning of February sixteenth. And so, after weeks of agonizing, the dreadful decision was made by Mark Clark on the fifteenth to bomb the ancient monastery on Monte Cassino from which the all-seeing eyes of the German observers had held us at bay on the Winter Line, as they did now from the Alban Hills. Then, early the next morning, the southern front would attack and finally take the demolished monastery, freeing the Air Force, by then having done its dirty job, to turn the tide at Anzio.

That was the scenario. We bombed hell into the Abbey—and the Germans dug into the rubble deeper than ever.

Against our three divisions augmented by the units guarding our flanks, General Mackensen had the equivalent of six on the line, with his 26th Panzer and 29th Panzer

The Abbey (*U.S. Army*)

Grenadiers poised to smash down the highway upon the 45th behind Hitler's elite Lehr Regiment.

At one-thirty in the morning of the suspected counterattack General Patton had a phone call from London that General Eisenhower wanted to see him at once. Driving through the night, he was there by 10:45. Alexander had concluded that Lucas and his staff weren't up to the crisis and "What we need is a thruster like George Patton." As Patton recorded in his diary, Ike told him, "You may have to take command of the beachhead in Italy and straighten things out." He replied that he was "willing to command anything from a platoon up in order to fight."[22]

Chomping at the bit, Patton donned his new battle jacket and ordered a brace of planes warmed up at the London airport to take him to Italy. But he foresaw trouble with Clark and his Fifth Army HQ and told Ike that he "was anxious to go, but that I must be backed up by him, as otherwise I would have my throat cut."[23]

By next morning Eisenhower had changed his mind and decided to replace Lucas with Truscott of the Third Division. "We were all very sorry that the show was called off," the disappointed Patton wrote in his diary, "it would have been very risky, but much honor could have been gained. No man can live forever."[24]

Blow it out yer ass, General.

To the haunting skirls of the Scots units' bagpipes that night of the fifteenth, we Thunderbirds of the 45th and on our left the Black Cats of the British 56th, which had just been brought up from the Winter Line, moved up to relieve their exhausted First Division, down to one-third strength.

For the second time the 36th Engineers traded foxholes with us. Our Second Battalion took over Limey holes square in the face of the anticipated enemy attack down the Via Anziate, the Rome–Anzio highway, with G Company on the left, E actually straddling the blacktop, and F in reserve in the gap between. Battalion headquarters, Medics and 158th Artillery communications moved into a labyrinth of caves in a shale bluff behind G Company, cavernous enough for vehicles and safe from shellfire and bombs.

Two miles south, the Via Anziate was crossed by an east–west road over an overpass, "flyover" to the Brits. Here our Third Battalion set up a second line of defense behind concertina barbed wire already rolled across the highway by the relieved Tommies. First Battalion was in reserve on its right at the edge of the Padiglione Woods, then the 179th, 180th, the Third Division, the 504th Paratroopers and First Special Service Force at the coast. The depleted British First and our First Armored Division were put in reserve.

Presumably the 157th was planted so squarely in the way of the expected Panzer tanks as a reward for stopping them at Salerno. Losses were already heavy. The Third Battalion commander, Major Boyd, had been killed, and Colonel Church was in hospital with pneumonia. The interim command of the Regiment was in the hands of his executive officer, Lt. Colonel Chester James, a big, beefy, beer-drinking National Guardsman.

Our forward regimental CP was set up inside the northern edge of the rather scrubby Padiglione Woods, half a mile or so southwest of the Overpass. That afternoon Les Gerencer drove Lieutenant Pullman over to the British First Division CP for maps of their minefields in the area our Second Battalion was taking over north of the Overpass. Pullman returned that evening:

> Goddam, here they came, the flares first, then the bombers. We just threw ourselves under the trucks. The bombs are comin' down, and here's Gerencer under one with me, and I says, "Les, what the hell was that racket?" And hell, it was our helmets hit together. He dove under one side, and I the other.
>
> A barrage hit at dawn while I was in the CP itself, which was sandbagged, and I said to somebody, "I've always wondered what would happen when they got as much artillery as we have, and I'm finding out now." This British brigadier came in, wearing his little beret and a very unusual badge, and of course he's putting me on, a nice young American lieutenant, with some story about a patrol he sent twenty miles behind the lines. Just then a shell from the Anzio Express arrives, and Jesus, there you are in front of a British brigadier, so you're not going to show fear, but you're just absolutely ready to shit your pants. All kinds of casualties, and his driver's hit and comes in with a piece of shrapnel in him, and says "I'm sorry, Sir," and collapses.
>
> About that time Maxie from Second Battalion shows up. "Ready to go, Jack?" Sure I'm ready to go out there in the cold, and they've probably run out of ammunition and so they quit firing. I didn't want to leave the dugout but I did, and we went up and guided some of the boys through those minefields.

Meanwhile, Pullman had sent Sergeant Dick Beech, Jerry Waldron and a third man to set up an OP around Second Battalion as far up Highway 7 as they could get. Jerry remembers considerable activity in the sky:

> We worked from about ten [at night on the fifteenth] until three in the morning laying two or three miles of field phone wire, all on foot, to a house that was directly behind the front lines where we found a British forward artillery observer and his radioman. He told us he was still awake because there was so much movement of all types on the German lines. Within thirty minutes, and just after we had checked in with the CP by phone, all hell broke loose. Dawn was breaking, and their artillery was all over us, the most concentrated on one front I'd ever faced, because we were way out ahead of the Overpass and to the left, out around E Company, not far from the highway. It was a rolling barrage ahead of the German infantry attacking down the highway. Within five minutes our phone line was blown out.
>
> The barrage lasted well over half an hour. I spent it on the floor under a table, while the Limey lieutenant's in his chair tipped back against the wall telling his man, "Let's see if we can get back with the radio and tell 'em what's happening," but it was no damn good either. He may have been Coldstream Guards, whose officers never hit the ground while under fire.[25]
>
> When the barrage was over both of us went on our scopes. A brief firefight ensued, and we quickly saw why our guys had been routed—a long, gray line of German infantry proceeding up the hill like Pickett's charge at Gettysburg. Dick

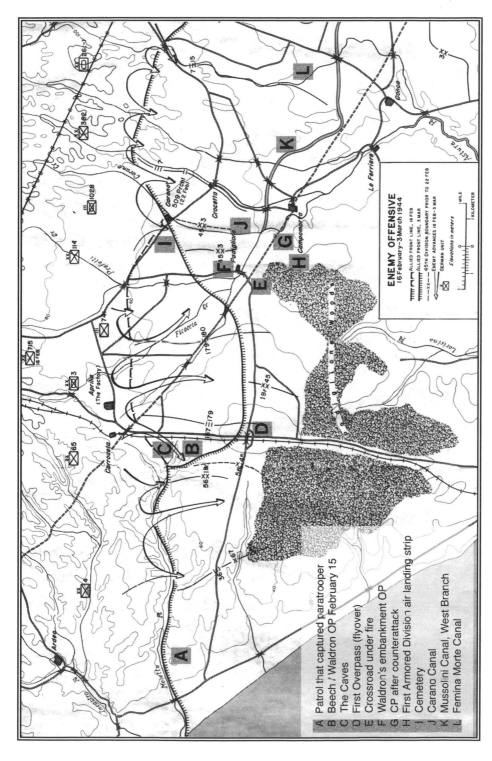

A Patrol that captured paratrooper
B Beech / Waldron OP February 15
C The Caves
D First Overpass (flyover)
E Crossroad under fire
F Waldron's embankment OP
G CP after counterattack
H First Armored Division air landing strip
I Cemetery
J Carano Canal
K Mussolini Canal, West Branch
L Femina Morte Canal

ENEMY OFFENSIVE
16 February–3 March 1944

ALLIED FRONT LINE, 16 FEB
ALLIED FRONT LINE, 3 MAR
— XX — 45TH DIVISION BOUNDARY PRIOR TO 22 FEB
ENEMY ADVANCES 16 FEB–3 MAR
GERMAN UNIT

Elevations in meters

1 MILE
1 KILOMETER

(Department of Defense, with additional information from author)

Beech and the British FO decided we couldn't defend anything, and it was more important that we get out and be the eyes and ears on what's happening. We pulled back some distance using dry drainage ditches for cover, and about an hour later, when the sun was up, were running down a gully—a main gully which the Germans were smart enough to shell. As we started up a side gully I was leaning back against the bank when a shell hit down at the intersection of the two. I said to myself, "Gee, that one missed me!"—when suddenly I got this pain in my shin. I'd been hit.

I could move, so we continued on, but it was stiffening up, and I'm limpin' along, and we get back to another house where there's an anti-tank gun peeking around the corner. We must have had an observation team there, but we were trying to find a new location that would have been a good one. And as we looked back a shell came in and removed the whole corner of the house and the anti-tank gun.

Eventually we got back to the Medics, who put me on a British hospital ship, and since I was one of the early wounded, it didn't leave for four or five days. We had tea morning, noon and night and four o'clock and a fifth time, and for years I wasn't able to drink the stuff. Back at Naples the wound was so small they didn't operate. No scar. Don't even remember which leg.

That house with the anti-tank gun behind it ... Dave O'Keefe had taken a couple of the young replacements to set up an OP in a small farmhouse in the same area north of the Overpass.

There was an anti-tank gun and squad there. Through this window on the east we saw Germans and tanks over toward the Factory, and I says, "Naw, we can't do anything here, let's go back into the other room away from the window." It was one o' my premonitions. There was a masonry partition there. No sooner had we left than there's a blast. We went back and the window was gone. One o' those tanks put a round through. That night we pulled the hell outta there. I kept the ole North Star over my shoulder, and we come up to the concertina barbwire the British had laid. "Halt!" We told 'em who we were and got through the wire and back to the CP.

Dawn was just breaking on the morning of the sixteenth as our infantry finished changing holes with the Tommies and tried to figure out where they were, where the Germans were, and how to lay in their fields of fire, when suddenly the whistles of incoming shells, the more distant rumbling and roaring, the end-of-the-world explosions and resounding thuds, the geysers of earth and stone, the screaming death ... and the universe imploded on them.

For an hour they hugged Mother under the worst barrage and bombing yet experienced by the Regiment. Then, as abruptly it lifted, and down out of the smoke clanked the enormous, roaring, clattering, squeaking Panzers with the Grenadiers trotting in their wake. Three were rolling right over E Company's left-flank platoon when a tank destroyer knocked out two and the third withdrew. The TD's machine gunner broke up the infantry assault until he ran out of ammo and they had to haul back.

The Overpass—underpass to hell (*Department of Defense*)

Though Hitler's vaunted Lehr Regiment broke and ran for their lives, wave after wave of Germans of stronger stuff charged down the Via Anziate and on either side behind a crawling shield of small arms and shellfire, tanks firing point-blank at whatever moved. Overrunning E Company, they snuck around the British and the 1/9th on Second Battalion's flanks, nearly cutting them off and forcing them to pull back.

Tanks attacking G Company on the bluff above the Caves were knocked out by our artillery, which at one point was reluctantly called down on one of the beleaguered platoons and cut the attackers to pieces, but they just kept coming, crawling through draws under terrible fire and leaping into foxholes for hand-to-hand battle with each *Amerikaner* as if it were a personal vendetta, finally forcing what was left of the platoon to withdraw.

In the afternoon Panzers eradicated a squad of men and a platoon leader. At nightfall three enemy companies resumed the attack against E Company through the ditches on either side of the Anziate. The left platoon was wiped out; a handful of men on the right of the highway still held on.

Hastily dug in the swampy ground and taking refuge in the tunnels left by the British in the east—west highway embankment at the Overpass, Third Battalion took a more prolonged shelling, bombing and strafing from everything the Germans had. Men were exploded; noses bled from the concussion; some of the wounded lay where they got it for two days before they could be reached. Medics and litter parties, drivers, Wire Section men from Regimental Headquarters repairing recurrently broken phone lines, all worked under constant fire.

Answering with 432 guns and 500 air sorties, we were locked together with our enemies inside a continuous, ground-shaking concussion of flying fragments of steel, buildings, vehicles, mud, bullets and bodies.

Returning from driving an officer up to the Second Battalion CP beyond the Overpass, Bill Caird ran over some barbed wire that wrapped around the drive shaft.

I got under with the wire clippers trying to free us, but the Germans were attacking, firing all around, so the officer says the hell with the jeep, and we walked back. At the CP, Colonel James comes out and wants to know who the hell are those guys up there on the horizon? And it's the Germans diggin' in. Dawn was just comin' up.

Meanwhile, Danny Boone's driving Mullenax and a crew to set up an OP in a house on the road not far from the one I'd been shelled and strafed off, when near the Overpass they run into shellfire. A fluke shrapnel hits the ignition key and disables the jeep. Mohawk and the boys hike on to the house, and Danny walks back to the CP to get a tow from Vern Dilks, who for once is ruffled.

When we got up there a coupla Sherman tanks right back of the Overpass had been hit and were burnin' like hell and ammunition goin' up, and a little further on some British Bren-gun carriers—it was a moonlit night—and you could see the bodies o' these guys who'd been killed, hangin' over the sides. We got outta there. I guess the Germans got the jeep. I was sweatin' blood.

When the CP was pulled back, Dilks and Emmett Oman were cruising around looking for a spot to dig in when a couple of tanks began throwing in 88s. Dilks:

They was hittin' stumps and stuff, and shrapnel flyin' all over. I heard one come right across the windshield, and by the time I got my butt outta there and was layin' on the ground, the second one come in, and what it didn't do to the back o' my left leg, like somebody hit me with a red-hot ax. Boy that medic was on the ball, shells bustin' all around, an' that guy standin' there cuttin' my pants off, dressin' it with sulfa. Might have been Emmett got hit by the same shell but I don't think so. We went to different hospitals in Naples, and he never come back.

Up in their house on the east–west road as the February sun rose wanly over the smoke of the developing battle, Mullenax, Nye, Trubia and the new men, among them Montford "Monty" Locklear (quiet, serious) from Ohio and a couple of even newer ones unnamed, were trying to establish an unobtrusive OP in the midst of other American and British artillery observers, a naval fire control party getting set up, a few military police, and some tanks rumbling around. To the Germans it must have resembled the Brandenburg Gate at rush hour. Pullman had just left after looking in and was worrying if he should pull them out of there. Shorty Nye wasn't too happy either:

Our troops was just in front of us, and there was these tanks of ours on the road. The Kraut artillery had already smashed the damn house, windows all out and big holes in the walls, and on the top floor a dead woman lyin' there. We had the OP in the back end so's not to be seen, lookin' through these holes where we could see Germans, one or two, or a half-track or a motorcycle go this way and that way and all over the place. There was four or five houses, and we was in the next one from the end.

There was two planes come over. One bombed our house, one the next one. We heard a HHHRRRMMMMMMM and that was it. A ZZZOOOOMMMMMM over here and then a BOOOOOMMMMMM, and when we heard the ZZZOOOMMM again we took off. Got about halfway down when we heard the first bomb hit the next house. The second one just got the back corner of ours, but the concussion knocked the shit out of everything in front, and in back everything was on fire. I mean we was just ready to go out the door. It was in a little cupola. That bomb turned us every which way. I said them sonsabitches are gonna shell us 'cause they'd shelled us before. I think I had three guys with me, and we hit for cover. Maybe I should of stayed, but I was all rattled up with that God damn bomb.

So we went back across the road into the woods. The CP was back in there with a bunch o' artillery an' every other damn thing. Then they started shellin' the woods. We heard guys talkin' an' found out they had a nice little cave, so we stayed there for about two hours and come out and went on back, and everything was deserted.

Dom Trubia thought they were going to use the house for an artillery OP and there'd been no time yet even to lay in a phone line.

I think I was the only one that didn't get a scratch. There was a British ack-ack gun in front of the house they'd been using for artillery. They burned up the barrel and were changin' it when the planes came over and dropped those 500-pound bombs, so nobody got a shot at 'em. After the medics picked 'em all up there was a major there gettin' out of his tank to come over to the house to ask us directions, I guess. He got a leg blown right off.

The medic asked me if I was all right, and I said I had an awful headache. Boy, the concussion just doubled the size of my head. So he took me back to the aid station, opened a foot locker where he had some good old American whisky and gave me a good slug and said that oughta help me, and if it didn't, come back the next day. My headache was gone, and all I could think of was that quart, so I told him I still had a headache, and he poured me another drink and says, "I guess your headache's gone now 'cause that's the last one you're gonna get from us!"

It was here that Valen Mullenax, the One-Man Army, Mohawk our Shield of Invincibility, had his Date with Destiny at exactly 1415 by his watch:

Three of our tanks came up there. Dive bombers came over. One bomb turned a tank over on its side. The other two bombs was right around the house, and one was about seven feet outside the big window I was looking out through at the German lines, and that's the one that smashed my chest, broke ten ribs, put three of 'em through the left lung and nearly hit the heart. A piece o' shrapnel or rock tore through my scalp. Pullman was up there and had just left. I thought Locklear was killed. I'd been breaking him in, a good man. [Monty and the two greenhorns were wounded.]

We was supposed to go out and get a prisoner that night, and this combat MP come up there and was gonna take him back. When they bombed us he was knocked down but wasn't hurt much. He come to and was lookin' around, and all them other guys was dead except I started to groan. He threw me over his shoulder with them ten broken ribs and made a run for a British jeep that was back in the woods. They threw me in the back, and he jumped in and they took off for their aid station.

They gave me a big heavy shot o' morphine and took me back to the field hospital. Two British doctors put me under a fluoroscope, and I was so full o' morphine I couldn't talk but could hear them, and they looked at each other and looked at me and at each other and said "This man should not be here. He's not even supposed to be alive according to his picture. He should be dead." Blood was running outta my mouth.

Three days later at the General Hospital at Naples the blood was all clotted. They couldn't get it out with a needle so I had to cough it up. That was about thirty days of misery. Every time I'd cough the blood them ribs would grind together. They just give me morphine every three hours for sixty days, said there's nothing we can do for that man except see what nature does. No penicillin, just morphine 'cause I didn't have any open wounds; it didn't break the skin where it caved those ribs in. Along toward the last they'd come with that morphine needle, and I'd get sick at my stomach 'cause it was building up in me. I had an aversion to it. When the ribs finally got to knitting, and I got up, this shoulder was hanging clear down to here, but that came back up. The three ribs was all healed on top of each other, and the shoulder muscles was all messed up. That's why they wouldn't let me go back to combat.

These six chaplains would come to my deathbed at various times tryin' to git me to join their church, and I says I won't be a hypocrite because I don't believe in everything you got in your different religions. I believe in the Creator and Jesus Christ and his true teachings but not in the doctrines the way they interpret them. My parents never enforced any church on me so I tried 'em all and compared what the ministers had to say.

When this here bomb hit it knocked me out so quick that I didn't feel anything, but when I came to I seen a big flash of light in my mind, and then all that pain hit me. That light in my mind has had one terrific bearing on me ever since, 'cause I know there's more in this world than we know about, and that there light always will be in my mind. I can use it any time. My channels has been opened to the metaphysical part of my mind from that day. That's how I got over my alcoholism. I used an analyzing research in my own mind.

Well, what the hell. We always did say it would take a bomb to bring down our Big Mo. Instead, it opened him up.

You were so barely ahead of the rampaging dragon that in an instant a flame could flick you to a crisp. In an OP house, you or whoever put you there was asking for it, and we were blown out of our share. It could strike anywhere. The bastards were all over us. Observation had suddenly ceased to be a spectator sport. To see was to feel. An OP or CP behind the line one minute could be on the front the next. Short of joining the fray with rifle and grenade, our dwindling Platoon was reduced to recon patrol liaison to confirm the positions and status of incommunicado flanking units, mainly the British Black Cats on our left.

From the day those burp-gun bees buzzed over my head on the mountain trail and the incoming mortar shells dropped between me and home, brain and body discovered an unfamiliar neural pathway that pointed toward survival. It was the saving irrelevance of my situation that by lucking out of the Camp Croft officer lottery I escaped the insane vulnerability of up-front field leadership, and that a second intervention rescued me from the crapshoot of riflemanship in Third Battalion under fire up there right now at the Overpass, if I'd lived so long.

Somewhere between my eyebrows and the back of my skull lurks the old, gray software of what I did or didn't do, what I endured, saw, heard or felt as a brash kid, you might say, thirty-five hundred miles from home sixty-four years ago. Yet to this day those neurons imprinted so long ago will not loosen their grip except for the few that perhaps randomly, then again perhaps not, seem to have eluded the bonds of silence or denial as if to reassure the rest: "It's all right. Calm yourselves. Go back to sleep. These scraps are enough to placate the incursions of his consciousness, and his conscience."

For example, there's this persistent image of the Tommies (as characterized by our fathers of the First War) of whom I wrote home when the crisis had passed: "I have the most profound admiration for the British. They're systematic, hard, dogged fighters. Under stress they're the coolest men I've ever seen, and they somehow manage to preserve a humor withal that is marvelous. Even on the front they shave and wash every day (our ears tingle!). An honor to fight beside them." (Well, not quite every day.) "Ragged, dirty, gaunt, and so beat," I remembered as an afterthought. And droll, as I wrote home some time later:

> One day one of the boys from our Company was passing by a battery of Limey 12-pounders that was about to fire a mission. Never having fired an artillery piece, he asked if he could pull the lanyard on one. "Right enough," they said. When the order came, all the guns roared except his. He tugged and tugged without success. Finally, after a heavy pull, it fired. He apologized for the delay, but the gunner said, "Oh, that's all right, ole boy. When Jerry thinks the last one's come in, 'e'll stick 'is 'ead up an' 'ave a look around, an' that's when we'll get 'im with yours!"

Yah, growled Dilks, "and come four o'clock in the afternoon, if the Limey artillery was backin' you up, ferget it, because they just gotta have their cup o' tea."

About that time Griff took me and Jimmy Dowdall on a contact patrol to locate a British unit on our immediate left. I recorded in my journal:

We walked through a steep-banked gully with good enfilade, then had to go over the top and race across a field some distance toward a lone house, in plain view, I think we figured, of the enemy. Very fearful of machine gun fire—ran like hell. Seems to me that from the house somehow we ran for another wadi, parallel to the front [it was the front] and found a Limey platoon, pretty exhausted, sort of half dug in and strung out along the bank. They were cheerful, glad to see us, made us tea. Kraut mortars came in while we were there, dropping more or less down the length of the wadi. The lieutenant then called the roll as apparently he did following each barrage the Jerries had been laying in every half hour or so day and night. They were a cool lot all right. We didn't linger for more than the brief amenities and the info we came for. They were London Irish Rifles of the Black Cat Division.

On the way over there we went past this British gun emplacement that was right behind this house and had to crawl along some ditches and dash across some open spaces, and when we got pretty close to their command post some Limey says "Git down! There's a sniper aboot!" This old boy with a handle-bar mustache was their commander, the London Irish. They got in some new replacements that looked like a bunch of Boy Scouts in their overcoats, awkward kids that didn't know what it was all about, and they'd been shelled in there and didn't know who they had or who'd got hurt. They were calling the roll off a roster. He told an orderly to get some tea for us. And then we talked business. We showed 'em the map, and they told us their situation.

But when we came back past that gun emplacement the house was flat, and some of the British were still there, some no doubt wounded. They'd emplace their guns on high places instead of defilade as we did, and of all places to put a gun, behind that house. The Germans just flattened it, and they acted like, "What happened? What do they mean, throwing fire in on us? What do they want to play that way for?" You could just assume that their party was going to end pretty quick, because when we went up there they were firing away, having a big time throwing lead at the Germans, and when we got back there it was over.[26]

Jim Dowdall:

When we established that we were Americans and not Germans the commander was giving some o' the men hell for not shavin'. There was a stream at the bottom o' this glen, and they had captured a badly wounded German and made him as comfortable as possible, but he was dying. While Griff was talking to the officer about where our position was, and trying to get theirs and where their machine guns were set up, we were back talking with the privates. One was Scottish and the other English, and had an argument about who had the better whisky. They asked me—they knew I was Irish somehow—which is the better? I said the English have the better ale but the Scots the better whisky. By God, they were delighted at that Solomon's answer!

One night soon after, Dilks drove Mickey Smith on a mission to check out probably the same London Irish and was impressed.

We stopped and hid the jeep behind some old half blowed-out building and went up on foot, 'cause at night you couldn't use it much. They had about ten rounds of ammunition and no big gun support. All they had was bayonets. They were jest sittin' there playin' cards an' drinkin', figgerin' as soon as the Krauts hit 'em they were gonna get killed or captured.

Maybe the same building with the gun. Did we blow their cover when we sprinted across that field (in sight of the enemy as we suspected), and paused at the house before continuing on to the wadi? A certain derring-do that sometimes characterized our closest allies elicited a certain ancestral resentment in Delmar Griffith, who took the Welsh view, just as Dowdall took the Irish.

> Regiment was just hungry for information, and three or four of us got out there in no-man's-land and ended up where the British, the crazy devils, had put their guns on a mound instead of defilade, with a trench, and abandoned it. We were about to set up an OP on a little elevation when the Germans sent in the worst barrage I was ever in. We were down in the trench with shells and the dirt flying in and the smoke so thick you couldn't breathe. I was scared. I thought, "Well, this is it, I won't get outta this one." They were zeroed in, but none of us got hit. I had thoughts I never had before. I just sorta condemned the whole of mankind. I wasn't prayin', I was cussin'.
>
> I went one stretch of fifty or sixty hours without a wink of sleep. Finally had a chance and came back to the CP where I had a shallow hole. It was after dark when I threw my blanket in and crawled in, and when I finally woke up along toward noon they'd shelled the area. There was a new shell hole right next to me, and I didn't even hear it.

What little we knew or guessed of what was unfolding up the highway, I had scant heart and energy, and no inclination, to record when it was over, except, twelve days later: "Second Battalion was pushed too far ahead, got trapped and surrounded, part of them living in a cave. Before they got out Jerry smashed them. They had 200 men left. Three of our new men, Mountain, Sumey, and Fleischer, went out on a detail to them and haven't been heard of since. Captured, I hope."

The second day of the counterattack, February 17, a battalion of the Sixth Armored Infantry moved into the gap between our depleted Second and Third Battalions. Captain Felix Sparks withdrew the fourteen left from his E Company and four others from H Company down the highway to a rise of ground two hundred yards to the left, where they dug in. Again the Germans attacked with tanks and infantry, this time against the machine guns of G Company set up so lethally on a bluff above the Caves that soon an X of bodies marked the paths of their crossfire, and the survivors withdrew.

Nevertheless, a wedge two miles wide and a mile deep had been driven between the 157th and 179th into which General Mackensen threw forty FW-190s and Me-109 fighter planes. The Sixth Corps responded with seemingly overwhelming artillery and anti-aircraft, plus big naval gunfire from two cruisers offshore, and 1,100 tons of bombs.

Ordered to stop the 14th Army at the concertina wire, I Company at dusk was barraged and then attacked by German infantry. The guys cut them down at the wire, only to face the direct fire of a trio of tanks. The remaining Krauts crept around and harassed them all night, but they held the line.

At daybreak on the eighteenth, K and L Companies and the already battered 179th tried to push the line back up to our now-surrounded Second Battalion, whose supply routes were virtually cut off, but they ran into fresh Germans preparing to attack and were pushed back.

Food and water were so low that a single K ration was serving three men. With priority for the wounded of both sides in the Caves, the G.I.s were boiling and drinking water from a small stream that ran red with the blood of dead Germans lying in the draw.

As darkness approached, F Company was hit by machine-pistol fire and grenades outside the Caves. Up on the overlooking bluff, G and H Companies laid heavy fire on the attackers, and our 158th Field Artillery was called upon for a thirty-minute barrage on friend and foe alike. The attack withered, leaving the area strewn with dead and wounded Germans … and how many G.I.s? That night a supply route was finally forced through, and our drivers and carrying parties got up with water, rations and ammo and back with about a hundred wounded.

Three of the carriers were probably those new boys in the Platoon, Mountain, Sumey and Fleischer, who joined just before the landing. No one recalls their first names, only Bill Caird, who with George Mountain, a kid of about eighteen, took off from the rest area outside Naples, got drunk, and roared back singing "Lili Marlene"; Topkick Bill Sevey racked their asses for waking everybody up. A relief party to the Caves was being made up that afternoon, and Lieutenant Pullman got the word to supply three volunteers.

> Naturally I'm not going to pick three of my old hands but three of my new ones. I barely remember Mountain, a little small kid. I've always felt bad about that. Did I just say "You, you and you, they need some help up there," and deliver three bodies to somebody, knowing full well the situation, and the very little chance of them getting in and out? But looking back, I'd do it again the way I did.

Killed? Captured? We never again laid eyes on Mountain, Sumey and Fleischer—just Mountain, Sumey and Fleischer to us.

The next day, February 19, the fourth of the 14th Army's counterattack, Mark Clark and his Fifth Army officers conceded among themselves that the Second Battle of Cassino—the attempt to break the Winter Line by driving the Germans out of the ruins of the bombed monastery, upon which the strategy of Shingle was predicated—had failed. Three times that day the enemy attacked the Anzio Beachhead across the plain and down the Via Anziate to the concertina barbed wire and the remaining men of I Company behind it, and three times they were cut down. Their dead and wounded and ours, including most of I Company's officers, lay everywhere in the fields and on the road and over the wire.

There was one more try to come. Working by twos and threes down the draws and ditches on the twentieth, the German infantry built up a line closer and closer to the barbed-wire barrier, when out of the blue they were hit with a mass barrage of seventy-five British 25-pounder guns and decimated to a few moaning wounded. Their furious retaliation was five hours of shelling on I Company's position.

It was the final German attack on the Overpass and the day of my training buddy Gareth Dunleavy's exit from the war. After landing at Anzio with the rest of us, his 45th Cavalry Reconnaissance Troop manned various relief and reserve positions, and at least once he and I were probably not separated by more than a few hundred yards. Not until five days into the enemy offensive, however, was the Troop committed to action, when late that sunlit morning a half dozen Recon guys were sent in a jeep and an M-8 armored car up either Highway 7 or the intersecting "Bowling Alley" road parallel to the coast to check if any enemy tanks had moved up. They dug in during the night preparatory to supporting another attack. Corporal Francis Accavallo drove the jeep, with Dunleavy beside him. Dun recalled to me:

> We'd hardly started out when an RAF Lancaster bomber prematurely released a load that barely missed us. We cursed and drove perhaps another quarter of a mile when an 88 exploded low over the marshland to our right. Accavallo signaled for a turn-around, but it was too late. The driver of the M-8 panicked and froze. Accavallo braked to a stop and shouted to the M-8 crew to get out and crawl under. We jumped into the ditch alongside the jeep. A second airburst was closer. The tank's gunner had zeroed in on us. I turned myself into an earthworm, with my face and belly down.
>
> The third shell exploded over our heads. Accavallo grunted and cursed. Years later I learned he lost his right leg. An agonizing pain ripped through my lower back and belly. I remained conscious long enough to see an ambulance on the road above, the first I'd seen so close to the front line, and I was on a stretcher. They musta given me a helluva lot of morphine, because it was a rough ride back, hurt like hell, and I didn't finally black out until I was on the operating table at the 93rd Field Evacuation Hospital.

The Caves, by combat artist Mitchell Siporin (*Department of Defense*)

Sometime before dawn I woke up on a cot in a slit trench. Screams, moans, and curses came from a German paratroop sergeant at the other end of the darkened tent who died before sunrise. A nurse was sitting there with me and told me that for hours I'd been repeating in a loud voice, "Sherman said war was hell." Nightly detonations of our ack-ack overhead terrified me. I shook and sweated and imagined that shells meant to destroy German bombers would fall back on our tent, rip through the canvas and inflict new wounds on me.

I had thirty-six pieces of shrapnel all up and down my back, in my chest, buttocks, gut, right leg and left elbow, something like 120 stitches. They took a fairly large piece close to the backbone out from the front, and decided to leave another in my chest, the one that sets off the metal detector at the airport every time I fly.

The following day the Queen's Infantry of the British 56th suffered seventy-six casualties from butterfly bombs as they tried to fight through to relieve our Second Battalion and had to withdraw. The British First Division relieved our Third Battalion, which in six days had 324 casualties, about 50 percent. Three officers and sixty-eight men remained out of 165 in I Company.

On February 22 the remains of Second Battalion relieved by the Tommies fought through to join the remains in the Caves.

An artillery driver reported that along the Via Anziate "we saw a German bulldozer digging a trench for the German dead. There were several piles of bodies, with about 150 or

Captain Felix Sparks
(*Department of Defense*)

more in each pile. There were also many hundreds dead along the route we marched—killed by our artillery."[27]

That night the Krauts attacked again, captured an F Company platoon and H Company's crews and heavy mortars, and liberated German prisoners.

At two o'clock in the afternoon of February 23, as the remnants of our Second Battalion began their withdrawal from the Caves—the walking wounded and guys with trench foot dragging themselves along in the rear—the Germans opened up on the retreating column, as it filed through the draws and ditches, with savage and prolonged machine-gun fire. Most of the men of G and F Companies in the lead were able to crawl along on their bellies and make their way back to safety, but the handful that remained of E and H under Captain Sparks, under heavy fire from close range, were killed or captured. Of E Company, only Sparks got away with what was left of the Battalion; he was joined two days later by Sergeant Leon "Doc" Siehr, who had fought forty-eight hours with the British after the broken unit was relieved. Captain Peter Graffagnino and his medics refused to leave the Caves and were captured with their wounded.

By February 23 the German command knew they couldn't break the Beachhead. The 157th moved back into Division reserve to reorganize and train replacements. General Lucas was officially relieved of the Sixth Corps to his relief and replaced with his deputy, Lucian Truscott, the former commander of the Third Division who was, as Blumenson put it wryly, "unlike Patton, sufficiently junior in rank to be no threat to Clark."[28]

Of the 713 enlisted men and 38 officers of Second Battalion, 551 and 23 respectively had been killed, wounded or captured or were otherwise unaccounted for. The counter-attack cost the 45th about 400 killed, 1,000 missing in action and 2,000 wounded—a total of 3,400 men.

In the first month of the Beachhead the Division's casualties were calculated at 5,709 men. The Allied forces lost 2,000 killed, 8,500 missing and 8,500 wounded. Enemy losses gaining a 1,000-yard bulge of drained marsh were believed to be comparable. Division artillery fired 129,732 rounds.[29]

On February 29, perhaps because it was Leap Year, the Germans attacked again, this time on the Third Division front, but were out-gunned, manifestly weaker, and repulsed. On March 4 General Mackensen's 14th Army assumed the defensive.

Back in hospital with time on his hands, Jerry Waldron answered a letter from my father received just before he went on the OP:

> I lost my steadfast belief that I was immune to German steel, receiving a couple of "Whistling Willie" gifts in the shin and under the arm . . . The hospital has been wonderful, both in rest and treatment, and they are even going to let me carry two small pieces in my leg to prove that I have been hit (allowing shrapnel to remain if small enough is a common practice of this war).
>
> Joe is the life of the platoon, and I think, if he was a very quiet boy before Army days as he says, you will find a changed man. He is, as you know, a natural mimic, and he kids everyone. The only guys who ever get mad are the guys who can't take it, and since you can count them on your ears, you don't care about them. Joe says that

he likes to see other people react to his words as he knows they will—a sort of moulding of personalities which is a game with him. He works this successfully on me, so I know, but I also know how to manipulate him, so it's all even here.

We both think we are with the best gang of guys in the Army; maybe this is because we face death every day with them. Both of us have sunk into the monotony of war and so we have become, in many ways, the machines that the Army wished us to be in the first place. War is just what Sherman said it was except he left out too many adjectives.

Not until February 29, for the first time in three weeks, was I able to get back to my journal:

The new front proved to be the hottest fighting this Division has ever seen. Scores of times I thought my time was up in the last ten days. It was one long nightmarish Hell. We went through so many terrific barrages, patrols, sleepless nights, I can't recount them all. Only bright spot was our close association with the British, a wonderful nation. Second Battalion was pushed too far ahead, got trapped and surrounded, part of them living in a cave. Before they got out Jerry smashed them. They had 200 men left. [Little had we known how bad it was.] *For several days there were ten men left functioning in the I&R. All the rest were wounded, sick, missing, yellow, or truck drivers.*

Wounded were Mullenax, Locklear and the two newer replacements with them; Waldron, Dilks, Oman; Dowdall for the second time, grazed on the head by a butterfly bomb and back the next day, bandaged up—as he laughed—like a Minuteman. Missing in action were Mountain, Sumey and Fleischer. Mills and Zapiecki were still in hospital, and one or two others may have been sent back sick. No one was yellow.[30]

Over the lifetime since, I've been able to recall but scraps, vignettes, reactive flashes such as the house we were shelled out of when the jolly Limey brass came parading up the drive, and the weird patrol with Griff and Jimmy to the London Irish, sweating out the clocklike shelling in their gully.

More shadowy yet is that black, bedlam night, bouncing through shell holes up to the line beyond the Overpass on some mission, flares bursting overhead, rifle and machine-gun fire all around, tanks rumbling, guys wounded, shells coming in and going over, and hightailing out like crazy through shell holes, mud and ruts with nothing but blackout lights that illuminated nothing.

Dimmer still, the afternoon a couple of us were wound up so tight that we hit the dirt at the sudden SSSHHHHH of an incoming shell, only to see when we picked ourselves up that it was a guy dragging brush to camouflage his dugout.

The rest, along with all those terrific barrages, patrols and sleepless nights that I couldn't recount, are buried beyond retrieval in the debris of war in my head. Why mine and not Zapiecki's and Mills's and Pullman's and Dilks's and Dowdall's and Waldron's and Caird's and the rest, I cannot fathom, for surely I've no more reason to repress those memories than they, or do I?

Especially our beloved Pullman, hospitalized with battle fatigue. In Kansas City thirty-four years later he and I talked about it.

Jack:

I wore out. Got scared. Took it too personally. I just got weak. I couldn't stand what was happening to my friends, and couldn't stand not doing my own job. I'd had it, and my breaking point was less than you guys.

They gave me some pills and put me to sleep for twenty-four hours, then to the 105th Station Hospital for a couple of weeks, then the 300th General in Naples. I was too personalized with you guys. Raised the same way you were, that you're supposed to do what you have to do in this world, you take care of your own and they'll take care of you, and that's not always possible, so you have some conflict when you don't do it. I feel that I let everybody down, and yet I know that it was an impossible situation. We were all lucky to get out of it alive, or at least not captured.

I think I deliberately got into hazardous situations, trying to prove something to myself, maybe not consciously all the time but maybe the same attitude that attracted me into the Army in the first place. That's why I say that these things are going to turn out good for everybody that participated in them. I think that you're looking at yourself also through our mutual experience, reassessing Joe Garland in relation to these things at the same time, because anything that I did affected you, and what you did affected me.

Joe:

I was never promoted, and I had this big thing about not sucking ass for it. In fact I didn't want the responsibility, because I'd have to stick my neck out, lead and not follow, and it would be riskier. Maybe I presented myself as smart enough, but how reliable? Sort of a cut-up. If I became a squad leader and was given a mission I'd have to try and do it, if on a patrol be up front, if walking into a minefield or ambush the one to go first. I guess I worked things out to follow orders, try to pull my part as a dogface, not do anything to bring attention to myself or get in a situation where it was really put to me.

We looked to you to protect our interests. We'd do our job, but you were the only buffer we had between the legitimate mission and the horseshit one.

Jack:

I worked very hard to avoid horseshit missions, and this is why the Army is set up this way, that you don't become too personal with your men. And yet if we hadn't had this relationship we wouldn't have been as effective as we were. So when I felt I wasn't doing my job anymore, I temporarily couldn't handle it.

That's probably where Griff, when he took over from me, was better, a little older and a little more dispassionate, essentially the difference between us, by temperament not an outgoing person. I imagine he was hurt underneath a lot more than we think. Always a little too uptight and a little too efficient, hasn't had a way to vent his emotions. But it got to everybody sooner or later, even to him.

My closing entry on the last page of my first journal notebook, February 29, 1944:

> One day I floundered through the clinging mud
> And came upon a strange and trampled path.
> With eager haste I plunged into the flood
> Of souls there streaming with a fiery wrath.
> A gripping band of flame soon seared my brain;
> My tortured soul in giddy swirls was swept.
> I knew not whence or where that giddy train
> Was tending, but I felt my soul had leapt
> The wall that parts the shadow from the light.
> I had a vision through the darkest cloud;
> A veil was lifted from my searching sight.
> My fate lies with the dusty, common crowd,
> For I must follow where it madly runs
> And save myself by standing by its guns.

Heil Hitler (*U.S. Army*)

(*Courtesy of Norman Maffei,* 158th Field Artillery. *Used with permission.*)

❖❖❖ 7 ❖❖❖

BLOOD-RED,
BLOOD-FED POPPIES

Anzio
February–May 1944

IF, AS I GASPED, it had been a nightmarish hell for the handful of us in the I&R still tottering about when the remains of the Second Battalion limped back from the Caves, what was
it for the guys entrenched in the path of Hitler's 14th Army?

Our 157th Infantry Regiment was taken off the line on the twenty-third of February
and shifted to the 45th's right-hand sector behind our 180th, east of the Padiglione Woods
where the First Armored Division was dug in. It was not so much for a rest as because practically half the Regiment had been knocked out staving off the full force of the German
counterattack. Heavy transfusions of jittery replacements were needed, and there was scant
time or inclination to make them feel at home.

We lost our bitch Boots in the move, and for her there was no replacement . . . until a
couple of weeks and a few miles later we encountered her trotting down a road.

With the leader who cared too much gone perhaps forever, our fate passed to Staff
Sergeant Delmar Griffith, as square-jawed in his devotion to duty and abhorrence of tom-
foolery as Jack Pullman was laid-back on the matter of living to live another day and in his
disdain for damnfoolery. Though he was among the youngest, Jack's coolness covered the
caution of a Scout leader (we were, after all, scouts), while behind the twangy schoolmas-
terishness of Griff, our oldest, lurked the gambling instinct of the gold prospector that was
above and beyond the call of our duty if not his, as he saw it anyway.

Of the new boss I reflected in my journal that

*he hasn't missed a day of action, has terrific wiry stamina for a man in his early thirties, is a fanatical
devotee of the West and outdoor life, filled with wanderlust. Tops on maps and knows the technique of
intelligence work to a T. His glaring fault is his inability to master men, to understand them and to*

209

completely appraise them, all of which Pullman had. The result is that work is not apportioned out
fairly, and his favoritism is obvious to everyone and is responsible for much of the jealousy and petti-
ness, all the more a paradox as he is vastly informed and really an intellectual.

Respite. What craved the inner man, or boy? Home. Ma and Pa. Just to let down and
feel alone in the middle of a war on Leap Year's Day:

I haven't found a single spare moment to write in the last fortnight, but I have a
breather now, and will try to catch up … When I sit down to write I very frequently
find that I can't convey to you my deepest thoughts. I have to discuss some of the
more superficial aspects of my life, and I know that I often miss the mark in telling
you what you want to know. Many of the details of "everyday life" I can't or won't tell
you. Life isn't "everyday" here anyway. When we're not working we're trying to rest,
sitting around, bulling, cleaning up, writing letters. All of us who smoke, smoke furi-
ously, almost with a vengeance. You will find me, however, a changed man when I
return—much more of an extrovert, more patient, more responsible—these my
virtues. More frank (perhaps more bellicose), a tougher outlook on life, worse table
manners (ever eat steak with a spoon?). You're always in my thoughts—even when
I don't seem to express myself fully.

A couple of days later:

Today is a lovely day, the first after many of rain and mud. Everywhere are spread
blankets, shelter-halves, clothing, shoes and whatnot, to take advantage of the
warmth. Spring is on the way. Many little buds, like crocuses, poking up through the
ground. Ernie Fried, one of our drivers, is standing next to me, in a pristine state on
a raincoat, taking a bath from a helmetful of cold water. I did the same two days ago.
The war seems more distant. Aside from the roar of planes and the noise of artillery,
I might be out on the farm. It's a rare day when one gets that feeling. Great to see the
bombers going over the enemy lines today, wave after wave of them.

Three more days and our reconstituted Second Battalion took over the holes of its
counterpart of the 180th. The front sagged now toward the Padiglione Woods in a stalemated bulge five miles wide and a little more than two deep, marking the last gasp of the German
counterattack. Quiet enough for breaking in the replacements, poor devils, and for me to
read James Thurber's *My World and Welcome to It* and Wordsworth's poems on his visit to Italy.
    As for the opposition, a 'Bird took an unmailed letter from a German's body and had
it translated.[1]

8 March 1944
My dear Brother Fritz:
    Just a quick letter as I do not have much time. I would write more if it were not
for the fact that these damned English and Americans, and especially the 45th
American Division, have had us in an uncomfortable spot.

The pigs attacked us rather suddenly. We had rather heavy losses and unfortunately were not able to get ourselves together in time.

I hope to receive the Iron Cross very soon, as I am on rather good terms with my lieutenant.

How is everything with you? These damned American dogs are bombing us more and more every day. I hope we will be able to defend ourselves from these devils, these asses, these fools—the Russians. Unfortunately, I have no envelope for this letter so I can send it to you but I will make or get one someway.

For a few days a damned American with a Browning automatic has been shooting at us. And what do you know—he spoke German. At first I thought he was a brother—a German soldier, but I was soon to be very much disappointed. He has already killed five of our men. If we ever get a hold of this pig we will tear him to pieces.

Our beloved Fuehrer sent us a telegram, telling us that we must have no fear about an American-English invasion—as our navy is too strong for them.

Well, I must close now as I have no more paper left.

> With much luck
> Heil Hitler!
> Hans

Pat "Let's Get Foolish" Farley was back with his Purple Heart to take over from Pullman as platoon leader again, his machine-gun-nicked knee on the mend. Jerry too, with a couple of small shell fragments in his leg and another removed from his armpit. And Zapiecki, up on the line again from the hospital in Naples, and "I'm hearin' bagpipes one morning at dawn and thinkin' the war's over! But it was just some Limey outfit movin' up to the front." And Jimmy Dowdall, with that broad grin, "there were the guys gatherin' around Andy in a circle to hear his stories when he came back, bendin' forrard eagerly, and every time he got to the funny part, they'd all straighten up laffin', like a sunflower openin' up."

And of course Mills: "This Red Cross girl asks Dilks 'What's yer name?' That was the worst thing in the world to ask him. He says to her, 'What the hell do you care? You ain't ever gonna see me again.' I says, 'Dilks, be a little civil if you don't want the doughnuts.' 'I don't want the doughnuts,' he says. 'Every time we take the doughnuts it means we're goin' back up an' half the guys gets killed.'"

And the lightly wounded Dilks, having drawn more than his driver's share of the Padiglione crossroads run, perhaps because he kept surviving it. "The Krauts would lay a barrage on that intersection every half hour, and if you were there and caught in the middle of it you were gone. When we were takin' water and supplies up to the OPs I'd look at my watch, and if it's 25 or 26 after I'd just pull over a few hundred yards down the road, and sure enough here it'd come—BLOOM, BLOOM, BLOOM—tear holes in the road, then after the last one, wait another five minutes and take off, an' yer all right."

We moved into possibly the very farmhouse Jimmy Dowdall thought the Germans didn't bother to shell because it was too obviously perfect for an OP. For a case of frazzled nerves, Dom Trubia was—relatively speaking—in forward observer's heaven.

The OP was upstairs, but the stairway was on the outside and exposed to the Germans on three sides. So we chopped a hole in the floor and down in the kitchen set up a table with a chair on top to climb up from, then dug up the kitchen floor on the wall side facing the rear for our dugout. It was like a second home to me.

You took a turn up there, Joe, and I came awful close to gettin' mad at ya. We had that beautiful captured scope and picked up a German dress parade. I didn't report it and you were put out with me that I didn't fire on 'em, and I tried to tell you they were out o' range. You called the CP and told 'em you had a fire mission and called for chemical mortars. Jeez, they gave you a round o' smoke, and holy Moses, it was so flat there it looked like it landed right in front of us. So then you had a 105 lay in a smoke, and it looked the same. Then I says, "Call for the Long Toms!" They had a range o' fifteen miles. They laid a round o' smoke and it was about halfway between us and this dress parade. That was the end o' your fire mission!

One night a Tiger tank rolled up and PISHEEOOO, he'd put 'em over my head and they'd fall in the CP. I tried my best to pick up that guy but couldn't. Captain Edwards called from the CP an' hollered, "Can you find that gun?" I said, "Which gun?" PISHEEOOO! One went over us, and POW, over the phone I could hear it hit. I says, "You mean that one?" He says, "Yer goddam right I mean that one!" I never did find that tank. He'd roll up behind a knoll and start firing, and I'd lay in some stuff over the knoll, but very seldom would he quit. Must be I wasn't hittin' too close to him.

On the fifteenth of March, back on the Winter Line, the Third Battle of Cassino was mounted to dislodge the Germans from the monastery that commanded the coastal lowland and bottled up the southern front in the mountains. Two days later I journaled cautious vent to the bottled-up emotions on our bottled-up Beachhead.

Our white phosphorus shells zero in around the enemy-held farmhouse. From aloft in the western rim of the Appenines beyond, the Germans keep track of our every pee. (*Department of Defense*)

A Flying Fortress (B-17) bomber drops a load. Ack-ack (anti-aircraft) bursts up ahead. (*U.S. Air Forces*)

News is beginning to look somewhat more optimistic. The Russians have gained nearly all of Russia back. They are 27 miles from the Dniester, having cut the last German railroad escape route in the Ukraine and are ten miles from Nikolaev. The Finns have til midnight tomorrow to accept or reject Russian peace terms. Three fourths of Cassino is in our hands, most of the fighting having a focus on Highway 6 to Rome.

Been reading old editorial comment on the Beachhead. Consensus seems to agree that we lost our initial advantage by not throwing in sufficient troops. Undoubtedly it was abortive, probably serving as bread and fishes for the clamoring newshawks. Obvious to us that all was miscalculated and badly planned. Morale has been low, mostly issuing from the feeling that we're victims of the bigwigs' incompetence. [One rumor had a shipload of chaplains' pianos misdirected to Anzio instead of ammunition.] *We pray for Cassino to break. Bets are even being made that the Russians reach Berlin before we reach Rome. Much talk of us fighting for an "ungrateful America."*

The third attempt to topple the Germans from Monte Cassino had failed by March 23, and a few brave robins up from the south provided us the only relief from that quarter. Homeward I grunted: "I'm getting mighty sick of this war, and I've seen all I want to of Italy or any other country."

And to Pete Sax in Harvard Medical School: "I saw a Fortress shot down the other day. How does that poem about the Phoenix go? One of the saddest and most majestic sights I've ever seen." Did the crew parachute? I don't recall. As spring touched this foreign land after the bleakest winter of our lives, contrasts yanked us this way and that, as I wrote home three days after the equinox.

At night the frogs set up a great croaking just as they do at Lincoln [a country town west of Boston where our family had a weekend cabin in the woods] in the spring, and there are a few small trees here and there that are bursting into blossom. So I guess Italy has an early spring after all, in spite of the snow still in the higher mountains.

Here nothing is more appreciated by the senses than a rare sunset, a warm day, a few spring flowers, or even a lull in the almost omnipresent din. One does not feel completely happy at these moments, but one does get wistfully nostalgic; complete happinesses in war seem few and far between. These interludes, more than anything else, are aids to perspective. Often enough, they give us the courage to see through and beyond the haze and smoke of battle, and the insight to forget ourselves as often as we can.

Over here we can never give ourselves completely to the beauties of something. There is always the tendency to compare them to even rarer beauties at home. Perhaps now you can understand my mixed feelings as I was standing, in comparative quiet, contemplating a gorgeous sunset, to have the whole scene marred by a burst of machine-gun fire on the lines.

Ah, the contemplation of a gorgeous sunset, the life of a trapped mole, or death ever-present at my elbow inspired or drove me to write:

MONOLOGUE IN A HOLE

That's it—stretch out your feet and shift your back a bit.
That lump of dirt hits the bottom of the spine.
Well, this is a little better. Except for those damn Long Toms.
Every time they fire a lot of dirt from on top of the logs
comes down and hits you in the eye. Christ, the noise
knocks your ears in down here—five feet under ground.
Must be the earth magnifies the vibration. Seismographic.

Hell, it seems I talk to myself more and more as the weeks
stretch into months on this sunny summer resort they call Anzio.
Particularly on nights like this when I'm all alone in the hole.
Jerry's off somewhere out there in the blackness on patrol.
Be more lonely than ever if he doesn't come back.

Every once in a while a shell floats in out of nowhere
and tosses a lot of mud and warm steel around—
close enough to the ground so it would feel uncomfortable in your
belly or your back or even in your head.
And what good's a helmet? Shave and wash in it.
Sometimes scratch the ground with it when you're in a hurry

to get inside Mother Earth instead of on her.
You can turn it upside down when you're loafing around
and sit on it, too. It fits the fanny, but you can't sit there
too long or the edges will start to cut off the circulation
and paralyze the butt.

I suppose it's safe enough here if nothing lands on top.
Damn little timber on this summer resort—at least where we are.
All we have here is brush, although across the field there's a
pine grove—where the First Armored is. They got better
protection—dug their holes right under their tanks. And if a
shell comes in over there it bursts in the trees—usually.
But a tree burst can get a lot of men when they're outside eating
or playing ball under the trees. Then the fragments come down
in a hail—all over the place.

While ago we took over that dugout the 155 howitzer boys had used
up the line. They had to build it mostly above ground.
If you dug down more than six inches or so you hit water.
But the walls were thick—they used shell cases filled with dirt.
And there must have been three feet of mud and crap on the top.
They said an 88 or something came in one day and landed square
on the roof. The man inside was bounced around and stunned, but a
feller standing outside was killed. Most holes aren't that good, though.

Kinda interesting the way things happen like that. Like that
deal a while back. Just a few days ago—or was it longer?
Just like now, we were back from the line for a day or two's rest.
We'd had supper and in a while it would be twilight.
So we were standing around with our messkits, shooting the breeze
and kidding and waiting for perhaps a little color in the sunset.
And we just happened to be looking out across that wide field
over in the direction of the pine grove where the First Armored is.

Along the edge of the grove they have a landing strip for the
artillery observation planes—the "division bombers."
Little flimsy bugs, they take their chance and putt-putt low,
almost in a stall, over the Kraut positions to see what there is to
knock the Hell out of. And when they find something they get the
guns on it by radio. Before long they got it plastered because
they're hanging right over it in a balcony seat.

Pretty soon twilight began to creep in, and while we were looking
that way for the sunset a division bomber came in and started to
circle. Getting ready to land. He wasn't so high. They never are.
Well, all of a sudden there was a crack and a burst of flame,
right where he was, and he disappeared.
Then there was a puff of smoke that drifted away with the slow
breeze, and pieces were falling towards the ground.
That's all there was to it.

Back a half-mile or so a battery of 240 millimeter howitzers had set up
and fired their first round to zero in on the targets for the night.
And it hit the little bug of a Division bomber.
Guess those shells weigh a hundred pounds or more.
Nothing left of the pilot, poor guy.

Sure, we were surprised and felt bad, and we talked and argued about it some
to try and get straight in our minds what happened so we could write
home about it later. But we didn't bother much about it. Hell,
there wasn't much use in wondering about that when a shell might
come singing in right then and get us all
while we were standing there wondering.
So we went into one of the holes and started a pinochle game.

Maybe if you just edge over a little to the right you'll miss that
damn bump of dirt. Goddammit, you did it again. You brush against
the side, and you get a peck of dirt down your neck every
time. One more butt and then get to sleep before some damn fool
pokes his head in here and wants you to go off on another damn
fool patrol. Just roll that field jacket a bit tighter under your
head, and maybe it'll be more comfortable.
And, for God's sake, stop talking to yourself.[2]

The Anzio dugout was a primitive simplification of the *abri* invented by the French in
World War I, a cave dug in the side of a trench for protection from gunfire. Now, as the
stalemate settled in, both sides burrowed to the extent possible before hitting the shallow
water table of the filled Pontine marsh. Greater depth was achieved on the slightly higher
ground. Defensive positions up on the line tended to follow the limited defilade afforded
by gullies and the embankments along roads and canals, principally the Mussolini Canal.
Foxholes merged into the more sociable but vulnerable trenches in which a few million of
our parents' generation had died, with occasional crude dugouts covered, for some pretext
of protection against a direct hit, with whatever limited roofing material could be foraged
under front-line conditions.

In a barrage Hank Mills had an admittedly "uncanny habit of jumpin' in somebody else's hole. Emmett Oman had a helluva hole he beat me to one day in a barrage, and I went in on top of him. He raised hell, and I said, 'What are ya bitchin' about? If it woulda got a direct hit, it woulda been me instead o' you.'"

When we were back at the CP with more freedom to move around by day and more access to building materials and other amenities, dugouts assumed thick roofs and even an air of hospitable coziness that was descended into by stooping down an earthen step or two and through an L-shaped entry trench to minimize vulnerability to wayward shell fragments. Mickey Smith hollowed out such an *abri* and wrote Edie that "I am a cave man again … Have electric light. And when it rains I also have running water." Likewise the burrow of my crew leader at the time, Corporal Dick Beech. As I wrote back to the States:

> It's a model home for the up-to-date dogface, about five by seven, three feet underground, covered with shell cases and around three feet of dirt. There are shelter halves as tapestries for the sides and branches and cardboards on the floor. *Esquire* girls adorn the walls, there is a box at the end for a shelf, and electric light hooked up to the jeep battery. Four of us—Dick, Bob Coleman, Jim Buckley and myself usually sit in here in the evening, play cribbage, make coffee (as Ernie Pyle describes in his column). A pretty good rest when we're off.

It was about this time that a couple of casualty replacements with a similar ring to their names but near-opposites in personality, Bob Coleman and Bill Belleman, had joined the Platoon. Bob was a sharp, good-looking guy from a big family in the northeast Pennsylvania town of Avoca, where his father worked in the coal mines and on the railroad. Married to his high-school sweetheart, Veronica Snopkoski, he was a tool and die trainee with a steel company in New Jersey when he was drafted. With I&R training, able and straight talking, appraising of gaze, he came across confident verging on cocky. We hit it off and for a time "roomed" together below ground, played cribbage, bullshitted and horsed around, perhaps when Waldron was out on an OP and we were back from the line.

Then on some damnfool kick during one of the periodic daytime shellings of the CP when we all dashed for the nearest dugout, Bob casually strolled around the area amidst the din and flying shell fragments as if walking on water and when it was over descended into our hole and called me chicken for taking cover. I fired back that he was a goddam fool, to which he countered—with surprising resignation for a guy just entering combat—that if the shell has your name on it, it has your number.

"A pretty good egg when he hit the outfit," I noted. "Knew his stuff pretty well, was a willing worker, had plenty of guts. Recently he's changed—become conceited and foolhardy. Thinks he's a candidate for corporal, and maybe he is, but Griff's favoritism reeks. Of course Bob has good qualities. He wants responsibility, and more power to him. He's a good observer. But his 'courage' borders on foolhardiness. I'm suspicious of his judgment and even more so of his ambition."

I was sort of bucking for corporal myself, thinking I was in pretty good with Griff, and resented the competition from this newly cast Ironhead over whom I had seniority. As for

"Living conditions at the front during the latter part of the Anzio campaign," wrote the caption writer who clearly wasn't there, "were much improved as the men protected their fox holes with sandbags, tarpaulins and camouflaged roofs. Fighting was light and living was leisurely, disturbed only by sporadic shelling and bombing." What bull. (*From* Anzio Beachhead, *1947. Department of Defense*)

ambition up on the front—for what? A posthumous medal? Realization that I wasn't even in the running set me to some soul-searching and conveyed more about me than about Bob. I journaled:

The corporal's rating apparently is between Jerry and Coleman. I feel as though perhaps I hadn't completely fulfilled my job here, to have a newer man rated ahead of me. I may not have made the close friends I should have, and my college is against me, too. As usual, I can't resist the barbed remark, and probably never will. I've sucked no ass, have stuck to my principles as best I could. If I've adhered to my hole sometimes, it's because I know there's no brave man when it's not necessary to expose oneself to artillery. I've done my job pretty well. If I can look the boys every one in the eye, what care I for the rating?

Later:

There's a certain distaste for Harvard men in the Army. [You don't say!] In college they taught me how to be a Harvard man. Now I've learned (I hope) how NOT to be one!

By contrast, lanky Bill Belleman, with his broad and ready grin, and I discovered that we brought out the ludicrous in each other and our circumstances in general with stand-up comic gigs for the amusement of the idle like an Amos 'n' Andy radio comedy routine and low burlesques such as belching contests stoked by the chow—that sort of slapstick. I decided he was "full of the small town jargon, adores the girls in a back-seat (of the car) way and fancies himself quite the dude. Has a wonderful vaudeville sense of humor, keeps us in tears and eats like a sloth. Partly because Bill's so good-humored and lackadaisical, Griff piles details thick and fast on him, hasn't much confidence in him because he's never given him responsibility."

On his urging I wrote a letter to a girl named Helen Bryan with whom he grew up in Salem, New Jersey, one of the two daughters of the Reverend Alison R. Bryan, the Presbyterian minister there. Bill represented her as a very bright, very funny, tomboyish and athletic girl of eighteen who'd roughhoused with his gang, played hide-and-seek among the vaults in the cemetery next to the pastorage, and joined them in throwing stones at passing boxcars in the railroad yard and shooting rats in the town dump with a .22.

To my surprise I received a timely reply from Miss Bryan, who to my fascination was born and raised for six years in Miraj, India, where her father had been a missionary and met and married her mother, a Scottish mission teacher from Edinburgh. One exchange led to another. How beguiling that she'd played under the eye of her *ayah*, or nurse, in the grove of banyan trees behind the mission and learned to swing from limb to limb with the friendly tribe of monkeys that made it their home, hence her guardian's nickname for her, "Little Monkey," or "Monk" to the wide-eyed Salem boys to whom she related the magical stories of her childhood on the other side of the planet!

Smiling Bill Belleman
(*Courtesy of Dominick M. Trubia*)

From Penn Hall, a Pennsylvania boarding school where she was preparing in the fall to enter Sarah Lawrence College for women in Bronxville, a northern suburb of Manhattan, "Monk" wrote her parents (her father was now an Army chaplain) early in May: "I had a letter from Bill Belleman the other day. He seems to have changed a great deal … much more serious. He's on the Anzio beachhead. A friend of his wrote me a wonderful letter a couple of weeks ago. I couldn't imagine who it was from until Bill told me. He's had three years at Harvard. English major and on the crew."

With unaccustomed *élan* I reported home on the eighth of May: "One of the boys gave me the address of a gal who's at Penn Hall in P.A. She wrote back and sounds like a neat number, so I'm going to keep up the correspondence and see what comes of it."

During the recent years of my adolescence there was a girl next door, but she was too next-door. There was one down the street, but she was too sexy and scared hell outta me. There was one with a funny last name, but Pa made fun of it. The one I was really crazy about went off to college and took chemistry, the very course and source of my academic downfall.

Now here was a girl (after a while we exchanged snapshots) an ocean and a war away I'd never even laid eyes on, and she had me in goosebumps.

⁂

We'd taken plenty of shelling in that CP to the east of the Padiglione Woods day and night through March and the first two weeks of April. Some was intended for us, some for the 105s and a battery of 155s dug in not far in our rear that landed short on us. The chance of a sudden barrage or air raid gave the bunched-up chow line the jitters. Dilks had a mock feud with the cooks, "who for some reason or other when I come through always gave me the lousiest piece o' meat, or I imagined they did. Once I hollered 'Luftwaffe!' and the guy threw his ladle down and headed for his hole, and I just walked over and picked out the best piece."

These chow-line antics narrowly missed coming to a negative conclusion the night the kitchen took a hit. According to Trubia "at breakfast time nobody hollered or blew any whistles, and Dilks headed down for chow as somebody was coming up and told him a shell blew up the kitchen. He starts laffin' and asks how many cooks got killed? The guy says nobody, they hadn't begun yet, and he says, 'Them sonsabitchin' Germans!'"

Another night something hit the supply tent and atomized the souvenir burp gun I thought I could strip and mail home in pieces. Yeah, sure.

Of course there were the rare dawn fogs of early spring when we enemies climbed out of Mother Earth and stretched and took a pee and brushed the teeth and drank in the cool fresh air, except that the fog might lift, just like that, leaving you out there as if naked in plain view of each other. Then what a run for cover!

On March 24, the day the 157th returned to action in relief of the 30th Regiment of the Third Division northeast of Padiglione, Corporal George Sylvester Viereck, Jr., the younger son of the Nazi propagandist and a member of the Platoon in the States who before going overseas was transferred to the Second Battalion intelligence section as an interrogator of enemy prisoners, was killed by mortar fire. His father, the avowed German agent, was in prison for violation of the Foreign Agents Registration Act. A buddy, Corporal Allen Bedard, interviewed by Flint Whitlock, remembers that young George "loved to play chess, and could debate on any subject . . . he looked like Sad Sack. Otherwise, he was a very conscientious soldier." That day, Bedard recalls:

> One of the soldiers yelled out that he had been hit. I went up and saw he had caught a piece of shrapnel. It just missed a vein but shattered his leg. While I was attending to him, George ran back to the CP and got a couple of guys with a litter and came back to where I was. We got this fellow on the litter and the four of us carried him. On the way back . . . the Germans lobbed in a couple of mortar shells. George got hit with a fragment across the temple. He died in our arms; he just bled to death. He kept asking us, "Please help me, please help me." There wasn't a thing we could do for him.[3]

Some who were in the Caves during the counterattack remember Viereck shouting to the Germans from one of the entrances. Frank Merchant, who'd recruited him to the I&R, was told by an eyewitness that "he called to the Germans in German and brought them closer, and his outfit gunned down a lot of them. I think this got them out of it for a while." Another version has it that he persuaded some to climb from their holes and surrender. He was in the small band that got out.

George Viereck's older brother Peter, in the Army in North Africa, would resume his career as a historian and poet after the war, winning the Pulitzer Prize for poetry in 1949 when he was thirty-three. Upon learning of George's death, he wrote an Elegy, to which he added a brief introduction fifty years later.[4]

> The word "Vale" (Latin for "farewell") was used on Roman tombstones. *"Ave atque vale"* is, of course, the phrase immortalized by Catullus in his elegy to his brother, killed fighting for Rome in an older war than mine. As a sergeant in the U.S. Army's African campaign in Tunis 1944, I was among the Roman tombstones in the ruins of Carthage when I heard the news that my brother was killed by a German bullet at the Anzio beachhead, near Rome. He and I had met last at Times Square, New York.

1. *"VALE"* FROM CARTHAGE
    (*for my brother, G.S.V. Jr., 1918–44,*
    killed fighting the Nazis)

I, now at Carthage. He, shot dead at Rome.
Shipmates last May. "And what if one of us,"
I asked last May, in fun, in gentleness,
"Wears doom, like dungarees, and doesn't know?"
He laughed, *"Not see Times Square again?"* The foam,
Feathering across that deck a year ago,

Swept those five words—like seeds—beyond the seas
    Into his future. There they grew like trees;
    And as he passed them there next spring, they laid
    Upon his road of fire their sudden shade.
Though he had always scraped his mess-kit pure
And scrubbed redeemingly his barracks floor,
Though all his buttons glowed their ritual-hymn
Like cloudless moons to intercede for him,
No furlough fluttered from the sky. He will
Not see Times Square—he will not see—he will
Not see Times
        change; at Carthage (while my friend,
Living those words at Rome, screamed in the end)
I saw an ancient Roman's tomb and read
"Vale" in stone. Here two wars mix their dead:
    Roman, my shipmate's dream walks hand in hand
    With yours tonight ("New York again" and "Rome"),
    Like widowed sisters bearing water home
    On tired heads through hot Tunisian sand
    In good cool urns, and says, "I understand."
Roman, you'll see your Forum Square no more.
What's left but this to say of any war?

                    (Carthage, 1944)

By the end of March days of warm sunshine were bringing out the first leaves. We saw magazine photos of Mount Vesuvius billowing smoke and belching forth ash and rock in contrast to the familiar wisps we had taken for granted when back in the environs of Naples. "I am rather enthusiastic," I wrote home, dreaming of peace, "about trying my hand at journalism, which in its higher aspects appeals to me immensely. It is hard to make plans for the future here."

Came spring even to Anzio, and with the Regiment again on the line, though the stalemated front was relatively quiet, we were back in the OP business, and Corporal Zapiecki was back in his ongoing sparring match with Sergeant Griffith, who regarded him as slightly insubordinate anyway.

Griff is taking me out to set up an OP one night, with Danny Boone driving, and he says, "Yah, we go right up here, and over here." Then—"HALT!" I says. "Wait a minute. Now I'M gonna go check." You know what it said on that sign? *ACHTUNG! MINE!* And Griff says, "We must be in the right place." And Boone says, "OK you guys, get off. I'll back up the jeep." "Like hell," I says. "You drove us up here. All you have to do is drive us back in them same ruts and we'll be OK!" And he drove us out of that field, and there was no OP that night.

The only Ironhead group photo on Anzio, photographer unknown. Mickey Smith, drivers Hank Johnson, Ernie Fried and Vern Dilks, Walter Wolff, Bill Belleman and Les Gerencer crouching in front. Mascot dog Boots somewhere around. (*Courtesy of Edith Smith*)

An OP that did materialize, and on as tenuous ground in the middle of a field near Padiglione, proved to be another test of reverse Teutonic psychology. Mickey Smith with Dowdall, O'Keefe and a couple of others moved into a high wooden shack sheathed with cornstalks, with attached pens for the sheep. The crew, or perhaps a bunch from the Third Division before them, rigged a platform high up against the forward wall where they could sit or stand and spy out unfriendly activity through peepholes.

A few sheep wandered forlornly around the place. O'Keefe dug down with his trench shovel eight or ten inches into the generations of hard-packed manure (hence The Sheepshit OP) that served as the almost smooth floor inside, and from this in-house foxhole gazed out through the door at the moonlight and up at the rats scurrying along the tie beams of the roof. During work hours much of our time on the platform was occupied with spotting and getting compass azimuths on German tanks firing, then working out the coordinates on the map for our 105 artillery crews to occupy themselves with counterbattery fire directed against enemy gun emplacements.

On March 28 Dowdall was up on the platform.

> I was countin' the shells the Germans were throwin' into this brick mill a couple hundred yards down from us, perfect for an OP but nobody in it, while we had nothin' but a few cornstalks between us an' them. We really got away with murder there. I called out to Mickey about seein' a Kraut tryin' to deepen his foxhole with his helmet and an ambulance with a cross on it behind him, an' somebody took another look: "Hey, they're unloadin' a machine gun!"

Just then a shell hit outside the shed somewhere. A stray fragment ripped through the wall and grazed the tip of Jimmy's left boot. He gave a yell and jumped off the platform to the floor and crumpled. His buddies rushed to him. Two toes were gone. Three hits since Sicily. Three Purple Hearts and you're out! They got him back to the Medics, who triaged him back and back and back all the way back to the USA and civilian life, where the pro-

foundly Irish Catholic Mister Dowdall, our lay Father, took to the road, somewhat awk-
wardly at first, and dropped in on all the families of his buddies he could find in the East,
including the Garlands and the Waldrons, to tell them what fine lads they had and bring
them the latest word, first-hand. Summing it up:

> The families I visited didn't have the tightness to lean on that we had in the Platoon.
> The thing that kept us fairly sane was a sense o' humor. We all understand how
> much Andy meant to us when a laugh was needed, but that didn't make him mean
> any more to us than the other guy.
>
> The Army experience was especially precious to me, the friendships, the anxi-
> eties about the future, about getting killed, that made the friends so dear. There were
> an awful lot o' young men in the Army like me who had gone through the
> Depression. I had feelings o' loneliness coming to the U.S., then leaving my family
> for the Army, an' then the breaks o' friendships made in this 'n' that camp. The war
> was not the high point o' my life. That was gettin' back safe 'n' sound to my family.
> If I were married it would be my wedding day, or the birth of the first child. But it
> was the high point in terms of summoning all my resources. The excitement was
> caused by the sense of danger. I was afraid, an' the guys I was with were afraid with
> me, but their fear made mine more bearable. That comradeship in the presence of
> danger was particularly precious to me.
>
> I never said the odds were gettin' lower an' lower. I was happy in that frame of
> mind that when it was over, it's over with an' let's get goin'. I never figured, "Oh you
> were lucky that time; well, wait 'til the next time."

I was temporarily with Nye's crew when we relieved Mickey's, and I took over O'Keefe's
geometrically carved hole (he had the instincts of a mining engineer). My first night I was
awakened by the tiny feet of a smallish rat scuttling nervously across my face, reconnoitering, no doubt, such a motionless body in such a neat grave.

A road crossing a half a mile or so behind us and to our left was under regular enemy
artillery interdiction of hundreds of rounds a day, though they didn't bother with our flimsy sheepshed that was obviously too obvious. We observed more than we deserved and
breakfasted properly, as always with Nye, on hot cereal washed down with real coffee and
topped off with canned rice pudding. After a few days Smitty's crew relieved us, with
Zapiecki replacing Dowdall and remembering everything.

> About twenty-five yards in front of us in the canal the guys didn't have nothin' else to
> do and were havin' a mud fight. There was a bridge there and we counted seven hun-
> dred an' twenty-four shells on it in one twenty-four-hour period. So on the sixth of
> April I was sittin' on my helmet countin', and Mickey was hollering through a window
> at these two guys, "Get back! Get back! Get away!" They didn't know what the hell he
> was talkin' about. They were in front of the shed and wanted to see what was going on,
> so they didn't get back as far as the Mussolini Canal, and here one shell comes over the
> shed, another one comes, and all we heard was SHHHH BOOM and I got hit, and my
> ears never stopped ringin'. If you were in my head now you could hear it.

It tore the map on the table all to hell, sheered the stock right off somebody's gun and put a hole in the gasoline can and it was runnin' out but didn't start on fire. Mickey was standing with his back to us and got knocked flat on his face. He picked himself up and shook himself, and when he saw what happened said for me to stay in the hole and went down to the canal and called Battalion and they called the CP. They couldn't get me out until dark.

Back in the hospital that was dug in three or four feet I had a patch over my eye, which was bulging out, and they told me to rest up a coupla days. No bed, just blankets on the ground. We're all sittin' around bullshittin', when they sounded the alarm. Put out the lights! And boy they're on target! BOOM BOOM BOOM. Everybody's runnin' around, and I'm on my hands and knees, where the hell am I gonna go? And a bomb landed outside. I bumped into a pole, and my helmet landed on a guy's foot. He's screamin' bloody murder, thought he'd lost his foot. The bomb landed twenty or thirty yards away and killed a doctor and a Red Cross nurse in a hole where they were dug in.

Next day they took the stitches outta my head. It was a jagged piece o' shrapnel about the size of a shoe nail, missed my eye by a hair and stuck in my skull. The doc couldn't find it, and I says, "Gimme yer finger," and we scratched it. He gave me a shot on either side of the eye and took a pair o' pliers and yanked it out. It felt like he was takin' my head off. Then I went to see Jimmy in the hospital.[5]

The day Andy got nailed I made my first entry in three weeks: "The Anzio Express has been stopping off here in the CP lately. Makes a hole about as big as a bomb. [More likely delayed-fuse 88s.] Here we're sure there will be no alleviation til invasion. Thus, it may be proposed that we 'fight it out on these lines if it takes all summer.' Morale is at the lowest ebb due to the stalemate."

Low morale indeed, as measured by "The Chimera—April 6, 1944, Anzio," tossed off in forty-five minutes of acute homesickness:

I see New England's purple, pine-clad hills,
Her rushing, whispering, snow-lined streams,
Her rippled lakes, fish-laden, lying simmering
Like a patch of velvet by her soft brown meadows.
I hear the buzzing, sleepy insect drone
That hangs about her pinewood farms
Which, wooed and ravished by a fickle weather,
Sit couched behind lush buttresses of purple lilacs
That tumble down the flagstoned yard
And overpower the picket fence.
I feel the restless shuffle on her crowded, winding streets
And gaze upon her sooty buildings, signs of strength;
I sense the pulsebeats of her mighty heart
Whence courses the lifeblood of a young and brawny land.

I also see her sturdy folk, grown straight and gnarled
As an ancient apple orchard,
And nourished by the bitter fare
Of sweat and toil and hardiness of thought.
All these things and many more
Appear before my half-closed eyes.
It is a fleeting, flirting glance of love
That takes me from the screaming shells
And thundering, jabbing, roaring guns,
That wafts me far away from dirt and scum,
From Death and gaunt Despair.
It is a magic charm that once possessed
Was never loved so much as now
When it is but a yearning.
It is a land of quiet wisdom,
A face of calm above the raging storm,
A place of balance in a giddy world.
Thus as I seek in vain to clutch
My vision through the battle haze,
I feel myself retreating like a beaten foe.
The vision shudders, melts and fades away,
And I sink back into the blackness of the fray.

Jerry Waldron had been shifted a couple of miles northeast from his OP on the road embankment near Padiglione to a farmhouse on the 45th's right flank behind the small settlement of Carano, where an enemy supply road crossed the Carano Creek, one of several that fed into the Mussolini Canal to the south. The lines ran through here and along the creek for a short distance, mostly across open ground providing little or no cover.

The key to the Carano front was a cemetery with numerous monuments and vaults, including the once-impressive tomb of Menotti Garibaldi, son of the great revolutionary leader, who campaigned with his father and died in 1903. With their usual bent for the macabre, the Heinies made this ancient burial ground into an elaborately trenched strongpoint of death, bristling with almost unreachable machine-gun nests, known to all as The Cemetery.

The farmhouse was about 150 yards behind our lines, which were so close to theirs, and the ground so flat, that only one or two men a night could be rotated out. Some spent days at a time out there and had to piss in their holes or attract machine-gun fire. To get supplies up to the line, a guy had to crawl up on his belly at night, sometimes under fire, dragging food, water and ammunition that he flung at the holes.

When I was on this OP later I was amazed it hadn't been leveled. Family photographs still hung on the walls, for twenty thousand civilians were evacuated south by the Navy during the campaign. Directly behind the house was a battery of camouflaged 4.2-inch

A 4.2-inch chemical (read poison gas, just in case) mortar with rifled barrel for accuracy and high angle of fire for distance (*U.S. Army*)

chemical mortars firing high-explosive shells but switchable to poison gas (hugely stock-piled on the outskirts of Naples just in case), and farther back some tank destroyers. While Jerry was in this farmhouse I was for a few days on an OP to his left, probably the "Sheepshit." We were in phone contact via battalion or regimental switchboard.

Jerry:
There were some haystacks out there. I turned away once, and when I came back it looked as if there was a gun sticking out of one of 'em. We were in contact with the TDs behind us. They had no trained forward observers and told me if I saw anything, fire away at it. So we fired every so often on this haystack to knock it off and see if it was a gun or they'd stuck a fence post or something in it to make it look like one. I swore there was a German tank in there.

Joe Garland:
From the other OP I could see where you were firing and got on the phone and said, "Jerry, that tank's made o' plywood!"

Jerry:
We never did get it outta there.

Caird:
One day Jerry said there was something looked different, and it took him all day to figure out that there was one more stack than yesterday. He called for incendiary fire from the chemical mortars; they burned 'em up, and sure enough, the Krauts had a gun under one of 'em. Same OP fired practically all day on this target, and just before dusk, when the dust settled, we see these two Germans get out of the rubble and run

like hell. Another time some guys were out in front of the OP. We hollered what the hell were they doin' out there? And they said they were lookin' for stray mules for a bareback mule derby bein' organized in the rear.

Jerry:
For weeks that house where we had the OP stood there intact with as many as thirty-two guys at one time, and then Griff was out checking around and walked up in broad daylight. A wonder one of 'em didn't shoot him. After he'd gone the Krauts hit it and chased everybody out.

Back from the bombed hospital as fast as his flat feet could carry him, Zapiecki took a turn on this OP overlooking the Cemetery and as usual, strange happenings arose around him.

This one guy with the chemical mortars behind the house was a brute. We had the scope in the window, and the Germans were in the Cemetery. He'd aim the mortar and take a armload of shells and say "All right now, watch!" And he'd run down the stairs, drop 'em in the mortar and fire 'em one after another and then back up the stairs and look through the scope. "Aha! That was a good one! That was a good one!" He'd put a cluster of six of 'em right there in the Cemetery.

What the Germans did to the hospitals of their wounded foes, by design or otherwise (*U.S. Army*)

Andy Zapiecki and Jack
Shannon jousting with
bayonets in a stateside
training camp (*Courtesy
of Andrew Zapiecki*)

There was a barn connected, with a big trough for the animals. At one end
somebody dug a tunnel down underneath that trough. One evening we're standing
around after being on the scope all day, and one of the dogfaces comes up and did-
n't realize it was a clear shot there from the Cemetery and lit a cigarette. It wasn't two
seconds when a burst o' machine-gun fire split some bricks off the house. We knew
what was coming after that and went for the tunnel, and the first guy didn't know
you went down and had to make an angle, and he got stuck.

My old buddy from when I was in K Company, Jack Shannon, a sergeant now,
was coming back from the dentist and asked me how everything was going, and I
told him what some guy told me, that you could cover twenty-six machine guns on
the map of the Cemetery with a dime. He says, "I'll tell you, I'm not gonna get far.
I'm gonna throw in the towel and surrender to the first German I see," but he never
did. The first time he stuck his head out he got killed.[6]

April 9 journal:

*Easter. The Anzio Express has been consistently hitting our hospitals, and they have also been bombed,
with a number of casualties, and it does seem deliberate. The enemy can't push us off the beachhead, but
he can make it mighty uncomfortable for us as long as the invasion holds off. About the latter there is
great speculation, particularly since it is our only hope of a letup. The Channel coast of England has
been closed, as has all transportation and communication between Great Britain and Ireland. The time
seems to be at hand.*

*The last two nights have brought rather heavy air raids. Friday night they strafed and dropped
butterfly bombs (we got two of their planes), while last night they did the same. One plane swooped so
low over the dugout I expected to be blown sky-high.*

The same day I finished Laurence Sterne's *Tristram Shandy*, the huge eighteenth-century
parody on human nature and the military that had been on my underground reading list
for four months, and wrote home in Shandian vein that "a new helmet liner is my Easter
bonnet!" Sweating filthily in our winter long johns, we longed for the summer underwear
that had not yet been issued. "I've stopped smoking for a while, just to see whether I can
do it; this is my second day, so I guess it can be done." Youthful hope sprang eternal.

In March the docs had cut the half-cast from George Furber's arm mangled by a German slug while he was with the Rangers in the January battle for Cisterna. On April Fool's Day he was back on the Beachhead with the Sixth Company of the Second Regiment, U.S.-Canadian First Special Service Force reorganized out of parachutists, rangers and commandos under General Robert T. Frederick. They were put along the Mussolini Canal on the right flank, First and Third Regiments on the line, with Second in the rear pulling outposts and patrols in rotation about once a week. George claimed to have enjoyed himself, and I don't think he was shittin' me either, but who knows?[7]

After seventy-eight days on the line, the 45th was relieved on April 15 by the Third Division, whose holes we moved into in an extensive, towering pine grove cooled by the sea breeze, a rest area on the southern shore of the Beachhead as far from the action as they could get it. Waldron, Caird and I took over "a veritable palace" of a dugout. They showed the movie *Buffalo Bill*. We wallowed in chocolate pie, doughnuts, applesauce, pork chops and French toast, and for the first time in almost three months "peeled off another layer of winter dirt" in the showers.

We played touch football (after I tussled with Farley I ran square into a tree and scraped my face) and softball, which produced a couple of Hank Mills sliders:

> In left field there was a big gun emplacement where they'd moved the gun out. Musta been eight feet deep. Somebody hit a fly ball, and I went back and had it all the way and was ready to tuck it in my hands, and I backed into that goddam hole and disappeared and didn't think I was ever gonna get out! One time I was battin', had two strikes on me, an' the guy threw a ball inside that almost hit me on the head, and the umpire says, "Yer out!" And some Kraut up in the hills yells, "You vass robbed!"

And I journaled:

The Second Front should be imminent. Huge convoys of troops are arriving in England, and the Luftwaffe sometimes is unable to get a single fighter in the air against raids (although they sent over thirty-four here in broad daylight about a week ago). Time magazine gives figures on the Red artillery barrage of November 19 at Stalingrad, 5,000 dug in, three and four hundred to a mile along the Volga and the Don. When it lifted, tanks, infantry and cannon plunged into the holes. The guns had fired 689,000 shells, destroyed 160 batteries, 293 machine-gun nests and 322 fortified points, killed 9,000 Germans.

April 23:
Seen some shows, had a pretty good time. A small dog got its head stuck in a water can—they got it out with oil. Mail very slow as mail ship was sunk the other night. Went to Memorial Service this AM. Very disappointing—not a particularly eloquent tribute to our dead by the chaplain, who's a Texas circuit preacher. We have the Victrola playing waltzes.

President Roosevelt was running against Tom Dewey for a fourth term.

The President, I think, is overconfident about our adherence to him. Moreover there is a large percent-
age of men who don't care much whether they vote or not. I suppose much of this attitude is due to a
certain anathema attached to everything political at home, a general feeling of disgust about the devil-
may-care attitude of the public, "It's all over but the fighting." After all, only a tiny fraction are vitally
connected with the men who live and die.

We were sleeping now under mosquito bars and head nets and popping anti-malarial
Atabrine pills, a daily reminder of the disease that still lurked in the Pontine Marshes
pumped dry via the canals ordered by Mussolini in the 1930s that supposedly eliminated it.
Not for another sixty-three years did research reveal that in late 1943, anticipating the invasion by the Allies and in retribution for Italy's surrender to them, the Germans reversed the
pumps, flooded the canals and reintroduced the *Anopheles* larvae in enormous quantities.[8]

Like the occasional incoming shellfire such as the tree burst that showered shrapnel
down on the rest area and wounded a guy in the chow line, there was no escaping the
Deadly Presence on and beyond the Beachhead.

A more intriguing intimation was the ever-in-the-offing, so come-hither, so American
voice of Mildred Gillars, *alias* Axis Sally, picked up on the jeep radio from Rome, but presumably originating in Berlin.

She plays American jazz records, sings and talks (very good for our morale, contrary, apparently, to
what Herr Goebbels thinks [Joseph Goebbels, Hitler's notorious propaganda minister]).
Advised us to surrender, that we will be well treated, and our wounded will receive immediate attention
and a very comfortable train ride. She maintains that Americans aren't getting both sides of the story.
The naiveté of the German propaganda machine is a constant amusement to us.

It stumped Dilks that "ole Sally knew exactly where we were, what day we got there,
and said 'I'll tell you when you're gonna leave.' One time she said 'We killed enough men
to make up one 45th Division, we captured enough to make up another, and we got enough
in our hospitals to make up another. I don't know where they all come from.'"[9]

After ten OK days at what we called Whispering-Pines-by-the-Sea, the 45th packed up
and returned to the lines on April 27. We relieved the Third Division's 30th Regiment in our
old CP. In recognition of past risks or anticipation of future or both, 30 percent of the I&R
(why only 30 I disremember) was awarded the new Combat Infantry Badge depicting a rifle
against an elongated laurel wreath. "A rather gaudy bauble. Should be good for a couple of
beers after the War. Looks like a billboard. I got one. Hope the Heinies don't see it from afar!"

I've forgotten what renewed hazardous duty was my lot, but Waldron was sent up
somewhat to the right of the previous OP from which he'd directed fire on the haystacks, a
vantage of the sort that the old gold miner Griff prospected out for his boys to man. To get
to this shallow hole Jerry was jeeped to the edge of the woods, then crawled a couple of hundred yards along a shallow ditch with telephone wire, phone and spotting scope to the brow
of a rise from which he could see the Cemetery. "There was a bunker out there, with a few

Germans sunbathing and wandering around, and I had fun chasing 'em around the grave-stones with shellfire."

Mills was out with him once, and for Hank it was a beacon moment.

Crawling out we musta got spotted because they laid a sonofabitch of a barrage on us. Up to that time I had a tendency when things got tough to get a little unwound, and it was so bad that I believe I woulda got up and got the hell outta there. Jerry just put his hand on my shoulder and says, "Everything's gonna be all right. Take it easy now." We were in the hole when they opened up and did everything but hit it, kicking dirt in on us. If I'da got in the ditch they'd have put a direct hit on it. We were spotted, but we rode it out.

From that day on I was entirely different. I don't think I ever again got overly frightened. That day was a turning point in my life. Jerry Waldron took me from a kid to a man. I never to this day have ever forgot. I used to say I wish I could be like him.

Hank's unflappable buddy Dilks exerted his own steadying influence on our Wise Guy, as we've seen, but more as a lightning rod.

Dilks:
If yer in the wrong place at the wrong time yer gonna get it, and if yer in the right place yer all right. Hank was pretty cool before Anzio, when he started gettin' jittery as hell. One night we were in the dugout—you're outta there and they kill ya—and he yells "The bombers, the bombers! Hey Dilks!"—knockin' me 'cause I was sound asleep. He's tryin' to light a cigarette and his hand's shakin'—"Goddammit Dilks, the bombers, the bombers!" I says, "Well, if one of 'em hits us it hits us. Whaddya gonna do? Go to sleep." But he couldn't see it that way.

Then he steadied out after a while. We was drivin' up on some mission, and I felt funny that day, and he asked "Got to ya?" and I says, "Ah, Mills, it ain't fer us to wonder why, it's fer us to do or die." "GOD DAMN," he says, "you cut out that damn shit!" I was jes' kiddin', but he didn't go for it.

Mills:
Dilks just didn't give a shit. He was unflappable. Most excited I ever seen him was when a guy set down a box o' C rations right where he was, and he had it in his mind he was gonna get one with a chaw-clate in it, and I never seen him move so fast. He beat everybody to the box to get the chaw-clate. I said to him, "I never seen you move like that before." He says, "I never wanted a chaw-clate like that before." His favorite expression was NAHHHH, and that was a mouthful.

April 28 journal:

Getting a sunburn. Everything green. Heard couple of cuckoos (never before). Swarms of insects in the evening. Finally getting beer brewed by a Budweiser brewmaster in Naples, supposedly 2/3 litre every two weeks. Our keg is sitting down at the kitchen waiting for a spigot, as there are only four for the

Intermezzo amongst the whispering (or whistling when an unfriendly shell crashed in) pines. Our single break from the front going on four months. (*U.S. Army*)

Regiment. Jerry and I have a fine hole now. Nearly three feet of dirt on top, a curved entrance, and a window made out of a C-ration box for light and ventilation. Juniper boughs on the floor make it smell like old home week!

Likely the dugout I dubbed The Bedpan with a sign at the entrance. Good news from home: Gareth Dunleavy is up in a wheelchair, more or less deshrapneled.

April 29 journal:

Last night the Jerries raided heavily, hitting the British pretty hard. They dropped a whole stick of antipersonnel bombs between us and the Medics' tent, hit a tank by the 1st Armored, and lost at least two planes. We have one OP out and have to send out motor patrols every night looking for paratroopers.

This was probably the night Andy's Victrola got it in that same tent. Having cranked and uncranked across the Atlantic and through three campaigns just behind the front lines, surviving barrages and bombings, Old Vic died honorably in the tradition of the company bugler of yore, exiting with echoes in my ears to this day of "The Open Road" and "Buckle Down, Winsocki."

Journal:

I have very few ideals in the war. If there's a Jerry tank firing at me or my buddies, I want to bring artillery fire on him and knock him out before he does me. Kill or be killed. Anything else is out of this world. If the soldier votes—good—if he doesn't, so what? He's a political tool at best.

The general situation on the beachhead is fair. There is a terrific amount of rear echelon now piled up to facilitate supply, repair, etc. Artillery is ample, and generally there is little difficulty in getting missions fired on. We have 240s [240-millimeter artillery] *and an airport not far away from here. Naval guns still supplement. The Germans comb the beachhead with tank fire mostly, and what the tanks won't reach the Anzio Express works on, with a range of twenty-seven miles, a half mile inaccuracy, probably explaining why hospitals get hit. For this reason smoke machines lay a heavy smudge over ammo dumps and heavily trafficked roads.*

On the line both sides, to a certain extent, are making use of night and day positions, the enemy perhaps more than ourselves. Their MLR [main line of resistance] *is in front of their houses in our sector. During the day they remain in the houses and at night they move forward, perhaps only a few yards, to dug-in positions. They have the advantage of houses which are excellent protection for reinforced machine gun positions and screening for tanks.*

Back up on the line the Germans had settled into sniping at us from their fearsome Tiger tank with its terrifying 88 around the corners of these houses and even haystacks, or perhaps from inside both, as Jerry had convinced himself. Such target practice with a three-and-a-half-inch shell aimed and fired as from a sharpshooter's rifle at 3,500 feet a second whiled away the idle hours on the upper hand of the stalemate.

One vividly blurred day I was caught in the sights of an enemy tank while I was on some forgotten mission to contact an adjoining unit, as I hurried solo toward a tree-lined road perpendicular to the front. They spotted me and must have figured I was a messenger, as I believe I was. One after another the shells screamed in as fast as the crew could reload while I dashed erratically from tree to tree, ducking unscathed behind each as half a dozen or so 88s burst at my heels until the hunters tired of the chase.

Bill Caird had a similar experience as a running bull's-eye:

> I brought some maps up to one of the battalions on foot and had to go through a big empty field to get to the draw where their CP was. I was going back to our OP and was coming down this road when SSSSSHHHH WHAM—an 88 went over my head and landed in the field. Didn't think anything of it, you know, when SSSSSH-HHHH WHAM—another one. Four of 'em come over—and jeez, that sonofabitch is firin' at ME! And sure enough he was. The guys were on the OP laffin' like hell!

So I hit the dirt and crawled the rest of the way. It was just one of those days when they were firin' at anything that moved.

Yeah, big joke. And Dilks:

Lotta times takin' stuff up to the OP—and there's a tank ov⸺ ⸺a start easin' up on your 'celerator, then mashin' down, 'cause ⸺ ⸺eep goin' at thirty or thirty-five that damn gunner'll turn that turret an' get right in time with yer speed an' git yer after a while. The only chance you got is keep changin' yer speed 'cause I've seen guys git hit sideways BLOM, one o' those 88s jes' plow right into 'em. We useta say we had the eighty-eightitis. Those Shermans of ours were obsolete before they come off the drawing board. They was jest junk with that old 75 on 'em.

No, there was nothing apocryphal about the oft-cited duel between a German Tiger with its 88 and a U.S. Sherman with its flimsier armor and stubby 75-millimeter. The Sherman fired first and the shell went clang. Then the Tiger blew the Sherman's turret off.

"Anzio was the worst," pronounced Shorty Nye, who saw it all. "You couldn't even git out of a foxhole without gittin' shot at with an 88. They didn't fool around with rifles."

Faced with such overkill, I upgraded my personal armament from an M1 rifle to the much-sought-after Thompson submachine gun, whose firepower I doubled by soldering two ammunition clips together backside-to and reversed, so that when one had been emptied I could pull it out and insert the other for a total of sixty hard-hitting .45-caliber slugs—"and damn glad of it," as I told my journal. "It's the best tight-spot weapon we have. I thank God I haven't had to fire at the enemy as yet, and hope to continue that way."

Nothing was more feared on the Beachhead than the overpowering German Tiger tank with its rapid, direct-fire 88-millimeter cannon. On the first of March we faced an estimated thirty-two Tigers, fifty-three 75-mm Panther tanks and around eighty of the medium-sized, more maneuverable Mark IV assault tanks. (*U.S. Army*)

I never did have to aim my Tommy gun and squeeze the trigger because in fact I'd been calling the shots and firing on the enemy for months—just not pulling the lanyard that ignited the powder that sent the big death-dealing shell on its way.

✢ ✢ ✢

It's May Day. The Russians are celebrating their Revolution by driving the Germans out of the Crimea. We're not rejoicing in our fourth month of being bottled up on the infamous Anzio Beachhead by these persistent troublemakers on the hills up there, but I manage to smile wanly homeward:

> Weather continues fine, and there are a number of wild flowers around I don't recognize. Colonel Church has been making pipes from brier he picked up in the fields. Many of the birds sing all night long, even more than in the daytime. This place can be sunny after all. The dust raised by a vehicle can mark out a road for miles, although of course it works both ways. I was up half last night, so I'll quit for now.

As the sun climbed higher over the Beachhead with the advancing Italian spring, the rising heat waves produced vague and shimmering images in the scope, observing from hardly any elevation as we were, much less so for the enemy inspecting us from the higher altitudes. It was hard enough to gauge distances over a terrain so flat and lacking in distinguishing features and distorted by the effect on depth perception of our monocular scope, while for the German observers in the hills beyond, with their high-power binocular range finders, the Beachhead was spread like a topographical map.

"Down in the doldrums again or as usual," I wailed to Pete Sax. "We just seem to butt our heads against a damn stone wall over here, and it's so hopeless and disappointing that

A sketch by Bill Belleman while I sat on a case of K rations, cleaning my Tommy gun and smoking a butt

I wonder whether it will ever end. I'm sick of trying to spot tanks that like to blast hell out of me and everybody else. I'm sick of it all and I wanna go home!"

May 9 journal:

We've moved up into the 180th's old CP, at the [Mussolini] canal, and have two battalions on the line. The plan was to stay up ten, go back five, but I hear we're moving again the 11th. Rumor has it on our right . . . Saw a fellow for the first time the other day who came over on the boat with me. He's in the 179th I&R. Somebody previously had said he was killed, so I was quite surprised.

Quite all right. Three more days:

At 11 last night an attack was launched on the entire southern front. The 8th Army is heading west, and the 5th north along the coast, and they will meet above Cassino and drive north.

This was Operation Diadem, the long-awaited spring offensive. After the initially promising Anzio landing failed to cut off the German rear above the Gustav Line, General Alexander decided to launch a breakthrough up from the south, timed just ahead of the Normandy invasion and followed by the breakout of the Beachhead forces to accomplish finally their original mission of giving the Germans a pinch of their own pincers, that is, to cut off the northward escape of their 14th Army.

The 34th Division and the balance of the First Armored Division had landed at Anzio, as had the British Fifth to relieve the worn-out 56th, plus fourteen thousand casualty replacements in March alone. Alexander thought he'd made it clear to Mark Clark, who was to confine his attention and command to the Beachhead operation, that when the time came, Truscott's Sixth Corps would strike off to the northeast and apply the stranglehold on the Germans in the south to Highway 6 at Valmontone.

But Clark had his fingers crossed behind his back while allowing his superior the impression that Truscott would head for Highway 6 unless a compelling reason arose to go for Rome. *Unless.* Mrs. Clark's Christmas present had yet to be bought, let alone delivered. The hell with defanging Hitler's 14th Army. *Mark Clark* deserved Rome, *Mrs. Clark* had been waiting for Rome for almost five months, and *his* Fifth Army had fought and died for *Mark Clark,* not to mention his wife. *Mark Clark* would conquer Rome, and Rome would be the *Clarks'* before the Normandy landings seized the world headlines.

Continuing my May 12 journal entry:

We are attacking here in three or four days, preceded by a 72-hour barrage of all the guns on the Beachhead, all 1,600 of 'em. The Brits are supposed to fire 3,000 tons of ammo. Almost all guns have finished moving up and are very closely dug in far forward. 105s are as close as 500 yards to the lines. The attack is probably to be directed at Cisterna by the 3rd [Division], and the schedule calls for 1½ miles first day. I guess it's intended to sweep right on to Rome. We expect the [Normandy] Invasion any day. 2nd Bn. will be on the line, and the other two will undoubtedly come up as the attack progresses.

Tomorrow night Jerry and George Ruder [a blond, good-looking, self-assured young replacement from Philadelphia] *go out to 2nd Battalion OP to pick out an OP in enemy territory. We will set up our own soon, calling for 1,000 sandbags, and the Colonel is supposed to direct operations from there. The 1st Armored is supposed to be putting 500 tanks in readiness, and the 36th has landed two combat teams, one trained in street fighting.*

They are calling for prodigious efforts in behalf of the forward CP. They wanted 8,000 sandbags, got 3,000, had to go back to the ammo dump and empty out shell boxes. They want 500 logs, and we've been cutting all day for the past three days and building at night. I hope the attack will be so successful that the enemy will be forced to withdraw from the Factory with his guns for fear of being flanked. Lately he has been using two crisscrossing searchlights at night to guide his planes to a certain spot.

The foregoing recklessness is long-ex-post-facto court-martial evidence of why combat soldiers were forbidden to keep diaries. The protest that the notebooks were stashed away with my meagre underground effects at the CP would have provoked outrage in a military court faced with the capacity of the Wehrmacht to overrun our positions, as recently demonstrated in the vicinity of the Factory.

But we didn't attack in the expected three or four days. The Fourth Battle of Cassino had gotten off to a melancholy start on May 11 as the Poles were beaten back from the ruined monastery with heavy losses. Then the British were able to establish a small bridgehead across the Rapido River while the French Expeditionary Corps under General Juin fought into the mountains beyond the Garigliano to a position commanding the Liri Valley. Three days into Diadem the Germans had no recourse but to begin pulling back from their coastal line to avoid being flanked by the French and the expanding Rapido bridgehead of the Brits as the Eighth Army wheeled to threaten Highway 6 above Cassino.

Kesselring moved his crack 29th Panzer Grenadier Division, then the 26th Panzer, south from Anzio to the assistance of Mackensen's beleaguered 10th Army, but too late. On May 18 Monte Cassino, the uselessly battered linchpin of the campaign, finally fell to the heroic Poles, whose motivation to kill Germans had been smoldering for four and a half years . . . indeed fanned by the presence up there ahead somewhere of Smiling Albert, Hitler's man in Italy, who had commanded one of the two massive Luftwaffe flyovers that ripped their beloved Poland apart from the air on September 1, 1939.

For six months the Germans had held on to Monte Cassino, and thereby the entire Winter Line, before the ancient monastery was shelled and finally bombed, and afterwards in the rubble, against everything and everyone the Fifth Army could hurl at them.[10]

As for my private, albeit first-class, strategic conjectures, a wordless week followed while I returned to the closest action I desired, the bare record of which is in my journal of May 19:

Went out on the new OP. It is about three fourths of a mile from the front with a splendid view of our sector, including the cemetery. Saw movement around the cemetery and laid in [an artillery barrage] *on them. I spotted gun flashes south of Velletri, found what I believe to be the spot on the map and made an overlay for S2. The 155s are checking up. Hope it's confirmed.*

Back at the CP was a letter from home mentioning one from Andrew Welch, a handsome and popular Roxbury Latin School classmate and athlete, inquiring about my war service in his role as secretary of our Harvard class. "What the deuce is he doing that he has time to handle such matters?" I snapped. What indeed? At the time he wrote me, Lieutenant (JG) Andrew J. Welch, Jr., was just about to ship to the Pacific for submarine duty with *USS Snook*. A year hence almost to the day, on April 8, 1945, Andy and his eighty-three shipmates went missing with *Snook*, probably somewhere off Okinawa. In her nine Pacific patrols in two years she was credited with sinking twenty-two enemy ships totaling 123,600 tons and damaging another ten.[11]

Andrew Welch (*inset*), the *USS Snook* (*top*) and its crew (*bottom*) (*Collection of the author, U.S. Navy*)

Rest in peace, Andy, and all you guys.

Looking for something, anything, to do between boredom and dread of the inevitable call to attack, I tackled the manifestly simple plan in the Italian edition of the *Stars and Stripes* for a dogface's dugout-built radio requiring nothing more than a cigar box, a razor blade, some wire and a set of earphones to be borrowed from the Radio Section. The razor blade served as a crystal over which one moved the end of the wire until a frequency responded. The role of the cigar box, and where I got one, escapes me.

"It gets static but nothing else," I complained to my journal. Two days later: "I finally managed to get my radio going for a while today. I got some Italian music, but on every station there was some Frenchman butting in with a line of chatter. It's on the blink again tonight." I think I brought in Axis Sally once before it blinked for the last time.

May 20 entry: "The southern front began a full-scale attack a few days ago. Indians and Italians on the right, Eighth Army in the middle, French and American 85th and 88th [Divisions] on the left. The front was advanced some 10 or 15 miles, many towns taken, the Gustav Line cracked, Highway 6 crossed, over 5,000 prisoners. They are now meeting stiff resistance at the Hitler Line. We have been giving the enemy a nightly TOT lately, apparently all set for the attack." (The most fearful employment of massed artillery was "time on target," concentrating the massed fire of multiple batteries to land simultaneously on numerous already interdicted German installations.)

As if mocking the sons for the sins and sacrifices of the fathers, by the third week of May the lush vernal green of the Pontine Marsh was hemorrhaging great orange-red gushes of poppies that stain my memory most starkly in the vicinity of the Femminamorta Canal. In front of us, the Dead Woman. To our rear, Campomorto, the Field of Death. All around us, Antium, the battleground of the ancients. John McCrae said it in 1915:[12]

> Take up our quarrel with the foe:
> To you from failing hands we throw
>   The torch; be yours to hold it high.
>   If ye break faith with us who die
> We shall not sleep, though poppies grow
>   In Flanders fields.

Ten months later, writing home, I was nearly overcome by the image of the fields, and fields of blood-red, blood-fed poppies, on the Beachhead of Anzio as I looked back:

> With what a mixture of hope and sadness I viewed the coming of spring. It seemed unusually fresh and sweet, such a strange breath of renewed life in the midst of death and barrenness. All my life spring had been the season when life seemed especially lovely and hopeful, the time of year when I took a fresh grip on the matters at hand. But last year I was terribly impressed by the notion that Nature was mocking us by showing us how dear life really was, while at the same time she redoubled her

threats to snatch it from us. I shall always look back on it as the most poignantly tragic spring I have ever experienced.

May 22 journal:

Tonight is the eve of the attack, due to begin 4:30 tomorrow morning. It's now 9:15, and the British are laying in heavily on the left. Possibly they are feinting at the Factory, as a number of flares are going up already, and it's not quite dark yet. The 1st Armored has been moving up steadily for the last three nights and will be ready by morning. Some 600 tanks on the Beachhead. The 45th is making the initial attack. On our right is the 34th, then the Third. The 36th has landed and is in corps reserve.

The show is being timed perfectly. The advance in the south is moving steadily. Cassino fell about the 19th. Fondi, on the coast, fell last night, and today's news bulletin has us fighting in Terracina, 23 miles from our right flank. Undoubtedly they've broken through by now, and the country between Terracina and Littoria, according to the map, is ideal tank terrain.

This marks the start of the momentous phase of the Italian campaign. When we get Rome, we will have taken, I believe, the largest city so far captured by the Allies in the war. I am seeing history in the making.

On the brink of the Breakout. Our tanks beyond. (*Department of Defense*)

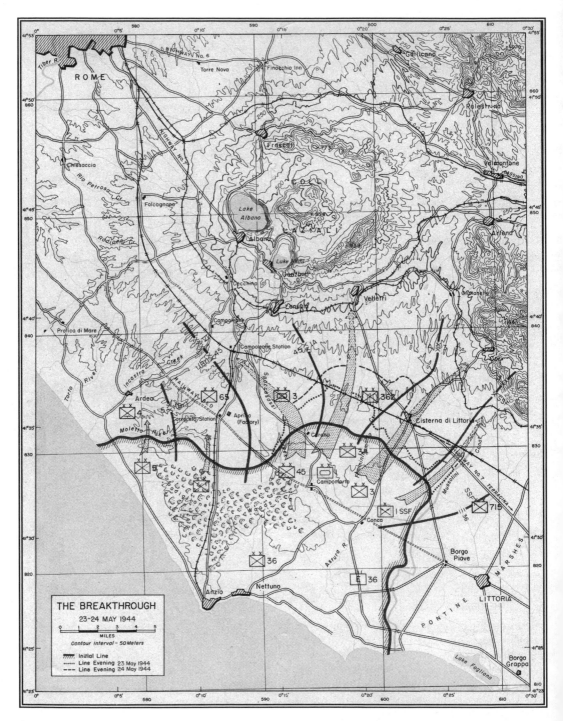

THE BREAKTHROUGH
23–24 MAY 1944

0 1 2 3 4 5
MILES

Contour Interval – 50 Meters

Initial Line
Line Evening 23 May 1944
Line Evening 24 May 1944

(*Department of Defense*)

✦ 8 ✦

"Here They Wuz
an' There We Wuz"

Breakout
May–June 1944

Ready for Breakout H-hour on the twenty-third of May, Jerry Waldron was out on his OP with another Ironhead in the hole on the rise of ground to the left of the Cemetery, the one he had to crawl to so as not to be spotted. "It was a great place to watch from. All this artillery was sitting there wheel to wheel, and I said to myself I'm gonna see a great part of history made here. Things just never came up to my expectations. I saw a lot of action, our troops attacking, but didn't really see the Germans."

Nor did I; back in the CP on the twenty-fourth I wrote: "Yesterday at dawn the attack was launched, preceded by surprisingly little artillery. The evening before, the British had reportedly preceded a twelve-man patrol with a terrific barrage." *Surprisingly little artillery?* Where did I get that? Dilks swore every gun we had just let go, and the whole ground shook. And Trubia couldn't figure how the Krauts survived it. Anyway, I continued:

Our First and Third Battalions attacked, and First managed to get several hundred yards on the other side of the railroad. They commenced to dig in, ready to push again when our flanks catch up. Third Division attacked early this AM. Highway 7 has been cut along a 2,000-yard strip, and as last heard, we were within a half mile of the city square of Cisterna. No real news yet of the British on our left.

The 45th took over 300 prisoners yesterday. They were young and old—one kid of 17 looked about 14. Among them were captured Russians forced into labor battalions. Our heaviest casualties

---

Chapter title is the caption of a cartoon by Bill Mauldin. Copyright 1943. Courtesy of his Estate.

were from mines. Many of our tanks have been disabled by mines and have also run off the road. Supposedly our Shermans engaged a unit of Mark VI's yesterday afternoon. We lost 15 tanks, knocked out three of theirs, one with a bazooka from L Company. Our next objective is, I believe, Velletri. The whole thing has begun well here, our own battalions advancing some three miles.

The southern front has forced a break through the Hitler Line and is pushing on towards us. They can't be much more than 15–20 miles away now. So far we've encountered amazingly light resistance in our sector, and there hasn't been the really great increase in enemy shelling I expected.

Had I been up on the line that morning I'd not have found the resistance among the survivors "amazingly light."

While the British feinted across the Moletta River on the left (recognized right off by the enemy as a diversion), the Third Division pushed on beyond Cisterna toward Valmontone with the 34th and First Armored protecting its left flank, while the 45th attacked through Carano and the Cemetery strongpoint northwest toward Campoleone on the Anzio highway north of the Factory.

The going was terrible. Our First Battalion on the left reached its objective, a knoll south of the railroad embankment that ran southeast from Campoleone, but the Germans counterattacked, and B Company nearly lost a platoon. Meanwhile, Third Battalion moved forward behind a rolling barrage with L Company taking the brunt, as described in the citation for the Congressional Medal of Honor awarded Technical Sergeant Van T. Barfoot:

Yeah, history in the making. The walking wounded, stumbling back and tagged for triage. American casualties the first day: 334 killed, 1,513 wounded and 81 missing. (*Department of Defense*)

…With his platoon heavily engaged during an assault against forces well entrenched on commanding ground, Sergeant Barfoot moved off alone upon the enemy left flank. He crawled to the proximity of one machine gun nest and made a direct hit on it with a hand grenade, killing two and wounding three Germans. He continued along the German defense line to another machine gun emplacement and with his Tommy gun killed two and captured three soldiers. Members of another enemy machine gun crew then abandoned their positions and gave themselves up to Sergeant Barfoot. Leaving the prisoners for his support squad to pick up, he proceeded to mop up positions in the immediate vicinity, capturing more prisoners, and bringing his total count to 17. Later, after he had reorganized his men and consolidated the newly captured ground, the enemy launched a fierce armored counterattack directly at his platoon positions. Securing a bazooka, Sergeant Barfoot took up an exposed position directly in front of three advancing Mark VI tanks. From a distance of 75 yards his first shot destroyed the track of the leading tank, effectively disabling it while the other two changed direction toward the flank. As the crew of the disabled tank dismounted, Sergeant Barfoot killed three of them with his Tommy gun. He continued onward into enemy terrain and destroyed a recently abandoned German fieldpiece with a demolition charge placed in the breech. While returning to his platoon position Sergeant Barfoot, though greatly fatigued by his herculean efforts, assisted two of his seriously wounded men 1,700 yards to a position of safety. Sergeant Barfoot's extraordinary heroism, demonstration of magnificent valor, and aggressive determination in the face of point-blank enemy fire are a perpetual inspiration to his fellow soldiers.[1]

By the end of the second day those two towns shimmering in the hills that had been lording it over us since January, Cisterna and Velletri, were taken or nearly so, and patrols from the southern front and the Beachhead met on the coast road. The Germans were falling back from their entrenchments reluctantly, buying time for the stubborn withdrawal of their main body from their mountain strongholds to the south.

The night of May 26, the fourth day of the breakout, Griff got us out on an OP to follow the action behind L Company, which was to attack in the morning. Dick Beech was in charge, with Bobby Coleman, Dynamite Thatcher and Garland.

I journaled about the events of May 26–27:

Got out to the hill finally, about 2–300 yards south of the railroad and 200 yards behind L Company. TD's and tanks were right behind us. The ground was like rock, and we dug til 4 in the morning. Got down 1½ feet with a bulwark of two layers of sandbags around the edges—no roof. That day observation was excellent. No luck on the radio (they had changed the channel and not told us, so we had no communication).

At about 1045 a terrific barrage began, and at 1055 one of the TD observers told us an attack was coming off at 1100, which it did. 2nd and 3rd battalions moved out westward along the railroad. It was the first attack I ever saw. They were followed by six tanks that preceded the 2nd wave. The boys encountered no resistance until they were about 200 yards from the north–south road on our left. Then the enemy opened up with machine gun and tank fire. The boys were pinned down til our tanks got direct fire on a group of houses at the end of the road.

It took them about an hour to get by one house. I was making a log while Bob was observing. He saw one of our boys mow down four Jerries with his Tommy gun. Also saw rather large numbers of enemy coming out with their hands up. We followed the attack until 1230, until our tanks were out of sight, when three tanks on the mountain opened up on the road in back of us and the hills around us where tanks were continuously moving up and down and firing. They laid in on us from 1230 until 9 that night. Must have thrown in 300 rounds. We couldn't move out of the hole. I pissed in a tin can while Thatch pissed in his helmet. Several rounds landed within 15 feet of us.

Towards dark they must have spotted us, for they threw several air bursts at us. One burst ten feet in front of us and six feet in the air. A small piece hit Bob in the leg. Earlier I got nicked in the knuckle [by an aluminum fragment of fuse about the size of a pea from one of the air bursts overhead], *drawing a little blood. The TD behind us got its radiator knocked out. One man hit in the family jewels and another in the chin. That was the worst barrage I was ever in. I thought my time was up. God saved us—how, I don't know. We suffered heavily, but gained a couple of miles.*

There it was again: *Gott* showing His impartiality on the field of battle. To this day He hasn't deigned to confide how or why He saved us or whether we deserved it, eyewitnesses to a battle spread out before us, and incommunicado with S2. For security, our field radios were assigned a daily change of channels, and not until we made it back to the CP did we learn we'd been sent up on the hill with the wrong channel, or that perhaps we were tuned in on the next day's, hence nothing but static. I suppose I turned in my tactically useless log. We (or Kilroy, the G.I.s' legendary fall guy) blew it, and we damn near got blown to wherever He might ordain in the bargain.

Late that day, or maybe the next, after the action moved on, we found a knocked-out, burned-up enemy tank and two or three dead tankers just off the road in the gully behind us. Moving up with Mickey Smith's crew, Dilks saw "that big ole Tiger tank turned over just off the road in the bottom of a ravine. Guess the crew all got out except one guy, you could jes' see his feet where the tank come down on him and jes' squashed him. Boy what a ugly-lookin' thing, the tracks wide as this table. Musta been backin' up during the night. That gun was about twelve feet long."

Probably the same Mark VI that under shellfire that day made for a thirty-foot gully occupied by K Company in shallow caves, overturned and landed in the bottom upside down. They shot the crew. Well, ancient memories differ.

As do versions. Only two days later I wrote Pete Sax, "You can imagine that I have finally pulled out of my funk. It won't be long now . . . The other day I was shelled for nine hours steadily, pinned down. Had 'em land ten feet away and got nicked in the hand." Already in my head they'd given it to us half an hour longer and five feet closer.

That morning, as we peered uselessly over our sandbags at the boys of K Company charging the tanks and machine guns, General Mark Clark dropped the other shiny shoe and told Truscott to turn the weight of the Sixth Corps—the 34th, 36th, 45th, First

Armored and First and Fifth British Divisions—on his personal glory road to Rome, leaving only the Third and First Special Service Force to push on toward Valmontone and Cassino-bound Highway 6.

More from my journal on May 27:

This morning we pushed again. F Company apparently had it easy by the railroad. They hit no resistance until all of a sudden tanks and machine guns opened up point-blank. They began to dig in—but in the middle of a mine field. Upshot is—eleven men left accounted for in the company. Every single officer wounded, some killed. A complete slaughter. It makes me want to cry.

Cori, Cisterna and Littoria have fallen. Also rumored is Frosinone. Supposedly we push tonight, again tomorrow. We're moving west behind the Factory, and will probably join with the British to cut it off. That goddam area is holding the whole beachhead up. We're about 15 miles from Rome, and the Germans say they may not make a stand there. Mines are the biggest problem. They're everywhere, all over, many of them plastic. Casualties will be very heavy.

And not just F Company. The weight of the counterattack of tanks and infantry against Second Battalion fell on E, with twenty casualties before our artillery and TDs forced them back.

May 28:
We pushed again last night and this morning made a concerted drive with the British. The 180th got in behind Aprilia and the Factory has fallen. As last heard, we were in the region of Lake Albano, 12 miles from Rome and approaching Valmontone. The French are nearing Frosinone (and may have taken it by now).

[Apparently I was unaware that Third Battalion attacked successfully to the left of the 34th Division, which lagged against heavy resistance, exposing the Battalion's flank on a 1,500-yard front to a counterattack that was stopped by nightfall only after I Company lost two platoons, probably captured. L was hard hit and ran out of ammo, and K was scattered.]

The previous night, I made note, Jerry Waldron had taken a crew out to follow today's situation, and I wondered where he was and how they were doing, contrasting his situation and mine, by now a safe distance behind the lines. He and his crew were sent forward to the old railroad embankment, where they saw the results of a tank battle, the German overturned and ours knocked out. On the night of the twenty-eighth, they were out again. Jerry:

In the dark we kept passing through guys and asking where the front lines were, finally got to where they said we're the front. We found what must have been a station house with a semaphore, got up on the second floor and figured we were all set, out in front of the lines.

In the morning they kick off and we're not on the front! We saw quite a bit but should have been farther out. We called back and said they've moved way ahead of us, which meant we blew it.

We were running up alongside the railroad, hurrying to get caught up, and
came to a gully where they must have been fighting hand-to-hand, thirty or thirty-
five bodies on both sides, and then we get up to a bunch of shell craters, and we're
running along in and out of them, and some sonofabitch in a tank with an 88 starts
shootin' at us. That was exciting. We finally caught up with the troops on a ridge and
saw some action.

No wonder the confusion. The First Armored Infantry were shifted over in the night
to relieve our battered Regiment at dawn on May 29, resulting in great congestion as the
Thunderbirds, many of them casualties from mines and tank shellfire, sought cover and
packed into the gullies just behind the line.

Then the unthinkable happened. An enemy shell struck the bluff on the steep reverse
slope of the most crowded of these refuges and caved it in, causing an immense landslide of
earth and rock that crashed down on the guys packed in at the bottom. At least a hundred

Cisterna (*U.S. Army*)

and sixty of the injured were evacuated, and there is no record of the number of dead under the rubble.

Was I in that gully soon after? A dark shadow of it, no more, haunts the back of my memory, and I cannot say. It may have been the Regiment's worst single day of the war. The guys weren't even up on the line. Not a word of it in my journal. I must have been struck dumb by the ghastliness of it.

What I did do at the end of that horrible day was write home I'd heard from Helen Bryan that she was spending the summer in Boston. "She sounds interesting, witty and brainy. I'd like to know her when I get back, and how!"

Then back to the banal: "Flies have bothered us more than mosquitoes here, and the dust from the roads is incredible, like a sandstorm."

Mark Clark's employment of his expressed doubt that Valmontone could be taken in time to cut off the German pullback from the south in order to rationalize his compulsion to throw the heft of his forces toward Rome did double duty as self-fulfilling and self-serving prophecy. What could Truscott do with one division and the Special Service Force against the whole staunchly retreating German 10th Army? Especially considering that though Highway 6 was the best, it was not their only escape route, as Clark believed.

So while Kesselring's two armies held fast, one enemy division after another streamed up Highway 6 to bolster the next stand, the Caesar Line in the mountains above Rome. The chance to make a break in the Italian campaign was lost, to Churchill's dismay and anger.

Then came a break for Clark. On May 30 a patrol was sent out from the 36th Division to probe around behind and to the right of the hillside town of Velletri, the key aerie and crossroads supply line to the German Anzio defense from which their observers had been scoping our every move for four months at their leisure. Sneaking up the slope of Mount Artemisio in what should have been wildly hostile territory, the 36th guys found nothing. In a rare oversight, the enemy had failed to occupy this strategic high ground overlooking the town from the back side.

The 36th took Artemisio over in strength and repulsed the inevitable counterattack (how rare to hold the upper hand in Italy!). Somebody had the sense to throw the 85th Division, just broken through from the southern front, on the right of Velletri, and the 36th and the rest of the Beachhead forces into widening the bulge on the left, and Rome lay ahead.

As Velletri was falling to the 36th and the temporarily attached 157th on the first of June, Griff walked Bobby Coleman, Dynamite Thatcher and me, with Dick Beech in charge, before the sun arose to an OP that seemed to have one advantage over that equally exposed ridge on which we'd just spent the day hugging the dirt. It was already dug—by a large bomb on what we called a bare-assed (naked of anything to hide behind) hill—I've no recollection where except maybe a hundred yards back of one of our rifle companies holed in on the slope of the gully in front of us.

We had time to dig little-bitty, scrunching-up foxholes into the sides of the bomb crater. Mine was about nine o'clock facing the Krauts, who spotted us and lobbed leisurely mortar shells our way for the next sixteen or so hours. One, for me, was the luckiest of the war. It struck on the level above the cozy burrow I was huddling in, no more than five or six feet from the edge of our bomb crater, flinging the shrapnel horizontally a few inches above my helmet.

Each time we tried raising our radio antenna to contact S2 back at the CP they saw it and dropped in another shell, so we gave that up. So no contact for another useless day. Never saw a German or any other action. Nothing to report if we could have, so when night descended we snuck off. When we'd dragged our asses back to the CP, which by then had been advanced to the Campoleone railroad embankment, Zapiecki commented: "Another useless OP up on another bare-ass!" Stubborn ole Griff heard him and responded by sending Andy out with another crew to the same hollowed-out bull's-eye.

What fucked-up fixes we got or were got into! Bobby Winburn, a straw-topped farm boy and recent replacement from Missouri, was sent off as the vulnerable lead man on a patrol under Shorty Nye to contact one of the battalions on the line for some purpose, the new guys being of course more expendable than the old. Bobby:

> They give us the password, but at battalion they give us a different one. We was goin' down a big draw in the moonlight, worst time to be out, through these shadows. Shorty was middle man and I was forward. Coupla times we stopped, and he said I was up too close. Next time we stopped in the shadows, and I waited an' waited maybe ten minutes and didn't hear nothin', and they'd gone.
>
> I'm alone with some joker behind me from the CP guards who'd wanted to go on a patrol. We didn't know where we're goin' 'cause nobody tole us anything. So we keep in this draw and this guy says "Let's capture us some Germans." I says, "You want to, you go ahead, but not me."
>
> We come up out of a draw to a vineyard and git challenged by a guy with a machine gun set up there, and of course I give him the wrong password. Only thing saved us was the other three guys that went on ahead said there's two guys comin'. So we set up an OP on a hill where our aid station was on the back side down the road. We were unloadin' stuff, and in comes a shell. The Jerries saw all these vehicles comin' an' not goin' out and decided sump'n was goin' on. There was no ditch so I hit down by the side o' the jeep. Shells breakin' all around. I looked down where I had my head next to the wheel, and there was a flat tire. Musta got hit. They let up, so halfway up the hill where I was carryin' this five-gallon water can and some other stuff, I took my helmet off to set on, and it had a dent you could stick yer fist in. Then I got scared.

Meanwhile, buddy Waldron and his small crew were jeeped to Velletri with orders to follow the situation as the 157th pushed on toward the small town of Genzano on the shores of Lake di Nemi, four miles on the Via Nuova toward Rome. Jerry:

> We were out ahead of the troops, had liberated a German scope and were set up in a good position when they started to shell. We retreated under cover, and the infantry came through and liberated the scope from us. We were pissed off because we had a helluva better use for it than they did. We were on the forward slope, and

the Germans were ahead of us on this ridge, with a road between. Our troops passed through us going up the hill. When they cleaned out the ridge we went up, and they're attacking up this road, and we're jumping from ridge to ridge above them and surprised there was no resistance.

We're going toward Genzano on this ridge and along a stone wall, being very careful, reporting back on the radio, able to look right down into the town which was about five hundred yards off, all hell breaking loose, people getting out, and then they told us to get outta there and leapfrog in another direction because that was all they needed at that point. Next thing we know, our guys went up over that same ridge and got the living shit kicked out of 'em. The Germans hadn't bothered with two or three like us; they were waiting for them. We got out of there, but I'm pretty sure we brought it down on them. I don't know that there were any great casualties, but we'd reported back there wasn't anything out there, and gee, everything broke loose. The rest of the way into Rome we were just following along.

Following along in pursuit of the Germans for the first time since I'd been in combat was as new an experience as war itself, fraught with the excitement of pursuit for a change, tension over the imminence of the unexpected such as the innocuous-looking field planted with land mines, the lone shell fired as if over the shoulder, the fanatic sniper and the suicidal ambush for the *Führer.*

But perhaps most unnerving of all, the sight and smell of the rotten fruits of victory, the roadside litter of mangled equipment, trucks, tanks, the riddled, bloated, putrefying bodies of horses, cows, dogs, and the sprawled, ungainly, surprised, peacefully sinister corpses of our late enemies in those uncomfortable, ill-fitting, ridiculously Teutonic dead-leaf-green, blood-clotted, shit-spattered uniforms into which the Wehrmacht had molded its millions of squareheads. And over it all the sickly-sweet perfume of flesh welcoming the succulent maggots of Mussolini in the June-day sun, inviting the gorge up into the back of your throat, except that being an American citizen-soldier from across the sea, you swallowed hard like a good Boy Scout, got out a butt, smoked hard, pissed in a bush and passed quickly on.

I'd seen the broken boys and bodies lugged back down from the mountain and across the marshes, the smashing by the Huns of everybody and everything that stood in their way or didn't, no matter, and the wished smashing of everything and everybody else including me and all the Ironheads and all the rest of the Regiment and the Division, Corps, Army and Navy, President Roosevelt, our women and children and all the non-Huns of the world (though we knew little then about the special places for the Jews), and our civilization, past, present and future.

But this was my first sight of what we could do to them, because these Kraut bastards, the best kill-or-die soldiers in the world, had held us at gunpoint in these mountains and on this plain, not giving a stinking foot, for seven solid months.

Poor buggers. There but for the grace of Mark Clark . . .

Then we skirted the Via Anziate that we knew simply as The Highway, and The Overpass, and The Factory, and The Caves where Hitler had hurled them down on us and the doggies had hurled them back and died or been smashed or captured, and we jeeped through Campoleone so near and yet so far, across the once-uncrossable billiard-table and up into the grandstand from which they'd watched us like ants underfoot.

In the once-fair resort of Velletri we Willies and Joes of Bill Mauldin's beloved 45th paused to look back down in wonder on the plain below and the sea beyond, and echoed his Willie and Joe as they echoed us on a ledge beside a knocked-out Tiger tank in one of his most eloquent cartoons, and looked back for a moment and gasped: "My God! Here they wuz an' there we wuz."[2]

Then, through a cameo cemetery of bloody green grass and bullet-spattered marble, littered with unburied body-parts of former enemies now merely the dead, we moved on along the road that led to Rome.

The cost to the 45th Division alone in the Sicilian and Italian campaigns: 2,110 killed, 2,094 missing, 6,777 wounded, 26,838 injured. Total 37,819.

June 3: "Already we've pushed several miles west along Highway 7 and are now at Lago di Nemi, just this side of Genzano. When we move another mile it will be downhill all the way to Rome. Today we got up to the front lines, and they threw 120 mm. mortars at us. A sniper left behind shot at us. Somebody captured him and he's upstairs, arrogant S.O.B. Christ, why didn't they shoot the bastard? More Russians taken yesterday. Damn nice kids. Mostly taken two years ago as civilians and forced into labor battalions. One was from Rostov and captured at Sevastopol."

In his late teens maybe, our snotty prisoner sneered that they knew from their radio that the Luftwaffe was at that very moment bombing Manhattan.

For two more days, between plodding along on foot in the heat and dust and shuttling in the regimental trucks, we moved up toward the west side of Rome behind the clanking tanks. The 180th in the lead was the first to cross the Tiber River south of the city.

June 5:
Yesterday Genzano was mopped up, Albano taken, and the Regiment rested last night here, west of Albano, in the division CP of the 4th German Paratroopers [our old nemesis on the left flank of the Beachhead from the beginning].

Rome just fell, having been declared an open city. The 8th Army came roaring up from the south, and the entire German line is now pulling back on the verge of collapse. The 157th moves up today to the left of Rome on the Tiber. I guess the 45th, as usual, is being deprived of the honors. Nevertheless, regardless of whether we've been robbed of the spectacular climax of the campaign, we can feel proud and satisfied that we plugged and plugged throughout, that several times we saved the situation, and that we're as responsible as anyone for building the road that leads to the pot of gold.

July 5 letter home:
I can hardly make you realize the way we felt when we finally attained the hills and looked back on the plain where we had been held for over four months. No wonder the enemy stopped us there. He could sit up in his porch at Velletri with a glass of brandy at his elbow and fire at any target he felt like. Our men fought like demons when the day finally came, and small wonder. Our Regiment saved the beachhead in

February, as you know, and held perhaps the key position in the attack. We're pretty damn proud of the boys.

June 7 journal:
We went around to the left of Rome, crossing the Tiber, a muddy stream about 100 yards wide, and going into the open, rolling wheat fields dotted with rather prosperous farmhouses. At one dairy the people were celebrating, giving out as much milk as we could drink. I had three-quarters of a quart, first in

"My God! Here they wuz an' there we wuz."

(*Copyright 1943 by Bill Mauldin. Courtesy of the Mauldin Estate.*)

General Mark Clark rides importantly into Rome, ignoring his orders to turn east and intercept the German northward withdrawal from the Cassino Line. He was, after all, a cousin of General George C. Marshall, who was running the show. (*U.S. Army*)

a year. Yesterday morning Thatch and I took off with a couple of field artillery boys and got into Rome, or rather, to the outside part. Wide boulevards, ancient ruins, waving citizens.

We've lost contact with the Germans. Nobody seems to know where they are, though a couple of planes were over last night. One reason may be that France was invaded yesterday morning by about ten airborne divisions, landing inland in Normandy somewhere. Apparently other landings were made simultaneously, and more are to be made. Landings involved 4,000 ships, and there are over 11,000 planes ready to go at a moment's notice. Perhaps we have really passed the hump in Italy now that the great moment has come. Perhaps, even, the Germans will retire completely from Italy under the pressure of invasion.

Perhaps, perhaps, perhaps ...

June 11:
The Division is in rest now (Corps reserve, I guess). We're just a few miles out of Rome in a gully [in the vicinity of Casalotti and Porcareccina]. *Country around here is typical of the National Geographic type of Italy. Gently rolling wheat fields as far as you can see, scattered farmhouses, almost all prosperous. It is entirely undamaged, as it has been since we left Velletri. Natives are either unfriendly or protest that they are "Communisti." There are plenty of dairy products if Griff will let you out of sight.*

On the roads north of Rome retreating Germans have left huge convoys burnt out. It seems that some were caught by plane almost bumper to bumper, while others ran out of gas or some similar trouble and were scuttled. I saw several SPs [self-propelleds] *intact, also a few tanks. Everywhere are dead horses, shot by the enemy. The Germans are still withdrawing, leaving heavy demolitions and mines and rear guard action. Civitavecchia has been taken, and by now, probably Viterbo. The 8th Army* is running into more trouble but still pushing. The invasion forces are described as "secure," and a decent strip of Normandy coast is in our hands. In my opinion the Germans will surrender when the first square foot of their territory is taken. The immediate object apparently is Paris, which will have tremendous effect on morale in addition to strategic advantage.

This afternoon General Eagles is to award decorations to the Regiment, while on Wednesday Clark will award the Presidential Unit Citation to 2nd Battalion in front of the Regiment, first division of this War to receive the honor.

Reflecting the same day on the dismal role of the I&R in the breakout from the Beachhead:

In a fast-moving situation OPs are generally not of too much use. As soon as you get the situation from S2, set up your OP and commence to observe, everything may have passed out of sight. Any OP to be successful may have to be moved several times a day, and even then it may not be worth it. Our best bet is to follow the companies in the attack and to radio back the situation as it is encountered—demolitions, mines, and whatever rear guard action there may be. Moreover, much of our work may be contact. Patrols go out to contact units on our flanks, or even our own units when the situation moves so fast that the companies lose contact with battalion or regiment. In this type of movement there are invariably pockets of resistance here and there. Often as not these are behind our lines. They may be houses the tanks have bypassed to let the infantry mop up, or they may be Heinies who have lain low to do a little rear area roughing it up. Also there is the inevitable trouble with snipers left in towns or houses. Snipers and a tank or two, or mines, can make all the difference in the world in delaying action.

So our OPs of the previous two weeks had been pretty useless, and Jerry's account of playing tag with an elusive front line was typical of our generally vain efforts to keep abreast of the action. As for the close to five months on the dug-in *there we wuz*, I wrote, "every minute, night and day, held fear of the artillery. It was as close to hell as this war will ever see."

Or that I would anyway.

(*standing*) Mills, Smith, Wolfe, Dibble and Harry Ramge; and (*squatting*) Nye, Beech and Coleman. Headquarters Company clerk Ramge had just joined the I&R to see more action. (*Courtesy of Dominick M. Trubia*)

✦ 9 ✦

THE DOGFACE AND THE DUCHESS

Rome, Salerno and Naples
June–August 1944

June 13 journal:
Our lines at the farthest point are some 70–80 miles beyond Rome. The German 14th Army is still
in rout, more so all the time. 8,000 Germans were taken in Rome in the hospitals. Prisoners in the
offensive alone must be nearly 20,000 by now, while casualties are approaching the 100,000 mark.
As yet the enemy has apparently not made any plans for setting up a defense line. [Wrong!] *The*
Air Corps has cut their retreating convoys to ribbons every day. New rumors have it that our 36th
and 34th divisions are being completely re-equipped, while the 3rd is to go to Anzio for amphibi-
ous training.

France, here we come. I guess we're in it to the end.

WELL, THE VAINGLORY that seduced Mussolini to his alliance with Hitler was his downfall and the self-inflicted tragedy of the nation that proclaimed him *Il Duce.* How poignant
in the end were their hallucinations and how operatic the retribution heaped upon the
bipolar Italian people and their wondrous land and civilization as they reaped the weeds of
their hapless aggression a thousandfold.

Yes, we dogfaces had mixed feelings about Italy and the Italians, the extremes of terrain and climate, of beauty and desolation, of tenderness and violence, of generosity and
exploitation, and the latent and not-so-latent hostility and duplicity of these our recent
enemies in this war and allies against the same ruthless foe in the last.

Our Italian strategy was the outcome of the justifiable fear held by the British, whose
memories of Dunkirk were still fresh, that a rematch across the Channel would be a repeat

of the unspeakable losses in the trenches of 1914 to '18, if not of the nightmare of Dunkirk itself. Yet how John Bullishly thick-headed to invade Sicily from the south, inviting the Germans to withdraw at their leisure to the mainland while preparing the most masterful defense of the entire war in Europe on the very home soil of the treacherous ally that had betrayed its partner in a last-minute surrender to the invaders at Salerno.

We never would drive Hitler's men from mountains that towered more unassailably by the mile. Churchill's "underbelly" spin and the outrageously planned Anzio landing were the cigar-and-brandy dreams of an armchair war buff. That his generals and ours actually fell for such nonsense was one of the patently avoidable tragedies of the war. The Italian campaign cost the Germans in blood and steel, but there's not the slightest historical evidence that it affected the outcome of the war in Europe on either the Eastern or Western Fronts by an hour, and it may well have delayed it.

In their immediate postwar memoirs two of the most experienced American correspondents in Italy, Eric Sevareid of the Columbia Broadcasting System and Herb Matthews of the *New York Times*, agreed that the campaign should have halted in the Volturno Valley, at most no farther than Rome, and that, as the former wrote, "it was all a frightful waste of lives and machines which could have been put to more fruitful use somewhere else."[1]

Sevareid took General Alexander to task for his

> . . . canard that we had never had more than a "slight" numerical superiority over the Germans at any time in Italy. He meant that the Allies had very few more *divisions* than the Germans, omitting to mention that the numerical strength of the average German division there was one half to two thirds of our own, that our air supremacy was around twenty-to-one, and that our supplies of tanks, artillery, and transport were enormously greater than the Germans'. And, most important of all for the final assessment of the Italian campaign, he admitted that the Germans had diverted only five new divisions into Italy from other areas—one, I believe, coming from Yugoslavia. In May his officers had made it clear that the Italian mission would be a failure if we merely forced a slow German retreat and did not oblige the enemy to divert large forces. So it seemed to me that on their own scales the Italian campaign was weighed and found wanting. It was not due to stupidity on the part of generals or to lack of valor on the part of fighting men; it was due to the impossible terrain of Italy itself, which made it possible for a third-rate army to hold off a first-rate force with one hand. But Italy's terrain was not an unknown quantity when the original decision to proceed up the peninsula was made. Who made this decision, where and why, has never been explained to the Allied peoples. I have heard it said in high places that the campaign was the "remnant of Churchill's abandoned Balkan strategy."[2]

Matthews went further, writing that "Marshall Alexander confessed to me and others, early in the campaign, that his original idea was to take Naples and Foggia, and then strike across to the Balkans. Evidently, Stalin vetoed that idea and the Americans backed him, although Churchill apparently wanted to go through with it."[3]

All the while, the Russian killing machine was devouring Hitler's divisions, spitting out the bodies of his soldiers by the tens of thousands and of his generals by the dozen. In Italy we knocked each other off one by one and inch by inch, we the cannon fodder, the realization of which I saw inscribed by the "enemy" prisoner on the bunk as I approached manhood on the cattle boat.

And what did this agony of military masochism cost the Allies in lives alone, and the deluded Italians and their homeland that would never have become a battleground had not we chosen to make it so, and what was gained? Hour by hour and day by day the uselessness and waste and degradation of Italy eroded everything and degraded everyone.

All this bears repeating and repeating, lest we forget, because the common soldier who had to do their fighting and their dying in Italy knew all along, of course, and without the aid of hindsight, that those who were calling the shots were neither shooting nor shot.

Or, as my father had written way back when he was my age, watching the first great slaughter in Europe from afar,

> Another commands your destiny.
> Are you less fitted for that task than he?

A week after the fall, capture or liberation of Rome, depending on your vantage, the 45th was still encamped in the countryside. The twelfth of June was fair and very hot. "I just finished a couple of games of pingpong with Griff," I journaled, "and found it as beating as an hour of tennis at home. Jack Pullman was around today, although I missed seeing him." He would soon be put in charge of the Fifth Army's mules. Hank Mills filled me in:

> Jack showed up, and all the guys were sayin', "Hey Jack, howya doin' pal?" and Coleman says to me, "What the hell is everybody makin' a hero outta that guy for? He was chicken, he took off, couldn't take it." And right away I says, "How do you know? You wasn't here long enough before to even know the guy."
>
> Bobby Coleman was a good friend o' mine, and I says to myself there's only one place that coulda come from, the Field Marshal, Tim O'Shenko. I gave that name to Griff. The Russians under Marshal Timoshenko were startin' to kick the shit outta the Germans, and I said we have a Irish platoon leader here, Marshal Timothy O'Shenko, and you know he hated my guts.
>
> I used to really zing him. We were standin' around one time, and I let on I don't see Griff an' says, "There was an awful scrap up here today." He useta have a favorite sayin', "There was an awful scrap up here today." And he says, "Yeah, what happened?" And I says, "Two lootenants from C Company got into a fight." And he says, "If you'd pay more attention to what's goin' on and less attention to yer goddam screwball ideas maybe you'd be better off!" I says, "Aw, you take this shit too seriously."

I did what I had to do. I wasn't lookin' for no Medals of Honor or no Distinguished Service Crosses. I was goin' to bring Mrs. Ruth and Frank Mills's boy back home. I didn't do anything dishonorable. But Griff was bitter. I feel a guy can give it to me and I can give it back, but I don't like somebody to take advantage of me due to his position, which Griff tried to do. He tried to get me transferred to a line company after Anzio, and Pat Farley says "You're doin' it outta spite because you don't like the guy," and vetoed it.

Many times I felt like takin' off. I never did. I was so goddam scared I couldn't even light a cigarette. I had enough pride to know that sooner or later if I made it I'd have to say to myself, did you take off or didn't you? If I had to get shot I didn't wanna get shot in the back runnin' away. I had to admire the Marshal, a cool customer. Whether he was lucky or not I don't know, but Griff wasn't a guy that got overwhelmed with what was goin' on—maybe the kind that made us do as well as we did.

Of course Mills was the Platoon wise guy, and ole Griff had no time for wise guys. Hank never could resist sticking out his chin and up with yer dukes, just to see who'd fall for the feint.

We was breakin' outta Anzio. One bright morning they had this little fire and were cookin' coffee an' shootin' the shit. I screwed the top off a grenade, poured the powder out, screwed it back on, walked over into the crowd, held the grenade out, pulled the pin an' dropped it. Jesus, they were jumpin' over trucks, under trucks, over bags. Everybody says "Hank blew his top, he finally went haywire," and I split a gut. It was a very chickenshit thing to do, and they wanted to beat the shit outta me, but I said, "Aw you guys can't take a joke." It wasn't no joke. It was a helluva thing to do.

Which may have had something to do with Griff's attempt to get him out of his hair. But to a line company? The salt mines? The death sentence. You didn't do it to your worst enemy. And then there was Zapiecki.

Three different times Griff sent me up to what was supposed to be the line with a crew, and we get there and what goes on, where is everybody? They're behind us. I come back madder'n hell. "Didn't you tell me to go this far and jump off from here and go to there? How could you do that in yer right mind? There was nobody there." "Well," he says, "they got there, didn't they?" I says, "Yah, over a half hour after we did. Then here comes the point guy and wants to know what we're doin' there." "You're overcautious," he says. "Look Griff," I says, "you watch your life, I'm watchin' mine. I don't think I'm overcautious, I just want a whole skin when I get outta this." But he wanted us to always take the direct approach. You can't do that.

And Bob Winburn:
Most of us wasn't takin' any chances we didn't have to. Seems like on an OP

everybody jes' took over an' run it like it needed to be. We knew pretty much what to do and not to do. If the leader was gone, somebody else did it. Somebody's gotta do it. Griff was careless about puttin' a crew out on an OP an' leavin' 'em. Didn't make any difference how careless he was for his own part, but when he got us in trouble, that was sump'n else.

Long after, ole Griff:
I don't think outside of Ankcorn we had a commander who paid any attention to the function of the I&R Platoon. They threw every dregs from the Regiment in there. It was a catchall. We got a lot of 'em that weren't qualified. It's a wonder we functioned as well as we did, being disregarded as much as we were. I got to the point that I just despaired and was just stringing along. There was too much to buck for me. I wish I could have observed an I&R in an outfit like the Third Division in a regiment of the Regular Army, and I have no doubt there would have been a very striking difference. It would have been a more disciplined outfit.

It was demoralizing to me. I might be dragging my heels on some of the policy, the way the Platoon was run, but you can't buck it, so I went along and did the best I could. I wish we'd had a good strong Platoon leader, but it would probably stem from the regimental commander. Colonel Church was an old Army man, and the I&R was a new concept to him. I don't think he took or had the time to get acquaint-ed with its true function. As long as the information kept coming in, he never ques-tioned the mechanics of it. What we needed was a good line company officer who was combat-trained and wasn't too overzealous of using the combat function which we weren't supposed to perform.

We never had a guy like that. Pullman and I were never what you'd call close. He was all right. I sort of felt I never did know why he left the Platoon. I never could understand battle fatigue. I'm not very sympathetic with anybody that can't take it. I don't know where Farley came from. But I think we were a dumping ground.

Joe Garland:
I'm glad I was dumped there.

Griff:
Well, I always had a pretty good opinion of you. Thought you were pretty gutsy. You didn't mind sticking your neck out. You weren't lazy, and we had some gold-bricks. What did Hank Mills ever contribute? Him and a lot of others I could name. He was pretty popular, but in my book he was way down at the bottom. Kinda insubordinate, no enthusiasm for real action, dragging his heels all the time. When you have personnel like that you can't make a person over. What are you gonna do?

Zapiecki and I were never close except in training camp. I liked his love of music, and he was a lot of fun. He did more or less what he wanted to do, and did a lot of work for the I&R. I have to hand it to him. But he sorta picked his spots.

Garland:

You've got to have a Zapiecki in a group of soldiers to relieve the tension and make them laugh.

Griff:

It's more necessary to some than it is to others.

Garland:

You stand above ordinary men in that respect.

Griff:

I think Woodhams, if he would have hung on, would have been chosen ahead of me. He had qualities of being a buddy and getting along with men that I never had. I think he was real I&R timber. I was more austere, roughing it and hardship and such as eating K rations and living what would be uncomfortable for some other people. I never dragged much along like some of the guys did, or had to eat or bed down like they did. I know that stuff can be enjoyed, but it was never very important to me. I don't think I was too popular, except with some fellers; there were some I just wrote off.

I have a feeling that I didn't know too much about handling men. I tried to set an example, and maybe that was about as far as I could git. There wasn't anything I'd ask a man to do that I wouldn't do myself. It's been more or less a tendency of mine to do the work for the other guy. Not that I'm reluctant to delegate authority, but I usually take over and do it from the old adage that if you want it done right, do it yourself.

I've seen fellers actually paralyzed with fear, just rendered helpless. Generally the Platoon behaved like soldiers should. The I&R had guts, but I've seen a case or two where they'd get almost to the point of whimpering, kind of possessed by self-pity—"I just can't do it." You try to kind of jack 'em up by reminding 'em how cowardly they are: "Are you a man or a mouse?" You know, Patton even resorted to slapping. An occasion or two I had to kind of buck 'em up and did it by being more or less rough on 'em. I got from the grapevine that ole Griff had no feeling for his men.

We had men killed and wounded, and I don't know really what I was supposed to do. You can't take too much time to grieve about losing a man. In fact, I think if you would succumb to grief over losing a man you'd probably lose yourself. It wasn't that I was indifferent, but I think some of the guys thought I was hard-hearted.

I never thought about getting killed. I knew there was always a possibility. I got the feeling after a while that I was crowding the law of averages because a lot of 'em were dropping out and gettin' knocked off, and there were times when I wondered why am I spared? There were guys with wives and kids getting it, and it doesn't seem like justice. But I never let it bother me. I didn't do any worrying, thank goodness. I'll always wonder just how good we were and how much better we could have been if it had been insisted on by the Colonel. I'll never know. But we could have been worse, I know that.

Which, from Griff, was sort of a backhanded compliment at that.

Zapiecki on the coolness between himself and Griff:
That was Jack's doing. He lived with us, knew exactly what to say, like "you fuckin' Polack." He knew how to insult you, and you liked him for it, and Griff never did.

And Mills:
If I had a second family the Platoon has gotta be it. A hundred years old, and I'll never forget that I belonged to the I&R.

The Ironheads. Les Gerencer peered and leered through his glasses at the screwed-up absurdity of it all, Meatless Tuesday telling how Lieutenant Francis Patrick Farley put the arm on him after Anzio to be his dog robber, his orderly.

He was supposed to censor the Platoon's outgoin' mail, and the guys were comin' to me an' sayin', "Jeez, it's still there after three, four days!" I told Jim Buckley, who was company clerk by then, "Jeez, look at all the mail I got, and that goddam Farley won't sign it," and he says "Sign his name," so I did, and half of 'em I gave to Farley an' he still wouldn't sign 'em. I ended up puttin' his name on about 75 percent of the letters.

Yeah Griff, we coulda been worse.

June fifteenth, sunny and hot on the plain west of Rome, was the day of the much-ballyhooed presentation by General Mark Clark of the Presidential Unit Citation to our Second Battalion for its heartrending role in the Battle of the Caves. For some forgotten reason I was picked to bear our "Eager for Duty" colors known as the guidon in front of the massed survivors of the 157th in parade array, standing at attention with Colonel Church and General Eagles and their staffs.

As the tall manipulator of our fortunes with the familiar hawk nose approached, and I stood rigidly with the long flag shaft thrust forward at the prescribed angle, something came over me.

I dropped it. Almost as fast, I retrieved pole and banner and resumed my stance, heart pounding. I suppose that on behalf of my Regiment my subconscious had momentarily gained the upper hand and directed me to commit at that moment in its history a simple, uncomplicated Freudian slip.

Ignoring my gaffe with the staff, our *History* reported that General Clark presented the Presidential Unit Citations on behalf of President Roosevelt to the Second Battalion and I Company for "fortitude and intrepidity . . . [in] the finest traditions of the Army of the United States" in the Battle of the Caves and "made a ringing speech promising that the men of the 157th would be in on the final march into Germany." Added our official *History* remarkably unofficially:

... There was very little cheering. The 157th had seen too much to inspire very easily. Given their choice, they would gladly have sat out the march into Germany.

Tech Sergeant Jim Rutledge of L Company summed up the general feeling bluntly in a later ceremony. Awarding Rutledge the DSC [for crawling forward under fire to dig out and rescue men who had been buried alive in their foxholes by shellfire during the Caves battle], General Clark said:

"Rutledge, I've heard a good deal about you."

Replied Rutledge:

"Yes sir. And I've heard a good deal about you, too."[4]

Having played a material role in the liberation of Rome, the challenge now facing the Thunderbirds was how to enjoy the fruits thereof since General Eagles had ordered the prize off-limits to the foot soldiers. Jerry Waldron:

Our Colonel Church got Colonel Funk of the 158th Field Artillery to trade trucks, which of course had the unit identification on the bumpers, to take the men in, figuring they'd really earned it. Eagles tells Church all you can see is 45th in Rome, and he's trying to find out who's sending 'em in. Church says he wasn't, "Here's my training schedule right here"—which is why he was the oldest lieutenant colonel in the Regular Army.

But Church said what got to him was when about one in the morning he'd be sleeping in his tent out by the road they came back on, and he'd hear this yelling and screaming and then "SHHHHH, we're goin' by the colonel," then, "Fuck the colonel!" and he says, "I'm sticking my neck out for these guys, and they're sayin' 'Fuck the colonel!' on the way back!"

No, our old CO didn't take himself overly seriously. Jerry claims to have been there the day one of the colonel's staff went up for a ride with a pilot from the Air Force base at Bari, and they buzzed our rest area. "Church was just coming out of his tent when this P-38 dives right down over his flags and pulls up the last second, and he says to his aide: 'Go get that man! He came within twelve paces of the flag and didn't salute!'"

Befitting a Harvard man, my first order of business in Rome, indeed my only business there, was to pay a courtesy call on The Duchess.

The dogface had been set on course for the Duchess when back in the States the imminent success of the Anzio landing was assumed. Some well-meaning or black-humored relative had sent me a Christmas necktie; I wrote home not long before the counterattack that "perhaps I can wear it to see the Duchess when we get to Rome."

Long before she was "the Duchess," the beautiful young Fernanda Rocchi married a Russian named Riabouchinsky around 1915. Her second husband in 1919 was Robert Goelet of the wealthy New York family, at the time a captain with the American Expeditionary Force in France. After their separation, she returned to her native Italy in 1939 and married the Duke of Villarosa. Her son Robert Goelet by her second marriage was now with the Navy in the Pacific. His wife and daughter were living in Boston, where my father was little Fernanda's pediatrician. Anxious about the Duchess's situation in occupied Rome, and learning from him that his son was a soldier at Anzio, the Goelets hoped I'd be able to look in on her at the address they asked him to forward to me.[5]

General Eagles must have backed off his ban by then because I got a pass to Rome, where I found that she'd moved. Being a scout of course, I scouted down her rented town house, confirmed by the brightly polished brass door plate: *Duchessa di Villarosa, 7 Via Donizetti*, whacked the well-shined knocker, and was admitted by a liveried butler to a drawing room that may have been in the style of the late Empire, quite in contrast to my recently vacated quarters in the Bedpan not thirty miles distant.

Presently the Duchess herself swept in, a striking woman of perhaps fifty, quite unfazed by this unbathed apparition from the recent Beachhead, this mere Pfc., hardly your expected conqueror, or liberator, or bemedalled officer at least, who had spruced himself up as best he could with water of dubious origin from an upside-down helmet in a field outside the city somewhere.

"I saw the Duchess finally," I duly reported to my sire. "She is very charming and attractive, speaking perfect English. I'll have to tell you her story some day; it's out of Oppenheim [E. Phillips Oppenheim, prolific British thriller novelist]. Met her other son (or nephew?) who also speaks English perfectly, and am going to hit the high spots with him. She is desperate for news. Knows nothing of her son or family, wants all the news she can get and a photo of her grandchild. You can do this through me, or perhaps directly with her."

Her man brought in a couple of glasses of wine, or perhaps cocktails and little crackers, and in due course I withdrew, promising to return for the weekend with whatever edibles I could cadge from the mess sergeant. My hostess, in common with about everyone else in Rome who was not in perfervid collaboration with the occupying Germans, was on rather short rations.

The humorless Griff or whoever was responsible for my liberty must have been intrigued with my account of this modest encounter with Roman nobility, for I got a second pass, this time for an overnight, and showed up at the appointed hour with a field pack of tinned and packaged army chow, fit, if not for a king, certainly for a Duchess in gustatorial distress. Her man received me with enthusiasm and made off with the forage to the kitchen, for I was expected in time for Saturday lunch.

We were joined at the table by her two sons, or perhaps stepsons, Luciano and Paul, whom I found "very nice if a bit too sophisticated and Anglified." In an intimate but noble dining room we were seated by the butler, now clad in immaculate white with green and gold braid and serving gloves. Soup was already at our places in the widest and most exquisitely gilded plates I'd ever seen, exuding a tempting and vaguely familiar bouquet.

And then, when the soup was cleared, what all had been waiting for, the *pièce de résistance* from the viands catered intact from the USA by the Hero of the Day! And with a glow of satisfaction on his face, and a renewed spring to his step, in comes the flunkey with a silver-rimmed platter doubtless handed down through generations of dukedom, in the geometrical center of which crouched the most mouth-watering chunk of Spam I'd seen in an entire week.

That afternoon I was presented to a blond, handsome chap of perfect manners and English, introduced as Count David York, who explained he'd been a member for the past three years of the Swedish legation but had been displaced from the Excelsior Hotel on Via Vittorio Veneto, tops in Rome and therefore taken over as a Fifth Army officers' club. He was staying with the Duchess in the old-fashioned sense, I gathered. "A very sincere and interesting fellow," I thought. I was given the impression that while representing a neutral country, York perhaps had been supplying Allied operatives in Rome with enlightening information as to what the Germans might be up to, in the manner of the mysterious "Swedish traveler" cited in news dispatches from unlikely places. Or—who knows?—the reverse.[6]

All the more intriguing is my hurried journal note of June 28: "While in Rome she was known to be antiFascisti and was blacklisted by the Germans. She played a deadly game of associating with German officers, gaining information from them, and at the same time harboring escaped Allied officers in her house." I remember nothing more.

Once when I couldn't get a pass, Jerry carried a note from me and confirmed later that the Duchess "explained that, you know, you had to survive, and she left me with the impression that she'd walked a tightrope and probably had been gracious to them as she was to us." In a letter home June 20 he added:

> We chatted about 15 minutes about the Germans and the food situation. She fits the picture of a duchess as I pictured one. I felt perfectly at ease all the while, which may be due to her graciousness or to my feeling that every Italian, no matter who he or she may be, is inferior to me. Anyway, this plus the fact Trubia managed to become friends with the Prince of Savoy made the I&R high in the ranks of society—in spite of no bars on shoulders.

Dom Trubia and the Prince of Savoy? Egad, I don't remember that.[7]

Late Saturday afternoon or early that evening Luciano and Paul brought me along to a party somewhere in the great, mysterious, romantic, holy, dangerous city, a party like many where the wine flows, a party that lodges in the vault of my senses as a swirling blur of foreign voices, loud and liberated, and of foreign faces, noble faces, faces finally free of fear, the faces of Rome's and no doubt Italy's most elevated crust. It was a fitting party for a Pfc. to be escorted to by the heirs of an Italian Duke who had just emerged from hiding, for indeed Luciano had until recent days enjoyed the protection of the Pope himself as a member of His Holiness's Noble Guards, by definition and duty bound within the Vatican walls— until the exodus of the Germans, anyway.

And that is how two weeks after the liberation I met in all that din and cocktail chatter two other brothers, handsome young fellow Guardsmen of Luciano's about my age, the

Princes Nicolai and Dmitri Romanov, grandnephews of the murdered Tsar Nicholas II and grandsons of the sister of Queen Elena of Italy, who had been spirited to the Vatican when the Gestapo was rounding up all the Russians it could find in Rome.

We talked of . . . who remembers? Did we roam the streets that night, move on to another party, the brothers Romanov and Villarosa, and I whose only brothers were the Ironheads? Perhaps, but probably not. The princes had been liberated, in a manner of speaking, and I had more of liberation to be a part of.

Next day Luciano took me to St. Peter's. I dispatched homeward a lengthy description of "the most beautiful sight I ever saw or expect to see. The magnificence, and in many cases, simplicity and great grandeur, take your breath away, and I understand how so many are converted to Catholicism when they first see it."

Outside, in the great square of St. Peter's, a sister came up and pressed on me a small St. Christopher's medal that I carried with me for the duration and long after until, to my unbelief, I lost it.

Wandering through St. Peter's, Dave O'Keefe and some G.I.s had "about the first audience the Pope gave in the Sistine Chapel or a little room just outside it, and I held up my rosary beads and he touched 'em!"

"Rome is tremendous," I wrote home, "and I could see only a jot of it. It is a city of wide boulevards, flanked by palaces of all ages, ruins or vestiges here and there, piazzas galore. The Tiber runs through the center, a muddy stream which has been made beautiful through the years by merely making use of the fact, architecturally, that it is a river. I am sending pictures taken in a street and a note from the Duchess, as she is rather anxious."

One photo of me swinging along purposefully was inscribed to Miss Bryan with appropriate irony: "How can we lose with men like this?" She reciprocated with several heart-tumbling snapshots that I treasured in my wallet until victory was ours and beyond.

By the third week of June we were on trucks, shifting time into reverse as the 45th convoyed back to the Beachhead, back to Anzio, and then we were back to sea on an LCI, and back, back past Naples from which we had embarked five months before, and back to Salerno for the second time in eleven months, now in peace but once again with amphibious intentions, back in the Seventh Army, now under Lieutenant General Alexander M. "Sandy" Patch, who had commanded the 14th Corps at Guadalcanal at the end of 1942.

Something was certainly afoot. The Thunderbirds were bivouacked exactly where they'd landed the previous ninth of September. Was it someone's black humor? From the bitter, bloody beach we trekked through the now-peaceful countryside and encamped outside Battipaglia, a mile or so from the den from which the Panzers roared down on the 157th that terrible sixth day in Hitler's all-out thrust to split *that* beachhead.

We were told we had been enrolled for a ten-day session at the Invasion Training Center back on the beach, as of the Fourth of July, courtesy of Uncle Sam. We were not told what for, that the 45th was to have the honor to participate in Operation Dragoon, (changed from code name "Anvil," which the Germans were believed to have caught on to), namely the invasion of Southern France.

"Southern France, I suppose," I had journaled. Top-secret stuff.

Anyway, the 45th was out from under Mark Clark and *his* Fifth Army, along with the likewise battered Third and 36th, which followed us down from Rome a week or so later.

We swam in the cerulean waters of Salerno Bay so recently red with the blood of Yanks who never had a chance to wonder why, and we played volleyball under the now-heavenly sun of southern Italy, haunched down on the slope after supper for good old American black-and-white movies cast on an outdoor screen, and grabbed off passes to pile into six-by-six GM trucks for the ride through Salerno to the ruins of Pompeii at the southerly foot of Mount Vesuvius, buried under the epochal eruption of 79 A.D.

June 27 letter home:

> The city is only half excavated—four square miles are dug up and it's quite a walk. In 36 hours 36 feet of ash fell (and three or four inches of fine grey ash fell since the last eruption). The houses follow a standard design (the wealthier ones)—open-roofed patio with pool and adjoining garden surrounded by pillared and roofed terrace, rooms being around the terrace. In many respects the buildings and streets are quite similar to the poorer sections of modern Italian towns. Lead plumbing was used, pipes being of lead strips bent into a cylinder and crudely fused. Even stopcocks. An interesting sidelight is the Roman attitude toward sex. There was no shame connected with brothels—in fact prostitution was quite legal, and Pompeii was known as the pleasure center of the Roman Empire. Phallic symbols were used to point out the way to the red light district. It is amusing that mythology quite easily dispensed with the unRoman sentimentalism of Christian morals.

For all but the most archaeologically minded of the touring G.I.s, in fact, the Roman attitude toward sex was unavoidably rather more than a sidelight. Not merely stopcocks were used, but cocks—mightily erect ones a couple of feet long, pointing the way to pleasures long anticipated, chiseled in bas relief plaques in the corners of dozens of structures. And once at destination one found, high on the walls of the happily excavated chambers of happiness, wondrously preserved frescoes instructing in the available postures of liaison beyond any need for the spoken Latin.

Back at the entrance to it all, the all-American boy/soldier was assailed, coming and going, by a shouting, pushing throng of entrepreneurs with "Hey Joe! Wanna cock-an'-a-balls? Only fifty lira! Cock-an'-a-balls here! Solid silva! Hey Joe! Nice souvenir! How 'bout? Hey, fifty lira!" Miniature cock-an'-a-balls in silver or an approximation, complete with elegant chain for a necklace to send home to wife, girl, Sis, Mom or Grandma as a memento of the ancient—and contemporary—Roman attitude toward sex.

What I did buy was a small and rather more aesthetically elevating watercolor of a fresco from the House Vetti in Pompeii by Gallo Giovanni (who would make his name as the official artist of Pompeii) depicting a cherub in a chariot drawn by a pair of prancing antelope. All I had the liras for, and I mailed it home along with the Kraut helmet (where'd I get *that*?) I'd stashed away in my barracks bag.

As our amphibious training got under way, Hank Mills, Dom Trubia, Dave O'Keefe and I found ourselves in the reorganized crew of Sergeant Mickey Smith, just returned from hospitalization in Naples initially for gallstones but discharged after a bout with dysentery and a rematch with malaria. Perhaps out of consideration for Smitty's still-rocky condition, and the fact that I was the only one who hadn't landed under fire, I was able to record a couple of days into the exercise, which was aimed at replacements anyway, that "so far we've ducked it."

Not for long, however. We were attached to First Battalion, and midway into the exercises I noted that we'd been told to remove our Thunderbird shoulder patches,

and rumors are very diversified as to our future. The CO of the 180th called together his NCOs and told them that they are going to Naples and then on a 21-day boat trip to a spot not so bad as the French beaches nor as bad as the Italian front. The CO of the 179th says ships are stocked for 28 days. A boat-load fresh from the States says there are signs all over Devens, "Welcome Home, 45th." One man's guess is as good as another's—England, Cherbourg, Norway, Yugoslavia? At least it doesn't appear yet as though we were making a beachhead.

I can't imagine why not. When the invasion training was over I debriefed myself: "First day we boarded LCIs [158 feet, ram up on the beach, the 200 amphibians file ashore down two fore and aft gangways], lay around in the harbor. That night, very rough, we boarded LCIs and transferred with great difficulty to an LST, after stoving a small hole in her side. At 5 next AM we got on LCVPs [Landing Craft, Vehicle, Personnel] from the LST and landed. That night we again boarded LCIs and transferred to LSTs for regimental problem. Landed next morning on LCVPs and ran through a screwed-up problem."

And as an afterthought concerning the nameless maps of an anonymous coast that we were solemnly instructed to commit to memory: "We knew designated underwater obstacles, pillboxes, terrain features, roads, houses, etc., matched our real objective, though we weren't told where and seem to have been the last to be let in on the war's worst kept secret."

Ironheads we surely were, yet accomplished goldbricks, for I managed to get away to the Verdi Opera House in Salerno for a performance by an English road company of J. B. Priestley's *Laburnum Grove*, which I found "an excellent satire on the English middle class," and we found ample time to swim and horse around on the once-dreaded beach, enough to apologize to my confidential notebook for the recent absence of confidences:

Perhaps it's not that I have been so busy. Rather, it's due to the fact that I am more and more one of the boys and spend more time fooling around. At the beginning of the beachhead I was quite unpopular, I hear. I hadn't yet, apparently, succeeded in completely adjusting myself to living with men under terrible strain. Just enough of college was left in me to make me critical and a bit supercilious, I'm afraid.

The Russians are past Vilno and considerably less than 100 miles from Prussia, and have begun an offensive in the south. Caen has been taken. Here we are hitting the Gothic Line and the greatest

resistance since the fall of Rome. This line consists of 6000-foot peaks and is considered the strongest
natural defense barrier in Italy. We are making some headway but are still a few miles short of Leghorn.

Done with our ten days of invasion training, the Regiment moved a few miles south
through the old Beachhead still littered with shattered monuments to our invasion of Italy,
and into the pyramidal tents, complete with cots, of a seaside rest camp near the monumental temples of Paestum, erected there by the Greeks from Sybaris who founded
Poseidonia, 600 years before the birth of Christ, and who knew how to please themselves
while pleasing their gods.

Gorgeous weather, showers, mess hall, Red Cross snack bar, demobilized Italian soldiers doing KP, cleaning the tents, policing up the area and odd-jobbing, movies, swimming, games. The only inconvenience, I journaled, was the "Vesuvial ash from the recent
eruption three inches thick in some places, very fine grey cinders, a little larger than coffee
grounds; hear it will multiply crop yields for years." Still, we hadn't had it so good since the
States. Altogether the perfect place, we voted, "to sweat out the rest of the war." Spotted
commando buddy George Furber trudging along in a column with full gear, exchanged
shouts, and they passed on up the dusty road.

Man, he could have it.

July 14 letter home: "I have no news I can reveal ... If Joe Stalin doesn't slacken his pace,
it will be all over before we know it. Germany, of course, will try to make a separate peace
with Russia, but this won't come about. (Bryan writes that she's going to drop in on
Garlands ... Want to hear what she's like)."

"An apathy or sort of mental torpor has been growing on me," I complained home. "I get
little enjoyment and less satisfaction out of life. I seem to be living a hopeless existence.
Nothing to look forward to, no really close friends in the outfit. Wherever I go I feel thwarted."

But armies come, and armies go, and after a sybaritic week on the shores of the
Tyrrhenian, the 45th trucked back north through Naples to Qualiano, a crossroads six
miles equidistant from the city and the sea. Here in the "Dust Bowl," where the heat held
unabated with no rain (how opposite from the Winter Line), we repitched our pup tents
amidst the olive groves, and sweated it out.

The Colonel talked to some of the NCOs, including Griff. We're going on an assault operation from
here, hitting a beach where rather poor resistance is expected. Apparently there are not large numbers
of troops there and not good troops, either. It is expected that we will penetrate at least ten miles before
any organized resistance appears. There will be mountains. He says it will probably be easy going.

Our latest venue offered a varied Neapolitan fare. Passes were liberal, and for certain
home events such as admission to the pup tent on the edge of our bivouac in which a young
local woman made not exactly free with a succession of about forty panting guys in an
impatient line out in the field, they weren't required. What more can I say, what less should
I say, about the degradation of war, which by definition leaves no winners?

Heading the menu in Naples was the fare at the renowned San Carlo Opera House near the docks which, after cleaning up the bomb damage, the Brits had reopened the previous November 15, only six weeks after the city's liberation, with, according to the program, "Italian dancers wearing brassieres and G strings, an Italian band playing the latest American popular successes in swingtime, and an Italian tenor singing 'Come Back to Sorrento.'"

By the time we hit town enough of the former singers, musicians and backstage people of the old San Carlo had been rounded up to restore the glorious operas of Italy to its lofty stage *voce piena*, and hundreds of thousands of Allied soldiers and sailors had filled and refilled its two thousand seats. The three I took in while we awaited our fate, *Traviata*, *Pagliacci* and *Cavelleria Rusticana*, sing and soar in memory, shards of sunshine and even hope amidst the storms of war and its aftermath that continued to ravage the length and breadth of this joyous and tragic land.

The drama was not all inside the San Carlo; outside its almost soundproof walls, Babel reigned. Out on the hollow, echoing, shuffling Via Roma di Napoli the world of World War II streamed up and down and in and out of the alleys, the bars, the cafes, the cathouses, the joints, the trinketries, the galleries, the black markets. Like cops everywhere, the MPs aloofly shouldered their way against the current—all back and forth like a turgid tidal creek, as purposelessly (except not to die) as lost souls at home and far away from home could mingle and part forever, listless and loveless as when they met, all victims of war, as time would prove, all losers, no winners.

One relevantly irrelevant image of that pulsating aorta overpowers the rest. As a couple of us leaned against a building on the bank of the sidewalk stream one afternoon for a smoke and to observe as idly as possible the tide run in one direction or the other or both, our interest was caught by a pair of dogfaces who'd taken up a stand on the other side of this main drag, facing each other across the sidewalk.

As we watched they raised and lowered their right hands a foot or so above the sidewalk, crouching and rising and crouching again in unison as if holding a thread between them. And the listless and the loveless, by the ones and twos and fours both ways, lifted up their feet to step over one more hurdle in the way, and with nary a grin, not even a smile.

Meanwhile, I had to do something about the Duchess. I couldn't just abandon her to Spam amidst the plush ironies of Via Donizetti. I remembered hearing that the Sixth General Hospital commanded by Colonel Thomas Goethals, father of my oldest friend Hank, who had gone in the Army (but not the infantry) with me from Harvard, was moving from North Africa to Rome. I wrote the eminent Boston obstetrician and colleague of my father (his father, General George W. Goethals, supervised the construction of the Panama Canal), bequeathing to him the *Duchessa di Villarosa* and enclosing letters from her son and daughter-in-law for the distinguished Colonel to hand-deliver.

My pen pal Helen (a.k.a. Monk) had written her parents then in Hattiesburg, Mississippi, where her father was an Army chaplain, that this friend of Bill Belleman's on Anzio is "terrifically intelligent with a sense of humor that is just killing, and his letters are

Dressed for lunch with the Duchess and as up for a bottle as for battle, I'm snapped by a street photographer in Rome (*left*). To the unseen but dreamt-of girl of eighteen back home (*right*) I mail a memento across which I've scrawled self-deprecatingly, "How can we lose with men like this?" (*Collection of the author*)

always well-written and his incidents well-chosen. He said he would be very pleased if I could stop in and say hello to his family, but not to feel obligated. I have an idea that it would be a very nice thing to do. It isn't out of order is it?"

It wasn't, and on the eleventh of August, with a school friend in tow, Monk traveled at my family's invitation from Boston to the adjacent suburb of Brookline for dinner. "Lovely people," she reported to Hattiesburg afterwards. "Of course, they are very proud of Joe and naturally interested to know what manner of woman be I. They were quite amazed, so it seems, when Joe wrote about me. They said he'd never been interested in girls at all—(that somewhat answers your question as to why he doesn't have a special girl at home)."

Never interested? Ma and Pa must have been running interference, because they knew darn well I'd gone ga-ga a few times, and they thought Monk was something else.

With the summer off before entering Sarah Lawrence College, she persuaded herself that it was her patriotic duty to get a defense job, which she found on a radar assembly line at Raytheon, an hour's ride by subway and trolley car from Boston in suburban Waltham. Her top-secret assignment was to test radar bulbs by plugging them in as they paraded by and tapping each with a sort of cork lollipop to test its efficacy.

Between her commuting costs and mandatory payroll deductions for benefits and union dues, my overseas girl friend discovered she was netting next to nothing and retired after a week of it. Her next job was with a useful little agency called Little Useful. Among other assignments Monk read to a nice blind lady and found someone to repair Harvard President Conant's fishing creel.

Back across the ocean on August 11, the day the sparkling young lady was meeting my family:

Several days ago we came down to the staging area and made a dry run on our LCI. Yesterday we got on the boats for good, and we're lying in Salerno Harbor now preparing to start. The Russians haven't moved much, but we have cut off Brittany and driven down towards Chartres. Our tanks are now less than 65 miles from Paris! Undoubtedly we will land in Southern France. We put in for currency exchange today.

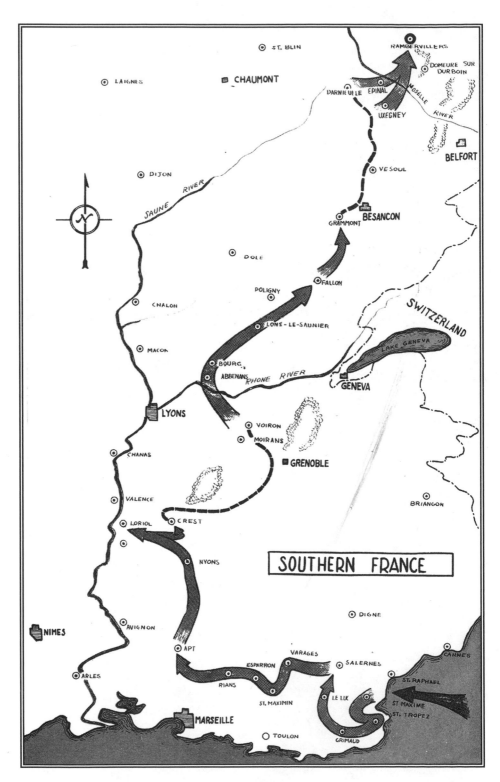

(*Department of Defense*)

✦✦ 10 ✦✦

FORTUNES O' WAR, MY ASS

France: Ste.-Maxime to Varages
August 1944

OUR LCI THROBBED AND GROANED and rolled and plunged toward the Strait of Bonifacio between the island bulks of Sardinia and Napoleon's Corsican homeland. We were stuffed into one of the 41 workhorse LCIs in the fleet of 221 vessels from transports on down, not including naval support, bearing the 45th Infantry Division on the fourth and final assault of its amphibious destiny.

Similar Seventh Army task forces carried old comrades and new in the 36th on our right and the Third on our left, and to their left, General Jean de Lattre de Tassigny's First Army of Free French bent on the liberation of Marseille, Toulon and points between and beyond.

We all made up the Allied Sixth Army group under General Jacob Devers, 33,000 of us and 3,300 vehicles in the 45th alone with all its support units, although probably not many more than 2,500 from our 157th and 180th Regiments, which would be the first to hit the beach, with the 179th in floating reserve. For all the comfort we could take in such company, we in that LCI among so many might as well have been alone on an empty sea. One small bomb from above or a single shell from a shore battery could blow us out of the water.

"Anvil," the abandoned code name for the assault on the French underbelly, was no less descriptive than "Overlord" was for the Normandy invasion, the object being to entrap the 230,000 *Boches* in the First and 19th enemy Armies under Generaloberst Johannes Blaskowitz in the south and southwest of France they were charged with occupying. Anvil's replacement, "Dragoon," means to compel into submission by violent means. So much for high-brass semantics.

The operation had been postponed when there weren't boats enough to float a second landing in France, and up to the last minute Prime Minister Churchill, from his bombproof war room, pressed Eisenhower to cancel it altogether in favor of another attempt at a big push in Italy or a Balkan invasion. The PM argued, out of what Ike viewed with his usual restraint as more political than military considerations, that southern France would be a slow and bitterly fought campaign, and there were adequate ports of entry on the Channel.

But in the end the Supreme Yank prevailed upon Sir John Bull that Marseille was urgently needed as another port, that intelligence showed southern France was thinly occupied by German forces and that a rapid thrust would not only protect the right flank of the northern advance but could cut off their escape as the two Allied armies joined in a pincers above Switzerland.

The tactical point of our immense swarm fell to the Seventh Army under General Patch, whose sector covering forty-five miles of the Riviera west of Cannes was most favorable for the approach to the Rhône and the drive up its great valley intended to link up with our eastward-roaring Third Army under Patton, thereby dragooning General Blaskowitz and his necessarily fleeing armies of occupation.

For ten months I'd been an Ironhead, a veteran in a manner of speaking, but not of Sicily or Salerno. This was my first landing with an assault division, next to Normandy the biggest of the war. On August 13, the day German air reconnaissance spotted our huge convoy, setting the 11th Panzer Division into motion toward the Rhône from Bordeaux, I made my last journal entry for two more months.

We have francs now. H-hour is 8 AM Tuesday. We land in a small bay between Toulon and Cannes, with the town of St. Maxime for an objective, I guess. As usual, orientation stinks—nobody knows anything. Our boat lands approximately H plus 2. A few hundred yards to our left is a small defended peninsula which can rake the shore, and barbed wire is fairly heavy as are mines. We may have trouble on a sandbar offshore. Again, nobody seems to know. I suppose I&R's big job is to find the CP and await orders.

While we were laying over in Salerno harbor the boys had an amphibious whore up in #1 hold who came out to the ship by rowboat. I've seen everything. It's a smooth trip so far. We arrive at a Corsica harbor this PM, I think, and wait 30 hours to get under way again. I'll close now and won't write again til I get the chance in France.

Our convoy didn't lay over for thirty hours in the Strait of Bonifacio but got under way again the next morning, August 14, and with almost two hundred miles to go, swung northwest for France. Our LCI was about the size of a large fishing boat. Its engine throbbed as it strove through that day and all night to deliver us to our beach, and so did our stomachs and our hearts. But no sign of the Luftwaffe, thanks to our bombs on its airfields.

"Never before," wrote Samuel Eliot Morison, the Navy's war historian, "had an amphibious force embarked so fit, ready, and full of *élan* as this one for the invasion of

Provence." Speaking on behalf of Willie and Joe, by your leave, Admiral Sir, I can say that
we were fit and ready for the next boat home, but as for *élan*, forget it.[1]

What the hell, H plus two. Not the first wave nor even the second. A whole two hours
after the bombardment stops and the fun begins. Maybe the guys would have the beach
cleared by then. Sure they would! We turned away from picturing them on the attack with
their guns, bayonets, bandoliers, grenades and full combat packs and gear, jumping off the
ramps into the surf up to their waists in a hail of fire, taking the shit for us.

Thus we few thousands variously in harm's way (prissy euphemism) sweated it out
again, surging onward toward occupied France, drawing minute by merciless minute closer to 0800 on Tuesday, August 15, 1944, when the Scoutmaster-in-Chief would glance at
his watch, stick the whistle in his mouth, and draw his breath.

Then each and every one of us who as mechanically as a single round had been shoved in
the chamber, and the bolt pulled back, and the rifle aimed, and the trigger squeezed, BLAM,
were on our way, as insensible of our destination and destiny as the bullet of its target.

For myself, all that lingers of my own particular trajectory on what must have been a
memorable morning is a ghostly aftertaste somewhere on the palate of my memory, a *bouil-
labaise* of dread and resignation, savored with a *soupçon* of oily bilge and a dash of *mal de mer*.
"Air recon doesn't show too much," I tried to reassure myself. "Probably a fairly easy landing." I know we bulled about whatever wasn't on our minds, swilled coffee, and
chainsmoked, flicking our Zippos with trembling, nicotined fingers. Dave O'Keefe, who
didn't smoke and generally remained maddeningly cool, played game after game of miniature pegboard chess with "Vawlter Voolff," perturbably off on the next rendezvous with his
former *Landsmänn*, while dukes-up Henry Mills advanced to the Practical Joke Playoffs.

> This tall, thin, cocky bastard of a jeep driver took the CO_2 cylinders outta my life pre-
> server. Somehow I found out that if I'da jumped over the side and squeezed 'em, I'da
> went clear to the bottom. He started to laugh, and I told him "I've got a notion to
> punch you right in the mouth." And I've never seen Dan Boone so hostile. He was
> sittin' there and says, "Yeah, you sonofabitch, if he don't I think I will; that was a ass-
> hole trick." I never thought Danny was ever gonna punch anybody.

Later Danny confided to Hank: "If I don't make it home by Christmas, I'm never
gonna." He wasn't alone on that one.

Two months later. October 8 journal:

*There's been a continual melee since the landing at France with next to no chance to enter anything in
the journal. The opportunity has finally been forced upon me by inactivity and boredom, and I'm now
propped up in a very uncomfortable position in the 300th General Hospital at Naples. All the events
that took place in France must be related from memory. Some are happy, some sad.*

*We landed at Sainte Maxime in the Gulf of St. Tropez on the 15th of August at H plus two—10 AM.
The night before, a couple of islands* [Iles d'Hyères, southeast of Toulon] *containing heavy coastal*

defenses had been neutralized by the First Special Service Forces. Shortly previous to H-hour airborne troops [First Airborne Task Force] *had landed behind the main Riviera defenses (which included anti-glider and paratrooper obstacles—heavy poles set in likely landing spots).*

The softening-up preparatory to H-hour was terrific. We watched wave after wave of bombers [1,300 on the invasion front] *pass overhead through breaks in the thick, early-morning fog* [as they had for two weeks]. *Tremendous salvos from the naval guns rocked the LCI and then the rocket ships tore loose, a sight which I missed.* [I can't imagine why. The massed rocket salvos by the hundreds from the specially fitted LCTs that had been transferred down from Normandy, intended to detonate land mines on the beaches, sounded like the end of the earth for ten minutes until one before H-hour.]

We expected the landing to be something along the lines of the Normandy deal. Nothing could have been more remote. There had been a few rounds of mortar fire on the beach, just a bit of machine gun, and that was all. The troops had driven well in from the beach when we waded ashore, and the only resistance met was a rather stubborn pillbox in the town of Ste. Maxime, which was soon reduced, and we swept inland to begin the amazing campaign that brought us to Belfort within three weeks.

At the east end of the 45th's three miles of beach Admiral Morison found a 220-millimeter gun (made by Bethlehem Steel for the French in 1918) camouflaged to look like the garden of a nearby villa, with rosebushes carefully painted on the concrete.[2]

Eric Sevareid of CBS News went in with the 45th on an LST that carried Dragoon's only radio transmitter available to correspondents, while Herbert Matthews of the *New York Times*, with the outfit at Salerno, was back with us. Sevareid wrote of our landing in *Not So Wild a Dream:*

> ... I could not quite believe it could all be over so quickly, so easily as this ... I felt almost disappointed. The soldiers did not.
>
> ... The dry hills beyond the beach and the coastal road were burning in several places, and a pink pleasure villa showed a wide hole where a shell had gone clear through. The road was already choked with traffic, and bands of prisoners, their hands in the air, were marching toward the water line. Already army signposts were stuck in the sand, and soldiers were directing traffic with a wave of the hand. The cement wall, five feet thick and eight feet high, had proved a poor defense. The first waves had surmounted it with ladders, and sappers had blown a great breach in it through which we rolled as easily as if we were entering the gate of a city—or a nation. A few trees were sprawling on the streets of Saint-Maxime [*sic*], and a few lengths of telegraph line were draped over hedges and fences. Three American Negroes sat in the shade against the stucco wall of a bistro, guarding a batch of prisoners from the master race. A white soldier was stretched out by the road with his shoes off under a bright green beach umbrella. Another was methodically moving through a vineyard filling his helmet with fat, bronze grapes. A girl of about thirteen, wearing an American helmet cocked over her long yellow hair, was trying, between spurts of self-conscious laughter, to pin a bunch of bright flowers to the shirt of a raw-boned infantryman.

Rocket ship with launchers for 1,000 rockets (*U.S. Army*)

Wading in from the LCI (*Department of Defense*)

There were not many civilians around. They watched us with an intense expression of curiosity, and they smiled easily, but there was no wild demonstration in this place. It was clear: the shock of the battle had stunned them, some of their friends had been killed, and they were just a little disappointed that we were not French.[3]

Just before embarking from Italy Jerry Waldron's map-reading ability and good judgment elevated him from the I&R to S2, the regimental intelligence section.

We got ashore and marched up that road from the beach as fast as we could for three or four hours, broke to have lunch and never finished because they made us get up and hit the road again. They had so many vehicles along that road we had to get up and take more ground so they could get more on! I remember a chaplain coming back with a prisoner, very pleased. It was like old home week in every town we came to because they were so happy it wasn't down around their ears.

It all went off as close to clockwork as anyone had seen in this screwed-up war. The seventh wave of Thunderbirds was ashore by 0910, barely more than an hour after H, and without a casualty. By the end of the first day the 157th alone had 356 prisoners, with only seven casualties, all wounded. After thirteen months in the war the 45th was finally in on the winning of it. The Heinies were on the run.

Our first day in France. Dibble, Richardson, Mills and Smith (Richardson and Smith wearing the required U.S. identity shoulder patches). (*Courtesy of Dominick M. Trubia*)

"Merci! Merci! cher Yankee!"
(*U.S. Army*)

Over the next couple of days we sped through the main drags of those first Riviera towns, Ste.-Maxime, St.-Tropez, Grimaud, Vidauban, past the stuccoed block houses, the blur of joyful citizens waving and shouting from the sidewalks and the windows, the beautiful beautiful girls, the flowers and wine and kisses and embraces and salutes and fiercely shaken hands. And then back in the countryside, trying out my schoolboy French at one farmhouse and then another with the glib assistance of one more preferred shot of *eau de vie*, the "white lightning" that struck headfirst, or glass of apple "champagne" because the *Boches*, as it was explained, had departed hurriedly, after goosestepping the length and breadth of *La Patrie*, with all the genuine bubbly they could steal.

One day the two Hanks, Mills and Johnson the driver, were jeeping through the countryside on some errand when Johnson found a motorcycle in a barn, got it gassed up and running, and asked Mills to take the jeep back to the outfit while he rode the two-wheeler. Mills:

> So I get back, and Griff says you go back there and tell him to get back here right now or he's outta the Platoon. So I went back and here's Johnson with his shirt off so he won't get grease on it while he's workin' on the motorcycle. He got it out on this road that was crossed by a one-track railroad on nothin' but a cinder bed. He musta got it wound up because when he went off the hard top on the turn, he tole me, he was up high enough in the air to look down and pick the spot where he was gonna land, which was on cinders on his arm and side. I got him in the jeep and got him back and Griff threw him out too, but had a change of heart and brought him back. That's the one time he wasn't mad at me; he was madder at Johnson.

Hank Johnson and his jeep
(*Courtesy of Dominick M. Trubia*)

Typical Johnson, like Pullman's story of the night in Italy when the runt turned in after washing up in his helmet, "and he heard something, looked out there in the blackness and thought he saw a wild dog. Got his gun, BAM! he hit it, and it jumped. BAM BAM! It kept jumpin'. BAM BAM BAM! 'I got the sonofabitch! I got it!' Hell, he went over and his helmet had a dozen holes in it."

Ah, the Champagne Campaign!

By the eighteenth of August we'd penetrated northwest about forty miles from the beach toward the Durance River, an eastern tributary of the Rhône. Having liberated the country town of Salernes, First Battalion had moved on without difficulty to Tavernes, along with the regimental CP and most of the I&R. The town square, with its typically drab and sobering monument to the townsmen who had died in the First War, fringed by the ancient *église*, the *mairie*, *boulangerie* and a couple of hole-in-the-wall *cafés*, was the by-now-usual but never-to-be-tired-of scene of liberation, libation, osculation, gesticulation and celebration of the departure of *les Boches* and the noisy, disorderly arrival of *les Américains*, with much milling around, clanking of tanks across the cobblestones, roar and rush of vehicles, shouting in English and French, and general running about.

After three days of it since landing I was more conversant with the natives, linguistically at least, than the rest of the Ironheads and had been urged and pulled by several voluble *Tavernesoises* into a cubicle cafe and seated at a table upon which was set with great ceremony a bottle of *anisette*. Glasses were brought, and a pitcher of water. A dollop of the clear, sweet, licorice liqueur was dumped in each, then a douse of water that to my amazement alchemized the mixture as white as milk, followed by a toast to liberty and the Americans and the French Resistance, the Maquis (meaning literally a thick underbrush found on the shores of the Mediterranean, especially in Corsica) who were emerging in force all over the countryside. I remember our moment of fraternity graphically because I'd detested the taste of licorice since I rejected my first cloying stick of it as a child. I took a deep breath and did my duty.

Outside in the square, Captain Edwards, the regimental intelligence officer, and Lieutenant Pat Farley, our sometime Platoon leader, were organizing a triumphal reconnaissance into Varages, the next town a few miles on. Farley, the tactician of the "Let's Get

Foolish" patrol that got half his platoon pinned down by machine-gun fire and his knee grazed by a bullet at Salerno, had avoided dealing with such a gang of individualists since his return from hospitalization that near-calamitous day. But he and Edwards had been quaffing the heady fermentations of victory and were avid for another go. They'd get up a bunch of Ironheads and liberate Varages!

Three or four I&R jeeps were already lining up in the square when a couple of very agitated *maquisards* from the FFI (*Forces Françaises de l'Intérieur*, de Gaulle's guerrillas of the resistance) were rushed into the cafe to tell me that Varages was one of the "take-a-stand" delaying points on the road to the main Rhône highway along which the enemy was pulling back, and "buzzing with Krauts," as I recalled in my journal.

There was no time to find out what the hell was going on in Varages. Rushing out of the cafe into the square, I confronted the two officers with the intelligence, hot from the next town, that it was loaded. The two waved me aside with assurances that *their* sources reported no Germans, and it was gonna be a cinch. They suggested, short of ordering me, that I join in the fun. Mickey's crew hadn't been roped in, so I declined, as did Dave O'Keefe, who figured "they wanted to get into town first, and the women would come out and throw flowers and bring out bottles of wine, *vive Américains.* I didn't need that."[4]

Not for another fifty-two years, when on a return to France I began to piece fragments of it together from veteran Maquis, did any of us have an inkling of what had been going on up ahead before the two patriots burst into the cafe with their warning.

The previous day FFI Guerrilla Group 18 under Jean Peronne ambushed a pair of German motorcyclists on the road from Brue-Auriac to Varages, killing one, and wounding and capturing the other, who told them a German convoy (which in fact failed to materialize) was en route to the town.

Hiking through Salernes. Next stop Tavernes. (*Department of Defense*)

As Farley and Edwards were preparing to get foolish, a second Maquis unit, Guerrilla Group 19 under Paul Bertrand, from their OP on the Barjols–Varages road spotted Germans advancing on the town and opened fire in a skirmish that lasted about an hour until they broke off for fear of being surrounded. Meanwhile, the enemy occupying Varages took three townsmen hostage and were on the point of shooting them even as Mayor Colomb, an appointee of the Vichy government, pleaded on their behalf.

Back in Tavernes as many as five jeeps, including a couple in the rear that may have been First Battalion, left the square and drove out on the road to Varages, keeping considerable distance between them.

In the lead was Lieutenant Farley, with Danny Boone beside him driving. Farley's dog robber, Les Gerencer, and George Ruder were in back with the 50-caliber machine gun that had been mounted just before leaving Italy. How the others lined up is not clear. Hank Mills seems to have been in the second jeep; Dom Trubia was toward the end of the parade, as were Captain Edwards and his driver, Gene Oates, with Ruder's buddy Bob Richardson, Bill Stratton and probably others in various jeeps along the way.

In the countryside approaching Varages the patrol met a man who made them understand that the *Boches* were still in the town. This may have been Jean Borgogno from the neighboring town of Barjols on a motorcycle.

In spite of this repeat warning the I&R patrol proceeded around a bend and across a low bridge, and as Boone drove over a rise suddenly came upon a group of Germans piling up a roadblock of furniture and barrels they'd dragged from a nearby house. Startled, they raised their hands in surrender, all but one who ran for the town. According to the French account, Jean Borgogno got behind a wall and joined the Americans in firing at the fleeing soldier. It appears that the Ironheads were not firing, remained unaware of his involvement at this point and supposed the shot or shots came from a trigger-happy dogface somewhere in the countryside.

The gunfire alerted a German machine-gun nest ambushed in a freshly dug grave in the town cemetery behind a high masonry wall on the left of the road. With a clear field of fire up the road around the end of the wall, the gunner opened up. Everyone jumped from the jeeps into the ditch by the roadside—everyone but Ruder, who rose up trying to get the heavy machine gun on Boone's jeep into action. Apparently the surrendering Germans changed their minds fast and took to their heels for the town.

Almost simultaneously a German fired at least one rocket from his *Ofenrohr*, or stovepipe launcher, which struck the passenger side of one of the jeeps.

When they had surprised the roadblock, Pat Farley had told Gerencer to hustle back and find Captain Edwards, presumably to get some support. But when the German machine gun opened up, Les ran back to the jeep and grabbed his rifle while Ruder sprang to the Ironheads' own machine gun. Then, instead of following the others in the deep ditch, Les sprinted along the exposed side, and as he crossed the bridge his gun was shot out of his hand.

As George struggled to get the machine gun into action, a burst from the German machine gun in the cemetery ripped across his stomach and he pitched forward, grabbing at his guts with both hands.

Lieutenant Farley told his driver—exactly as he had at Salerno—to get out of the ditch and back up on the road to turn the jeep around. Leaping into his seat, Dan swung to the left, spun the wheel and backed up; as he was turning toward the rear, the machine gunner in the graveyard riddled him under the right arm and in the neck, killing him instantly.

The premonition of three days back of young Danny Boone from Santa Rita, New Mexico, was on the mark.

The same burst or another killed Jean Borgogno, the French freedom fighter. He was thirty-six, married and a father. No one was even aware of him, probably because he was crouched behind a wall.

After jumping out of the jeep bringing up the rear, Dom Trubia crawled back in the ditch until he was around the curve, then ran back to a couple of tanks clattering along the road to Varages, providing cover for the riflemen of A Company who were moving through the uplands field to flank the town from the right. The tanks were already beginning to draw some fire, so he joined A Company. "We got to a clearing, and I pointed out the positions to them, and boy, we got peppered again. Such an awful feeling to hear those machine-gun bullets whiz past your ears."

Hank Mills, too, made his way back to A Company.

I asked the commander if he could help us, and he was gonna do what he could, but he wasn't gonna go runnin' up the road like a wild man and put his troops in jeopardy to save a bunch o' glory-hound bastards that had no business bein' up there anyway. I walked side by side with him up to where the action had taken place, and everything was cleared. The jeep was still there, but the roadblock and the Germans was gone. It was over. It was a delayin' action, and they wanted to get the hell outta there as bad as we did.

The people of Varages came out and carried Danny to a nearby house and laid him out until Graves Registration got around to taking him back.

Sergeant Griffith had gone back to the Engineers for maps, and I was there with him after he returned.

Griff:
They brought Ruder back in the jeep on his way to the aid station. He was sitting upright with his arms around his stomach. I could see from the pallor in his face that he was probably a goner. Never got to say anything to him. I never did see Boone or his body. That upset me terribly. I knew him well. I think it was Farley asked me to write his folks and tell them something about the circumstances of his death. I'd heard all the details but didn't try to recount them exactly.

Zapiecki:
We tried to get Trubia to go to sleep and gave him pills, and he walked around shakin' his head and cryin'. I went to the Medics to get more pills for him, and there was Ruder, layin' and half sittin', and the doctors, they just wrapped him up. The

first slugs musta hit him in the stomach, and he put his hand there where he got hit, and another burst just shattered him. He was tellin' me how much his stomach hurts, and I went back in the tent and asked the doctor, and he says we can't do nothin' for him, his guts are all ripped out, and it's only a matter of time. He was dead before morning.

Before they started George asked me if he should go, and I says, "Whaddya want, another bottle o' wine? Take a look in the jeep trailer; there's some in there."

And Trubia, we gave him so many pills to sleep we couldn't wake him up.

Trubia:

I broke down and had to be sedated and was in the hospital for a couple of days. Boone had a quick smile, an all-right guy. After the war when I was in Philly I called Ruder's family, and they invited me to their house in Germantown. Stayed for supper and gave them pictures of George and myself.

Mills:

George Ruder was a very, very impetuous young man. A good man, a helluva good man. You believe I'm cocky? Hey, he made me look like Little Orphan Annie. He would tell ya he was gonna win the Medal of Honor. And he wasn't bullshittin', he really meant it. And if he woulda made it through this incident, he mighta.

Bobby Richardson, his buddy, was the exact opposite in personality and everything else. Good man, except when Ruder got killed it ruined Rich. I don't remember how he got out of the Platoon, but later he was a supply sergeant at the replacement depot at Thaon.

For the price of a jeep a guy got killed. That was not the first time that happened to Danny. I'll never forgive 'em for gettin' him killed. Maybe that's more than I should say, but what a helluva waste. And for George too. I didn't know him well, but I was close to Boone.

As these things go, the big machine gun that had never been fired by anyone in the Platoon was so caked with road dust since the landing that a couple of days earlier, while cleaning the breech mechanism, someone had screwed up the reassembly. Too late it was found to be missing the left bolt handle and inoperable.

And the sequel.

Dibble:

Farley and Edwards came down and gave us hell for actin' like somethin' like that never happened before, and were makin' very little of it. Everybody was in a bad mood, and Farley more or less was gettin' the blame for the whole damn thing, which I think was probably right. There was bad feelings, and they knew it, and they came down and gave a big talk and said they didn't want to hear any more about it. Tryin' to play hero, and it didn't work out that way.

Zapiecki:

This is one of the things why I hated Edwards so much. He called us together and says, "You fellers are actin' kinda strange toward us because of what happened. You, Zapiecki, you're the oldest one here. Why is it?" An' I told him, "That was a god-damned foolish thing to do, to go out there an' try an' get a coupla bottles of wine an' have somebody killed off like that." He says, "fortunes o' war." And I says, "fortunes o' war, my ass."

Trubia grieved for us all, Zapiecki raged. At last our luck had run out. Except that it wasn't luck. And it wasn't once but twice. But Pat Farley was such a forgivable fellow.

The first two Ironheads confirmed to have been killed in action were awarded the Silver Star for gallantry, as posthumously as you can get. Seven Germans were killed in the action and buried, with Gallic irony, in the cemetery of their victims.

A final irony. The confrontation at the roadblock appears to have been the distraction that allowed that trio of hostages in Varages to escape execution by the Germans, a trade-off of three for three. Fortunes o' war.

Left: Norby Boone "taking a bath" in his helmet on the front bumper of his jeep, Anzio. *Right:* Bob Richardson, George Ruder and Bob Coleman in Italy just before the southern France invasion. (*Courtesy of Henry G. Mills and Dominick M. Trubia*)

Henry "Hank" Siaud and Roselyne, his wife-to-be, August 1945 (*Courtesy of Henry F. Siaud*)

"The Links of the Chain"

Rians to Livron
August 1944

From Varages the Regiment drove east toward the Durance River and the town of Rians in pursuit of the withdrawing Germans at a rate that kept leaving the supposedly forward-looking I&R far in the rear.

"It was in Rians," I journaled a few weeks later,

that I was in the town square with Griff waiting for Third Battalion to jump off. About two miles behind the town the artillery guys had set up and were apparently registering their guns now and then about a mile beyond the town. Lord knows why, because the Krauts were way off.

Suddenly a farmer came running up in a terrible state of agitation, and I asked him what was the trouble. He said our guns were shelling his house and insisted that the enemy had left long ago. I finally contacted the Third Battalion artillery liaison officer, and he located the source of fire and called it off. It had been these medium guns, and they'd picked this man's house to register on. The saddest part was that his family was there. I got hold of the medics, and they promised to send out a crew to see if there were any casualties.

All this time Griff had been impatiently calling me to go back to the CP. When I had done all I could I joined him, and he jabbered about a war going on, and it was none of my business about civilians, etc., etc. I blew my top and told him that by God, this war might make heartless machines of some men, but it would never do that to me, and it was the least I could do for these people who had suffered so much for our cause. He asked me why I didn't join the medics, and I said I had a damn good mind to. Later, he came up and told me to forget it, which seemed to me a little like putting the cart before the horse.

The Links of the Chain (*Les Maillons de la Chaîne*) is the abridged memoir of Henry Siaud of the French Resistance who volunteered to fight with the I&R.

From Rians we crossed the Durance on a pontoon bridge over a hundred yards long erected by the engineers in about three hours [our bombers had destroyed the old one to hold up the enemy withdrawal], *passing through Pertuis, a very pretty and neat little town, and stopped at La Tour d'Aigues, where we had around two days rest. Here Shorty Nye, Thatch, myself and others found a farm where we got dozens of eggs, fruit and milk for a few C rations. Thus introduced to the family, we were invited for gala suppers two or three times. Another French family came, and the two daughters of the farmer were centers of attraction. We had feasts in the best French tradition, and I was forced to hold conversation throughout with* les vieux, *while the rest of the boys made time with the girls, who found non-French-speaking Americans infinitely attractive.*

Hank Mills, on the other hand, remembers when he and I encountered an elderly lady who offered us sparse supper and wry advice about her neighbors. "An old aristocrat, all she had was beans and something at this big long table. You told her I was a New York gangster, and she believed you and kept looking at me, a baby-faced twenty-year-old, like, 'Don't take no silverware.' She spoke perfect aristocratic English and told us, 'Don't let the people fool you; they treated the Germans the same way when they were here.'"

La Tour-d'Aigues—plain La Tour to the locals—was a typical old Romanesque small town in the countryside of Provence that we liberated on our dash northward from the sea,

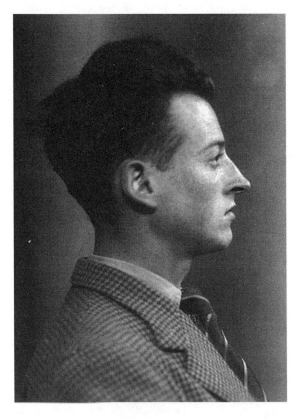

André "Andy" Joannon, 1944
(Courtesy of André Joannon)

to all appearances untouched by time and the Occupation, and hardly even by the war. About thirty miles north of Marseille, it presented as unique a face as Varages and scores of others that don't exist on Michelin's road map and are content not to. And like hundreds of others from the Rhine to the Pyrenees, La Tour-d'Aigues and its citizens had grappled for four years with the presence of the occupying Germans and with their own consciences.

Having witnessed the Dantean dilemma of the Italians under the boot of their former allies, and the mixture of resignation and opportunism with which they viewed us as their "liberators," many of us were quite swept off our feet as we rushed into the interior of France with no more than an intimation of the struggle between resistance, passivity and collaboration except for a chance encounter in a cafe during our own brief occupation of La Tour-d'Aigues.

Lieutenant Foolish Farley and a couple of the boys were having a drink when three young Frenchmen walked in. The big guy introduced himself in good English as Henry Siaud, a long-time member of the Resistance, and his friends as André Joannon and Francis Chaudon. With his broad, open features and ready smile, Henry was barely nineteen; André, who spoke almost no English and had just joined, was twenty-three, spare, somewhat reserved and more Gallic in features and manner. These two wanted to volunteer with us to fight the *Boches*.

Ever casual, Farley looked them over, and of course needing replacements for Boone and Ruder, told them to check with their parents and get back on the double because we're moving out. And so "Hank" and "Andy" became *Têtes de Fer* in G.I. uniforms, eating G.I. chow, bearing American arms, but to the Germans, French civilians in enemy uniforms who would be shot on sight.

Thus for the first time, appropriately in France, our war truly embraced the liberated. Thirty-nine years later, in 1983, Henry Siaud wrote *Les Maillons de la Chaîne* for family and friends, a vividly personal, honest and compassionate saga of his revered father who was the embodiment of the patriot of France in two wars, of his own early life, of the poignancy of defeat, the humiliation of occupation, the finally irresistible rise of resistance, and the redemption of victory. I translated it as *The Links of the Chain* and include extensive exerpts, the first published, in this volume. It expresses, as perhaps only a courageous and deeply patriotic Frenchman who loves America and Americans can, what we Yanks were doing in France for the second time in a generation.[1]

The Links of the Chain

Henry Siaud (1925-2006)

My grandfather, Théophile Siaud, was born in 1857, widowed, and married Louise Brun of Crestet around 1888. He was from a large family in Malaucène that prospered in olive oil. His own grandfather, Casimir, married Michel, one of whose ancestors had been made a noble by the king.

Around 1891 he went to Canada to buy hides with another man, bringing his wife and young daughter Marie. My father, Casimir, was born near Winnipeg in 1893, his brother Henri a year later. The hides business didn't do well, and Théophile lost twelve thousand francs, thanks to his dubious partner, and had to ask for advances from his brothers in France. He tried raising wheat, but a few days from harvest a snowstorm and intense cold ruined his crop.

They moved to the Yazoo valley in Mississippi and tried raising livestock until a flood on the river destroyed everything, so in 1895 they boarded ship for home. Théophile was very seasick. The drunken ship's doctor gave him the wrong injection, and he died, leaving Louise with three small children.

My grandmother had a small family property at Crestet inherited from her father, known as Grand Brun, Big Brown, because of his great height and strength that brought him some notoriety in the region. Yet he was a composer, and his unique daughter Louise was a wonderful piano virtuoso. Trying to make ends meet, she sold the property to family friends at Crestet and bought small grocery stores at Nyons and Vaison-la-Romaine.

Papa had many happy memories of life at Vaison and worshipped his mother, who after the death of her beloved Théophile rejected all offers of marriage with the avowal: "A woman who has been married to a Siaud never remarries."

Papa was apprenticed to a pharmacist, Ganichot, at Vaison, interested in clocks and film projection at a time of great technological advances, but who left the pharmacy for the Army in 1913 and was gone until 1919. At the outset Papa asked his colonel for a transfer from his regiment, which was to be assigned to the Dardanelles, so that he could be nearer his widowed mother, but was refused. Insisting, he was threatened with prison and transferred at the last minute when the colonel had a fit of apoplexy and relented. Back in France, he was a truck driver with a unit of motorized artillery at the front.

He told us many stories—of the shell that smashed in at the foot of the table where they were playing cards in their bunker, but didn't explode; and the one that buried him and a comrade alive, and the others who dug them out who thought their plight so funny that they fell to laughing, which the two of them stopped with a couple of buckets of cold water; of his deafness due to a shell exploding too close; of the day he was spotted in his truck by an enemy observation balloon that followed him for several kilometers, directing shellfire on him. His five years of war at the front shaped the rest of his life. It would be said of him that "his was an iron hand in a velvet glove."

After occupation duty Papa was demobilized and returned to Ganichot's pharmacy, meanwhile having met Mama, Seraphine Bernard, who was working as a cashier in a hotel, having spent five of the best years of her life as governess of the two children of a rich family in Italy. After a while Grandmother Louise sent a letter to Grandfather François Bernard asking the hand of his daughter for her son Casimir, and they were married in 1922. Formidable parents who raised us three in the belief in God, they tried to inculcate in us by example and counsel a sense of duty, the courage to confront obstacles, strength of purpose, especially honesty in all circumstances material and moral, frankness and fear of nothing save God. Papa was profoundly Christian. And the religious education of their children was paramount.

Ganichot as he grew older became increasingly risqué and flighty, which bothered Papa with his young wife, and in 1923 he accepted the offer of Maurice Esseyric to work for him opening his cinema at Nimes. Then arrived Laure and Monique, and me in 1925.

At the approach of the Second War my parents wanted me to have a career in agriculture, and I suspect that they secretly dreamed of one day recovering the little property at Crestet that Grandmother Louise had sold, and installing me there. But just a few days before my departure for the school they were told that it was going to be requisitioned by the army and turned into a military hospital in anticipation of a repeat of the slaughter of the First War. For them it was a hard blow, while I was glad to see my absence prolonged, and in the meanwhile took some courses with a retired professor at La Tour, where we lived, in mathematics, physics, chemistry, history and geography.

The debacle of June 1940 hit us like a thunderclap. I was at La Tour at this dramatic moment. I read the newspaper avidly every morning with a young neighbor of my age, André Brest, and would imagine strategies of counterattack for the French armies, a pincer in Sedan, the return of those who had been surrounded from Dunkirk, finally the Armistice that Marshal Pétain demanded on the 15th of June. This stopped the hostilities in our country under conditions that were so resented by all of us. As for me, I wept.

Casimir Siaud, a Poilu in World War I
(*Courtesy of Henry F. Siaud*)

Our dark years set in. Food became limited. Petrol almost entirely disappeared from the pumps and was reserved for doctors or indispensable official services. We began to hear talk of a dissident general named de Gaulle who had gone to England to continue the fight against the Germans, condemned to death by the government then in place under the presidency of the ex-hero of Verdun, Pétain.

Like many from the preceding war, Papa had joined the Legion of Veterans under the banner of the Marshal but was expelled for his outspoken support of de Gaulle at a time when there were the first glimmerings of the Resistance. In March 1941 I was enrolled by my parents in an agricultural school at Rians. The headmaster was pro-Pétain, as were most of the other pupils. Emboldened by Papa's example, I announced that I was a Gaullist and incurred the jibes of the others, whom I taunted with my shouts of "Vive de Gaulle!" They would chase me in the evenings after school and caught me once, pinned me down and were starting to strangle me when one told the others to leave off. I got up and shouted after them "Vive de Gaulle!" I did so much damage to my tormentors that I earned a reputation as a fighter. The anti-Gaullist taunts ceased, and I made some good friends out of it. We were always hungry and related to each other our dreams of food, caught a cat and got the Italian cook to boil it for dinner, and once fried a snake. We stole cherries and chickens at night from the farmers and cooked a chicken in hiding and had a feast with black-market sardines.

The combination of poor nutrition and overwork sickened me with lung congestion in June of 1943, and my parents took me out of the school in Rians on the recommendation of Doctor Roux and sent me to Savoy with my Uncle and Aunt Blumet on the Italian and Swiss borders for three months. The Germans were replacing the Italians occupying Savoy, and on a bicycle ride I saw the first soldiers. It was very hot. The military convoy had stopped by the roadside. Some small green wagons were parked in the courts of the houses in the valley, and the glorious soldiers of the Wehrmacht were sunbathing, stripped to the waist. Some were playing nostalgic tunes on their harmonicas. A little later we were stopped by the soldiers in another convoy, some swimming in the Isère River. There was an old house in ruins, and one of the Germans asked in bad French if it was due to English bombing. I told him not true. On our return my uncle said to me, "They took you for one of their own with your brashness!"

I ate prodigiously and in October, fully recovered, was back at La Tour but not to return to the St. Maurin school. On the map Papa and I followed the war which continued to rage on the Russian Front, where the Germans retreated more and more. He was thoroughly involved in the Resistance, between receiving coded radio messages from London that were understood sometimes with difficulty because of the jamming by the Germans, and the parachuting of arms and other matériel, always at night of course. There were also contacts with groups of saboteurs for the distribution of matériel. The management of the store of arms that found its way into an old farm outside the parish was assumed by Papa principally. Everything was stocked in an immense, unused wine cistern that you got to by a trap door.

Meanwhile the Germans were installing themselves at La Tour-d'Aigues. They lodged all over the place, including a school in the Bourgade quarter. I frequently observed their behavior, and it must be recognized that aside from considerations such as the concentration camps, the massacres of the Jews—indescribable and unpardonable exactions that were not the work of the regular army men—these guys were perfectly correct toward the population. This was not the case with the Gestapo.[2]

The men were for the most part strong, blond young fellows, very athletic, who always marched through the village in cadence, singing martial songs, sometimes in combat uniform, helmeted and armed with bandoliers, sometimes in shorts and stripped to the waist, returning from gymnastic exercises in the surrounding country-side, but always singing and hammering on the ground with their black boots. They had a proud gait and impressed the population.

Papa didn't want me to be outside watching them pass, so that when I heard the troops in the distance, arriving singing, I went in, climbed up to the front room and watched them through the closed shutters. I could not help comparing their strict discipline and their general appearance with the French soldiers who passed through in the winter of '39–'40, before the debacle, of whom the least one can say is that they had rather the air of a band of dowdy plunderers, noisy ribald fellows with their ragged uniforms, singing bawdy songs and not at all manly, returning from guard parties in the cafes of the village. They were far from the appearance of the Poilu of '14–'18. France between the two wars, what you have done with your children!

One must admit that it was not surprising, after all, that the Germans had conquered all of Europe, had gone up to the gates of Moscow, in Africa into the heart of Egypt, in Greece, in Crete. With armies made up of young fellows like these that I saw marching, behind my closed shutters, no, there was nothing surprising about it.

I got a job for a while cutting wood in the forests, and at this time I realized that the son of a noted person in the region was always turning the subject to the Resistance and asking seemingly harmless questions, and was suspected of being a collaborator. This was early spring of 1944. The Germans were losing the war. Those we observed seemed nervous, and the French Militia were more and more surly. The Germans occupying the village left in the direction, it was said, of the Russian Front.

Meanwhile, at Papa's insistence, I was seeing less of my good friend from school, Jean Schmitt, son of refugees from Lorraine. The Schmitt family was more or less suspected of connivance with the enemy. The Resistance was active in sabotage operations. All this created an atmosphere of total insecurity, people mistrusting one another, and one felt as if there were a powder magazine underfoot. Doctor Medvedowsky, father of my good friend Jean-Louis and his sister Nelly, had been found in a neighboring wood, his body riddled with bullets, after his arrest by the Militia for having treated a wounded Resistant, and after having been terribly tortured, as the marks on his body showed.

In this troubled and dangerous atmosphere, Papa, in his anti-Germanic intransigence, would not let his son associate with a boy whose family was thus suspected. I was heartbroken, because I loved Jean dearly. When he came to look for me they told him I wasn't there. Jean understood what was going on, and after a while I saw him no more.

In fact the Schmitt family disappeared one fine day. They lived on a steep road near Dr. Medvedowsky's villa. According to the neighbors they loaded up their two cars one night and vanished, without doubt furnished with the necessary identity cards. I do not believe that they had committed pro-German acts. They were refugees from Lorraine, having fled the occupation of their region. Speaking German, they were able to obtain the necessary permits to move around, particularly at night.

Besides, had they not helped my good friend Francis Chaudon to escape from the Youth Dockyards where he had been conscripted by force like many young Frenchmen? While one of the two Schmitt brothers stayed at the wheel of his car, hidden behind the trees, engine idling, ready to go like the wind if necessary, the other brother and their mother parleyed in order to give Francis time to secretly meet them.

If they had truly been collaborators with the Germans, would they have taken such risks? Why, then, their hasty departure which so resembled flight? Quite simply without doubt because, knowing the suspicions about them, they didn't want to risk incurring useless and perhaps bloody consequences of something of which they were innocent.

In 1946 I found a trace of the Schmitts at Nancy, where the family was living, from day to day intact, thank God, a bit Bohemian, talking among themselves in their Teutonic dialect, the children playing cards with their father while pounding their fists on the table, swearing like pagans. We didn't talk of the last days of their stay at La Tour, which might have ended tragically for them were it not for Mme. Schmitt.

On May 13, 1944, a hard blow occurred: the Militia arrested a Resistant, a talkative one, in a bistro in Pertuis, and after being tortured he finally revealed the existence of the arms cache at La Tour-d'Aigues, without, however, revealing any names.

On vigil, Papa and [fellow Resistant] Mr. Raspail were in the cache preparing plastic sabotage bombs. Papa's great regret in retrospect was not to have at least taken home or elsewhere the package containing five million francs received a few days earlier by parachute from England; they were safer in the cache than at home, where we risked search any minute.

In the next hour the Germans, alerted by their own militia who accompanied them, encircled the village. A bunch raided the cache, where they discovered to their amazement a whole arsenal of war and naturally the treasure of five million intended to supply the needs of the Resistance forces. In real paper money of the Bank of France, printed . . . in London!

Papa and I as well as the others, fortunately, had been warned by Mr. Raspail when the first soldiers had been signaled, and feeling instinctively that something was happening, we fled across the field behind the house. In the panic that ensued we rejoined a group of escapees behind the Long Wall, part of the periphery of La Tour. There I lost Papa from view and met again with a group of a dozen men, including the son of the local chief of the Resistance, Ritou Signoret. I wanted to stay behind to find out what had happened to Papa, but Ritou opposed it, assuring me he'd be found with another group.

Across a vineyard, already warm from the springtime sun, frequently on our stomachs, our little group moved, stooped or running, for almost an hour. I didn't know exactly where we were. I was very worried about Papa, who had been suffering in his leg and couldn't run very fast. I was also concerned for Mama and my two sisters staying at the house, that the Militia or the Germans might take them away. At the beginning of our flight we heard machine-gun fire that came from the village, then short and sharp bursts that stopped, followed by several shots. All this was very disturbing.

We spent the night in the dark in the hayloft of an old barn in the open country, with nothing to eat or drink, listening to the sounds outside without sleeping. Signoret tore up his identity papers into little pieces in case we were taken. We talked all night, creating possible scenarios of what might be going on all this time in the village.

Toward five in the morning we left, after assuring ourselves that nothing abnormal was going on outside, famished, paralyzed with cold, and went off toward another barn, also isolated, where we tried to figure out how to find the others who had fled like us. This barn wasn't very remote, and we didn't walk much. We first ran across a watchman crouched in the vines who had us advance up to the barn where we found a crowd of people who had fled and were as chilled and distressed as we were.

There, with joy that can be imagined, I found Papa, who gave a sigh of relief at the sight of me. There was also Francis Chaudon. A little later, around six, a man arrived from the village and told us the Germans and Militia had gone. Everything they found in the cache had been carried off by truck, but no retribution had been taken against the village. The volleys we had heard had been fired by the German soldiers at one who had been fleeing who had been lightly wounded. He owed his survival to the *sang-froid* of one Philibert who fled with him and told the wounded man, while raising up himself, "Don't budge; stay there." He raised his arms in a sign of surrender and appeared to be coming back until he saw the Germans turning their attention elsewhere.

All our group, perplexed and worried, hesitated to return, but Papa decided to try to get back to the house where Mama, Laurette and Monique were alone, probably worried about us. We got back furtively across the fields around seven. Mama was at the height of her distress but quickly recovered her calm at the sight of us.

Sunday passed without incident. We remained on a permanent *qui-vive*, ready to return to the fields at the slightest alert. In the evening, now furnished with warm clothes and some food, Papa and I set out again to sleep elsewhere, but this time in the open. We spent the night with an important group of men in the copse of a pine grove five or six kilometers from La Tour. I slept very little, Papa not at all. In the morning around four or five it was very cold. Everybody was silent and apprehensive. I believe Papa was especially afraid for me.

He made his decision in the night: he and I would leave La Tour the next day for some time. We would go to Vaison to the Tissots without saying anything to anybody. It was a little worrisome to leave Mama and my two sisters alone, but the circumstances of the moment made it sure that the Militia and their German masters would be looking for men capable of handling arms in order to make reprisals.

Upon arrival at Vaison, as agreed, Uncle Tissot phoned Mama that "the small and large packages had arrived safely." A few days later Papa got a phone call requiring his immediate return to La Tour without me; it was word of the Allied invasion of Normandy on June 6, with a coded message from London asking for stepped-up sabotage. The next day, in spite of the supplications of my uncle and aunt that I stay, I took off on my bicycle the 106 kilometers to La Tour.

I returned to my job in the Town Hall, though not very regularly. Things seemed to calm down a little. Nothing more had happened since the discovery of the cache. The local Resistants resumed their clandestine activities more than ever, little by little and prudently. The last months of the Occupation in our region, that is, until the moment of the Allied landing on the French beaches in the Mediterranean on August 15, were punctuated with incidents and events, if not as dramatic as the discovery of the cache, at least as dangerous.

The rate of air drops increased. Other caches were found. Almost every day, cars left from one knew not where, racing through the village like the wind, Resistants in flight or returning from sabotage operations, sometimes pursued by the Militia. Papa was on guard more than ever to be careful on his nocturnal missions.

One day the Germans surrounded the village by surprise. Few succeeded in escaping. Papa was sick in bed. Two SS entered the house with a militiaman and ordered him to come down. They yelled, *"Aus, aus, komme, schnell!"*

Mama opposed them fiercely, truly fiercely; the term is not too strong, for she could become very ill-natured in a case like this. Doctor Roux was brought immediately by the Militia, confirmed the illness, declared the sick man could not be moved. This was not entirely true, but the undesirable visitors didn't insist.

As for me, I was taken to the court of the Town Hall where there were already a hundred men or more. In our midst was one of the regional leaders of the Resistance who we knew was always armed in his travels. Luckily they didn't discover his weapon. After about an hour Mayor Berthezenne arrived with a German officer and a soldier interpreter. The officer warned us not to hide terrorists but to denounce them to the authorities, and if necessary, the German Army would exercise terrible reprisals. All the while, soldiers were all around, with machine guns pointing at us.

At last we were released, fortunately without a search, a few of us with only a check of our identity papers. I rushed to the house to reassure Mama and to see that all was OK with Papa, and went back to saunter in the streets, where the Germans were leaving.

Another day the Militia arrived without the Germans, did some damage, ransacked a bar, and took a mother and her two daughters and some others to the Town

Hall for interrogation. In the street I could hear distinctly the howls of suffering of those arrested and tortured inside the Town Hall. A little later—there were about a dozen of them—they were taken away in a truck surrounded by Militia with machine guns. Their clothes were torn and their legs were bleeding.

One gloriously sunny day at the end of June or beginning of July the sound of thunder suddenly split the sky. I rushed outside. People were running everywhere. What's going on? Looking skyward, I could see an immense armada flying from east to west on a bombing mission, we learned later, against German military objectives around the railroad station at Avignon. The preparation for the landing in the South of France was beginning.

The spectacle was fantastic, impressive of power. And then all of a sudden we could make out the tac-tac of machine guns in the azure sky. Two Luftwaffe planes were trying, a little ludicrously it seemed to us, to do some damage to this enormous flight. That also is impressive. And dangerous too, even for those on the ground. Indeed, a machine-gun bullet struck the trunk of a tree on the road from Grambois, coming out of the village, near the house on the height of Devarennes-Goutard.

Then suddenly, smoke from the tail of a bomber, and immediately bright specks all around the hit plane. In a few minutes, in a din of motors turning in space, it crashed a few kilometers from La Tour, in the direction of Grambois, a few meters from a farmhouse. The bright specks were the crew jumping in their parachutes. Not all, alas!

I jumped on my bicycle and rushed toward the thick smoke from the wreck. There was already a crowd, including a German truck. Useless to describe the fright of the farmer! For the first time I saw in the half-burned debris the star of the U.S. Air Force and some characters in English.

But there was a strange and very disagreeable odor of burning. In the garden, completely ravaged and strewn with smoking debris, leaning against the wall was what was left of a man, cut in half, the lower part only, one leg folded back, the other half torn off, all still smoking from the fire. This was the strange odor, the odor of burning flesh. It was a horrible and unbearable spectacle, but I could not take my gaze from what a few instants earlier was a very living man, doing the duty of a fighter, doubtless phlegmatically chewing some gum, and now, there, just as dead, for France, willingly or involuntarily.

Farther on between the rows of potatoes, a bloody hand torn off, then a fur-lined shoe without the foot, the buckles torn off, handwritten on the upper part, ROBERT SWANZY. Peace to the soul of Robert Swanzy![3]

The mayor of La Tour was charged with the burial of the mortal remains of the aviator in the village cemetery. A forbidden little ceremony was organized secretly, and a vague funeral oration pronounced by one of the Resistants present.

The wind wasn't very strong, and the parachutists were rescued by the FFI and hidden in a cave near Mirabeau until the troops landed in August.

August 15 was a fête day, and we went to mass in the morning; in the afternoon there was a procession with candles and many flowers in the park of La Ferrage near the lower village. But this August 15 was not like the others because, as the morning radio announced, the Allies had finally landed on the shores of the South of France, near Ste.-Maxime and St.-Raphaël.

So there was a great insurrection. At last we were going to do something on the great day. Indeed, at the moment of the landing (we didn't know it yet for good reason) a list of thirty-three names of Resistants from La Tour had reached the desk of the Chief of the [Vichy] Militia at Avignon. An action was under way to arrest and shoot them all.

At the head of the list appeared: "Siaud, father and son."

We learned this a few days after from a Resistant escaped from the jails of the Avignon Militia. No one ever knew where the denunciation came from, although there were suspicions of the son of a family of peasants living a few kilometers from La Tour who had been beaten by the FFI during a surprise raid on their house.

Anyway, we had a narrow escape. The Militia and their German masters now really had something else to do, an enemy army advancing from a landing to fight—and not much time for "terrorists." But Papa, who told me about it, and I hove gasps of relief.

The FFI went into action, gathering at the site of the last parachute drop near Pipailler on the road to Mirabeau, distributing the arms—some of the chutes later were made into dresses for their wives—and I took a rifle, a Sten machine pistol, with ammo for both, and enough grenades to have blown up my parents' house.

Still there, the revered machine-gun nest forty-seven years later (*Author photo*)

The last arrivals in the group, running and sweating, told us of having been machine-gunned by a German vehicle going along the road a few minutes after they had been on it, while they were in the open, climbing a hill.

My friend, my brother, André Joannon, was with us. We were simpatico and kidded around and swore at each other and so on. He was a royalist, and I, influenced or not by his inclinations, did not feel in disagreement with him. Loaded with guns and ammunition, we returned to La Tour by truck, where we were a sensation with the population, in the streets and out the windows. I decided that under the circumstances I should get out my Scouting cap, forbidden by the Occupation authorities, which I thought gave me a martial and military look. We slept at my house that night with all our war matériel under the bed.

In a day or two there was an alert. An isolated group of Germans had been seen in the gorges of Lourmarin, and volunteers were asked to give chase. There were about twenty of us, armed to the teeth with rifles, grenades, machine pistols, and so on. One of our leaders, a big, redheaded fellow, originally Polish, with gold-rimmed glasses, an intellectual type, in shirtsleeves, was looking for a driver for a motorcycle unearthed somewhere. André presented himself as an accomplished motorcyclist. I'm not sure he'd ever touched one before, but war is war. He mounted the engine and after many kicks got it started with a tremendous cloud of acrid smoke. The leader started off, and they went along, followed by the truck.

Arriving at the gorges of Lourmarin a little later, on the lookout, each of us realized how truly vulnerable we were in our truck. A single grenade thrown from the top of the gorges, or a well-placed machine gun, would have liquidated all of us before we knew what had hit us. We stopped our vehicle in a bend near where the Germans had been. Alas, our emptyhanded return to the village was hardly glorious, and I was very disappointed.

We were next ordered toward Pipailler where we took up a position on the side of the road to cut off an eventual retreat by the German troops from around Mirabeau. A young fellow of twenty whom nobody knew, armed to the teeth, had joined us. He told us he had come from the region of Lambesc where he belonged to a group of FFI who had been decimated by the Germans in a fight. His face wore marks of a tragic engagement.

We were led by some men with some military experience, including Francis Patard, a reserve lieutenant originally from Commercy, a refugee with his family from the debacle of 1940. We were stationed on a line of three or four hundred meters where we dug individual holes that encircled a machine gun served by three or four men.[4]

We spent the rest of the day in an initiation in the manual of arms and real firing exercises with mounds of earth for targets! In the afternoon we were inspected by the local leaders including Papa, Signoret and others. The first night in the open, on guard in our holes, I don't think anybody slept. In the distance, in a direction hard to tell but seeming to come from around Aix-en-Provence, we heard sounds of cannonading, which would mean that the next day we might be in a full-fledged battle.

Next day fatigue parties were organized for provisioning water and so forth, and guard duty. The weather was splendid and warm. The sounds of the guns had died down. Toward the middle of the morning I came back from a water party three hundred meters away when there was a sudden alert. On the road, a little lower down and in the direction of Mirabeau, had been seen a column of soldiers marching on each side, with, in the middle, what one took in the distance for a tank but was in fact a truck.

Someone shouted "The Germans!"

I let go my two pails of water and ran, bent over, toward my hole where I had my gun. The machine gun was quickly adjusted at an approximate angle of fire, and just as the signal of "Fire!" was about to be given, suddenly a silhouette appeared on the road which gesticulated and came toward us, shouting something no one could understand, especially considering the distance. As he approached, still running, his shouts became entirely distinct. He was yelling "It's the Americans! There they are! The Americans!"

And it was in fact the advance elements of the American troops. One can hardly imagine how close they came to a massacre!

In spite of orders to the contrary from some of our leaders, several of us ran out on the road to meet our liberators. I was finally going to be able to use my linguistic knowledge. [He'd been tutored in English on his father's orders by an internee named Heed.]

On our arrival on the road the column stopped for a few moments. They were handsome, young, big, with a well-nourished look, open and attractive, dynamic and calm at the same time, chewing gum nonchalantly. They weren't like the German soldiers, rigid and tight in their uniforms. Theirs were khaki, and not gray-green; their boots with leggings kept shut with two buckles had rubber soles that were silent as they marched on the macadam, unlike the Germans with their great hobnailed boots. The shape of their helmet was a little like that of the German helmets, which was why we identified them erroneously in the distance.

I put my first question in English. "Where do you come from?" To my great surprise, they appeared to understand me since they replied something that I didn't understand. Not immediately, in any case—only next day! Certainly their accent was different from Mr. Heed's.

"Sicily, Italy, Anzio, Cassino," they replied. They wore on their left shoulder an insignia representing a golden eagle on a red background. It was the boys of the 45th Infantry Division of the Seventh American Army, commanded by General Patch, as I learned later. On the top of the right arm they wore a brassard, a star-spangled banner identifying them as American.

A few minutes later they resumed their march toward Pertuis, and we went back to our positions.

A little later in the morning there was a real parade of tanks, trucks, cannon, amphibious vehicles the Americans called ducks [DUKWs], engines of all kinds, and also the curious little vehicle with four-wheel drive, the famous jeep that we admired so much. It was a war chariot, very maneuverable, equipped with radios and jerry cans of gas, which the G.I.s drove sportily and nonchalantly, chewing their eternal gum.

This enormous quantity of matériel paraded past all day. That morning we were still a territory occupied by the Germans, and with arms at hand we waited, a little nervously, and now, a few hours after this "time of anxiety," four years of Occupation was ending, the constraints, the suffering of all kinds, the humiliations, the fratricidal strife, the lies, the torture inflicted by the occupiers and certain of our own countrymen, and well, it was all over, we were now on the other side of the barrier, this new side so embodied in the immediate by the incessant flow of matériel and of our liberators.

In mid-afternoon an important unit of artillerymen came to set up exactly on our positions, their batteries put in place pointing this time to the west. We were surrounded by soldiers, jeeps and GMC trucks. We had some hesitant conversations with our liberators, the G.I.s. We discovered K rations, small packages in a paraffin box containing in condensed form a complete individual meal, chewing gum, vitamined chocolate bars, powdered coffee, packages of lemon for instant drinks, small stoves the men heated their coffee or cooked fried eggs on, finally, white cigarettes, Camels, the most sought after, Lucky Strike, Chesterfields, Philip Morris, Raleigh, the less prized. My God, what sudden abundance, superabundance, after so many years of privation and restrictions!

The jeep radios played modern tunes we didn't know, boogie-woogie, swing, or the more nostalgic numbers of Glenn Miller. All this alternated with conversations between radios in voices in nasal accents.

And to us, with our miserable holes on the hillside, in the middle of all this sudden richness coming from so far and so quickly, all this had something of the unreal. We savored a little of everything, talked a little randomly, so great was our joy. We were liberated from the German oppression, and there reigned in the air an inexpressible expression of extraordinary liberty.

All the while, the parade continued tirelessly on the road. But, Sir, where does it all come from? And what organization, what logistics—a word invented in 1944 by the Americans for the support organization for the fighters—what mastery required to advance like this in an unfamiliar country? The men did this work as if it were so simple, as if they had always been doing it.

The night passed without the road transport stopping for an instant, sometimes with the characteristic sound made by the treads of the tanks on the asphalt, a muffled rattling with squeaks, then some GMC going down the grade, giving an impression of power with the motor throbbing, and thus without headlights and without stop.

Next day our neighbors of the night broke camp. Jeeps, guns, GMCs, Dodge command cars, all left in perfect order in the direction of Pertuis, sliding into the traffic on the road that stopped for an instant to let them pass.

The next morning, having no more reason to stay there, since we were liberated, we went back to La Tour-d'Aigues and paraded . . . triumphantly, arms in hand, while the populace acclaimed us as . . . great victors!!

I felt a bit embarrassed, a repression, a frustration, since our combat (!!) was limited to almost firing on friendly soldiers! For me, this parade was a bit of a masquerade. Before the monument to the dead, there stood all the leaders of the Resistance, including Papa, who watched us pass by. Then the recent past suddenly arose, and I felt a certain pride. That compensated a little for my frustrations of these last days.

The FFI and the FTP (which had a revolutionary tendency) hardly mingled, regarding each other with little friendliness. The FTP tried to take control of the Town Hall. Tension mounted. One day as we were waiting for something or other near our assembly area around the Place du Château, the leaders got in a dispute, the pitch rose, each rushed to his machine gun, and there was almost an encounter. Fortunately nothing happened, things calmed down a little, and the Communists, seeing that they would have to make a big deal of it, didn't insist and renounced their project.

Meanwhile, the village had been literally invaded by G.I.s and their impressive matériel. They were everywhere, in the streets, the fields around about, the courts of houses, the houses themselves, in a great fraternization with exchanges of all sorts. The soldiers were looking especially for eggs and fruit of which the people made them presents. They received in return cigarettes, chocolates, gum, and everybody was happy! Soldiers perched on vehicles were bombarded with fruit, grapes, peaches, apples, melons, to their delight, everything coordinated by immense MPs at every intersection.

That evening the Café Gogglio on the Place du Château was filled with civilians and soldiers. One of the soldiers, a big fellow, broad shoulders, with blue, laughing eyes, black hair almost shaven, played at an old piano in the big room some wild songs unknown to us but which quickly became popular. Others accompanied him singing. Everybody stamped, laughed, chewed gum—suddenly in such abundance!—that the G.I.s got at the canteen with their cigarettes. A wild atmosphere!

An evening or two later at the cafe, André, Francis Chaudon and I met three G.I.s sitting at a table, including an officer, a big fellow with a relaxed air. We discussed with them while smoking their cigarettes that we might join them. The lieutenant, named Pat Farley, said "Why not? Go find a gun and come back; we leave in a quarter of an hour."

We had given up our arms during the day, and they were stacked in a barn on the road from the cemetery, duly guarded by two or three men including Francis Patard. What concerned me was that without the knowledge of my parents I had hidden under my bed a rifle, some cartridges and grenades, having decided not to give them up.

Francis didn't want to join us. André and I ran to the cache and explained to Patard the situation, and he gave us each a machine pistol and clips. We felt in full possession of our resources again—it seemed to us we were naked without arms— and rejoined our three Americans who had waited for us. We had asked Francis Chaudon to warn our respective parents of our departure, but not before tomorrow, for then we would be far away, and no one could catch up with us.

All five of us jumped in the jeep. It was almost eleven, and we drove through Pertuis, where our three tough guys paid a visit to some women of slight virtue, while André and I waited in the jeep. Toward one in the morning we passed back through La Tour. In view of the house, where no doubt everyone was asleep, I had strange sensations of pain and remorse. What were my dear parents going to think?

But we were already on the road in the direction of Manosque, going like an arrow, the wheel having been taken by the lieutenant. It was very cold. Near two we arrived in what we distinguished in the darkness as being an avenue of trees, where soldiers were sleeping, some in individual tents, some simply rolled up in their blankets. Neither André nor I could sleep a wink all night, it was so cold.

Early, around six, a sergeant called Shorty Nye because of his small size got out his little gasoline stove, pumped it, and made coffee which he shared with us with biscuits. The rising sun finished warming us and gave us a bit more optimism. The rest of the group regarded us with curiosity.

The unit with which we embarked on this adventure was called the "I&R," that is, Intelligence and Reconnaissance Platoon belonging to the 157th Infantry Regiment of the 45th Division, wearing high on their left shoulder the patch which portrayed the "Thunderbird," the bird of thunder. The whole unit adopted us immediately most congenially. André became "Andy" and I "Hank."[5]

Around ten everybody took off in the vehicles. André and I were with others in a Wehrmacht car with seats on each side of the rear, without a bonnet. It was a prize of war, an Auto Union in perfect running condition. On the floor, between our legs, were packages and a lot of strange stuff.[6]

Our convoy went toward the north by the Route of the Alps in the direction of Sisteron, which we reached several hours later, to the acclamation of the populace. There was a good deal of damage. American paratroopers had been dropped in the area the morning of D-day, and murderous fighting seems to have ensued.

We profited from this triumphal acclaim, without any act of glory, just being present! In an outburst of joy, wanting to respond to the acclamations, I threw my Scout cap in the air, and it fell in the crowd! Someone grabbed it with eagerness and ardor, thinking no doubt that he had in his hands a precious historic souvenir coming straight from far-off America—until, while examining it closer, he discovered the mark of the store, La Hutte, Marseille!

That night we bivouacked in the little town of Serres. Next morning before departure we saw on the road that overhung us a convoy of military trucks taking German prisoners south. It had a strange effect on us to see these soldiers of the Wehrmacht, so proud and full of arrogance a few days earlier, and now with the crestfallen and miserable air of all prisoners of war. Later, at Crest we bivouacked in a deep trench bordered by high trees and received our baptism of fire in the form of a German Stuka—one of the rare last planes of the Luftwaffe still in combat— which machine-gunned us, hedge-hopping the tops of the trees with a deafening roar of the engine and tac-tac. Nobody was touched.

Sergeant Griffith—a guy with a studious look, rimless glasses, brushed light brown hair, always with a slightly frowning air and not seeming to have a very good

Clockwise from Griffith at 7, Winburn, Coleman, someone, Joannon and Zapiecki in the heat of the French summer (*Courtesy of Dominick M. Trubia*)

rapport with his men—initiated us during this short sojourn in the handling and maintenance of the M1 rifles with which they had supplied us. After many taking-aparts and putting-togethers under the critical and bantering eye of Griffith, we knew the gun in the least detail. On his order we got rid of our Sten guns and buried them in the woods nearby, and got uniforms as well as regulation boots. We washed them first of all (they were not new) and put them on before our departure the next day for a new destination, not yet all dry. We had now become true G.I.s![7]

Angling northwest toward the Rhône after our brief rest at La Tour-d'Aigues, as I reconstructed it in my journal:

Our steady and nearly unopposed advance continued and increased tremendously in pace. The days were cram full. Several towns a day would be liberated by a battalion alone, and our work consisted of somehow trying to maintain a feeble contact between the companies and Regiment. It was sometimes useless, for we would have three or four radios out on relay. So unexpected was the entire situation that once (around D plus 10) we were in reality past the point of D plus 30 or 40. Troops rode on whatever they could find—jeeps, ducks, six-by's, tanks, TDs, artillery, and quantities of captured Jerry vehicles. At one time the CP was 100 miles behind the leading battalion. Incidentally, we couldn't move until we had the gas. Third Battalion was attached for quite a while to Task Force Butler [made up of ele-

ments of the assault divisions under General Frederick B. Butler] *that raced ahead as a sort of flying column, a reconnaissance in strength.*

While the Third Division and some French troops sieged Marseille and Toulon in direct assault (where the enemy had expected us to land, as I learned from captured letters later), we went north and then cut west toward Avignon and the Rhône, forming a semi-encirclement of the cities from the east. In the first stages of the campaign the main objective was to cut off the 19th Army which had been most-ly around the ports, and which was attempting to escape up the main Rhône highway towards Belfort [the Belfort Gap in the Vosges Mountains between France, Switzerland and Germany]. *Our entire left flank throughout France (to the left of the Rhône) was about cleared by the FFI. Probably the main reason for the phenomenal success of the campaign was Patton's Normandy breakthrough which raced across northern France and threatened to cut off all enemy troops in southern France.*

From La Tour d'Aigues, about August 25 we took a long trip of more than fifty miles north to Serres, travelling through the breathtaking French-Italian Alps above Nice. As we entered the Swiss Alps (Basses-Alpes) we noticed that the architecture showed the influence of the chalet, all frills and gingerbread. At Serres we found ourselves some hundred miles behind the battalions with practically no gas.

That night we loaded into a couple of jeeps, armed to the teeth, and hung on for dear life guarding General Church [promoted to brigadier general August 1] *to the line at Nyons. It was a beastly ride through the Alps which grew higher and higher. We clung precariously to the sides of mountains, skidded around hairpin turns at 50 MPH, through tunnels, down straightaways at 70. How we made it without turning over I don't know.*

[Hair-raising. No lights but the blackout bulbs on the CO's jeep which glowed about as incandescently as a cat's eyes in the dark. We had to keep up with his driver, a madman but as deft as Barney Oldfield.]

It was now the crucial moment to slice through to the Rhône just below Valence and cut off the 19th Army which had evacuated the southern ports and was racing for Belfort. Our 36th had run into a spot of trouble around Nyons where a holding force of a panzer and infantry division had been placed to protect the Rhône highway. We came up to their aid, going to Crest on the Drôme and then to Allex where we hit heavy resistance only a few miles from the highway. Through this delaying action a large part of the enemy force escaped, but it was a great satisfaction to know that a convoy of over 5,000 vehicles sev-eral miles long was caught on the Rhône road by planes and artillery and completely knocked out.

The story of Crest was typical, I imagine, of the terrorism that reigned all over Europe. An elderly lady who lived along the main road told me this, and the tears flowed from her eyes. I thought she would collapse. Approximately a division of Germans had been passing through when the Maquis came down from the surrounding hills and attacked them, inflicting rather heavy casualties. Then they retired again to their mountain retreats. The Germans went wild. They combed the countryside taking every bite of food, burning and otherwise destroying all the crops. They beat, raped, tortured and killed women, killed babies, ransacked hospitals and lined up as many of the men as they felt like. Then they ransacked all the private houses in the valley, destroyed all farm machinery and burned three out of every four dwellings. Finally they lined up the length of this long road and systematically shelled and machine gunned the houses along the road. Thousands upon thousands of Frenchmen were killed in this "incident" which was repeated hundreds of times in France alone during the four years of occupation.

In our pursuit of the campaign trail in 1991, Henry Siaud and I encountered no one in Crest who knew what we were talking about. Five years later, I read Eric Sevareid's reporting in *Not So Wild a Dream* of the German massacre of the people of La Chapelle-in-the-Vercors, the principal mountain retreat of the Maquis in the south between Crest and Grenoble, and was struck by the similarity.

Some time earlier the Germans had sent two divisions into the Vercors to end the incessant raiding by the Maquis by wiping them out, and if not by that means, by inflicting such reprisals on the civilians in the region as they vainly supposed would terrorize the Resistance into passivity. Sevareid and other correspondents who came upon what was left of La Chapelle got the story from the priest who had been forced to witness the execution of twenty-two noncombatant men and boys besides the sixty *maquisards* who died resisting. Then the by-now-drunken Huns looted and burned or blew up all but four of the ninety houses in the town. A few miles south of La Chapelle they hit the hamlet of Vassieux, where 137 died.[8]

❧ ❧ ❧

So it is more likely that the old lady of Crest was telling me with some exaggeration of the massacre at La Chapelle, or collectively of the unspeakable terror the hobnailed barbarians visited on the region of the Vercors. My memory nags me that either her story was so graphic that over time I telepathized myself into the ravaged town up on the slope, or that somehow I in fact did pass through and paused at the remains of La Chapelle on the way to or from Crest.

Letter home on August 26, first chance in twenty-four days: "At last I can write and say I'm perfectly OK and, as you must know by now, in Southern France. Wherever we go, they give us a tumultuous welcome, take us into their houses, give us food and their best wine. The Maquis and FFI are really helping us tremendously. My French improves all the time, so that by now I can converse with any Frenchman I see on about any subject and get most of what he says."

Two days later Second Battalion drove the Germans out of Livron, just east of the Rhône, a few miles northwest of Crest. "While on the OP in a cave during the height of the battle," I journaled, "I came down with malaria with terrific chills, sweat, fever, headaches and malaise [which may be why I remember nothing of the fighting]. I went to the 9th Evacuation Hospital. I must have had the fever latently for a long time before we left Italy, and it showed itself after I'd been unable to take atabrine for a couple of weeks in France."

The day I left with malaria Captain Edwards and Lieutenant Farley came looking for me to transfer from the I&R to the regimental intelligence S2 staff. But I was off to the hospital, and Harold Dibble got the job.

Helen wrote her parents on September 16 from Sarah Lawrence, where she was a freshman, that "after not having heard from Joe Garland for more than six weeks, I finally got a letter from a hospital in Southern France. He has malaria. His letter was very strange, no transition, not much concentration on the point he was discussing, and not at all like him. I guess he must have been in quite a state."

The malarial fever was pure fire, sunstorms flaring from inside outward, where I lay in my shorts in that evacuation hospital somewhere in France, until the sweat spewed from every pore. Then as suddenly the chills rose up from my depths, cold as death under my drenched and steaming skin. Nurse! Nurse! And blanket after blanket was piled on my chattering body until a momentary equilibrium of exhaustion had been achieved. Then the fever again. Off were flung the covers, the blizzard doused the flames, then the bed-rattling shakes, the interim of torpor like the eye of the hurricane, resurgence of the fire, flung and yanked this way and that in the clutches of a mosquito called *Anopheles*, noted earlier as having been reintroduced by the Huns to the rewatered Pontine Marshes.

Moderately severe case of Anzio malaria, the doc said, erupting weeks after we left the Beachhead and had quit or forgot or weren't given our daily anti-malarial Atabrine pills, but after a week I wrote home that I was only a little unsteady on my pins.

And in my head too, adding that "I'm only hoping the war will be over by the time I get back to the outfit, although it really doesn't make too much difference. I'm sure the campaign will be wound up before the real mud comes. The news grows better apace, while the German empire grows smaller. All the underground of Europe seems to be active, or ready to spring up in arms the moment we cross the frontier."

Brothers in arms once again. The motley members of the French Forces of the Interior (FFI) in southern France. (*U.S. Army*)

$$+\!+\!+\ 12\ +\!+\!+$$

WITH MY SHIELD, OR ON IT?

Lyon to the Vosges
August–September 1944

FROM THE NINTH EVACUATION HOSPITAL I was shifted to the 11th and then the Seventh Army Convalescent near Ambérieu, from which I took off daily with a couple of guys from the 36th Division for the city of Lyon, about thirty miles to the west, "riding along on my French and meeting several French people who enthusiastically ordered us to stay with them if we ever got back."

Which we planned to do, because the next stop was the just-opened Replacement Depot for Southern France in a drizzly, chewed-up field outside Grenoble, where a just-unhospitalized doggie had the option of dragging ass through the mud until someone got around to packing him into the lurching rear of a six-by-six truck for summary shipment back to the front, or taking off on his own behind his thumb—officially AWOL, but hell, heading back to hell and not the rear.

My remaining traveling companion from the ill-fated 36th Division and I had no trouble rationalizing a more leisurely approach to the call of duty and death and were as conscientious about returning to the fray in our own good time as a couple of kids taking the long way to school. The Champagne Campaign bubbled on as far as we knew, and we'd hardly be missed taking a couple of extra days to live it up just a little in Lyon. So we casually walked out of a camp—so new and primitive that the chicken echelon of the Seventh Army hadn't yet roosted there—and took to the countryside, just a coupla G.I.s on a hoot with our thumbs out. I journaled:

We hitched an open Jeep ride and crossed over the Rhône into the west side of Lyon. The bridge was lined with crowds, and the streets and squares were black with people who were all apparently expect-

ing someone. I thought I might as well make something of the moment, so I raised up a bit and began nodding and smiling and waving. Quite a response, too. We dropped off and joined the crowd. It had assembled for General DeGaulle, who presently came sauntering down in those great strides of his, accompanied by his entourage. The crowd went wild, and there were tears in his eyes as he waved and acknowledged their tribute. He is a very tall man, commanding, and French to the bone. He looks a little older than he is, and one can see the years of fighting and the years of waiting in his face but not his bearing.

Well, we looked up a young woman 36th had met and with another from his outfit stayed in her flat for a week while she did all the cooking, the three of us guys sleeping on a mattress on the floor. Josée de Lerys lives on in memory from my studio photo of a very French, theatrically upswept blonde with penciled eyebrows and clinging lashes, glancing over her shoulder coquettishly, and inscribed:*A mon bel Américain que j'estime beaucoup, je dédie mon meilleur souvenir—Josée de Lerys.* A singer and a patriot. She put up and put up with three dirty G.I.s for a week. *Ah, ma belle Française que j'estime beaucoup, où êtes-vous maintenant?*

From my journal:

Lyon was the biggest and best city I've run into overseas (not as big as Rome, but a much better time). It was full of Parisians who'd fled south. Most people told me it was a dull, staid place, and perhaps it was, compared to Paris or Nancy. The inhabitants appeared to have taken a continuous holiday since their liberation, swarming the streets, the squares, the cafes, the shops. There were as yet very few Americans there and almost no MPs. We were enormous objects of curiosity wherever we went. I wore my helmet and people stared and pointed and talked everywhere. Everybody wanted to examine the helmet. In the shops one could buy anything—evening gowns, furs, electric fixtures, furniture, antiques, everything—except food.

In our special haunt we began putting salt in our beer. The head waiter came around with raised eyebrows and summoned the waiters and waitresses. Customers turned and stared incredulously. I told them it was good, and they tried it. Pretty soon the whole restaurant was agog, laughing, salting their beer, and looking at us and smiling in the most confidential manner. One man leaned over and asked whether pepper was good too.

We met multitudes of people in the cafes who introduced themselves and invited us to dine or drink with them. Also a couple of girls whom we dated several times. One night we made a rendezvous with them at a night club and ate a simple dinner of omelets, spaghetti and white wine for four. The bill was $32—1800 francs.

Those girls, they were pretty and, yes, innocent—sisters perhaps, pals anyway, and we met them in a cafe or while strolling the esplanade that accompanies the Rhône through the city. I badly needed a shave, and with no barber in sight nor a safety razor to be found, bought an old-fashioned straight razor such as my father used, and a small leather strop to keep its edge as I'd so often seen him wield his man-sized strop with such skill—and upon my bare backsides too, in acknowledgment of some boyish backsliding.

Slipping into the restaurant lavatory *à la* phone booth, I lathered up with cold water and a filthy bar of soap and snuck up on my features with that bare blade of the enemy's Solingen steel, as had been done unto me but never before by me unto myself, followed by a slightly bloody wash with cold water from the tap, dry off with toilet paper, and *voilà*! Bring on *les jeunes filles*!

In the stillness of the evening following our rendezvous, we two chance couples lounged arm-in-arm and hip-to-hip, but no closer, along the Rhône, liberators and liberated once removed, in the semi-abstract. The reflections of the liberated lights danced again upon the great river of France. With what bittersweet intensity we embraced, we chance couples destined nevermore to meet.

Then we unknowns escorted those gentle girls arm-in-arm to their doors and returned to our mattresses on the floor *chez Josée*. We may have been dogfaces, we two, but *mon Dieu*, for one evening we were gentlemen! Besides, I was petrified, for the first time in my life, by my potential for passion. Do two elderly ladies of Lyon still remember a couple of love-starved young Yankee soldiers very, very far from home?

Journal:

After a week in Lyon we were very broke, and it was a sad parting, to leave all this comfort, happiness and urbanity for the front and our old life. We hitched to Bourg, which the Regiment had taken in my absence, and put up at the swellest hotel in town with sheets, elevator, spotless room, restaurant, etc., which cost the three of us 90 francs. Next morning we hopped a truck to Besançon and separated there, as we could see by the signs that our outfits took different roads.

On some back street, perhaps of Besançon, I was directed to a woman in a drab flat who with resignation and perhaps some private amusement conducted me through the ritual of The Passage. It was a rapid passage, nervously explosive, and yet for all that, as enlightening for a case of arrested development, common enough in the generation of '44, as the occasion called for. Whether toll was levied or it was a complimentary ride tendered out of pity or patriotism or both, my mind is a blank and just as well; luckily, no toll was taken.

The loosening of the loins intimated so magically on the bank of the Rhône led to the libidinous letdown. I don't think it occurred to me that the *Boches* probably preceded me, but more for her sake than mine I hope not, for I witnessed in the streets of France the young women, branded as collaborators, with their shamefully shaved heads.

Does an old dame remember a young soldier, so innocent, so inept, so far away from home? Not likely.

I look back almost with disbelief at my readiness to detach this paradoxical Passage from my sporadically developing romance with Monk, realizing now that it was but the extension of the soldier's personality-protecting rationalization of the incompatibility of the physical and psychic worlds of life and death, fantasy and nightmare, hope and resignation into which I had been thrust. Here was a quite unremarkable, pre-sexual-revolution bit

of acrobatics resorted to by most of us neo-Victorian Willies and Joes for whom any relationship with any woman under any circumstances of war was destined to be no more (and
perhaps no less) than one's pitiful due on the threshold of Kingdom Come.

Having traded another installment of the troubles of a boy for those of a man, I hit the
road again and hitched a ride to Vesoul, where I stayed the night with the family of the
Alsatian food commissioner, who had befriended me in a bar. The next day, September 21,
I moved on and was airing my thumb by a bridge when the foolish Lieutenant Farley, of all
the millions in France, came jeeping by and picked me up. Of what did we talk? I have no
memory.

The night my Teutonic malaria had erupted on August 28 the 157th was relieved and
shuttled about a hundred miles through Grenoble to beyond Voiron near the Swiss border.
Colonel Walter P. O'Brien succeeded our newly starred General Church, who had led the
Regiment since Colonel Ankcorn lost his leg after Salerno. A very decent old soldier (we
thought of him as old; he was fifty-two), Church was elevated to assistant commander of
the 84th Division then arriving in France.

The Champagne Campaign was now like a dream of home. The Germans streaming
from the south toward the escape corridor of the Belfort Gap in the Vosges Mountains were
being squeezed between our advancing Seventh Army and Patton's Third and had their
backs to the Fatherland. One of our company commanders was killed and another badly
wounded. Our Third Battalion CO, his operations officer and several men got it in an
ambush and weren't found until the main body moved up two days later.

Early in the morning of the thirteenth of September, Second Lieutenant Almond E.
Fisher was leading his E Company platoon in an attack on a strongly defended hill near
Grammont, about twenty miles west of Belfort, when they came under heavy machine-gun
fire. Working his way forward alone, Fisher killed the entire crew with his carbine. A few
minutes later they encountered another enemy machine gun. Again crawling up alone, he
blasted out the crew with hand grenades. An hour later they were stopped again by intense
fire but under his leadership wiped out the enemy pocket.

Yet the enemy fire intensified. When a bypassed German climbed from his foxhole and
tried to wrest a rifle from one of his men, Lieutenant Fisher whirled and killed him with a
burst from his carbine. Thirty minutes later he ran across an open field under intense fire
and knocked out another nest. Continuing to lead his men against yet another machine
gun, he pulled the pins from the platoon's two remaining grenades, and carrying one in
each hand crawled across open ground under heavy fire to within fifteen yards of the
emplacement, flung them, demolished the gun and killed the crew. His men had hardly dug
and replenished their ammunition when the Germans launched an all-out counterattack.

> Attacked by superior numbers from the front, right and left flanks and even from the
> rear, the platoon in bitter hand-to-hand engagements drove back the enemy at every
> point. Wounded in both feet by close-range machine pistol fire early in the battle,
> Lieutenant Fisher refused medical attention. Unable to walk, he crawled from man

to man encouraging them and checking each position. Only after the fighting had subsided did [he] crawl 300 yards to the aid station from which he was evacuated.[1]

Thus concluded his Congressional Medal of Honor citation.

While I malingered around Lyon, Hank Siaud and Andy Joannon rode the whirlwind of their choice. The Regiment was about halfway between Bourg and Bezançon in full pursuit of the backpedaling enemy when Hank saw his first battle-dead *Boche*, as he recalls in *The Links of the Chain*:

He was stretched out beside the road on his stomach, covered with a bloody G.I. blanket. I was upset by this vision to the right of the road that was bordered by great trees whose leaves were falling already, autumn approaching, under a gray sky somber with heavy clouds, with the sound of the guns not far off. All around, debris of all sorts littered the ground. No one risked staying in the open in this sinister place where from time to time a shell fell, throwing up the earth everywhere. A terrible vision of war. A German, to be sure, this body, but a man just the same.

In the course of this pursuit, André and I occasionally gave the addresses of our parents to farmers to let them know we were OK. I often thought of them, gnawed a little by remorse over their anxiety. We found on our return three months later that they had heard nothing about us, and Papa had gone to Marseille, where with the aid of a friend of André he had tried to get news of us through the Quartermaster General of the American Forces at Delta Base, but they didn't know what combat unit we were with.

We participated in patrols—between the great movements that were always announced by "we move"—never together in case of bad luck, with four or five men with a sergeant and sometimes the lieutenant, arms and ammunition in hand, and the portable radio. Our usefulness was especially our knowledge of French, which permitted us to interrogate people about the presence or movements of the enemy here or there.

Toward Rambervillers, which was still in the hands of the Germans, we came on patrol to a fir forest, cautiously, as there was danger from mines which the enemy had buried in the region. The forest was a veritable tangle of trees burned, sheared, knocked down, branches broken, pieces of all sorts of matériel, broken guns—I can't say whether German or American in view of their condition—German helmets, etc., all scattered everywhere, with shell holes, everything ravaged, empty cartridge casings around hastily dug foxholes, a nightmarish vision of a furious battle.

At the edge of this forest, camouflaged behind some felled trees, we were able to observe with the scope a small concentration of Germans moving near another forest. I had already seen some, but this was the first time I had seen them so close, six or seven hundred meters. We signaled immediately by radio and, mission accomplished, returned carefully and rapidly to our base.

One evening we were in a big house occupied by only two young girls, one twelve, her sister eighteen or nineteen, very pretty. Willingly or not, their parents weren't there. The sisters were neither frightened nor scared away by the presence of all these men. The older, decidedly not shy at all, spent practically all night in a corner of the room where several of us were trying to sleep, on the floor, embracing and kissing with one of the guys without once going farther (at least while they were there)!

This was not especially shocking except that I was disagreeably surprised to hear the elder say to her young sister, who was missing none of it—ignorant that two Frenchmen were present—"I find that Johnny resembles Karl, but he kisses better than him!" Karl was a German soldier who, like us this evening, had been in this house ... The night watch!

One Sunday afternoon Bill Belleman, a good buddy speaking a little French (who had flirted with a very pretty girl from La Tour when we were not yet acquainted with him, Pierette D., whom I knew well and for whom I had a little infatuation!), told us that a Catholic Army chaplain passing through was coming to hold a mass.

It was a beautiful sunny afternoon in the hollow of a meadow where the men had built an altar with boxes of wood covered with a white cloth. They gathered, one knee on the ground, praying. I was impressed by the spectacle of them, bare-headed, arms and helmets at their feet, praying fervently in the silence of the country only broken by the distant sound of the guns, responding in their language to the solemn invocations of the priest. This mass, under the circumstances—out of danger temporarily as we seemed—reaffirmed again my religious convictions.

That a people strong, generous, young, should send their sons so far to fight against oppression, victorious already after so many battles since North Africa, slowly climbing through Italy, inexorably approaching the heart of Nazi Germany— that these sons present here on their knees, in all humility before their Creator, our God, continued their battle, once this moment of spiritual release ended, moved me profoundly, and one could only render glory and grace to this God. This I did in joining in the common prayer.[2]

"Back from the hospital and with the outfit, fit as ever," I wrote home on September 22. "Spent all yesterday afternoon reading my mail. Awfully glad you saw Helen (or Monk). Do you really think she's nice? For my part, I'd be willing to tie up with her after the War. From all I can gather we dovetail together in about everything."

Even as I wrote of intercontinental romance our Third Battalion was crossing the Moselle River near Igney, only to buck into hard counterattacks, while our First was pinned down all day in the first real woods encountered in the war—different, difficult, fraught with the unknown, with ambush and with shellfire bursting in the trees overhead.

We moved on to Igney, where I was put on the CP radio while Shorty Nye set up an OP in the town of Thaon. This may be where his crew was in the church steeple, as Zapiecki tells it, and "Nye's down in the square all by himself fixin' up eggs—always with butter— when BOOM! an' plaster's flyin' all around. The Krauts hit the church, naturally. And that's when I come in to see what's goin' on, and here's Nye—'Dirty sonsabitches!'—and he's tryin' to wipe the plaster off the eggs."

Meanwhile Dick Beech, by my account, "set up an OP just across the Moselle immediately after we crossed. Vern Dilks had driven Griff out to Thaon, which was believed free of enemy, to reconnoiter for a likely OP spot. He'd parked on the road while Griff went into town and was sitting under a tree half-dozing when he heard a buzzing and looked up just in time to see four Krauts on two motorcycles come racing hell-bent out of the town towards our lines."

Dilks:

The second motorcycle had a Kraut in uniform drivin' with a guy who could have been one but was in civilian clothes, forty or fifty yards off. I was left there all alone with that damn jeep. I think I had a BAR with only two magazines of ammo. I was gonna start shootin', then I figgered hell, I'll wait 'til these guys in the crew get back 'cause they'd left me alone by this ole building and took off on foot. The Krauts didn't bother me, didn't turn off, went straight into the town and were there about a half hour. I could see 'em watchin'. They knew I was there.

I took the gun and was around the corner, and if they make one turn I'm gonna wait 'til they're a lil bit closer an' then empty the damn thing, but they didn't. They jest whooped along an' kept right on goin' back. They might have had some girl friends in the town when they were stationed there and come back to see 'em or been reconnoitering. They probably knew exactly what they were doin'. The road went down beyond a little knoll where there coulda been a coupla tanks, so I figgered to jes' keep cool 'til the guys come back. They'd told us that town was evacuated, but those bastards was there yet, probably jes' waitin' fer orders to pull back, 'cause they didn't seem to wanta fight. I could see their burp guns hangin' across their backs.

Skirting Belfort to our southeast, we were now driving north toward Epinal around the western edge of the Vosges Mountains that defined the southern limits of Alsace-Lorraine and separated us from the Rhine and Germany itself by less than sixty miles. From my journal:

I'm afraid the rainy season has started in, a slow drizzle most all the time. Luckily, here most of the roads are asphalt and in good condition, so I don't believe the days at Venafro will be repeated. There was a rather short and bitter fight in the woods to the northeast of Epinal, and then we moved into Girmont and on to Dogneville, where we set up the CP.

I was on the radio (Griff, I think, had definitely reached the conclusion that I wasn't worth a damn any more, and I reckon he was right), and I invited myself into the house of the village curé, who was very cordial and put four of us up there for a couple of nights in huge thick feather beds, with those enormous goose-down pillows as big as a mattress.

I had some interesting conversation with him. He'd fought in the last War at St.-Mihiel and told me something about the battlefield there and at Verdun. He'd been crippled for about fifteen years due to an automobile accident, but though one leg was completely stiff, he rode his rounds on a bicycle. He had a fine, sardonic sense of humor and high courage and common sense. He embodied for me the real attributes of a minister. No cant, no rant.

Preceding our entrance into the town he'd passed through German bivouac areas, strongpoints and positions, caring for the wounded and giving last rites. At the same time he gathered detailed information on strength, positions, units, etc., and passed it on to us through the FFI. Back in '40, when the Germans had first occupied the town, they had contrived to knock over the steeple on his church, which had fallen through the roof of the main part. The townspeople had patched up the stump but could get nothing from the enemy to rebuild it with. He showed me his plans for a new and magnificent steeple to be built after the war and the secret, cramped space above his rectory ceiling where he crouched to listen on his banned radio to the BBC broadcasts to the French.

On September 27 we bid an almost filial farewell to the fatherly curé and moved on to the next small town of Padoux, which had been liberated by Third Battalion a few hours earlier with little difficulty. Pausing en route to relieve myself behind a small stable adjoining one of the houses, my eye caught the still-legible regimental designation that a doughboy passing through during the First War had scratched on the inside wooden wall, perhaps after pausing there with the same aim.

We came to an abrupt halt at the very northeast edge of Padoux, where the last small stable attached to the last small house faced broad fields beyond which lay the edge of dense woods, and out of sight beyond them the large town of Rambervillers, our next objective and the scene of bitter fighting in the First War. Our riflemen were all around, waiting to resume the attack. Zapiecki and Mills and I were setting up an OP in the loft of the stable that we hoped would command a broad view in the direction of the Germans, whose presence we were to determine after placing our scope at a window about four by ten inches conveniently located in the thin wooden wall under the tiled roof.

Hardly had we climbed the rickety ladder, which was about eight feet long, and begun getting our bearings in the hay when here comes the familiar distant BOOM of an unfriendly gun, and the first of a clump of shells screamed down around us with the usual shattering and scattering results. The wooden loft of a flimsy stable that stuck up like an obvious OP was no place to be in a barrage. Hank hit the top of the ladder on the scramble, Andy and then me right behind, all three of us not backing down but as if racing down a flight of stairs.

Halfway down, Zapiecki missed a rung and fell back against the ladder, which broke, dropping him on top of Mills, who by then was in a heap on the stable floor. With the upper half of the ladder gone out from under me, I plunged from the loft in a free-fall, catching my left shin on the teetering but still-upright, fractured end of the lower half of the ladder, and joined the pig pile in the shallow cellar.

Hank helped me pull up my pant leg, "and I knew then you were gonna be gone a while. You were hurt pretty bad, but not enough you couldn't walk. You had a helluva torn shin, but the blood wasn't just pourin' outta ya. I was kinda wishin' I had it."

My shin was ripped open to the bone for about six inches, pulled apart by the muscle spasm in a wedge nearly two inches across, and yes, an unheroic "wound" arguably the result of enemy action compounded by a rickety old ladder. Writing home:

Andy helped me into the cellar of the house adjoining the barn. There the French family gave me a bit of cognac and wanted to bandage me, but a line company medic fixed me up. When the shelling had lifted Hank drove me back several miles to the CP, where I was rebandaged, taken via ambulance to a clearing station, thence to an evacuation hospital for a couple of days.

I was evacuated to an air evac hospital near St. Loup and then flown to Marseille, where I spent the night in another air evac hospital and flew to Naples. Around a thousand miles, I should say, all because the unexpected swiftness of the campaign had kept the hospitals slated for France back in Naples.

My first plane ride was on my twenty-second birthday, leaving the battlefields of France twelve months to the day since I sailed from North Africa for the battlefields of Italy. From my bed in the 300th General Hospital in Naples I recalled the journey on Red Cross stationery (I'd left without my journals, which Jerry Waldron gathered up for safekeeping) with the enthusiasm of a St.-Exupéry.

Flight was steady, though occasional air pockets caused the plane to rise and sink, giving one much the sensation as riding in an elevator. The most amazing and utterly novel sensation was created by the panorama of the earth below. Hills seem to come up at you and then recede into the valleys, and there is nothing comparable to the sight of cliffs, gorges and rivers, particularly when they are sharply accentuated by shadows. Marks of civilization were not so unique to the eye since I had seen so many aerial photographs. It is the third-dimensional quality which is so utterly unlike anything we see on the ground. Since there is nothing about one in the air to give a sense of perspective, the ground itself and all its features seem animated and continually flowing and heaving. Truthfully I was not quite so excited by it all as I had expected. Probably because I was on a litter and not feeling too chipper.

This was the workhorse C-46 fitted out with stretchers. Though my torn leg hurt like hell, I propped myself up on an elbow and twisted to peer out the nearest window. I'd lost my helmet somewhere between hospitals, which I rationalized as an omen that without it I was fated not to survive a return to combat.

This concluded my contact with France, the happiest six weeks I've spent in the Army. From first to last I was enchanted by the country and the people. My feelings are of admiration, wonder and understanding.

The country itself was, by and large, hardly damaged by the war. In Midi it is rolling, green and fertile, much like the Connecticut Valley. Although the majority of farms have thatched roofs, the interiors are spotless, plastered, comfortable, like the inside of a New England farmhouse. The cities such as

Lyon have broad avenues, fine and ancient public buildings, and street after street of restaurants and sidewalk cafes. The center of every town is its square and fountain, and every town has its Boulangerie, Poste, Coiffeur, Mairie and Ecole, and of course the village church. More often than not the town hall and the school are in the same building.

The men wear berets, sometimes knickers or shorts. The women tie their hair in a kerchief and often, too, wear shorts. Everyone who can, rides a bicycle, of which there are many. There are a few motorbikes and a very few gas cars. The girls everywhere are gorgeous, coquettish, but virtuous. Of wine there was plenty. The best had been hidden since '40 and was brought out for us to be drunk from on top of a tank or while resting on a rifle. Bread was black and rationed, but a new wheat crop was expected. Dairy products were not abundant, but could be found nine times out of ten on the farms.

There was, nevertheless, a singular and very noticeable piece missing. That was the young manhood of the nation, millions of whom were prisoners of Germany, in the Resistance, or with the Free French. Every woman one met had some male relative or close friend in Germany, every young man in good health (formerly, at least) had been captured and escaped, or had some desperate run-in with the Germans.

The joy of these Français when we liberated them is beyond description. So much was unsaid. They expressed externally to the extreme what lay underneath, but they could never touch bottom. Four years of oppression could not be broken away from in a day. They could not give vent to all that had been pent up within them for four years in a single outburst. They could only weep and laugh, dance ring-around-the-rosies with the boys in the square, go from soldier to soldier with their best wine (they had nothing else to give), invite us into their homes to establish our CP's and OP's, to set up our radios, to rest our weary bones, and to fight the enemy from. Their men, women and boys felt that the least they could do was to pick up every weapon they could lay hands on, run every risk they could to pave the way for us and show us the way afterwards.

One wonders, after all, who should be grateful to whom. The curé who spied on the enemy in the midst of his work, the sous-officier who was captured and taken to Germany, and who escaped and made his way 300 miles back to Lyon in order to help the FFI, the young student and former prisoner who carried millions of francs in a shabby old bag all over Lyon to pay the necessary expenses of the Underground—and they are beyond words in their gratitude to us.

Thus I viewed France and the French from my hospital bed back in Italy.

I'd carried a gun into action from November 8, 1943, when I was first shot at in the Apennines of Italy, until September 27, 1944, when I was last shot at in Padoux as we skirted the Vosges in France eleven months later, and never once squeezed the trigger. Jack Pullman took a shot at a German across Comiso Airport after the landing in Sicily and may have killed him. Bill Woodhams knocked out an oncoming tank with a bazooka rocket at Salerno and came as near as fate would have it to being blown out of the building. George Ruder tried to fire a broken-down machine gun at Varages and was killed. Dilks had the chance to knock off a couple of unsuspecting enemy motorcyclists and was too surprised to do it.

When the Germans' barrage hit we were about to search with our field glasses, through a small window that had been under the peak of the roof over the loft, for their positions far across the field on the left. (*Author photo*)

The fallen G.I. and Madame Albert and her son at the door of their home/stable (*Collection of the author*)

A few feet from where I stand, the guilty ladder's successor (not pictured) leans uncertainly against the loft. (*Collection of the author*)

We Ironheads were not a killer platoon, and yet, how many casualties had we been responsible for as scouts for the guys up on the line and as forward observers for our artillery, how many enemy, how many civilians?

Forty-seven years passed and the likelihood of locating the stable of my salvation as we continued on our recapitulatory *retour* with Hank Siaud seemed remote. It had been on the edge of Padoux, but surely the town had expanded into and across that broad meadow beyond the far reach of which the Germans had lurked and waited. A gas station or two for the motorist chancing by, a modest supermarket and a few more houses must have crept across that inviting real estate, and the house and the stable would have been unrecognizably absorbed at the very least, since the French seemed loath to raze anything left standing after the passage across their landscape of two devastating wars in less than twenty-five years.

But as we drove slowly down the Epinal–Rambervillers road through the village, Padoux ran out just as suddenly as it had in 1944, and *voilà*! The same house with the same stable, the same sentinel over the same long fields, the same distant woods beyond! At the kitchen door we were greeted by a weathered, handsome woman of my vintage. Hank explained our mission. She opened the stable door, and I exclaimed, "This is it!"

There it was, loft and all, and Mme. Suzanne Albert recalled how that twenty-sixth of August so long ago, when she was twenty-two, she and her family took shelter in the cellar of the house as the war passed through Padoux, then heard nothing, then voices, strange voices . . . then *"Les Américains! Les Américains!"*—the soldiers of liberation, and the people pouring into the streets, and cheering and hugging and laughing and weeping—and then the *Boche* shells ZEEE-RROOMMING in on us all, and back to the cellars.

Suzanne was sure I was the first Yank ever to revisit Padoux and picked us some flowers from her garden, pressed still in an album of photos.

G.I.s of the 45th Division!

Many thanks for your nice leaflets! So you think that we deserve some rest and an occasional leave, do you? Well, what about the blisters at your feet? We don't mind not getting any leave just now. You don't get any leave either. All that matters to us is that

You Won't Get to Berlin.

You have been told the war would end in autumn. Your division, well known to us since the days of Sicily and the Anzio-Beachhead, did not achieve anything spectacular so far. Quite a number of your fellows, however, have kicked the bucket. Pretty tough for the replacements who never dreamt of having to cross the pond, isn't it? Your pals told us how much they "enjoyed" fighting. No wonder

They had no idea whä : they were fighting for!

One of them said that he had been FIGHTING FOR FREEDOM He didn't seem to be one of the brightest boys.

You left your freedom behind

with your folks at home, your parents, wives, children, girl-friends of whom you keep such a lot of photos.
Slugging it out in the mud you have a good chance to be killed or maimed for the sake of war-mongers and profiteers who once more contrived to stay at home.

Your buddies are glad to be out of the mud. They are sure to return home safe and sound. They have taken the short-cut. You still have a long way to go. Keep alive, if you can. For remember

You are still wanted . . . for JAPAN!

German propaganda leaflet (*Courtesy of Henry G. Mills*)

⁺⁺⁺ 13 ⁺⁺⁺

"We Will Meet You All Again"

Rambervillers, the Woods and Back in Naples
September–December 1944

The day after I dropped out of the loft and the war, German resistance stiffened. Rambervillers, scene of a terrible battle of World War I and a strategic crossroads strongly fortified by the enemy, was under siege, with heavy fighting southeast of the town and in the forest north of Padoux.

Observation approaching this forest was nigh impossible from open fields with scant elevation from which to see anything more than trees and with equally sparse cover. On September 29 Griff sent Mickey Smith and Shorty Nye up ahead anyway to look for some rise of ground where they could set up an OP. What followed erupted from Shorty's sealed memory as I dug it out of him at his home in Fostoria, Ohio, with Andy Zapiecki thirty-three years later.

> We went up and looked around, and right in front of us was nothin' but trees, trees, trees, trees and trees, no matter which way we looked was trees. Mickey and I got up there and crawled up to the line, and we looked an' looked an' looked, and he says, "What the hell, I can't see nothin' but trees!" Well, we started down on this side and then went right back up again, 'cause if you got down five or six steps below the crest you couldn't even see the trees. So the next hill was lower but there was nothin' but woods. Where we was was jest a bare pasture.
>
> Shellfire was comin' in on the crossroads below us most of the time. Altogether we walked the distance of about two blocks, gradual, jest grass, a pasture was all it

---

Chapter title is from a 1943 poem by Bob Coleman.

was. No place to hide, no trees, no nothin'. Ain't no way they couldn't have seen us. Just a grassy hill, no rocks or anythin' on it.

The stuff started comin' in, and we both of us dropped. We was layin' side by side. Had to be a rocket. If it had been an artillery shell it woulda blowed the hell outta me. We were about a foot apart. How come I got dirt from neck to asshole an' never got a scratch? Dug a lil hole right smack between Mickey's legs and never touched me. I was close enough to him I could lay my hand on him. He had his legs right close together, and that saved the concussion from me, 'cause everything was gone, there wasn't nothin' but bones from here on down. Lit right in there.

I said, "Mick, come on, I'll pull you down here until we get underneath the cover." "Dammit," he says, "I'm in too much pain. Just get the hell outta here and git me some help!" We was up there about half a city block or sump'n like that, an' I crawled on my hands an' knees down to the jeep. I laid beside the jeep an' got it started an' was layin' on the ground while the shells an' stuff were comin' in 'cause I was scared to git in. But I got it turned around an' jest jumped in an' flew, an' when I got to the edge of the village I shut the motor off an' run the rest of the way.

They tole me to go to the Medics, and the medics says, "OK, come with us." An' I says, "I'll give you the location right on the map." They says, "We can't help it. If he's as bad as you say he is he'll die before we find him. You gotta help us." I tole 'em, "Well, they're shellin' hell outta things." They said, "We don't care. You gotta come along with us or we'll never find him." I says, "All right."

So we jumped in the ambulance an' went an' parked down where we had our jeep before. We went up the hillside. Course they wasn't shellin' at that time, but I expected them to any second. The two medics—you know, Mickey's a pretty good-sized boy— each one grabbed hold of a arm an' a shoulder, an' they said, "Grab his leg." An' I says, "No I CAN'T!" They said, "You GOT to! We GOTTA have help!" So I closed my eyes and grabbed ahold of him. That's all there was, bones broken all to hell an' everything, but there wasn't no meat or anything on 'em. That's when I got sick. An' we got back, an' that was all I knew for about three days. Somebody gave me a jug o' whisky.

They gave Sergeant Smith more than a dozen transfusions. One leg was blown off at the knee, the other nearly so, and he was hit in a buttock and a shoulder. There was no alternative but to amputate both legs above the knee. Zapiecki:

Here comes Charlie Nye. He's cryin', tears comin' down. "Mickey got it! Mickey got it!" The medics didn't think he was gonna live. Two days later about ten of us went back to the hospital at Epinal. Mickey was holdin' on to the German field glasses he had. We were like curious kids. We picked up the blanket, and his legs—the stumps were cut off—they had a bar in between. They told him he lost one leg and so much meat gone from the other he said you may as well take it off. Then he smiled half-heartedly and says to us sump'n like he was happy he was going home on account of he'd never seen his daughter and never thought he'd live to see her.

Sergeant Delmar Griffith, as I well knew, had a way of taking or ordering his men out on bare-assed hills and leaving them there without being overly concerned whether they might be in plain sight of the Krauts at sun-up. Mickey getting it out there like that, and Nye almost—Zapiecki's old buddies from Ohio—really got to Andy, who'd been through the mill as much as anyone, wounded in the head, ulcers, jaundice, flat feet, and going on thirty-two, the oldest guy in the Platoon next to Griff.

> Griff woke me about three in the morning and wants me to get my crew together and go on that OP, and I asked Nye what happened. He says "He put us out there, and we couldn't stick our heads up." Nobody wanted to go there. So I says to Griff, "I'm not gonna go over there, not on that bare-ass hill, because Nye tole me about it." I says, "If you wanna go I'll go with you." So he says OK, he'll go with me. So we're on the road—and I swear to God this is the truth—he says, "I gotta go see Second Battalion, stop the jeep." I says, "Well, where's the OP at?" He says, "It's out there, out there. You'll find the scope and everything there."
>
> When he left I says to the driver, "Turn this jeep around, we're going back." So we went back. In the meantime the guys took Rambervillers that same day. Griff comes up to me and asks did I go up on that OP? And I says, "No I didn't. You know yourself that I said you and I would go. The scope and everything is still out there." And you know, he never did recover that scope.

Andy's refusal to take his crew to a suicidal position on a hilltop, one that had just cost the Platoon so dearly, and Griff's evident backing off on his promise to go with them, escalated their confrontation to Bob Coleman, who had been promoted to corporal over more senior Ironheads and who, with Sergeant Dick Beech, was regarded as a favorite of the Platoon Sergeant.

Early in October they had a gripe session. Andy:

> Coleman didn't like the idea that Griff would tell me to go someplace but I wouldn't go the way he said. I would look at the map and try to get a position above where the enemy was at so I could look down on them without exposing myself. And he says, "But you can't do that, Andy. You gotta be more aggressive." I says, "Aggressive is a soldier that's fightin', but if you want to gain information about the enemy you've got to be secretive. You don't want to let 'em know what you're doin'.

That was it. Andy had had it and went to his old friend Colonel Ralph Krieger, who had helped Pullman organize the Platoon.

> I says to him, "I want outta this outfit. I've had enough. I wanta be treated fairly like everybody else." And Krieger says, "I know, Andy, you saw the way Mickey was hurt, and you figger you're gettin' a dirty deal. I'll write you a slip. Take a rest for a coupla weeks and you'll have a different view."
>
> I says, "You give me that slip, and you'll never see me again." And I went back, and the doctor lays that cold stethoscope on my chest and asks how long have I been over here? I says, "Twenty-three months more or less." "Aw," he says, "you've had enough. Let somebody else."

Well, they sent our ole Zapeck back to Italy and reclassified him out of action. He'd been a Thunderbird since six months before Pearl Harbor, an Ironhead for two and a half years, and in combat for fifteen months. So let somebody else.

✦ ✦ ✦

On the eighth of October, 1944, nine days after Mickey got it, Bobby Coleman was killed by an artillery shell. He was up front on an OP with Johnny Dunbar, Bill Stratton and Harry Ramge, our company mail corporal who had traded places with Jim Buckley before the Anzio breakout because he wanted to see more action. Harry was an office type, older, short and thickset and wore glasses. The last Hank Mills saw of Coleman Bob was trying to teach him the words to "The Rose of Tralee." "He'd sing it to me, and I'd never get it right."

Henry Siaud shared the Platoon's loss in his *Links*. "The previous day Bob was fooling around with André and me when we had an argument in English and dubbed each other 'Poor Guy.' This amused him tremendously. Kindness itself, inveterate laugher, generous, sharing with us his rations of good things, Bob was dead, like that, one day to the next, one minute to the other. An American, come from his distant land, asking only to live, who fell among us in a foreign land far from his own, from his family."

Veronica Coleman didn't get an account of the death of her twenty-year-old husband for nine more months, when Harry Ramge wrote from back home in Lima, Ohio, on July 14, 1945.

> My Dear Mrs. Coleman
>
> I am writing this letter to you, Mrs. Coleman, without knowing whether I am doing right or whether it would be better if I did not write it. Forgive me if I am doing wrong but I thought you might like to know.
>
> My name is Harry Ramge and I was in Headquarters Company 157 Infantry. I was in the I and R Platoon and was in Robert A. Coleman's squad. I was with him on the morning of Oct. 8, 1944, but I shall start before that.
>
> I suppose you know what kind of work Bob was in. How most of his work was as an observer of the enemy territory. Our platoon built a platform in some trees at the edge of a little woods about three quarters of a mile from Rambervillers, France, in order that we might observe the German lines. We dug a hole and covered it so that we would have a place to go in case we were shelled.
>
> Bob and his crew were sent out to this place to observe. Four men, Bob, Stratton, Dunbar and myself.
>
> Bob and I put up our tent close to a concrete wall around the woods and Strat and Dunbar decided to sleep in the hole.
>
> On the night of Oct 7 Bob and I went to our tent early as there was nothing else to do out there. We talked some time before going to sleep. We talked about many things, his experiences as an observer in the I and R in Italy and about his family. He told me about his wife and child, and showed me pictures of them. Talked about his

parents and said that he had had enough of this and would be glad when it was all over and he could go back to his wife and to the folks at home.

The morning of Oct 8th was a misty morning. For some reason I got up first and climbed to the platform but could see nothing because of the mist. When I came down Bob was there and said it would be some time until it would be clear enough to see anything over the lines.

We were standing there talking when a German gun started firing, the shells going over us and landing 500 or 600 yards back of us. This gun was the only one firing at the time, and as it was a quiet morning we could hear it distinctly. I can hear it yet—the "boom" of the gun as it was fired, the "eeeeeeee" of the shell as it came toward us changing to "aarrrrow" as it went over and then the "wham" as it exploded over along a road. Bob and I took the angle from which the gun was firing (74 degrees) and were counting the shells as they went over, all landing over along a road.

The gun fired again and we listened as the shell came toward us just as the rest had come. I remember that something flashed through my mind that this one was a little different when it exploded about 75 feet away.

A little piece hit me in the hip. It did not hurt, just felt as though someone had hit me with a hammer. I ran for the hole but did not go in because of my hip. I looked for Bob and saw that he had been hit and hit awfully hard. I could do nothing for him. No one could have done anything for him. I do not believe he ever knew what happened to him.

The shells had been going over us but for some reason this one landed close to us. It "fell short" as they say in the Army. Why it did no one will ever know. Since their shells had been going over us we had just listened to it come and made no effort to get down. It was just one of those things that happens in war.

I was sent to the hospital, then to the U.S. and was discharged on May 30th.

Things do not happen as they should. I was closer than Bob but only one piece hit me. Why it happened that way we will never know.

Robert Coleman was an excellent young man and was liked by all who knew him. His loss was deeply felt by the platoon, as a platoon and by every man in it, personally.

He was my corporal and my friend.

This letter may bring back memories that you have been trying to forget but I found his address in some of my papers and determined to write to you. I wanted you to know that he thought of you and his greatest wish was to return and be with you again. That wish was not granted but we don't know why.

I send my sympathy to you, Mrs. Coleman, and to his parents. If this letter has helped I am glad. If not I am sorry.

Sincerely,
Harry H. Ramge

While finishing his I&R training the kid with a future wrote a triumphal ode to his buddies as if he were already thinking of strolling around the landscape, daring an artillery barrage. Just before sailing off to war he mailed it home to the bride carrying the daughter he would never see.[1]

You can laugh in jubilation
About Communication
You can kid the I and R on how they ran.
But the thing that is our aim
Is to win this fighting game,
And in doing so to have a little fun.
When there's a battle and we're in it
You can bet your life we'll win it
For we've got the brains it takes to beat the foe.

Though our training is not through
We'll succeed in what we do,
And I'll whip the man who says it isn't so.
Our company gave us spirit,
And the world will someday have it,
For the spirited ones are going on the trip.
When we get there it's farewell
For we'll start araising hell
Just the minute we get off our transport ship.

Our thanks we give to you
Who has been a Company true.
We will show you what we mean when we get there.
Luck to all the gang we leave
And I surely do believe
There's a great day coming soon somewhere.

We will not say good-bye
We will not even try.
Because we're just going first to join the fight.
So hats off to all you men,
We will meet you all again,
And brothers I ain't kidding, you're allright.

⁂

Meanwhile, I was right back where we'd so longed to get out of, poor southern Italy of all the places in the world. The Champagne Campaign had simply outstripped the arrival and activation of a Seventh Army hospital of last resort in the France it was so rapidly liberating. Separated from my buddies (and equally unaware of what had happened to Mickey and what was about to happen to Bob), trapped in a bed in the Army's 300th General Hospital in poor Naples of all the places in Italy. Only slightly damaged, awaiting my turn behind the armless, legless and faceless flown across from France in a bandaged, maimed and bloody stream.

Maybe out of the war, maybe not.

Within a week my split left shin was scraped clean, the margins stitched back together, and the leg immobilized from hip to toe in an L brace. The Red Cross girl offered to mail home my Purple Heart if I paid the postage, so I borrowed it from the guy in the next bed, a Johnny Reb always good for a touch. Somebody found a guitar for him to play for the ward. He and another G.I. drew hard labor for some misdeed at Anzio and were told to fill in an eighty-foot well. They put boards across about two feet below the top, covered them with sheet metal, threw on some dirt, and their officer came around and was truly impressed.

The Purple Heart never made it. Maybe someone along the mail trail derailed it. A year later the United States of America came through with a replacement.

Seven hundred miles from Naples, having taken Rambervillers at the end of September, the 157th was gingerly probing the first really deep woods it had encountered in Europe, the western fringe of the Vosges forest that the Germans were turning into the equivalent of the jungle adopted as their own by their Japanese allies on the other side of the planet. The rounded Vosges Mountains stretch 150 miles along the western side of the valley of the Rhine from Basel to Mainz, corresponding to the Black Forest along the east in Germany. Both ranges descended steeply to the border river and away from it gradually and were heavily wooded. Between the rugged heights, the trees and the miserable climate this natural border barrier was said never to have been successfully invaded in the winter.

Consolidation and reconnaissance were called for, and for the next three weeks defensive positions were maintained to the north and east of Rambervillers while the battalions rotated through the town for rest and clean-up. Welcome as those hot showers were, they sent a shiver down the spines of our Fighting Frenchmen, Hank and Andy, already hardly distinguishable from Mauldin's Willie and Joe.

Henry Siaud and his *Links of the Chain* in my translation, continued:

> The showers were in a former German barracks. It was the first time we had washed since our departure from La Tour-d'Aigues, about two months. When we came out we didn't recognize each other, we were so clean! We could feel the recent presence of the Germans. The walls were covered with inscriptions, swastikas, a big framed photo of Hitler. I felt that the Boches were still truly very near.
>
> We were billeted for a while in the empty rooms of a school run by the Sisters. Progress was especially slow. The Germans had found this wooded region easier to defend, with places to dig in, and they bombarded Rambervillers ceaselessly, day and night. The woods to the south were full of our men and equipment. We met columns of soldiers going up to the line or coming back, tired, dirty, muddy, silent. At the crossing of two roads in the middle of the woods a group of G.I.s was firing a field mortar. Regularly, untiringly, every few seconds, a mortar shell went off to sow death among the enemy a few hundred meters away.

We were awakened in our schoolhouse one morning by the whistle of shells, followed by explosions directly in the area. Everybody ran for the big cellar on the other side of the playground that served as a shelter for the Sisters from the bombardments. Some civilians, children, Sisters and soldiers were already there. The noise of the detonations outside was deafening. It lasted about half an hour, then ceased completely. Everybody waited for a while before going back up to the open air.

But having a pressing need to relieve myself, I went up rapidly, before the others. At the moment of my leaving the WC, I heard the long, typical whistling. Knowing I hadn't time to get to the cellar, I threw myself down behind a metal post in the playground, just in time. At the precise instant I hit the ground the shell burst exactly five meters from me, at the foot of the church wall bordering the court on that side.

I remained for a few moments with my face glued to the earth, my hands on the back of my neck, getting all kinds of debris on my body which rattled on my helmet. In the minute that followed, I heard the voice of André, who knew where I had gone, calling "Henry, Henry, where are you? Are you OK?"

I ventured an eye toward the court where an enormous cloud of smoke and dust didn't allow me to see him. While getting back to the cellar I told him everything was OK. Shorty Nye made some disapproving remarks on my imprudent sortie, punctuated by some swear words about the "fucking Frenchman!"

Our stay at Rambervillers lasted several days. We were gone alternately with André on observation patrols to the east. A few kilometers away we could see on the heights at night St.-Dié burning. It was sinister. The old central church in Rambervillers had suffered damage from the bombardments and was occupied by wounded civilians. I saw the heart-sickening spectacle of them stretched out on the floor, old people rattling their last breath, children crying, mothers imploring or silent as the good Sisters and a few nurses lavished their ministrations, sometimes the last.

During our rest period a mobile kitchen under a tent assured us of three hot meals a day. We discovered pancakes, doughnuts, eggs and bacon fried for breakfast, boiled chicken with preserve, orange marmalade which made André tremble with indignation but which I found not bad. Sweet desserts, cake, coffee, milk. All hot. We had the impression of returning to earth after these months in mid-air, at war.

In the barrack Les Gerencer had a phonograph he found somewhere on which he played most of the day his favorite record, which he sang badly with his voice a little off, "Beautiful, beautiful brown eyes, beautiful, beautiful brown eyes—I'll never love blue eyes again," drawing disapproving jibes from the wings. Others played poker on one of the beds in which the Germans had slept a short while before us.[2]

Back in Naples I grumped to myself that

bad weather seems to have commenced in earnest. The Italian front is completely bogged down, and the 7th Army drive has slowed to almost a standstill, bucking heavy counterattacks and artillery. The enemy is determined to hold the southern anchor at Belfort. The 7th is drawn up through the Vosges Mountains on the western border of Alsace-Lorraine. The French told me just before I left that winter is extremely fierce throughout the region. Aachen has fallen, and we are driving for the Saar. Progress there is measured in yards against fanatical resistance.

The Russians have taken Belgrade, and Allied landings in Greece have, with the help of the Resistance, almost succeeded in clearing the entire country. Hungary has been tottering towards a complete break with Germany, while the Reds have penetrated into East Prussia against fierce opposition. Biggest news is the invasion of Leyte Island by MacArthur and the smashing defeat of a majority of the Jap fleet during the landings. Still, the Germans look as though they were good for this winter, at least.

By mid-October the skies enveloped the Vosges with downpours and impenetrable ground fogs. Action was reduced to reconnaissance patrols until, inevitably, the offensive must be resumed. Our regimental *History* caught the mood of dread and death:

> The replacements came up with the rations. They were "broken down" like so many K's, like so many five-gallon cans of water, and sent to the individual companies.
>
> They sat on the wet, muddy slope of the hill and listened to the platoon sergeant talk to them ... talk quietly and grimly.
>
> "You're gonna be tired," he said.
>
> "Goddammed tired!
>
> "You're gonna be wet and miserable.
>
> "You're gonna jump off at dawn and fight all day and dig in in the dark.
>
> "And then you're gonna jump off again the next morning.
>
> "You're gonna be disgusted and sick and scared.
>
> "You're gonna be fighting the German army, the weather and the damned woods.
>
> "You're gonna wanna lay down and die ten times a day.
>
> "But ... somehow ... God knows how ... you're gonna find the guts to go on."[3]

The 157th jumped off again on October 25 toward the town of Raon-l'Etape. The *History* continues:

> Intermittent rains soaked everything. The attackers climbed hills and fought down the reverse slopes. They were wet. They were tired. They were hungry. But that was nothing new. They'd been wet and tired and miserable before. What was new was the stealthy, nerve-wracking movement through dense woods with visibility limited to ten or fifteen feet. What was new was the continued tension on every step of the way. It was sometimes a relief to be fired on, for fire gave some location of the enemy. Every tree was a possible enemy stronghold, every bush could screen an enemy machine gun.
>
> "If we only could see the bastards," was the constant mutter of the attackers ...
>
> The rains and cold grew worse. When the [bed]rolls did come up, they were soggy masses. Men who dared to take their shoes off, slept with their socks under them in the hope of drying them out by morning. But too often enemy troops infiltrated at night, fire fights broke out, and the extra time spent fumbling for shoes could spell the difference between life and death. So more men were evacuated for trench foot, and the old Venafro-Benevento pattern evolved again.

They went on. They attacked and dug in and attacked again. They gulped down the hot coffee that came up with the rations and chewed the cold, leathery hamburgers that offered some relief from the continuous K's. They learned to advance quietly in a woods where a slight sound carried hundreds of yards. And no matter how tired they were, they put some kind of covering over their holes at night. Tree bursts were a constant hazard and the only protection against them was a roof. One man found what he thought was a pile of empty shell containers and covered his foxhole. He discovered the next morning that . . . [they] were filled with live ammunition.

Mail was delivered on the front lines and the men read rain-soaked copies of their hometown papers. They read of home town optimism, plans for V-E Day, and sweeping ridiculous statements of a quick victory. They read long analysis by armchair strategists who wiped out German resistance with a bold stroke of the typewriter. They questioned new men who had left the States the previous month and heard that the war was practically over. The reaction was bitter and profane and heartfelt. These men had seen friends blown to pieces an hour before and fought for the ground under their feet yard by yard. Their pants were caked with the mud and dirt of France and the blood of the men who died beside them. There was no optimism, no jubilation, no plans for a V-E Day in the snow-covered Vosges Mountains of France that November . . .

. . . No man slept the night of November 6th. For continuous mortar fire fell in the area and foxholes had become swimming pools. The wet, weary troops occasionally threw themselves on the muddy ground beside their holes in a weird parody of sleep. When a shell whistled they automatically rolled into the three or four feet of water for what protection it offered.[4]

During the first week in November the 100th Division had been moving up only a fortnight after landing in Marseille from the States, green as they come. After repulsing a fierce enemy counterattack on the seventh, the 157th was relieved by the 100th's 399th Regiment, and the 45th, with eighty-six days on the Seventh Army's main line, moved back southwest of Epinal to around Bain-les-Bains for a rest.

For the Thunderbirds it had been four hundred miles in a comparative breeze from the beach to Rambervillers, but from the beginning of October through mid-November a mere fifteen. In the jungle-like woods it was impossible to tell direction without a compass. The men rarely saw a target, and a squad leader saw hardly more than two or three of his own. Between heavy rains, constant shellfire and the woods, keeping roads and communications open reminded the veterans grimly of Italy. In another throwback to the First War, carrier pigeons—more reliable, if slower, than wire or radio—took flight from Division with messages. Because the Germans let combat patrols come so close that our artillery couldn't be brought to bear, we had to send our patrols ahead of the main body to draw fire.

The objective now was to crack the enemy's winter defense line, penetrate the Vosges passes and clear them out west of the Rhine. The Seventh Army aimed for Strasbourg, capital of Alsace, annexed by Germany in 1871, returned to France in 1918, and retaken in 1940. Though not especially strategic, Strasbourg's return had symbolic meaning for the French.

The objective of the First French Army on the Seventh's right was the German bridgehead around Colmar from Strasbourg west to the Vosges and south to Basel, the "Colmar Pocket."

Shorty Nye was snug in his hole when

Griff says, "I gotta go to Second Battalion CP" or someplace, and I says, "Go ahead," and he says, "I want you to go along with me," and I says, "Why the hell do you want me along? They ain't no sense in both of us gettin' killed." He says, "You're goin' anyhow." I says, "OK, if I have to, dammit, I'll go."

So we went up, and they was shellin' hell out of it on both sides. Griff was walkin' along jest like nothin' ever happened—you know Griff. Got up to the CP and they was beatin' hell outta them too. He got his business done, and I was down talkin' to the soldiers there, and they said, "Why in the hell don't they GET US THE HELL OUTTA HERE? We cain't even see nothin' to shoot at."

They was on the down slope of a hill, and there wasn't nothin' in front of 'em but trees, trees and trees. All they was gittin' was artillery fire. The guy was tellin' me, "they wanted us to attack and we refused." The whole company refused. Soon after, a fresh outfit come in, and they attacked and the Krauts pulled back. They had everything covered, didn't give us any sleep, kept within a mile of us all the time. That's what makes it tough. You cain't get any sleep, you cain't think, and the tireder you git the more you cain't think or do anything.

Trubia (*Courtesy of Dominick M. Trubia*)

Nye (*left*) with unidentified scout (*Courtesy of Dominick M. Trubia*)

Another time they told us to recon a woods about half a mile wide and a mile long, beyond the woods our guys were in, a valley about a city block in between. When we started back we got the shit shelled outta us, and it was coming from our side. We tried to get through to 'em on the radio to see who the hell was firing on us 'cause they had us pinned down, but we never did get 'em to stop. We could hear the Germans in the woods talkin' and laffin', and one of our guys who understood German couldn't make it out but said they were laffin' because our guys was shellin' us, not them. Every time they'd slow down we'd back up a lil ways and finally got outta there.

Convalescing back in Naples, I wrote Pete Sax in Boston that "I'm afraid I'm going a bit ga-ga over this gal I've been writing to ever since Anzio. She seems to have her claws in me, a not unpleasant feeling. I guess anything can happen when I get back."

By late October my shin was healed, with only slight pain in the leg, and I was in shape to return to France and the front. But Captain Secor, my surgeon, was working on my reclassification for limited service. My having a well-known medical man for a father appealed to his sense of fraternity, and I didn't discourage him. I never asked whether Doctor Garland pulled strings or tried to, but I was looked in on by two or three medical colonels who happened to be friends of his. I expect he got on my case when he and Ma opened the wire on Friday the thirteenth announcing I'd been hurt. Perusing his journal fifty years later I found that he'd approached his Harvard classmate, Massachusetts Congressman Christian A. Herter, who "had no luck" with the War Department.

On October 31 I exulted homeward: "I'm getting Class B, limited service, so I'm through with combat. You better have a celebration!" Next day I was discharged from the hospital to the Sixth Replacement Depot for reassignment, the one we first replacements had founded in Mussolini's Racetrack the year before. "I know it's a great load off your minds, and now at least I know I'll get back unless I fall down an elevator shaft or something! Boy, oh boy! I just hope and pray for the safety of the men who have to stay up there, because I know all they have to go through."

My father rejoiced. "Are we pleased and relieved! I can imagine your own feelings; probably somewhat mixed—a little regret at leaving the Ironheads and the front, and a good deal of relief at being through with all the mud and discomfort and hazard. You've had your year of it and taken it in a way that's made us constantly proud of our parenthood. Congratulations!"

Having been raised in a family whose sober Republicanism was taken for granted, in my first election on the soldiers' ballot I voted a fourth term for FDR, my Commander-in-Chief. In mid-November I noted in my journal: "The 7th Army is stuck in the woods, and Griff writes that it is the most miserable weather he has yet seen." By now I had learned of the Platoon's most recent casualties, Mickey and Bob. Around this time I dined with Captain Secor, and reported home perhaps unwisely that I "helped him consume a quart of Calvert, over which I got quite high and after which I got quite miserable!"

Griff in Germany
(*Courtesy of Dominick M. Trubia*)

Officers and gentlemen got a whisky ration or at least an alky/pineapple juice mix from the battalion surgeon and mess sergeant. The dogface might see a can of beer every few months, otherwise "Dago red" or rotgut. Hence my miseries, which drew a low-proof caution from Pa to take it easy with the booze. Sensing the way the wind blew, I wrote his wife that "in all my life I haven't been really 'bottled up' more than three times, and that includes my army time. In four months at Anzio I had exactly one glass of wine, and since early fall I haven't had more than a small snort once or twice a month. I detest being drunk or even quite tight; it gives me a feeling of physical and mental revulsion. I never have and never will turn to drink as an outlet."

Brave words.

The Naples Racetrack where we pioneer spares had founded the first replacement depot a year earlier was the clearinghouse of the Italian campaign, an encampment of pyramidal tents, mess halls, supply backups and everything else required to sort out green replacements on their way to their dates with destiny, hospitalized wounded being returned to the same Racetrack, and guys like myself lucky enough to be reclassified out of it and awaiting whatever. I was put to work with saw and hammer in a crew making crude doors in an attempt to tighten up the pyramidal tents against our second Italian winter.

It was almost as much fun as pitching a pup tent in the middle of Grand Central Station during rush hour. The sole redemption was the retreat into fantasy of the evening movie shown on a big screen set up squarely in front of the main grandstand when the weather favored.

I was about halfway up the stands one night, and as they were changing reels some jerk flipped a lighted cigarette butt from an upper row. As this spark arced high over the stands someone whistled like a bomb coming in. Most of us had been on the receiving end of shellfire and were various degrees of psycho anyway, so there was mass panic as the bleachers jumped up as one man and pushed and shoved trying to get down to earth and take cover somewhere in what might or might not be an air raid but no one was gonna take a chance. One guy trapped in the uppermost row just jumped off the back thirty or forty feet and broke both legs when he hit the dirt.

Back in France the 45th was nearing the end of its two-week respite, and our pair of unpaid *Têtes de Fer* the end of their volunteer service to the two old allies. The new French government was anxious to detach for its own growing army young patriots who had joined up with the Yanks.

Henry Siaud finished linking his chain that November:

> Toward the end of our rest we were near a village not far from Epinal in some wooden huts in the deep forest that had served as shelter for the Germans a little earlier. Big wood stoves glowed inside and warmed the damp and cold air. It rained almost every day, a freezing rain that looked almost like melted snow. Then one beautiful day, in preparation for the return to the front, they began to distribute winter equipment, lined boots, heavy socks, long underwear, wool caps, heavy gloves, and warm, quilted parkas.

Before André and I received our equipment, Pat Farley called us together and told us, "Sorry, boys, but the French government wants all Frenchmen that joined the U.S. Army to go back home, so I'm afraid you have to go."

So our epic was going to end here.

A little sad at leaving the friends with whom we had lived so many good moments in difficult, dangerous, painful times, we got our things together. The village policeman had been told to find us civilian clothing, which we put on over our uniforms.

At the moment of our final good-byes to those we believed we would never see again, we felt that they envied our return home—and at the same time regretted to see us leave. Roughly and without ceremony, Shorty Nye gave us a collection of a little more than three thousand francs taken by all the guys in the Platoon, which would assure our survival until our return to the South. After our awkward good-byes, a Dodge truck took us to Epinal.

Where are you, dear friends, dear comrades, so generous, so kind, such cut-ups, looking for pretty girls, living in discomfort in the cold, raining nights, often in the open, sometimes in the straw of barns, more rarely with a farmer, on the ground, all dressed, gun at your side, but warm and sheltered for one time?

Have you all gone back home, safe and sound?[5]

Ah, the high jinks and the laughs and the wild, wild stories, the gentle hyperbole and the explosions of disbelief, the fun and laughter, the lightness, the esprit, were fading. There was less and less of what anyone wanted to remember as the Germans fought with the bitter taste of the very desperation they'd inflicted on their helpless, hopeless victims at the beginning of it all when they were riding roughshod.

The Ironheads were never the same after the soul-searing worst of the enemy counterattack at Anzio with the departure of Jack Pullman, who wanted no part of being an officer; Mohawk Mullenax, the one-man army laid low; thrice-wounded Jimmy Doodle, our Irish padre, out of it; Shorty Nye and his horrors and his saving lil black bag; my special buddy Jerry Waldron promoted up and out; and then in France the final exit in dread and disgust of Andy Zapeck, who'd kept us in stitches for ever so long; and the ghastly brush with death of Mickey Smith, the calm at the center of every storm; uncounted other casualties too, quiet ones; and Griff, bitter and blunt to the end and after. But over it all Dan and George and Bob, so brutally and abruptly killed except that it was all so brutal and abrupt.

Especially Pullman, who simply wore out. The cool, wiry, talismanic presence of Jack, jes' plain Jack, who'd fashioned our purpose and knit us all together, watched over us, back twice to us from the hospital, saved us for another day, agonized over us and wept for us.

It all faded farther and farther into the no-man's-land of the gut as the killing and maiming of body and soul just kept on and on and on, driven and sucked in toward *Deutschland über Alles*.

Would I have said the hell with a scar on my shin and gone back to the front if Jack had still been in charge or if Jerry were still with the Platoon? I might have. Yes, I might. Others who were hurt plenty more did. But given that premonition on the plane ride back from

France that I'd not survive if I did, and the unsought chance of reclassification out of it all, I don't know. I just don't know.

At the end of November General Eagles was injured by a mine that got his jeep, as Colonel Ankcorn had been after Salerno, and was succeeded as Division commander by Major General Robert T. Frederick, who headed the First Special Service Force in Italy and then the now-deactivated First Airborne Task Force that parachuted into southern France in the invasion. The Regiment pushed on through the Alsatian Plain into the northern Vosges, clearing Lembach on the Maginot Line on the third of December.

With the Rhine up ahead, every man under fire had to wonder who'd be the next to get it without having the least effect on the foregone conclusion. Nervous Hank Mills still had nerve enough to be driving up to the front one day with a hitchhiking rifleman when

> they dropped a shell right behind the jeep that blew four holes in the back, a hole in the gas tank, put a piece o' shrapnel through this guy's left arm and engulfed us in smoke. I got down the road another fifty feet and looked at the windshield, and here's a hole no more than four inches to the right of my head. I looked down and a fragment had torn half of the sleeve outta my jacket.

Nearing Germany, Mills and Dilks and a couple of others were moving up on the road with the advance point when they were pinned down by incoming shellfire. And at it again.

Mills:
Dilks said to me, "You know, I think I'm hit." I says, "Well, you don't think yer hit; yer either hit or yer not. If yer hit you know yer hit, and if yer not hit yer not hit." He says, "Well, I'm hit." He shows me his jacket, and there's this big hole. So I unzipped it and pulled it down. Sure enough, he had a hole you could lay yer finger in where it just tore a piece o' meat right out and kept on goin' but didn't take no bone with it. I took him back to the CP, and they dressed it and kept him there on light duty.

Dilks:
It was wintertime, an' I had so damn many clothes on that the piece jes' barely grazed my underarm. At the Medics I thought, "Boy, I'm goin' back." I didn't know how bad it was, couldn't see under there. Then the medic said, "Aw it ain't bad" an' give me a shot o' whisky an' dressed it nicely an' said "You come back here every day an' get a fresh dressing," an' I got teed off, figgered hell, he wouldn't send me back, an' I never went back again.

Mills:
A month later we got up into this little town and established an outpost. Dilks was shavin' outta his helmet. Had on a T-shirt, undershirt, and two or three sweatshirts, and he was standin' beside me, and I got this smell, and I says, "Jesus Christ you stink. How long's it been since you took a bath?" "A coupla weeks ago or whenever," he says. "How long's it been since you had that shoulder dressed?" I says. "Aw," he says, "I never bothered."

The shirts had spots where they were startin' to soak. We pulled 'em off, and the bandage, my God, was dirty. I lifted it up, and it was nothin' but gangrene. I got him down to the Medics. The guy looked at it and asks when did it happen? He says, "Aw, I dunno, about a month ago."

Dilks:
They still wouldn't send me to the hospital. "You ain't got no fever, we'll take care of it." It was a week and a half before I finally got rid of it. It was my fault. I shoulda went back. It was jest healin' up when I went back to the hospital at Strasbourg because I'd turned yeller with the jaundice.

While my old buddies were returning to action after a couple of more weeks of rest with no sure future, back at the Racetrack awaiting reassignment I was toying with the novel idea that mine had been given back to me.

"Writing of one sort or another has the strongest appeal for me, but I'm not sure to what extent my abilities go," I wrote to myself.

My vocabulary is far more restricted than I should like, and my thinking is not as clear and quick as I know it should be, nor is the liaison between mind and pen really steady and efficient. Thoughts run unpredictably either ahead of or behind the written word, and I dislike intensely having to resort to a superficial and far-fetched style of wit or fantasy in order to be readable. I've never set my hand to fiction to any degree, though I might have more success than I think there. My powers of observation don't satisfy me. Nonfiction such as biography, criticism, even higher journalism, is the devil to get started in, but that can't be a deterrent. Everything else worth while will be too.

Acknowledging the arrival of a pack of sixty-four letters that had been trailing me from APO (Army Post Office) to APO: "Monk outdoes herself in belles lettres, even wrote me three days in succession when I had malaria! I like her better all the time and find myself entertaining novel thoughts for the postbellum period in connection with her. I never thought I'd be stricken through the mail. I'm afraid she has more brains than I, but I think I can handle her in my own masterful fashion." And to medical student Pete Sax: "My 'affaire du coeur' is sometimes enigmatic, constantly frustrating, and very fascinating. If she is like her letters when I see her, I'll tread the aisle with her. However, she must be agreeable to such a permanent arrangement. I'm gettin' old."

How accommodating of me.

To myself December 6: "The 7th has captured Strasbourg. The 7th and the French 1st are both sweeping across the plains of Alsace to effect a junction at Colmar. It's extraordinary that I've gone haywire over Monk. Damned if I see how a man can be on the slippery brink of falling in love with a girl he knows only through her letters, but it's happened. I'll surely hit the curb when I first see her, but I'm a trifle scared how she'll react—probably take to her heels."

Two days later to family friends: "Perhaps what bothers me most is a completely washed-out feeling. The spice of life seems to have flown away, and only the chaff is left. I'm

Monk
(*Collection of the author*)

smoking like a chimney, and ten months on the line have given me a nervous tic in the right eye. Rheumatism has caught up with me in damp weather. You have no idea what the change in tempo involved in leaving the line does to one. However, I reckon it'll wear off eventually."

It didn't. Five weeks in limbo with time on my hands, the guys I left behind still getting beat up, another bleak European winter coming on, an endless war, and me out of it. Christmas drew nigh, and lacking a card I sent home cheery personal greetings: "The wind is blowing through the cracks of this so-called 'winterized' pyramidal tent like mad, and there's no way to get warm except to go to bed. So after I've finished this and tossed off a note to Monk I'll hit the hay (and it's only 6:30!). We're all anxious about the breakthrough, but it will wear itself out. There are a few Xmas trees tacked up here and there around the area, but somehow it all seems a little unconvincing."

Oh well, I wasn't the only doggie laying around on my recycled ass in the same old Racetrack through which thousands had been cycled up front and back over the past fourteen months since we spare parts pitched our tents amidst the sheep. On Christmas Eve I wrote my usual note to Santa. Lacking a chimney, I sent it westward across the Atlantic.

> For the second time I'm spending Christmas in the traditional setting of the Nativity. The spirit of the day is not always as sublime in a soldiers' camp as one might expect at home. The chowline still has to be sweated out, and alcoholic revelry here and there thrusts itself intrudingly into one's mood. The sharp command, the hoarse shout, and the obscenity continue as on any other day. One concludes that apart from mere religious dogma the day is observed in the light of the strength

of past associations, events, friends and loved ones. So it is with me, and my heart reaches out over thousands of miles to my family. Thus I can picture the old Christmases and look forward to the new.

Enough of such bonhomie. Poor, ravaged Italy eked out another miserable Yuletide as 1944 lurched toward its bloody finish, and "I'm sitting here on the edge of my bed with my overcoat on and another one over my knees as a blanket, writing, as usual, by the flickering light of a candle. It is windy, cold and rainy."

It worked. Ma wrote back that she was feeling guilty in front of the fireplace, thinking of me huddled in a tent with only a candle for warmth and light.

Three could play that game. In a Boston department store, Pa wrote, "I picked out a lovely 'mouton' coat of sheared sheepskin, soft as beaver and very reasonable in price, and brought it home as pleased as Punch with myself, Ma made me pack it up and take it back. 'No fur coat til after the war.' Was my face red! And you say you don't understand women."

Yup, now that I was out of it the Old Man was beginning to let up and let down. But not Ma. She should have let him give her that coat. He'd worked like the beaver it was as soft as, taking care of sick kids days, nights and weekends to pay for it, and it was very reasonable, and c'mon Ma, it was only sheared sheepskin anyway. Enough of that New Hampshire Calvinism, both of you.

Early in the new year the Army's official *Stars and Stripes* published a "sonnet" of my own that I'd scribbled and fired off to the paper a few weeks before.[6]

The Last Shot

"Who fired that shot?" they wildly cried—
"The shot that won the war!"
But all they saw was a ghastly tide
That flowed on a foreign shore.
Again they screamed, "Who fired that shot?
That shot that beat the Hun!"
But the only reply was the putrid rot
Of bodies that lay in the sun.
"Who fired that shot?" once more they roar'd—
"The shot that stopped the foe!"

But all they heard was the voice of the Lord
From the voiceless grave below:
"That was no shot, but the Crack of Doom
As it sealed forever the hero's tomb."

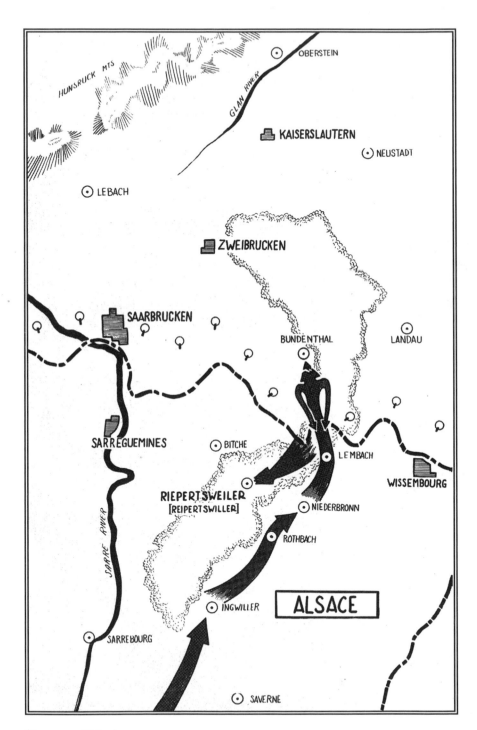

(*Department of Defense*)

✦✦✦ 14 ✦✦✦

AMBUSHED AT REIPERTSWILLER

The Bulge
December 1944–January 1945

> Their's not to make reply,
> Their's not to reason why,
> Their's but to do and die.
>> "The Charge of the Light Brigade,"
>> Alfred, Lord Tennyson, 1854[1]

ON THE SIXTEENTH OF DECEMBER the retreating Wehrmacht pulled itself together and smashed back in the final, dying blitzkrieg against the advancing liberators of Europe that would go down in history as the Battle of the Bulge. The entire Western Front shook from the shock waves. Just south of the Bulge the 45th was holding down the northern flank of the Seventh Army, and here, once again since the Panzers almost split the Salerno and Anzio Beachheads, all hell chose the 157th to break loose upon.

In Alsace it was blowing and snowing. With their backs now to their border, the Germans planned to use France's Maginot Line, so futile against their blitz of 1940, to blunt the Seventh Army's attack while they withdrew to their own Siegfried Line, equally as confident of its unbreachability.

The fulcrum of the French Maginot was the Ensemble de Bitche, or plain Bitsch in the Franco-German of the Alsatians, four large and interconnected forts at the key transport junction of Bitche that rendered it the strongest point in the modern Maginot Line and a key in France's defense since the seventeenth century. The original stronghold on a great jut of rock dated back at least eight hundred years. Bitche was at the head of the Lower Vosges Mountains. Northward the forests thinned into open country. The fort's guns, unlike most of the Maginot, could be turned about-face against France itself, and the German commander (son of a bitch that he was) was said to have been under orders to fight to the last man.

On December 12 the American 44th and 100th Divisions attacked the Maginot Line at Bitche in an all-out assault backed up by intensive air strikes, artillery and armor. Three days later, northeast of Wingen, the 180th of the 45th was the first Seventh Army unit to cross into Germany and come up against the outer works of the Siegfried Line.

The next morning of the sixteenth, A Company of the 157th crossed and tacked placards on trees inviting those who followed to "Shit on Hitler's Home." Once over the border, the 'Birds found the outer defenses deceptively light because after little more than token resistance the Germans were racing back to the concrete and steel, the blockhouses, trenches, massed guns and cutting crossfires of the Siegfried's formidable *Westwall.*

The same day, only eighty-odd miles to the northwest, Field Marshal Gerd von Rundstedt suddenly smashed through the Ardennes with twenty-four divisions, including ten armored, overran six American divisions (some inexperienced and some resting from battle) and punched a bulge in our lines thirty-five miles deep and sixty wide.

Even as the Panzers roared toward France for the second time in four years, the 157th took the small German town of Nothweiler overlooking the outer Siegfried Line and advanced to take Bundenthal on the Line itself, which was found to be protected by an anti-tank moat, covered on three sides by enemy positions in the hills and on the fourth by pillboxes impregnable to artillery, as our astonished forward observers observed when their shells bounced off the concrete.

Working through intense fire, two platoons each from First and Second Battalions managed to probe out crossings of the water-filled anti-tank ditch and infiltrated the town, only to be surrounded in the buildings they'd occupied. A fifth platoon was trapped in a cemetery but escaped when a patrol got through to it.

By day the enemy knocked down the buildings around them. By night, with rations running out, the trapped G.I.s liberated some penned rabbits and vegetables but quit cooking when the smoke attracted shellfire. They concocted a mix of hog meal and half-rotten apples. A Russian forced-laborer brought them some water but never returned. They held off the Krauts from the upper stories, but every attempt at their relief was thwarted by ferocious fire.

On December 22 two men escaped back to the lines. Next day, following a barrage so intense that it temporarily silenced the pillboxes, the pair took a twelve-man patrol back into Bundenthal through a designated safe path in our shellfire pattern and led the way out for the seventy-four left alive after a week facing annihilation, including wounded who were shouldered or lugged on blanket stretchers.

Hitler's final fantasy had Rundstedt's blitzkrieg driving a wedge of discord and discouragement between the Americans and British that might somehow enable the shift of significant forces to the Eastern Front against the Russians. It evaporated the day after Christmas with the relief of surrounded Bastogne, whose electrifying defense by the 101st Airborne Division was distilled in General Anthony McAuliffe's rejoinder to the German surrender ultimatum: "Nuts!" Meanwhile the Seventh Army was ordered to abandon temporarily its offensive and hike left to pick up slack as Patton's Third Army moved over to hammer the Bulge.

On New Year's Day, as our Intelligence had warned, the Germans mounted a major counterattack against the Seventh Army before it could regroup. Consequently, the 45th and 100th Divisions were ordered to pull back from the Siegfried Line, including the Bitche forts that had fallen to them on December 20. The 157th had to retreat to the Maginot Line, which it manned from the fourth of January through the twelfth.

Lined up against the 45th's stretched-out front were major elements of four German divisions. They were reinforced on the fourth day of the attack by the hitherto-untested fighters of the Sixth SS Nord Division fresh from occupation duty in Finland, fanatically Nazi, trained in mountain and winter fighting and clad in white fur-lined clothing and insulated boots. The enemy strategy now was to occupy the territory around the villages of Philippsbourg and Reipertswiller as springboards for a drive toward Strasbourg intended, in turn, to block the Seventh Army objective of moving the U.S. divisions on the right of the 45th to take this major city from the north.

After another unusually heavy enemy attack the 157th was again withdrawn, this time to the hilly Lichtenberg Forest on the southeast of Reipertswiller, a hamlet at the edge of the woods too insignificant except for the finickiest of cartographers. On the thirteenth it relieved the 276th Infantry of the 70th Division under shellfire. By preempting the high ground overlooking Mouterhouse and the valley to the east, the Regiment was expected to prevent an enemy breakthrough down from the forested hills to the main highway leading to the Alsatian Plain and Strasbourg.

The outlook was bad for the 'Birds, whose already thinned ranks were beset by the bitter winter. Worn out from weeks of desperate fighting without pause for replacements, each of the three battalions of the 157th was down about two hundred from its near–six hundred strength, facing the full-clout 11th Regiment of a fresh SS division defending the Fatherland, dug in on the high ground, and backed, as immediately became apparent, by a variety and accuracy of massed artillery such as the veteran Americans had never before been up against.

On the fourteenth the 157th and 180th were to converge on the ridge beyond Reipertswiller. The battle plan called for the 180th and then the 179th to line up some distance on the left of the Third Battalion of the 157th, while the old Anzio comrades of the 36th Combat Engineer Regiment would attack on the right of First Battalion.

The Third and First jumped off, with the Second in reserve. Colonel Felix Sparks, who had taken over Third Battalion after its commander was killed, was shaken up when his jeep hit a land mine just before the start but resumed command after his executive officer was wounded. Sparks thought the shellfire his men ran into the heaviest he'd seen in nineteen months, including the Anzio counterattack and Battle of the Caves. They dug in.

Next day the attack was resumed. Only Third Battalion made its objective of two ridges connected by a saddle and moved into the holes vacated by the SS. They had succeeded only too well and were about 150 yards ahead of their flanks, a vulnerability immediately realized if not indeed invited by the withdrawal of the Germans, who counterattacked fiercely and beat back every attempt to bring the rest of the American line up with the Third.[2]

Determined to hold on to this ridge lest our domination of the hills enable us to break through to the north and swarm down on their massed supporting artillery in the Mouterhouse Valley, the Germans had stonewalled First Battalion as it attempted to advance on the flank and hit Company K with a counterattack that left fifty enemy dead in its immediate field of fire. "Those damn Heinies came in rushes," said one wounded rifleman. "Their dead were piled up like cordwood in front of our positions." Only two, identified as from the 11th Regiment of the Sixth SS, were captured; one thought that a hundred of his *Kamaraden* were killed and only seven got away. After dark a supply detail got through and evacuated a few American wounded.[3]

The Germans kept up massed artillery, tank, mortar, rocket and machine-gun fire on our positions on January 16, maintaining frontal counterattacking pressure on the Third Battalion while infiltrating around its flanks. Companies C and G of First and Second Battalions moved up close in an attempt to reinforce somewhat the exposed right and left flanks, making it five companies on the line. The infiltration only strengthened. By mid-afternoon I and K Companies reported enemy in their rear.

But it was the devastating accuracy of the shellfire on its positions that turned the tide against the embattled Third Battalion.

Jerry Waldron, then in our S2 regimental intelligence section, remains convinced our attack had been drawn to the ridge line because our intelligence indicated that it appeared to be the target ground, some two or three miles north of Reipertswiller, of the artillery training range of the German military camp at Bitche, where he believes that for years enemy guns must have been thoroughly zeroed in for practice firing on or near the ground occupied by Third Battalion.

A rare Signal Corps photo of the isolated town of Reipertswiller under enemy fire. Note the water-filled shellholes. (*Department of Defense*)

Those guys firing on us were the instructors on the range, and that's why they select-
ed that spot to try and pinch off all our troops that were beyond us going toward
Strasbourg. And if they could have knocked us off they would have cut off three or
four divisions that could never get out this road which we were defending and which
was back of the ridge we were on. You had to go over this road to get your heavy vehicles into Strasbourg, and our troops might have got out but they'd have gotten all
our vehicles.

So they brought down the Sixth SS Division. We replaced a green division there
and were sacrificed to hold the line. What the world doesn't know is that in the
Battle of the Bulge they were trying to chop off those divisions that were ahead of
us at Reipertswiller.

In crisis mode now, an ad hoc "provisional composite regimental company" was hurriedly organized early that evening under Captain Robert Cannon of Anti-tank Company
as a reserve unit in an attempt to keep Third Battalion's supply route open. Two anti-tank
platoons of twenty men each were posted to guard the trail up. Lieutenant Pat Farley of the
I&R was put in command of fifty Ironheads, guards and MPs, with orders to occupy the
ridges behind them.

The role of the Ironheads in the battle of Reipertswiller emerges from recollections
more episodic than ever, sometimes of a fleeting moment in the thick of it—more often on
the fringes. No one foot soldier or even regimental scout and observer in such a staggering
encounter survived it with more than a chaotic montage of blinding mental short-circuits
and a burned-out fuse box.

Hank Mills was following a road around a hill, when "suddenly around a bend there
was a bunch o' Germans off to one side setting up guns or something, not more than a
hundred yards off. I dropped my head way down in my ribs and kept walkin'. They saw me
but never reacted. Musta figured anybody that stupid wasn't worth bothering with."

Bobby Winburn was with somebody in a hole.

Winburn:
The 88s were tearin' up the woods pretty good an' kept gittin' closer. Last one was
about fifty feet away. The guy with me took off an' I went back to another hole, and
then we went down on a road, about fifteen or twenty guys ahead o' me. A light tank
come up. We hit a bunch o' Germans at a roadblock. One o' the CP guards was leadin'
off, an' they ripped him right down the middle. We stayed right there, formed the line
there 'til next day when we went back to the CP, an' that's when they started pullin'
'em out. You couldn't trust anybody you saw 'cause some o' the Germans had our uniforms on. You'd hear a dog barkin' once in a while. I hadn't seen a dog in two or three
months. Lotta Germans wanderin' around. In the woods, the wind blowin', leaves
rustlin'. You'd swear it was people walkin' around but you couldn't see anybody.

Shorty Nye:
We had I&R, the Wire Section, cooks and CP guards. Nobody knew how to fight
hand-to-hand. We was dug in on the back side of a hill. It was early in the evening

after dinner, and we went this way with this little small biddy-ass tank, and Griff
went that way where the road split. We just went so far when a machine gun up on
the top of the hill started firing down. The tank fired back, but they wounded four
or five guys. That's where one of the CP guards got his ass shot off. They loaded the
wounded up on the tank, and it went back, and there we was, stuck out there, no
tank, no nothin'.

Farley says, "Dig in!" I said, "Lieutenant, we're only a hundred yards beyond
our God damn holes where we're in deep in a cliff, and why in hell should we dig in
here in no-man's-land where it's all rock?" He said, "Charlie, maybe you're right.
OK, everybody fall back to our original positions." So we did, and a coupla days later
we got relieved.

They gave Farley and Griffith the Silver Star for valor. No one recalls the occasion, but
the latter had no use for the former: "He was never much of an I&R leader. He turned into
Colonel O'Brien's stooge. He'd hang around the CP, and anything come up, he was really
anxious to volunteer, which meant Griff. Probably the only person I can really say I hated.
Lord, I've seen him panic. He just had no guts."[4]

The Platoon Sergeant was too harsh. Pat was easygoing and likeable, easy to warm up
to, easy to let off. The schoolteacher/prospector was as hard and unforgiving as the Wales
of his ancestors. It wasn't guts that Lieutenant Farley lacked; he could have drawn limited
service with his wounded knee after the Salerno fiasco and avoided returning to face his
men and hazardous duty. It was judgment, and he was lazy and traded on his good nature.

The day after this pickup company was organized it tried to fight through the steel ring
of the SS to the Third Battalion. From an OP Dom Trubia directed artillery in an effort to
maintain a fire-free path through enemy positions in his buddies' way. Griff and a bunch
started off along this trail on a night patrol with Captain Cannon:

> We ran into more artillery and mortar fire than I ever saw in the war and got pinned
> down by machine guns. They practically mowed that forest down. We never did get
> there. A round or two struck a tree ahead. We could hear it coming. I flattened
> myself, and Cannon sort of halfheartedly squatted down. Someone said let's go, so
> I got up, and there was Cannon in front of me. I reached down and got ahold of his
> shoulder and shook him and said, "Let's go, Captain." He kind of gurgled, and that
> was the end of Captain Cannon. He was dying. We left him there, and the medics
> brought him down.

Although the records fail to show that the provisional company effected a link-up,
Griff remembered otherwise.

> Some of us went up at night to take food and medicine to Third Battalion, and we
> got ambushed along this trail, and a sergeant got shot. The rest of us got through
> and got some provisions up there and then pulled out. Dark o' night, and I didn't
> know where we were going. I was about ready to throw in the towel. Tired more than
> anything, tired. Cold, cold. Gosh, a lot of the guys got knocked off.

Bill Caird was one of those who got through. He'd had it, but not for long.

> The shelling and small arms fire were terrific. We were in a fight with the Krauts. I
> think I had a Tommy gun, which was ineffective at the distance, lost the radio I was
> taking up but made it back and broke down. They sent me to the Medics for a rest
> cure for a couple of days, then back to the Platoon.

That night Lieutenant Willis Talkington of Third Battalion's Pioneer Platoon loaded
up a light tank with rations, ammunition and medical supplies and plunged through the
surrounding Germans. The next day, January 18, his tank tried to return and was knocked
out by an enemy rocket. The tankers were killed or wounded, but the wounded lieutenant
made it back to his lines.[5]

This was the fifth day of the battle, with cold more bitter than ever, laced with snow
and rain. So deadly were the German guns that the medics could no longer get to the
wounded, who crawled to their holes and prayed for help. The uncanny marksmanship of
the incoming shellfire left little doubt that it was being directed by radio from enemy infil-
trators who were by now reckoned to be in at least company strength or more between the
surrounded battalion and the American main line.

The SS grew more furious with every attack. In a desperate effort to rescue our First
Battalion, the entire Division artillery pounded the advance to no avail. Fire met fire, and as
the American infantrymen were forced back, the enemy swarmed all over. Only thirty from
Company G got out, leaving the triumphant enemy in a position to pour it harder than ever
on the exposed flanks. An attempt by the 179th to help fared no better. They, too, were
pinned down.

There was more. Third Battalion's Anti-tank Platoon had tried to attack with two
armored scout cars from the 45th Recon Troop but withdrew with them when platoon
leader Lieutenant Charles LeFebvre was shot through the head—all but Staff Sergeant
Bernard Fleming's squad, which was pinned down in a shell crater:

> My squad was in a ditch with three enemy machine guns on us. I asked for a volun-
> teer [Pfc. Lawrence S. Mathiason] to get aid. He got only about fifty yards when a
> machine gun killed him. I asked for another [Pfc. Emmett L. Neff] and he got about
> ten yards before he was shot through the legs. I went out and dragged him behind
> some cover, then yelled to the others that I was going to the rear myself. I don't know
> how I made it, but I did. I saw Col. Sparks and told him what happened.[6]

During that fifth day, twenty-four American 105s fired 5,018 rounds on the German
positions with no perceptible effect. Surrounded, all wire lines blown by artillery, the five
infantry companies maintained communication in code.

> By this means they could notify battalion and regimental headquarters of their
> plight, of the counterattacks which they repulsed, of the enemy infiltrating constant-
> ly behind them, of their steadily diminishing slender reserves of strength due to casu-

alties and lack of supplies, of the ceaseless destruction wrought upon them by the
enemy's artillery, mortar, and rocket fire to which they were subjected on the ridge . . .
    . . . it was apparent that the surrounded units were no longer within any sort of
physical contact, and that they might never escape.[7]

In a state of high alarm, Colonel Sparks asked his Regimental Commander's permission to pull back in line with the First Battalion on the right and the 180th on the left.
Colonel O'Brien concurred but had to clear it with General Frederick at Division. Thirty
minutes later he got his answer.

It was emphasized that the beleaguered companies had not fallen into a trap . . . That
they had to remain there as long as possible and finally be engulfed was part of the
fortunes of war. It would mean greater danger to the Allied front and more lives lost
if the enemy had regained the positions in the dominating terrain . . .
    . . . The Commanding General ordered the Regiment to hold its position as long
as possible in order "not to show its weakness."[8]

Every effort to break the surrounding grip of the SS during the sixth day, January 19,
came to naught. Tanks were thwarted by the steepness of the ridge and great trees felled in
their only path. An air supply drop was aborted by sleet and snow.
    From Jerry Waldron's S2 report for that crucial day:

The enemy again employed his infantry to attack our front line units, with the pri-
mary mission of breaking through our lines and the secondary mission of infiltrating. In each of his three attempts today, one at 0715 hours, the second at 0740
hours and his last at 1525 hours, his main effort was hurled back by Company K,
Company I and Company L. But in each instance, infiltration was accomplished.
This infiltration has enabled the enemy to build up a line of estimated company
strength in which a number of automatic weapons are emplaced and which is out-
posted by machine gun positions. In many places in this line, enemy forces are dug
in under the rocks on the slopes of the hills and because of the accuracy of the
artillery and rocket fire brought down when any attempt is made to dislodge these
troops, it is believed that there are artillery observers in this line, providing the
support-fire so necessary to its existence.[9]

The next day, the seventh of the battle, two consecutive attempts in miserable weather by the remainder of the 157th, the 179th, and the 411th Regiment of the 103rd Division
to break through were beaten back. It was two days after General Frederick had commanded the Regiment not to show its weakness. Now he directed it to pull back "preparatory to
being relieved of its mission in order to reorganize."[10] That afternoon Colonel O'Brien
ordered the men left in his six trapped companies—there were now no more than 125—to
about-face and attack southwest through the Germans in their rear at 1530 hours.
    Two hours and ten minutes later Pfc. Benjamin Melton and Private Walter Bruce from
Company I staggered into the Third Battalion CP. They gasped that every man left behind

had been killed or captured, and were evacuated with nervous exhaustion. Melton reported later:

> . . . Ammunition was scarce but we made progress until the enemy artillery zeroed in on us. Some of the men were blown to bits and I saw one officer get a direct hit and just disappear. I was knocked to the ground several times by the concussion of exploding shells but I wasn't wounded. We saw that we weren't going to be able to get out so we went back to our holes where we at least had a little protection. Somehow the Germans sent word to us to surrender by 1700 hours but I remembered reading about the massacre at Malmédy and I didn't want to stay there and be killed in cold blood. Together with Pvt. Walter Bruce and another fellow whose name I don't remember, I set out to try to get back to our lines. The other man was killed by machine gun fire but Bruce and I . . . kept halfway up the slope of the hills and stayed away from all paths and trails. We saw some shoepac marks in the snow and followed these for a while. Then we saw a shelter-half which was covering a foxhole. We laid low until a G.I. looked out from beneath it. You can imagine how glad we were to see that guy.
>
> The enemy artillery and mortar fire out there was the worst I'd ever seen. At least three-quarters of the men on the hill had a wound of some kind and a few had two or three. Until the last day we placed the wounded in holes with the other wounded so that men who weren't hurt could guard them and give them aid. We had no medical supplies, no food and no heat to melt snow for water. Once we found a box of rations underneath an ammunition pile. We gave the rations only to the wounded.[11]

By Felix Sparks's count, five rifle companies, elements of three heavy weapons companies, and five forward observer teams from the 158th Field Artillery, comprising seven company commanders, about thirty platoon leaders, and some six hundred enlisted men, were casualties of the 45th's costliest battle of the war. No one ever knew how many Thunderbirds died, or were wounded, or captured, or went missing in action. In a footnote to their official account of the battle, Army historians stated only that "regimental casualties for the month included 32 killed, 244 wounded, 472 missing, and seventy known prisoners of war," a total of 818.[12]

A historical analysis, however, concluded that 141 men of the 157th were killed, 345 wounded (not including those captured), and about 450 captured, for a total of approximately 940.[13]

❧ ❧ ❧

In 1986 two Frenchmen exploring the battlefield with a metal detector discovered the remains of Private Roger H. Caron, D Company, of Nashua, New Hampshire, identified by his dog tags in what appeared to be his foxhole in the area of his company's machine-gun section; his helmet, cartridge belt and boots were missing. Six months later they unearthed the body of Private Homer D. Wadlow, L Company, of Pilot Knob, Missouri, in the company's final position, buried under rocks in his uniform and helmet, with his dog tags and wallet. Both soldiers were returned home for final burial.[14]

Inexplicably virtually passed over in the Army's history of the campaign, the battle of Reipertswiller was the costliest in the annals of the 157th. The Regiment had been crucial in stopping Hitler's all-out attempts to drive to the sea, split and destroy the two Italian Beachheads. Much later in Alsace, with the outcome of the war now assured, it can be argued that had the Germans broken through the valiant, sacrificial defense of the surrounded Third Battalion, they might have been able to threaten the Seventh Army's advance south on Strasbourg with temporary cut-off, if not encirclement, conceivably delaying, at least, the final day of reckoning. As it was, the SS were so battered that they were withdrawn from the line a few days after the 157th.

Jeremy Waldron, whose eyes were fixed on the S2 situation map throughout the long battle, believes that the 157th was recommended for its second Presidential Unit Citation for the heroic stand of the five rifle companies and their supporting units on the ridges above Reipertswiller, but that the initiative "was deep-sixed by the High Command because, to award it, they would have had to admit that about fifty thousand troops should not have been there in the first place."

✧ ✧ ✧

As time passed, Felix Sparks searched for MIAs in the cemeteries of France and among the living at home with scant success. In 1987 he revisited Reipertswiller for the second time in the intervening forty-two years with his wife, Mary. The retired commander of the Colorado National Guard, parent of the old 157th, was a brigadier general now.

> . . . The small villages in the area look much the same, except that the war damages have been repaired. The positions occupied by the five rifle companies are still outlined by many foxholes. The German positions and machine gun emplacements are still visible. Empty and rusting M-1 clips are to be found everywhere. The area is heavily forested, and a brooding silence prevails. Our guide informed us that wild boar and deer inhabit the area. As I stood on the final position occupied by K Company, bitter memories of the battle flooded my mind.[15]

Some of the thrust of that bitterness emerged in General Sparks's reflections on General Eagles's replacement by General Frederick, whom he rather invidiously described as "a coast artillery officer who had never before served in either the infantry or an infantry division."

> . . . However, he was the commander of the 1st Special Service Force during part of the Italian campaign. After the fall of Rome, the 1st Special Service Force was disbanded. This event left General Frederick and most of his officers at loose ends. The unfortunate loss of General Eagles provided Frederick and his people with the opportunity to move in on the 45th Division. This they did in a big way.

Shortly after Frederick's arrival on the division scene, the division staff was reorganized, with several of the experienced division staff officers getting the boot. A new assistant division commander was brought in, Colonel Paul Adams, formerly of the 36th Infantry Division. One of the former Special Service officers was sent down to our regiment to take command of our Second Battalion, although he did not arrive until after the Reipertswiller battle.

And so the stage was set for the disaster at Reipertswiller.[16]

At the opposite end of the chain of command was Frank Merchant, forever an Ironhead, who missed Anzio, was returned to the Regiment in time for the Southern France invasion, and was hospitalized out of it as the Champagne Campaign wound down. He remained an astute observer of the military scene who never lost his distaste for it. As a retired English professor at Union College in Barbourville, Kentucky, he wrote me some thoughts on the Reipertswiller tragedy and other matters forty years later on February 23, 1985, and although (and possibly because) neither of us was there, I find them illuminating:

> This was the worst damage inflicted on us by any opposing ground forces, I believe. The casualties were suffered by what may have been our "best" battalion, the Third. It was never over-used since it seemed Colorado National Guard policy to put "foreigners" (easterners) into the other line units, especially the First Battalion, which included B Company (in part a punishment company). Third Battalion, finally commanded by Sparks (once Ankcorn's adjutant), was to my mind a bit more intelligently and energetically officered than the other units. But it was rammed into what amounted to a desperate German ambush. I suspect there was lack and disregard of preliminary reconnaissance, very likely on summary orders from above—up to Corps and Army. It may have been that at that time every approach beyond company patrols was disregarded. I assume that Sparks, who knew better, was by higher authority rammed ahead.[17]

Felix Sparks's epitaph for his lost battalion: "How fragile is the thread of life and how futile is the waging of war."[18]

And Sergeant Delmar Griffith's: "I got to thinkin' this is the most foolish, messiest business that mankind could ever git into. You git bitter. Awful easy to git bitter. I was pretty demoralized, as much as I ever was, around Reipertswiller when we lost the Third Battalion."

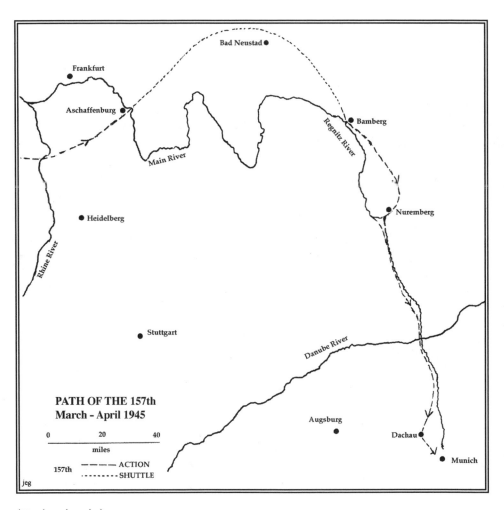

PATH OF THE 157th
March - April 1945

(Map drawn by author)

⁂ 15 ⁂

MAJOR LAMBERTH'S
GÖTTERDÄMMERUNG

The Siegfried Line to Nuremburg
January–April 1945

ALL CUT TO HELL BY THE FRESH and fierce SS, the 157th limped to the rear for a massive intravenous of replacements and in only ten days was back on the line near Reipertswiller relieving our 180th, the static situation having afforded a lull for breaking in new men. On February 17 the Regiment was relieved by the 42nd Division and shuttled back to Rambervillers for a month of rest and practice at river-crossing and pillbox attack, broad hints of what lay ahead.

In mid-March the reconstituted outfit was trucked to an assembly area near Sarreguemines. A few miles to the north bristled the Siegfried Line; much farther to the east lay the Rhine. On the left was the 180th, the 179th in reserve, the Third Division on the right. The new mission of the Seventh Army was to drive the Sons of the Fatherland back home across the Rhine, starting in two days.

Since we Ironheads sailed away from the stalemate of Italy, where we were on or close behind the line and shared some of the shit and plenty of the shelling, the war had outrun us as it had even the rifle companies until the Germans escaping southern France planted their backs to their border and turned on us again with the familiar snarl.

Out of it, with plenty of pull via Doctor Joe Garland from the Army contingent of the Boston medical establishment in Italy, I was classified as a medical technician reassigned from the limbo of the Racetrack Replacement Depot to the four-hundred-bed 154th Station Hospital in the Volturno Valley on the north bank of the river between Caserta and Santa Maria, about fifteen miles above Naples. The Commander was mild-mannered Major William Tecumseh Sherman Thorndike, a medical friend of my father and namesake grandson of the Scourge of the Confederacy in the Civil War.

Well, whaddya know? From Harvard pre-med to dogface to ward boy—lowest of the low—on the third of January, 1945, armed with bedpan, urinal and dynamite pills for some poor plugged-up bugger who hadn't had a dump for a week and then cleaning up after him. And making beds.

I followed the fighting back up front with the vicarious avidity of a deserter on the lam.

By now General Rundstedt's drive to split our forces had penetrated more than forty miles into Belgium. Outnumbering us two or three to one, he was throwing in giant Ferdinand and Royal Tiger tanks, and our planes were grounded by the weather. Still, I figured, "Kesselring tried the same thing in February. He can't succeed because he hasn't the means to keep the stuff rolling, and he hasn't the stuff to roll. He's creating a huge bulge, the base of which will undoubtedly be hammered away at from the north and south. Evidently we'd taken a calculated risk in shifting troops south to Patton and Patch for the drive into the Saar and Alsace. It was just one of those things where the line had to be weakened in a spot not considered too vulnerable anyway in order to strengthen a push in another spot."

Continuing my journaled cogitations on such grand matters, I was struck, reading Emil Ludwig's biography of Napoleon, that "to unite Europe it was necessary for him to soar above the nationalism of Europe, yet to accomplish his purpose he must, as a national leader, assume the nationalism of France. He was torn between these two necessities from the beginning to the end."

Tragically for history, Hitler cared less for learning from it than for making, or breaking, it.

For my part, as the action distanced itself from me, I retreated from it. Moving from the homeless confines of the Neapolitan Racetrack to the tame routines and distractions of the hospital, I followed the news and drew the battle lines on my map like any other distant spectator but knew nothing of my old outfit's costliest encounter ever until Reipertswiller was history.

Distancing is as essential in the continuum of war for those who remain as for those who are distanced. Observe its unfolding in this brief *entr'acte* between Reipertswiller and the advance into Germany from the 157th's *History*.

> It was like a blood transfusion.
>
> Replacements came by the hundreds to fill the gaps of the lost six companies. New men from the States: fresh, alert, cocky—along with older non-coms from adjacent units, fighters wise in the way of combat infantry to add the seasoning of experience.
>
> And like a period of convalescence was the quietness of the line around Wimmenau. It was a life-saving interlude following the blood transfusion.
>
> The regiment healed fast.
>
> And feet were itching for the feel of German soil again.
>
> And the old cry sounded out:
>
> "Adolph, count your men."[1]

Thus with the coolness of the surgeon—or the general—does the military historian-on-the-spot put it behind him only months in his past, because the fighting unit, like the corporation and the church and society itself, remakes itself, and he is chronicling, as am I, not for the dead but for the living, for the survivors, and for the survivors of the survivors.

So the day had come when hope outweighed dread, and parents and son could relax their familial grip on the upper lip and admit that each had been trying to support the other by not letting on. My mother's forty-ninth birthday was coming up, and I sent her greetings from afar:

> Really, Mum, all I want to do is to remind you again that I'm not very demonstrative as a rule and apt not to express all that I feel. But occasionally I want to tap a little deeper into the well of my feelings and tell you how I miss you and the family terribly. You don't know how you've been a tower of strength to me over here, particularly in the darker days when hope was nearly exhausted. So I'd like to say on your birthday what I feel all the time and to ask you to remember what I usually leave unsaid.

And a few days later, on January 28, I logged:

Biggest news of the war is that the Russians are less than 100 miles from Berlin. With the taking of Warsaw a couple of weeks ago, they jumped off on a terrific all-out drive sparked by Marshal Zhukov. They shot a spearhead to Breslau, another one around East Prussia and to the sea, isolating some thirty divisions there. Upper Silesia has been cleared and almost all of Poland, Tannenberg taken and Koenigsberg besieged. Poznan, not far from the German-Polish border, has been surrounded by Zhukov, who had driven straight through central Poland with his armored columns.

As yet the Germans have made no real stand, and the Russians are driving on the entire front with three and a half million men. It is impossible to be otherwise than optimistic. It looks like a drive that may be momentarily checked in a desperate, frenzied last stand, but it is such a colossus, such an avalanche, that in spite of all my abortive and generally wrong predictions of the past, I think the end is very near.

By mid-February I'd talked Major Thorndike into trading pisspots and bedmaking for fresh air as a driver and was behind the wheel for the first time in two years. From my journal:

I've moved down to the motor pool and am living in a big kitchen tent with concrete floor, high sides, tables, radio, etc. Very nice life indeed. I have my own ambulance, a Dodge in beautiful shape with a honey of a motor. Got my license a few days ago and have been driving a six-by [the Army's heavy-duty, all-purpose, GMC two-and-a-half-ton truck sometimes called a six-by-six, or just six-by] *and a three-quarter-ton weapons carrier. Good bunch of boys here. Yesterday went out on an emergency call up a mule path to the top of a mountain where two 155s had overshot the forward slope of a practice firing range and landed on the reverse in a village, killing one civilian and wounding two.*

Another ambulance had picked them up already—wild ride. It's a marvelous sensation to be driving hell-bent down a narrow road with a Military Police escort to clear the way.

The Russians were only thirty-five miles from Berlin. Budapest fell. The Big Three met at Yalta. Manila was virtually in our hands. Twelve hundred planes plastered Tokyo. But my elation over the war news and my release from the wards to the open road were short-lived. Right off I was struck with crippling pain in my legs and back. Three days later I had to be lifted out of bed and taken to sick call, where the medical captain told me he could find nothing clinically wrong, that I was having a nervous breakdown, and go back to duty. I must be imagining all these aches and pains.

Having complained before Christmas that "sometimes on damp days my legs ache like thunder," I diagnosed my problem as the sudden onset of arthritis or rheumatism from the months in the mountains of Italy and so wrote my medical parents. "Very sanguine about the outcome of these acute arthritides, especially following fatigue and exposure," Doctor Garland replied after consulting his specialist friends in Boston. "They may take a bit of time, but they always clear up completely and usually leave the victim as good as ever."

My hospital, however, put me in the psychiatric ward. For days I couldn't raise myself up in bed and had to call a ward boy to turn me from one side to the other. I was a lousy patient. March 3 letter:

> I weary of hearing these rear-echelon commandos spouting off fourth and fifth-hand stories they've heard about the war as if they were their own. They're the type who rush to join up with the American Legion or VFW and try to run the country. You rarely hear from the man who's been fighting the war.
>
> I haven't the feeling that I've done my job in this war by any means, because a man has never done it here until he's so incapacitated that he can do nothing more. I feel out of it, and I don't feel motivated so much by intense patriotism as I do by the fact that the men on the lines must fight on while I, by a mere lucky break, have been withdrawn. I wish that I could help them in some tangible, satisfying way, and no matter how comfortable and secure this life is, that compulsion is always in my mind.

Three days later:

> I can stand up for only a few minutes until my knees ache and pain so that I have to go back to bed again . . . Jerry writes again. His sense of humor has enabled him to keep his grip for so long. I have the greatest admiration for him. I am suffering heavily from ennui here and would get up if I could. I'm treated as though I were a child and can find out nothing about opinions on my case.

March 10:

> The news today is wonderful. The 1st Army has made a crossing in strength of the Rhine, just below Remagen, after taking Cologne a few days ago . . . The bridgehead

is now secure and more than five miles deep. The Krauts were caught with their pants down again … Prisoners are pouring in, and the enemy seems to be on the verge of disruption. "Military experts" are in ecstasies of amazement and optimism as usual … The Russians are driving on Stettin and Danzig and are less than 30 miles from Berlin. Half of Mandalay is ours, and nearly all of Iwo Jima.

I'm now up and about and hankering to get out. With all this big news that feeling comes back to me again. Wish I could be up where things are going on instead of sitting here on my dead ass.

Jimmy Dowdall, thrice wounded and twice returned to action, the prototypical Irish bachelor living with his parents in Jackson Heights on Long Island and reluctantly running an elevator in Rockefeller Center over in Manhattan, knew the distance and the pull, and replied to a letter from my mother the day after St. Patrick's Day:

His wish for a return to the I and R does not surprise me. I've often heard combat soldiers state that the farther back from the front the more restless they became and the more impatient with their surroundings and company … Even now there are times when the thought of being redrafted and sent back to the I and R is not unpleasant. It is a strange feeling—this feeling of loneliness to fellows who have been with combat outfits.

Ever since that last day under fire in Padoux I've felt that a leg split on a broken ladder wasn't quite a wounded one, that the Purple Heart I got for it was borderline (never mind that it was part of a chain of events due to enemy action as if I'd taken a hit), and that my limited service reclassification despite eleven months in combat was a cop-out on the guys I left behind. For fifty years I saw my pain and immobility after becoming a casualty as an occult psychogenic manifestation of guilt verging on cowardice, reinforced by having been consigned to the psycho ward. Or it may just as well have been a transient infectious disease manifested by acute arthritis-like symptoms.

No matter. After fifty years of latent combat post-traumatic stress disorder (PTSD) that blocked my recognition of it and my ability to tackle the guts of this volume, it began to sink in that every survivor of combat endowed with a shred of compassion since men have gone to war feels some measure of guilt to be alive and must ask himself why he was spared when he thinks of comrades who weren't. Not to make too fine a point of it, I'm relieved now to be thoroughly glad to have survived. I owe completion of this work in large part to an evening of intense enlightenment thirteen years ago with Boston psychiatrist Jonathan Shay, MD. His compassionate bridging with intensely suffering Vietnam War survivors through his work with the Veterans Administration led to his pioneering recognition in the 1994 landmark book, *Achilles in Vietnam*, that the Greek poet Homer described essentially the same behavior among the combatants in the Trojan War some 3,200 years ago. Dr. Shay postulated—correctly, I believe—that each of us who has been to war "in harm's way" over the centuries has stood, high or low, on some rung of the aftermath's haunting "ladder of guilt," if only for having come out of it alive.[2]

✣ ✣ ✣

To clear the enemy out of the Saar Pocket in the rich industrial Saarland west of the Rhine, Patton's Third Army was to drive across the Moselle and then strike south while the Seventh attacked north between Saarbrücken and the Rhine to form between them a giant pincers. The 45th was on the left with the objective of smashing through the Siegfried Line again, this time to take Homburg. The Third Division was on its right.

The Thunderbirds jumped off March 15 near Sarreguemines. The Germans fought a token delaying action while falling back to the pillboxes of the Siegfried Line behind the irregular formations of pyramidal "dragons' teeth" tank barriers of concrete and ditches that zigzagged across the landscape. On the seventeenth, behind a rolling barrage and with the help of armor and air strikes, the 157th once again banged on the West Wall of the Third Reich. So well planned and rehearsed was an operation projected to take weeks that in two days the invincible had been vanquished:

> . . . The tanks were stopped at the Dragons' Teeth where they opened fire on bunkers and pillboxes, trying to button them up as the infantry moved in. Under cover of this slugging, the doughs crawled up to the apertures, and went to work with hand grenades, flame throwers and demolitions.
>
> . . . If a man hesitates, if a man falters, if a tank pulls back, a lot of men die. But there was no faltering, no pulling back here. Men lost limbs and lives in that attack, but from its start there was never a doubt of its success, and the enemy must have realized that as he saw them come.[3]

First and Second Battalions led off. Company C was the first to break through behind Corporal Edward G. Wilkin of Longmeadow, Massachusetts. Twenty-seven years old and the father of a young son, Wilkin was about to earn the Regiment's fourth Congressional Medal of Honor for outstanding valor under fire, posthumously.[4]

> . . . Heavy fire from enemy riflemen and camouflaged pillboxes had pinned down his comrades when [Corporal Wilkin] moved forward on his own initiative to reconnoiter a route of advance. He cleared the way into an area studded with pillboxes, where he repeatedly stood up and walked into enemy fire, storming one fortification after another with automatic rifle and grenade, killing enemy troops, taking prisoners as the enemy defense became confused, and encouraging his comrades by his heroic example. When halted by heavy barbed wire entanglements, he secured bangalore torpedoes and blasted a path toward still more pillboxes, all the time braving bursting grenades and mortar shells and direct rifle and automatic weapons fire. He engaged in fierce fire fights, standing in the open while his adversaries fought from the protection of concrete emplacements, and on one occasion pursued enemy soldiers across an open field and through interlocking trenches, disregarding the crossfire from two pillboxes until he had penetrated the formidable line two hundred yards in advance of any American element. That night, although terribly

fatigued, he refused to rest and insisted on distributing rations and supplies to his comrades. Hearing that a nearby company was suffering heavy casualties, he secured permission to guide litter bearers and assist them in evacuating the wounded. All that night he remained in the battle area on his mercy missions, and for the following two days he continued to remove casualties, venturing into enemy-held territory, scorning cover and braving devastating mortar and artillery bombardments. In three days he neutralized and captured six pillboxes singlehandedly, killed at least nine Germans, wounded thirteen, took thirteen prisoners, aided in the capture of fourteen others, and saved many American lives by his fearless performance as a litter bearer. Through his superb fighting skill, dauntless courage and gallant, inspiring actions, Corporal Wilkin contributed in large measure to his company's success in cracking the Siegfried Line. One month later he was killed in action while fighting deep in Germany.

I ask myself, almost in disbelief, what drives or pulls such a guy?

Once breached, the Siegfried crumbled as the inflexible Maginot had five years earlier. On March 19, the fifth day of the assault, the 45th poured through and swept on across the Saarland and a hundred miles to the Rhine, which was reached at Westhofen on the twenty-third. The 179th and 180th crossed the river almost unopposed, with the 157th in reserve, and once again the Thunderbirds were in pursuit of a Wehrmacht falling back into unaccustomed disarray, this time on its own soil, mile after mile a repeat of the Champagne Campaign except now no champagne, no hugs and kisses, no dancing in the deserted streets, only white flags in place of swastikas. In town after town eighty thousand enemy were trapped in the closing of the pincers on the Saar west of the Rhine by the Third and Seventh Armies.

From the Rhine the objective was about fifty miles to the ancient academic town of Aschaffenburg on the east bank of the Main River at its confluence with the Aschaff fifteen miles southeast of Frankfurt-on-Main. While the foot soldiers of the 45th mopped up in their wake, Patton's tanks of the Fourth Armored Division roared to the Main and in a piece of luck found an intact railroad bridge across which on March 25 they established a bridgehead between Aschaffenburg and its near neighbor down the river, Schweinheim.

Meanwhile, having gained a tankhold on the far side of the Main, General Patton sent down the order to organize out of the Fourth Armored a self-sufficient expedition to dash fifty miles farther into Germany to Hammelburg, break into Oflag XIIIB, an officers' prisoner-of-war camp outside the little town, break out as many captured American officers as the vehicles could carry and dash back triumphantly to his Seventh Army lines.

What only he knew, because the word had been passed to him top-secret through the highest Allied channels, was that his son-in-law, Lt. Colonel John K. Waters, who'd been captured while serving with the First Armored Division in North Africa in November 1942, was probably among the prisoners. "Hope to send an expedition tomorrow to get John," he wrote his wife, and he assigned an aide, Major Alexander Stiller, to Task Force Baum (as it was named for Captain Abraham Baum, its commander), equally top-secret, to target the boss's kin for rescue.[5]

Task Force Baum had 294 officers and men, sixteen tanks, twenty-seven half-tracks and three self-propelled 105s. There was to be no backup force and no air support. They were on their own. The ostensible purpose was to feint the enemy into shifting forces south, from the sector where the Third and Seventh Armies were to attack, move to the northward and in the process rescue as many officer POWs as possible from the camp. As Major Stiller told one of the planners, the expedition was also intended to make the liberation of 5,000 prisoners from camps in Manila recently engineered by the Boss's archrival for publicity, General Douglas MacArthur, "look like a Boy Scout hike."[6]

Patton's subordinates were aghast and warned him to no avail that such an isolated and unsupported venture deep into German territory would end in disaster. Shades of the 45th's ill-fated end runs along the north coast of Sicily so that his guts and the blood of his boys could beat Montgomery into Messina.[7]

Task Force Baum jumped off the night of March 25 and fought through Schweinheim with the help of its parent Fourth Armored Division, which then withdrew back across the Main River. After doing initial damage to isolated enemy forces astonished at the presence of such a free-lance expedition wandering about their countryside, and liberating 700 Russians to whom Baum turned over 200 captured Germans, it was all downhill. The Germans closed in through their spider web of familiar roads and terrain and harassed the invading column with such effect that when the Yanks the next day reached the gates of Oflag XIIIB, which readily surrendered, Captain Baum had only about 110 men and four of his ten medium tanks left.

Moreover, not only were there 4,700 prisoners, of whom 1,400 were American officers—many more than estimated—but in a momentary misunderstanding following the rescuers' arrival, Colonel Waters was so seriously wounded by a German rifleman that he couldn't join the exodus of POWs who rode or walked with the remaining G.I.s as the Task Force headed for home.

Among the prisoners were a number of 45th officers including three from the 157th who'd been captured by the SS on the ridge at Reipertswiller two months earlier, Lieutenants Richard Baron, John E. Floyd and William Meiggs. Baron, who with Baum in 1981 coauthored *Raid!*, an account of the debacle, wrote that he commanded a heavy machine-gun platoon from D Company in support of Company C and was one of only 176 prisoners who came off the hill that day.

Most of the POWs couldn't keep up with Task Force Baum as it tried first one way and then another, only to find each blocked by the enemy closing in, and were sent back toward Hammelburg and the prison camp on foot. Methodically tracking the depleted raiders as they holed up in some woods that night, the Germans silently brought up an overpowering force of armor and artillery, and when dawn broke, opened up on them. The remains of Patton's latest whim with the lives of his countrymen were scattered and destroyed in the hellfire. Total cost: nine dead, sixteen missing and presumed dead, thirty-two wounded, fifteen who made it back to the American lines, the rest captured, and no estimate of the number of "liberated" American prisoners killed.

Ten days later the 14th Armored Division of the Seventh Army liberated Oflag XIIIB and Patton sent his personal physician, the Third Army's chief surgeon, in a Piper Cub plane to evacuate his son-in-law from the camp hospital to an American army hospital. The rest of the hospitalized POWs were left in the care of a single medic for three more days, including Bob Zawada, who had a leg blown off when the Germans caught up with Task Force Baum in the woods, and the wounded Captain Abe Baum himself.

Patton to his wife, April 13: "... they are trying to make an incident out of my attempt to rescue John ... How I hate the press."[8]

The aim and fate of the General's Task Force Baum makes the fictitious mission of *Saving Private Ryan* in Steven Spielberg's powerful 1998 World War II motion picture look like a Boy Scout hike.

The day Task Force Baum was destroyed the 45th reached the Main River, facing Aschaffenburg on the other side. His colleagues promoted Lieutenant Pat Farley of the I&R to a staff captaincy, and Staff Sergeant Delmar Griffith was commissioned lieutenant in his place. The way Griff put it:

> When the leadership became vacant I was afraid a thirty-day wonder would git it. I never really thought about the prestige of a battlefield commission until back home it dawned on me that maybe it was kind of a mark of distinction. It was all practical-ly the same job as platoon sergeant. The war was about over when we crossed the Rhine. It was simply a chase. We didn't man many OPs. It was reconnaissance, espe-cially routing troops, scouting out roads, checking to see if tanks could go through, detail jobs like bringing back prisoners, helping the MPs.

My old crew leader Dick Beech replaced Griff as platoon sergeant, and Sergeant Charles Nye was shipped back to the States and home, having enough time in the Service, including overseas and combat, as gauged by the Army's priority point system. As Shorty looked back on it:

> There was never anybody killed in my squad the whole war, just Mickey and Mullenax got hurt. The good Lord was on my side. All I got was a piece o' shrapnel in my fanny, and that was our own artillery, I don't remember where. Went to the Medics and had it pulled out. No Purple Heart. I told 'em noooo way, jest thank you fer takin' it out and put a bandage on there an' ferget it. Only time I ever was touched. I hated that artillery. You couldn't fight back. You couldn't do nothin'. Every time a barrage started I made coffee from outta the lil black bag. I hadda be doin' sump'n.

Hank Mills drove the little good-luck guy back and out of it.

> We had an old captured German truck, and coming back I got lost. The guys are sit-tin' up in the buildings watchin' me take this German truck through the streets, and

they told me I was ridin' along ahead of the lines like nothin' was goin' on. I didn't realize it, and the Germans musta thought I was one of 'em. I finally got back to the CP, and everybody's laffin'. They showed me where I'd circled around through those streets and come back this other way. It was a focal point and the Germans wanted to hold it because there were a lotta artillery intersections.

This was the beginning of the battle of Aschaffenburg, the 45th's last major engagement of the war. A picturesque, red-roofed Bavarian hill town proud of its scholarly heritage, Aschaffenburg occupied the site of a Roman settlement and was presided over by a Gothic castle. In recent times, however, it had been performing triple service as a convalescent, replacement and officers' training center for the Wehrmacht. Now, whether ordered from on high or on his own, a certain Major Emil Lamberth, (initially thought to be von Lambert), one of those Wagnerian Nazis, felt inspired to launch a personal *Götterdämmerung* in the face of the *amerikanische Angriff* and take all with him to Valhalla from the heights of the Aschaffenburg castle from which he hurled this lightning bolt:

Soldiers, men of the Volksturm, Comrades:
    The fortress of Aschaffenburg will be defended to the last man. As long as the enemy gives us time we will prepare to employ our troops to our best possible advantage.
    This means: 1. Fight!
                2. Erect dugouts!
                3. And Barriers!
                4. Get supplies!
                5. WIN!!!
    As of today, everyone is to give to his last. I order that no one will rest more than three hours out of twenty-four. I forbid any sitting around and loafing.
    Our belief is that it is our mission to give the cursed enemy the greatest resistance and to send as many as possible of them to the devil.
                MAJOR VON LAMBERT [*sic*], Commanding.[9]

Although he had little artillery and no Luftwaffe at all, Lamberth had plenty of mortars, anti-tank guns and small arms, and young Germans in the officers school who knew the terrain and town intimately and set to work reinforcing buildings and setting up strongpoints and fields of fire. Aschaffenburg had as well an existing system of pillboxes for training purposes, a considerable cadre of fanatically indoctrinated Hitler Youth, and a population determined to defend their homes. Civilians desiring to leave were granted a brief grace period to do so, but thereafter the middle-aged Nazi in charge had a roving force of fifty SS troopers ensuring that the town was defended to the last man or else.

On March 28 our Second Battalion reached the Main River and crossed over the planked-over railroad bridge just south of Aschaffenburg that had been taken by the Fourth Armored Division and from which Task Force Baum had just jumped off. No one was informed of this or told that after helping the Task Force fight through Schweinheim the Fourth had pulled back across the river—or that an enemy division was on the way in response—or even that the east side of the river still belonged to Major Lamberth and not to General Patton. So when the Thunderbirds reached the opposite shore they were fired on by dug-in Germans.[10]

The clearing of the town fell to Second Battalion, and of smaller, contiguous Schweinheim to the Third. Lamberth evidently was running the defense of both. Our artillery blasted them. They fought back house-to-house. Our 155 Long Toms were brought in, their barrels were lowered, and the town's buildings were exploded. The Germans emerged from the rubble to snipe and fight on. With no sign of the Luftwaffe, our P-47s flew 176 sorties, dropped a thousand tons of high-explosive bombs and flaming, frying napalm, and strafed them with two million fifty-caliber machine-gun rounds. Their returning mortar fire was deadly. We retaliated by turning blocks into our own trademarked holocausts with flaming phosphorus shells from our chemical mortars. Old men and women and even girls threw grenades from rooftops and upper stories, and as the hated Yanks inched forward, snipers hid out to pick them off after they had passed by.

The avenging Thunderbirds were as overpowering as the Panzer Grenadiers had been in '39 and '40. Now the boot was on the other foot. The Master Race were defending their soil, their homes, their families, their towns, their heritage. The devil they turned loose had been turned on them.

G.I.s watched fleeing civilians who wouldn't fight mowed down by the machine guns of their own roving SS. Teen-age kids, fanatic *Hitler Jugend*, died in their holes before they would surrender. Lamberth executed an officer who claimed immunity from the fighting because he was Luftwaffe. Another who pleaded his wounds as an excuse was hung outside a wine shop with a placard round his neck:

> Cowards and traitors hang! Yesterday an officer candidate from Alsace-Lorraine died a hero's death in destroying an enemy tank. He lives on. Today—there hangs a

Our tanks in support of the 157th go after enemy snipers concealed in the rubble of Aschaffenburg. (*Department of Defense*)

coward in officer's garb because he betrayed the Fuehrer and the people. He is dead forever.[11]

In this kind of street fighting the I&R had no part. A recon patrol was no more than asking for trouble; there was little to observe amongst the buildings, even from an OP, with the exception of one set up in a church steeple near the Main River by Dom Trubia, Les Gerencer and Jerry Waldron, who although now with S2 still yearned for the action. Their three versions illustrate the glacial effects of time on memory.

Trubia:
I'd called for some P-47s to come in and strafe, and of course they opened up way behind us and came over the steeple with their guns still blasting away. Les thought they were going to get us. He jumped up in the middle of the bell tower and conked his nose on the bell.

Gerencer:
It was in the outskirts of Aschaffenburg, a railroad station down below. I didn't see no P-47s, just this plane of ours, a Piper Cub, comin' over, and some Kraut in the station opened up wid a machine gun and Christ, he hits the tower, and I happened to be right in the opening, and had my head out, and PWWRRNNGGG I felt a burn right across my nose. You can still see the mark. When it gets cold it gets white. Jeez, I moved down to the steps and felt my nose, like a burn, jest a little blood, jarred my head a little bit. Put some salve and a patch on it, that's all. When I was goin' down the stairs I bumped my head and my helmet come down an' hit me on the nose again.

Waldron:
I was with Les when he got his nose skinned. I think he turned away just at that moment, and if he hadn't he woulda been dead. They had sent him and me up in this church not five hundred feet from the Main River. We could see our guys moving up through Aschaffenburg street fighting, and our planes strafing just ahead of 'em, sometimes not more than fifty yards. Below us along the river was the 45th Recon Troop, and there was a place where they had to run across an opening between some houses to get to the kitchen, and a German across the river with a twenty-millimeter flak gun would open up on 'em. This was a big irritation.

Finally one of the guys says we know where he is. He got a mortar out of the bottom of their supply truck and set it up. They wanted to fire a round of smoke, but the guy grabbed an HE [high-explosive shell] and was dropping it down nose-first when someone grabbed him, and they turned it right side up and fired it so the observer could see where it would land. It went in the hole where the German was and knocked him out. I claim that's the greatest shot of the war. Just pure luck.

On the last day of March and the fourth of the battle, a Piper Cub flew over battered and smoking Aschaffenburg and dropped a curt ultimatum to Lamberth beginning, "Your situation is hopeless. Our superiority in men and material is overpowering," outlining the conditions of unconditional surrender, starting with the raising of a white flag over the castle, and concluding: "Should you refuse to accept these conditions, we shall be forced to level Aschaffenburg . . . The fate of Aschaffenburg is in your hands."[12]

No white flag fluttered over the ruins. On April first the 179th and 180th Regiments bypassed the besieged towns and moved on through the German countryside against sporadic resistance, leaving the 157th to finish the job. Dive bombers and artillery plastered the defenders, but they wouldn't quit.

The next day Third Battalion mopped up Schweinheim and for the first time moved into the east end of Aschaffenburg. The opposition was crumbling.

A United Press correspondent described the finale:

Battered Aschaffenburg fell yesterday because the fanatical Nazi commander finally lost his nerve and sent a U.S. private to tell the Americans he had had enough.

Monocled Major Lambert [*sic*], who was so popular with his own troops that they nicknamed him "*Schweinhund*" [swine dog], sent an American soldier, who was taken prisoner three days ago, with a German captain toward the American lines at 0400 hours to tell the Yanks he was willing to surrender the remaining troops who were still holding out.

The two men were forced to retreat before a hail of artillery fire the first time, but at 0730 hours they tried again and were picked up by Yank outposts at the southern end of town.

Col. Walter P. O'Brien, commander of the U.S. 157th, instructed the German captain to tell Lambert to display white flags from the turret tops of the command post and out of every window before 0900 hours.

There were 30 tense minutes to wait and then just as 0900 hours was about to strike, the castle door swung open and Lambert appeared with an immaculate high-peaked Wehrmacht cap, well pressed trousers and riding boots. He stepped out followed by 100 officers and men bearing numerous white flags of surrender.

They marched in a column down the broad Obernau road leading south, through the city, toward the American lines. At the outskirts the column was received by the U.S. military police commander.

Lambert admitted that the German spirit was broken by the crushing forces of guns, planes and fighting men hurled at them for the last six days.

O'Brien ordered him to return to the heart of the city accompanied by an American platoon to instruct the remaining Germans to give up. Lambert walked back to each enemy resistance point with the message: "Everything has ended for us—it is time to come out and surrender."[13]

Around 1,620 Germans were believed to have been killed, and 3,500 were taken prisoner. The American casualties are unknown.

The next day all was quiet on that particular sector of the Western Front, and the 157th Infantry Regiment for the second time since Reipertswiller went into reserve for reorganization. For another ten days it would bring up the rear of the 45th on a sweeping

arc northeast around Brückenau and Neustadt, then southeast and south toward industrial Bamburg and Nuremburg.

Organized resistance rapidly fell apart as piecemeal German forces tried here and there
to make a stand. Like Schweinhund Lamberth, the survivors were deciding not to die for
the *Führer* after all. *Adolph, count your men,* as the doggies were grunting.

Back in Italy, if I was aware of what my old outfit was going through at Aschaffenburg
I made no record of it, news reports and my regularly updated battlefront map notwithstanding. The hospital acquired a Navy jeep that needed body work but had a good engine.
"I feel better now that I can cruise about the countryside with the wind and the dust in my
face," I almost gloried in a letter home.

> Red as a beet driving around in my open jeep in beautiful weather. The holidays have
> been marked particularly by Easter parades, all of them alike in their peculiar reli-
> gious symbolism. As the main body of the procession (consisting of a Madonna and
> Child float surrounded by dignitaries, children, etc., in various costumes) approach-
> es town, it is preceded by a troop of barefoot men, women and boys. The women
> wear a white, loose dress, while the men and boys have a satiny, matador-like cos-
> tume with a sash, all moving at a dogtrot down the highway!

Always in the back of my mind was my limited service status. Reexamination for continued Class B or back to 1A was coming up. "If I could get back to the old outfit rather than
some other one," I mused, "it wouldn't be so bad"—which must have given the home folks
a nasty turn. My father, reacting:

> The fact is that glad as you are to be off the line, you've kind of got it in for yourself
> for not being up front with the 45th, instead of skippering a four-legged grasshop-
> per over the hills and dales of sunny Italy. Who can tell whether your breaks have
> been good or bad, lucky or unlucky? Make the best of the present and what it brings,
> and keep a long view for the future.

April 12 journal:

*Can't keep up with the situation. The 7th Army is about 30 miles northwest of Nuremburg… Spring
is coming over the land again, with hot days and dust, cool nights … I finally got a tarp and bones
made for my jeep, gave it a coat of paint, tightened up the bolts, welded it together here and there, and
named it* Yvonne *for Charlie Dassori's daughter* [he ran the motor pool], *and* Helen. *It's in pretty
fair shape, and already I've put on over 1000 miles driving between here and Caserta.*

I'd just had word from my father that Helen and her cousin Jane Edmondson had
stayed with my family while in Boston from Sarah Lawrence for a concert with the Harvard
Glee Club. God, a songbird too! My jeep would proclaim my happiness (and Charlie's) for
all *our* world, anyway, to see.

The Jeep (*Collection of the author*)

April 15 (Sunday) letter home:

Friday was a sad day for me; I felt almost as if it were a personal loss, and it must have seemed much the same for millions of others. There is no doubt about it—the President, though born an aristocrat, came to symbolize the cause of the Common Man perhaps more than anyone else in our generation, and he was taken away at a time when his wisdom was finally beginning to sink home in the minds of people the world over. It goes without saying that he was one of our greatest Presidents in one of the most difficult periods of our history. I'm not sure that an even more difficult one isn't at hand, and we've lost a pilot upon whom, I for one, didn't realize how much I relied.

From Pa April 12:

This afternoon late, eclipsing all other news, has come that of the sudden death of the President, a great man and a great leader, and as nearly indispensable as an individual could be at the present time. I was glad of his election although I didn't vote for him, but, with an eye towards the present not unexpected calamity, I'm sorry more considerations of a statesmanlike level weren't given to his probable successor ... Well, regardless of how we may have disagreed with him on some matters, he was one of our truly great men, and certainly our man on horseback at the time of our latest and perhaps greatest jeopardy.[14]

Six days after the President's death, Ernie Pyle, who with Bill Mauldin was THE champion of the dogface, was killed by a Japanese sniper's bullet on some worthless island in the Pacific called Ie Shima. That same month Howard Gleason, another of my Harvard naval classmates, who, like Andy Welch had volunteered for submarine duty in the Pacific, was lost with all hands. A third classmate, Second Lieutenant William J. Wolfgram, was killed in action in Italy.[15]

"More and more taken with journalism as a career," I wrote home. "I'm inspired by the saga of Ernie Pyle."

About this time I got a pass to Rome with Steve Ference, a lean-and-hungry, twice-wounded veteran of the Third Division working as a ward boy at the hospital, ("pretty shaky as am I, so we naturally fell together"), and hunted down Andy Zapiecki, now a motor pool dispatcher bossing and exchanging favors with the Italian drivers and living in style in a hotel.

"Saw the Duchess and I'm sick of her," I wrote home April 21. "She's going back to the States shortly, taking all the luggage she wants (which will beat about 15 soldiers out of passage), and when she gets there is sending for her son. A hypochondriac and as patronizing as a queen—paid $490 for a gold cigarette case for him 'as a little present.'"

Back with the Ironheads our disenchanted *Jugend Junge*, Walter Wolff, had finally come into his own with the cracking of the Siegfried Line and the 45th's arcing sweep through the tottering *Vaterland* after Aschaffenburg. On several occasions Waldron was sent ahead into the next town with him to "restrain him, I guess."

Walter'd get the burgomeister out there and whip him around and have the place straightened out in no time. Once Dilks got mad at him over something or other—Walter knew how to be maddening—and he finds a grenade and gets all the powder out, or thinks he has, walks in, Wolff's in bed, he pulls the pin and says, "Walter your time has come!"—and tosses it in the bed with him. Of course all the powder wasn't out, and Jesus, the building was filled with smoke, but he only gets a scratch.

Dilks:
I was always doin' stupid things like that. The first grenades had dry powder, and you could unscrew the cap and dump the powder out, then screw it back, throw it, and in five seconds it would go POP. I'd done that a coupla times when the guys was eatin'. But they changed that powder to some kinda paste, which I didn't know. A lot of it stuck inside when I threw it, and it blew that feather bed all to hell, feathers flyin' all over, and the ole German woman was tellin' me she's gonna have me pay for a new comforter. But what I was worried about was Wolff layin' there in the bed. It landed only about two feet from his head, and I says to myself, that's when I stop foolin' around. The guy coulda got killed jes' me horsin' around.

Gerencer:
The German lady who owned the house lived a coupla houses away and come in and

seen this and was gonna report everybody to the company commander, so they had a collection and gave her a bunch o' money.

Dilks:
It was a real solid building, like a caretaker's cottage. They all said, "You're the last one in bed. You turn the light out." So I jes' shot. Missed the light an' grazed the ceiling. I fired two or three times before I finally got it out. One o' those cheap pistols made in Czechoslovakia. Half the time it misfired, wasn't worth a damn.

Gerencer:
Me, Wolff, Dilks and Trubia went out with a recon outfit that had the trucks with 57s [57-millimeter guns] and jeeps with machine guns. We'd met 'em and asked could we go wid ya? Trubia was always wantin' to try things, devil-may-care, and says how about lettin' me on one o' them machine guns? The guy says sure, and we're goin' up the road, nothin' there, and we come to this spot where there was woods and a red barn and a red house on the left. So the lieutenant put the spotlight up there and the binoculars an' says, "I see sump'n! Out there!" And Trubia opens up with that machine gun and strafes the house, kept holdin' the trigger. Finally the lieutenant says, "Stop that firin'! Ya wanna burn the barrel out?"

So we went down a little more, and there's a German comin' outta the forest, and he had his hands up like this, and this guy in the armored truck wid the 57 on it, he let loose a shot, hit the guy here in the middle of the chest and blew his arms right off. He musta done it accidentally.

After that we got outta the column. Trubia says let's go back to the farmhouse he shot up. So we went back, and them guys from the recon outfit kept goin'. We went in the barn, and Wolff started to climb up the ladder. All of a sudden there's ten or twelve Germans come outta the loft wid their arms up. We held 'em down there, and searched all over, and got twelve or fourteen pistols outta the deal, but we had to take 'em prisoners—one was a major—back to headquarters wid us.

And then there was Jeep, the last of the Platoon's doggie mascots, with a special feeling for Jerry, who had a special feeling for him:

Somewhere before Nuremburg we got hung up by an outfit that was holing up on a ridge, and we were trying to take it. Colonel Brown, the Exec, a short little guy, decided he couldn't wait for a company to come up. He'd found a tank to attack, and Headquarters Company, though not all the I&R because we had crews out, was to fan out and go up on either side of this road. I was on the left flank, way over on the side, and had a carbine and thought there's somebody in that tower over there. So I was firing to keep him down, and I broke a lot of glass as we went up the hill.

Little Jeep, the size of a cocker spaniel, black and tan mongrel, rode in the jeep, and everybody got attached to him. Every time I hit the ground he'd come over and lick my face. A bullet went through my jacket, and I cursed that dog. Whoever was on my right and I went up, and we captured a German in the trench, couldn't have been more than sixteen or seventeen, and took him back. He'd been firing and was the last resistance. His rifle had one bullet left, and he couldn't get us both.

I thought right there that if I had to do this all the time I wouldn't make it back. The tank overcame the ridge, and that was the last action I saw in the war. Jeep was right in the middle of it, poor little soul.

The real sad part of it came in a later town where an armored car was backing up, and Jeep panicked, and I can see the wheels going over him now. I guess I took care of him about as much as anybody—at least I was the one he was kissin'.

By mid-April the 45th had half-cleared the German communications center of Bamberg and with the Third and 42nd Divisions was driving on to Nuremburg, where Hitler had staged the annual conventions of his National Socialist Party since 1933. The Regiment circled around the city clockwise and attacked from the southwest. After some stiff resistance and house-to-house fighting, this Nazi symbol was effectively cleared April 20, Adolf Hitler's fifty-sixth birthday.

For the always-quirkish Ironheads, and for Walter Wolff in particular, there had to be one brief and bizarre footnote to the story of Nuremburg, one empty echo of the thunderous *Sieg Heil*s that shook the stadium not so long before, and it has to be related by my old buddy Waldron since neither of the participants can be found.

"Wolff got maybe Hank Johnson to drive him around the running track in the tremendous Nuremburg stadium where the Nazis put on their shows, himself standing up in the back of the jeep like Hitler. They were the only ones in the whole damn stadium as far as they knew, and somebody took a shot at Walter, they never knew if a G.I. or a German. They got outta there fast."

April 29 journal: "The 45th took Nuremburg, the 7th Army has crossed the Danube, is about to reach Munich, has reached the Austrian border . . . The Russians are leveling Berlin house by house. Retribution of a nation on a city. Very good. Radio rumor today is that Himmler has offered capitulation to Great Britain and U.S. We've given him until Tuesday to include Russia. Reports say that Hitler has died of a stroke."

From Nuremburg it was a race between the veteran 45th and the recently arrived 42nd to take Munich, and between enemy units to surrender to anyone but the Russians, and to cap all POW stories, Dom Trubia swore that he and a couple of other Ironheads captured a regiment of Austrian cavalry after Nuremburg.

I didn't know what the hell to do with 'em. Called the CP, and they said just bring 'em right on up the road. We made 'em dismount, get rid of their weapons and turn the horses loose.

I knew then that the war was coming to an end because they were surrendering in wholesale lots, and I really became nervous. I thought, oh God, I hope some trigger-happy German doesn't kill me now, because it's over, and yet they just had to keep trying instead of surrendering. They had to get that last shot in.

Those were my toughest days. I'd reflect back on people that were in and out of the Platoon and try and recall some of the replacements that didn't last too long. We

You asked for it, Nuremburg... (*Department of Defense*)

... But pity the old women of two world wars. (*Department of Defense*)

had about twenty-eight full-strength and must have run through a hundred before it was over. I felt awfully despondent. There were only about five of us old guys from the beginning left actively running patrols. I had this horrible feeling I was gonna get killed. I couldn't shake it. I thought what an awful, awful time to die, after I've been through all this, to die as the war ends.

When it did happen I could hardly believe it was over with and I still had my skin intact. I never spoke to anybody, but I imagine everybody else felt the same way. In those last few months the doubts set in. I'd always been a devout Catholic and still am. Faith was very sustaining. Every time Father Barry set up services I felt so good to be able to go or receive communion. But toward the end I didn't see much of him. I'd go to German service in some town, and even though it was German I still felt comfortable, like I understood everything they said even though I didn't.

I felt I had a guardian angel that was with me all the while, but I had a fear of being captured, being abused, and used to think to myself, "Oh my God I don't want to be abused," and this is why on two or three occasions, if I had any brains at all I would have surrendered, but I didn't because I had this terrible fear of being abused. I saw some of the stuff we did to the German prisoners, not intentionally, but we didn't have enough food to go around and stuff like that, and knew they were in worse shape than we were in, and I knew darn well I wouldn't be getting any three square meals a day.

I heard tell that somebody from the 36th got captured, and the Germans had him up around Rome. He escaped, went to a Catholic priest and asked for asylum, tried to get into the Vatican. The priest got him in, and when we took Rome he came

The Jeremy R. Waldrons: like father, like son. (*Courtesy of Jeremy R. Waldron*)

out and told the story that if you would work for the Germans you got three meals a day, and if you didn't you only got two—coffee, or rather chicory, and a slice of black bread for breakfast, and supper was cabbage soup and black bread.

This kept preying on my mind, that I don't wanna be abused.

My particular buddy Jerry Waldron, we all agreed, had it together as much as anyone in the Platoon. Colonel O'Brien wanted to send him back to Officers Candidate School, but Jerry wanted to go home and follow his father in the law.

Coming out of an Ivy League college I thought I was a step above everybody else, but the great thing I learned from the war was that there are a lot of guys who can do a lot of things better than I can. The Platoon did a wonderful thing for me—made everybody dependent on everybody else. I was probably fated to go the infantry route because I wanted to get really involved in the war and to do what my dad had done. Throughout my time under fire that was a source of strength. I didn't want to do anything that would be a blot on the Waldron name.

I don't think I ever had the feeling that I wasn't coming back. I felt that I was going to be as lucky as my father was. Our Platoon was sent out to get the information, which was all-important. There were rare times when we had to stand and fight, and so if you got stopped over here you'd try to work around there to get it, but if I'd been in a line company where you had to keep attacking I'd have had a wholly different impression. I had the feeling that if the first shell or bullet got by me I had a very good chance of avoiding anything else happening.

I never did feel that a shell ever had my number on it. I did some praying. There was a place at Piedimonte with a beautiful view, and I used to go up there in quiet meditation. And there were other places along the way that I'd go. I must admit that when I came out of the service I was much more religious than when I went in. I did feel I'd been lucky and that somebody had watched over me. I don't know why I thought I was gonna make it, but I did.

My mother had inquired a month earlier, a little tentatively: "Do you have any opportunity to get to church, and what sort of a fellow is the chaplain? You've said nothing since you went overseas about any contact with chaplains or church services, and I hope that doesn't mean you've had none." She went on to outline for me a four-point program she'd read about for bolstering failing faith.

I'm afraid I didn't give my wonderful Ma a very satisfactory response.

Medics search for survivors in boxcars (*Courtesy of U. S. Army Military History Institute, Carlisle Barracks, PA*)

⋙ 16 ⋘

DACHAU

What, at Last, It Was All About
April 29, 1945

> I would swear my hand on the Bible that if I had not gone
> through it I wouldn't believe it.
>
> Morris Rosenwasser

AT LAST, AFTER TWENTY-TWO MONTHS of the worst of war, the weary Thunderbirds staggered south through Germany. Now all that lay between them and Munich, where the Devil had hatched his worst, was the peacefully picturesque old Bavarian town of Dachau.

Ten miles north of Munich, and within sight, sound and stench, the world's prototype concentration camp had been placed in operation in the outskirts of Dachau on March 22, 1933, as a repository and death chamber for "undesirables" and political opponents and victims of the Nazi Party, most conspicuously Jews, and for purposes of human experimentation.

Adolf Hitler had been Chancellor of the Third Reich for seven weeks and Franklin D. Roosevelt President of the United States for eighteen days. The New Order and the New Deal.

Dachau's creator was Heinrich Himmler, a schoolmasterish-looking former chicken farmer of thirty-three who was running the SS (the *Schutzstaffel* elite guard) and about to take over the Gestapo (the secret police)—his *Führer's* twin agencies of terror.

When after a couple of months the clumsy murder of several prisoners aroused one of the last public protests to ruffle the New Order, *Reichsführer* SS Himmler replaced the camp's first commandant with Theodor Eicke, who went on to develop for Dachau's SS Totenkopf (Death's Head) guards the code of blind obedience to orders, fanatical hatred of the prisoners as enemies of the State, and systematic brutality and genocide that would breed hundreds of camps and institutionalize millions of murders as a way of death.

Here were invented and refined the New Order's "progressive" methods of punishment and torture, Doctor Sigmund Rascher's novel and fatal experiments with the decompression and freezing of inmates for Hermann Goering and his Luftwaffe, and the sophisticated gas chambers and ovens with their by-industries of soap manufacture, lampshades and so forth using body parts such as oil and skin.

Here were trained the like of Himmler's chief bureaucrat of the "Final Solution" Adolf Eichmann and the most exalted commandants of many of the more notorious concentration camps that followed Dachau's pioneering lead. And here were imprisoned such undesirables as the former French premier Léon Blum, tried but never convicted by the Vichy government of responsibility for France's defeat; Kurt von Schuschnigg, Chancellor of Austria during the *Anschluss* defeat; and Pastor Martin Niemoller, imprisoned since 1937 for opposing Hitler's preemption of German Protestantism.[1]

Twelve years and about a quarter of a million prisoners after the modest beginning of a facility designed for a mere five thousand, when the handwriting was on all German walls but those of the *Konzentrationslagern*, a certain Hungarian Jew, Morris Rosenwasser, age twenty-one, was being railroaded into the camp in a boxcar to join a population of by then around forty or fifty thousand.

It was now toward the end of March, 1945, and the sweep of the 45th Division through the Reich was being held up in Aschaffenburg by the monocled Major Lamberth. Although no one except a few top brass knew it or had even heard of the camp, Dachau was on the agenda of the 157th.[2] Thirty-six years later, Morris Rosenwasser contacted the 157th Infantry Association to offer the hospitality of his hotel in Miami Beach to veterans of the American unit that had liberated him and his fellow inmates of the camp. In Florida I recorded his story.[3]

Morris Rosenwasser's Road In

I was born in Ivbran, a town of eight thousand near Budapest with thirty-two Jewish families. When I was eight I was a Talmudic student in Hebrew in a small town eight kilometers from mine. One day I came home for a holiday. We had a big room, two beds, a door to the store, big table with eight or ten chairs. My brother, twenty-one, is going up and down the room with a little book, and he says, "Good morning" and then "Good evening," translating from Hungarian. He was a tough kid. In Europe the big brother is in charge.

So I goes to my father, who was fifty-seven years old, and says, "Pa, what is Izzy doing?" He says, "Young kid, you wouldn't understand nothing. Leave me alone. I got my own troubles. You don't have to know what's going on." I says, "Pa, I'm asking you a question. What's he studying?" "It's a long story," he says. "Times are not so good. Anti-Semitism is beginning. Izzy has to go in the army. We have an Uncle Herman in the Bronx in New York. I wrote to him that if possible he should send papers to your brother, and he will go to America." "Really? Izzy to America? When I grow up I'm gonna go to America too."

Morris Rosenwasser
(*Author photo*)

Those were the days when the Rhode Island Red was being introduced to Europe as a good-quality meat and egg producer. Whoever in 1932 had fifty chickens had the Almighty in his hands. I had an older brother who's not alive. He didn't survive the camps in Russia, with four children and his wife in the gas chamber. He was partner with another brother in a store, the biggest and the best, you could get everything. They had the coop of fifty chickens with all the trimmings, special diet.

I says, "Pa, I'm gonna go to America, marry an American girl and have a farm." But he gave me the big deal that I'm gonna have a lamb to raise. He had customers who were sheepraisers. I was crazy for animals. When it was calfing time I went into the room of the cow to try to help get the calf out. I was a genius in that, and my father resented every step of it, because all he wanted was for his kids to be religious Jewish boys and girls. If you spoke Hungarian language in my father's house on the Sabbath you got beat for it. If you sneaked in a book to read in Hungarian language you got beat. "Take the training," he said, "the Bible, read it, study, nothing of the nonsense with cowboy stories."

So I go back to school. I was never a good student, but since that day in my mind was America, an American girl and a farm. My brother never made it to America. My uncle wrote home a letter from the Bronx to my father: "Abraham (or Adolph they called him). Adolph, forget about it. America is not religious enough for your children, so don't send them." And that was for my father good enough. "My brother wants to keep my child religious. That's the way I want it, so forget about America."

You could be in America a bookworm, pray the whole day, and nobody's gonna bother you as long as you got enough to live, so why did he write his brother that his nephew would not be religious enough in America? Because he himself was not religious.

In Hungary when you reached twelve you must go half a day each Sunday for six weeks summertime military training, maneuvers, target practice, marching, push-ups. I was a platoon commander of my neighbor Christian boys, and one day this kid, he was a nobody, a private, stayed at my gate with a make-believe wooden rifle and says, "Morris, you can't get out of here." And I says, "Why not? Who's gonna stop me?" And he says, "Me! I got orders. Remember you used to give me orders I gotta obey? Now I got orders."

It didn't penetrate to me. I says, "Joseph, if you don't let me outta this gate I'm killing you right here on this spot." He didn't have nothing to defend himself with except a wooden rifle. And I went to my brother's stable and took a pitchfork with four strands pointy as a needle. "I knock your brains out," and I'm turning around and running with it.

My mother is outside, and she says, "What's going on?" I says, "Joe wouldn't let me outta the gate." "Where do you want to go?" "In town. This is my country, my farm, he's gonna tell me what to do, Joe, dumb Joe who dunno what two and two is? I'm gonna kill him. They're gonna kill the Jews," I says. "I'm gonna kill him."

She gave me a slap in the face. I put the pitchfork away, went into the house and nothing happens. But if my mother wouldn't have stopped me I wouldn't be here to tell this story. They would have pulled me up in the middle of the marketplace and cut me to pieces. Which was the way to survive, to run away, to stand still, to take orders. Sheer luck that was somewhere given to you that your destiny was to survive or your destiny was to die. That's the only thing I can think of and believe in. Turn into a partisan, go and fight, maybe the first bullet would have been mine.

On April 15, 1944 I was called into the state labor camp in Košice (Kassa in Hungarian), Czechoslovakia, controlled by the German army. Wherever they needed workers they'd call for them. The same day my whole family was taken from our home and put in the ghetto. All the Jews were taken together. They could take so many belongings, so much food. Everything else confiscated with the excuse of the government that it was wartime and you were going to a labor camp.

I had five brothers and four sisters. My mother, two sisters, my uncle and eighteen nephews and nieces were all exterminated in Auschwitz. We are now four brothers and two sisters, all in America.

Košice was in 1938 in Czechoslovakia. Hungary occupied it in a big battle my brother fought. But when Hitler got too big for his boots he said the Jewish boys are no good for fighting, so he made slave laborers of them. From one hour to another, one uniform to another, they became nobodies. I stayed there approximately four weeks.

We were clearing, fixing things, digging trenches, and saw a lot of German soldiers coming back with civilians, many Polish and from wherever, in pretty bad shape. Lots of music, lots of entertainment, lots of booze. Boxcars passing by with people locked in trying to scream in Yiddish, Rumanian, Hungarian, and we just looked like sheep standing there, a hundred sixty in the unit.

When one guy says, "That's my wife there and my children, standing in the window!" whoever was in charge says, "Don't let him go! You're responsible for every person!" This train was heading for Poland, ninety to a hundred in a wagon, some almost dead. No food, no water, no nothing, and here's this guy screaming his head off he wants to go. Finally our lieutenant says, "OK, go! Go! They're your wife, your children, go!"

There we got the first idea of what's going on. A dirty thing, this going to work in a factory. It's a bluff, but never extermination! There was Polish Jews who came to Hungary with Christian papers calling themselves Polacks running away from the Russian army. My brother was a sergeant in the Hungarian army who showed us a picture, in 1942 I think, of how they were taking the Jews out from the small towns, letting them dig a hole, then machine-gunned and bulldozed them in. You wasn't trying to be a Partisan or resistance person, didn't have no ammunition, didn't have no gun, didn't have no nothing. Just a plain dummy religious Jew trying to be religious and make a living every day from business, work or whatever, mostly business.

In May we were called into a textile factory near Budapest and worked there as handymen. Food was excellent. One day I got a postcard printed in German, signed by the family name Rosenwasser. There was a postmark on it, but who cared? Who would have known where it came from? "We are all fine. We are all healthy. We are all working. God bless you. Next time we will write more." That's all I got. We just lived by rumors, just of what Polish Jews or Hungarian army personnel was willing to talk, what they were doing to Jewish people in the Ukraine, in Poland, in Latvia, in Czechoslovakia.

The Hungarian Jews were left to the last to be persecuted. July passes by. August passes by. There is rumors the Hungarian government is gonna fall, and a total Fascist government is gonna take over. I was my lieutenant's housekeeper, cook, shoeshine boy, whatever you wanna call it in the American army. I made my old man—he should rest in peace—pretty good meals. I asked a Hungarian lady, "Lissen, for money are you willing to cook a nice private meal for my lieutenant?" So, lucky I had three officers from my neighboring towns, a corporal, a sergeant, a staff sergeant. The corporal's family were fishermen I bought fish from in the town where I went to the Jewish school, and I made up to this fellow, this *Landsmann*, which gave me a little advantage, a little bit rubbed off. So maybe he could do me a little favor sometime.

One day I received a letter from my brother who was in another camp somewhere. He says, if you can get to Budapest, here's the address of Miss So-and-so who will give you fifteen pengös, which was at that time three dollars. I went to my lieutenant for a pass to Budapest to see my brother's brother-in-law's girl friend. A Jewish woman with a bogus birth certificate—some other woman's—could hide forever as long as the other one didn't come along and say, "That paper's mine. This is a Jewish girl," and they would take her and shoot her.

He says, "OK, here's your pass. Be careful. Don't do foolish things. Don't try to run away."

But I was already technically three months in jail, without freedom, and I wanted to see how it is to be free. I went for the trolley car, but before I reached it they spit on me and called me filthy Jew. I took off my yellow band that I was supposed to wear on my arm, and my yellow star and my army cap, and put on my beautiful black hat, and I was dressed just like a peasant boy from the bottom of the best Hungarian family. Riding boots and pants, short coat, that was the style. Nobody could tell that I was Jewish.

So I go in and get my fifteen pengös. The girl tells me, "As soon as I am giving you the fifteen pengös you are disappearing. I don't want you here." I took the money and walked out. In the street I hear this shouting behind me to stop, but I didn't think it had anything to do with me and kept on going and heard it again, and then a shot, and I looked around, and it's a German soldier. He comes up and wants to see my papers. I don't have any, and he takes me behind a wall and says, "Drop your pants." So when he sees I'm circumcised he took me to the headquarters, and they give me a going-over.

So when I don't show up for my lieutenant before the curfew he notifies the headquarters to be on the lookout and finally gets me released. But after a while I got shipped out.

I got three or four pounds of the sugared coffee ration they gave us and walked out with nothing else. They put us on a train with German SS, about three Red Cross wagons, and Hungarian soldiers. We reached the Austro-Hungarian border a day or two later, twenty-eighth of December. There was rumors that the front was ahead of us and we can't cross by rail. Either they're gonna execute us here now, or they're just gonna let us go over. Whoever is gonna win the place where the train is is gonna have us, Russians or Germans, and they change back and forth in the night, even a coupla hours.

We stayed there not too far from Vienna about two days. I ask the Hungarian sergeant, "Lissen, there's some frozen cabbage leaves in the field. Would you let me down to pick 'em up?" He says, "You got some money?" So we all get together eight hundred pengös. He let me down, and I got nine leaves, and he bangs me with his rifle, so I went back to the car. Either he got scared from a higher officer or tried to tell me I was gonna run away. I brought back the leaves, and everybody grabbed some and I didn't even get a taste.

We got to Vienna. I sold my bar mitzvah watch, got a piece of salami, a piece of bread, and got into the car and got some hot coffee. The Hungarians were left behind, the German SS took over, and New Year's Night, 1945, we reached Buchenwald concentration camp, I dunno where it is, in the German area of Poland.

When we arrived I think there were 680 left alive from 4,200 of us. They stepped on 'em, shit on 'em, beat on 'em. I was very depressed, full of lice, hungry, survived on a spoon of this coffee concentrate I had with me. There was a body standing right there next to me, fifteen days we were standing together.

We get off the train into a big office line. Belongings, valuables—the most important things we got to give up—watches, rings, a silver coin, a gold piece or a knife or a thousand pengös. And they even made records of it. I thought it was a real legitimate place. The inmates, they were shaving you, disinfecting you, chasing you from one place to another, dunking you like in a swimming pool with some kind of solution, another one with another solution, handing out wooden shoes, striped prison uniform, cap.

I had a red beret, like a French beret, because I always had a problem with a head cold, and my beautiful suit in my backpack that I brought along with me from Hungary. I hear somebody talking Hungarian. Ah, my own language! I can talk! I spoke very good Yiddish and Hungarian, and if a German came along I could understand 50 percent. He's a fat guy. We came from fifty, eighty miles apart. He says, "I'm not Hungarian anymore. I'm French because I lived in Paris." He says, "I'm in charge. Somebody has to do the dirty work, and I'm none of them. Have you got anything to exchange for food?"

So I gave him my beautiful high boots, and he gave me a slice of bread I think. We were sleeping fourteen in a bunk, everybody on the left. You wanted to sleep on your right, you woke up, "Hey, everybody on the right!" It come about one o'clock in the morning, and they woke us up and started beating us with sticks and poles—bang, bang all over.

Get up!

What's this?

Food is coming.

Food?

We gonna celebrate.

Every time they ask you to volunteer for something you should go. So in the kitchen I look at this guy and look at him and look at him. He didn't recognize me. Men, boys, nothing but skin and bones. He was the son of the cantor leader in my town who was in charge of the ritual slaughtering of the animals. I said, "You are Moshe?" He said, "Who are you?" I said, "You don't recognize me? I don't look that bad!" Then I found out that for religious purposes he never ate anything but dry, soft kosher bread and potatoes. That's all he ate. If there was in the soup a little fat or a little piece of meat, he never ate it.

So we had our New Year's supper after I found this boy from our town, and he told me the true story of what happened on Pentecost. My whole family arrived that day at the Auschwitz concentration camp, and everybody that was not in shape, children and all, to the left and the gas chamber and finished. Good-bye, that day in April 1944.

The sad story is I'm here and he is not. After Buchenwald I haven't seen the kid never. But I found out his younger brother survived the concentration camp and was taken to Sweden and came to the United States and attended the Baltimore rabbinical school and became a rabbi here.

A few days after we got out of Buchenwald we were asked to volunteer for transport work and were put in boxcars, forty-five to a boxcar. Pretty comfortable. Bunks, an oven in the middle. Pretty good covers. Little by little we tried to fix up, such as shoes that they should match and be walkable. Whoever was a shoemaker volunteered to fix shoes, guy who was a tailor to make and fix clothing.

The SS commander got together some six hundred people into eighteen or twenty boxcars, plus the German officers' plush living quarters, and I think between forty and sixty soldiers. Food was very minimal. Working was from six to six or as the sunset allowed. We had a locomotive constantly hitched up to our train. If the Allies bombed the tracks, and it was a decent distance, they pulled us

Three prisoners in Dachau (*Courtesy of the 45th Infantry Division Museum*)

in, and bing-bang, we fixed it up. Headquarters in Offenburg, near the French border.

We were out from the end of January until almost the end of March, when the Allied troops were not far from the Czech border. I was in Nuremburg also with this train. We were under a prisoner like me, not a soldier but a Christian, not a Jew, who wore a little red insignia which meant he was a communist. First of all, he was a homosexual. Second, he was a terrible-tempered man. If you knew how to play into his hand he was a beautiful guy. Go and steal for him cigarettes, vitamins, from this tremendous depot in Offenburg with four of everything that you could think of from ammunition to baby powder or cologne or vitamins, wine, cheese, clothing, jewelry, you name it that they don't have it. A depot for everything that the Red Cross supplied through the Swiss supposedly for the prisoners. The Allies came and bombed it.

Then one day we left the train and marched. We didn't know where the hell we were going. We heard many stories. The Allies came, a couple of little planes, bing-bang, they drop a few packages, little bombs and machine-gunning, people running around stealing between the boxcars. There is cheese, there is wine, there is liquor, I don't know what. You gotta watch out you shouldn't get killed. Up in the towers is the SS watching that you shouldn't run around and steal.

A buddy of mine hid himself under the boxcar, and the impact came, and the boxcar sprung up and the wheel landed on his stomach. He's hollering, and in a few seconds he just died. That day we lost I think seventeen people and one German soldier also, and we buried them in the railroad area in a mass grave, just slide them in there bing-bang. I was one of them that did the job.

And as we're marching there is a rumor from the German soldiers that they're gonna execute us. This German Christian guy who's a communist, he didn't have a chance to run away so easy either. If a German officer wanted to give him a chance he could go away because he spoke fluent German, could not be recognized, had civilian clothes, could have escaped. And the same for the SS officer. If he didn't want to be taken prisoner by the Allies all he had to do was throw his officer's clothes away and walk. Besides, as an officer to carry out his duties of the High Command, he was not a bad man. He never tortured us. If anybody tortured us is the lousy German guy who I'm talking about, the one who was a prisoner like me but he was not Jewish.

The rumor come around that our SS officer said he don't believe that in six-hundred-some-odd Jewish boys there isn't gonna be somebody who's gonna attack his squad. He's gonna execute us. He's afraid of us. Somebody's gonna grab a gun away from a SS, and they gonna start shooting back. So he says the best thing is to get rid of the bunch of Jews and throw 'em into Dachau.

We was not too far away from Dachau. He threw us in. Let us go. The night before we went, my civilian commander, this German prisoner who was a prisoner with me, he disappeared.

We went into Dachau, they closed the gate, and we didn't know what the hell is goin' on. Approximately the end of March. We were put in barracks, given some food. We saw conditions inside, unbelievable. Clean, mind you, every barrack was clean. But people were just plain skeletons, nothing but dried-up fifty-pound, sixty-pound skeletons and hollering for water in every nationality you can name, Italian, French, Jewish, German, Polack, Russian, Ukrainian, any language in the world.

Then again, you have to go to work if you wanna exist and get ahold of a piece of food, something, try to steal the sick people's piece of bread that they used to get for a ration.

One day they needed work, I volunteered. I went out I think two or three times to the gas chamber. Put the people on a flatbed wagon, push them to the gas chamber and feed 'em in. I saw a Polish Jewish boy working with me, took a piece of metal from his pocket—and these guys were all alive that we took to the gas oven to burn up—and he just took a piece of the hind, the skin is hanging, there is nothing else to cut, and this skin he just carved it out from this live guy and he's chewing on it.

I says to him in Yiddish, "What the hell are you doing?"

"Look at the big-shot Hungarian that arrived yesterday," he says. "He's gonna tell me what to do. When you gonna be seven years like I am seven years from one hell to the other, you'll cut your own finger off and you'll eat it. 'Cause you think that's how you gonna survive. I guarantee you six days you gonna be here and you'll be doing the same thing like I am."

Oh, I see baby, wait a minute, this job is not for me. Who is that to tell me that I'm gonna tell somebody, hey, I don't like this job. Somehow it was that I had luck and I volunteered after I came back from that job to clean the rooms, bathrooms, so-called water fountains that wouldn't shut off, and I remained on that job. Inside job. No more out in that crematorium, gas chamber or whatever it was.

One Saturday afternoon we have rumors that the whole place is gonna be dyna-mited, that somebody sneaked out and got in contact with you guys and told 'em, "If you are not hurrying up here this camp is going up in smoke with thirty thousand prisoners." Anyhow, around noontime a little plane showed up. Bang, there is bombs going off. I says this must be mad unless it's a German one camouflaged with American or British insignias on it. They're bombing us, they're gonna wipe us out. But we heard backfire from the guard itself, and saw tanks moving in and out from the camp. Oh, they're running, the officers are running. There's something going on here. We saw a big German tank moving out the gate. We said this is something, they're running away. They're trying to save their own skins, or maybe there's a bat-tle or whatever.

The Road of the Thunderbird

Jumping off from Nuremburg on April 21, the 157th split into semi-autonomous, company-strength task forces, with tanks, anti-tank guns, mortars and 105s, and cut loose against spotty opposition in a swath through the German countryside, leading the 45th Division's race with the 42nd for Munich. In five days the 'Birds covered the fifty miles to the muddy brown Danube and crossed in assault boats and over a pontoon bridge under enemy mor-tar fire. Munich lay only forty miles ahead.

At about this time Heinrich Himmler ordered evidence of atrocities at the Dachau camp destroyed, and seven thousand or so inmates were marched out on foot. To ensure their disappearance into *Nacht und Nebel*, the night and fog of Nazi oblivion, prominent political prisoners including Pastor Niemoller, Blum and Schuschnigg were moved to the Niederdorf camp in the Tyrol for execution by the SS; they were rescued in the nick of time by American forces on April 28.[4]

On the twenty-sixth, three hundred miles to the north, the Russian army was driving toward the Chancellery in Berlin where Hitler and his mistress Eva Braun were holed up in his bunker. On the twenty-eighth the 157th was in the outskirts of the town of Dachau.

Two hundred miles to the southwest Mussolini and *his* mistress were caught by Italian partisans near Lake Como as they tried to escape to Switzerland, shot and hung by their heels in the main square of Milan. "Finito Benito," I wrote in my journal.

The next day, April 29, Adolf finally took Eva for his bride, deep under earth that shook with the blasts of Soviet shells landing almost overhead. Our Company L occupied Dachau town while K pushed toward Munich, and Colonel Sparks was abruptly ordered to divide his Third Battalion's mission and proceed immediately to capture a concentration camp outside the town, post an airtight guard, and allow no one to enter or leave. Sending L Company off to join K for Munich, he brought I Company up from reserve to head for the mysterious camp. Having no idea what to expect, he decided to go along himself.

Horror

Acting evidently in anticipation of I Company's mission, Lieutenant Delmar Griffith of the I&R Platoon put together his final patrol of the war and started off by jeep down the road that according to his map led from the town to his assigned objective, whatever it was. Les Gerencer was with him, Dom Trubia and an unidentified fourth. They appear to have been the first American soldiers to be witnesses.

> Griff:
> When we approached there was a railroad siding outside of the enclosure with some box and cattle cars. There were inmates in the cars just practically dead, just living corpses. We found out later they had been evacuated from some other concentration camp, brought into Dachau, and they hadn't had time to take them within the enclosure or really didn't care to. They were just left there to die.

Down the railroad track (*Department of Defense*)

We were right outside and knew it was being defended. Maybe we drew fire but I don't remember. We went back and reported.

They didn't stop to count. According to a subsequent tally, 2,310 corpses from 39 boxcars were spilled out along the tracks and roadbed.[5]

Gerencer:

We went right up to the gate by those boxcars—arms, skeleton faces, jest piled up any which way and fallin' outta both sides at random. Then a woman came runnin' down from around the gate, outside, appeared outta nowhere in a light fur collar coat and a round hat, and stopped in front of the gate and was hollerin' somethin' at us an' pointin'.

That woman hollerin' and that sight there musta got to Griff because he stopped the jeep and decided not to go in. We turned around and as we were goin' back heard rifle shots, like up in the windows, couple from this side, couple from that side. Got back to the CP in the town, and Colonel O'Brien said we shouldna even been up there.

Trubia:

We were supposed to see if the bridge was out. Got down there, and it was not out, and there were all these bodies piled up alongside this railroad track just over the bridge, and I said we better turn that truck around and get ready to retreat.

I looked around and just could not figure what was going on. There was this high wall, like it was part of an estate. I tried to get up to the gate to look through,

U.S. soldiers view the Dachau death train (*Courtesy of the United States Holocaust Memorial Museum, and County of Allegheny, Division of Photography*)

and I just . . . my stomach wasn't just right from seein' all those dead bodies, and I thought the hell with it, I've had enough of this.

   We got back in the jeep and went back. I told Edwards what we'd seen, and he accused me of drinkin' again.

Meanwhile, a second I&R recon patrol was dispatched from the town, and Bobby Winburn was on the jeep.

Winburn:
We had come into Dachau and set up the CP where they had some rooms in a store or sump'n, an' somebody said they wanted us to go out an' look over the concentration camp. Some sergeant was with us from a line company for a while, a driver— not one of our regulars—who spoke German, myself an' another guy, four of us. We went out through the town an' come to a creek. The bridge was halfway blowed out, but we could git across with the jeep, an' we come to a railroad siding with about forty boxcars full o' dead people. The doors was open, an' they was jest stacked. We went along on this pretty good-sized highway, an' there was the gates to Dachau, with a concrete area like a circle where you could turn around. About fifty feet from these big closed gates a civilian on a bicycle come chuggin' along, wavin' to us. Our driver could understand him, an' he said it hadn't been taken, and there was SS troops there. So we said thank you an' turned right around.

   Goin' back to the CP we run into an officer who said, "Where you guys been?" We said we was sent up to look at Dachau, but it hadn't been taken. He said, "I know. I'm supposed to take it." We said, "Well, have at it."

Presumably Winburn encountered I Company preparing to advance on the camp with tanks in support. In the meantime, a third I&R patrol had been organized under Bill Caird, with Hank Mills, and Bill Belleman driving, to scout out the camp, when Trubia reported in to the CP and was told to go along and guide them back "as punishment because the night before I'd been drinkin' and raisin' hell." There seems to have been some confusion as to whether I Company had already reached the camp.

   Mills was in the back of the jeep.

Mills:
We had to drive out and double back on the highway to get to the camp. We drove down a straight road, and the railroad siding ran parallel to it on the left to the gate. The cars were right up to the gate, crammed with bodies, bodies fallen out and layin' on the ties and the rails, stark naked. They hadn't begun to bloat and decompose, and it was a warm day, the smell just startin'. I'm almost certain there was no children in the cars. They'd been systematically packing them in.

   I didn't really believe all the stories they told about the Germans until I seen what was layin' right before my eyes. Right then I knew the whole two years overseas wasn't wasted. If we'd been held up again like we were at Aschaffenburg for four or five days they would have disposed of a helluva lot more people. They were tryin' to get rid of the evidence, and we got there in time to stop them. I think the bodies on the train were being brought in for disposal.

All of a sudden, when we were about a hundred yards from the gate, they fired on us from a stone archway where they had a machine gun. We jumped into the ditch only about a stone's throw from the bodies and were pinned down for fifteen or thirty minutes when I Company comes up the road and the company commander says, "What the fuck are you guys doin' here?" We told him we understood he had the camp secured. He says, "We're just comin' up now."

We all went in at the same time, no resistance, right by the railroad cars, right into the chambers, and right to the ovens, the clothing piled on one side and a pit full o' human bones on the other. That was the first time I believed the Germans were exactly what they said they were. There was bodies everywhere. The prisoners was walkin' death, sunken eyes, nothin' but skin drawn over bones, seventy pounds or less. They'd been systematically starved and could barely navigate. Probably all been dead if we hadn't got there when we did.

I was only in this one gas chamber, like a big shower room with jets on the wall. Outside the guards could look through and operate it. I remember sayin' to myself: It's time to go home. I wanna see my mother.

In fact, there was an initial spasm of resistance from the guards in the camp towers. When a ten-foot fence topped by electric barbed wire and surrounded by a moat gave way under the pressure of a mass of inmates, two SS tower guards fired down on them and were instantly riddled by the aghast G.I.s. According to the 45th Division's history:

> ... Scores of SS men were taken prisoner and dozens killed, as German guards were eliminated in a swift fire fight. Then Poles, Frenchmen, and Russians working outside that grim barbed-wire enclosure seized American weapons and turned on their captors, killing many more.
>
> The yard behind the high barbed-wire enclosure was bare as a Swiss Red Cross representati e and two SS officers, in place of leaders of the camp who had fled, came out of a building bearing a white flag ...
>
> ... The Division eliminated a number of dogs of vicious temper and great size which apparently had been used to keep the prisoners in fear.[6]

Griff returned behind I Company.

Griff:
I never saw anything like that scene there in those railroad cars, but inside it was one of indescribable horror. Those inmates were so happy. They were dirty and unkempt, and they'd come up and try to embrace you. We were told that they were typhus-infested, and it was kind of hard to push them away, but you felt a revulsion, you know. I'll never forget that, how happy they were to be liberated. I don't know whether they were Jews, no doubt some Jews slated for the next bath. I wanted to see the gas chambers, but they placed them off-limits right away and wouldn't

allow any unauthorized personnel inside the enclosure. The Medics and other units took over.

Jerry Waldron drove up in a jeep with Colonel O'Brien, the regimental commander.

Waldron:
We'd had no briefing about concentration camps. It was just a name. Some had been liberated in the northern part of Germany, but we didn't know about it, we didn't know about the ovens, and we certainly didn't know there was one here. We were in this race with the 42nd Division. Regimental Headquarters knew the camp was there and sent the first I&R patrols out to find out what the situation was. They moved I Company out because they thought it could handle the camp alone.

Then out of the blue are these freight cars on the siding outside and inside the camp, bodies stacked in them, jammed in them, legs sticking out, some hanging out in all directions, some on the ground, they'd been in such a rush trying to clean it up. That's what happened, out of the blue from the General on down.

As we started in the gate, this reaction began to come over me, that I can't believe it. How could they do this? I didn't see the ovens. Whoever I was with didn't want to make the tour. But you just wanted to do something. You didn't know what. You'd never been quite all that sure why you were fighting, but by God, when you saw that, you knew. Even today my stomach is turning.

Revenge

Trubia:
We went back and through the gate and found out what it was. We looked at the gas chambers, the furnaces, went into the infirmary where there was a mother and child, and rigor mortis hadn't even set in yet. The Germans were killin' these prisoners right up to the last minute. I saw a prisoner take a guard by the arm, pull his arm out straight, and the other guy hit him with a cane and broke his arm, and then they tried to twist it off of him. That's when I lost my breakfast. They just went wild. They tore the Germans apart by hand, just tore 'em apart by hand. Oh God, I couldn't sleep for a week.

Winburn:
About an hour after we got back to the town they come after us agin'. They sent about six of us up. "Go back to Dachau. They're shootin' up the guards. Go git 'em out before they shoot any more."

Everything was open by then. We went about a hundred yards in. There the guards was, about fifty of 'em. We lined 'em up four abreast. I was right up by the front on one side. There was two or three of 'em shot up. I tole the others, "You better help 'em if you want outta here." They'd got 'em out in the street there when we got there. No idea how many'd been killed. Then we took 'em back to the town.

On the right where we went in we passed that shower where they gassed 'em, with the piles o' clothing. We were only in there for twenty minutes or so, jest enough time to git these guys lined up an' git 'em out. One SS trooper, a young kid, was scared to death we was gonna shoot him. The prisoners looked like they was starvin' to death, but we jest didn't git to stay.

Griff:
When the G.I.s, the rifle troops, saw all that they were out for revenge. They went berserk. It was shocking, but I didn't have any feelings at that point. I don't think I could have been surprised at anything. I say I was shocked. I was more or less, but not shaken. Just couldn't believe that anything like that could happen.

Mills:
A lot of the guards had seen combat and were unfit for it and had been put there with some SS. One of 'em was grabbed, and three or four prisoners took his arm and held it straight out and beat it with a cane until it fell off. I seen it.

One guard shot in the stomach come staggerin' over, clutchin' his belly and croakin' *"Wasser! Wasser!"* And Bill Belleman grabbed him by the arm and flung him against the wall. I grabbed Belleman and hauled him off. "You don't do that to a guy who's helpless, no matter what!"

I Company's orders were to secure the camp, be sure the prisoners were not released on their own, that they were medically cared for and fed and made comfortable. It wasn't even a full combat company because they were short on replacements. They isolated the guards in a concrete enclosure like a garage with no roof. Sparks had told a machine gunner to guard them, and when he turned and walked away he heard him open up. He ran back and kicked him off the gun. The guy says they're tryin' to get away.

Waldron:
This guy on the machine gun was just bent outta shape by what he'd seen. When I got there guards were sitting up in various stages, blood all over the place. I thought some guys in I Company had just gone off their rocker and tried to punch the daylights out of these guards. I wasn't aware they'd shot up anybody. I got there late and wasn't long enough in that area to find out anything. Then I went down to the crematorium area and went through another traumatic experience, one of joy perhaps. Here they were clamoring for food but you knew I Company had saved people from death. I was almost a little bit high.

I can see those guards stretched out, some of 'em against the building, stacked up against it. I didn't really focus because I was so upset, but there was so much blood around that it couldn't be just beatin' 'em up. It had to be shooting 'em.

General Frederick was standin' there and lookin' at 'em, and somebody says to him, "What are we goin' to do about it?" I don't remember just what he said, but the gist of it was—what could you? They didn't punish I Company because we all felt the same. We were just wild.

What had happened? In the very last days of the war, after nearly two years of heroic and honorable fighting, was this a latter-day Chivington Massacre, a reversion in the face of revulsion to the dark Indian-fighting and strikebreaking chapters of the old Colorado Militia and Guard?

Colonel Sparks offered no excuses for the men under his command but stress, horror and outrage to the breaking point.

> As the main gate of the camp was closed and locked, we scaled the brick wall surrounding the camp. As I climbed over the wall following the advancing soldiers, I heard rifle fire to my right front. The lead element of the company had reached the confinement area and was disposing of the SS troops manning the guard towers, along with a number of vicious guard dogs. By the time I neared the confinement area, the brief battle was almost over.
>
> After I entered the camp over the wall, I was not able to see the confinement area and had no idea where it was ... [It] occupied only a small portion of the total camp area. As I went further into the camp, I saw some men from Company I collecting German prisoners. Next to the camp hospital, there was an L-shaped masonry wall, about eight feet high, which had been used as a coal bin ... The prisoners were being collected in this semi-enclosed area.
>
> As I watched, about fifty German troops were brought in from various directions. A machine gun squad from Company I was guarding the prisoners. After watching for a few minutes, I started for the confinement area, taking directions from one of my soldiers. After I had walked away for a short distance, I heard the machine gun guarding the prisoners open fire. I immediately ran back to the gun and kicked the gunner off the gun with my boot. I then grabbed him by the collar and said: "What the hell are you doing?" He was a young private about 19 years old and was crying hysterically. His reply to me was: "Colonel, they were trying to get away." I doubt that they were, but in any event he killed about twelve of the prisoners and wounded several more. I placed a noncom on the gun and headed for the confinement area.
>
> It was the foregoing incident which has given rise to wild claims in various publications that most or all of the German prisoners captured at Dachau were executed. Nothing could be further from the truth. The total number of German guards killed at Dachau during that day most certainly did not exceed fifty, with thirty probably being a more accurate figure. The regimental records for that date indicate that over a thousand German prisoners were brought to the regimental collecting point. Since my task force was leading the regimental attack, almost all the prisoners were taken by the task force, including several hundred from Dachau.[7]

A Signal Corpsman took a widely republished photograph from behind the machine gunner and four American soldiers, showing four of the German prisoners standing before the wall, two with their hands up, and an indeterminate number sprawled on the ground, dead or wounded. Feigning? Not likely.

Sparks's count was disputed by Howard A. Buechner, one of his medical officers and, curiously, a close friend, in his 1986 book *Dachau: The Hour of the Avenger*, wherein he reprinted the preceding account written for members of the Regimental Association of

The last massacre at Dachau. Any one of us might have done it. (*U.S. Signal Corps photo by Arland B. Musser*)

Prisoners about to beat a guard with a shovel. Bodies against the wall. (*U.S. Signal Corps*)

which Sparks was founder and secretary. Buechner, however, claimed with no supporting evidence that exactly 520 guards were executed, including 346 on orders of the late Lieutenant Jack Bushyhead, I Company executive officer, whom he called "the Avenger."

Following with his driver what appeared to be I Company's route in, Buechner wrote that he heard sustained machine-gun fire for about a minute, then what sounded like .45-caliber pistol shots.

Though he'd been told by Sparks not to enter the inner enclosure, curiosity drew him there. Peering around the end of a wall, he related, he observed Lieutenant Bushyhead on the flat roof of a low building, beside him one or two soldiers with a machine gun. In the foreground were several armed G.I.s, including a machine gunner. Across a courtyard before a long, high wall, according to Buechner, was a row of "perhaps 350 fallen soldiers" and three or four inmates in striped clothing, armed with .45s, walking among them and shooting those still alive in the head.[8]

Elsewhere Buechner stated that 346 guards were killed. Nowhere did he provide documentation for either figure, indicate that he conducted a body count or identify anyone else who did so. There appear to be perhaps fifty guards, standing or on the ground, in the Signal Corps photo, which is evidently not inclusive, however. Dr. Buechner quoted Lieutenant Bushyhead as responding to his incredulity: "Doc, have you been to the crematorium? Have you seen the gas chamber? Have you seen the box cars? Have you seen the little [emaciated] people?"[9]

As reconstructed by his medical officer, after Colonel Sparks had restored order among his men following the machine-gun massacre, he set up a temporary CP outside the camp and gave Buechner permission to enter the outer area within the walls in case there were any of his wounded men to be treated, but not the inner enclosure.

Meanwhile, Lieutenant Walsh marched I Company off to join the rest of the Battalion in the attack on Munich, leaving a few men with his executive officer, Bushyhead, to guard the captured guards. It was then, Buechner wrote, that Bushyhead, finding himself evidently in charge of the camp, ordered the Germans to line up against the wall and his machine gunners to mow them down, providing the inmates with the pistols to finish the job.

Allowing for those who had fled at the approach of the Americans and been replaced by an SS company from the outside, and a number of imprisoned soldiers who were impressed as guards, the German garrison at Dachau stood at 560, according to Buechner's arithmetic—the number that the newly arrived camp commander, Lieutenant Heinrich Skodzensky, had tried to surrender to I Company. Of this total, he calculated, 520 were "executed in one way or another" by the men of I Company and the armed inmates that day, including those shot in combat by American soldiers and the machine-gunning halted by Sparks, and the 346 allegedly executed on orders of Bushyhead.[10] Sparks wrote of Buechner's work:

> To the best of my knowledge, the book contains an accurate reconstruction of the events which took place at Dachau during the time of liberation, with the exception of actions attributed to Lieutenant Bushyhead and the number of German casualties.

I had never before heard of the alleged actions of Lt. Bushyhead, and I doubt that they took place. The book also records the number of German guards killed during the liberation as 550. It is my firm opinion that the actual number killed was less than fifty.[11]

Jerry Waldron, who arrived on the scene immediately after, confirms that about fifty guards were killed. Why Howard Buechner would escalate this damning figure to the tenfold greater shame of his outfit can only be speculated.

Under orders to let no one in or out, having just halted a massacre of prison guards, concerned that the press of prisoners would force the gate between their inner compound and the outer camp, and along with his men in a state of shock, Sparks was close to the end of his rope when a trio of jeeps led by Brigadier General Henning Linden, deputy commander of the 42nd Division, got through the main gate and appeared before him. Tagging along was Marguerite "Maggie" Higgins, a young war correspondent for the *New York Herald Tribune*, dressed as a soldier. According to Sparks, the General was explaining to him that she wanted to interview inmates who were prominent anti-Nazis when she unaccountably ran over to the inner gate and removed the crossbar.

The prisoners surged forward. Sparks ordered his men to fire over their heads and rush the gate. They did and closed it again. He already resented the 42nd, a famous WWI outfit on the line only since December that was apparently vying with the 45th for Dachau and on occasion elbowing into his battalion's sector en route. General Linden's appearance on the scene was the last straw. Sparks:

> It had already been a most trying day. I therefore requested the general and his party to leave and directed one of my men to escort them from the camp. The good general was a dandy who carried a riding crop as his badge of authority. As my man approached the jeep, the general laid a blow on the man's helmet with his riding crop. I then made some intemperate remarks about the general's ancestry and threatened to remove him and his party from the camp by force. He then said I was relieved of my command and that he was taking charge. I then drew my pistol and repeated my request that he leave. He left, but only after advising me that I would face a general court-martial for my actions.[12]

Seventh Army took over Dachau, and Buechner claimed that General Linden initiated court-martial charges against Sparks, Bushyhead, himself and several other Third Battalion officers and enlisted men for failing to prevent or halt the massacre of the guards.

A few days after the liberation, Sparks wrote, the 45th's General Frederick told him he thought he could handle the matter of the charges but meanwhile was relieving him of his command and sending him back to the States until it blew over, when he would have him reassigned to the Division, which had been alerted for the invasion of Japan.

Decades later Sparks claimed in his *157th Infantry Association Newsletter* that with three trusted men he was sent to Le Havre, where he was arrested by an MP officer with orders to escort him to Seventh Army headquarters near Augsburg back in Bavaria. Noting to the

MP that his men were armed, Sparks claimed, he talked him into allowing them to travel on their honor and learned upon arrival (after a few days' pause in Paris) that his case was in the hands of General Patton, who had just taken over from Seventh Army as military governor of Bavaria.

> The following morning I reported to General Patton's Chief of Staff and arranged for an appointment with the general that afternoon. At the appointed time I reported to the general. He then said to me: "Colonel, I have some serious court-martial charges against you and some of your men here on my desk." I replied that I had never been advised of any specific charges but that I would like to offer an explanation of the events that took place at Dachau.
>
> The general paused for a moment and then said: "There is no point in an explanation. I have already had these charges investigated, and they are a bunch of crap. I'm going to tear up these goddam papers on you and your men."
>
> With a flourish, he tore up the papers lying in front of him and threw them in the wastebasket. He then said: "You have been a damn fine soldier. Now go home." I saluted and left. The whole interview lasted perhaps three minutes. I then rejoined the regiment in Munich and heard nothing further about the matter.[13]

As for charges that Buechner had failed to halt a massacre or treat the wounded, they were dismissed following an initial inquiry, Sparks wrote, while the others charged were summoned to Patton's headquarters, questioned and dismissed. Lieutenant Bushyhead, Buechner claimed, was brought before the General himself, who questioned him, then ordered the investigating officers to appear with the entire evidence they had gathered, burned it in his metal wastebasket and had the affair stricken from the record.

The roles of the veteran and war-weary 45th and the relatively fresh 42nd Divisions in the liberation of Dachau, the circumstances and extent of the massacre of the German prisoners, the confrontation between Sparks and Linden, and the aftermath remained for decades matters of inside conjecture until Sparks in 1984 distributed his version to the 157th veterans. That touched off a bitter standoff with the 42nd camp as to which division liberated Dachau—however tainted by massacre that "liberation" was—and concerning Sparks's and Buechner's veracity, which continued into the next century following publication by the late General Linden's son in 1997 of his exhaustively researched *The True Account* of a monumental event that should have been the occasion for unqualified joy.[14]

A jeep patrol of Ironheads was the first to approach the concentration camp and come under fire, followed by two more and our I Company that gained first entry. Exhaustive postwar research unequivocally demonstrates that Lieutenant Colonel Felix Sparks's Third Battalion of the 157th Regiment of the veteran 45th Division was the first to subdue the guards, enter and liberate the inmates of this prototypical concentration camp. The record shows that the 222nd Regiment of the recently committed-to-action 42nd Division under Brigadier General Henning Linden, after overrunning fierce enemy resistance en route, penetrated another sector of the camp, played a major role in subduing and restoring order to the camp and arranged and accepted its surrender, and that no other U.S. units or individuals—as has been claimed from time to time—were on the scene or involved.

The massacre (and there is no other word for it) in the coal yard of the lined-up and unarmed enemy guards by the overwrought young machine gunner assigned to guard them was in straight-out violation of the Geneva Convention yet wholly understandable in the world of unprecedented horror into which the American soldiers walked that spring day and discovered at the last minute, a week before the surrender of Germany, for what they had been fighting and suffering and maimed and traumatized and dying.

For no one can it have been more traumatic than Felix Sparks, who rose through the ranks from making a buck on the side as part-time snapshot processor in his training days to barely escaping death or capture in the Battle of the Caves at Anzio, to the command of an infantry battalion ambushed beyond his control at Reipertswiller, to losing control of his men in the horror of Dachau (and how could he not have under the circumstances?) and to being relieved of his command in the very last unworldly days of an almost continuous war in which he had fought valiantly for nearly two years.

"How fragile is the thread of life" would reflect this citizen-soldier who moved on to a career of public service in Colorado, and how futile is the waging of war."[1]

What Did the People Know?

> Children pedalled past the bodies on their bicycles
> and never interrupted their excited chatter.
>
> News report[16]

Waldron:
I think we stayed overnight in an inn there in Dachau, the first time I slept in a real feather bed that came right up over me. I couldn't believe what I was hearing back at the CP, and I went out there and BANG, there it was. I came back and talked with the people in the inn, and they said they didn't know about it. But it was perfectly obvious to me that that was what they would say and that there probably wasn't much that they could do about it.

Mills:
The people in Dachau had to know about it; you could smell the stench there. I always had the impression that the Germans were different from us; they would carry out an order whether it was right or wrong. I don't think you could get an American to operate a gas chamber. You might get an element to do that, but not wholesale units to try to wipe out a section of the population. They did it to kids, to women, the sick, like they were nothing.[17]

Griffith:
I took some snapshots of great piles of corpses in the so-called showers. I sent them home to my mother. There was in our town a German family that ran a meat market, the Boehms; I went to school with the boy. Real nice family. She took those pictures

U.S. soldiers force Hitler youths to view their leaders' handiwork. (*Courtesy of USHMM, and National Archives and Records Administration, College Park*)

in and showed them to Mr. Boehm, and he looked at 'em and shook his head and said, "I believe it now. I can see it here. But I didn't think anything like that could happen, didn't think the German people could stoop so low." Wish I had 'em. They got away from me. Don't know who got 'em. Someone must have realized they had a little more significance than I did.

Then the military government took over and engaged in a Nazi hunt. At that point you couldn't find any Nazis or Nazi sympathizers. All the German civilians denied ever having any affiliation with the Nazis, and they didn't know anything, played dumb, afraid of retaliation of course. And I sometimes wonder just how much they did know. If they did, they were powerless to speak their conscience. I don't think they would sanction or condone such things as extermination of the Jews, but they went along with it. For some reason or other they went along with it. They were powerless to resist.

Trubia:
The people in the village did not really know what was going on behind that wall. After we pulled outta there the commander of the 42nd lined them up and marched them through, and I guess they really went to pieces when they saw what had been

happening. I took about three or four rolls of film of it and was going to send it home, then thought they might get lost and gave 'em to a German photographer in the town to develop. Every one of 'em was spoiled. I coulda killed him. That sonofabitch sabotaged me.

Waldron:

On the fences were all these emaciated prisoners trying to get out, and I think they made the mistake of feeding them some of our rations which they weren't able to digest, and finally they had to bring in the medics and bring 'em back with soups or whatever.

Rosenwasser's Road Out

By 4:45 in the afternoon the American soldiers were inside the gate. And we started to steal canned food, pork and all kinds of meat. Diarrhea. What's going on here? Somebody poisoned us. We poisoned ourselves with the food we aren't used to, cold canned goods, meat just swallowed. It took about three days until the Red Cross came in, and they collected all the food from us. We only got biscuits, coffee, peas, cereals, cookies, liquids. And we are hollering, "Hey wait a minute, baby, you are worse than the Germans. Finally we are liberated. We wanna piece o' bread, a piece o' meat. All you giving is cereal and cookies?" We don't understand the logic until it was brainwashed into us that we had to start a new life, eat like babies, our stomachs cannot take what we want, and eventually we'll get used to it, the food, and be able to eat whatever we want.

This is the story of the liberation of Dachau.

The firing was on from noon until four or four forty-five. Definitely you were bombing either after somebody got the idea that this is a mess here and then you discovered this is Dachau concentration camp. Them sonofabitches, they didn't give up fast, them SS tower guards. We saw the whole firing. Outside they were bombing, enthusiastic and everything. We saw the crossfires and everything going on, and all of a sudden we are already dragging the prison commandos, not so much soldiers but civilians, Polish or Russian, Ukrainian, German company commanders who were in charge of us, and they were some of them meanies, and we wanted to tear 'em apart and get 'em, and I tell you that morning I almost felt sorry that the Americans came.

I stood by a lineup of German prisoners from the ones you got there when you liberated the camp. They were goin' to do the work whatever you guys wanted 'em to do. The guys smokin' cigarettes. One of our guys goes in there, you know, "We are the victors now. We won the game." This German smoking the cigarette, he says to them in German, he says, "Hey, yesterday when you lined up in your platoon, did your officer allow you to smoke?" I dunno whether he answered him or not, but by the time he asked him the question he gave him his fist. Then come by an American soldier, get up there with a rifle, pointing at the Jewish boy. "None of your business. Get the hell out of here!"

I tell you I was bitter, very bitter. I wasn't a revenge man. If I had been I would have taken stones and tried to kill this guy, despite that the Americans are staying there behind their rifles. Besides this little incident, nobody ever thinks anything but the Germans were treated much better than we were. Number one, we didn't know why they were treating us to the food like this. We couldn't understand it why couldn't we get food? Number two, we saw the treatment that a German soldier who was yesterday the enemy of me and the enemy of the American soldier is treated better than I am. More treated, more food, more liberty, more humanitarian to him than to me.

So I tell you that as a Jew I can't take it as nothing but anti-Semitism. If these American soldiers know that we are Jews then they haven't got the right to say that, because I don't think we were 10 percent Jewish in there.

Mostly Polish, Russian, Ukrainian. Only about two thousand and I don't know how many hundred Jewish people in there.

I would swear my hand on the Bible that if I had not gone through it I wouldn't believe it. And today that the people don't believe it, it's a sad story. I regret it very much the people who don't believe it, because this tells you that anything can happen, and the person, the shoe is not on his foot, will never believe it and will never accept it.

Concentration camp comes, and two things is important in my life. One is to fill up my stomach, and one is to get to America. This willpower of that dream, that determination that I wanted to succeed in life, this helped me to survive more than anything in the war. Everything came true, and it's continuing yet because I'm not finished with my destination.

In December 1945 I took off from Hungary and it took me four years through Austria, Germany and France to arrive in the United States, to the dream, with a dollar and forty-five cents in my pocket. I arrived as a rabbinical student in Cleveland, Ohio, in June 1949, spoke pretty good English, jumped the fence in four weeks. By December my cousin in New York gets me a job as a necktie presser, 6,800 a day for twenty-eight dollars a week, sixty-five people in the room—open the window, close the window and put on the fans, everybody to his own crazy feelings. I go home at night to a hole with a family with three kids and share the bathroom, and my bones are brittling. I say this is not for me, and I jump the fence again.

Meet an old Czech friend from Europe with a Jewish cousin with a chicken farm in Kingwood, New Jersey. My friend takes me to Howard Clothes to get a brown, white-stripe suit for thirty-two dollars to go for a job in. When I speak Yiddish the owner lets me take it for five dollars a week. This is America! I can't believe it! I go to the farm like a new man, out of prison . . . chickens, dogs, cows, fruit trees, flowers . . . this is my whole life!

The boss on the farm was a gentleman of gentlemen, escaped from Poland to Russia, lucky, just plain lucky. Nice beard, wife, two children, big farmhouse. She was a little messy in the kitchen, but what a cook! I was a Hunky, used to the best cooks, best food. Polack! What does a Polack know how to make a meal? But when I ate the first one, I says, "Baby, all the Hunkies can go and hide. This Polack maybe is good enough for me."

When the boss saw how I went for the hoppers and cleaned up the chickenshit and freshened up the mash he said, "Hey, you wanna job?" and I says, "That's what

I came out for!" He offered me twenty-five a week with room and board, one of the family, cash money in my pocket! Everything else is free! Unbelievable! Went back to New York with my friend, told the necktie foreman to shove the job and paid off the last five dollars on the suit.

Like they say in Europe, "Go to America. You pick up gold on the sidewalk." It's truly that way, but nobody wants to look. Only the guy who suffered and lost everything, and he came here with nothing, is the one who's willing to pick up the pieces and go with the freedom and the opportunity that is available in this country. Put your shoulder next to it, and America will back you up 'til the last penny . . . unless. Someday there will be the same story. Things will change here, and history will repeat itself. I dunno if it's gonna be here, or Russia, or Israel or wherever. History will repeat itself, and everything is worthless. My father worked for some fifty-odd years, and nine children, and by the time he died he didn't accomplish in fifty years like I accomplished in fifty hours here in America.[18]

An Incomplete Record

Dachau Concentration Camp
(drawn from the *History of the 157th Infantry Regiment*)[19]

Survey of Internees by Nationalities, April 29, 1945
> Forty-one national, ethnic and political categories including 9,082 Poles, 4,258 Russians, 3,918 French, 2,907 Slovenes, 2,539 Jews, 2,184 Italians, 1,632 Czechs, 1,173 German Nationals, 848 Belgians, 670 Hungarians, 558 Dutch, 8 British and 6 Americans.

Total internees: 31,432

Internees Processed

1933–1939 (card index)	60,000
March 1940 to 26 April 1945 (card index)	161,930
Three weeks before liberation (incomplete records)	7,000

Total: 228,930

Natural Deaths, 1945

January through April (card index)	14,700

Executions
(Partial figures. Most complete records destroyed three weeks prior to liberation)

Jews brought in from other camps for execution	
June 20 to November 23, 1944	29,138
Non-aliens (Germans from foreign countries)	
October 1940 through March 1945	16,717

A cheer for U.S. troops, April 29, 1945 (*Courtesy of USHMM, and National Archives and Records Administration, College Park*)

The Hofbräuhaus in Munich (*Department of Defense*)

✦ 17 ✦

THE LAST PATROL

Munich
April 30–May 7, 1945

IF BLOWING THE LID OFF DACHAU revealed to the dogfaces who liberated its 31,432 survivors of Teutonic bestiality what the hell they'd been fighting about since the beaches of Sicily, what did it reveal, if anything, to the citizens of Munich who had been spicing their beer with the human smoke when it drifted down on them from the ovens?

The units of the 45th that weren't preoccupied with the concentration camp bore down with the 42nd ("Rainbow") and 20th Armored Divisions from the north and northwest on the city that spawned Nazism, while the Thunderbirds' admired brother division, the Third, after taking Augsburg, swung up from the south to get in on this final chase of the monster to its lair.

As elements of the Third and 42nd penetrated into the center of Munich on April 30, the 45th's 180th was stalled all day fighting two battalions of last-ditch SS holed up in their barracks on the northern fringe of the city. The Storm Troopers raged like beasts with lowered ack-ack and machine guns in a dying snarl of ferocity and had to be dug out, room by room.

In the city proper, however, clumps of civilians ranging from genuine underground to opportunists teamed with knots of Hitler's deserting soldiers in street fighting against the few organized defenders, captured the Munich radio station and secured the bridges while a delegation of residents advised the American conquerors that efforts were under way to persuade the remnants of the Wehrmacht to forgo Valhalla and spare what was left.

Munich had reaped the hurricane. Seventy-one Allied air raids in four years had destroyed 10,600 buildings, 30 percent of the city's housing, left 550,000 homeless, cut the population nearly in half to 480,000, but killed only 6,500, for it had been spared firebombing as its once-favorite son had not spared Rotterdam and Britain.

That very afternoon of the last day of April, as his special city fell to the Allies and the dreaded Russians approached to within a block, Adolf Hitler retired with his Eva Braun to the inner close of their bunker under the Chancellery in Berlin. At 3:30, eighteen days after the death of his archenemy, President Franklin Delano Roosevelt, the *Führer* picked up his pistol, stuck it in under his mustache and pulled the trigger, and his wife of a day swallowed her poison.

Those faithful to the last carried the bodies up to the garden, threw them in a Russian shell hole, doused them with gasoline, torched them off and stood at attention.

Coming up, as an ironic fate would have it, was May Day, by the mock celebration of which in 1933 Dr. Joseph Goebbels, Hitler's most loyal Minister of Propaganda and chief mythmaker, had lulled Germany's trade unions into being taken over the next day by the Nazis. Goebbels ordered his six children brought in from their play to the bunker and poisoned, somewhat to the last-minute misgivings of their mother, and then instructed his SS orderly to shoot him and Frau Goebbels. The corpses of the family were burned hastily and less completely in the same garden.

Overwhelmed by the Seventh Army, Munich surrendered. Our First Battalion, delayed for a few hours while it liberated eight thousand inmates of one of several satellite concentration camps in the outskirts, rejoined the Regiment. The 45th was assigned to garrison the city, the 157th taking the north central section, the 179th the eastern and the 180th the southwestern.

Back with the I&R, Bobby Winburn's crew had the distinction of copping the Platoon's final batch of prisoners.

> That German-speaking sergeant and driver plus Trubia and Gerencer and me, we captured seventy-five enlisted men and ten officers in this little-bitty town on the way to Munich. They jes' come out and all give up. I believe they thought we was the lead element of a column comin' in—but we wasn't! I don't think they'd have given up if they knew we was the only ones. I was bein' real nice with 'em, 'cause I got seventy-five men over here, and Les's got ten officers over there, and the sergeant and driver went back to git more vehicles, and Trubia's runnin' around lootin'! An hour or so later a column come through, and some lootenant jumped all over me for lettin' 'em sit around. I wasn't about to git anybody mad! Their guns was still all around the place! There's a time to be that way, and a time not.

Henry Mills and his buddy Vernon Dilks were targeted and missed again, this time for the last time, as Hank retold it.

> Munich was a little on the wild side. Dilks and me pulled in between these high-rise apartments, and we're settin' in the jeep. I happened to be drivin'. All of a sudden CRACK, and some Kraut puts a bullet through the windshield right between him and me. I rolled out on my gut and crawled around the corner of the building, and he did the same.

Dilks:
I remember it vaguely, got shot at so damn many times. I wasn't used to it and drank about two gallons o' that damn German white wine and went pop, gone. They thought I was dead. Gerencer threw three gallons o' water in my face an' I never woke up. He said it was three days before I did. Only way he knew I was alive he could feel my pulse. And that brandy from the warehouse at Aschaffenburg. We threw our gas masks away, everything, and had about ten cases on the jeep. You'd get so drunk with that stuff you'd wake up in the morning and take a glass o' water and be bombed again, jes' like that.

Gerencer:
While we were billeted in the Munich police station we had a big party. What a party! Champagne, Cointreau! Man! Guys were passed out in the gutter next day, on the sidewalks, in the middle of the square.

At the beginning of his climb to power Hitler agitated and organized with his clique and gang of toughs among the three biggest beer cellars in Munich, the Hofbräuhaus, Löwenbräukeller and Bürgerbräukeller. A few blocks southeast of the central Max Joseph Platz, the Hofbräuhaus, with a main hall that could hold two thousand, was the site of the first large-scale meeting of the Nazis in 1920. From the Bürgerbräukeller (unceremoniously to be razed in 1979 to make way for a shopping center), Hitler launched the Beer Hall Putsch in 1933 that, though momentarily unsuccessful, paved the way for his career.

Jerry Waldron was awarded the doubtful honor of The Last Patrol.

Colonel O'Brien told me the 42nd Division was gonna get in and take over the Hofbräuhaus where it all started unless we were there first, and he wanted me to have the honor of leading the patrol to occupy it for our CP. I hadn't taken a patrol for months. I don't remember who was with me, but I do remember that right then it came over the wire that the SS opposing the 180th fought to the last man in their barracks, and all I wanted to do was get home!

We had a little short captain in a long trench coat from Allied Military Government assigned to us who looked and walked like a duck. He said he wanted to lead the patrol. I said to myself, "Be my guest." We had maps of Munich and had been briefed. You went down an L-shaped street with the beer hall at the dead end of it, and I'm saying, "Oh bully, if they fought to the end in the barracks they're gonna have somebody sittin' on the steps of their shrine with a machine gun."

So we're going up the sides of the street and the Duck is out in the middle, and I said, "Captain, you better get over near a building here, because this may be a little exciting." He says, "You're not in charge of this patrol. I'm gonna walk down the middle of the street." And I said to myself, "Fine, fine, they're gonna take a shot at you first and that's gonna give us all time." So we turned that corner, and there's the Duck waddling down the middle as if he were leading a parade, all the rest of us hugging the buildings, and I'm waiting for those guns to go off. It was quiet as a tomb, and I think, "Oh Jesus, they're lettin' us walk into this."

About halfway down there's a civilian in a doorway, and I began to feel better. We got to the beer hall and nothing happened. Then I'm thinking about booby traps around, and again with this idea that I wanta get home, I didn't go in to loot it and got no souvenirs!

But as it turned out, at the same time our interpreters were out there finding Hitler's apartment [a nine-room flat in Prinzregentenplatz] and liberated his complete silver service and brought it all back, kept the good pieces and divided some of the rest with guys in Headquarters Company, and I came out with three silver coasters with the initials AH. My wife has been mad at me ever since we got married because I gave two to a girl I thought I was gonna marry out on the West Coast after I got out.

One of the boys from Headquarters found a can of paint and daubed it up there where Adolf got his start, a couple of feet high right between two of the arches.

CP 157 Inf
45th Div

Hank Mills was lounging in front of the CP:

These guys come down with photographers and officers and start paintin' the Rainbow of the 42nd on the front, and I asked what the hell's goin' on? He says we're capturing the Munich beer hall, and I said we captured it two days ago. He asks what outfit you with? And I said the 45th, but it was all over and our guys were walkin' around town lookin' for women.

Back at the hospital in the valley of the Volturno I tracked the ending of the war in Europe with the wistfulness of the benched player.

On the 29th all enemy forces, both German and Italian, in Italy and southwestern Austria, surrendered to the 15th Army group. Yesterday it was announced that all forces in Denmark and adjacent islands, Netherlands and northwestern Germany had surrendered to Monty. Berlin fell, and the entire pocket on the Elbe surrendered to the 9th Army. The news has just come that forces facing Devers's 6th Army group have surrendered, effective tomorrow, which will give up what's left of Austria. Reports have it that all forces in Norway have surrendered, or are about to. This leaves only the enemy forces in western Czechoslovakia, consisting largely of Bohemia, and Partisans have already begun to take over Prague. Thus there is one remaining pocket of Germans.

Admiral Doenitz announced that Hitler had died of shock a couple of days ago and that he is the new Fuhrer, as appointed by Hitler the day before his death. A high official captured by the Russians said that both Hitler and Goebbels have committed suicide in the Reichschancellery, but their bodies haven't been found.

So—several million Krauts have surrendered in the last six days. I give it only a few days or hours more.

On the third of May the 179th relieved remaining units of the 157th at Dachau. The 157th and its attached 191st Tank Battalion were assigned to the entire garrisoning of Munich. The 180th was to set up and administer POW camps for more than 125,000 prisoners.

And there the guys were, wherever they were, in on the winning as they deserved. I was feeling almost terminally sorry for myself. Fortunately, I kept to my journal.

Notes regarding the daily physiological activity of a certain unicellular organism, viz: J. E. Garland—

Physically and mentally I feel sick and lower than a snail's ass. I've just finished with a lousy sore throat and five-day headache. My stomach kicks up, and I have no appetite, no ambition whatsoever. Sometimes I feel myself going nutty. I'm losing my self-control, getting more nervous. I don't know how much longer I can take it before I go completely off the beam end. I'm just a turd on a rock [!], so completely and absolutely useless to the Army and everybody except officers and nurses who need a chauffeur. I wish I knew what's to become of me.

What became of me, as I wrote Pa, was that

I've acquired a dog. She's a black and brown, airedalish sort of hound, with white paws and an endearing manner, so I call her Boots after our old platoon mascot. I bought her yesterday for a pack of cigarettes from an Italian woman. Boots is beginning to learn her name, holds her water til she's outside, and knows that the box under my bed is hers . . .

The war is taking on the aspects of the finale of a tragi-comedy. Landsmann Hitler has apparently been lifted into the arms of his own peculiar breed of Valkyrie amid the strains of a Wagnerian dirge. Von Rundstedt has been captured, and all the

Dibble holds a piece of Hitler's silver,
from the same spoils of war as Waldron's.
(*Author photo*)

talk is of unconditional surrender. Soon, soon St. George will place his foot upon
the filthy dragon's neck and raising his sword cry "Kaputt!" May the pictures of
Buchenwald, Nordhausen, Belsen and all the rest be shown across the length and
breadth of the USA. Now let them compare the Jap and the Hun. Whose horns are
longest now?

    P.S.: 9:30 PM. The news has come that the war is over here in Italy. Dad, it's been
a helluva long road, and I'm damn proud of the part I've played here in this goddam
Dago country. Beyond a question of doubt it's been one of the toughest campaigns
in military history.

The Thunderbird Division on May 6 was put in command of the entire Munich area
with responsibility for the welfare of the civilian population and thousands of displaced
persons from all over Europe. The 157th Infantry Regiment continued to garrison the city.

    On May 7 I wrote home that I'd chauffered Major William Tecumseh Sherman Thorndike
from his hospital where I was a driver into Naples so that he could celebrate victory in
Europe in the Officers' Club there.

Great excitement reigns everywhere, particularly here in town this evening where
I'm waiting for the Major in the jeep. Victory has come and everyone is wild, though
I can't work myself up too much about it. I have a feeling of satisfaction but not one
of terrific elation.

    (Later) I'm continuing this later in the evening while I'm still waiting for the
Major who's at a dance. The streets here are filled with paper, books, junk, cans, toilet paper, water and what not, where the Eyties were suddenly becoming patriotic
after we ended what they started ... All in all, the soldiers here are taking victory in
a very sensible way.

And I was too. Somehow it seemed right, sort of cleansing anyway, that the ex-
Ironhead with the new scar on his shin should be sitting in the jeep with *Helen* nicely let-
tered under the windshield. In the parking lot of the Officers' Club, high above the Bay of
Naples. Almost exactly where I'd been with the other roistering replacements that omi-
nously magical evening a year and a half earlier. Writing home while the Major toasted vic-
tory with the armchair brass even as the last of the ole Ironhead buddies somewhere up in
Germany drank themselves silly on booze liberated from the Krauts who stole it from the
Frenchies.

    My momentary atonement, I suppose, for not being there.

Personnel Statistics of the 45th Infantry Division*
July 10, 1943 to May 7, 1945

Drawn from *The Fighting Forty-Fifth: The Combat Report of an Infantry Division*[1]

	KILLED	WOUNDED	INJURED	MISSING	TOTAL	REPLACEMENTS
SICILY	302	717	2,728	167	3,914	1,923
ITALY	1,808	6,060	24,110	1,927	33,905	13,780
FRANCE	1,178	5,269	12,285	1,449	20,181	7,532
GERMANY	362	1,683	2,446	72	4,563	1,639
Total	3,650	13,729	41,569	3,615	62,563**	24,874

* Full strength about 14,300, of whom some 7,500 were front-line soldiers

** Total casualties: 60,023 enlisted men and 2,540 officers

Ironheads. Gloucester, Massachusetts, Fourth of July, 1979. (*Left to right*) Garland, Griffith, Zapiecki, Pullman, Mills, O'Keefe, Waldron, Dowdall, Merchant. (*Collection of the author*)

··· 18 ···

"Would You Think There Was War at the Heart of Love?"

Europe and Back in the USA
1945–2008

A COUPLE OF WEEKS AFTER my solo celebration of Victory in Europe in the officers' parking lot above the Bay of Naples my shin was so well healed that to retain my limited service status my guardians at the hospital redefined my incapacity as psychoneurosis, I suppose on account of the baffling crippling of my legs. "I'm not terribly violent yet," I reported home. "Give me another six months, and I'll froth at the mouth for you!"

Of course the amusing psycho news brought a chins-up response from Ma.

> Whatever is keeping you from feeling whole again, I'm sure we can set you right somehow, and soon. One by one the awful, terrifying possibilities are being eliminated, and you can see the way opening up, I'm sure, to returning to an opportunity to make and shape your life again.
>
> I'm very grateful that you've had the satisfying experience of really getting to know a girl like Helen. Of course we've not known her well nor seen her much; and you really know her much better than we. But you say she evidently thinks you're tops, and that is something for you to hold on to, and cherish.

My father being on a fishing trip in Maine, his always-protective wife added that she wouldn't show my letter to him until I sent clarification, which I hastily and rather sheepishly attempted:

Chapter title is from a 1979 poem by Frank Merchant.

There's been an alarming amount of hogwash in the States about psychoneurosis, but the fact is that it runs the gamut all the way from near-insanity to mere nervousness. The latter is about my case. I'm only rather nervous, restlessly so, I mean. It's absolutely nothing to be alarmed about, for I've been that way ever since the first days on Anzio. It manifests itself by extreme restlessness, the inability to stay still, fairly heavy smoking, shortness of temper (frequent "blowing your top", just a way of getting off excess steam). Just about everybody who comes out of the infantry alive is that way, varying only in degree, and it will obviously wear off to a great extent in civilian life and through the process of adjustment. That ease your mind? I'm perfectly frank and holding nothing back. I'm just war-weary, that's all.

Little did I or anyone else know. So she showed Pa my letter and wrote back wondering that anyone who saw combat could think of anything else, "but of course the human mind and body can get over those things, especially young ones."

Meanwhile her reflective husband counseled their "rather nervous" son:

You have done your sober duty as a citizen-soldier, and when that duty is discharged your real life begins again. This is trite and comes poorly from a parent, but while you are waiting don't let your time be too much wasted ... After a year in civilian life you will look back on your army life as a strange interlude, but one in which much of your positive character will have been built.

   We will not again inhabit the world or see the social systems reappear that flourished before the world upheaval of the first half of the twentieth century ... There's going to be considerable equalization, and the wise people will adjust themselves to a world where the wealth is much more equally distributed than now ... I can imagine no worse basis for a lasting friendship with Russia than the oft repeated predictions that we'll be at war with her inside of fifteen years. We, with our bank accounts, are just so afraid of the Russian influence and the possibility that we might have to share prosperity with the working classes that we can't bear it.

After all the finagling to get into the Medics and then my impatience to get home and get on with it, I took a notion that once back in the States I might try getting assigned as cadre in a camp somewhere teaching combat intelligence. Four days after V-E Day, I wrote to myself: "Terrain in China may in many respects resemble closely what we've been accustomed to in Italy. It's just been promised that landings will be made on the China coast. I'm rather attached to this notion, as I'm not sure at all that I will even accept demobilization, if offered, until the end of the Pacific War."

China? The brass was talking Japan. *Not accept discharge?* Psycho all right.

A few days later were reaped early dividends from the hidden legacy that would haunt the battlefields into the next century: "Four Italian children have been hurt the last couple of days, one seriously (amputation) by mines. I imagine that with early summer plowing and mowing the people are venturing farther afield and thus walking into them."

In Naples while on some mission I met a gorgeous *signorina* and made a date to take her to a dance at the hospital. After a couple of numbers, I wrote home wrathfully, "she says excuse me and runs off to some other guy she knew, and that's the last I saw of her. I took off to bed at 11, because I knew darn well that she'd play up to me around the end of the dance for a special ride home (the other girls had to ride to and from in a truck). Although everyone said she was the knockout of the party, these hunkies are all the same. Hope Monk can raise my ideas of women above the gutter level."

Ma was incensed.

I think perhaps you don't understand about the give and take of social relationships with women. You tell them off because you don't get their undivided attention. I can't believe that it's always their fault. And moreover I resent your saying you "hope Monk can raise your opinion of women above the gutter level"! Come, come!

Pa too.

Sorry you don't like women whom, not infrequently, I find not unattractive. We all at home particularly like Miss Bryan who is, however, a happy extrovert and will probably continue to find the world at large stimulating and interesting, regardless of where she places her affections.

"Letdown, a feeling of uselessness and superfluity and boredom" were getting to us all, I complained home. "The heat has been absolutely wicked. We're in a bowl with mountains on all sides, and all the hot air in Italy, including that from the Parri cabinet, heads this way. The boys say it's worse than the Persian desert, and it soared into the 100s there. I'll have to take off my skin and sit around in my bones."

Up in Germany the Thunderbirds were moved from Munich into the Bavarian countryside. Veterans with high service points were readied for shipment home and replaced with newer men transferred in from the Ninth, 103rd and 14th Armored Divisions, which meant that a rejuvenated 45th was to be redeployed back to the States for refit, retraining and the invasion of Japan.

Now attached to the 103rd Airborne Division of Bastogne heroism and hoping to get home to enter Harvard Law School in September ahead of the influx of veterans, Corporal Jerry Waldron caught me up in a letter on July 25.

Dilks is cooking in I Company! Bill Caird saw him the other day and for the first time he was not bitching. Alas—Dilks who laughed when he heard the kitchen had been hit and cried when he heard none of the cooks were injured—a cook!

Damn it, Joe! You should not have been reclassified. After you left and after we left Rambervillers, we did not have one casualty ... But in the end, of course, you are alive today, and you might not have been had you been here ... Your diary is still with me, and I intend to return it personally to your parents. I am quite proud of myself—I have not looked inside it since I took it out of your things. I've just returned from four days in Paris, had a good time, saw everything but was alone. I wish you'd been there. We could have really done the place.

Having turned in my Helen/Yvonne jeep for a three-quarter-ton weapons carrier, the beamy predecessor of the postwar pickup, I was towing a monstrous, brakeless delousing machine to Caserta one day when my truck's brakes let go while descending a long grade toward the Volturno River, where the road up ahead turned ninety degrees to the right along the bank. All I could do was keep ahead of the damn thing and pray not to jackknife as we picked up speed. It was either into the river or make the turn, which we whipped and skewed around, almost upsetting, before careening along the level to an equally abrupt turn to the left and over a narrow bridge to the other side, where we drifted to a stop on the gentle upgrade. My last close one of the war.

I reported home August 5 that "I've started a course in 'Modern News Reporting', an Armed Forces Institute self-teaching course contained in one book, and all I'm doing is reading the book." And in five days: "I'm getting more and more interested in the book on journalism and am just about settled once and for all on that for a career."

August 8, two days after Hiroshima, one before Nagasaki: "The great thing now is the atomic bomb. It doesn't take much imagination to see the possibilities, good and evil. I don't expect much will be made of it that is good during our lifetimes, but another war will be the last." Two more days: "The radio has just announced that the Japs are ready to toss in the towel if we will save their Emp's dishonorable face ... We may as well leave them to their own devices on their islands; they will diligently tend their little rock gardens with the knowledge that the atomic bomb resides with the United Nations [oh yeah!]. I doubt very much that the Nips are as fond of their ancestors as they would have us think."

Back home, while visiting in Vermont, Doctor and Mrs. Garland dropped in on my friend Helen, vacationing from college and counseling at a camp for underprivileged girls in West Dummerston, where she was teaching them songs ranging from "Flaming Mamie" to "Lift Thine Eyes."

"Monk wrote very enthusiastically about your visit," I reported back, "and claims she was all excited and flustered and that everything will be perfect if I'm anything like you, a fact of which I'm perfectly aware."

Already we were hearing of massive layoffs from war production and were afraid returning vets would be at a serious disadvantage in the labor market. "We don't want privilege; we only ask for an even break and equal opportunity. It's a time of urgency. I'm impatient as the devil to finish off my education, get started on my career and raise a family. Right now the bit hurts more than it has in thirty months. I chomp."

August 26, another letter: "Today Allied forces are scheduled to begin landings in Japan, and the final surrender will take place on September 2, when the papers will be signed on board the battleship Missouri in Tokyo Bay."

✧ ✧ ✧

Time crept on. The baking mid-summer of the Infernal Valley, as we called the Volturno, gave way to the early rains of September. My somatic or psycho aches advanced again and then retreated. The 154th Station Hospital was inactivated, and we were attached to the 300th General in Naples where I'd languished a whole year earlier. They took away my weapons carrier, gave me a big ole "six-by," and made a man-of-all-transport of me, running shuttle between the 17th General Hospital and Naples. "It gets pretty tiresome lifting nurses in and out of the truck," I wrote home.

We counted the days. October 15 letter: "I'm seriously thinking of making a book out of my diary, submerging the earlier and later parts and concentrating on my year in combat. I'll probably write less about my actual combat experiences than about the people and the country and the things I saw and what I thought." Hmm.

My final home-bound V-mail of the war, November 5, 1945:

> This is the last letter I'll write. We came down here to the depot Saturday and finished processing yesterday, getting our clothes check, customs inspection, and flu shots. We're in barracks between sheets and on pillows.
>
> Some of the men in the company are already getting orders (they started coming in about an hour ago) and there are two transports in the harbor now, the Sea Snipe and the Sea Scamp, which they're going to load tomorrow. Hope I get on one of 'em but don't know for sure. Should be embarking in the next day or two.
>
> I'll see ya—
>
> Love, JEG

On the seventh of November *Sea Scamp* steamed out the Bay into the placid Tyrrhenian, leaving Napoli and Salerno and Venafro and Anzio behind, and into the Mediterranean, past the Bloody Ridge of Sicily and by the bleak coast of Africa and the dirt of Bizerte and the dung of Oran, gliding under the overpowering hulk of Gibraltar still there—Ceuta a small, smug string of neutral lights across the Strait to port—and after twenty-six months back into the Atlantic. No convoy. Just *Sea Scamp* and us.

Home, and Monk, here I come!

The excitement that mounted by the mile and the hour, the good chow   wow, what chow! And my bunk snugged the farthest aft, right over the CHURN CHURN CHURN of the propellor shaft. And when we hit the great gale in mid-Atlantic, and *Sea Scamp* plunged her bow into an Atlas Mountain of a sea that coursed under her hull and lifted that great flailing prop clear out of water, her stern and me in my bunk vibrated up and down with every labored turn of the screw in the air—WHUMP WHUMP WHUMP! Then the gigantic sea rolled aft under us, and as *Scamp* settled on her broad rump, and those prop blades hit the ocean again, her whole stern shook so you'd think she was gonna toss you right out of your sack and pop every rivet in her and just split apart. But only CHURN! CHURN! CHURN! until the next big one, and here we go again!

Monk, here I come!

We churned back on November 18 to Newport News, where so many of us had embarked, so many never to return. Like all the other weary guys I wired home my safe arrival. Same old Camp Patrick Henry. Same old steam train pounding and belching cinders back up the same old Southern Railroad. No evidence of bombing or shelling en route, no bullet-ridden stucco, no rubble, no burned-out anything, no bodies, no ragged kids pimping their sisters.

Devens, as chilled and drab as ever. Phoned home, and there were Ma and Pa waiting for the call, hysterically calm. Must avoid unseemly emotional response. Processed out, certifiably breathing, as processed in by Army stock clerks: OD uniform with attached ribbons, Purple Heart and Combat Infantryman's Badge, hash marks and overseas bar on sleeve; personals; petty loot, namely Kraut helmet, GOTT MIT UNS belt buckle and enemy machine-gun ammo case; 10 percent monthly disability pension for scar, left shin; honorable discharge.[1]

Last chow in Service, still nervous. Thanksgiving dinner 1200 hours, Thursday, November 22, 1945 at Fort Devens where it all started. Train back to same old North Station, Boston. Met at 1715 by Pa in family sedan. Through Brookline Village, up High Street, left on Allerton to number 28, still there, at 1800 hours, into driveway, same front yard where I dug dandelions, same ole gray-shingle Victorian house, same little cairn terrier squirming with joy, same Ma rushing out the door. Huge hugs and kisses, possibly tears, and same up-country-style home cooking again after thirty-two endless months or was it years? Two turkey dinners in one day! The chowhound is back.

Helen and pals were cooking a turkey with her mother in a rented cabin in the woods of Katonah up in New York's Westchester County. I phoned and left the Big Word of arrival at Sarah Lawrence College. Chaplain Bryan, father, was still in Europe. So The Returned Hero was paraded before his uncles, aunts and old family friends at home.

Telephone contact made with The Girl. Heard for the first time, her voice was even more magical than her treasured letters, and a date was arranged. The next Tuesday chowed with ole buddy Jerry Waldron, who came up for air from his first-year law studies at Harvard. Then conferred with an undergraduate counselor about re-enrolling to qualify for the BA degree at the end of the year.

A civilian a week to the day and as jittery as an expectant bridegroom, I swung on the Merchants Limited at Boston's South Station and was clickety-clacking off for New York, Grand Central Station, the Information Booth, the Big Clock. Wow! And Monk, who'd be wearing her short fur coat and a nervously expectant expression. We'd know each other instantly, of course.

We did, and the next day we were engaged to be married—sometime.

Doctor Garland's journal, Thursday, December 13, 1945:

> Joe has been home three weeks today and engaged for two weeks to Helen Bryan, the nicest and sweetest girl that one could possibly want to welcome into a family. She has been up from New York on two of the intervening weekends, and Joe is going down tomorrow. We hope she'll be back for a good part of the Christmas holiday. This brings happiness to us all.

Pa and Ma and me. Pa snapped Ma and me, then I snapped him, and Ma pasted Pa on her other side. (*Collection of the author*)

Joe (*left*) and Joe with his Old Model T (*right*) (*Collection of the author*)

I wouldn't be back at college for two months, the G.I. Bill gratefully paying for the balance of my education. The Nicest and Sweetest was in full swing at college, president of her class *and* the student body, undefeated tennis champion, the most vivacious and popular on the campus, and concentrating in international affairs, a field in which we both now had some perforce platonic experience. I was a couple of hundred miles away with no car, and with nothing to my name except the pittance I'd been knocking Uncle Sam down for since March 11, 1943.

A catch-as-catch-can romance it was, of continued separation, long train rides, borrowed cars, stolen moments in an era when even engaged couples didn't live, let alone sleep, together—all under the ceaselessly unobtrusive eyes of our elders who were rightfully suspicious that at any moment the hot blood of the pent-up young veteran might burst all proper bounds.

So we talked, we walked, we drove somewhere when we could borrow a family car, we romanced, we dined and danced at Cafe Society Downtown (or was it Uptown?) and were partied by her adored and adoring namesake role-model Aunt Helen Bryan in New York. We slipped into the Horseshoe Bar to hear jazz fiddler Joe Venuti and pals in an after-hours gig, and on New Year's Eve were partied by the neighbors back in Brookline.

But I was still ticking on a hair spring. Like Griff, back home in Denver, watching a movie on the Battle of the Bulge, when "all at once there was this scream of a shell coming in, and I just left my seat and hit the aisle. I felt real silly."

And Pullman, walking along a Manhattan sidewalk when "a load o' coal went down one of those sidewalk chutes, WHOOSH like a shell comin' in, and I picked myself up out of the gutter but didn't feel too bad because down the street about twenty-five yards another guy was doin' the same thing, and we looked at each other. He'd been there." And in Germany, readying to come home, Jerry Waldron had been ahead a few paces in a column on parade before the 103rd's General McAuliffe when a truck backfired. "I went down on one knee and looked back, and there were most of the guys, stretched out on the street."

Psycho, undiagnosed, ununderstood, untreated and unwelcome in polite civilian company.

In February of 1946 I was back in a Harvard classroom with a couple of degree credits for basic training in the Infantry, a laugh but I'd take anything. Monk and I tried to see each other on weekends but with a full load of my own, it was tougher than ever. She even sat in on one or two lectures with me. Jack Pullman (briefly in New York) and I swaggered nonchalantly into the Sarah Lawrence dining room with her during lunch hour one day and created a sensation—early "heroes" back from overseas.

Wheels I had to have. A patriotic used-car dealer in Brookline Village at the foot of the hill from our house sold me a 1923 Model T Ford sedan flivver for seventy-five bucks, and after a lesson in the astronomy of the planetary transmission, the ex–Army truck driver drove it home. The old tires were in tough shape, but a plaintive letter to the Firestone people from the new vet reactivated the molds. Soon my tin lizzie had new rubber to go with my black paint job, and Monk and I were chugging around Boston, lording it over the traffic, and off as far as the family cottage in Gloucester one fine day, the objects of many an astonished and sentimental glance.

Chaplain Bryan was mustered out of the European Army of Occupation as again the Reverend Bryan and in May moved with Helen's retiring and sometimes seemingly secretly amused mother with the softest Scots accent from Bronxville to Cambridge, where he was the new Protestant chaplain at Harvard and the Massachusetts Institute of Technology and preacher at the Harvard Divinity School. Tall and somewhat austerely Presbyterian, he was persuaded, I believe, mainly by his sister Helen and brother George, to bring Presbyterian surveillance to this matter of his younger daughter of twenty and the urgent ex-soldier three years her senior who had few if any prospects in the offing and neither the means of footing the remainder of her education bills nor of supporting the two of them should they fly off into wedlock at any moment.

In June I was still working toward an August degree when my fiancée of twenty finished her junior year and on short notice was posted off with a college friend for a cooling-off summer vacation in Texas and Mexico. I was stunned. As the end of my formal schooling approached I sought work as a newspaper reporter in Boston and elsewhere in New England, only to be dusted off with the postwar catch-22, "Come back when you've got some experience."

Farther afield I must look. My Harvard degree arrived in the mail. Mrs. East, the elderly widow of a Harvard professor, offered to pay my expenses to drive her west in her car to her winter home in La Jolla, California.

Monk returned from Mexico. Try as we might, destiny had us on different tracks. She was on the right and rational main line. A lifetime older in matters of life and death, I was emotionally stunted, and like an overgrown kid had to have it all, everything we'd put off, everything we'd been deprived of, everything we'd fought and died for, if not right now, tomorrow at the latest.

Urgency, for me as for so many of us, had become a way of life and urgently remains so.

It was a breakup so awful that it's taken its place with the worst of Anzio back in the surrounded caves of my mind. I was beside myself with frustration and rage at everything that came between us, which was what had brought us together, the war, the war, still the war. I demanded back her engagement ring. I angrily returned the enchanting green wool sweater she'd knit for me. I demanded back all my letters to her since that casually hopeful note from my Anzio hole more than two years earlier, all the pourings-out of myself. I gathered all the letters of growing knowledge and support and love the dear girl had written me those seventeen months, and I burned the lot in an unrehabilitated fury.

That's why there has been almost nothing herein of what passed between us in our long-distance wartime love affair. What had Pa jotted in his diary when I was seventeen? *Gaining definitely in poise and control although he still has his outbursts.*

The Nicest and Sweetest Girl that one could possibly welcome into a family was of course aghast. I drove Mrs. East west. Monk was sure I'd look back. After knocking on newspaper city room doors from Denver to L.A. to San Francisco, Portland and Seattle, I landed as a beginning reporter with the *Minneapolis Tribune* starting that December.

While pausing in Minnesota, I fell for a very attractive and interesting daughter of the wealthy neighbors of my father's college roommate in Winona, Rebecca Choate, a Vassar graduate in chemistry working in a laboratory at the Mayo Clinic in Rochester. Once back home, I sold my Model T for next to nothing, bought a 1930 Model A business coupe for around 150 bucks from my Uncle Phil Lewis and drove west for my first postwar job.

Four months later ("Will he ever grow up?" Pa asked his journal) Becky and I were married. As he'd cautioned after that explosion over a *signorina* from Naples, "Miss Bryan is a happy extrovert who will probably continue to find the world at large stimulating and interesting, regardless of where she places her affections."

We met once again in 1948. I was by then on the staff of the Associated Press in Boston. Helen was with the National Student Association arranging transport for young Americans to travel, study and work in Europe as part of the rebuilding of international connections severed by the war. She dropped by for an hour, as sublime an extrovert as ever.

Thirty years passed. The middle-aged Ironhead had evolved from newspaperman to free-lance writer. It was early in the summer of 1978. Becky and I had bought, rehabbed and occupied a large, airy former vacation house on the Eastern Point shore of Gloucester Harbor with our two daughters. She was now a research scientist in biochemistry at the Massachusetts General Hospital in Boston. Our tracks had predictably diverged (shades of the fourteen in organic chem that changed my life). Peggy, our elder, was married, a nurse-midwife with the first of her three children; Susan was heading for social work. I had written a number of nonfiction books based in the lore of America's oldest fishing port, home to generations on my father's side, to which I had come home. Now fifty-five and looking to my own experience for inspiration, I picked up on the idea, first expressed back in Naples before boarding *Sea Scamp*, of making a book of the journals Jerry Waldron had guarded, never once opened and brought home to me.

Perusing my scribblings, so many of them hurried and sketchy, and studying my bulky exchange of letters with my parents, I knew I must find all the surviving Ironheads I could and get their stories as the mortar for the bricks of my own. Or so I thought. Dowdall, Zapiecki and Waldron were all I'd been in touch with since the war; Jimmy and Andy had maintained a few contacts and had some ancient names and addresses.

While preparing to get under way with tape recorder, camera and a nip of tongue-loosener I remembered a surprise phone call a few months back from Helen, then living in Hastings-on-Hudson, New York, above the great river just north of Manhattan, with her second husband and her four grown children by her first, from whom she'd been divorced for fourteen years. Her older sister Janet had learned through their aunt (as fate would have it, a summer neighbor in Gloucester) that I was a writer. Helen had a well-known yacht builder friend with a well-known ego who wanted me to do a book about him. I demurred.

Some months later the phone had rung again. Her eldest daughter had just broken up with her Grand Passion, and Helen had told her of her own Lochinvar riding off into the west with Mrs. East seven years before the young lady was born.

So I wrote inquiring if after my tour of the Ironheads I might drop by Hastings and interview *her*? Under the circumstances a bit much perhaps, but she replied that she'd be in

Europe with her husband, a passenger steamship line executive, and back home in time, and come on by.

Ranging from Connecticut to Colorado, my circuit was explosively productive. Nearly all the old soldiers had suppressed what they didn't want to relive ... but there was something about my project, perhaps the way it echoed the comradeship in the face of common danger as I touched base with one after another like some sort of messenger from the past. Dams of memory and emotion overflowed. No longer my book, it was ours.

On the fifth of July, 1978, after interviewing Bill Caird in Connecticut, I drove on to Hastings-on-Hudson, where my former fiancée greeted me warmly in her large, airy, historic home overlooking the river and the Jersey Palisades. She had the day all planned.

First a drive up the Hudson and across the Bear Mountain Bridge to West Point for animated catching-up over lunch at the Thayer Hotel—her two marriages, her grown Carlson children, her sixteen years as close friend and associate of anthropologist Margaret Mead in the early stages of the international environmental movement, her work in the field as a nongovernmental observer at the United Nations; and mine as journalist, writer, newspaper union organizer, and so on and so forth as Waldron liked to say.

Then to the West Point museum for an evocative look at the World War II exhibit, and back to Hastings to prepare dinner for daughters Anna, Janet and Alison and son Rob Carlson, all in their twenties, all friendly and delightful, and her cordial second husband, John Reurs, a Dutchman raised and educated in the States but hidden in Rotterdam during the war.

She recalled no specifics of our correspondence, only her growing anxiety for my safety on the front. Next morning I took my leave for Gloucester. Somewhere on the interstate in Rhode Island I pulled into a rest area, turned off the ignition and wept.

We tried to preserve our marriages, but it was not to be. Our separate bonds had long been slackening. Our own, broken so abruptly and apparently irrevocably so long ago, were mysteriously reknitting day by day. By October Becky and I were separated, then Helen and John, and our divorces followed.

Another year had gone by when Monk and I were hosts at Gloucester to the first reunion of the Intelligence and Reconnaissance Platoon of the 157th Infantry Regiment, 45th Division, from the second through the fifth of July, 1979. Jimmy Dowdall, Delmar and Sophie Griffith, Frank and Chris Merchant, Hank and Jean Mills, Dave and Katie O'Keefe, Jack and Wilma Pullman, Jerry and Joan Waldron, and Andy and Julie (his Italian war bride) Zapiecki. From the Colorado National Guard Griff had borrowed the big regimental flag. We raised it on our flagpole, *Eager* (on our own terms now) *for Duty* (temporary) once again.

Then we all had a sail around the harbor in my old sloop, and when nobody was looking, not even the skipper, ran into a steel navigation buoy about the size and shape of a small missile rising out of the depths. No damage of course, for we were the Ironheads.

Then Monk fixed a banquet, and we told oft-told tales, and raised tearful toasts.

In December Helen *née* Bryan and I appeared before the town clerk of Redding in Connecticut and signed our license to be married in January in the country home of her old

On the beach at Naples (Florida!) Christmas 1978
(*Collection of the author*)

Joe and Helen Garland, with a smile and a wink from
Ma and Pa *in absentia* (*Collection of the author*)

friend Martha Pate. The invitations were out, the flowers and the lobster and champagne
ordered—and, with about a week to go, I came down with cold feet.

In any but a soap-opera script this would have been the second and final breakup of a
wildly improbable romance—but Helen and I worked back to the line of scrimmage, as I
enjoyed putting it rather too archly.

So on the twenty-ninth of October, 1981, thirty-six years after we were engaged, Monk
and I were married at three in the afternoon by Freddy Kyrouz, the Gloucester city clerk, on
our front porch overlooking Gloucester's great harbor. She was fifty-six, and I was fifty-
nine, neither of us exactly in the first blush. My beloved Uncle Phil Lewis, now eighty-
seven, stood up with us. No other family, no guests, just us.

Almost two years earlier Frank Merchant had penned

FOR JOE AND HELEN

Would you think there was war at the heart of love
and that conflicts graved, as they formed, this frozen diamond?
Some tender emotion falls, pressed in old books like flowers
but I claim pangs, from years-old flying splinters. The clear glass
    I picked from skin I've saved today while the pollen's vanished.
    Again think the bullet's no drowsy buzz
    in a grove where I wandered.
Light made us aware, beyond a hill, before a dawn
that bombardments were our day, in whatever terror.

Think of folly—a private mistaken as bleeding from mulberry juice
and caught in the tree he plundered—
and how old rules are gone
and how keen feelings should rise, in every night's great lightning
no matter how much a rifleman has sworn,
    "I need never fear again." But he could love if he lived.
Will time admit
this lasting jewel encloses a woman and a man
and there's surrender to memory
long after the victory celebration, parades and burials?
Be reassured
if you have gotten through a war
with hurt or murky fright
that on some day
you may possess yourselves.

(Epithalamion)

May this day, a diamond discovered
glint from the old war and terror.

Wear it on your hand, her brow
as you stand in new time
facing down both suns past and vacant nights.
And you have outlived even escape, even the armies' triumph
to see your own land. May you long retain it.
                    xox
           11-8-79 Frank Merchant

We *have* faced down both suns past and vacant nights, we thank our lucky stars, we Libras. Eighty-five I am now, herself eighty-two six days later. And we've outlived even escape.

Oh yes, about the sweater Monk knit for me that I hurled back at her so long ago. She raveled it and shoved the crinkly green yarn in a bag and stashed it away somewhere out of sight and mind. Forty years passed, and something happened in her life that reminded her of it. She dug it out, washed and straightened the yarn, and reknit it with a Thunderbird on the right shoulder.

And here's something else Monk just dug out and knit again for both of us and all of us from her bottomless bag of memories, a dream going back sixty years to the early spring of 1945, as the worn-out Thunderbirds trudged that final road from Nuremburg to Munich.

While at Sarah Lawrence taking two courses in international affairs that naturally involved the war, I had a dream so vivid that it has never left my mind, though some of the details have.

I was inexplicably in Germany in the tree-shaded old suburban part of a city, hiding among deep and vibrant blue hydrangea bushes that lined the path to a house and surrounded the foundations. Somehow I "knew" that very blue hydrangeas were typical of Germany, though I'd never been there and don't recall being told that they are.

The hydrangeas allowed me to approach an open porch door where awnings and curtains and other off-season equipment were stored in a closet. I was a little embarrassed about trying not to lose my gold compact with powder and powder puff because I should have been more focused on my real purpose, which was eventually to enter a huge stadium on the outskirts of the neighborhood, where Hitler held rallies, and I had to take great care to conceal the big gun I was supposed to fire when I got there.

The frustrations were that I might be found in my hiding place and that I didn't really know how to handle such a gun very well, although I had been taught to fire .22s and BB guns as a twelve-year-old in Salem, New Jersey! And then I continually had to powder my nose, silly girl!

It may be that you wrote about the two of your guys touring the empty stadium at Nuremburg and getting shot at. [I couldn't have; didn't hear about it until years later, from Jerry Waldron.] But when I managed to get to the stadium, it was empty, and my dream ended.

Obviously I was dealing with the stark contrast in male/female roles for people my age in the war. I was living almost a normal college life and doing frivolous things like painting fingernails and thinking about cosmetics and going to New York City on dates, even though they were all in uniform. While my courses would have taught me about the military situation, it would have been your letters that gave me the most direct contact.

Twenty-nine years ago in 1979, on the final day of that I&R observation post on the shore of Gloucester Harbor, our Bard so distant and so near and dear, expressed it for all of us Unknowns when he wrote

AT JOE'S REUNION
    Frank Merchant 11063257

The sea inside and out of the house:
watch by watch the clock-bells
lift and drop us, so we seem to float
past ordinary time.
The pictures have sails outspread;
the rocks were painted still

waiting for storm, loaded with gulls;
models in a case lie on a painted sea
where an unknown mariner is becalmed—
he may see us, while we are not keen enough to peer down
                              into his adventure, or his world.
We have stirred up the past in waves,
a rumble of talk, no saying goodbye
no regrets for healed wounds, the strain of youth.
Unheeded fireworks went up during battle stories
while we stopped a day, stretching history
with a look over death
paving elegy for others.
Gentlemen, you've come back holding your papers
but may as well turn them in
since you need them not, while the historian
establishes your anecdotal roles:
    Know from them
    there will be no discharge.
        I&R Platoon, 157 Inf., 45 Div.
        1st and 35th year Bivouac Reunion
        Gloucester, Mass. July 5, 1979

In Memoriam

During the course of the war, four men in our Platoon were fatally wounded, all of them in France. Two were lost in the ambush at Varages, along with a French *maquisard* then unknown to us. Another would survive the war but ultimately succumb to the hit he took at Rambervillers. It was nearby that the last of the Ironheads to give his life for liberty was killed by a German shell.

Norby Boone and George Ruder

Alerted by a newspaper report of the 157th Infantry Association's coming observance of the fortieth anniversary of the landing in Southern France, our adopted Free French fighter Henry Siaud, living in nearby Marseille, turned up out of curiosity at the Draguignan Military Cemetery in August 1984. There he met Jerry Waldron, one of the veteran Ironheads who'd flown across for the occasion, who told him of the book I was working on. We corresponded, and the following summer he and his wife Roselyne, and his pal André and wife Florence Joannon, flew to the States, visited Helen and me and took in the Association's annual reunion in Denver. Here, with Roger Humann, another Frenchman who'd volunteered to fight with the Regiment, Hank and Andy were awarded the Colorado Meritorious Service Medal on behalf of the Governor. Helen and I reciprocated the visit in 1991 and 1994.

After forty-seven years I remained haunted by the mystery that shrouded the heroically futile deaths of Danny Boone and George Ruder. The main purpose of my return to France in 1991 was to follow the campaign trail from Ste.-Maxime with Hank Siaud as guide and interpreter, and to identify positively, if we could, which town on the road to the Durance

André Joannon and Henry Siaud, who
joined the Yanks fifty years before to
drive the *Boches* from their homeland
(*Author photo*)

River was the scene of the ambush. I'd forgotten the name and was struck by Dom Trubia's
clear memory of the approach to the German roadblock and the machine gun concealed in
a cemetery on the left of the road.

Arriving in Tavernes that April, there it all was, the shaded town square, the monument
to the dead of other wars, the church tucked in behind, the stucco house fronts, the tile
roofs and the cafe where the two underground Resistants had burst in. And there in the
square we bumped into Germain Sauvaire, who remembered that in the next town of
Varages on that day the *Boches* were preparing to shoot several hostages (the number had
escalated in the telling to as many as forty over the years) for the killing by the FFI of one
of their soldiers.

We drove on in gloomy anticipation until beyond a bend in the road we came to the
sign "Varages," then over a rise the first houses, and on the left, a walled cemetery.

The wall seemed too long; it would have blocked a machine gunner's field of fire to the
road. A closer look revealed that in the intervening years a new, lower section had been
added to the old cemetery in the direction from which our patrol came, and the wall had
been extended; from an open grave at the road level in the original graveyard a gun would
have swept the approach to the town after all.

Out of the cemetery with its ornate remembrances and simple tributes, out of a freshly
dug grave awaiting the legitimate occupant, had rattled the fire of death.

Earlier that day we had paused at the overwhelmingly moving American Military
Cemetery in Draguignan, just off what the French people honored as our "Rue de
Débarquement" and only a few miles inland from the beach.

For one who had absorbed the attrition of casualties by ones and twos and tens and
twenties and forties for months, who had just identified the bloody spot in the road where
the first of my platoonmates were slaughtered, the sight of thousands of white crosses held
aloft by the souls buried beneath the green, green grass in the precise files and rows of an

army on parade was beyond the comprehension of the moment. Here and there amongst this multitude of comrades, dead in a common cause, lay many a Thunderbird, including not a few of the 157th, the "Eagerness for Duty" attributed to them finally assuaged.

We searched in vain for the crosses of Norby Boone and George Ruder, nor could their names be found in the office registry of all those buried here.

Then the superintendent explained. There were no records in France, not in any of the military cemeteries, nowhere at all, of the Americans who died for the nation's liberation, no crosses, nothing if their remains had been returned to the United States at the request of their next of kin, as perhaps half of them had.

No wonder that when I'd found and seen what memory shrank from I hurried on past. Varages was my first re-encounter with all that killing and death after fifty years, and I, though miles back that day, a part of it. Could I have prevented it? Of course not, and yet...

Three years later, in 1994, Monk and I planned a return trip, this time to "navigate" a chartered houseboat through the Canal du Midi with the Siauds in September, a few weeks after the fiftieth anniversary of the Champagne Campaign. I asked Hank to inquire of the mayor of Varages if the town would permit the surviving buddies of the two Thunderbirds who had died in the German ambush that day to have a modest memorial plaque placed in the outside wall of the cemetery at our expense. I knew nothing then of Jean Borgogno.

But Mayor Jean-Pierre Goudal would have none of it. Instead, he rallied the Municipal Council and commissioned at his town's expense a *stèle commémorative*, a strikingly sparse slab monument and pedestal of cast concrete, eight feet high, created by Jacky DuBois, a local artisan. Upon this was affixed a large, colored ceramic plaque (Varages formerly had an illustrious ceramic tile or faience industry for four centuries). Executed by Yvon Caturani of the town, it depicted the crossed Tricolor and Old Glory above our regimental and

The monument marks the stretch of road where our patrol ran into enemy machine-gun fire.
(*Collection of the author*)

Hank, with Andy standing by, reads the account of the action of August 18, 1944. (*Courtesy of Henry F. Siaud*)

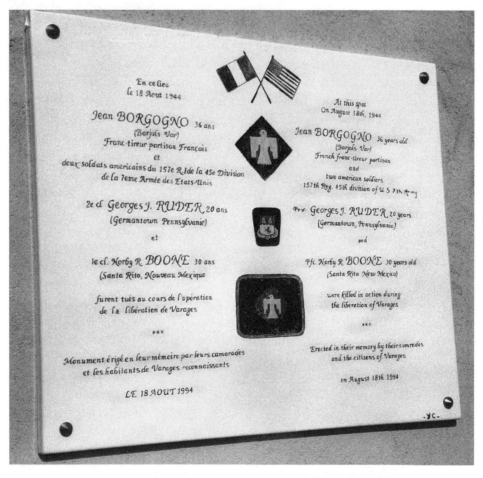

In Memoriam (*Collection of the author*)

divisional insignias, and to the left in French and the right in English the names of Jean Borgogno, "French franc-tireur partisan," followed by "two American soldiers, 157th Reg. 45th division of U.S. 7th Army," George Ruder and Norby Boone, and their ages and home-towns, all "killed in action during the liberation of Varages." "Erected in their memory by their comrades and the citizens of Varages on August 18th 1994."

Here was a sad surprise, a Maquis, Jean Borgogno, killed in the cemetery ambush, a comrade of whom none of the I&R on the patrol was aware. What a crossroads of time, memory, irony and ambiguity.

The memorial monument was placed on a specially prepared patch of park with a bench across the road from the cemetery and dedicated on Sunday, the twenty-first of August, 1994, as part of *Les Cérémonies du 50ème Anniversaire de la Libération de Varages* follow-ing a tribute to all the dead of the Liberation at the war memorial in the town square. I pro-vided enlarged snapshots of Danny and George in the field, Borgogno's widow a portrait of him, that were displayed and presented to the town. Henry Siaud donated a memorial wreath on behalf of the surviving Ironheads in America and read my translated account of the action that day. His old friend André ("Andy" to us) and the widow and grandsons of Borgogno were on hand.

Remarks were delivered by Mayor Goudal; Max Dauphin, the local representative of the French Resistance Veterans Association; and retired Colonel John Williams, veteran of the 82nd Airborne Division living on the Riviera and representing the American Legion of Provence. The French Navy sent Admiral Lancastre and a color guard.

The ceremonies were followed by a collation, then fireworks (*Grand Feu d'Artifice—Spécial Cinquantenaire du Débarquement—Tiré par PYRAGRIC*) and closed with a grand ball.

A month later we motored with the Siauds and Andy to Varages and inspected the memorial with Mayor Goudal and other patriots responsible for such a moving tribute to these particular three, and to all the rest of them, known and unknown to *La France*, who gave their lives for her liberation from the *Boches*.

Mission accomplished.

Mickey Smith

Edith Smith and their nine-month-old Carol Ann were living with her family in Somerville, a suburb of Boston, when the telegram arrived from the War Department on the sixteenth of October, 1944, regretfully informing her that her husband, Sergeant Stewart Smith, had been wounded. Eighteen days it took. The next day, as luck would have it, came a V-mail from Mickey himself.

> Sorry I havent been able to write for quite some time, but I've had a little accident. I've been wounded again and unfortunately lost a couple of legs. I'm fine though, so dont worry at all. I'll probably be seeing you soon. It was quite painful at first but I hardly notice it any more. The boys are all swell and come to visit me as often as they can. I dont want you to feel badly, as I dont, and nothing is as bad as it seems. Excuse

the writing as I am laying down flat. I will write again as soon as I find time. I am moving from one hospital to another.

> Lots of love, Mickey
>
> PS/ I received the cake from Carol Ann

He broke the news to Edie's sister for her to soften the blow. At her home in Sarasota in 1978 Edie told me "the censor crossed out only where he wrote that he lost his legs, but only lightly, and I think he meant that if Mickey wanted me to know, I was to know. Mickey made up his mind in that first letter that he was going to live with it, and he always did. And he never was disabled, and I never thought of him as that."

Living so close by, Edie had already been in touch with my family, who had only received the wire about my humble tumble four days earlier. She phoned right off, and my father, writing me with relief, postscripted: "Very distressed about Smitty. Can I get any more word about him back for Mrs. S?" In the same mail he posted Lieutenant Colonel Langdon Parsons, a Boston surgeon who was executive officer of the 52nd Station Hospital in Naples and whose children were patients of his, on a search for Mickey in the hospitals there.

My mother wrote on October 28 that she was in frequent touch with Edie; could I confirm the loss of Mickey's legs?

What went around came around on October 30 when I wrote home: "Colonel Parsons was around yesterday and told me about Smitty which is the first I've heard of it. I hope to God it's not as bad as Mrs. Smith thinks. He is one of the greatest guys I've seen in the Army."

Colonel Parsons found him in the 45th General Hospital within a few hours, because the following day I wrote that "he came around this PM, and we went over to see Smitty. He's cheerful as ever and making out pretty well."

As I approached his bed it hit me to see how flat the sheets were where his lower limbs should have been. In a play on the sawed-off buddy Nye who'd saved his life Smitty grinned "They're callin' ME Shorty now!"

"Although he's lost an awful lot of blood," I continued to Ma, "he's regaining color and hasn't too much pain. Both legs were taken off just above the knee, having previously been blown off by a shell which landed between them. He has a wound in his buttock and in the shoulder, neither of them bad at all. This all sounds pretty grim, but you should see him. He's the kind of guy who can't be licked, and I expect he'll be climbing trees and jumping fences in a few months. Tell his wife what a peach of a husband she has and not to worry a bit. He'll be home shortly."

Mickey was shipped out of Naples on the third of November, arriving back in the States six days later and at the England General Hospital in Atlantic City on the eighteenth.

On December 6 he took pencil in hand and from a prone position wrote my parents an affectionate letter about their son along with a jocular appraisal of his own situation:

Stewart "Mickey" Smith
(*Courtesy of William E. Woodhams*)

Mickey, Edie and Carol Ann
(*Courtesy of Edith Smith*)

Received your very nice letter and thank you for the compliments although I don't deserve any of the nice things you said about me. Edith and I are very happy to be together again and I'm having a most enjoyable time with my daughter. I'm a pretty lucky fellow to still be alive and have such a family to come back to. Losing my legs has temporarily upset my apple cart but when I get going again I'll be just a streak of lightening. The Doctor declared war on me today because I was out of bed. They took my wheelchair away and he told all the nurses to see that I stayed in bed. You'd think I was crippled the way they treat me. Well I guess that's life.

They gave him Christmas off and operated again on December 28, three months after the blast on the hill. "Stitches taken out Jan 10," he entered in his notebook. Edith told me:

At England General he did most of his work with other paraplegics. One who had lost his hands said he'd be Mickey's legs, and Mickey was his hands. He inspired lots of men there. He'd decided he was going to live with what had happened to him. I never really noticed that he had a low point. When he'd go around in the wheelchair [with a blanket on his lap], little old ladies would come up to him and tell him to thank God he had his legs, there were so many others that didn't. I think he made up his mind in the hospital in Italy, maybe even in Southern France, that he was alive and he was going to make the best of it. The shrapnel in his back and rear healed and never bothered him.

He never did speak much about what went on in the war, and I didn't pursue it unless he wanted to talk about it.

One of the things he had to do to get out of the service [on February 21, 1946, after seventeen months of hospitalization and rehabilitation] was to wear his artificial legs home and wear them all the time. So he went from Atlantic City to Boston. At Philadelphia he had to go down one flight of stairs and up another to change trains, and he never ever said one word to me. When we got to Boston his stumps were raw. He called the next day, and they came in an ambulance and took him in and fixed them up.

So when he came back they had to operate again and take more bone off, and he had to heal all over again. He wore the artificial ones for dress only, really, and could walk with them very well, but the first thing he did when he came back from anywhere was take them off.

A newspaperman from Sylvania, Ohio, came down to the England General to see Mickey and wrote a story about the hometown hero, and the people raised a fund and built the Smiths one of those ranch homes for the returning veterans that proliferated across the American landscape after the war. Convenient for amputees. Basements rarely, so that everything was on one floor including kids, dogs, and the Dy-Dee can of soggy diapers reeking with ammonia on a hot day. One summer they painted the exterior, Mickey taking the lower berth, hiking around on his rear end, Edie the upper. He passed his driving test in the spring of 1947. *Driving?* Explained his proud wife:

He had a knob on the wheel, with hand levers on rods that came down to the accelerator and brake pedal, and automatic transmission. He never needed any help. He'd go out, put his wheelchair in the back seat, did the whole thing by himself. He helped me; I didn't help him. He hated to see me staying in the kitchen too long, and he'd come out and help me. He didn't want any help, and I didn't ever have to give him any help. He would do for me, not that I had to do anything for him.

Driving? Back in nearby Toledo with his Italian bride Julie, Andy Zapiecki was impressed by the ease with which he'd grab hold of the jamb over the door and swing himself into the driver's seat.

Andy remembered the night the Smiths were over visiting when Edie went into labor. "Mickey's going about fifty down a crowded avenue with lots of lights when the gas and brake pedals got stuck. He managed to turn off the ignition, fixed the problem and got her to the hospital in time." About half an hour later their first son Jimmy was born—May 19, 1947.

The next summer the Smith family drove east, Mickey at the wheel, to visit Edith's family in Somerville, and they stopped by for supper. The driver's door opens, and out my old sarge slides onto the street on his butt, with the same big grin and crinkly eyes. He shook hands with a grip of steel and then hiked himself up the walk on his rear, using his arms as crutches. Darnedest display of pure will I ever saw. He hated Uncle Sam's legs for sure.

Having already qualified as an Army radioman, Smitty took a correspondence course in radio and television repair and set up shop at home, then in various appliance stores. They vacationed in Sarasota in 1953, and Mickey fell for Florida. No more Great Lakes/Winter Line climes for him. They sold the Sylvania house the next year, bought a lot on the inland waterway of Sarasota, lived in a rental while their dream house was being built there, and occupied it in June of 1954 while Mickey began a new job in a cabinetmaking shop. And as Edie told me with a sigh, "the only bad thing about it was that at least he had to slow down in the winter in Sylvania, but he was going twelve months here, and it was too much for him."

But it was The Life at last! The laid-back west Florida style, the climate, the semitropical setting, the miles of beaches, the inland canal behind the barrier reefs and islands, the fish and wildlife, and the great Gulf beyond, all was a mecca for folks who had earned some rest and respite, and for paraplegics, of which there was an ample postwar surplus. Retired Ironhead Stewart Smith was an inspiration for the many friends he made among the other amputees fighting the stifling effects of pity. His wife:

You know, Mickey had a lot of rhythm in him. In Toledo he joined the Squarewheelers Club; they formed a circle and squaredanced in wheelchairs! Once down in Sarasota he jitterbugged with a girl on television, both in their wheelchairs! Another time a man came down from Sylvania and took him up in his biplane, and after two hours he was soloing it.

He kept a boat down at his dock at the foot of the yard on the canal, a wooden Lyman that he bought unpainted and finished up himself. That was his love, gettin' out fishin'! When he took another paraplegic friend they'd wheel down onto the dock. Mickey'd pull himself out of his wheelchair onto the bow, sit up there and lift his friend out of HIS wheelchair onto the bow and into the boat! And then they'd go off and fish in the bay or go on to the Gulf for the day.

In June of 1957 Smitty was parked on a hill when a driverless truck parked above him rolled down and hit his car and threw him over on the passenger side. The truck's brakes had let go. He thought somebody was in the truck and kept blowing the horn. He wasn't even bruised.

But often he'd wake up in the night and his legs, the nerves, would just seem to bang up and down. The medication for that was a shot of Canadian Club. He spoke many times of the phantom limb; he'd feel the foot he didn't have, itching. I don't think he ever got over that. And he had trouble with kidney stones, I think due to what happened to him, to his circulation, but never complained.

On February 21, 1958, Mickey had a heart attack, a coronary. I think he might have already had one because he complained of pains in his arms at work in the cabinet shop, where he drove in and back every day, a full day. The doctor told him to stay in bed (he didn't want to go to the hospital) and thought that as long as he behaved himself he'd be all right. But after a week he wanted to get up, which he did. He lived just one month.

Just fishin' (*Courtesy of Edith Smith*)

On March 22 he had a heart attack at one in the morning, another at about ten-thirty, and the one that took him at three o'clock. There wasn't much anybody could have done then.

Joe Garland:
What if you'd nursed him and he'd lived another five years?

Edie:
Well, that would have been another five years.

Joe:
But what about the quality of his life and the intensity with which he lived it by doing for himself?

Edie:
I've often thought of that too. I don't think he would have wanted to be helped. He always wanted to be self-sufficient and do for himself, and he did.

Joe:
For the first time, when he got the coronary, he saw the possibility of having to limit himself.

Edie:
Right, and then he just wasn't Mickey. He didn't want to have to stay in bed. He didn't want to be told he couldn't do this, that or the other thing when he thought he could. He'd hear somebody go down the canal in a boat, and he'd say "Wait for me! I wanta go fishin' too!" So I don't know whether he could have.

I thought that with so many new medical things Mickey would get through his coronary. I really wasn't worried. I thought it would heal and he'd be back to himself again. So that, really, when he got those three that day I couldn't believe it. I thought when he got the third attack he'd come out of it just like he came out of the other two.

He never, ever, acted disabled, and I never thought of him as being that. He could do anything that any other man could do, and he did it. When you think he jitterbugged on TV! How many men in wheelchairs could jitterbug on TV? He had a good philosophy of life, really.

When I got his letter that time the only thing that was frightening to me was thinking how terrible that operation must have been when they took his legs off. Not knowing, not being there. And then to think, oh I hope and pray nothing happens between getting back from there to here, and I just prayed every day that nothing would happen because I didn't care, really, as long as he came back. That was the only important thing to me.

Mickey was thirty-eight when his wounds overwhelmed him.

✧ ✧ ✧

Nine months after our Sergeant Stewart Smith died, his widow went to work as a temporary typist for the First Federal Savings and Loan of Sarasota, later the United First Federal, and over the years worked up to Teller, Head Teller, and Administrative Assistant to the Treasurer.

Carol Ann, born as we prepared to land at Anzio, was graduated from Florida State in Tallahassee and married Joseph Patrick Lynch. She went on to teach school in southern Georgia while her husband worked as a sales representative for Western Auto. They had a son, Michael Patrick.

On July 26, 1966, a friend of Edie's older boy Jim persuaded him to override for the first time his father's repeated orders to stay away from motorcycles, which Mickey regarded as deadly, and try his for just a quick spin down the street near the Smith house. Tentatively Jim climbed on, started up, and had gone a block or two when he was hit by a car and killed instantly. He was nineteen.

Doug, their younger boy—a tall, strapping fellow with a great beard who loved sailing and the sea and made his living by it—was drowned on April 14, 1986, in a fight outside a seaside bar a week after he and his wife Karen were divorced, but before the judge had signed the decree. He was thirty-four.

A couple of days before Thanksgiving three years later, Edith wrote me from the house above the dock on the canal: "Doug's two are growing up too fast. Rachel is five and Justin seven. We go to movies and plays together and they stay overnight with me on weekends. Their mother took them to the beach to throw flowers in the Gulf in memory of their father's thirty-eighth birthday in October. Rachel called me that night and told me."

In her 2003 Christmas card Edie wrote: "My lovely daughter Carol died of a heart attack just like Mickey on May 16. That's my whole family gone. Carol had taught school 35 years. We are having it very cold here. Will be so happy when it warms up. All the best for the New Year. Love, Edie"

Bob Coleman

In 1978 I located Veronica Coleman in Avoca, Pennsylvania, a few miles west of Scranton, and phoned her at the ladies' garment factory where she worked. We met at her trim house during her lunch hour. Warm, obviously strong, somewhat reserved. A photograph of her uniformed young husband of less than two years greeted me in her entryway, and there were others all about. She hadn't remarried.

Bob's widow told me that after he was buried in the U.S. Military Cemetery at Epinal she requested that his remains be brought back to the Cemetery at Gettysburg. He was reburied not far from where President Lincoln delivered the Address, which gave me a start—on my way to Avoca the previous day I had swung by the battlefield on the spur of the moment, walked up to the cemetery and paused by the Lincoln monument, where I must have been only a few paces from Bob's grave as if drawn there. Most of his belongings went somewhere out in the Midwest, she said.

> The War Department wrote me that they were blood-stained and asked if I wanted them, and I said no. Film was rationed, and the druggist would save me a roll every month, and I'd take pictures of our little girl Phyllis and send them. In the last one she was nine months old, standing at the gate. It came back with his blood on it. He'd carried it with him when he was hit.
>
> I've worked all my life, supported my daughter, made up for what the Army didn't give, which wasn't too much. We survived. To keep close to her I went to factory work where I could name my own hours, go to work after she went to school and be home when she came back, with days off when she was home. She went to Marywood College in Scranton, graduated in chemistry, married Robert Dodds and has two boys.
>
> Bob wrote me that all he wished was that when he came back nobody would ask him what he saw or what he went through.

Veronica was discouraged about the state of the union in 1978 and wondered if all the sacrifice of the war was worth it. Friends were telling her they didn't think they'd bother to vote; she scolded them that her man had died for the privilege. As her lunch hour drew to a close, she lamented "the life that never was" for her handsome, headstrong young husband killed by a German shell thirty-four years before, five weeks short of his twenty-first birthday.

But that life it was, and Bobby Coleman lived it to the limit.

We will not say good-bye
We will not even try.
Because we're just going first to join the fight.

And because he was buried back home in the United States at the request of his young widow, there is no record in France that a guy from Jersey not old enough to vote gave his life for its liberation.

Robert F. Coleman, 1944 (*left*) and Veronica Coleman, 1978 (*right*)
(*Courtesy of Veronica P. Coleman, and Author photo*)

"*You'll get over it, Joe. Oncet I wuz gonna write a book exposin'*
the army after th' war myself."

(*Copyright 1943 by Bill Mauldin. Courtesy of the Mauldin Estate.*)

Postscript

Intelligence & Reconnaissance from Afar

AROUND 2002 OUR AIR FORCE invented a seven-pound, plastic, remote-controlled model-size airplane called Desert Hawk. Launched by two guys with a bungee cord, it was equipped with engine, battery, radio, day-and-night cameras and minicomputer and could fly, precisely maneuvered at a remote distance from the ground, for more than sixty minutes at twenty-five to fifty miles an hour while transmitting images of what it saw. Since then, I imagine, satellite-based imaging has supplemented, if not actually replaced, Desert Hawk and like devices.

These developments have medievalized our old techniques for spotting targets and directing artillery fire and aerial bombing, infinitely more effective than we Ironheads in the dark of night on our bellies in the rain and mud with dirty binoculars and a field telephone that was barely working if the wire hadn't been blown up by an incoming 88.

Child's play alongside satellite-based global positioning of nuclear bombs on any target in the world. Along with our headlong toying with our earthly environment and our childlike fascination with war, we may as well toss in the towel sooner as later. Or can we do better? Yes, we can.

We better.

NOTES

For books cited in Notes, full publication information is contained in the Bibliography.

CHAPTER 1: COME BACK WITH THIS SHIELD, OR ON IT

1. Though faithful to his meaning, the "soft underbelly of Europe" is a popular misquote attributed to Winston Churchill and his fixation on attacking the southern coast of Nazi-controlled Europe. According to *Brewer's Famous Quotations: 5000 Quotations and the Stories Behind Them*, people seem to have merged two quotations from the PM, "exposure of the under-belly of the Axis" and "the soft belly of the crocodile," both referring to the Italy strategy (Rees, 139).

2. Garland, *The Youngest of the Family*, 171.

3. Ibid., 5.

4. I hadn't read Erich Maria Remarque's anti-war novel of the German trenches and had never heard of *Under Fire* or *Her Privates We*, the searing novels of the Poilus and Tommies of the First War by Henri Barbusse and Frederic Manning.

5. Even as we were being bent to the military, the Army was issuing its *New Infantry Drill Regulations* for officers, updated to April 15, 1943 with some surprisingly (in retrospect) sagacious "Guides to Leadership," such as:

> The environment and education of the average American soldier have laid great emphasis on his value as an individual; in order to get the most out of him, you must treat him as such ... Keep your men informed. Nothing irritates American soldiers so much as to be left in the dark regarding the reasons for things. There is much about Army life that is new to the majority of them—old customs and traditions and strange ways of procedure for which there are good and cogent reasons ... Sound psychology and long experience

indicate that the American soldier responds best to leadership which appeals to his pride in himself and his organization . . . Discipline cannot be founded on the fear of punishment alone—such discipline seeks to compel adjustment and only arouses opposition. True discipline is based on willing cooperation, which springs from knowledge, idealism and a sense of duty . . . Any red-blooded American soldier instinctively resents abuse, and it often drives him to acts of apparent insubordination when, as a matter of fact, he is actuated principally by a hatred for the NCO who, under the cloak of authority, has violated the American principles of fair play.

6. Curiosity drew me back to Spartanburg in January 1987 en route to Florida. There was scarcely a trace of the Camp Croft that shipped out 182,000 of us. South Carolina had bought 7,000 of its 19,000 acres for Croft State Park in 1949, mainly the range impact area; most of the rest went to private developers. Virtually all the Army buildings had been razed. I was bewildered. The warden directed us to a country road behind the park and through the scrub brush owned by a textile mill to a lonely blacktop that intersected those very abutments, as remote and overgrown as Mayan ruins. I climbed down through this jungle into the pits where the bullets had zinged overhead forty four years before. The target numbers were still there on the concrete.

Back home, I wrote Senators Strom Thurmond and Ernest Hollings (a staff officer with the 45th Division during the war) suggesting they push for designation of that portion of the old rifle range as a National Historic Site under the National Park Service, being as close as the nation could get to a bona fide monument on American soil to the dogfaces of World War II. Thurmond's staff forwarded some preliminary research. Hollings did not reply, and I heard no more.

7. Hitler, *Mein Kampf*, 616, 618.

8. Most of the mountain fighting in Italy was over, pursued by ordinary infantry units, when the 10th Mountain Division, which had been ski training in the States, saw its first action in the Apennines in January 1945.

9. In a rare effusion about such matters, an Army history conceded as much after the shooting was over. "There were some few Liberty ships that had already been partially converted for the purpose of bringing prisoners of war to this country . . . [which] were immediately available as transports . . . Troops were embarked on ships which had just been fumigated to rid them of the vermin left there by the prisoners of war" (Wheeler, *The Road to Victory*, 124–5, 127).

10. What we didn't know was that Ciano to the Germans was a hated name. Admiral Count Constanzo Ciano, whom the college memorialized, was a hero of our Italian allies in the 1914–18 war against the Kaiser. Count Galeazzo Ciano, his son married to Mussolini's daughter Edda, mistrusted Italy's Axis partner, opposed his father-in-law's deepening involvement with Hitler, and was one of a cabal of Fascist leaders that overthrew the Duce in July. In three more months Ciano would be tried in Verona and shot for treason.

11. Forty years later, now a pawnbroker in Houston, Furber dropped by to visit during a trip back to New England, Texas drawl and all, about eighty pounds heavier, with a case of vodka in his trunk for extra fuel. Not your typical Harvardian. He recalled:

You fellers got to realizing what the damn war was about, and what it involved, and why git yore ass in a worse sling. I said, "You chickens! You sonsabitches an' bastards! I'm goin'!" So I went. The major used negative psychology—"Yore gonna be killed if you join us" and all that—which would generally get 'em in, but it turned you and the others off. I dunno. It jest sounded good to be goin' in the Rangers. I looked at it this way: we're infantry, and we're gonna be dogshit and sit up on the line. You git into an outfit like the Rangers, they send you on a dirty job, and then yore gonna be pulled back off the line and be treated like kings. That was my philosophy.

So I went for a personal interview, and the major said, "Now lemme see if you understand what the situation is. You and I are alone up in the mountains. We capture fourteen prisoners. I turn around and tell you to shoot 'em. Whaddya do?" I said "I shoot 'em." He said, "You weren't brought up to do that." I said "I wasn't brought up to go to war." He said, "Lemme take another instance. You and yore best friend are out on the battlefield. His guts are ripped up. No way he can survive, but he wants to eat. The only food you got is for yourself. Whaddya do?" I said "I don't give him any." He said, "That isn't the Christian way to live." I said, "No, but I gotta live."

My mother didn't bring me up to go to war. I promised her I wouldn't go into the Paratroopers, but of course she woulda died if she'd known I was going into the Rangers when I went.

12. Dunleavy:

A grizzled old sergeant told us we were to become the pioneering demolition platoon of the Troop. Didn't take long to figure that the new boys were to go out in front of the whole damn Division and clear the land mines. Fortunately I never had to sweep or lay them. In case of retreat we were supposed to blow up the culverts and the bridges, and in advance to clear mines for the Troop and subsequently the infantry. A motorcyclist would come up with a piece of paper, and within twenty minutes we'd have some god-awful thing we were up against. That's all I ever knew. I don't know why it took me so long in life to realize that one should always ask questions, and I never did, and I never knew what we were supposed to be doing or where we fitted into the whole situation. Nathan Crystal, our champ boxer on the *Samuel Ashe,* and his buddy Steve Graber, were assigned to the Troop with me and were killed on a patrol soon after.

CHAPTER 2: YEAH, "EAGER FOR DUTY"

1. Zapiecki on his family:

There was two sides to our family, quiet and bigmouth. I took after my mother. She'd go to the butcher shop, and he useta turn his back, and she'd say, "OK, you pull back a way! I wanna see what yer cutting fer me! Lemme see what yer doing there! Lissen, I'm paying you money, right here, and I wanna know what yer giving me, and if I don't like it I'll throw it in yer face!" And the butcher after that never gave no trouble.

My father's idea of a peaceful day was lemme alone. He'd light up his cigar, and when it got too low he stuck a toothpick in it and held it that way, never bothered nobody, and the only friend he had was my uncle. Ma'd say to us, "I don't care how late you stay out, but when that church bell chimes at ten-thirty, you're gonna be in church."

The Old Man was at Standard Steel and Tube until 1926. Got up every day at four-thirty, my mother at five, just common labor all he ever did in his life. The factory was moving out. He didn't understand. Ma said, "You tell 'em you quit. You've worked long enough." So he retired and worked as a janitor for the church, shovel the coal, ring the bells for mass and extra for funerals, and us pitching in fer him. After five or six months Ma went to the priest and says, "Never mind. The boys are doing most of it, and he's getting too stoop-shouldered to work."

She'd saved all that money, ten dollars a week board. The house was all paid for. All these people on my block ever believed in was, "I wanna own my own house, sit on my porch and watch the world go by, and don't let nobody bother me." All the ethnic groups were strong for keeping to themselves. They'd parade up and down. Say the grass wasn't cut. The Old Man would come home and say, "Everybody got their grass cut and you didn't cut it? Get right out there and trim it up, and with little scissors." And if you ever took a shortcut across somebody's grass and got caught, man, you really got it.

2. "News from Old Friends," an editorial by Harold B. Johnson, July 16, 1943 in *The Watertown Daily Times*, Watertown, New York, 4.

3. Griffith:

I was a bit disillusioned with all the made jobs during the Depression and thought I would just take off for the West and start a new life. In Denver I ran across a guy that worked in the gold mines in Alma, east of Leadville, which had been brought back to life when Roosevelt raised the price to thirty-five bucks an ounce, and he gave me a letter to the superintendent.

They were hiring muckers, ore shovelers, but I didn't git on and went to work building high voltage line from Climax over in the Mosquito Range until the snow drove us out, and then they put me on all winter 'til the next spring.

A lot of Kansans, Okies and Arkies had been uprooted, blown out of the dust bowl, and had hit the road, and when the price of gold rose, they landed up around Alma, where with a shovel and a sluice box you could dig out beans at least, placer mining, washing gold out of the sand and gravel. We got a lease from the owners of the Como placer, right next to the Alma placer, me and my buddy Art Discoe and another feller. Everybody up there said, "Boy, you're in clover! You were lucky to land that lease!"

The long and the short of it was that they dug and timbered their shaft down fifty feet, struck a little gold at bedrock, then drifted sideways until they came up against the boundary of the adjoining lessor and had to quit. Next they got a lease for a hydraulic operation, and just as they were taking out twenty ounces a week at thirty-five dollars an ounce in the summer of '37 the owner canceled their lease, and Griff got a job as shift boss for an outfit reclaiming old ore dumps from the days when they shipped only the best by wagon to the smelter at Leadville.

4. Pyle, *Brave Men*, 62.

5. Bradley, *A Soldier's Story*, 118. Bradley and Blair, *A General's Life*, 174.

6. Blumenson, ed., *The Patton Papers, 1940–1945*, 269. Talk to 45th Division, June 27, 1943.

CHAPTER 3: OPERATION BARN DOOR

1. In another six years Admiral Kirk would be the United States Ambassador to the Soviet Union.

2. Brigadier General Felix Sparks, organizer and secretary of the 157th Infantry Association, was Colonel Ankcorn's adjutant, a lean young Arizonan of twenty-five drafted into the Regiment out of law school after making second lieutenant in the old Citizens Military Training Program in 1939. Writing his reminiscence of the Sicilian campaign for the *157th Infantry Association Newsletter* ("Forty-Five Years Ago—Sicily to Venafro [July–Dec., 1943]," Fourth Quarter 1988, 4) he added the following riveting postscript, which he wrote "has never before been reported but which has been etched in my memory for all of these many years":

> The convoy commander was a naval reserve officer who was usually addressed as "Commodore." As we approached our disembarkation station seven miles off the Sicilian coast, the convoy came under fire from Italian shore batteries. At the time, I was standing on the ship's deck with Colonel Ankcorn. I was the regimental adjutant, and the colonel used me to carry messages to the various parts of the ship. As we stood on the deck in darkness, we could tell that the ship had suddenly changed course and was heading back to sea. Without saying a word, the colonel made his way to the steel ladder leading to the bridge of the ship. I followed him.
>
> As we entered the bridge cabin, the colonel said to the commodore: "Commodore, why are we heading back out to sea?" To which the commodore replied: "We are coming under fire from the shore and I am taking the convoy out to a safer distance of eleven miles." Colonel Ankcorn then drew his pistol, placed it against the head of the commodore, and said: "Commodore, our scheduled station is seven miles offshore. Now you turn this convoy around and get back on proper station." The commodore made no reply to the colonel, but he issued orders for the convoy to turn around and get back to the seven-mile station. The colonel and I then returned to the deck of the ship. I never heard the incident mentioned again.

Not only had the regimental commander's armed confrontation with the convoy commodore that Sparks thus describes never been reported, the U-turn of Transdiv 5 back to sea had never been reported. These alleged events appear in neither the Army's, the 45th Division's nor the 157th Regiment's official histories of the Sicilian campaign, nor in the Navy's by Admiral Morison, and none record hostile shellfire from shore. When I asked Jack Pullman, who was in the wardroom of the *Charles Carroll* that day, about Sparks's account, he said he recalled no such maneuver; likewise, none of the other members of the I&R Platoon aboard that day that I was able to contact had any memory of the ship changing course.

At the behest of Captain Charles Todd Creekman, Jr., Deputy Director of the Naval Historical Center in Washington, a search of operational reports of the Sicily landing, including Captain Bailey's, was conducted by John C. Reilly, Jr., Head of the Center's Ships History Branch, who wrote me on March 6, 1998 that he could find no evidence of the maneuver or confrontation on the bridge, although "reports written after an action can 'fudge' matters for any number of reasons. Perhaps, at the time, no one was in any position to keep a running tally of what was happening, and matters had to be reconstructed afterward, with the help of fallible memory. Perhaps those concerned soon had other urgent business in hand, and simply needed to get their reporting out of the way as quickly as possible. And, I must admit, there is always the chance that reports may be so written as to make something—or someone—look better than was actually the case."

With that in mind, Reilly inspected the *Charles Carroll*'s deck log for the day of the landing and found no references to course changes. His conclusion: "A look at the extant operational reports of the Sicily landing does not appear to substantiate the account given by General Sparks."

3. Bradley and Blair, *A General's Life*, 171.

4. Admiral Sir Andrew Browne Cunningham, commanding the invasion's naval forces and observing from a destroyer, lauded the operation as an amazing feat of success (Eisenhower, *Crusade in Europe*, 204). Morison, in his *Sicily—Salerno—Anzio* (143), makes it plain that the Navy's handling of the 157th's approach and landing left much to be desired. The worst of it was that the code-breakers had learned that the Hermann Goering Division posed a threat, but in order to protect Ultra (the British deciphering effort), the American command had told the boys they faced only a few enemy technicians, "a cruel deception on our own forces," as General Bradley admitted years later (Bradley and Blair, *A General's Life*, 176).

5 Replacement Jeremy Waldron had the same reaction in Oran on his way to joining the I&R in Sicily when a captured company of the Afrika Korps came marching down the road in hobnail boots, singing *"Horst Wessel."*

6. *The Fighting Forty-Fifth* states without elaboration that Thunderbirds and paratroopers killed each other (Bishop, Glasgow and Fisher, 21–22). The *History of the 157th Infantry Regiment* doesn't mention casualties at all. In a singularly magnanimous post-mortem, the 82nd's General Matthew B. Ridgway said that responsibility for the lack of discipline and liaison was so hard to fix that he only hoped the lessons had been learned.

7. Bradley and Blair, *A General's Life*, 188.

8. Blumenson, ed., *The Patton Papers, 1940–1945*, 293. Diary, July 19 [1943].

9. Ibid., 289. Letter, GSP, Jr., to Beatrice, July 16, 1943.

10. Ibid., 295. Letter, GSP, Jr., to Beatrice, July 20, 1943.

11. Related by Jeremy Waldron.

12. Dramatically smaller and lighter than the .45-caliber American Thompson submachine gun, the 9-millimeter German machine pistol, named "Schmeisser" after its original designer and manufacturer, was equipped with a steel rod folding stock and a 32-round magazine. Fired in short bursts at the rate of 1,100 rounds a minute, usually at close range, this feared weapon was a "burp gun" to the guys on the receiving end.

13. Blumenson, ed., *The Patton Papers, 1940–1945*, 270. Diary, July 3 [1943].

14. Ibid., 307. Diary, July 30 [1943].

15. Ibid., 306. Letter, GSP, Jr., to Middleton, July 28, 1943.

16. Reynolds, *The Curtain Rises*, 211–212. Palermo, August, 1943.

17. Bradley and Blair, *A General's Life*, 221. The massacres were suppressed for decades until revealed by Bradley.

18. Blumenson, ed., *The Patton Papers, 1940–1945*, 432.

19. Bradley and Blair, *A General's Life*, 221.

20. Green, *Superior Orders in National and International Law*, 131–32.

21. Bradley and Blair, *A General's Life*, 220–21.

22. Ibid., 221.

23. Blumenson, ed., *The Patton Papers, 1940–1945*, 431. Letter, GSP, Jr., to Beatrice, March 24, 1944.

24. Ibid. Letter, GSP, Jr., to Beatrice, April 4, 1944.

25. Listening to his harangue of the Eighth Division in Northern Ireland in March 1944, Edward C. Williamson, an officer, "had the distinct feeling that Patton came close to advocating the killing of prisoners" (Blumenson, ed., *The Patton Papers, 1940–1945*, 430).

    Historian Eric Morris wrote that some believed that in Sicily the 45th "had taken the dictates of 'Blood and Guts' too much to heart. The Panzer Division Hermann Goering accused the Thunderbirds of shooting prisoners. This elite force of Panzers was regrouping just north of Naples and anxious to square accounts with the Americans" landing in the Salerno invasion (Morris, *Salerno: A Military Fiasco*, 19).

    The 45th Division History is silent on the whole dirty business, but observes of German prisoners taken in Sicily precisely as the suppressed massacres occurred: "They fought desperately to keep from being captured. They said that they had been told Americans castrate and kill all prisoners. Some prisoners of war even suggested that we drop leaflets over the German lines telling them about the humane treatment of prisoners" (Bishop, Glasgow and Fisher, *The Fighting Forty-Fifth*, 24).

    Perhaps it was not by oversight that Bradley made no mention in his memoirs of the German massacre of American prisoners at Malmédy during the Battle of the Bulge eighteen months later.

26. The Associated Press, "Capture of 'Bloody Ridge' Told by Boys Who 'Dood' It," July 30, 1943.

27. Mauldin published nineteen cartoons and two columns from the *45th Division News* in Palermo as the *Sicily Sketch Book*. The crudely printed pamphlet was distributed to the grim delight of the Seventh Army G.I.s and the near-apoplexy of General Patton, who suspected that the ragtag Willie and Joe were subversive of his brand of soldiering. He tried vainly through the rest of the war (even griping to Ike, who merely laughed) to have the immortal pair evicted from the Army newspaper *Stars and Stripes*, failing even in a personal confrontation with Sergeant Mauldin to get him to shave them.

28. Bradley and Blair, *A General's Life*, 199. Patton's order to Bradley to expend men to beat Montgomery to Messina is omitted from Martin Blumenson's account in *Patton: The Man Behind the Legend, 1885–1945*, 202, wherein he quotes his subject as merely telling his subordinates: "This is a horse race in which the prestige of the U.S. Army is at stake. We must take Messina before the British."

29. Pyle, *Brave Men*, 46.

30. Ibid., 49.

31. Ibid., 48.

32. Ibid., 51.

33. Blumenson, ed., *The Patton Papers, 1940–1945*, 315.

34. Garland, Albert, *Sicily and the Surrender of Italy*, 428.

35. Bradley and Blair, *A General's Life*, 198.

36. Morison, *Sicily—Salerno—Anzio*, 218–19.

37. Eisenhower, *Crusade in Europe*, 181.

38. Bishop, Glasgow and Fisher, *The Fighting Forty-Fifth*, 35. Close of General Patton's speech to 45th officers and men near Bagheria, Sicily, August, 1943.

UNKNOWN SOLDIERS

39. Forty-seven years later, at eighty-seven, Bob Hope was still at it, entertaining the troops sweating out the beginning of Operation Desert Storm against Iraq in the Saudi Arabian desert at Christmastime, 1990. He died at one hundred in 2003.

Chapter 4: Sure, General, You Bastard, Five Days to Naples

1. Bradley and Blair, *A General's Life*, 204.
2. "Amalfi" (written in 1875), stanza 7, lines 3–4. In Flight the Fourth of the Birds of Passage series. Longfellow, *Poetical Works*, 92.
3. Blumenson, ed., *The Patton Papers, 1940–1945*, 344. Diary, September 1 [1943].
4. Lewis, *Naples '44*, 16, 22.
5. Blumenson, ed., *The Patton Papers, 1940–1945*, 352. Letter, GSP, Jr., to Beatrice, September 13, 1943.
6. Matthews, *Education of a Correspondent*, 424.
7. Ibid.
8. Ibid., 423.
9. Bishop, Glasgow and Fisher, *The Fighting Forty-Fifth*, 50. Letter dated September 16, 1943.
10. Levi, *Christ Stopped at Eboli*, 4.
11. Smith et al., *History of the 157th Infantry Regiment*, 181.
12. Matthews, *Education of a Correspondent*, 424.
13. Somewhere in this mess, as a lieutenant with one of the divisions, a Harvard classmate was killed, Julian B. Clark, Jr., one of thirty who died in the war. He was a year and a half older, left Cambridge for the Army in July 1942, was commissioned in chemical warfare and was sent overseas in April. I remember him from his photograph in our yearbook. Nice-looking guy from Ridgeland, South Carolina. "In spite of his quiet temperament," somebody wrote of him in our first class report four years later (or maybe because of it), "Julian succeeded in winning many friends who will remember him especially for his kindliness and engaging humor." Three weeks in combat, and zap.

Chapter 5: The Underbelly

1. Blumenson, *Salerno to Cassino*, 312.
2. Bishop, Glasgow and Fisher, *The Fighting Forty-Fifth*, 61–62.
3. Smith et al., *History of the 157th Infantry Regiment*, 49.
4. "You should have tried smoking those Raleighs ten years later," remarked my younger friend, ex-Captain Thomas Halsted, after reading the manuscript of this book. "We were still getting vintage 1944 K rations in 1955."
5. Diary of Major General John P. Lucas, November 14, 15, 16, 1943. As excerpted in Blumenson, *Salerno to Cassino*, 249.
6. Blumenson, *Mark Clark: The Last of the Great World War II Commanders*, 146. One wonders what induced a distinguished military historian to write such a strange biography of such a vain mediocrity. Blumenson offers little to substantiate his title and plenty of the scorn with which Clark was regarded by the British, the press, colleagues such as Patton, and us dirty dogfaces in the dregs of *his* war. After the war Clark was in the headlines as an extreme right-wing racist supporter of Senator Joe McCarthy.
7. On the left of the First Rangers was the Fourth Ranger Battalion for which the recruiter who came looking for suckers after we set up in the Racetrack had enticed and goaded George Furber and

Leon Domaszewicz. Years later, I asked Furber how many Germans he thought he got in combat. His capsule account made my blood run cold.

> The first one I ever knew I killed was when I was first scout and leadin' the Battalion goin' up in the mountains above the Volturno. This happy-go-lucky German with his rifle on his shoulder was comin' down, all by himself, musta thought he was walkin' back down to headquarters. He saw me and was goin' for his gun. And that's when I learned how to shoot a Thompson submachine gun, 'cause I always used to carry it like this, with my fingers right up to the trigger. We jest came around a lil bend in the path. He was about ten feet away, and I jest fired. Well, my gun walked right up [if you didn't bear down on a Tommy gun, the recoil drove the butt down and the muzzle up, and it climbed], and his face jest disintegrated.

"What the hell kind of a sensation was that for you?" I asked. "Did it shake you up?"

> You know, it didn't bother me a bit. I've never had any qualms about it. I'd got him. He didn't git me. The only thing that worried me was my firing, if I'd alerted any Germans up ahead, so I was extra careful after that. Generally they'd let the first scout by. If I missed something and he spotted it, my second scout would give me a catcall, and then I knew, shit, I was in trouble.

"How about prisoners? Did you take prisoners?"

> Not unless they wanted 'em. Up in the mountains—I'm sure you had the same thing happen—we'd git a bunch o' prisoners, always send a BAR gunner with a coupla men to take 'em back, an' you know, they'd git fifty or a hundred yards away an'—RRRRRRR—come back. "They tried to git away an' we had to shoot 'em." An' you knew damn well they didn't, but who the hell wanted to go down the mountain an' back up again. So they took 'em a nice distance so they didn't smell up the camp.

8. At the end of the war, when Pullman was up in the Po Valley in charge of captured German horses eventually given the farmers so they could plow and plant, he ran into a German artillery captain who remembered very well the Americans above Viticuso, looking down their throats and shelling them every time they moved, and who thought he might have laid in the round that got Jack and Jose.
9. Morison, *Sicily—Salerno—Anzio*, 319.
10. Eisenhower, *Crusade in Europe*, 204.
11. Dunleavy, interview, 1982, and his "Hitler Count Your Children: Personal History."
12. When I rediscovered Mohawk in 1982 at the regimental reunion in Denver, where he was living, he was sixty-eight and the courtly and portly self-ordained Dr. Valen J. Mullenax (AD, Rev'd, MscD). Pullman and I spent an afternoon with him, and Jack wrote me in December:

> I have of course now recovered from the afternoon session on Tejon Street ... Mullenax is a real victim of the all too human propensity to tidy up the story, sanitize the

"Battlefield," play the might-have-been game. With details of course, and who is to say 2000 years later that it was or wasn't ten thousand people who were fed with eleven loaves and seven fishes.

What is the basis of Mullenax's legends? Is it the Angel Gabriel, the spirits that talked to Christ in the wilderness, Buddha on his mountaintop, Mohammed in the desert? Or, was it the gods who came down to design the Pyramids, build Andean space stations, cause countless likenesses of themselves to be sculptured on a small island in the mid-Pacific? Add all the little bits and pieces, personalize the myths with names, and you have a program tailormade for a Striver like Valen J.

I strongly suspect that if you dig back deep enough in his gene line you'll find a first or second-generation American circuit preacher. Perhaps we'll hear of him yet, leading a group to the Top of a Mountain, in California no doubt, hopefully awaiting the Second Coming.

And yet, yes yet, the very prophets that Mullenax believes in may have interfered . . . I would have liked to have discussed a few of these things with the Mohawk, but heavens, he might have converted me.

13. Blumenson, ed., *The Patton Papers, 1940–1945*, 369. Letter, GSP, Jr., to Beatrice, November 7, 1943.
14. A few ridges away, Gareth Dunleavy didn't have to go on patrol in the snow and mud with the 45th Cavalry Recon on New Year's Day because an unspoken truce prevailed.

So we stayed holed up in two or three houses in this rotten, stinking little medieval village, where I was told to take Tom Craig, an artist with the Army, on a tour of the damage.

I took him up to a house that had been blown out by our shellfire. He had a camera with him. I looked in and said, "Here's something you might like to see." An armor-piercing shell or something horrible had come right through the door. It was a German squad of six or seven men. The leader had sat down and probably propped himself up against the side of the fireplace, and his head was off, in his lap. The men were lying around, dead and terribly chopped up.

Craig took one look and turned around and disappeared as if the mountains had swallowed him up. I never saw him again and was all alone walking back down.

The Moroccans had tried that same Hill 895 all over again . . . en avant, au secours . . . and we're sitting there chewing on our New Year's turkey brought up in the vacuum containers when there's this clip clop, clip clop, clip clop, and Christ, this long mule train is coming down slung with body sacks, and every single one's got a goum, and then they stack 'em like cordwood within a few feet of where we're tryin' to eat. Must have been thirty bodies.

These Arabs and French noncoms and officers had a very different attitude toward life. We were much more protective and defensive and careful. We learned very quickly that there wasn't any point in marching up the side of a hill like a goddam fool working his way through an infiltration course back in the States. This was absurd. We'd go out on these patrols in the late afternoon day after day and come back—and there'd be two or three guys gone—in order to find out how things were and line things up so the Moroccans could go up the next morning and get themselves slaughtered again.

Chapter 6: Whale On the Beach

1. Thirty-five years later, while visiting Vernon Dilks at his home in Sarasota, Florida, I recalled the accident of his old buddy Mills. "Yeah, he got mad as hell at me, but I couldn't stop laffin', he looked like such a idiot [uncontrollable laughter]. The guy kicked the boilin' water [laughter], and it went all over him [laughter], and he got up an' took his pants off [laughter], an' danced around like a stupid drunken idiot [laughter]. Helluva thing to laff at [laughter]. I just couldn't stop [laughter], an' he got so mad at me for laffin' [uncontrollable laughter]."

2. Incident recalled by Andy Zapiecki.

3. Diary of Major General John P. Lucas, January 9, 1944. As excerpted in Blumenson, "General Lucas at Anzio," in *Command Decisions*, 333.

4. Diary of Major General John P. Lucas, January 10, 1944. As excerpted in Blumenson, *Salerno to Cassino*, 355.

5. Blumenson, ed., *The Patton Papers, 1940–1945*, 400. Diary, January 20 [1944].

6. Morison, *Sicily—Salerno—Anzio*, 346.

7. Colgan, *World War II Fighter-Bomber Pilot*, 65.

8. Ibid.

9. Ibid., 67–68.

10. Morison, *Sicily—Salerno—Anzio*, 346.

11. George Furber:

> They let our Third Battalion go into Cisterna, and then as we came up they had us almost surrounded by machine guns. But we jes' laid down for the rest of the night so we could see in the daytime what was goin' on.
>
> When daytime come, Colonel Murray was right beside me, and we were talkin' on the radio with Third Battalion. They were completely surrounded, and the Germans were advancing on 'em. So Colonel Murray said we'll spread out and make an attack in a big sweep. The minute we started they pinned us down. So smarty me, I told him we oughta have a bayonet attack. Good idea!
>
> I was firin' my M1 with the bayonet on, and they hit it first, knocked the butt against my cheek, and then as my arm was up in the air the bullet went in around the bone and came out and knocked my knuckle off and picked me up a hundred an' eighty degrees and threw me directly back. Leon Domaszewicz got hit in the thigh and couldn't walk and tole me that Red Gillig [another of my fellow Croft trainees] just a short way from us got it right between the eyes. A bunch got it on that sweep. The Germans were only two or three hundred yards away.
>
> After the medic got through with me I went into the irrigation ditch off the Mussolini Canal, maybe two or three feet deep, where we could pull the boys in, and laid out there and helped with the wounded and those I could do anything with, givin' 'em morphine and a drink o' water. When it got dark the wounded who could walk went back to Ranger headquarters. That's the only time I saw Colonel Darby actually crying. Major Miller was killed, and he knew it was a wipeout. The Third Battalion was gone, and here the Fourth's gone, and the First's about all that's left.
>
> Back in the hospital in Naples I was operated on and in a half-cast until March, and when they took it off it was real gooey and started to stink. The orderly had to leave, and the nurse wanted to, and the doctor too. It hadn't smelled, but it would itch and I'd scratch

the bottom with a coat hanger. But I had this tremendous scar and asked the doc, "What the hell is this? When I came in I didn't have but two lil holes." He said, "If it had been shrapnel we wouldn't have done a thing, but with bullets you hafta clean it." I'm soakin' it and there's lil black threads, and he says, "That's good. Pull 'em out. They're nerves."

For years it felt dead, but the nerves have all grown back. You can bullshit the VA and say goddammit my arm hurts and I can't use it. But as far as lifting, there's no disability, and I've always been lefthanded. Never had any compensation. It looks worse than it is.

12. We never could get the unit nomenclature of the Brits straight, even after Pullman explained that a regiment enlisted in the traditional fashion from one county was split up for the Second War amongst several brigades in order to retain pride of identity while preventing the sort of wholesale wipeout that had divested so many areas in the UK of the cream of their young men in the First War.

13. It didn't occur to me until one day sixty years later while taking a reflective shower that when his *Kameraden* found Fritz shot dead and without his gun they might logically have assumed he was killed while unarmed. And I'd hiked away from that grisly scene with his bloody Schmeisser, and his blood on my hands for which I was not responsible but that no shower can wash away.

Poor Fritz. He died for *das Vaterland* fighting the Yanks from across the sea and the Brits from across the Channel while he and his associates devastated the land of the despised Italians who'd betrayed his beloved *Führer.* Irony without end.

14. Smith et al., *History of the 157th Infantry Regiment*, 55.

15. Churchill, *The Second World War*, 488.

16. Hibbert, *Anzio: The Bid for Rome*, 129. Originally the "Leopold" and also known on the Beachhead as "Anzio Annie," this monster could be fired and then backed along the railroad to concealment in a mountain tunnel. Only twenty-six years earlier Annie's progenitor shelled Paris. The only one to survive World War II, this biggest of all guns was shipped to the U.S. and is on display at the Army's Aberdeen Proving Ground in Aberdeen, Maryland.

17. Ibid., 88–89.

18. Ibid., 89.

19. Blumenson, ed., *The Patton Papers, 1940–1945*, 414. Diary, February 12 [1944].

20. Writing home: "I observed for our 105s and probably damaged a tank and took care of a number of personnel." Waldron wrote my father about the same time that "our Platoon has more or less gone back to its main work of observation, and Joe immediately distinguished himself by knocking out a tank at three miles, putting one HE [high-explosive shell] on the front end and one on the rear—fini de movement around tank."

21. Matthew Arnold, "Dover Beach" (written in 1867), lines 35–37. From Lieder et al., *British Poetry and Prose*, 1181.

22. Blumenson, ed., *The Patton Papers, 1940–1945*, 415–16. Diary, February 16 [1944].

23. Ibid.

24. Ibid., 415–16. Diary, February 17 [1944].

25. In his amiable satire *The English Gentleman* (39–40), Douglas Sutherland writes in his chapter "The Gentleman at War" of "those two very gentlemanly gentlemen at the Battle of Waterloo, the Duke of Wellington and his second-in-command, Lord Uxbridge.

"'By God, I've lost my leg!', remarked Lord Uxbridge.

"'So you have, by God,' remarked his chief as they continued to ride into battle."

26. Christopher Hibbert, the Oxford-educated historian and author of *Anzio: The Bid for Rome*, was a captain in the London Irish Rifles in Italy.

27. Bishop, Glasgow and Fisher, *The Fighting Forty-Fifth,* 81.

28. Blumenson, ed., *The Patton Papers, 1940–1945*, 416.

29. Bishop, Glasgow and Fisher, *The Fighting Forty-Fifth,* 81. Division equipment losses for February included four Piper Cubs, 21 tanks and 17 tank destroyers as well as "88 trucks, 16 trailers, 34 anti-tank guns, 159 machine guns, 61 mortars, 101 [BARs], 364 rifles, 109 carbines, 219 pistols, 12 Tommy guns, 674 bayonets, 398 trench knives, 228 binoculars and 122 wrist watches."

30. As one of the ten, I so regretted that gratuitous *yellow*, which upon reflection, unlike General Patton, I found foreign to the spectrum of fear in war, that I expunged it a couple of years later while transcribing the journal.

Chapter 7: Blood-Red, Blood-Fed Poppies

1. "A Final Letter," *157th Infantry Association Newsletter*, Fourth Quarter 1987, 7–8.

2. Jerry Waldron and Les Gerencer were co-witnesses with me that evening. While I was under the impression that the Piper Cub was struck by a 240-millimeter shell, Gerald E. Nicholson of Manchester, Massachusetts, told me in 1982 that he was with a 36th Field Artillery battery of 155s the day they hit the spotter plane.

   Clifford E. Kinney, pilot of an observer Cub with the 933rd Artillery Battalion supporting the 45th on the Winter Line, recalled in his privately published memoir *The Life and Adventures of a Liaison Pilot in World War II*, hearing a slightly different version, namely that during a lull one of the artillery battalions prepared to zero in its guns on a base checkpoint and ordered its "liaison plane to take off and proceed to a position for adjustment." The Piper Cub reported "ready to adjust" and was hit by the first round (33).

3. Whitlock, *The Rock of Anzio*, 179. The most thorough and graphic history of the 45th.

4. Peter Viereck, "1.'Vale' from Carthage" (written in 1944; first of "Two Elegies"), in *Tide and Continuities: Last and First Poems 1995–1938*. Fayetteville: The University of Arkansas Press, 1995. Reprinted with permission of the author, who died at eighty-nine in 2006, and the publisher.

5. Hospitals were bombed or shelled by the Germans, not necessarily by intent, on at least ten occasions in spite of the prominently displayed red crosses. Medical staff casualties alone totalled over 500 within one four-month period (Blumenson, *Anzio: The Gamble that Failed*, 165).

6. Zapiecki:

> Shannon was a good soldier, but it was too much for him. The thing that hurt more than anything was that they didn't understand guys like him. Jack wasn't really a soldier, he was a draftee, a printer for the *Denver Post,* a good basketball player, a happy-go-lucky guy, and every time he would lead his men into combat something would happen to him. Like at Salerno, he disappeared, rolled down a hill about sixty feet, hurt his back and hit his head on a rock, and they were looking all over for him. There was a layer and layer and layer on top of a guy. You took it every day, every day. What chance did he have in a line company?

7. George Furber:

On outpost we just stayed and watched, with a telephone back to the line. Ace, King and Queen patrols worked routinely up and down the front line, while Jack pulled the unexpected tricks like knocking out machine-gun nests. During the day First and Third would lob mortars in the enemy minefields; I guess the Germans couldn't figure out why because there was no one out there. Then at night someone would sneak out and mark the safe way, and we'd follow the paths through and back.

The Germans were jittery, and in the dark we'd sneak around and they'd start shooting from a nest and give themselves away. We'd get behind 'em with canvas bags with eight sticks of explosive all hooked together with a primer cord, put on a long fuse, slip the bag in there and back off, and the concussion would kill all the men down inside and generally ruin the gun.

On one patrol we went about a mile behind their lines way over by the sea, way back into a German camp and got one tent away from Kesselring's. We didn't know at the time he was there, but we could have captured him. We were sneaking in and just slitting the throats of the men as they lay in their bunks. They thought they were back in the rear echelon. We had the Ranger commando knife. Wheechew! Stick the knife in real quick in the throat, put your hand right over his mouth and slit up his esophagus. We had these stickers made up—"The worst is yet to come"—and pasted 'em on their faces and bodies.

Oh Jesus, they dreaded us, didn't like night at all. Called us the Devils in Baggy Pants from the big pockets to carry all our rations. It got to where if a German brought one of us in he could go home!

The Germans in a house had a slit trench for a latrine a ways off, and we'd wait 'til some sonofabitch just about got to it and then start firin', missing to see which way he'd run, then go after him—or wait 'til he got shittin' and make him jump into the trench. We were dirty bastards. Training for Anzio north of Naples, Red and Leon and I would go buddy with three Troop Ten British Commandos to a restaurant, and depending on who's to pay, shoot out all the lights, grab the waiter or waitress and put the forty-five to their head and scare the shit outta them. Two of the Commandos came from the country in England, and one was a Cockney and you couldn't understand him, but they were a good bunch and we had a lotta fun with 'em.

But I'm sorry to say sometimes we jest murdered people. We had a boy called Scoopshit Brown, one of the best scouts ever, could tell from the manure what everything was—rabbit, donkey and all that—but had syphilis and was eventually gonna die from it. One night we were walkin' down this street in Naples and met some poor civilian. "Ah you sonofabitch!" he says, an' puts a knife right in his gut and rips him up. We became cannibals. We were ready to kill anybody or anything.

Joe Garland:
So you came out of all the mayhem without nightmares or terrible feelings of guilt?

Furber:
Maybe I'm hardnosed or something, but it didn't bother me. Lots of guys, their first kill, they didn't wanna knife. "I'll stand guard." Didn't bother me a bit. You hafta be fast. One

sonofabitch make a bit o' noise and it's gonna wake the rest, and you're in a hotbed because you're behind their lines and outnumbered.

Garland:
We didn't get into that kinda stuff on OPs and patrols. The idea of slitting another guy's throat . . . you didn't think, Jesus, how the hell can I do it?

Furber:
No. Joe, I did it, and I'll have to admit it didn't bother me a bit. I just did it, and in a grue-some sort of way I enjoyed it. I haven't killed a person since the war, and I wouldn't, but the enemy, it's him or me. If I don't get him, he'll get me.

Garland:
I'm sure I'm responsible for some deaths of Germans, but it would be by directing artillery fire, that kind of thing, which is pretty long distance and impersonal. You hadn't been involved in any violence before the war, had you?

Furber:
Oh no, no.

Garland:
And you haven't since?

Furber:
No, it was wartime and what we had to do. Course some of those raids where we slit the throats weren't necessary 'cause we didn't get anything out of it.

8. Snowden, *The Conquest of Malaria*.
9. The Allies of course had their own radio news (never "propaganda") beamed to the occupied countries and Germany, and both sides waged a lively battle of the leaflets from the air over the other's front lines. I have a genuine-looking German reproduction of a dollar bill that when opened up reveals a message appealing to French anti-Semitism: CE DOLLAR A PAYE LA GUERRE JUIVE . . . L'Argent n'a pas d'odeur, MAIS LE JUIF EN A UNE. (THIS DOLLAR HAS PAID FOR THE JEWISH WAR . . . Money doesn't smell, BUT THE JEW DOES.)
10. Back home in Toledo after the war, Zapiecki, the second-generation transplant from Poland, bumped into the simple answer.

My butcher a few years after the war was a German paratrooper shot in the leg on the Russian Front with a scar about a foot long. They told him they're gonna put him in a nice place where he can rest up. He was at Cassino from beginning to end, and he never got a scratch. I says, "Howdja do it?" "Vell," he says, "ven ve hear da planes everybody goes in da holes. Ven da planes are finished, come out da holes OK. Nobody get hurt." They proved that you *can't* bomb a guy out of a position unless it's a direct hit. The dogface still has to do it, overrun the position, dig the guy out, kill or get killed.

11. See Chapter 15 Note 15 for more about Andrew Welch and the *USS Snook*.

12. Lieutenant Colonel John McCrae, MD (Canadian Army), "In Flanders Fields," (written in 1915), lines 10-15. From the Project Gutenberg Etext of *In Flanders Fields And Other Poems*.

CHAPTER 8: "HERE THEY WUZ AN' THERE WE WUZ"

1. Smith et al., *History of the 157th Infantry Regiment*, 181.

2. Caption of a cartoon by Bill Mauldin, copyright 1943 by Bill Mauldin. Courtesy of the Mauldin Estate. Taking a break from a disarmament conference a few miles south of Rome at Nemi in 1976, my friend Thomas A. Halsted, then a U.S. specialist, hiked with a couple of friends through Genzano and into Velletri. "As we trudged along," he writes,

> as you did thirty-two years before (though we were without pack and rifle, going the opposite direction, and had bathed more recently), we looked southwest and downward to the Tyrrhenian Sea. I could clearly make out Anzio, 20 miles away, at the end of the straight-as-an-arrow Via Anziate. Knowing only vaguely of the history of the Anzio Beachhead and the months of agony that followed before the breakout, and years before I met you, I relied on my best-remembered source of the lore of the Italian campaign, the drawings of Bill Mauldin. I looked down on the broad plain below and recalled one drawing clearly, Willie and Joe doing the same, one of them saying, "My God! Here they wuz an' there we wuz." Imagine my astonishment when I read in your manuscript that this very site was indeed the locale for Willie's and Joe's—and Bill's and Joe's—epiphany.

CHAPTER 9: THE DOGFACE AND THE DUCHESS

1. Sevareid, *Not So Wild a Dream*, 427.

2. Ibid.

3. Matthews, *Education of a Correspondent*, 422.

4. Smith et al., *History of the 157th Infantry Regiment*, 182, 97.

5. From *Who Was Who*.

6. *The Register of Swedish Nobility* does not record a David York during the war or since.

7. To my regret, I failed during our interview in 1979 to ask Dom Trubia about the Prince of Savoy.

CHAPTER 10: FORTUNES O' WAR, MY ASS

1. Morison, *The Invasion of France and Germany 1944–1945*, 247.

2. Ibid., 264–65.

3. Sevareid, *Not So Wild a Dream*, 431–32.

4. Declining the invitation to join the patrol to Varages was O'Keefe's sensible swan song. A few days later there was need for a draftsman in Division G4 (planning), and Dave was transferred back to safety.

CHAPTER 11: "THE LINKS OF THE CHAIN"

1. Siaud, *The Links of the Chain (Les Maillons de la Chaîne)*. Reproduced by Henry F. Siaud privately in 1983 and included here in my translation with his approval.

2. In the late 1990s appeared a graphic exhibit, "Extermination War: Crimes of the Wehrmacht 1941–44," documenting the regular German Army's mass slaughter of Jews, Gypsies and pris-

oners of war in the former Soviet Union and the Balkans. It toured sixteen cities in Germany and Austria before opening in February, 1997, in Munich, the birthplace of Nazism, where it raised a particular hue and cry. Hannes Heer, the curator of the exhibit assembled by German historians, was quoted by the Associated Press as stating to *Der Speigel* magazine that contrary to the widely held view by older Germans (that while the SS carried out the Holocaust, the Wehrmacht stuck to fighting enemy soldiers) the regular army was in fact responsible for the noncombatant deaths of between 9 and 11 million people. ("WWII display stirs ire in Bavaria," Associated Press dispatch in *The Boston Sunday Globe*, February 23, 1997).

3. Robert Swanzy was twenty-six. His younger brother David of New Orleans, whom I contacted in 2006, visited La Tour-d'Aigues with his wife in 1996 researching a book about Robert and the downing of his B-24 bomber. He interviewed the nine surviving crew members and fifteen living Resistance fighters who saved them. He hopes to publish his book in 2008.

4. During a visit in 1991 to the scenes of '44 with the Siauds we drove along the same approach to La Tour-d'Aigues, turning off a quiet dirt road in the country and parking partway up a low, meadowed hill. "Hank," as we'd come to call Henry, led us a short walk to the crest, where I instantly recognized a rough rectangle of rocks as their machine-gun emplacement of forty-seven years before. A large metal shed had been built between the Maquis redoubt and the road, blocking what would have been their first sight of the column of Thunderbirds. Parallel with the road, in the brush a few yards beyond and down the slope, he found to his surprise the small semicircle of rocks he had piled up around a slight depression, all that remained of his foxhole. The farmer who owned the land must have been aware of the significance of the place, for nothing had been disturbed in almost half a century.

We proceeded to the comfortable farmhouse of Félix Reynaud, a retired vintner of La Tour-d'Aigues who had been a leader of the Resistance. Here a few old *maquisards* had gathered for refreshments and reminiscence with us. We heard an amusing and moving account from Madame Reynaud of one or two of her husband's escapes from the *Boches* and were presented with several vintage bottles of Reynaud La Tour-d'Aigues before moving on to an official reception in the *mairie* and a tour of the ancient town, which, like most others in the path of the Champagne Campaign, had changed little since the war.

5. Besides Siaud and Joannon, at least five other French civilians of record and probably more joined up to fight with the 157th in the Southern France and Vosges campaigns: Roger C. Humann of St.-Michel-sur-Meurthe and Jean B. Pierre of Chaumont in D Company, Georges A. Cau of Aix-en-Provence and Francis L. Escartefigues of Marseille in A Company, and Pierre Bompar of Gap in Third Battalion Headquarters Company.

6. Back at Vidauban, I had recalled in my journal, one of the battalions "surprised the German garrison, had a firefight and captured most of them. It was here that everyone was picking up enemy vehicles. We got a trailer and personnel carrier (a converted Belgian sedan), both of which were very useful when given G.I. markings. All these facilitated movement when we could get gas."

7. "It was open season on Germans in France and men, women and children, armed with ancient hunting rifles, M1s, horse-pistols, anything that would shoot and kill the conqueror, roamed the hillsides and valleys. Returning from the front, they cheered the Americans, shook hands all around and related their experiences in voluble French. Patriot patrols accompanied the battalions and small FFI groups searched the mountain passes and valleys, flushing Germans

from their scattered hiding places. Information provided by the Marquis [*sic*] proved vital to the rapidly moving regiment" (Smith et al., *History of the 157th Infantry Regiment*, 102).

8. Sevareid, *Not So Wild a Dream*, 449–50.

CHAPTER 12: WITH MY SHIELD, OR ON IT?

1. Smith et al., *History of the 157th Infantry Regiment*, 180.

2. Siaud, *The Links of the Chain* (*Les Maillons de la Chaîne*).

CHAPTER 13: "WE WILL MEET YOU ALL AGAIN"

1. Untitled poem by Bob Coleman, written in 1943 and reproduced herein with permission from his wife, Veronica.

2. Siaud, *The Links of the Chain* (*Les Maillons de la Chaîne*). With the Siauds on the campaign trail in 1994, we paused for lunch in Rambervillers, a large town that already, as we bore closer to Alsace, looked more heavily Teutonic than French. After some reconnaissance Hank Siaud found the school of the Sisters, bustling and abuzz with young girls, and then the courtyard, and the spot where the shell landed that left him prostrate, and finally the essentials, less the walls, of the very pissoir of his urgency that morning.

3. Smith et al., *History of the 157th Infantry Regiment*, opposite 111.

4. Ibid., 115–19.

5. Siaud, *The Links of the Chain* (*Les Maillons de la Chaîne*).

6. Joe Garland, "The Last Shot" (written December 10, 1944), *The Stars and Stripes*, January 1944.

CHAPTER 14: AMBUSHED AT REIPERTSWILLER

1. Alfred, Lord Tennyson, "The Charge of the Light Brigade." (written in 1854), lines 13-15, memorializing events in the Battle of Balaclava, October 25, 1854. From the Project Gutenberg EBook of *Beauties of Tennyson*.

2. The *History of the 157th Infantry Regiment* states that Third Battalion was 1,500 yards ahead of its flanking units (Smith et al., 131)—an impossibility, as Waldron, who was working the situation map in S2, points out. The extra digit must be in error.

3. Waldron believes the density and unabated frequency and ferocity of the enemy attacks, and the reserve capacity that produced continual replacements, suggest that the Sixth SS Division may have committed more than its 11th Regiment against the 157th.

4. When I was interviewing Delmar Griffith at his home in Denver in 1978 I asked him for the specifics of his Silver Star citation. He rummaged around but couldn't find it, and the matter dropped.

5. Willis Talkington was awarded the Silver Star.

6. Smith et al., *History of the 157th Infantry Regiment*, 134. The identities of Mathiason and Neff were tracked down by retired Colonel Hugh F. Foster III of Carlisle, Pennsylvania, who has made a study of the Reipertswiller battle.

7. Bishop, Glasgow and Fisher, *The Fighting Forty-Fifth*, 142–43.

8. Ibid., 142–44. After the 157th was relieved, Sparks recalled in the *Association Newsletter*, General Frederick visited his battalion area. "He was quite friendly, but I was in a dark mood." He told the 45th commander that if he had it to do over again he'd go against his orders and pull his battalion out while he could, "and a few other remarks besides. He was not pleased" ("A Return to Reipertswiller," *157th Infantry Association Newsletter*, Third Quarter 1987, 4–5).

In *Sparks: The Combat Diary of a Battalion Commander*, xvii, Emajean J. Buechner, wife of her subject's battalion surgeon Howard Buechner, writes:

> ... the order to retreat should have been given five days earlier. Major General Robert T. Frederick ... did, however, have himself awarded a medal for this infamous massacre. There was a commendation written for Lt. Col. Felix Sparks for the Congressional Medal of Honor, but it became lost in red tape. Sparks did win a second Silver Star. Very shortly after the battle, Sparks stood before the General, and with tears streaming down his grime-smeared face, he said, "If I had to do it over again, I'd go against your orders and pull the battalion out while I could." Very harsh words were exchanged. Perhaps there was a deliberate effort made to side-track his citation. The truth will never be known.

Other accounts indicate that Sparks was recommended for the Distinguished Service Cross, not the Medal of Honor, that the DSC was disapproved and he was awarded the Silver Star.

9. Smith et al., *History of the 157th Infantry Regiment*, 135.
10. Bishop, Glasgow and Fisher, *The Fighting Forty-Fifth*, 145.
11. Smith et al., *History of the 157th Infantry Regiment*, 135–36.
12. Clarke, *Riviera to the Rhine*, 521.
13. Felix Sparks, citing statistics sent to him by Lieutenant Colonel Hugh F. Foster. "Reipertswiller Book," *157th Infantry Association Newsletter*, First Quarter 1988, 8.
14. Sparks, "MIAs," *157th Infantry Association Newsletter*, Third Quarter 1987, 6, and "Recovery of MIAs," Fourth Quarter 1987, 8.
15. Sparks, "A Return to Reipertswiller," *157th Infantry Association Newsletter*, Third Quarter 1987, 5.
16. Ibid., 4.
17. Frank Merchant to Joe Garland, February 23, 1985.
18. Felix Sparks, "Epilogue," *Operations Near Reipertswiller, France, January 14–20, 1945*, March 31, 1982, 5.

CHAPTER 15: MAJOR LAMBERTH'S *GÖTTERDÄMMERUNG*

1. Smith et al., *History of the 157th Infantry Regiment*, opposite 137.
2. Shay, *Achilles in Vietnam*. Dr. Shay's sequel, *Odysseus in America: Combat Trauma and the Trials of Homecoming*, examines the strikingly comparable problems facing the contemporary war veteran in his efforts to reintegrate with society.

The first investigators I know of to apply psychiatric methods to the study and treatment of combat and post-combat stress in modern warfare were Roy R. Grinker and John P. Spiegel of the U.S. Army Air Force Medical Division in the North African campaign. Their insightful and pioneering findings among "psychologically wounded" ground force soldiers were published as the monograph *War Neuroses in North Africa* in 1945, followed the same year by *Men Under Stress* (Blakiston), a full-length analysis of the Army Air Force combat crews under severe stress and its long-term effects.

Not long ago I encountered a singular example of the well-known reluctance of my surviving fellow combat veterans to "talk about it." I was chatting on the subject with a much younger retired Army officer who had entered the priesthood and was recently consoling the family of a WWII infantry veteran who had just died. Lamenting the old man's absolute refusal to discuss his experiences, they were dumbfounded to discover among his closely guarded mementoes the Congressional Medal of Honor for extreme heroism in battle. Every time I tell the story it chokes me up. It was obvious that in circumstances where he must have killed so many to save so many he felt torn to have survived, let alone receive the Medal of Honor.

3. Smith et al., *History of the 157th Infantry Regiment*, 143.

4. Bishop, Glasgow and Fisher, *The Fighting Forty-Fifth*, 11. The same day, March 18, Lieutenant Jack L. Treadwell, commanding officer of Company F in the 180th, singlehandedly knocked out six pillboxes and took eighteen prisoners. He was awarded the Division's eighth Medal of Honor.

5. Blumenson, ed., *The Patton Papers, 1940–1945*, 665. Letter, GSP, Jr., to Beatrice, March 25, 1945.

6. Baron, Baum and Goldhurst, *Raid! The Untold Story of Patton's Secret Mission*, 38.

7. Charles B. MacDonald in *The Last Offensive*, 281–84, writes that General Manton Eddy, CO of the XII Corps, deplored Patton's scheme to send an entire combat command and insisted on a small task force that General William Hoge of the Fourth Armored Division believed would be destroyed but was overridden by Eddy. Baron, Baum and Goldhurst's *Raid!*, the later work by eight years, on the other hand, claims the notion of the smaller force originated with Patton, and that Hoge objected when the order was transmitted by Eddy, who went back to Patton but failed to dissuade him.

8. Blumenson, ed., *The Patton Papers, 1940–1945*, 675. Letter, GSP, Jr., to Beatrice, April 13, 1945. Sources for the story of Task Force Baum include: Baron, Baum and Goldhurst, *Raid! The Untold Story of Patton's Secret Mission*; Buechner, Emajean J., *Sparks: The Combat Diary of a Battalion Commander*; MacDonald, *The Last Offensive*; and Blumenson, ed., *The Patton Papers, 1940–1945*.

9. Smith et al., *History of the 157th Infantry Regiment*, 148.

10. Felix Sparks recorded in the *157th Infantry Association Newsletter* ("Aschaffenburg Battle," Second Quarter 1982, 3) that his Third Battalion attacked March 27, the Second the 28th, and the First the 29th, contrary to the Regimental and Divisional histories, which have the assault launched by the Second Battalion on March 28.

11. Bishop, Glasgow and Fisher, *The Fighting Forty-Fifth*, 163.

12. Smith et al., *History of the 157th Infantry Regiment*, 154.

13. United Press dispatch, "Aschaffenburg's Major Tells Private: 'We Yield,'" April 5, 1945. General Sparks stated categorically in the Association's *157th Infantry Association Newsletter* ("Aschaffenburg," Fourth Quarter 1986, 2) that Major Lamberth and his entire staff surrendered to him as commanding officer of Third Battalion, not to Colonel O'Brien.

> . . . Present at the time were a couple of lieutenants from regimental headquarters and some soldiers from G Company, along with my command party. I collected about fifty pistols from Major von Lambert [*sic*] and his officers which I loaded in my jeep. I then ordered von Lambert to tour the area with me for the purpose of inducing the surrender of the remaining German positions. This he did willingly. Upon the surrender of the final German positions, I then turned von Lambert over to the regimental lieutenants, who took him back across the river to the regimental CP where perhaps he surrendered to Col. O'Brien in a more formal manner. Col. O'Brien was never in Aschaffenburg at any time while the battle was going on or at the time of the initial surrender.

> The Third Battalion commander's presence at the surrender is not noted, however, in the United Press dispatch or in the unit histories, indicating that it was likely accepted by his immediate superior, the commanding officer of the 157th Infantry.

14. "Business conditions in general remain as bad as ever if not worse," my father had complained

in his journal in December 1932, "despite an overwhelming Democratic landslide in the last election. Roosevelt elected; probably not a strong character."

I saw FDR only once, when I was going on fourteen. A member of the Class of 1915, my father took me to the Harvard Tercentenary, the 300th anniversary of the founding of America's first college, in Harvard Yard in Cambridge. The date was September 18, 1936. President Roosevelt, Class of 1904, sat through the afternoon's ceremonies in his top hat, umbrella-less in the cold drizzle, dauntless and grand in his composure and good spirits. For three terms, with millions of others, I viewed the only President of my growing-up as an awesome figure of authority and hope through the Depression and the New Deal and then the war.

15. Andy Welch was a natural leader in my twenty-five-member Class of 1940 at the Roxbury Latin School for boys in Boston, admired by students and faculty alike and one of three RLS classmates at Harvard who asked for the submarines. Lieutenant (JG) Welch was assigned to *USS Snook* for her ninth patrol, off the south coast of China, clearing Guam on March 28. On April 12, about two hundred miles east of northern Formosa and four days after her last radio contact, *Snook* was ordered to stand lifeguard duty for British aircraft carrier–based air strikes against the Japanese. Presumably while surfacing *Snook* was torpedoed on April 8, her last radio contact, by one of several enemy subs later sunk in the area, and took some eighty-five submariners and officers to the bottom, including Andy.

Like Welch, Howie Gleason was one of those shining personalities who seemed to exemplify the best in every respect, all-around athlete in football, hockey and crew, expert mariner who'd sailed the New England coast, sensitive, appreciative, a lover of life who just naturally drew classmates and faculty to him. Completing his training and truly eager for duty, he drew the submarine *Trigger* in the Pacific as captain of the gun crew, and in that same fateful month of April *Trigger* was lost with all hands during a patrol in Japanese waters. Howie left his widow Elizabeth, whom he'd married on his graduation.

On April 16 Lieutenant Willie Wolfgram was the second of my Harvard classmates to be killed in action in Italy. He was with the 10th Mountain Division. Before college he was graduated from Northwestern Military Academy in Wisconsin. "This was reflected in the squared shoulders and immaculate dress that were his trade marks," according to the *1947 Report of the Harvard Class of 1944*. "He was a born leader of men, and a person we are all proud to have known."

CHAPTER 16: DACHAU

1. Shirer, *The Rise and Fall of the Third Reich*, 984–86, 988–90; Sydnor, *Soldiers of Destruction: The SS Death's Head Division, 1933–1945*, 8–21, 42–47; Buechner, Howard, *Dachau: The Hour of the Avenger*.
2. The most gripping account of the liberation of Dachau appears in Flint Whitlock's first-rate *The Rock of Anzio: From Sicily to Dachau: A History of the 45th Infantry Division*.
3. Author's taped interview with Morris Rosenwasser, May 4 & 5, 1981, Miami Beach.
4. Shirer, *The Rise and Fall of the Third Reich*, 918.
5. Buechner, Howard, *Dachau: The Hour of the Avenger*, 89.
6. Bishop, Glasgow and Fisher, *The Fighting Forty-Fifth*, 185.
7. Buechner, Emajean J., *Sparks*, "Dachau and Its Liberation," 141–42. At the Asssociation's Denver reunion in September, 1982, General Sparks showed Jim Dowdall and me a copy of the Signal Corps photo from a publication with a caption alleging that the guards lying before the wall had all been shot. He repeated his belief that they'd thrown themselves on the ground

moments before when the shooting started.

8. Buechner, Howard, *Dachau: The Hour of the Avenger*, 84–92.

9. Ibid., 95–99.

10. Ibid.

11. Felix Sparks, "New Book," *157th Infantry Association Newsletter*, First Quarter 1990, 4.

12. Buechner, Emajean J., *Sparks*, "Dachau and Its Liberation," 143.

13. Ibid., 147.

14. It was fifty-two years afterward that the late General Linden's son, retired Army Colonel John H. Linden (West Point, 1945), entered the lists with his 1997 self-published book, *Surrender of the Dachau Concentration Camp 29 Apr 45: The True Account*. Colonel Linden served with the 42nd's Airborne Artillery, serving staff duty with the Army Chief of Staff and Joint Chiefs of Staff, and retired in 1968.

In this carefully documented study, liberally illustrated with numerous revealing and hitherto-unpublicized photographs, John Linden and those who assisted him retrieve the reputation of his father and the 42nd from the dismissiveness of Colonel Sparks and his adherents respecting their role in the liberation of Dachau. While freely agreeing that I Company of the 157th's Third Battalion bore the brunt of the brief fighting involved in the subjugation of the guards and the physical liberation of the prisoners, they present solid evidence that Dachau's official white-flag surrender to General Linden and the 42nd and much of the restoration of order was engineered by him and his aides, a Red Cross official, inmate representatives and SS officers in the administrative section of the camp.

Further, the book argues that: (1) When Linden and his party arrived at the gate area being secured by the 157th, Maggie Higgins, disguised in German army winter gear, turned up in a *Stars and Stripes* jeep and was unknown to him. (2) Linden's tap on the helmet was for an evidently drunk Thunderbird who was shaking a pair of leg shackles at inmates and further exciting them. (3) Sparks did not force Linden out of the camp with his .45, and in fact the General made no mention of such an episode in his testimony during the Inspector General's investigation of the massacre. And (4) if Linden filed court-martial charges against Sparks, there appears to be no record of it.

With respect to Sparks's movements subsequent to April 29, Colonel John Linden's *The True Account* asserts that (1) Sparks was in fact relieved of command of the Third Battalion on April 30 by Headquarters of the European Theater of Operations (ETO), and reassigned to its Assembly Area in Rheims and Suippes, France, where Army day reports list him as present for duty and where he was unavailable for questioning from May 8 through July 14 while the massacre and his conduct in Dachau were investigated by the Inspector General. (2) Sparks seems not to have traveled to Le Havre, as he claimed. Both his interpreter and his driver have stated in letters to Linden that they did not accompany him to Le Havre, nor could his runner, who was in Munich at least until May 12, have done so.

Blumenson's *The Patton Papers, 1940–1945* (718–26) places Patton in his new headquarters in Bad Tölz, about twenty-five miles south of Munich, from May 24 to June 4, when he flew to the U.S., returning July 6.

Hence, after reviewing both Linden and Blumenson sources, it appears that (3) Sparks could not have met with General Patton in Augsburg on the day he claims, June 10, because on June 4, Patton departed for Paris from his new Third Army HQ (that on May 23 he had moved to Bad Tölz), and on June 7, flew home to Boston on leave, returning July 5. (4) There appear to have been no court-martial papers to tear up. And (5) Sparks all the while was assigned to the ETO assembly area, as attested by the day reports listing him as present throughout the period in question.

Lt. Colonel Joseph M. Whitaker, Assistant Inspector General of the Seventh Army, reporting on June 8, 1945, on his May 2 investigation of "Alleged Mistreatment of German Guards at Dachau," found that seventeen SS prisoners had been shot and killed at the wall "under the personal supervision of Lieutenant Walsh" of I Company, who herded four other German soldiers who had surrendered to him into a boxcar where he shot them, and that three still alive were finished off by one of his men.

Colonel Whitaker stated in this June 8 report, within a day or two of Sparks's claimed interview with Patton at Augsburg, that Sparks is "now with Assembly Area Command . . . [and] because it has been impossible to contact him for his testimony, conclusions as to his responsibility are not drawn in this report."

It's worth an aside that if the interview with Patton had come off as reported by Sparks, it would have been the sort of episode Patton customarily noted in his diary or in a letter home. Yet there is no reference to the Dachau massacre or to a meeting with Sparks in Blumenson's Volume II of *The Patton Papers* covering the war years.

Attempted cover-up of the massacre? So it appears, and no apparent evidence that Patton was involved or even aware of it. Felix Sparks's assertion that General Frederick, for whom he had expressed such disdain, sent him home via Le Havre to take the heat off Sparks doesn't square with the record, notwithstanding that the 45th commander may have had a hand in his immediate transfer to the Assembly Area at Rheims to sequester him (and the chain of command) from the IG's troublesome inquiry.

The early histories of the campaign credited the 45th with the liberation of Dachau. In its later official history, however, the Army awarded the distinction to the 45th *and* the 42nd. In 1991 the Center for Military History issued a correction stating that the 42nd was chiefly responsible. When then-retired General Sparks conceded that the 42nd played a role, the official record was again altered to make it *jointly*.

The same year there appeared Emajean J. Buechner's *Sparks: The Combat Diary of a Battalion Commander*, the vanity press biography/autobiography of "one of the truly great heroes of World War II" (back cover). The cover features the grim visage of a tough-looking soldier with a lieutenant colonel's oak-leaf insignia on his helmet, in battle mode—not Lieutenant Colonel Sparks, however, as it's apparently intended to convey, but the head-and-shoulders close-up of a Marine corporal of the Korean War charging past the camera with his gun, followed by another soldier, reproduced and modified without credit or attribution from the noted photographer David Douglas Duncan's *Yankee Nomad: A Photographic Odyssey* (NY, 1966), page 299, as discovered by Jack Pullman. The corporal's stripes have been erased, and the oak leaf drawn in on the helmet.

"He is of the mold of a MacArthur, a Patton, and if you will, an Alexander," Mrs. Buechner wrote of her subject, "who wept because there were no more worlds to conquer" (*Sparks*, xix).

BULL. Felix Sparks died at ninety in 2007.

15. Felix Sparks, "Epilogue," *Operations Near Reipertswiller, France, January 14–20, 1945*, March 31, 1982, 5.
16. Bishop, Glasgow and Fisher, *The Fighting Forty-Fifth*, 185. Unidentified reporter.
17. See Chapter 11, Note 2 regarding the German traveling exhibit "Extermination War: Crimes of the Wehrmacht, 1941–44."

18. Rosenwasser interview, May 4 & 5, 1981, Miami Beach.

19. All figures drawn from Smith et al., *History of the 157th Infantry Regiment*, 166–67.

CHAPTER 17: THE LAST PATROL

1. Casualty statistics are drawn from Bishop, Glasgow and Fisher, *The Fighting Forty-Fifth*, 195. Footnote regarding Division strength is from the Author.

CHAPTER 18: "WOULD YOU THINK THERE WAS WAR AT THE HEART OF LOVE?"

1. My 10 percent disability pension was around eleven dollars a month. A year or so later I was summoned to the Veterans Administration office in Boston for routine physical examination to determine continued eligibility. When I protested to the doctor that there was nothing wrong with my left leg and I didn't feel entitled to a dime, he stared at me in disbelief, allowed that I was the first vet he'd encountered who asked to be taken off the rolls, and told me to go home and not be a damn fool. By 2008, between politics and inflation, Congress had raised me to $117 a month for a barely visible six-inch scar inflicted by a busted French ladder on my left shin sixty-four years ago. But I ain't complainin', and at twenty bucks an inch neither's my leg.

SELECTED BIBLIOGRAPHY

Anzio Beachhead: 22 January–25 May 1944. American Forces in Action Series. Washington, DC: Historical Division, Department of the Army, 1947.

Baron, Richard, Major Abe Baum and Richard Goldhurst. *Raid! The Untold Story of Patton's Secret Mission.* New York: Putnam, 1981.

Bishop, Lieutenant Colonel Leo V., Major Frank J. Glasgow and Major George A. Fisher, eds. *The Fighting Forty-Fifth: The Combat Report of an Infantry Division.* Baton Rouge, LA: Army and Navy Publishing Co., 1946.

Blumenson, Martin. *Anzio: The Gamble that Failed.* Philadelphia: J. B. Lippincott Company, 1963.

Blumenson, Martin. "General Lucas at Anzio." In *Command Decisions,* edited by Kent Roberts Greenfield. Washington, DC: Center of Military History, Department of the Army, 2000.

Blumenson, Martin. *Mark Clark: The Last of the Great World War II Commanders.* New York: Congdon & Weed, Inc., 1984.

Blumenson, Martin. *Patton: The Man Behind the Legend, 1885–1945.* New York: William Morrow, 1985.

Blumenson, Martin, ed. *The Patton Papers,* Volume II, *1940–1945.* Boston: Houghton Mifflin Company, 1974.

Blumenson, Martin. *Salerno to Cassino.* United States Army in World War II: The Mediterranean Theater of Operations. Washington, DC: Office of the Chief of Military History, United States Army, 1969.

Bradley, Omar N. and Clay Blair. *A General's Life: An Autobiography by General of the Army.* New York: Simon and Schuster, 1983.

Bradley, Omar Nelson. *A Soldier's Story.* New York: Henry Holt and Company, 1951.

Buechner, Emajean J. *Sparks: The Combat Diary of a Battalion Commander (Rifle), WWII, 157th Infantry Regiment, 45th Division, 1941–1945.* Metairie, LA: Thunderbird Press, Inc., 1991.

Buechner, Howard A. *Dachau: The Hour of the Avenger; An Eyewitness Account.* Metairie, LA: Thunderbird Press, 1986.

Churchill, Winston S. *The Second World War: Closing the Ring.* Boston: Houghton Mifflin, 1951.

Clarke, Jeffrey J. and Robert Ross Smith. *Riviera to the Rhine.* United States Army in World War II: The European Theater of Operations. Washington, DC: Center of Military History, United States Army, 1993.

Colgan, William B. *World War II Fighter-Bomber Pilot.* Manhattan, KS: Sunflower University Press, 1988.

Duncan, David Douglas. *Yankee Nomad: A Photographic Odyssey.* New York: Holt, Rinehart and Winston, 1966.

Dunleavy, Gareth. "Hitler Count Your Children: Personal History." Manuscript, 1995, on deposit in the Military History Collection of the Brown University Library.

Eisenhower, Dwight D. *Crusade in Europe.* Garden City, NY: Doubleday & Company, Inc., 1948.

Garland, Lieutenant Colonel Albert N. and Howard McGaw Smyth; assisted by Martin Blumenson. *Sicily and the Surrender of Italy.* United States Army in World War II: The Mediterranean Theater of Operations. Washington, DC: Office of the Chief of Military History, United States Army, 1965.

Garland, Joseph, M.D. *The Youngest of the Family: His Care and Training.* Cambridge, MA: Harvard University Press, 1932.

Green, Leslie C. *Superior Orders in National and International Law.* Leyden: A. W. Sijthoff, 1976.

Hatlem, John C.; compiled by Kenneth E. Hunter, with the assistance of Margaret E. Tackley. *The War Against Germany and Italy: Mediterranean and Adjacent Areas.* United States Army in World War II: Pictorial Record. Washington, DC: Office of the Chief of Military History, Department of the Army, 1951; reprinted 1975.

Hibbert, Christopher. *Anzio: The Bid for Rome.* Ballantine's Illustrated History of World War II, Battle Book No. 15. New York: Ballantine Books Inc., 1970.

Hitler, Adolf; translated by Ralph Manheim. *Mein Kampf.* Boston: Houghton Mifflin Company, 1943; renewed 1971 by Houghton Mifflin Company.

Kinney, Clifford E. *The Life and Adventures of a Liaison Pilot in World War II.* Albuquerque, NM: C. E. Kinney, 1998.

Levi, Carlo, translated from the Italian by Frances Frenaye Lanza. *Christ Stopped at Eboli: The Story of a Year.* New York: Farrar, Strauss and Company, 1947.

Lewis, Norman. *Naples '44.* New York: Pantheon Books, 1978.

Lieder, Paul Robert; Robert Morss Lovett; and Robert Kilburn Root, eds. *British Poetry and Prose: A Book of Readings.* Boston: Houghton Mifflin Company, 1928.

Linden, Colonel John H. *Surrender of the Dachau Concentration Camp, 29 Apr 45: The True Account.* Elm Grove, WI: Sycamore Press, 1997.

Longfellow, Henry Wadsworth. *Poetical Works in Six Volumes*, vol. 3. Boston: Houghton, Mifflin and Co., 1904.

MacDonald, Charles B. *The Last Offensive.* United States Army in World War II: The European Theater of Operations. Washington, DC: Office of the Chief of Military History, United States Army, 1973.

Matthews, Herbert L. *Education of a Correspondent.* New York: Harcourt, Brace & Co., 1946.

Mauldin, Bill. *Mud, Mules, and Mountains: Cartoons of the A.E.F. in Italy.* Naples, 1944.

Mauldin, Bill. *Up Front.* New York: Henry Holt and Company, Inc., 1945.

Morison, Samuel Eliot. *The Invasion of France and Germany 1944–1945.* History of the United States Naval Operations in World War II, Volume XI. Boston: Little, Brown and Company, 1957.

Morison, Samuel Eliot. *Sicily—Salerno—Anzio: January 1943–June 1944.* History of United States Naval Operations in World War II, Volume IX. Boston: Atlantic Monthly Press, Little, Brown and Company, 1954.

Morris, Eric. *Salerno: A Military Fiasco.* New York: Stein & Day, 1983.

New Infantry Drill Regulations. U.S. Army, April 15, 1943.

Pyle, Ernie. *Brave Men.* New York: Henry Holt and Company, 1944.

Rees, Nigel. *Brewer's Famous Quotations: 5000 Quotations and the Stories Behind Them.* London: Weidenfeld & Nicolson, 2006.

Reynolds, Quentin. *The Curtain Rises.* New York: Random House, 1944.

Salerno: American Operations from the Beaches to the Volturno, 9 September–6 October 1943. American Forces in Action Series. Washington, DC: Historical Division, War Department, 1944.

Sevareid, Eric. *Not So Wild a Dream.* New York: Alfred A. Knopf, 1946.

Shay, Jonathan, MD, PhD *Achilles in Vietnam: Combat Trauma and the Undoing of Character.* New York: Atheneum, 1994.

Shay, Jonathan, MD, PhD. *Odysseus in America: Combat Trauma and the Trials of Homecoming.* New York: Scribner, 2002.

Shirer, William L. *The Rise and Fall of the Third Reich.* New York: Simon and Schuster, 1960.

Siaud, Henry F. *The Links of the Chain (Les Maillons de la Chaîne).* Written by Henry F. Siaud in 1983 and reproduced privately; translated by Joseph E. Garland and excerpted in *Unknown Soldiers* with Siaud's permission.

Smith, George P., Robert LeMense, Jack Hallowell, Al Morgan, Joe F. Meis and Irving Kintisch (eds. and authors). *History of the 157th Infantry Regiment (Rifle): 4 June '43–8 May '45.* Baton Rouge, LA: Army & Navy Publishing Co., 1946.

Snowden, Frank. *The Conquest of Malaria: Italy, 1900–1962.* New Haven, CT: Yale University Press, 2006.

Sutherland, Douglas. *The English Gentleman.* London: Debrett's Peerage, 1978.

Sydnor, Charles W., Jr. *Soldiers of Destruction: The SS Death's Head Division, 1933–1945.* Princeton, NJ: Princeton University Press, 1977.

Viereck, Peter. *Tide and Continuities: Last and First Poems 1995–1938.* Fayetteville: The University of Arkansas Press, 1995.

Volturno: From the Volturno to the Winter Line; 6 October–15 November 1943. American Forces in Action Series. Washington, DC: Military Intelligence Division, U.S. War Department, 1944.

Wheeler, Major William Reginald, ed. *The Road to Victory: A History of Hampton Roads Port of Embarkation in World War II,* Volume I. New Haven, CT: Yale University Press, 1946.

Whitlock, Flint *The Rock of Anzio: From Sicily to Dachau: A History of the 45th Infantry Division.* Boulder, CO: Westview Press, 1998.

INTERVIEWS

HEREWITH ARE THOSE I TRACKED DOWN in the 1970s and '80s for an exchange of memories about the war, with the exception of Jimmy Dowdall, Jerry Waldron and Andy Zapiecki, with whom I'd always maintained contact. All the men were Ironheads save for fellow infantry trainees Dunleavy and Furber and for Dachau survivor Rosenwasser. So far as I know at the time of this writing, out of all the Ironheads only Jimmy at ninety-six, Doug Studebaker (whom I replaced after he was badly wounded in the Salerno campaign in 1943) at eighty-seven, Jerry at eighty-seven and I at eighty-five survive.

William R. Caird	Frank Merchant	D. Douglass Studebaker
Veronica P. Coleman	Henry G. Mills	Dominick M. Trubia
Harold R. Dibble	Valen J. Mullenax	Helen W. Vollhardt
Vernon Dilks	Charles E. Nye	Philipp F. Vollhardt
James J. Dowdall	David J. O'Keefe	Jeremy R. Waldron
Gareth W. Dunleavy	Jack T. Pullman	Robert C. Winburn
George P. Furber	Morris Rosenwasser	William E. Woodhams
Lester Gerencer	Henry F. Siaud	Andrew M. Zapiecki
Delmar W. Griffith	Edith Smith	

ROLL CALL

Brigadier General Charles M. **Ankcorn** was retired from active duty in December 1944 and died in 1955 at sixty-two.

Richard A. **Bashore** died in 1987.

Richard G. **Beech**'s last known address was in Reading, Pennsylvania, but my letter was unanswered. He died in 1991.

William **Belleman** is reported to have married, remained in the Army for a hitch or two as an investigator and spent most of the rest of his career as a detective with the Baltimore Police Department. He died sometime before 1978.

The Reverend Alison R. **Bryan** served as pastor of several Presbyterian churches in New Jersey and New York before his retirement. After the death of his wife Marion in 1973 he married Edith Fargo of Frenchtown, New Jersey, where he lived until 1992, nine days after his 101st birthday. He was the third-oldest living graduate of Princeton.

William R. **Caird** was a telephone company installer and equipment tester until his retirement to Unionville, Connecticut, with his wife, Marion, who had a daughter by a previous marriage. Bill died in 2005 at ninety-one.

Major General John H. **Church**, while Assistant Division Commander of the 84th Division, was wounded for the third time in February 1945 heading Task Force Church, which spearheaded for several days the drive of the Ninth Army into the Rhine Valley. Chief of the U.S. Military Advisory Commission at the outbreak of the Korean War, he took over the 24th Division in 1950 when his predecessor was captured. In 1951 he assumed command of the Infantry Center at Fort Benning, Georgia, retiring in 1952. He died in 1953 at sixty-one.

His World War I Distinguished Service Cross citation: "Knocked down and rendered unconscious by the explosion of a shell early in the attack on Cantigny, he staggered forward as soon as he regained consciousness and insisted upon resuming command, thereby giving a striking example of fortitude to his men."

Jose G. **Contreras** died in 1968.

Harold R. **Dibble**, an accountant with Uniroyal Chemical in Connecticut, lived with his wife, Grace, in Waterbury. They had four sons. He died in 2000 at eighty after a long illness.

Vernon **Dilks**: "I had 110 points, enough to fly home instead of takin' the boat, and what'd they do but bring back that damn Fifth Division that was in Iceland all through the war—only casualties they had was when they fought each other—and they accumulated all those points just settin' there five or six years, and hell, they took all the airplane seats." Vern was a house painter in Sarasota, Florida, when I found him with his wife Kathryn in 1978, but I've lost track of them.

James J. **Dowdall** worked for the Post Office at LaGuardia Airport in New York for twenty-six years until his retirement in 1973. He signed without reading my release-for-publication form for interviewees. At ninety-five, nearly blind and looked in on by his adoring family, Jimmy lives an avuncular bachelor's life and relives the days of the Ironheads in his family home in Jackson Heights, New York.

Gareth W. **Dunleavy**: "As I grow older the whole experience seems somehow to get more important, and I have more time to think about it than in the first thirty years when I was too busy getting my career established. I don't feel bad about the whole thing and suppose I have a bit of pride that I did it and came out unscathed more or less, and that I did it for reasons that might not have been very good but that were at the time something I felt I had to do." He retired as Professor of English and Comparative Literature at the University of Wisconsin-Milwaukee, where his second wife Janet was also a professor and where he was chairman of the Department of English and an internationally recognized and widely published authority on medieval and Irish literature, with a special interest in Chaucer and Joyce. The Dunleavys were awarded first-ever man-and-wife Guggenheim Fellowships for study in France, coauthored *Douglas Hyde: A Maker of Modern Ireland* (Berkeley, CA, 1991), and moved to Exeter, New Hampshire, where Janet died in 2000 and Gareth in 2004 at eighty-one. He had a son and daughter by his first marriage, a stepdaughter with his second.

Ernest **Fried**'s whereabouts are unknown.

George P. **Furber** was a pawnbroker in Houston, Texas. He died in 1996 at seventy-one.

Joseph **Garland**, MD retired from the practice of pediatrics in the Boston area in 1947 to become Editor of the *New England Journal of Medicine*, from which he retired in 1967. He was the author of numerous articles and several books on the practice and history of medicine for professional and lay readers, including a memoir, *A Time for Remembering*, and was awarded honorary degrees by Tufts University and Boston University and numerous international honors. He and the former Mira Crowell were married fifty years on September 20, 1971. In August of 1973 he died at eighty. My beloved mother followed him in May 1974. She was seventy-eight.

Lester **Gerencer** was working as a clean-up man and cutting-machine operator for Ingersoll Rand in Phillipsburg, New Jersey, in 1978, divorced, with three daughters, and hoping to retire in 1981 when I found him. No word since.

Delmar W. **Griffith**: "I never did presume to even speculate on the advisability of this or that maneuver in the war," he told me. "There were foul-ups for sure, but I was never enough of a strategist to be critical. The whole idea of fighting just got to be, well, what did we get out of it? The Vietnam War was a foolish undertaking, and unless it should come to a defensive war

I just wonder if you can arouse the patriotism in the people like you could a generation ago. They didn't have to go to any great effort to indoctrinate a soldier to git in that fracas."

He and Sophie Prisner, a teacher, were married in 1951 and had two sons and a daughter. He had retired as a successful building contractor in Denver when I looked him up in 1978, and he was just as lean and angular and acerbic as ever, though betraying signs of mellowing around the edges. He died in 1985 at seventy-four after a long siege of Parkinson's disease.

André **Joannon**, after returning home from the I&R, got a job with the Army's Graves Registration combing the French countryside for dead G.I.s. Andy married Florence Montgolfier, a descendant of Pierre Montgolfier, the French papermaker whose sons, Jacques and Etienne, invented the balloon in 1783, retired from the management of his family wine dealership in Marseille and died in 2007.

Henry W. **Johnson**'s whereabouts are unknown.

Montford **Locklear** retired as a government communications technical expert in Dayton, Ohio, after forty-six years.

Frank E. **Merchant** was discharged after being hospitalized , from the Vosges with trench foot, and subsequently launched upon a varied career as journalist, publicist, author, poet and teacher. He retired in 1976 after sixteen years as a respected and maverick Professor of English at Union College in Barbourville, Kentucky, where he died in 1991 at eighty. His wife Christine and son Karl brought his ashes to Gloucester to be consigned to the deep from my boat. After an appropriate reading the container was dropped overboard but declined to sink, instead floating away as if wafted by the playful spirit of the departed, who could almost be heard to chuckle. Starting up my sloop's engine, I gave chase. We retrieved the floating box, opened it properly this time, and scattered Frank's earthly and earthy remains to the Atlantic on the shores of which he had spent many a joyful day in his youth.

Henry G. **Mills** returned to Altoona, Pennsylvania, to a job with the Pennsylvania Railroad as fireman on a steam locomotive, then worked up from lineman to foreman with the municipal electric company. "One thing about bein' a lineman, when you're up on top o' the pole yer the boss. We had an old sayin' that you don't put things on a pole and make it look like a pitchfork full o' hay. I could have very easily paid for a much better home, and had what I wanted, than live where I do now. Jean Marie and I had to make the decision: Do we buy ourselves a big, fancy house or do we dress our kids [three girls and a boy] the way we want 'em dressed and feed 'em the way we want 'em fed and educate 'em the way we want 'em educated? We can't do both, and when my kids was growin' up they always knew their mother was home." Having survived two coronary bypass operations several years apart, Hank retired with Shirley, his second wife, whom he married after the death of Jean Marie in 1987. He died in 2001 at seventy-eight.

Valen J. **Mullenax**, while taking a variety of correspondence courses ranging from engineering to physics, journalism, philosophy, psychology, economics, law and Bible history, worked in the postwar years variously as a carpenter, attendant nurse in a mental institution, stitcher, shipping clerk, millwright, machinist, security guard and other pursuits, mainly in the West and Midwest. By the time of our 1982 reunion he had become proprietor of Metaphysical Science and Design Drafting Services in Denver and was offering classes in Revelatory Religion of Reality and Mind Power Dynamics. He wrote me after the reunion that he was composing "the Philosophy and Doctrine for the Revelatory Religion of Reality which is based on the true life and teachings of Jesus and scientific facts, as we know them today. So you see I have my work cut out for me, and some opposition also, as some people do not like to face the truth." Our One-Man Army died in 1985 at seventy-two.

Charles E. **Nye**: "Hard to remember when you're tryin' to forget." Shorty (or Chuck) worked in production for Autolite in Fostoria, Ohio. After Chucky Joe (Charles, Jr.), he and Madge had two more boys. He retired to Lake Placid, Florida, where he died in 1991 at seventy-five.

David J. **O'Keefe** after the war trained as a draftsman with the Farrell manufacturing company in Connecticut and was in charge of its plant maintenance in Rochester, New York. He and Katie had three daughters and two sons. She died in 1985. He retired with his second wife, Christine, to Marston Mills on Cape Cod, Massachusetts, where he died in 2001 at eighty-three.

Emmett H. **Oman** died in 1975.

Jack T. **Pullman**: "Back in the States," Jack told me, "I thought about going to school but was too lazy, went to New York and loafed around, then to Birmingham, Alabama, and back home to Kansas for a few months, then out to Denver. Got married and took on two stepdaughters and had to go to work for a year and a half in Colorado with the Climax Molybdenum Company, from there to Oklahoma for my in-laws making nitroglycerine. Went up to Tri-State Oil Fill in Illinois and made nitro and shot wells for five years. Due to a technological breakthrough they no longer had to use nitro to raise oil from the rocks, so went back to Climax for another nine years doing construction, timbering, training new hands. Then in light construction for myself in the Leadville area. Divorced in '69. Had a daughter, Virginia, and a son Jack, who was in a destroyer for three tours off 'Nam, and like us, 'got to see the elephant.' Left Colorado and moved back to Kansas and bought a few houses, fixed 'em up and sold 'em. Eventually tired of that, married Wilma in Kansas City and gained three stepsons, then went to work there for the city as a building inspector, and more or less semi-retirement since then."

Wilma died in 1979. The following year Jack married Hazel Coe, who died in 1996. He made his home with his daughter Ginny in Kansas City and died after a long illness in 1999 at seventy-eight.

Harry H. **Ramge** died in Lima, Ohio, in 1970 at sixty-nine.

Cyril H. **Reynolds**, whereabouts unknown.

Robert **Richardson**, whereabouts unknown.

Morris **Rosenwasser** worked and saved and parlayed his twenty-five a week into his own farm with three thousand chickens. He and his New Yorker wife, Florence, had two sons, worked and borrowed and parlayed it all into the Duane apartment motel in Miami Beach in 1981, to which he issued an open invitation to any of his liberators in I Company to be his guests and where I interviewed him. Regrettably we've lost touch.

Henry F. **Siaud** was recruited by André as an interpreter with the Army's Graves Registration unit locating the bodies of American soldiers. Back in "civilian" life he worked for twenty-five years as a maritime shipping agent, then another sixteen likewise for an international chemical company before retiring to Marseille in 1990 with his wife Roselyne. Hank and "Lily" had four daughters and a son. Our beloved French buddy died at eighty-one in 2006 after a long struggle with Parkinson's disease.

D. Douglass **Studebaker** sold newspaper advertising, life insurance and real estate, mainly in Colorado, forming his own small company in industrial sales before moving to Alaska, where he had charge of recreational facilities for the Sohio Alaska Petroleum Company's facility at Prudhoe Bay. Doug and Thora Louise Rose eloped in 1942. They had four daughters and a son.

He retired to their home in Anchorage. Thora died in 1996, just short of their fifty-fifth anniversary. Doug "hangs on" at eighty-five with his family nearby.

Robert **Thatcher**'s whereabouts are unknown.

Dominick M. **Trubia** married Lucretia Piraino from his hometown in 1946. Aspiring to a career in teaching, he found he could make twice as much bartending. They had three children while he sold life insurance in the South, then returned to Perry, New York, where he got his teaching degree in 1962. Dom was the most beloved mentor in the Perry public schools when he retired in May, 1978, due to ill health. When I traveled to Perry to interview him that September he was gaunt from the cancer he'd been battling for years, but the old zest shone through. He died the following April at fifty-five.

Philipp F. **Vollhardt** took early retirement in Redding, Connecticut, as an engineer in the aerospace industry, where he specialized in guidance systems and worked on the Hubble space telescope. He and Helen had five children. Their eldest, Philipp, went through the Reserve Officers' Training Corps program at the University of Connecticut, was assigned to the infantry, trained with the 82nd Airborne Division and was sent to Vietnam, where the small unit he commanded was ambushed while on convoy on February 2, 1971, and he and a sergeant were killed by a rocket.

Helen: "Two men in uniform came to the door with the news. It took so long for Philipp's remains to come home. The children had planned a surprise party for our twenty-fifth wedding anniversary on the seventeenth, and the surprise party was the funeral on the thirteenth. Saint Patrick's Church was packed; they were out on the steps. We got a letter he sent one of the neighbors, and at that point he wasn't enthralled with it anymore, felt we shouldn't be in Vietnam."

Phil died in 2004 at eighty-four.

Jeremy R. **Waldron** joined his father's law firm in Portsmouth, New Hampshire, after his graduation from Harvard Law School, and retired in 1996. I was best man at his and Joan's wedding in 1961. They have a married daughter. A dedicated golfer and Rotarian, Jerry is an esteemed civic leader in Portsmouth and a founder of "Strawbery Banke," a national prototype of historic district preservation in the colonial downtown waterfront area. In 1995 my closest old buddy collapsed while giving a luncheon talk. He was revived twice after being pronounced clinically dead, underwent six-way cardiac bypass surgery, and thirteen years later claims his golf game is better than ever, notwithstanding (but perhaps partly on account of) a prior hip replacement. His faith and assistance in *Unknown Soldiers* have sustained me for sixty years.

Robert C. **Winburn** retired to his home in Overland Park, Kansas, after a career as a diesel mechanic with an interstate trucking company. He and Dorothea had two daughters. He died at sixty-nine on the fiftieth anniversary of D-day in 1994 after a year's bout with cancer.

Walter R. **Wolff** visited several of the Ironheads on a motorcycle after returning from the service and hasn't been heard from since.

William E. **Woodhams** worked at the Denver Mint after his return to Colorado, then for the Federal prison in Denver, where he had charge of much of the outdoor work for inmates, counseling and helping them develop skills they could use back on the outside. Bill had a daughter by his first marriage and a son by his late second wife, Selma. Retired since 1965, he died in Omaha, Nebraska, at eighty-seven in 1999. I wish I'd served with him.

Andrew M. **Zapiecki**: "When Rome was captured we were riding around in the jeep looking for someone to do our dirty clothes, and here's a little girl on a fence, and she says, 'Maybe, if you get soap. I'll ask my mother.' So the next day we came to pick 'em up, and here's Julie (her name was Juliana Agostini, and she was twenty) ironing my shirt, and damn if she didn't burn a hole in it."

But Andy didn't forget, and the next winter, after he was sent back from the I&R in the Vosges and reassigned to a motor pool in Rome, he commenced serious romancing. He and Julie were married in the fall of 1945, and he brought his war bride back to Toledo, Ohio.

"I went back to the American Can Company where a guy got me interested in the union, went to a few meetings, ran for secretary and won and in '47 ran for president and won. And I didn't have to work. If you were president you showed up for an hour or so and got paid for the whole job. My brother was working at the Post Office and said try it, so in '49 I took the exam—and got off the gravy train to go there and work, which at that time was rugged. So in three more years I get interested in the postal workers union, and ten years after, I'm still president. At the beginning, you say boo to the postmaster you get fired, so you could see how it progressed."

"Zapeck" retired in 1977 to grow tomatoes in his backyard patch in Toledo and maintain a commanding presence at the Polish neighborhood watering place he founded when he returned from Italy with his lovely Italian wife Julie. He called it the Commodore Club because that sounded good, and told uproarious stories about his fifty-five months in the Army at home and abroad. They had a son and two daughters. But he grew more obdurate as his health failed. They separated in 1989, and Andy died in 1993 at eighty.

Unless otherwise noted, all photographs in this section are by the author.

Bill Caird   Harold Dibble

Vern Dilks, with souvenir shrapnel

Jim Dowdall

Gareth Dunleavy

George Furber

Joe Garland a few years ago, with a few early drafts
of this book

Les Gerencer

Delmar Griffith

Frank Merchant

Hank Mills

Val Mullenax

Shorty Nye

Dave O'Keefe

Jack Pullman

Doug Studebaker

Dom and Lou Trubia, shortly before his death
in 1979

Phil Vollhardt (*Courtesy of Helen W. Vollhardt*)

Jerry Waldron (*Courtesy of Jeremy R. Waldron*)

Bob Winburn

Bill Woodhams

Andy Zapiecki

LIST OF MAPS

INDEX

Other books by Joseph E. Garland include:

LONE VOYAGER

The Extraordinary Adventures of Howard Blackburn,
Hero Fisherman of Gloucester

THE FISH AND THE FALCON

EASTERN POINT

GLOUCESTER ON THE WIND

America's Greatest Fishing Port in the Days of Sail

BEAR OF THE SEA

THE NORTH SHORE

A Social History of Summers
Among the Noteworthy, Fashionable, Rich, Eccentric
and Ordinary on Boston's Gold Coast, 1823–1929

THE GLOUCESTER GUIDE

A Stroll through Place and Time

DOWN TO THE SEA

The Fishing Schooners of Gloucester